THE
hockey
compendium

THE hockey compendium

NHL FACTS, STATS, AND STORIES

JEFF Z. KLEIN AND KARL-ERIC REIF

M&S

National Library of Canada Cataloguing in Publication Data

Klein, Jeff Z.
    The Hockey Compendium

Based on: Klein and Reif hockey compendium
ISBN 0-7710-9575-9

1. National Hockey League—Miscellenea. 2. Hockey—Miscellanea.
I. Reif, Karl-Eric II. Klein and Reif hockey compendium. III. Title.

GV847.8.N3K54 2001   796.962'64   C2001-901982-3

We acknowledge the financial support of the Government of Canada through the Book Publishing Industry Development Program for our publishing activities. We further acknowledge the support of the Canada Council for the Arts and the Ontario Arts Council for our publishing program.

Design by Ingrid Paulson
Typeset in Minion by M&S, Toronto
Printed and bound in Canada

McClelland & Stewart Ltd.
The Canadian Publishers
481 University Avenue
Toronto, Ontario
M5G 2E9
www.mcclelland.com

1 2 3 4 5   05 04 03 02 01

Contents

To my mother, my sister, and my father, for all they've done for me,
in bad times and in good, with love, always.

— JZK

To Beth, with daily astonishment and all my love,
and to Jones, who couldn't stay for the end of the game, and is missed.

— KER

Foreword

It was at Dave Bookman's apartment in 1989 that I first encountered the powers of Klein and Reif. Our evening's plan was for Bookie and me to meet Clarkie and Dobson at the Cheap Trick show at the Opera House, then watch the Habs-Islanders game later at a nearby bar. I think Cheap Trick were on their reunion tour, but I'm not sure (like Dave Lowry or Bobby Dollas, they might have never stopped playing either). Bookman lived with Tim Mech in the east end of the city. Tim had just started a new band called 1:38. When I asked him what the name meant, he told me that 1:38 was the time left on the clock when the Americans scored the winning goal to capture the gold medal in 1980. Both Bookman and I thought this was weird because Tim wasn't really into sports. The first time Dave and Tim's band, The Bookmen, toured Canada, Dave insisted that they plan their return dates scheduled around the 1987 Canada Cup. Tim protested, because he was anxious to get home to his girlfriend, who'd confessed infidelity over the phone, but Dave was adamant about following the fortunes of the national team. They spent hours driving from prairie town to town looking for a hotel room that had cable, all the while tuned in to a scratchy, barely audible radio signal, Bookman listening hunched over, his hands gripping the wheel.

I'd met The Bookmen that summer at the Canadian Independent Music Festival in British Columbia. I remember spending a gloriously drunken evening with Dave on Commercial Drive, recalling the hockey highlights of our youth, whipping ourselves into a frenzy thinking of all of those games and players and goals and what they'd meant to us and our lives. Sometimes you just connect with a person, and sports is often the conduit for feeling close to people you've only just met. That's what happened that night in Vancouver, and it was the reason why I was hanging around Bookie's place, preparing to head downtown and take in the Trick.

While sitting on the couch, I happened to open a copy of *The Village Voice* that Bookie had lying around the apartment (Dave always kept an array of rock and roll mags and sports tabloids – not to mention the three major dailies – hanging around his pad). The paper flew open to the last page, where a cryptic headline stared up at me in thick black type:

BE AFRAID
BE VERY AFRAID

I asked Bookman, "What the frig is this?"

"Sports. The *Voice* has sports," he said, chewing on a chocolate finger.

"C'mon."

"No, really. It's good. Check it out."

I became engrossed in the story, a prognostication on the Rangers' dubious playoff chances. The article was written by two fellows, neither of whom I'd heard of. There was something strong and immediate about their prose, and it hit me like a brick to the head. My first impression was that it was the first hockey writing I'd read that had swearing in it. Not to disparage the old class of hockey scribes, who favoured colloquialisms like "fadoo" and "goldarned" and "teed off" when we all knew what they really meant, but Klein and Reif wrote the way Bookman and I talked. Their language was funny and irreverent, yet serious, too. It possessed the same tone that Dave and I had used that night in Vancouver, and that thousands of fans around the world use at doughnut shops, gas stations, bowling alleys, and outdoor rinks when discussing what their team did or didn't do or hasn't done or never will do. You could tell that they believed, as I do, that the only thing that really mattered about hockey was everything. Their work was salty, yet sensitive; funny, but weighted. It was infused with an understanding of the absurdity of the sport, its magic, its ability to pull us together and tear us apart, the fickleheartedness and frailty of loss and triumph, and the drama, pathos, converging storylines, and memory trips that inform every play, game, and team, sometimes as rich and compelling as a Proustian epic. Well, maybe not Florida versus Columbus. But you get the idea.

A few years later in Toronto, Bookman and I hosted a college radio show called *High and Outside*. Dave would gripe about the potholes on Vaughan Road; we'd comment on the previous evening's scores; and the engineer in the control room would roll smoke and lay in Jonathan Richman records underneath. One day, I called *The Village Voice* and got Jeff Z. Klein on the line and asked if we could interview him on the air. He said that we could, and after a while, Jeff became a regular on the show. At first, it was hard to comprehend the notion that my two favourite hockey writers were Americans, but as we discovered talking to Jeff, both he and Karl came from Buffalo, which explained a lot. Southern Ontarians and Buffalonians share television and radio stations, so it was no accident that much of their writing was informed with cultural references to which we could relate. This is not to say that Karl and Jeff could have come from Ontario. I believe that their style was the result of having viewed the game from the other side of the window, thus bringing a unique perspective to the game, allowing them to see what Canadian writers couldn't, making for a fresh approach to a weary trade.

Our relationship with Karl was less instant. The first time I met him, he reminded me of Animal from the *Lou Grant* show. While both he and Jeff were products of the counterculture, Karl was more of a freaky dropout. He wore his baseball cap low on his head and spoke in long Buffalonian slurs about players I'd never heard of, calling up stats by rote. But Karl's savant made for a highly prolific run at *The Village Voice*. At one point during the paper's sporting heyday, he took to composing comics based on recent events, producing memorable works such as "The Messiah," a strip about Mark Messier's pious quest to lead the Rangers to their first Cup in over 40 years. Around the same time, both he and Jeff wrote about the Buffalo Bills, who were in the throes of losing four consecutive Super Bowls. While the Bills provided awful hardship for fans in upstate New York (and parts of Southern Ontario, too), they yielded some of the duo's most stunning prose. Jeff's rant "Buffalo Bilious" is one of the most visceral pieces of sports writing I've ever read.

After a few years, Bookman and I stopped doing *High and Outside* (these days, Dave is griping about potholes on a legitimate station, and I've gone off to write my own books about the ice ballet). It seems as if the two of us have less time for the universe of pro hockey than we once did. Besides, it's hard to keep up with so many teams and players. Bookie and I have long since departed that era when Monday was TSN hockey, Wednesday was the Leafs, Thursday maybe the Sabres, and Saturday the Leafs or the Habs. I don't even buy the *Voice* anymore, ever since they pulled their sports section to make space for phone-sex ads, though they did reinstate it a few years afterwards, with less effective results.

But despite these changes, the work of Klein and Reif still represents an irreducibly profound time in my life. James Joyce is like that, too, only he never wrote about hockey. It's for that reason that this second *Compendium* means so much to me. It's why I consider it not only an indispensable tool in understanding all those contemporary teams, players, and games that so few of us have time for anymore, but also a representation of the kind of literature that altered my perspective on the game, and in no small way helped me focus better on becoming the hockey fan, and sports writer, that I am today. And even though Bookman and Clarkie and Dobson aren't calling as often, reporting late scores, conveying the goals or fights that they saw on television, or debating whether pro hockey will live or not live into the next decade, I feel strangely comforted knowing that a few things still exist that allow me to rekindle those days when they once did: Cheap Trick keep on touring. And Klein and Reif are still writing great books.

This is one of them.

Dave Bidini
Toronto
April 2001

Introduction

"Hello, caller, go ahead."

"Yeah, hi, um . . . *why keep statistics?*"

The questions don't come much more blunt or basic than that. It was actually asked of us several years back by a caller to a phone-in sports radio show on which we were guests. Guests, in fact, because we were busy making the media rounds in support of our first book, the original *Hockey Compendium*.

That was 15 years ago, or thereabouts, if you'll pardon our statistical inaccuracy. National Hockey League teams were combining for a fast and sloppy eight-goals-and-change a game, a callow youth named Wayne Gretzky was in the midst of his mind-boggling revision of the NHL record book, regular-season overtime had only recently been reintroduced. In an NHL slightly overpopulated with 21 franchises, the four-time Stanley Cup champion New York Islanders were still a major power, having only just been dethroned by Gretzky's Edmonton Oilers. Yep, it was a different world then. Shoot, Gordie Howe had retired for good only a couple of years earlier. And our manuscript was scratched out in longhand and hammered out on a typewriter, not a computer, and our women, clad in animal skins, tended the fire to cook the mastodon we'd killed to feed our tribe.

Strange to think so much is different just 15 years later, but as large a difference as anything from that time to this is the perception of statistics in hockey. Football and, especially, baseball, almost from their beginning have churned out reams of numbers in dozens, hundreds, of statistical categories, devoured hungrily by their fans, easily digested, and memorized and enshrined as touchstones of performance in those sports. Baseball fans, for instance, had an intimate shorthand rooted in that game's most treasured numbers – 714 . . . 56 . . . 2,136 – Babe Ruth's career home-run total, Joe DiMaggio's consecutive-game hitting streak, Lou Gehrig's consecutive-games-played mark, and hundreds of other figures at their mental fingertips. But hockey, on the other hand, had traditionally tabulated only the most basic stats and delivered them to the fans almost grudgingly.

Basically, hockey, and hockey fans, lacked six fundamental things that were a given in other sports:

- a wide and complete variety of statistics in almost every conceivable category;
- easy access to the whole scope of those stats – as tabulated, measured, and freely distributed by the league – through the full range of media: newspapers, magazines, books, radio, television, and even sports cards;

- a reasonably stable number of teams playing seasons of relatively consistent length over the history of the sport;
- a wise statistical tradition of measuring performance not just by raw numbers but by percentages (such as batting average, earned run average, fielding average, yards-per-carry, points-per-game, won-lost percentage, and so on);
- a culture of statistics that made the numbers not a complicated, headache-inducing ordeal, but a convenient, accessible second language in which every fan was fluent – and more than that, established an understanding that no one statistic by itself could establish the full worth of a player; and
- a sport-wide ethic – maintained from the top down, from the league office and the players themselves even to the casual fan – that held that the game's history and traditions were to be treasured and that statistics were vital to articulating achievement in the sport and keeping its history alive.

Hockey culture, certainly on the first five counts, had none of those things. Neglect of record-keeping was noted as a problem as far back as 1902, when Harry Trihey, star centre of the Stanley Cup champion Montreal Shamrocks and president of the Canadian Amateur Hockey League in which they played, reported his frustration in a letter to the rest of the league:

> I regret exceedingly having to draw your attention to the poor support in keeping an official record of matches, which the secretary of this league receives from too great a number of referees. Instructions to referees are quite clear, that they should forward to the secretary of the league a report of the match during which they officiated, embodying the names of the players and officials, and the result of the contest. I must report that not more than 50% of the referees during the past season complied with this request. As a consequence the league finds itself without a bona fide official record of the matches and players who participated therein.

When we discovered hockey as kids in the 1960s and '70s, it was literally impossible to get hold of any statistics beyond goals, assists, points, penalty minutes, and goals-against average. The culture of hockey, in fact, had so long been limited by those unsubtle, bare-bones numbers, it had become numb to the notion that any more incisive statistics were needed – suspicious, in fact even resentful, of the very idea that better, more complete statistics might be useful or possible.

When Lloyd Percival's landmark *Hockey Handbook* was first published in 1960, coaches and hard-core fans latched onto its dissertations of strategic matters – positional play, breakout patterns, and so forth – but skimmed past its novel statistical examinations of things like ice time and shooting percentage. Plus/minus had been developed by the Canadiens in the 1950s, but even though its use had become widespread among NHL clubs by 1970, the actual numbers were closely guarded by individual teams; it was a juicy tidbit back then just to hear the rumour that some journeyman player was underrated and actually had an extraordinary plus mark. When in the late 1970s and early '80s, New York–area fan Vince DeMarco calculated save percentages – they were actually referred to as "goaltender fielding percentages" – the hockey media trotted them out not as a revelation, but as an amusement, an immense but neurotic effort in Chinese calculus that could have little practical use except as a diversion for the game's "figure filberts."

Just as frustrating was the hockey media's inevitably embarrassing misuse of any stat outside of the traditional pantheon of hockey numbers. This team, then that, was proclaimed the greatest offensive force in the history of the league, for example, solely on the basis of the fact they'd just broken the NHL record for goals in a season – ignoring the fact they'd averaged fewer goals per game than some earlier team that had played a schedule only half as long, or that evolving rules and styles through the history of hockey had wildly enhanced or severely hindered the ability of teams to score, depending on the era in which they played. One team or another would be acclaimed on any given night for its remarkable record of almost never blowing a lead it took into the third period, ignoring the fact that every team – even the worst, on the rare occasions they actually had a lead to protect after two periods – rarely blew that lead in the last 20 minutes. Considering how often and how badly even the simplest stats were mishandled into producing misinformation that ran counter to common knowledge and common sense, perhaps it's just as well they weren't relied on more, and little wonder they were regarded so dubiously.

Maybe it's the lack of statistical tradition in hockey that led to the basic misapprehension that the numbers were an end unto themselves – columns of numerals that existed for their own sake, and not as a vital tool to reveal the true quality of performance. But now, more than ever, beyond illuminating the real value of a particular player or the real worth of a particular team, statistics also have an additional role: keeping alive the names of the legions of players and teams that, over the course of more than a century, have skated and struggled and made the game what it's been and what it is, that have thrilled and disappointed and entertained, that have lived out their dreams or fallen short, that have left us all with countless stories and memories, legends, and footnotes, and that in one way or another have forever left their mark on hockey.

Today, though, the last of the six counts we mentioned above has been aggressively abandoned by the NHL – the league that should be most responsible for protecting and preserving the game's history and traditions. Today, the names and achievements of even the game's immortals are unknown and meaningless through most of the United States, and seem to be slipping out of mind even in Canada. They're being lost amid the bustle of a sprawling NHL carnival that's been a blur of breakneck overexpansion, franchise relocation, cartoon robots, gigantic, charmless new arenas, corporate luxury suites, blaring rock music, licensing, merchandising, mascots, and Nashvilles and Carolinas and the Minnesota "Wild." Given that, it seems to us that any excuse for rolling out the stats and the names of an earlier age is welcome and worthwhile.

In Canada, a few ancient watershed figures, like Joe Malone or King Clancy or Newsy Lalonde, the Patricks or the Conachers, the Dawson City Seven or the Montreal Maroons, survive in the consciousness, and the heroes and the heritage of more recent eras, still in living memory, are part of the fabric of hockey and the fans' experience. But in the States – in a culture where hockey has at best been a regional sport, no matter how many ill-conceived Sun Belt expansion franchises the NHL has foisted on us, in a sports culture that's been so X-tremized, so designer-sport-inundated that the NHL is perceived to have no more history or credibility than indoor soccer, Arena Football, roller hockey, or pro skateboarding – most fans outside the northeast and the Great Lakes region labour under the vague impression hockey was invented out of whole cloth in the early 1980s when Gretzky first laced up his skates, and that the Leafs or Canadiens have no more history or tradition than the Mighty Ducks of Anaheim.

Make no mistake, this isn't as far-fetched as expecting some adolescent fan in Tampa Bay to be able to tell you about Ace Bailey or Aurel Joliat; the lack of awareness of what's gone before, even of major figures and events, is endemic even within the hockey community. As Blackhawk star Tony Amonte inquired, when asked by his coach to be Team U.S.A.'s answer to Paul Henderson: "Who the hell is Paul Henderson?"

Under the NHL's current administration – one with no roots in hockey whatsoever, one having no familiarity with, nor any respect for, all that's gone before – the legends of the game, all the tradition and history, don't even register as an afterthought. Even the administrations that preceded it assumed the NHL's heritage was a given and did little if anything to maintain or promote it.

There's a scene in that staple of 1960s adolescent adventure-fantasy, *The Time Machine*, that reminded us of the whole thing. Rod Taylor, as Victorian author/time-traveller H. G. Wells, lands in the year A.D. 802,701, expecting to find fantastic advances in art and technology — but instead finds the Eloi, a passive, childlike, intellectually dead "culture" incapable of telling him anything about their world. "I can learn all about you from books!" Taylor declares. "Books will tell me what I want to know!" He's led to the library in the Eloi's central habitation, a huge crumbling ruin of a futuristic building perhaps millennia old. But upon eagerly grabbing the first book at hand, it crumbles to dust in his fingers — as does every book on the shelves, having been left unattended, unappreciated, and carelessly exposed to the elements for centuries. "Yes, they *do* tell me all about you," growls Taylor, who then shouts at his gormless young guide: "*What have you done*? Thousands of years of building, and rebuilding – creating and re-creating – so you can let it crumble to dust!" Taylor turns away in disgust. "A million years . . . men dying for their dreams – *for what!*"

The league and the fans, however, are immensely fortunate to have had men like Ron Andrews and Benny Ercolani working conscientiously in the NHL Information and Communications departments over the last 20 or 30 years, saving the details of the game's distant and recent history, so that we don't have to get all worked up like Rod Taylor did. When we first began digging into NHL stats, back in the 1970s, to learn more about the game we'd become obsessed with, we quickly grew frustrated with the lack of information available. It was easy to blame Andrews, then the league's chief statistician, and we asked ourselves why the hell more, and more incisive, stuff wasn't available, and what the heck he was doing when so much material had to be at his fingertips. It wasn't until years later that we learned the whole story. When Andrews took on the position gradually during the 1970s, his reaction to the NHL's record-keeping must have been one of overwhelming dismay: half a century's worth of scoresheets, stats, and game reports, just tossed pell-mell into dozens of second-hand cardboard boxes, scattered at random and stuffed into the back of various closets and cubbyholes throughout the NHL offices. Andrews deserves the lion's share of the credit just for revamping the operation, organizing all those thousands of pages into a remarkable statistical library.

From there, the NHL's information section has become one of the league's few real success stories over the last 20 years – assembling a wealth of data rivalling that in any of the other major North American team sports, archived in a well-organized, accessible office staffed with people who've always been ready and able to provide the most arcane information promptly and courteously.

Ercolani, the NHL's current chief statistician, and his small staff have been of immeasurable assistance to us over the years, and we have to tip our hats as well to Gary Meagher, NHL vice-president of Public Relations and Media Services. Meagher was kind enough to give us a tour of the facility when we finally visited in person a few years back, and we have to admit that just holding the actual scoresheet from the first NHL game ever played gave us nearly as big a thrill as drinking from the Stanley Cup itself.

But what would Gary Bettman make of the opportunity to peruse the ornate, scrupulous Edwardian penmanship on that time-browned page? Actually, the idea of Bettman holding that fragile artifact in his sweaty little hands gives us the willies. He's out of the same mould as the Ziegler-administration NHL entity who told us point-blank, "Nobody gives a shit about Cyclone Taylor." And just so we're all clear on the league's attitude, that comment was made to us not with a sense of loss or dismay, but with a self-satisfied contempt for everything about the game's history that Taylor could symbolize.

Given the league's utter disregard for the game's past, the information that could give fans a framework in which to understand hockey's history, and a handle on how to regard the names in the Hall of Fame, was as rare as hens' teeth. At the same time, the hockey media relied almost exclusively on anecdotal evidence, produced vague and subjective evaluations, and displayed a laughable ineptitude when it tried to trot out some unfamiliar statistic. We regarded this as a gross disservice to . . . well, to us personally, but to every hockey fan and to the game itself.

It was our exasperation with all that that led us, as fans who simply wanted to know more about the game, and about its teams and players, first to do some extensive but easy calculations using what little information we had at hand, then to parlay that into a newspaper column intended to tell our fellow fans what we'd figured out, and, we hoped, to elevate the level of the discussion. That in turn led to the original *Klein and Reif Hockey Compendium*.

The *Compendium* was embraced by many . . . well, several . . . well, okay, a tiny handful of fans and hockey media . . . but met with a fair amount of scorn and ridicule from a few pretty big veteran names in the media, who feared that the evil magic of statistics would somehow reveal their beloved Gordie Howe to be a wuss or something.

Fifteen years, and the landscape has changed. There's been an explosion of numbers in hockey. Ice time, tracked to the second. Complete breakdowns of even-strength, power-play, and short-handed scoring. Face-off percentages. Giveaways. Takeaways.

Are all these numbers just esoterica? Well, maybe. But just the exposition of real basics such as goalie save percentage and plus/minus, and their widespread acceptance among the fans and media, represents a sea change in the way hockey is thought about and talked about. We'd like to think the original *Compendium* had at least a little something to do with that. And, as well, with an increased interest in the game's history and hockey stats in general – reflected in the birth some years back of the Society for International Hockey Research and the Hockey Research Association, the ice game's admirable answers to the Society for American Baseball Research – and with a remarkable output, in just the last few years, of several excellent new hockey encyclopaedias and statistical volumes – one to which we were contributors, in fact, and many of them all but indispensable for fans with an abiding interest in the

game, and its past. With 15 more years of major-league hockey to assess and cratinloads of new and revised statistics having been made available to us since our last edition, not to mention the promise of hundreds of Canadian dollars for two years' worth of research and writing, we figured maybe it was time for a completely updated *Compendium* as well.

Back to our caller. Why keep statistics? We'll tell you now pretty much what we told him then: because they are the sole objective measure of team and individual performance, the means by which team and individual performance are objectively measured for all time. They provide the context with which to judge accomplishment. And all of us, as fans, are driven to compare one team to another, one player to another, not just within this or any given season, but across time and across eras. How well would the Islander dynasty teams of the 1980s have done against the Canadien dynasty teams of the 1950s, or the Canadiens of the '70s against the '50s Red Wings? How well would Gretzky have performed in the 1960s, or '50s, or '30s, or how would Howie Morenz or King Clancy have done in the NHL of today?

Without statistics, the questions would be meaningless on at least two counts: first, you'd have no context in which to put their respective abilities and performance, when the conditions under which they played were so radically different; and second, you'd be arguing in a vacuum, with nothing but subjective impressions to support your argument – if in fact you were even lucky enough to have seen all of them play. You might as well argue about who the greatest actor of all time was: Laurence Olivier? Edmund Kean? David Garrick? Anthony Hopkins? Frankie Avalon? Well, even leaving Frankie out of it for the moment, the same two problems make the question irresolvable. First, the qualities of performance that were prized in the mannered, 18th-century theatre of Garrick or the melodramatic 19th-century stagecraft of Kean would be derided as hilarious by the acting standards of today, just as the studied naturalism of Olivier's or Hopkins's film work would probably be regarded as painfully inept by audiences of centuries past. And of course, while Olivier's and Hopkins's performances have at least been captured for all time on film, to be judged and compared by audiences today and a hundred years on, there's no record remaining of Kean's work or Garrick's but for the subjective reviews of the critics of their day – when journalism itself was a far different thing.

Just the same: would Gretzky, or Paul Kariya, or Pavel Bure, have starred in the hockey of the '30s or '50s? Or would they have even had the opportunity to shine, as they have playing their free-skating game, playing instead under the restraints of the lane-bound, everyone-must-backcheck style in force in some earlier era? Would the great stars of the '20s or '30s, like Morenz and Clancy, have been able even to compete in the NHL today, given their diminutive physical size? Or would their great skating and playmaking abilities shine even more brightly, unshackled from the burdens of too much ice time and disciplined positional play, and set loose in the scrambly, talent-diluted hockey of the 21st century?

Not to get too artsy here or anything, but dance (hey, we only know this because one of us was going out with a dancer at the time we wrote the first *Compendium*; personally, we prefer the, ahem, "Canadian ballet" over in Fort Erie) has a history somewhat similar to hockey's in terms of its lack of documentation. For centuries, forms as varied as ethnic folk dances and the formal choreography of ballet were handed down from troupe to troupe and from generation to succeeding generation only by re-enacting the entire performance, which was then learned by repetition. It wasn't until the latter half of the 20th century, when Albrecht Knust and Rudolf Laban developed Labanotation, a written code for movement, that dance compositions could be recorded, copied, and archived, and taught, without the need for personal demonstration, free of the pitfalls of imperfect memory or subjective reinterpretation.

The lack of statistical record-keeping in hockey's past means immense amounts of information, and the insights they provide into the accomplishments of teams and players of the past, are lost forever, and at best available only in subjective terms. For instance, unless you're something of a hockey historian, you may be surprised to learn that the assist, that familiar and telling measure of a player's passing and playmaking ability, did not even exist as a statistic for the first half-dozen years of major-league professional hockey. Assists have been awarded at the remarkably consistent rate of about one-and-two-thirds on every NHL goal scored for the last 45 seasons. But changes over the years, in the official definition of what constitutes an assist, have seen seasons when helpers were handed out with an eye-dropper – less than one per goal until the early 1930s, less than half an assist per goal until the mid-'20s. How many clever passers from the early days of pro hockey, how many steady zone-clearing defencemen, are lost to history because the rules that were then in effect short-changed them any number of assists – and in turn the recognition of later generations of hockey fans, who find every forward of that era with puckhog numbers, goal totals dwarfing assist totals, and every defenceman with a string of zeros in his statistical table?

Even as recently as 15 years ago, some absolutely fundamental, indispensable hockey statistics had barely begun to be officially tabulated and distributed by the league – shots on goal and goaltender save percentages, for example. How can you possibly make a fair assessment of a goaltender's value without those figures? The standard, for decades, had simply been goals-against average, even though it's obvious to anyone who thinks about it that goals-against average is a measure of team, much more than of individual, performance. Who could ask even the best goalies, while playing behind the worst teams, to match the numbers of even mediocre netminders playing behind the best sides? Alec Connell or Jacques Plante or Ken Dryden or Martin Brodeur may have had the tiniest, shiniest goals-against marks, but were they, are they, really better than, or even as good as, Roy Worters, or Chuck Rayner, or Roger Crozier, or Dominik Hasek?

For that matter, Gretzky scored more goals in one season than anyone in history, but was that performance really better than Malone's famous 44 goals in 20 games, or the Rocket's immortal 50-in-50 campaign, or anything Espo or Mario or either of the Hulls ever did? Were his jaw-dropping assist totals really more impressive than the seemingly modest numbers of Joe Primeau or Bill Cowley, or even Bobby Orr's own record-shattering marks? Were Gretzky's Oilers really the greatest offensive force of all time? Did the Red Wings' 62-win season a couple of years back really mark them as the best regular-season side ever? Were the Canadiens' five consecutive Stanley Cup championships really the greatest playoff achievement in history?

You may think you know. You may know someone who thinks otherwise. It's been wisely said that "a single fact can spoil a good argument." Let's get us some facts.

1.

History of the Major Leagues

To the Wayback Machine, Sherman. We're heading for the remarkable year of 1908 – the first year in which one all-professional league established its pre-eminence over all other leagues. In this chapter, we'll be looking at the tumultuous changes through the years in the number of teams involved at the highest level of competition, and at the roller-coaster ride of inflation and depression in goal scoring that has been caused both by the varying numbers of teams and by changes in rules and style of play, and get an idea of how those numbers have in turn affected team and individual performance.

Our focus is exclusively on what can be described as major-league professional hockey. So even though a lot of long-time fans may think that excludes the NHL of at least the past four or five years, the entire history of the NHL is here nonetheless, as is that of its immediate linear ancestors, the Eastern Canada Hockey Association and the National Hockey Association. Included here, too, are the histories of several long-defunct rival leagues that can also make a fair claim to being major-league: the Pacific Coast Hockey Association, the Western Canada Hockey League, and the World Hockey Association.

This does mean, however, that we're skipping past hockey's pre-Stanley Cup Ur-history, and the amateur and semi-pro leagues that competed for the Cup for many years after its origin in 1893. For you newcomers to the game, however, just let us say that those were fascinating days. You would be doing yourself a great favour by searching out the stories of the birth and childhood of hockey in North America, and it pains us that we haven't the space here to tell you about them, nor about the International Pro League, the first all-professional hockey league, which operated out of Upper Michigan, the Canadian Soo, and Pittsburgh from 1904 to 1907, nor the Ontario Professional Hockey League, Canada's first all-pro hockey circuit, which operated from 1908 until 1911 – both of which could have fair arguments made for their inclusion as major leagues in this or future studies.

Nor, alas, is there room to detail the Stanley Cup challenges made by Winnipeg Rowing Club, or Rat Portage, or New Glasgow, or Port Arthur, or Galt; or Kenora Thistles who actually won it; or even the famous Klondike kids of Dawson City. And it's a shame we can't really justify rambling on about Mike Grant, Haviland Routh, Dolly Swift, One-Eyed Frank McGee, Graham Drinkwater, Gord Lewis, Clare McKerrow, Harry "Rat" Westwick, Weldy Young, Frank Stocking, Baldy Spittal, Hod Stuart, Harv Pulford,

Cecil Blachford, Fred Chittick, Dan Bain, Bouse Hutton, Moose Johnson, Ernie Russell, Blair Russell, Russell Bowie, Nick Bawlf, Art Throop, Pud Glass, Oren Frood, Owen McCourt, Walt Smaill, or the Power brothers – Rocket, Chubby, and Joe – or dozens of other players. It's too bad, because many of them are great figures in the game's history, many are interesting footnotes, and mainly because we just like saying "Oren Frood."

And we couldn't even begin to mention the Montagnards, or Sheriff John Sweetland, or Grand Trunk, or the Little Men of Iron, or the Countess of Minto. You'll just have to look them up yourself.

What we *can* talk about is the Eastern Canada Hockey Association.

The ECHA's 1908–09 season is a somewhat subjective choice for a starting point, but it is far from arbitrary. It is a point contained in the continuum that began in 1893 with the awarding of the Stanley Cup to Montreal AAA of the Amateur Hockey Association, the league which in turn became the Canadian Amateur Hockey League, then the Eastern Canada Amateur Hockey Association, and then the ECHA when it fully accepted professional players in 1908–09, and would soon become the NHA, which became the NHL. The CAHL's merger with the Federal Amateur Hockey League for 1906–07, spawning the ECAHA, established a single premier hockey league among several rival circuits. And the ECHA schedule for 1908–09 was extended to 12 games – up from 10 – which gives us 20% more hockey to work with statistically.

Rival leagues continued to exist – the Maritime League, the Quebec League, the Temiskaming League, leagues in the west based in Manitoba, Saskatchewan, and Alberta – and mainly the Ontario Professional Hockey League, which we've often been tempted to include in our survey of major-league hockey, but which we again leave aside here. The Trolley League, as the OPHL was better known, had teams at various times in Toronto, Brantford, Galt, Guelph, Berlin (now Kitchener), Waterloo, and St. Catharines. It boasted some of the great players of its day – Newsy Lalonde, Tommy Smith, Hugh Lehman, Bruce Ridpath, Skene Ronan, Eddie Oatman, and yes, Oren Frood, and more – and played schedules of 12 to 18 games, but the drop-off in talent after the big stars and a generally erratic level of play compel us to bar their inclusion here. For the same reasons we justify our rude snub of the International Pro League, which, we grant you, raises the question, when that same complaint can be fairly levelled at today's NHL. What can we say? Maybe in another 15 years when the next *Compendium* comes out. At any rate, there would be more rival leagues to come, which do meet our harsh standards for major-league status.

Now then, where were we? Ah, yes, the formative, evolving years for hockey, which was played under many different variations of rules depending on the region and the year. In 1908–09, hockey was a seven-man game – the three forwards, somewhat as we still know the positions, although to a much greater extent kept in lane-bound patterns; a rover, who had more latitude to freelance; the point and cover-point positions, whose responsibilities were confined almost exclusively to defence and who would evolve into the more modern defence pairing; and the goaltender, who used an ordinary narrow stick and was forbidden to drop to the ice to make saves. This restriction – a vestige of the rule, then already long abandoned, against "lifting" shots on goal – would soon be done away with. Hockey was still an "onside" game – no forward passing was allowed, and increasingly frequent changes to the offside rules over the next 20-odd years would radically affect strategy and scoring levels. Games were played in 30-minute halves. Rinks, some barely half the size of today's standard, often had boards less than a foot high; they featured natural ice, which was frequently dreadful as spring approached, and was generally rendered a field of snow by the late stages of any game. Players, including the goaltenders, took to the ice with the skimpiest of padding – cane shinpads were still in vogue for most players, cricket-style leg pads for goalies, and even hockey gloves were only a recent introduction. And teams rarely comprised more than eight men – the seven regulars, who played the entire 60 minutes or more, and a substitute, who usually made an appearance only in the event of injury to one of the others. Yep, things sure were different 15 years ago. No! Wait – that was 1908–09, and the ECHA.

With that scene in mind, feast your eyes on the table on the next page. There's the ECHA at the start of the time-line. Focus on two sets of figures here, and in all the tables that follow in this chapter, as the cornerstones for the context in which the game has to be seen. The first: the number of teams – and, by implication, the number of players – competing, and the length of the league schedule; the second: the average number of goals scored by both teams combined per 60-minute game, or the goals-per-game average (GpGA).

The ECHA in 1908–09 consisted simply of Ottawa, Quebec, and two Montreal teams – Wanderers and Shamrocks – playing a 12-game schedule. Two other Montreal-based teams had left in a huff at the start of the season, typical of the disputatious foot-stomping and franchise-folding that was an annual event in every league in this era. The rules, the personnel on hand, and the style of the day all favoured offence. Lots and lots of offence. The average game that year saw opponents combine for almost 14 goals, quite a contrast to the 5 or 5½ goals NHL teams have combined to put up since the mid-1990s. Shamrocks, the 2-10 tail-enders, averaged 4.67 goals per game; Quebec averaged 6.5, Wanderers just under 7, Ottawa almost 10. Except for Shamrocks, and a single three-goal game by Quebec, every team scored at least four goals in every game of the entire season; fully one out of three

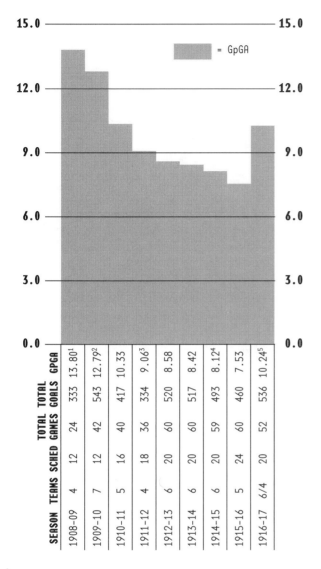

= GpGA

SEASON	TEAMS	SCHED GAMES	TOTAL GAMES	TOTAL GOALS	GPGA
1908–09	4	12	24	333	13.80[1]
1909–10	7	12	42	543	12.79[2]
1910–11	5	16	40	417	10.33
1911–12	4	18	36	334	9.06[3]
1912–13	6	20	60	520	8.58
1913–14	6	20	60	517	8.42
1914–15	6	20	59	493	8.12[4]
1915–16	5	24	60	460	7.53
1916–17	6/4	20	52	536	10.24[5]

1 ECHA 1908–09.
2 NHA 1909–10 to 1916–17.
3 Changeover to six-man hockey.
4 One scheduled game unplayed and forfeited.
5 Two teams (228th Battalion and Toronto Blueshirts) dropped out of league during season.

games saw a team hit double digits. As a result, Ottawa's Marty Walsh, regarded by many at the time as the best centre in the game, and who died in a tragic swimming mishap just six years later, led the scoring parade with 38 goals in his 12 games. Scoring came easy to everybody: Herb Jordan, Dubbie Kerr, Bruce Stuart, Harry Smith, and Bad Joe Hall all personally averaged two or more goals per game. As a footnote, the Trolley League averaged a similar 13.67 goals per game that year.

The profluent scoring at the dawn of major-league hockey is a little hard to fathom, given the small rinks that put the puck carrier within easy reach of defenders, the often miserable ice conditions, the primitive skates, and the fact these guys played the entire 60 minutes or more without substitution, which had to take more out of the forwards, skating end to end, than out of the defence, whose responsibilities were almost exclusively in their own end of the ice. What kept the goals pouring in were the prohibition against goalers falling to the ice, the dazzling stickhandling abilities of the forwards, and the rules that forbade forward passing, which could keep a team hopelessly bottled up in its own zone.

Such were the conditions of the day, and that's what you have to keep in mind when you compare scoring totals from different eras. Given the exact same set of circumstances, but pro-rating the ECHA schedule to a more modern 80 games, there's no reason at all to think Walsh wouldn't have scored around 250 goals or that Ottawa as a team wouldn't have amassed close to 800. However, as we'll see, the conditions under which major-league hockey was played would change profoundly in subsequent years – and there are plenty of reasons why there's just no way you can get a meaningful comparison of performance from different eras by simply pro-rating team and individual totals on the basis of games played. We'll get into that later.

Let's look at the following season, 1909–10, and the birth of the NHA. Don't worry, we're not going to examine every one of the past 83 seasons in detail – just a few critical campaigns along the way. There's a great deal about hockey's long-ago "Age of Disorder" that needs to be understood and brought into focus. After yet another fractious November meeting of the ECHA executive, with the annual charges and counter-charges about who signed whom, who's paying what, where the games will be played, and which new teams will be allowed to join, the result is that the league splits up – Ottawa, Quebec, and Shamrocks regrouping with two new Montreal clubs to form the Canadian Hockey Association; the new NHA forming with Wanderers as the cornerstone, joined by Renfrew, Cobalt, and Haileybury – all bustling towns in the days of the Ontario mining boom – and another new club off to an ironically uncertain and inauspicious start, Montreal Canadiens. Two weeks into the season, Shamrocks and Ottawa left the other CHA teams high and dry when they instead bolted to join the NHA after all. Sorta reminds us of a rotisserie league we used to play in.

The 1909–10 scoring parade, led by Newsy Lalonde and Ernie Russell, is a roll call of Hall of Fame enshrinees about 30 or 40 deep (which again raises the old question of just how many of these guys were really all *that* good and merit official immortalization – but we'll leave off that until later as well), and the hockey of the day is still conducive to almost 13 goals a game.

The 1910–11 season began with a court case that forced a change in ownership of the Canadiens franchise, which then absorbed the Haileybury team. Quebec returned and took over the Cobalt club, and Shamrocks resigned from the league altogether. As all player contracts were on a

History

one-season basis, the franchise movements accelerated the usual squabbles and bidding among teams for the rights to players, and the owners' unilateral implementation of a salary cap ignited threats by the players to strike or to jump to other leagues. Yes, so much has changed over the years, hasn't it? This year, though, is most notable for the introduction of three 20-minute periods replacing two 30-minute halves – an institution now so long in place and so much a part of the record book, that it is uniquely a part of hockey's identity. The suggestion, by some NHL and television executives in the last few years, that the league switch to a footballian arrangement of 30-minute halves and 15-minute quarters, should set on edge the teeth of every self-respecting hockey fan. Scoring took a bit of a dip, down to a "mere" 10⅓ goals a game. Old photographs, showing far more substantial goaltending equipment – including the earliest, most modest versions of leather leg pads and the paddle-type stick – offer some evidence why.

The 1911–12 season was a watershed year for hockey. The Patrick brothers, Frank and Lester, both star players through several CAHL, ECAHA, and NHA campaigns and Stanley Cup challenge series, moved west and established the Pacific Coast Hockey Association, with teams in Vancouver, Victoria, and New Westminster. They lured many other luminaries of eastern hockey along with them, more than enough to give the PCHA, tiny though it was, immediate major-league credibility. PCHA goalies were allowed to leave their feet to make saves. Pro rinks had been growing larger, and the arena built in Vancouver set a new standard – the first artificial ice surface in Canada, a full 210 feet by 85, and in a building that could seat 10,000. The PCHA played seven-man hockey, but back east, largely in response to rising player salaries – a handful of stars were making more than $1,500 for a season – the NHA decided to eliminate the rover position and play a six-man game. Also blaming salaries, the legendary Renfrew Creamery Kings disbanded as a franchise. The NHA adopted the goal nets designed by star netminder Percy LeSueur, which now featured a crossbar, and the rule book liberalized substitution and added more detail and definition as to what constituted a foul. Scoring in the NHA dropped by another goal per game, now a hair over nine goals a game; in the PCHA, the goals-per-game average stood at more than 11.

The NHA added two Toronto teams for 1912–13: Blueshirts, who eventually became the Maple Leafs, and Tecumsehs, who would soon fade from history. Confusing, we know. More changes of name and identity and more deaths and reappearances than in a daytime soap opera. The league also made one last flirtation with seven-man hockey – for one week in February of that season, when each of the six clubs played three games under seven-man rules – but after that it was gone for good in the east. Scoring began to stabilize at around 8½ goals per game, while the PCHA, which had added several top-notch defence players

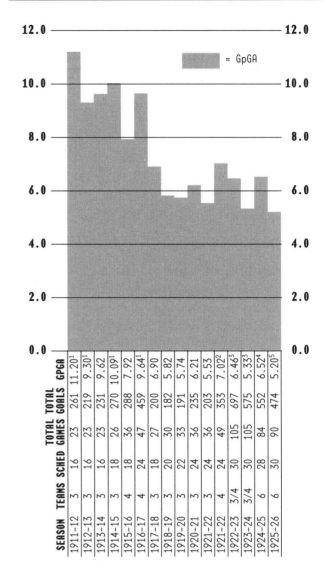

= GpGA

SEASON	TEAMS	SCHED	TOTAL GAMES	TOTAL GOALS	GPGA
1911–12	3	16	23	261	11.20[1]
1912–13	3	16	23	219	9.30[1]
1913–14	3	16	23	231	9.62
1914–15	3	18	26	270	10.09[1]
1915–16	4	18	36	288	7.92
1916–17	4	24	47	459	9.64[1]
1917–18	3	18	27	200	6.90
1918–19	3	20	30	182	5.82
1919–20	3	22	33	191	5.74
1920–21	3	24	36	235	6.21
1921–22	3	24	36	203	5.53
1921–22	4	24	49	353	7.02[2]
1922–23	3/4	30	105	697	6.46[3]
1923–24	3/4	30	105	575	5.33[3]
1924–25	6	28	84	552	6.52[4]
1925–26	6	30	90	474	5.20[5]

1 Final scheduled game of season not played, having no bearing on final standings.
2 WCHL's inaugural season.
3 PCHA (3 teams) and WCHL (4 teams) played interlocking schedule; totals for both leagues combined.
4 PCHA folded, two teams joining WCHL.
5 WCHL changed name to WHL.

by raiding NHA clubs, saw scoring drop by two goals a game, down to nine and change.

We've really put the magnifying glass on these early years of major-league hockey. We hope you're finding the game's history as fascinating as we do, and that you're perhaps learning a little as we go along. We do it for a reason – well, for several reasons, of course – but mainly to give you a perspective on how different the game was, very long ago, and how the game came to be stabilized and really perfected, and how it's threatened today by forces that would destabilize and pervert everything that required so many years and so much effort to create.

Frank Patrick's innovation, the introduction of the blue lines for the 1913–14 PCHA season, which for the first time demarcated the rink into zones and allowed forward passing, utterly changing the game's flow and strategy, is a pivotal moment in the game's development. Patrick and the PCHA were also the first to record assists – a practice soon adopted by the NHA, although neither league did much of a job of publicizing the stat – and the first to punish on-ice fouls with penalty time rather than fines. The NHA improvised a split-season format in 1916–17 to set up a post-season playoff for the league championship, an arrangement kept in place when it became the NHL a year later, but in 1917–18 the PCHA was the first league in any sport to implement a version of the seeded post-season playoff system in use ever since.

The PCHA proceeded merrily along despite the occasional franchise move; prevailing opinion had it that the overall quality of play in the West Coast loop was far superior to that back east. Meanwhile, as the signing war for players escalated, squabbling and bickering had reached a boiling point in the NHA. Unable to expel Blueshirts owner Eddie Livingstone, the other owners dropped out of the NHA together, leaving Livingstone and his team the only franchise in the league (Quebec and the 228th Battalion had shut down operations during the 1916–17 season). Other interests bought up the contracts of the Blueshirt players, renamed the club the Arenas, and joined the Canadiens, Wanderers, and Ottawa to reorganize as the new National Hockey League. Such was the august, formal birth of the NHL.

In its first two seasons, the NHL came to copy many of the PCHA's innovative features, including the blue lines, limited forward passing, permitting goalers to drop to the ice, forcing a penalized player's team to play short-handed, and the seeded playoff format. Both the NHL and the PCHA remained small, and in 1921, a third major league sprang up, the Western Canada Hockey League, with teams in Edmonton, Calgary, Saskatoon, and Regina. The WCHL began playing an interlocking schedule with the PCHA the following season, and the two circuits became fully joined under the WCHL title in 1924. The Western League folded after the 1925–26 campaign, however, leaving the NHL to stand alone as hockey's premier circuit, signalling the end of the Age of Contentiousness. The NHL had added the Boston Bruins and Montreal Maroons in 1924; in 1925 the Pittsburgh Pirates came on board and the Hamilton Tigers moved to New York to become the Americans. With the disbanding of the WHL, the NHL grew to 10 teams for 1926–27, with Chicago Black Hawks, Detroit Cougars (later Red Wings), and New York Rangers joining up. Also that year, Toronto finally changed its name to Maple Leafs after spending the previous seven years as the St. Pats.

Throughout the 1920s, the downward trend in scoring steadily accelerated, especially in the NHL, as you can see in the table. In fact, scoring diminished every single season there for nine straight years, from a hefty 9½ per game in 1919–20 to a minuscule total of 2.8 in 1928–29. The leagues

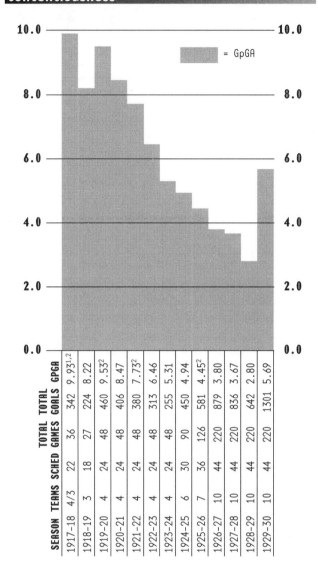

1917–18 to 1929–30 – The Age of Contentiousness

= GpGA

SEASON	TEAMS	SCHED GAMES	TOTAL GAMES	TOTAL GOALS	GPGA
1917–18	4/3	22	36	342	9.93[1,2]
1918–19	3	18	27	224	8.22
1919–20	4	24	48	460	9.53[2]
1920–21	4	24	48	406	8.47
1921–22	4	24	48	380	7.73[2]
1922–23	4	24	48	313	6.46
1923–24	4	24	48	255	5.31
1924–25	6	30	90	450	4.94
1925–26	7	36	126	581	4.45[2]
1926–27	10	44	220	879	3.80
1927–28	10	44	220	836	3.67
1928–29	10	44	220	642	2.80
1929–30	10	44	220	1301	5.69

1 NHL 1917–18 to 1999–2000; one team (Montreal Wanderers) dropped out of league during 1917–18 season.
2 Amount of overtime not verified.

had been responding with small adjustments to the rules on offsides and forward passing, intended to reinvigorate scoring but instead making it more difficult – the new rules only better facilitated teams' ability to clear their own zone, but not to move the puck in the attacking zone, where forward passing was still illegal. As scoring continued to plummet, other, more complicated rules were installed, "anti-defence" rules limiting how many players could occupy their own zone when not backchecking, penalizing ragging the puck, restricting the unabated increase in the size of goalie equipment, and so on, all to no avail. The 1920s are a microcosm of the conditions that have alternately enabled and frustrated scoring through the history of the game, the kind of thing you have to keep in mind every time you hear some commentator with a copy of the record book, but no clue about the game's evolution, marvel at Joe Malone's 44 goals in 20 games in the NHL's goals-by-the-truckload maiden season, or George Hainsworth's 0.98 goals-against average and 22 shutouts in 44 games in the goals-by-the-thimbleful 1928–29 season. Go to the blackboard and write one hundred times: *Statistics without context are meaningless.*

Demonstrating the lack of foresight and clear thinking that have become the NHL's hallmark, the league threw its hands up at the scoring drought and began the 1929–30 season by doing away with almost any restrictions on passing whatsoever. Scoring mushroomed, of course, but the game became a farce of goal-hanging forwards camped in front of opposition nets while play carried on at the opposite end. A month into the season, the NHL governors convened to work out a more sensible system. The first 66 games had produced an average of 6.91 goals per game; the last 154, 5.49. Further modification of the rules governing offside and forward passing, enacted for 1930–31, represent the rules essentially in place ever since, and for all practical purposes the arrival of the game's modern era. The only exception was the continuation of the rule requiring the puck be carried, and not passed, across the blue line when exiting the defensive zone. Regular-season overtime, which had always been played when regulation time ended with the score tied – but always as one or more full periods regardless of how many goals were scored – was limited to 10 minutes beginning in 1928–29.

We can't emphasize strongly enough how significant these years were, and still are, for hockey. From the late 'teens through the 1920s and with the dawn of the '30s, all the fundamental elements that make hockey the game we know and love clicked into place – universal acceptance of the six-man game, standardized full-size rinks, the four-by-six-foot goalmouth, three 20-minute periods, the modern offside rules – all the basic elements and basic geometries that have remained hockey's consistent, reliable parameters for 70 years. To make changes to what's been perfected is to make it imperfect. When you hear suggestions that the rink should be made 15 feet wider, or the goal 6 inches or 2 feet larger, or other such ugly malarkey that would radically alter the standards against which more than 70 years of performance are measured, you have to realize, to recognize, that these are the voices of philistines with no appreciation for the game or its past – and that at best, they are insane over-reactions to the natural fluctuations in scoring levels that occur no matter how stable the league. The NHL today finds itself in another scoring drought – nothing to compare with the late '20s, mind you – and the much-bruited notions for "fixing the game" are ghastly and nauseating. There are reasons for that drought, easy to demonstrate and easy to address, and none of them have anything to do with any misguided suspicion that the most fundamental elements of the game itself are somehow in need of "fixing."

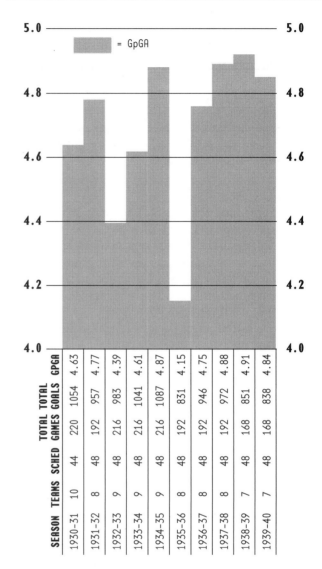

SEASON	TEAMS	SCHED	TOTAL GAMES	TOTAL GOALS	GPGA
1930–31	10	44	220	1054	4.63
1931–32	8	48	192	957	4.77
1932–33	9	48	216	983	4.39
1933–34	9	48	216	1041	4.61
1934–35	9	48	216	1087	4.87
1935–36	8	48	192	831	4.15
1936–37	8	48	192	946	4.75
1937–38	8	48	192	972	4.88
1938–39	7	48	168	851	4.91
1939–40	7	48	168	838	4.84

During the 1930s, a couple of tail-end franchises dropped out of the NHL, one to return briefly and drop out again, but the '30s were really an age of unprecedented stability for major-league hockey, an Age of Equilibrium. Scoring through the decade reflected that stability, staying in a consistent, narrow range of about 4.2 to 4.9 goals per game.

It would take the global upheaval of World War II to upset hockey's equilibrium, and the effects were soon seen. The war years were the "Age of Military Leave" for the NHL. Between 1939 and 1942, 90 NHL players enlisted or were drafted into military service, which surely helped the Allied cause but devastated the level of play in pro hockey. Quality defence players – goalies, rearguards, and forwards who could backcheck – always at a premium, were replaced by bush-leaguers, and play became sloppier and more wide-open as the war raged on. The 1939–40 scoring average of 4.84 goals per game soared, topping 5 a game in 1940–41 for the first time since 1929–30, topping 6 a game in 1941–42 for the first time since the mid-'20s, topping 7 a

History

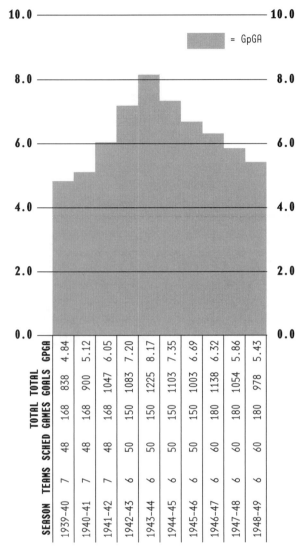

SEASON	TEAMS	SCHED GAMES	TOTAL GAMES	TOTAL GOALS	GPGA
1939-40	7	48	168	838	4.84
1940-41	7	48	168	900	5.12
1941-42	7	48	168	1047	6.05
1942-43	6	50	150	1083	7.20
1943-44	6	50	150	1225	8.17
1944-45	6	50	150	1103	7.35
1945-46	6	50	150	1003	6.69
1946-47	6	60	180	1138	6.32
1947-48	6	60	180	1054	5.86
1948-49	6	60	180	978	5.43

■ = GpGA

[1] We've included the figures from the preceding season and several that follow in order to emphasize the anomalous nature of scoring levels during the war years.

game in 1942–43 for the first time in 20 years, and busting the bulb on the thermometer in 1943–44 at more than 8 a game for the first time in more than two decades – a figure that wouldn't be rivalled for another 40 years.

One significant rule change occurred in this era: the introduction of the centre red line, which finally allowed teams to pass the puck from their own zone to a teammate in the neutral zone, rather than having to carry it out. This alteration is universally, but misleadingly, referred to as the signal moment of the game's "modern era," and inevitably described as "a move designed to speed up the game." In fact, it was only a small adjustment to the offside rules put in place for 1930–31. And it really didn't "speed up the game" so much as provide more back-and-forth flow and limit long spells of play at one end or the other. By allowing a team to clear its zone with a pass instead of a stickhandling foray or a clearing pass right back to the opponent, defence

was aided as much as offence, and the real beneficiary was the transition game. Also of note: regular-season overtime was done away with early in the 1942–43 campaign, mainly as a concession to wartime travel schedules.

After the disruption and horror of the war, you can't blame anybody for wanting to come home to something safe and stable. Hockey provided that, reliably, without change or interruption, for the next 22 years. This, of course, is the era remembered with such affection by older fans as the days of "The Original Six" – although since the NHL began with only four, and only two of them had survived, it's a bit of a misnomer; perhaps "The Age of Stasis" would be a more appropriate title. Post-war scoring levels descended almost as quickly as they had risen, and, once settled, churned on steadily, season after season, never varying outside a range of 4.8 to 6.1 goals per game for any season from 1947–48 to 1966–67, nor ever showing a change of more than 0.43 goals a game from one of those seasons to the next. There were no franchise failures, additions, or relocations between 1943 and 1967; no rule changes of any earth-shattering significance; practically the biggest change of note was the referees going from white sweaters to the familiar striped shirts in 1955. In a way, hockey reflected the conservative insularity of North American life in general during the Eisenhower–Diefenbaker years.

Having discovered the game in the first years of the expansion era that followed, we often rolled our eyes at the bland routine NHL hockey offered during the long days of the Original Six. But now, sharing the feeling of many fans that we're all suffering under the old Chinese curse that hopes we "live in interesting times," the stability and dependable familiarity of the Original Six seems a thing devoutly to be wished. Still, there were drawbacks; fondly as the era may be remembered in Toronto, Montreal, and Detroit, it probably seems a vast wasteland to fans in Boston, Chicago, and New York. The first three teams held a virtual hegemony in on-ice power from 1949 to 1966. Montreal never missed the playoffs during those years, Detroit missed just twice, Toronto only three times – while the Bruins, Black Hawks, and Rangers *combined* to finish higher than third a total of just six times, and none of them won a single regular-season title in that span. In fact, starting in 1942, Toronto and Montreal each won the Stanley Cup 10 times in the next 26 years, and Detroit won it 5 times. Chicago's surprising Cup victory in 1961 was the only interruption to the Leafs', Habs', and Red Wings' exclusive party. The handful of teams competing ensured a tremendous concentration of talent in the NHL, but relegated dozens of NHL-calibre players to lives in the minor leagues. Worst of all, though, insularity discouraged innovation. While the game was growing, evolving, developing in Europe and the Soviet Union, it was stagnating in the NHL. One notable exception: Boston's puck-rushing, forechecking, backchecking, seeing-eye-pass-dealing, heat-seeking-missile-firing backliner

History

13

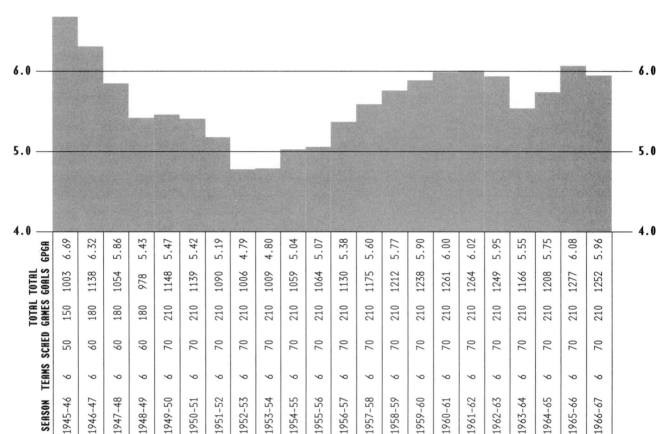

■ = GpGA

SEASON	TEAMS	SCHED GAMES	TOTAL GAMES	TOTAL GOALS	GPGA
1945-46	6	50	150	1003	6.69
1946-47	6	60	180	1138	6.32
1947-48	6	60	180	1054	5.86
1948-49	6	60	180	978	5.43
1949-50	6	70	210	1148	5.47
1950-51	6	70	210	1139	5.42
1951-52	6	70	210	1090	5.19
1952-53	6	70	210	1006	4.79
1953-54	6	70	210	1009	4.80
1954-55	6	70	210	1059	5.04
1955-56	6	70	210	1064	5.07
1956-57	6	70	210	1130	5.38
1957-58	6	70	210	1175	5.60
1958-59	6	70	210	1212	5.77
1959-60	6	70	210	1238	5.90
1960-61	6	70	210	1261	6.00
1961-62	6	70	210	1264	6.02
1962-63	6	70	210	1249	5.95
1963-64	6	70	210	1166	5.55
1964-65	6	70	210	1208	5.75
1965-66	6	70	210	1277	6.08
1966-67	6	70	210	1252	5.96

History

14

Bobby Orr, whose spectacular talent and sense for the game found him busy revolutionizing the defenceman's position and permanently influencing the way hockey would be played.

Given the greed and conservatism of NHL owners, it must have taken quite some job of salesmanship to convince them to relinquish their claims on hundreds of players in their systems and share the wealth with the six new teams those players would stock. But, apparently persuaded by the promise of new major markets in which to grow and popularize the game, and by the millions of dollars in expansion fees on the table, the NHL agreed to expand for 1967–68 – although expansion is really too modest a word. The league fully doubled in size, from six teams to twelve, adding the "Second Six" – Pittsburgh, which had been home to one of the IPL teams at the turn of the century and an NHL team in the 1920s; Philadelphia and St. Louis, which had both briefly hosted NHL teams in the 1930s; Minnesota, a bona fide American hockey hotbed; and Los Angeles and Oakland,

which had long minor-league traditions but were really chosen only to establish a West Coast presence.

Fears that quality of play would suffer with the sudden influx of new players were not realized; there were a hundred guys with major-league talent who had been excluded from the NHL simply because there hadn't been enough roster spots to go around, and league-wide scoring remained stable. Talent began to thin a bit with the overdue admission of Buffalo and Vancouver to the NHL in 1970. Dilution became an evident problem when the NHL added two more teams – Atlanta and Long Island – in 1972, and another two – Washington and Kansas City – in 1974. The third and fourth expansions were mainly pre-emptive strikes against the rebel World Hockey Association, which was formed in 1972. The WHA's 12 clubs lured away many of the NHL's star players, and journeymen as well, with the high salaries they'd been denied during the NHL's long monopoly. The war of attrition between the two leagues, the raiding of players, the battle for territory, was a raucous

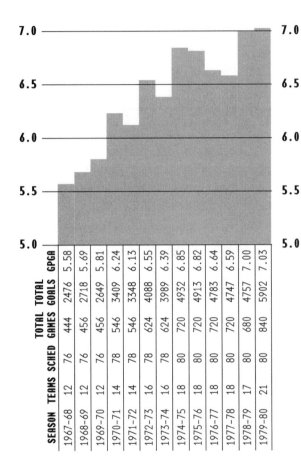

SEASON	TEAMS	SCHED	TOTAL GAMES	TOTAL GOALS	GPGA
1967–68	12	76	444	2476	5.58
1968–69	12	76	456	2718	5.69
1969–70	12	76	456	2649	5.81
1970–71	14	78	546	3409	6.24
1971–72	14	78	546	3348	6.13
1972–73	16	78	624	4088	6.55
1973–74	16	78	624	3989	6.39
1974–75	18	80	720	4932	6.85
1975–76	18	80	720	4913	6.82
1976–77	18	80	720	4783	6.64
1977–78	18	80	720	4747	6.59
1978–79	17	80	680	4757	7.00
1979–80	21	80	840	5902	7.03

= GpGA

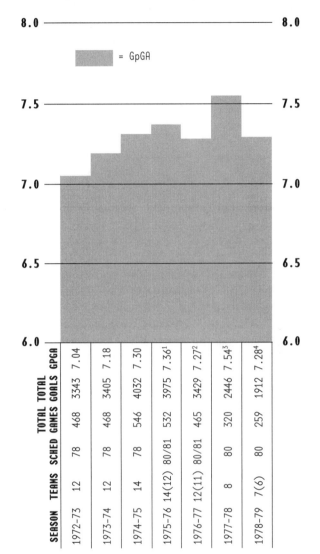

SEASON	TEAMS	SCHED	TOTAL GAMES	TOTAL GOALS	GPGA
1972–73	12	78	468	3343	7.04
1973–74	12	78	468	3405	7.18
1974–75	14	78	546	4032	7.30
1975–76	14(12)	80/81	532	3975	7.36[1]
1976–77	12(11)	80/81	465	3429	7.27[2]
1977–78	8	80	320	2446	7.54[3]
1978–79	7(6)	80	259	1912	7.28[4]

= GpGA

return to hockey's Ages of Disorder and Contentiousness. Regrettable things were said. Innocent lives were lost. Many were the Minions of Klortho who learned what it was to be cast into the Fiery Pit of Zuul in *those* days, we can tell you!

Between the WHA and the NHL's mad scramble to thwart them by putting new franchises in any remaining city in North America capable of supporting a team, major-league hockey grew to a bloated total of 30 teams – far, far too many to be supplied by major-league talent. Thank God we'll never see a situation like *that*, again, eh? As talent became ever more thinly dispersed, defence, as always, suffered most. Just as when the addition of new teams to the PCHA and NHA in 1916 siphoned the tiny pool of available talent, and just as when the war took top-flight talent away from the league in the 1940s, the introduction of lesser players again damaged the league-wide quality of defence, causing scoring to climb. Bush-league players who had been

1 Two teams dropped out during the season, requiring adjustments to the schedule that resulted in four of the remaining teams each playing one additional game.
2 One team dropped out during the season, requiring adjustments to the schedule that resulted in eight of the remaining teams each playing one additional game.
3 Each team played one game against the Czechoslovakian National Team and one against the Soviet National "B" Team, the results of which counted in the standings.
4 One team dropped out during the season. Each of the remaining six teams played one game against the Czechoslovakian National Team and one against the Soviet National Team, the results of which counted in the standings, as did a single game between one WHA team and the Moscow Dinamo.

allowed to invade the NHL and fill out expansion-era rosters watched as better players skated circles around them; their only resort was to hold, hook, clutch, and grab, and in the case of Philadelphia, to incite mayhem and thuggery as an intimidating tactic. The Flyers' pro wrestling strategies were wildly popular with millions of fans of questionable taste – gaining nationwide publicity for an NHL that had never been more than a marginalized, regional sport in the United States – and the league relaxed its enforcement of the rules. Other teams quickly followed suit; smart, clean, well-positioned defensive play began to

History

15

devolve into clutch and grab, and bench-clearing brawls were almost a nightly feature through the mid-'70s.

History is written by the victors, and in the war between the NHL and the WHA, you know who that was. The WHA wound up getting the blame for everything that was wrong with hockey in the 1970s, but the NHL's first serious rival in more than 45 years was really an overwhelmingly positive influence on the game. Twenty years down the road, the NHL would take witless pride in featuring the very things for which it had, in the '70s, condemned and derided the WHA – overexpansion, sloppy play, franchise relocations, and ugly uniforms, for instance. But the rebel circuit maintained competitive balance among its clubs and played its games with a panache rarely seen in the button-down NHL. Most commendably, and most influentially, it was the WHA that first turned its eyes to Europe in a search for talent; while its transatlantic hunt was born of desperation, it soon discovered the marvellous skills of the best players from Scandinavia and Czechoslovakia – and in signing them incited the influx of amazing European talent in the '70s that has continued to this day, to the benefit of the game and its fans. Plenty of the Europeans who played in the WHA and then the NHL were no better than the other North American bushers padding out rosters in both leagues, but the best among them brought with them the swirling, cycling, criss-crossing Euro-style of hockey. Its emphasis on skating and passing was an often beautiful contrast to the lane-bound, hard-nosed North American style, which had won the illusion of superiority with Canada's narrow victory over the Soviets in the heart-stopping Summit Series of 1972.

Euro-style hockey soon dominated the WHA, especially after a Winnipeg team comprising largely Swedish and Finnish players became the new league's most exciting team and won the first of its three Avco World Trophy championships. The NHL and the media had it that WHA play was a scrambly, wide-open affair, its inflated scoring levels marking it as indelibly minor-league. But in fact WHA scoring exceeded the contemporary NHL rate only slightly, and two years after the WHA surrendered, NHL scoring surpassed the WHA's highest mark and stayed there until the mid-1980s. The WHA, from its inception, also featured the return of regular-season overtime – ten minutes, as had been the custom in the NHL from 1928–29 until 1942 – but in a sudden-death format, as in the playoffs. Give the WHA immense credit, too, for putting a far larger share of the financial profits in the players' pockets, where it's always belonged; for putting more major-league hockey back in Canada, where it's always belonged; and for putting the smug, stodgy NHL on its ear, where it's often, if not always, belonged.

With the WHA facing financial collapse after the 1978–79 season, the NHL reasserted its monopoly on major-league hockey by admitting the four remaining charter WHA clubs

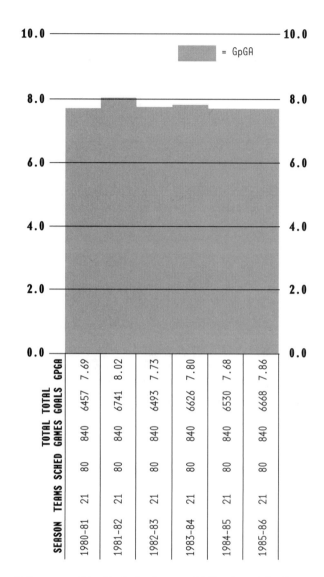

SEASON	TEAMS	SCHED GAMES	TOTAL GAMES	TOTAL GOALS	GPGA
1980-81	21	80	840	6457	7.69
1981-82	21	80	840	6741	8.02
1982-83	21	80	840	6493	7.73
1983-84	21	80	840	6626	7.80
1984-85	21	80	840	6530	7.68
1985-86	21	80	840	6668	7.86

– Edmonton, Hartford, Quebec, and Winnipeg. The former WHA teams, however, as a condition of joining the senior league, were first stripped of almost all their players by the NHL. Those players, and those from the two other disbanded WHA clubs, were returned to the NHL teams that last held their rights; the four WHA teams the NHL had taken in were then supplied by an expansion draft.

While the WHA teams had been dismantled and divided, though, the Euro-hockey influence, carried in its players, insinuated itself into the NHL. Under better conditions, this cross-cultural pollination might have been as happy a success as it had been in the defeated World league. But too many NHL teams and players tried to copy what they perceived as the freewheeling chaos of Euro-style offence while failing to recognize or understand the patterns within it – and defences, already reduced to a clutch-and-grab standard, were equally as baffled by forwards who refused to stay in their familiar lanes. All the nasty things the NHL had

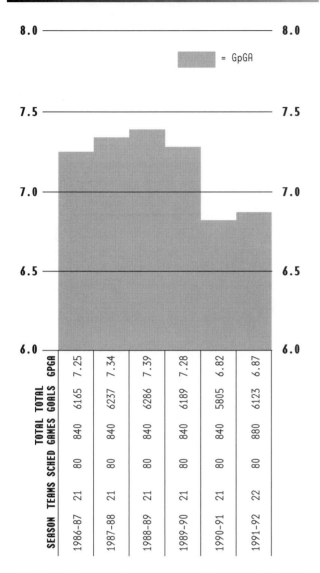

SEASON	TEAMS	SCHED GAMES	TOTAL GAMES	TOTAL GOALS	GPGA
1986-87	21	80	840	6165	7.25
1987-88	21	80	840	6237	7.34
1988-89	21	80	840	6286	7.39
1989-90	21	80	840	6189	7.28
1990-91	21	80	840	5805	6.82
1991-92	22	80	880	6123	6.87

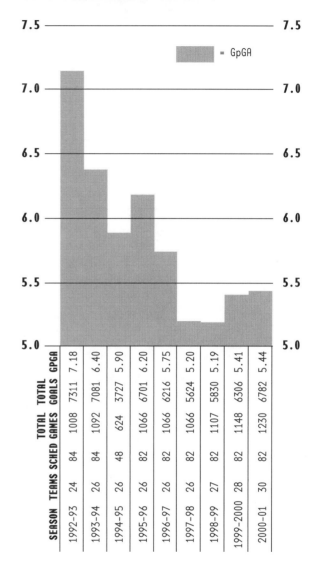

SEASON	TEAMS	SCHED GAMES	TOTAL GAMES	TOTAL GOALS	GPGA
1992-93	24	84	1008	7311	7.18
1993-94	26	84	1092	7081	6.40
1994-95	26	48	624	3727	5.90
1995-96	26	82	1066	6701	6.20
1996-97	26	82	1066	6216	5.75
1997-98	26	82	1066	5624	5.20
1998-99	27	82	1107	5830	5.19
1999-2000	28	82	1148	6306	5.41
2000-01	30	82	1230	6782	5.44

said about the WHA became true of the NHL in the early 1980s. Offences ran amok, and games often resembled the directionless, high-speed, slapdash, fire-at-will action of Air Hockey. But for the worst of the war years, the NHL hadn't seen goals being scored so freely and with such abandon since the league's infancy 60 years before. Following the WHA's lead, the NHL also reintroduced regular-season overtime in 1983–84 after an absence of 40 years, albeit an almost pointless, five-minute, sudden-death micro-overtime. And amid all this, feeding the scoring frenzy and feeding off it, there arose a single offensive force of unprecedented brilliance, the greatest and most influential player since Bobby Orr first left his mark of offensive genius on the game more than a decade earlier – a kid named Gretzky.

The goal-scoring fever broke in 1986–87, as several years with a stable number of franchises (and only one relocation!) seemed to bring order, an integration of styles, and an improved level of play. Scoring dropped by more than

half a goal a game, stayed closer to a healthy seven than a red and swollen eight – despite Gretzky's continuing exploits and the arrival of Mario Lemieux, the only player to challenge Gretzky's jaw-dropping raw numbers. Balance had been restored – or really, had restored itself. You knew it couldn't last long.

No, the NHL just couldn't resist diddling around again. Presented with a game as healthy on the ice as it had been in at least 20 years, the league quickly began working to destabilize the quality of the game, the one thing that the league should be concerned with above all else. While the groundwork for some of this was laid under the previous administrations of NHL presidents John Ziegler and Gil Stein, it's no coincidence that almost all of it has transpired during Gary Bettman's ensconcement as NHL commissioner. One expansion team in 1991–92, among the 21 established clubs on hand, could be accommodated, no matter how unnecessary or unwelcome it was, but two

History

17

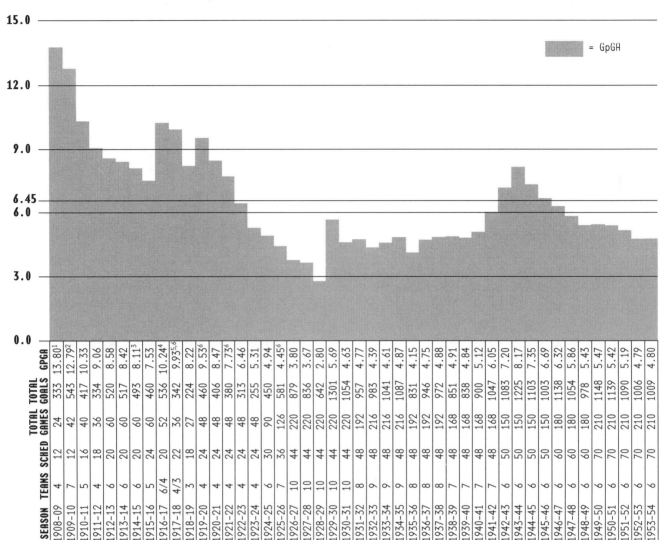

= GpGA

Season	Teams	Total Games Sched	Total Games	Total Goals	GPGA
1908–09	4	12	24	333	13.80[1]
1909–10	7	12	42	543	12.79[2]
1910–11	5	16	40	417	10.33
1911–12	4	18	36	334	9.06
1912–13	6	20	60	520	8.58
1913–14	6	20	60	517	8.42
1914–15	6	20	60	493	8.11[3]
1915–16	6	24	60	460	7.53
1916–17	6/4	20	52	536	10.24[4]
1917–18	4/3	22	36	342	9.93[5,6]
1918–19	3	18	27	224	8.22
1919–20	4	24	48	460	9.53[6]
1920–21	4	24	48	406	8.47
1921–22	4	24	48	380	7.73[6]
1922–23	4	24	48	313	6.46
1923–24	4	24	48	255	5.31
1924–25	6	30	90	450	4.94
1925–26	7	36	126	581	4.45[6]
1926–27	10	44	220	879	3.80
1927–28	10	44	220	836	3.67
1928–29	10	44	220	642	2.80
1929–30	10	44	220	1301	5.69
1930–31	10	44	220	1054	4.63
1931–32	8	48	192	957	4.77
1932–33	9	48	216	983	4.39
1933–34	9	48	216	1041	4.61
1934–35	9	48	216	1087	4.87
1935–36	8	48	192	831	4.15
1936–37	8	48	192	946	4.75
1937–38	8	48	192	972	4.88
1938–39	7	48	168	851	4.91
1939–40	7	48	168	838	4.84
1940–41	7	48	168	900	5.12
1941–42	7	48	168	1047	6.05
1942–43	6	50	150	1083	7.20
1943–44	6	50	150	1225	8.17
1944–45	6	50	150	1103	7.35
1945–46	6	50	150	1003	6.69
1946–47	6	60	180	1138	6.32
1947–48	6	60	180	1054	5.86
1948–49	6	60	180	978	5.43
1949–50	6	70	210	1148	5.47
1950–51	6	70	210	1139	5.42
1951–52	6	70	210	1090	5.19
1952–53	6	70	210	1006	4.79
1953–54	6	70	210	1009	4.80

1 ECHA 1908–09.
2 NHA 1909–10 to 1916–17.
3 Includes one unplayed, forfeited game.
4 Two teams (228th Battalion and Toronto Blueshirts) dropped out of league during season.
5 NHL 1917–18 to 1999–2000; one team (Montreal Wanderers) dropped out of league during 1917–18 season.
6 Amount of overtime not verified.

History

18

more in 1992–93 signalled the coming of the Age of Miserable Greed. Every new franchise was merely a new bank vault full of expansion fees – a new revenue stream for the other owners – and not a response to any realistic demand for new major-league hockey teams. Two more were added the following season, another franchise was slapped together in 1998, and one more in '99, and still two more made their dreaded debut in 2000–01 to a chorus of catcalls from throngs of fans already sickened by the endless dilution of the game. Nine new teams in nine years, almost 200 new players in the NHL who wouldn't have been good enough to play in the league had they been around just nine years ago. And while the NHL dissipated itself into a noisy haze – plopping franchises down in any

American city with a parking lot, enough grandstanding local politicians to wheedle millions in arena construction funds out of the local taxpayers, and a crazy owner to turn that heap of cash over to the NHL as an expansion payment – the league allowed teams to abandon cities where the fans actually knew and loved the game: Minnesota were thrown in the trunk of a car and driven down to Dallas in 1993, Quebec were kidnapped to Denver in '95, Winnipeg were dragged off to Phoenix in '96, and Hartford were shanghaied to somewhere in the Carolinas in '97.

Exacerbating the ugly spectacle, the NHL achieved parity with the other major sports in one area: team finances, player salaries, and management-labour squabbling. The owners locked out the players in the biggest labour dispute,

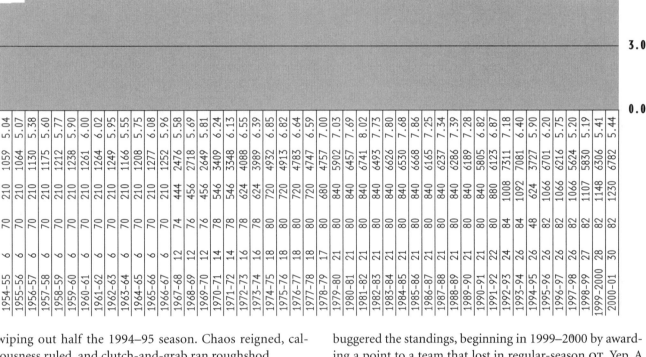

Season	Scoring Avg	Goals	Games	Games/Team	Teams
1954-55	5.04	1059	210	70	6
1955-56	5.07	1064	210	70	6
1956-57	5.38	1130	210	70	6
1957-58	5.60	1175	210	70	6
1958-59	5.77	1212	210	70	6
1959-60	5.90	1238	210	70	6
1960-61	6.00	1261	210	70	6
1961-62	6.02	1264	210	70	6
1962-63	5.95	1249	210	70	6
1963-64	5.55	1166	210	70	6
1964-65	5.75	1208	210	70	6
1965-66	6.08	1277	210	70	6
1966-67	5.96	1252	210	70	6
1967-68	5.58	2476	444	74	12
1968-69	5.69	2718	456	76	12
1969-70	5.81	2649	456	76	12
1970-71	6.24	3409	546	78	14
1971-72	6.13	3348	546	78	14
1972-73	6.55	4088	624	78	16
1973-74	6.39	3989	624	78	16
1974-75	6.85	4932	720	80	18
1975-76	6.82	4913	720	80	18
1976-77	6.64	4783	720	80	18
1977-78	6.59	4747	720	80	18
1978-79	7.00	4757	680	80	17
1979-80	7.03	5902	840	80	21
1980-81	7.69	6457	840	80	21
1981-82	8.02	6741	840	80	21
1982-83	7.73	6493	840	80	21
1983-84	7.80	6626	840	80	21
1984-85	7.68	6530	840	80	21
1985-86	7.86	6668	840	80	21
1986-87	7.25	6165	840	80	21
1987-88	7.34	6237	840	80	21
1988-89	7.39	6286	840	80	21
1989-90	7.28	6189	840	80	21
1990-91	6.82	5805	840	80	21
1991-92	6.87	6123	880	80	22
1992-93	7.18	7311	1008	84	24
1993-94	6.40	7081	1092	84	26
1994-95	5.90	3727	624	48	26
1995-96	6.20	6701	1066	82	26
1996-97	5.75	6216	1066	82	26
1997-98	5.20	5624	1066	82	26
1998-99	5.19	5830	1107	82	27
1999-2000	5.41	6306	1148	82	28
2000-01	5.44	6782	1230	82	30

Graph vertical axis labels: 15.0, 12.0, 9.0, 6.45, 6.0, 3.0, 0.0

wiping out half the 1994–95 season. Chaos reigned, callousness ruled, and clutch-and-grab ran roughshod.

The league so overextended itself, inventing franchises for its shortsighted cash grab – and, in so doing, grossly overtaxing the talent pool – that for the first time, expansion actually *lowered* scoring levels. Frustratingly effective defensive systems – the only resort for most clubs, the dearth of capable scorers and playmakers making it impossible for them to mount a wide-open attack – combined with an unprecedented neglect in enforcing obstruction fouls, an ironic zero-tolerance policy (ineffectively enforced by video surveillance, no less) on players trespassing in an enlarged goal crease, and the exponential growth in the size of goalie equipment, to reduce scoring to levels not seen in more than 40 years. On top of all that, the NHL sent forth its stalking horse for an eventual move to change six-man hockey to five-man "hockey" – reducing the number of skaters to four a side in regular-season overtime. Then the league even buggered the standings, beginning in 1999–2000 by awarding a point to a team that lost in regular-season OT. Yep. A point for losing.

Behold, now, the All-Time ECHA-NHA-NHL Scoring Table. The line running straight through the graph represents the average season scoring level over the 93 years of that ECHA-NHA-NHL continuum – and what, after all that time, through all the scoring gluts and scoring droughts, might be thought of as a sort of ideal figure toward which hockey tends – 6.45 goals per game.

The game's changed a lot over the years. It's different now than the balanced if diluted game it was 6 or 7 years ago, when it was different than the Air Hockey it was 15 years ago, when it was different than the fistic abattoir it was 25 years ago, when it was different than the insular, rugged, lane-conscious game it was 35 years ago, and so on. And you surely don't need our permission to have your own preference for a more wide-open style or a more physical, close-checking, defensive style, or some combination or some point in between. There really aren't any "good old days," in a sense: every era of hockey has had its frustrations, its irritations, its drawbacks.

We all can recognize, however, the difference between quality play, of whatever style and whatever level of offensive production, and boring, ineptly played junk, which is plainly what we have in a league expanded beyond solidity or stability. Until the 1990s, though, every era of the NHL had this, at least: a manageable number of teams (playing in cities with some tradition in hockey), with a recognizable cast of NHL-quality players (whom fans knew and could keep track of), playing games that at least seemed to mean something (that the players at least seemed to care about and the fans surely did) and which fans could afford to attend. Today, the NHL is 1,200-some dreary wrestling matches between teams in cartoonish uniforms, played in sterile new megaplex stadia that have replaced the game's old, character-rich cathedrals, and most of those games seem to be between Florida and Phoenix or Carolina and Tampa Bay.

There ya go. One more good reason to immerse yourself in the game's history instead of trying to work up any interest in what's happening in the NHL today. All right, let's do that. Now that we have a detailed context in which to place all the goals and assists, and wins and losses, and plusses and minuses, and shots and saves, let's get to what we came here to do: figure out which players and which teams have really been the best and the worst, the most overrated and underrated, and the most fun to think about as the Nashville Predators face off against the Mighty Ducks of Anaheim.

2.
Teams

Wayne Gretzky and Gordie Howe walk into a bar. Howe sits down and says to the bartender, "Put a drink in front of the greatest hockey player of all time." Gretzky sits down next to Howe and says, "Yeah, put a drink in front of the greatest hockey player of all time." The bartender pours two drinks – and walks away with them and out of sight. "What was *that* about?" Howe and Gretzky ask when the bartender returns. "You told me to pour a drink for the greatest hockey player of all time," says the barkeep, "so I did. And I served them to Mario Lemieux and Bobby Orr in the back room."

Ba-da-dum.

Then there's the one about the 1956 Canadiens and the 1986 Oilers . . .

Point is, everybody likes to argue – in a cordial, respectful way, of course – about which player is better, which team is better. Was Gretzky better than Howe? Is Lemieux better than Gretzky? Was Orr better than any of them? And wait, what about the Rocket, eh? You've probably got your own opinion already, and nothing anybody can say is going to change your mind. If you head down to the local arena, though, or the local sports bar, or, better yet, if you poke around the Internet, you can probably find someone making their own self-assured, impassioned case for Lindros, or Kariya, or

Darcy Tucker, or for the '98 Red Wings or the Leafs of 1967 or any Montreal Canadiens team *ever*.

Problem is, these debates inevitably fall back on some subjective, emotional viewpoint for support. Howe was better than Gretzky because he was so much tougher and had to backcheck! Gretzky is better than Howe because he played so much smarter, and just look at the numbers! Lemieux is better than Gretzky because he was so much bigger and wasn't surrounded by other superstars! Or, the 1980s Oilers were the best ever because they were so much faster and more exciting! The 1970s Flyers were the best because they were so much meaner and tougher! The 1960s Leafs were the best because they had so much more discipline and heart!

Well, as the old saying goes, you can't measure heart – nor for that matter can you weigh toughness, nor calibrate excitement, nor put hockey smarts on a scale. Nor should you try, nor put much stock in any of those grids that show up a couple of times a year in almost any hockey periodical purporting to do exactly that – breaking down individual players by various qualities, such as "skill" and "size" and "spirit," putting them all on a scale of 0 to 5 or 1 to 10, and always giving all of them equal weight in some sort of "formula" that just adds up those numbers and thereby pretends to provide an absolute rating for players or teams. These things are fine as an amusement, but they have as much scientific validity as adding up the letters in your first name to decode the secret message from the Wishing Well on the last page of the newspaper, and they're misleading and irritating when they try to pass themselves off as real statistics. If you think this team or that player is better than some other team or player, go ahead and say so, but don't claim you've "proven" it by showing that one rates a "3.5" for "hockey sense" and the other only rates a "3." Putting a number value on an opinion doesn't make it anything more than an opinion. Besides, you can't mix opinions and objective statistics into the same formula, and you can't just rush ahead with the assumption that "size," for example, is every bit as important as "skill." You might want to make the argument that it is, but you can't just go ahead and assume it.

And we wouldn't even try. You won't find dissertations in this book that leap right in and try to convince you that, say, the Boston Bruins of 1929–30 were a better team than the Detroit Red Wings of 1997–98, or the other way around either. That's not our objective – and a good thing for us too, because it's frankly impossible. It might be easy to say those ancient Bruins, even bolstered with another eight or nine decent players, would be run out of the rink by the recent Red Wings teams; it would be at least as interesting to conjecture that the Red Wings – sent back in time with only their 10 or 11 best players, suited up in the flimsy equipment and flat-bladed skates of the '20s, each man forced to play 40 or 50 or the whole 60 minutes, by the rules of the day in which obstruction was called by the book – would be left with their tongues hanging out against Boston Hall of Famers such as Marty Barry, Harry Oliver, Dit Clapper, Cooney Weiland, Eddie Shore, and Tiny Thompson. But we'll never know. There's just no way you could ever say for sure one way or the other how it would turn out. Because you can't lift a team out of its time; you can't pull it away from the context of the season in which it played. You can only measure it in the context of its own time and compare it to the teams it actually played against. That will indeed give you something meaningful, though: a useful and intelligently derived set of figures that serve well as a basis for comparison.

How to do that? Well, this a simple point at which to begin. Which was the best team in the NHL in 2000–01? The Stanley Cup champs? Well, fair enough, but that's a whole 'nother argument. Let's confine our discussion to regular-season achievements. The best regular-season team in 2000–01 was Colorado. The awkwardly named Avalanche rolled up 118 points in the standings over 82 games, earning them the cruelly underappreciated President's Trophy. In an 82-game schedule, it's mathematically possible to win every game and capture all 164 points available in the standings. So here's the formula familiar to fans of every other sport: winning percentage. For other sports, that's wins divided by games played; for hockey, it's points divided by points available. A team that wins every single game has a winning percentage of 1.000; a team that loses every single game (and does not manage to secure any of those idiotic points for being tied at the end of regulation time before losing) has a winning percentage of .000; a team that winds up with 82 points after 82 games has a winning percentage of .500. We're sorry if this sounds like kindergarten-primer explanations of basic arithmetic to you, but you wouldn't believe the kind of confusion and resistance that stuff every bit this simple found among some fans and media just 15 years ago, and we want to make sure everybody's up to speed.

So Colorado, without the four asinine bonus points they got for losing in overtime, were a .695 team in 2000–01 (114 points earned, divided by 164 points available, then rounded off). By comparison, Toronto, with 85 actual points, were a .518 club. Benighted Long Island, the league's worst, won at a miserable .299 pace. So what? Why can't we just look at the standings and the points in any given year? Because if we're going to try to make any cross-era, year-to-year comparisons at all, the wide variation in the number of games played by any team in any season makes that awfully difficult. For example, the 1995–96 Red Wings led the NHL that year with a 62-13-7 record – an NHL record for wins – and 131 points. A better rate of success than the 1977–78 Canadiens, who won 59 games and accrued 129 points? The '96 Wings played 82 games, though; the '78 Habs only 80. Detroit were beaten 13 times, Montreal lost just 10. Their winning percentages: Detroit .799, Montreal .806. Again, we apologize if this sounds obvious, but you can't give credit to a team or a player to whom circumstance has given more chances to reach a given total and take credit away from a team or player that wasn't afforded the same opportunity. The 1929–30 Bruins we referred to above played a 44-game schedule; even if they'd won *every one of them*, they'd still have had only 88 points. Had they in fact done that, we're pretty sure we'd all agree it would have been a more remarkable achievement than the '96 Wings' admirable 131 points and .799 winning percentage – or in other words (or other numbers, really), winning not quite four of every five games.

So raw points in the standings won't do, if we want to compare how much success one team had in one season to how much another team had in a different season. We have to use winning percentage.

The All-Time Best Single Seasons

Right then. Let's look at the teams that have had the very best seasons in the history of major-league pro hockey. Just one thing before we do that, however: if you started to sputter out a protest that it would be a lot harder to win every game over the course of an 80- or 82-game schedule than over a 44-game slate, your objection is sustained. The fewer games you play, the easier it is to win all of them (or lose all of them). On the other hand, there's not a single reason to think that a team good enough to win, say, 18 games in a 20-game season wasn't good enough to have won 72 games had their season been 80 games long. But we'll grant you that the longer the season, the truer the test of a team's ability. So we're making a 16-game schedule our minimum criterion for inclusion on this list. And sure enough, that does exclude three memorable sides that played at the dawn of the pro game: the 1908–09 Ottawa Senators of the ECHA, and the NHA's Montreal Wanderers and Ottawa Senators of 1909–10. Since their rosters were so small and their records so remarkable, we'll take a moment to describe the teams for you.

Ottawa rolled up a 10-2 record in 1908–09, good for an .833 winning percentage – the third-best of all time. The Senators featured Marty Walsh, Bruce Stuart, Dubbie Kerr, Billy Gilmour, and Edgar Dey at forward, Cyclone Taylor at cover point, one-eyed Fred Lake at point, and Percy LeSueur in goal; all of them but Kerr, Dey, and Lake wound up in the Hall of Fame. Ottawa, as new champions of the ECHA, were handed possession of the Stanley Cup by Wanderers, who had won the Cup the previous year and defended it successfully after the 1908–09 season against a challenge from Edmonton of the Alberta League.

Ottawa made a few changes going into the 1909–10 NHA season; the team now featured the great forward combination of Kerr, Walsh, and Bruce Ridpath, as well as Stuart and rookie Gordon Roberts (later *Doctor* Gordon Roberts, another Hall of Famer); the long-time defence pairing of Lake and Hamby Shore; speedster Ken Mallen; and LeSueur. The team went 9-3-0 in 1909–10, a .750 clip. As Cup champs, Ottawa had to defend it against challenges from both Galt of the Trolley League and Edmonton of the Alberta League before returning the Cup to Wanderers, the new champions of the NHA. Ridpath, like Walsh, would meet with tragic mishap; his career – though not his life – was ended when he was run over by a car in Toronto the following year.

The Wanderers went 11-1-0 that year – .917 – and would have topped the entire list with the best single-season record ever. In many hockey reference sources, the only evidence of the Wanderers' existence is their 1-5-0 record in the NHL's first year of play, with an asterisk noting they withdrew from the league after their arena burned down. It suggests a team pathetic in its ineptitude, lucklessness, and anonymity. All but forgotten as a result is the fact that between the heyday of the fabled Ottawa Silver Seven and the advent of the NHL, Wanderers were a perennial power in hockey. Ernie Russell, Harry Hyland, Pud Glass, Jimmy Gardner, and Cecil Blachford were the Wanderer forwards this season, Moose Johnson played cover point, Jack

Marshall point, and Riley Hern tended goal; Russell, Hyland, Johnson, Gardner, Marshall, and Hern all wound up in the Hall of Fame. Wanderers won their last ten games in a row; then, having been handed the Stanley Cup by Ottawa, they easily defended it against a challenge from Berlin of the Trolley League.

Now let's look at that list of teams since 1910–11 with the best-ever single-season records – and we'll put some flesh on those bones with a few words on the dozen best of them:

Top 20 Regular-Season Records
(minimum 16-game schedule)

RANK	TEAM	LEAGUE	SEASON	W-L-T	PTS	PCT
1	Boston	NHL	'29–30	38-5-1	77	.875
2	Montreal Can	NHL	'43–44*	38-5-7	83	.830
3	Montreal Can	NHL	'76–77*	60-8-12	132	.825
4	Ottawa	NHA	'10–11*	13-3-0	26	.812
5	Montreal Can	NHL	'77–78*	59-10-11	129	.806
6	Quebec Bul	NHA	'12–13*	16-4-0	32	.800
7	Montreal Can	NHL	'44–45	38-8-4	80	.800
8	Detroit	NHL	'95–96	62-13-7	131	.799
9	Montreal Can	NHL	'75–76*	58-11-11	127	.794
10	Ottawa	NHL	'19–20*	19-5-0	38	.792
11	Boston	NHL	'70–71	57-14-7	121	.776
12	Boston	NHL	'38–39*	36-10-2	74	.771
13	Montreal Can	NHL	'72–73*	52-10-16	120	.769
14	Vancouver	PCHA	'14–15*	13-4-0	26	.765
15	Boston	NHL	'71–72*	54-13-11	119	.763
16	Ottawa	NHA	'16–17**	15-5-0	30	.750
17	Edmonton	NHL	'83–84*	57-18-5	119	.744
18	Edmonton	NHL	'85–86	56-17-7	119	.744
19	New York Isl	NHL	'81–82*	54-16-10	118	.738
20	Philadelphia F	NHL	'75–76	51-13-16	118	.738

* Won Stanley Cup.
** An 8-0 Ottawa victory was charged as a loss after it was determined they had used an ineligible player. Had the victory stood, Ottawa's record would have been 16-4-0 (.800).

1929–30 Boston Bruins

You didn't think we happened to mention the 1929–30 Bruins after just picking them out of a hat, did you? No, we knew darn well that this Boston club had the best regular-season record of any team of the last 90 years. And, presaging the Big Bad Bruins of the early '70s, the first thing that strikes you about them is their overwhelming attack. The '29–30 Bruins rang up 179 goals in their 44 games, almost a goal a game better than the next-best offensive club that season, and a mark that wouldn't be surpassed until the advent of a 50-game schedule and the defensively porous war years. In an attempt to revive scoring, the NHL had made the desperate move in 1929–30 of striking down almost every rule covering offsides. The Bruins took better advantage than any other team.

Remember what we told you about the way NHL scoring had been steadily disappearing down the drain for nine years in a row in the 1920s, and how the NHL finally just gave up on trying to tweak the rules into producing more offence and instead just decided to let pretty much anything go? Passing across blue lines was still forbidden, including passing from your own defensive zone to a teammate in the neutral zone, but there was no restriction on players simply preceding the puck into another zone. Charles Coleman, in his incomparable, indispensable history of the game, *The Trail of the Stanley Cup*, paraphrases ambivalently derisive news accounts of the day: "The reporters said the new rules succeeded in every intended way, speeding up the play and contributing great excitement. However, whether or not the game should be called hockey was a question. In general it is a wild scramble from start to finish, strangely reminiscent of that honourable pastime called shinny."

It was now perfectly legal for one or more attacking players to camp out deep in the opponents' end – then wait for a teammate to carry the puck in, and pass it to them where they had the goaltender at their mercy. Bruin coach Art Ross, the legendary rushing defenceman and hockey labour activist of the pre-NHL days, had his players exploiting the new rules to their full advantage. Dit Clapper and, particularly, Cooney Weiland, were, in Coleman's words, "practically setting up light housekeeping at the side of goal creases." Weiland, the diminutive young centreman, a great stickhandler who couldn't be intimidated, wound up leading the league with 43 goals in 44 games; Clapper, the right winger, another youngster and a huge man by the standards of the day, was just behind with 41 goals. Together with left winger Dutch Gainor, who had by far the best season of his career here, they formed the Dynamite Line; all three finished in the top 10 among NHL scorers that year. Rookie Marty Barry, another gifted stickhandler, centred Boston's other forward line, flanked on the right side by veteran Harry Oliver – a great star with Calgary in the old Western League and the Bruins' leading scorer in 1927 and '29 – and on the left by reliable Perk Galbraith. Spare forwards seeing limited action were Bill Carson, Harry Connor, Bob Taylor, and ancient Mickey MacKay, a Hall of Fame legend with Vancouver in the old PCHA, who helped out here in the final season of his career.

While opponents were overwhelmed by Boston's scoring prowess, those Bruins were also ferocious in their own end of the ice. Boston's defence, likewise, was the NHL's best that season. Tiny Thompson, in the sophomore season of his Hall of Fame career, was impregnable in the nets, but the defence pairing in front of him was fearsome. The lanky veteran Lionel Hitchman, the first-ever captain of the Bruins, was the rugged but clean stay-at-home half of the duo; his partner on the blue line was Eddie Shore. If you know anything about the history of the game, you know about Shore, as storied a character – as a player and later

coach and team owner – as there is in hockey. Shore's penchant for berserker mayhem on the ice and his iron-fisted managerial style off it, however, have almost overshadowed his abilities as one of the greatest defencemen ever to lace up skates. Shore began as a forward with Edmonton in the WCHL and was snapped up by Ross when that league folded. Flawlessly positioned in his own end, Shore was a vicious body-checker up and down the ice, and a great offensive threat rushing the puck, leading NHL defencemen in scoring six times in his first nine NHL seasons. Seven times a first-team All-Star, Shore was four times the winner of the Hart Trophy. Harvard product George Owen, a long-time Boston-area amateur star, spelled the top pair, later joined by former Dartmouth star Myles Lane.

Bruins defeated every other team in the league during a 14-game winning streak that began in December, a record that would stand for 52 years. Later that winter, they won another 12 straight, a mark that stood as the NHL's second-longest for 41 years. Among Boston's handful of just five losses, three of them came at the hands of second-place Chicago. In the playoffs, the Bruins got past Montreal Maroons three games to one in a great, hard-fought series, and awaited the winner of the Canadiens-Rangers' best-of-three. Despite the absence of the injured Gainor, Bruins were heavy favourites to retain the Cup no matter whom they met in the best-of-three Final. It would be the Canadiens, who then easily took the first game, blanking the potent but uninspired Bruins 3-0 in Boston, with George Hainsworth getting the shutout. Bruins travelled to Montreal and mounted a far better effort, but again fell behind 3-0 and then 4-1 before really cranking it up, closing within 4-3 and putting up a great flurry at the end. But Boston couldn't get the equalizer, and just like that, their one-year Cup reign and their magical 38-5-1 season were over. The shorter the series, of course, the less the advantage for the favoured team, and a best-of-three format certainly didn't help Boston. As a result, the NHL went to a best-of-five format for the Cup Final starting the following year.

1943–44 Montreal Canadiens

The number two team on the list is also a team from a year of scoring turmoil in the NHL. The 1943–44 Canadiens rose to excellence amid a league-wide exodus of talent and the inflationary scoring that followed. During World War II, enough NHL players were away in military service to stock another six-team league. Every team lost players to the Allied cause; some, like the Rangers, were brought to their knees by the loss of talent. The Canadiens, however, were little affected, and the depletion of the other clubs, as much as the Habs' own newly burgeoning roster, left Montreal atop the NHL.

The Canadiens of the 1930s and early '40s, in fact, had been a dismally unsuccessful club on the ice; the days of the original Flying Frenchmen were long gone and the team had no more of a dynastic history or mystique than any other NHL franchise. Following back-to-back Cup triumphs in 1930 and '31 and a first-place finish in '32, the Canadiens spent a decade just looking for respectability. In the 11 seasons from 1932–33 to 1942–43, the Habs managed only three winning campaigns – one just a game over .500, another only two games over – and finished last or next to last five times.

French-Canadian ambivalence about the war, however, translated into fewer Quebecois enlistments, which in turn meant the Canadiens organization, with its strong Francophone talent base, wasn't as deeply affected as were other NHL teams. Ranger forward Phil Watson, that team's only French-Canadian player, was unable to obtain a border-crossing permit amid the war-time security measures, shortages, rationing, and travel restrictions of the day, and Montreal benefited again when, as a result, New York essentially loaned him to the Habs for the season. Paul Bibeault, Montreal's number-one goalie the previous two years, was among the few Canadiens who did enlist for military service, and no knock on Bibeault, but this too proved an unforeseen boon for the Habs. Faced with a limited choice of replacements in net, Montreal GM Tommy Gorman and coach Dick Irvin bypassed journeyman Bert Gardiner and teen-aged Gerry McNeil and settled on 28-year-old senior league star Bill Durnan. The ambidextrous Durnan would prove to be the cornerstone of what indeed became a Canadiens dynasty.

Montreal had something else new that year: a forward combination of veteran left winger Toe Blake, young centre-man Elmer Lach, and a ferocious rookie on the right side named Maurice Richard. Blake started out as a fiery winger for Montreal Maroons but never really shone until after he was acquired by Canadiens. He was by far the best thing they had going for them during the late '30s – three times an All-Star, leading the NHL in scoring, and earning the Hart Trophy while playing for a last-place club. Lach, the clever, wiry pivot, would have the first of five All-Star seasons in 1942–43, in a career that saw him overcome numerous injuries to also garner two scoring titles, the Hart, and a berth in the Hall. Richard, of course, was a force of nature on the right wing, one of the great goal scorers in the history of the game, and ascended to virtual godhood throughout Quebec and ultimately all of Canada.

Watson, the pepper-pot right winger, teamed with two nifty veterans – Ray Getliffe and Murph Chamberlain – to give Canadiens two extremely solid lines when most other clubs were lucky to still have one. Habs also got great production from a pint-sized pair of war-era one-hit wonders, Gerry Heffernan and Fern Majeau. Both were stars in the Quebec Senior League, before and after their stint with Canadiens; each played only two years in the NHL; and each put up impressive numbers in only the '43–44 campaign. Bob Fillion also contributed playmaking from the wing.

Montreal were thinner at defence. The top pairing was big Butch Bouchard, who would go on to the Hall, and little Glen Harmon, who proved himself a worthy rearguard through a nine-year career, though both were just kids in '43. Their back-ups were Leo Lamoureux and Mike McMahon, two well-travelled veterans of Quebec senior hockey, who were called up due to the shortage of experienced bodies and did not last much past the end of the war.

Montreal began the season with a 14-game unbeaten streak – an out-of-the-gate standard that would stand for 41 years – and went the entire year without a single loss on home ice. The Canadiens' depth at forward not only helped Montreal lead the league in goals-for, but their domination and Durnan's great work in goal also found Montreal leading the league in goals-against by an enormous margin. It carried Habs to a 38-5-7 mark, a record 25-point bulge over runner-up Detroit in the standings, and right on to the Stanley Cup. Richard exploded in the playoffs, scoring five times in one game as Montreal dumped Toronto four games to one, and notching a hat trick in one game and two in another en route to a sweep of Chicago in the Final.

1976–77 Montreal Canadiens

The Canadiens of '76–77 were in the midst of a four-year monopoly on the Cup, and on full merit; they played it clean, played it brilliantly, led the league in offence and defence, and there wasn't an area on the team that wasn't the best in the NHL. The Montreal attack came in ceaseless waves – swift, elegant right winger Guy Lafleur won the second of his three straight scoring titles, going on a 28-game point-scoring streak along the way; Steve Shutt, the smiling sniper, led the NHL with 60 goals off the left wing; both were set up by smooth, cerebral centre Jacques Lemaire. Big, rangy Peter Mahovlich and yappy Doug Risebrough centred second and third lines; like a good soccer team, Canadiens "packed the midfield with nippy little bastards" – skilful, hyperactive wingmen including Yvon Cournoyer, Mario Tremblay, and Rejean Houle, as well as the more sedate but equally determined Yvon Lambert. Bob Gainey, who always saved his best for the playoffs, teamed with centre Doug Jarvis on the Habs' tenacious checking line and penalty-killing unit. Quiet Murray Wilson provided checking depth at forward, as did sour-faced vet Jim Roberts, who also filled in on defence.

All but impassable on the blue line were the "Big Three" – looming, rock-solid Serge Savard, rugged yet nimble Guy Lapointe, and the ubiquitous rushing rearguard, "Big Bird," Larry Robinson, tough, tall, angular, and the author of a +120 mark on the season. American-born Bill Nyrop, Venezuelan-born Rick Chartraw, and Butch Bouchard's son Pierre also patrolled the Hab zone, and on the occasion an opponent got through all that to register a rare shot on the Montreal net, towering Ken Dryden was there to block and smother it, with Bunny Larocque giving him the occasional night off.

The Habs went 33-1-6 in the Forum, including a record 34-game unbeaten streak at home, and did it all with an unrivalled grace and élan. Canadiens swept St. Louis in four straight in the quarter-finals, polished off the up-and-coming New York Islanders in six in the semis, then dispatched Boston in a four-game sweep to reassert their claim to the Cup.

1910–11 Ottawa Senators

Ottawa showed little drop-off in 1910–11 from the dreadnought sides they'd iced in 1909 and 1910 and which we described earlier. LeSueur was still in goal; Lake, at point, and Shore, at cover point, were still the defence duo; and Walsh, Kerr, and Ridpath were still the top line. Bruce Stuart contributed little this time, in the final season of his career, but the only real major change for Ottawa going into 1910–11 was the departure of Roberts, who had enrolled at McGill University to begin his medical studies and would continue his great hockey career with Wanderers. His place was taken by Horace Gaul, who had had a superb year with Haileybury the previous season but did not prove much of a factor here, and, more auspiciously, by Jack Darragh. Darragh's first game as a pro was on New Year's Eve 1910, in the same game in which Canadiens goaltending legend Georges Vezina made his professional debut. Darragh scored the first goal against Vezina; both played their entire fabulous careers for the same teams with which they began; both earned their places in the Hall of Fame; both died prematurely – Vezina of tuberculosis in 1924, Darragh of peritonitis in 1925. Shore, incidentally, was yet another member of this club to die early, succumbing during the influenza epidemic of 1918–19.

On a happier note, Walsh and Kerr were one and two this season in NHA scoring, Walsh with 37 goals and Kerr with 32, each in 16 games, and Ridpath and Darragh were close behind. The Senators' attack churned out better than 7½ goals a game, fully two per game better than the next best side. Ottawa, in winning the NHA title with their 13-3-0 record, now took possession of the Cup from Wanderers, and defended it with little trouble against challenges from Trolley League champion Galt, and New Ontario League champion Port Arthur.

Also notable from the Ottawa club this season was a dispatch from the team's secretary, Martin Rosenthal, stating that he believed the publication of goal-scoring totals was "spoiling good combination play." He suggested a trophy be presented to the player with the most assists, even though at this point no procedure had even been devised for awarding assists. The following year, NHA president Emmett Quinn voiced a similar concern that "scoring rivalry led to hogging the puck," but as a solution suggested abolishing official scorers altogether.

1977–78 Montreal Canadiens

This was the follow-up edition to the 1976–77 Canadiens, who hold third place on this list. Despite the ample size of their modern-era roster, there were only two personnel changes of any real significance from the team that had won 60 games and its second straight Stanley Cup a year before: rookie Pierre Mondou took his place on the team as a smooth and effective two-way centre, and early in the season, Peter Mahovlich was dealt to Pittsburgh for the artistic but erratic young gunner Pierre Larouche.

The Canadiens rolled on, again healthy and injury-free, again leading the league in scoring – a total boosted by a lethally successful power play – again leading the league in defence, again producing the league's best record. In fact, the '77–78 Habs won just one game less and amassed only three fewer points than the '76–77 version of the club, and went on a 28-game undefeated streak along the way. This time Lafleur was the 60-goal man – the best mark in the NHL – and he won his third consecutive scoring title and second straight Hart Trophy. Canadiens waltzed to another Stanley Cup coronation, blowing away Detroit in five games and Toronto in four straight before meeting Boston for the second year in a row in the Final. Bruins put up a better show this time, tying the series at two games apiece on Boston ice after falling behind two games to none in Montreal, but Habs put it away with a pair of 4-1 victories.

Scotty Bowman established his overblown reputation as a coaching genius while running the Canadiens' bench through the 1970s; while his strategy of disdaining traditional three-man forward line combinations in favour of forward pairs with a rotating variety of plug-ins to complete the line was fairly innovative, Bowman has never once in his long and celebrated NHL career been challenged, nor challenged himself, to take charge of a team that wasn't ready-made to have a strong shot at least at reaching the Stanley Cup Final. The astounding talent he's had to work with over the years has done much more for him than he's done for it.

The real credit for keeping Montreal atop the hockey world from the mid-60s through to the end of the '70s has to go to general manager Sam Pollock. Montreal won the Cup in 1964–65, Pollock's first year at the helm, repeated the next year, and in all claimed the Ancient Tureen nine times in the 14 years Pollock had the GM's office. His best moves came during the early years of expansion, when he often dealt veteran journeymen to new teams in exchange for high draft choices, which he used unerringly to select young stars from junior hockey who promptly became superstars in the NHL. Looking back on some of those trades, Pollock appears to have been taking candy from babies, but he was dealing with veteran hockey executives. Pollock retired after the 1977–78 season, and the club he'd built won the Cup again the following year. While most teams would envy Montreal's two Cup triumphs in the 21 years since, they're a far cry from the relentless dominance Les Habitants displayed during Pollock's tenure.

1912–13 Quebec Bulldogs

While the Canadiens were busy designing a team for Montreal that was built on a foundation of French-Canadian talent, 160 miles northeast, down the St. Lawrence River in Quebec City, M. J. Quinn had already constructed a starring line-up of players of exclusively English and Irish heritage. Their league-leading attack featured a staggering one-two punch of Joe Malone at centre and tiny Tommy Smith on the right wing, each of whom produced one of the great individual goal-scoring performances of all time that season. Phantom Joe, as clean and sportsmanlike a player as he was quick and skilful, scored 43 goals in 20 games here for Quebec, presaging his famous 44-goals-in-20-games outing in the NHL's maiden season; Smith racked up 39 in 19 games, a feat he duplicated two years later. Reliable veteran Jack Marks patrolled the left wing, mammoth and affable Harry Mummery had cover point, and roughhouse Bad Joe Hall the point. Paddy Moran manned the nets in Quebec, as he did for 15 of the 16 years of his career, and Bulldogs were the league's toughest team to score on. Quebec relied almost exclusively on this starting sextet; Rusty Crawford, probably the best defensive forward of his day, was the only sub to make any real contribution.

For the second year in a row Quebec romped over a Stanley Cup challenger from the Maritimes – this time Sydney – and became the first all-professional club to win it back-to-back. Quebec's Cup triumph produced one of our all-time favourite hockey photos – their championship portrait. The entire team, in full uniform, is gathered in what seems to be a wood-panelled Edwardian office with a fireplace in the background. On the carpet in the foreground are the O'Brien Trophy, emblematic of NHA supremacy, the Stanley Cup, and between them the team mascot – not some stupid eight-foot-tall cartoon character, but a proper mascot, a real live English bulldog.

Good as these guys were, they were lucky that the series they played on the West Coast two weeks later was only an exhibition and not for the Cup itself. PCHA champion Victoria, with a powerhouse line-up of their own, including Goldie Prodgers and the immortal Lester Patrick on defence, star forwards Tom Dunderdale, Skinner Poulin, Bobby Rowe, Walt Smaill, and Bob Genge, and with Bert Lindsay – Ted's father – in goal, took the three-game set two games to one. The first and final games were played under western rules – seven-man hockey – the second game, under eastern six-man rules. Quebec had shown their ability with either style, going 3-0 during the NHA's mid-season one-week experiment with a return to the seven-man game, but their only win in the exhibition in Victoria was in that six-man second game.

1944–45 Montreal Canadiens

Like many of the teams on this list, the 1944–45 Habs were no flash in the pan. This was the follow-up edition of the 1943–44 team that ranks second on this list. They again won 38 of their 50 games, and again led the NHL in both offence and defence. Durnan remained the bulwark in the nets; Bouchard and Harmon remained the top defencemen, joined now by Lamoureux and fireplug Frank Eddolls. Getliffe and Chamberlain continued to provide depth at forward. Watson returned to New York, but his place was taken by Buddy O'Connor, the slick, mite-sized pivot. Young Kenny Mosdell, who would go on to a good long career, was called up to make Montreal three-deep at centre, and little Dutch Hiller, the much-travelled journeyman left winger, was reacquired from New York. O'Connor and Hiller both contributed 20-goal seasons here. Fern Gauthier had a career year, adding some scoring power from the right side. But this was the year the Punch Line landed a haymaker. Lach, Richard, and Blake were one-two-three in NHL scoring, and the Rocket blasted 50 goals in 50 games, the first man ever to reach that magical mark or even to exceed Malone's record 44.

Les Habitants stumbled on their way to the Cup, however, as Toronto gained revenge for the previous year's playoff meeting, knocking off Montreal in a great six-game semi-final. Canadiens, though, would reclaim the Cup the following year.

1995–96 Detroit Red Wings

The 1995–96 Wings were the first NHL club in a decade to flirt with an .800 season, and would have been the first in almost 20 years, and one of only eight in the entire modern era, to have accomplished it. They didn't; they fell a thousandth of a percent short. We won't rag 'em for that, though. A 62-win season was something fans in Hockeytown deserved. The Wings had been a very good club for several years leading up to this banner season, but hadn't had a single winning campaign between 1972–73 and 1987–88, and hadn't laid claim to the Stanley Cup since 1955.

The '95–96 club had great depth at centre, which keyed an excellent attack – but far from the NHL's best that year; Detroit's real strength was their mobile defence corps, which was the major factor in their league-best goals-against mark and gave them a marvellous transition game. The rugged Russian Vladimir Konstantinov was their best at the blue line; always superbly positioned, Konstantinov was remarkably strong and a vicious hitter, and could contribute offensively as well. His +60 mark was tops in the league by a wide margin, even though, not surprisingly, four of the NHL's best plus/minus marks belonged to Red Wings. Slava Fetisov, the 37-year-old legend of Soviet hockey, another of five Soviet-bred regulars in the Detroit line-up, was Konstantinov's mentor and a solid contributor at both ends of the ice as well. Paul Coffey, a puck-rushing star in Edmonton and Pittsburgh, was still the big point-producer from the Detroit blue line at the age of 34, and he'd actually learned to play a modicum of defence by this late stage of his celebrated career. The guy who'd emerge from this group as a star for years to come was the clean, nimble Swede, Nicklas Lidstrom, just 25 here but already one of hockey's best in his fifth full NHL season. Three more veteran stay-at-home rearguards, all well past 30 – Mike Ramsey, Marc Bergevin, and Bob Rouse – added reliable depth to the unit. Young Chris Osgood was adequate in goal behind this group, backed up by veteran Mike Vernon.

Up front, versatile Sergei Fedorov was the most productive scorer, clicking for a 107-point season while playing not only centre and left wing but seeing a little time on defence as well, igniting the power play, killing penalties, and chipping in clutch goals. Centre Steve Yzerman, at 30 and in his 13th season in Detroit, remained the Motor City's superstar, giving his unfailingly clean but tenacious effort at both ends of the ice and falling just short of a hundred-point year himself. Early in the season, Detroit acquired another ancient Russian star, 35-year-old centre Igor Larionov, "the Gretzky of Soviet hockey," who produced better than a point a game over the course of the year while enabling Detroit to ice an all-Russian unit of Fetisov, Konstantinov, Fedorov, Larionov, and youngster Vyacheslav Kozlov, who played on the wing as well as at centre.

Other major figures on the club were hulking, aggressive wingman Keith Primeau; 36-year-old winger and stinging gnat Dino Ciccarelli; yet another centre, young Greg Johnson; two lines' worth of checking forwards – clever old vets Bob Errey and Doug Brown, dogged youngsters Tim Taylor and Kris Draper, and combative Darren McCarty and Martin Lapointe. Stu Grimson was along for the ride as the archetypal gigantic lumbering goon.

Detroit ended the history of NHL hockey in Winnipeg when they closed out the Jets in the sixth game of their opening-round playoff series; Red Wings then found themselves down three games to two against St. Louis in the quarter-finals before getting off the mat to beat the Blues as well. Detroit fell, however, to the eventual Cup champion Colorado Avalanche in a six-game semi-final series, and would have to wait one more year before finally hoisting the Old Chalice themselves, for the first time in 42 years.

1975–76 Montreal Canadiens

Yes, yet another edition of those extraordinary Canadiens of the '70s. This was the one that inaugurated the Habs' four-year reign of unprecedented regular-season and playoff dominance. After winning the Cup six times in nine years from 1965 to 1973, Montreal, despite 45- and 47-win campaigns, were without the Auld Mug for two years while the Broad Street Bully Flyers smeared it with their blood-stained fingers. When hockey in its darkest hour needed a true champion, Montreal arose fresher, faster, and stronger than ever to take on the challenge.

Their NHL fourth-best offence in '75–76 was only 11 goals behind Philadelphia's league-high 348. Montreal's defence led the NHL, and they displayed a nearly flawless and admirably clean brand of hockey in an era when mayhem was running amok. Lafleur led all NHL skaters with 125 points, and his 56 goals were second-best in the league. Mahovlich totalled 71 assists, also second-best in the NHL, while amassing 105 points of his own. Shutt ripped in 45 goals, Cournoyer and Lambert 32 each. Robinson, Lapointe, and Savard were the heart of the defence, backed up this year by Bouchard, veteran Don Awrey, and, in his only year in Montreal, Jean Potvin, who by no coincidence had far and away the best season of his long, much-travelled career.

Mahovlich would be dealt to Pittsburgh two years later for Larouche, but almost all the guys here stayed on as the nucleus of the Montreal dynasty: Lafleur, Lemaire, and Shutt; Robinson, Lapointe, and Savard; Gainey, Cournoyer, and Lambert; Houle, Jarvis, Risebrough, and Tremblay – and of course Dryden and his stablemate Larocque.

Les Habitants were on a mission when the playoffs finally arrived. They dispatched Chicago in four straight, then tossed aside a tough and emergent Islander team in five games, setting up an apocalyptic showdown in the Final: the Forces of Darkness – the two-time Cup champion Flyers – against Canadiens, representing the Forces of Light. Montreal reclaimed the Cup with a four-game sweep of Philadelphia, and, having reasserted the supremacy of skill, speed, smarts, sportsmanship, and style over thuggery and clutch-and-grab, would not relinquish the Cup for another four years.

1919–20 Ottawa Senators

The great Ottawa teams of the earliest part of the 20th century earned the sobriquet "The Silver Seven" for their sterling performances in the seven-man hockey of the day; those players had already long passed from the scene, seven-man hockey had been relegated to the West Coast, and Ottawa had gone through several undistinguished seasons, when the post–World War I Senators underwent a renaissance and won a new appellation: "The Super Six."

The 1919–20 sextet was an impressive mix of versatile young veteran players. Up front, Frank Nighbor, the indefatigable centre, by every account the best defensive forward of his day and among the most gentlemanly on-ice performers as well, led Ottawa with 25 goals in 23 games. On his right side, almost equalling his production, was Jack Darragh, another clean player who at 30 was showing no signs of slowing down. Punch Broadbent spelled Darragh and alternated on the left wing with Cy Denneny. Broadbent, a feisty checker along the boards, banged in 19 goals, while Denneny, the young fireplug, equally ready to mix it up when necessary, banged home 16. The rambunctious duo became known as "the Gold Dust Twins," after the inseparable pair of kids that were the trademark of a popular abrasive clean-up powder. Thirty-year-old Eddie Gerard captained the Sens and was a stalwart on defence, rugged but clean and all but impassable. Paired with him was Sprague Cleghorn. Better remembered for his years with Wanderers and Canadiens and best remembered for his vicious, hyper-aggressive style, Cleghorn may have had his best season here with Ottawa, as he kept his legendary temper under control while playing up to his usual level as a fine defender and puck-rusher. George "Buck" Boucher alternated with Gerard and Cleghorn on the blue line and also saw time on the left wing. Guarding the nets was Clint Benedict, the showy, acrobatic goaltender whose frequent dives to the ice while stopping the puck had, two years earlier, caused the scrapping of the rule prohibiting goalies from doing just that.

In the four-team NHL of 1919–20, Ottawa, Toronto, and Montreal did not finish far apart in goal scoring, but Senators kept their own net tidier, to the tune of nearly two goals a game better, than runner-up Toronto. Winning both halves of the split-season format – 9-3-0 and 10-2-0 – Ottawa obviated the need for an NHL playoff, were declared champions, and prepared to face PCHA challenger Seattle. This would decide a Cup champion for the first time in two years, the previous year's Cup series having been cancelled due to the deadly influenza epidemic that claimed Joe Hall, Hamby Shore, and eventually Canadiens' manager George Kennedy, not to mention millions more worldwide.

Seattle journeyed east with a star-studded line-up of their own – Frank Foyston, Bernie Morris, Jack Walker, Bobby Rowe, goaltender Harry "Hap" Holmes – and in a closely contested series plagued with poor ice conditions, Ottawa won once under eastern rules and again under western rules, and Seattle then followed suit, tying the series at two games apiece. Ottawa took the fifth and final game decisively to win the Cup, and would win it twice more in the three years to come. Every single one of the eight regulars on this team has been enshrined in the Hall of Fame.

1970–71 Boston Bruins

Orr. Espo. Cashman, Sanderson, Hodge, Bucyk, McKenzie, Green, Awrey, Cheevers. *Man*, did we hate those guys. What can we say? We were kids, and besides, we didn't yet know what Philadelphia would spawn in the next few years. Boston fans, take our hatred as a badge of honour. The Bruins hit, and pounded, and grinded, and scored goals by the crateful. They didn't just beat you, they didn't just beat you up, they *buried* you under the proverbial relentless barrage of frozen vulcanized rubber. Bobby Orr scored goals off phenomenal rink-length dashes that defied description and sometimes the laws of physics, and when he wasn't doing that, he scored goals while masterminding the power play from the left point. Phil Esposito scored goals from the edge of the crease while setting the standard for immovable objects, and if he wasn't jamming them home there, he scored goals off muscular rushes of his own, opponents draped over him and falling away like kids off a runaway toboggan. Ken Hodge and Johnny Bucyk scored goals off Orr's and Espo's feeds and sweeping in on sudden dashes down the wings. Derek Sanderson and Eddie Westfall scored short-handed. Everybody scored. The Bruins shoved you around and then ran up the score. Or they ran up the score, then shoved you around if you objected. That they always came into your building in those nasty black sweaters just made them all the more maddening. Thirty years later, they have our undying respect.

Boston had already won the Cup, in 1970, for the first time in 29 years, and they looked even more impressive in '70–71. Orr, the spectacular 22-year-old defenceman, and Esposito, the burly veteran centre, were the lightning and thunder of Boston's fearsome attack. Espo was flanked on the right by the smooth Hodge, who'd come to Boston with Esposito and Fred Stanfield in a notorious 1967 trade with Chicago, and on the left by the obnoxiously irascible Wayne Cashman. The gentlemanly Stanfield manned the right point on the power play and centred the second line, with scrappy 34-year-old Pie McKenzie looking for trouble on the right wing and the beefy 35-year-old Bucyk cruising the left side. Sanderson, the devilish playboy centre, and Westfall, the button-down-flannel right winger, led Bruins to a record 25 short-handed goals on the year, and usually lined up with Wayne Carleton or Don Marcotte when they weren't killing penalties brilliantly.

On defence, Orr was supported by four tough, capable veterans – Awrey, Dallas Smith, Rick Smith, and Ted Green. And in goal, Gerry Cheevers, a favourite of the Boston Garden crowd, his mask beginning to sport the Magic Marker–indicated stitches with which it would eventually be covered, actually played far better than it looked like he did to most observers outside Boston. Another veteran, Eddie Johnston, was the frequent back-up.

Solid defensively, solid up and down the line-up, and with the game's best defenceman and top centre leading a seemingly unstoppable goal-scoring assault, the Bruins looked to be a juggernaut entering the playoffs. But in the opening round, Boston faced Montreal. Bruins took a 3-2

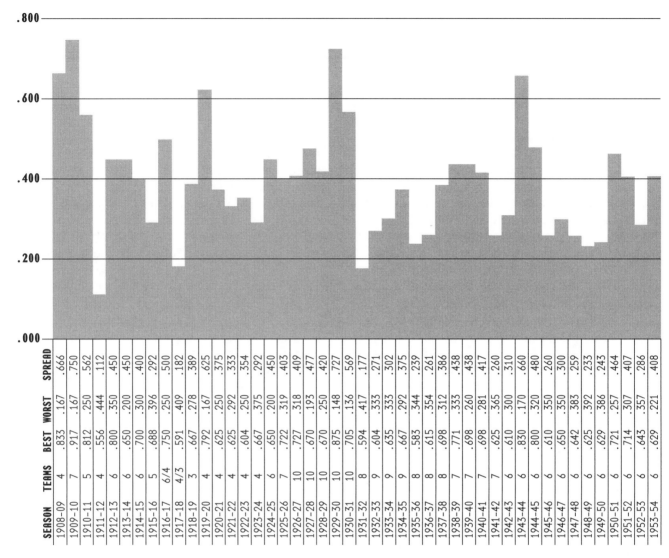

SEASON	TEAMS	BEST	WORST	SPREAD
1908-09	4	.833	.167	.666
1909-10	7	.917	.167	.750
1910-11	5	.812	.250	.562
1911-12	4	.556	.444	.112
1912-13	6	.800	.350	.450
1913-14	6	.650	.200	.450
1914-15	6	.700	.300	.400
1915-16	5	.688	.396	.292
1916-17	6/4	.750	.250	.500
1917-18	4/3	.591	.409	.182
1918-19	3	.667	.278	.389
1919-20	4	.792	.167	.625
1920-21	4	.625	.250	.375
1921-22	4	.625	.292	.333
1922-23	4	.604	.250	.354
1923-24	4	.667	.375	.292
1924-25	6	.650	.200	.450
1925-26	7	.722	.319	.403
1926-27	10	.727	.318	.409
1927-28	10	.670	.193	.477
1928-29	10	.670	.250	.420
1929-30	10	.875	.148	.727
1930-31	10	.705	.136	.569
1931-32	8	.594	.417	.177
1932-33	9	.604	.333	.271
1933-34	9	.635	.333	.302
1934-35	9	.667	.292	.375
1935-36	8	.583	.344	.239
1936-37	8	.615	.354	.261
1937-38	8	.698	.312	.386
1938-39	8	.771	.333	.438
1939-40	7	.698	.260	.438
1940-41	7	.698	.281	.417
1941-42	7	.625	.365	.260
1942-43	6	.610	.300	.310
1943-44	6	.830	.170	.660
1944-45	6	.800	.320	.480
1945-46	6	.610	.350	.260
1946-47	6	.650	.350	.300
1947-48	6	.642	.383	.259
1948-49	6	.625	.392	.233
1949-50	6	.629	.386	.243
1950-51	6	.721	.257	.464
1951-52	6	.714	.307	.407
1952-53	6	.643	.357	.286
1953-54	6	.629	.221	.408

lead in games and seemed to have the series in hand. But Montreal blew out the Bruins to square the series at three, then shut them down in the seventh game behind their big rookie netminder, Ken Dryden. Echoing the fate of the '29–30 Bruins, Boston's season came to a shockingly premature end. Montreal went on to win the Cup in 1971, and Boston would have to wait another year to reclaim it.

1938–39 Boston Bruins

All the great teams that put together the great seasons on this list have players and stories worth telling about, but we'll detail just one more, since it has a happy ending – they win the Cup, and no one dies tragically. This is another Boston team, the Bruins of '38–39, famous for the Kraut Line and Mister Zero.

The young "Krauts" – Milt Schmidt, Bobby Bauer, and Woody Dumart – were so called because all three were of German ancestry – Schmidt and Bauer were born in Berlin,

Ontario, Dumart in nearby Waterloo, and all three had played together for Kitchener, formerly Berlin, in the OHA. Schmidt, the centre, was as rough-and-tumble as he was skilled, and as likely to bowl over defenders and simply crash his way to the net as he was to stickhandle nimbly around them; his career would include an NHL scoring title and the Hart Trophy. Dumart, the left winger, was, like Schmidt, a big physical specimen, a good goal scorer and tough checker but unfailingly clean, an annual Lady Byng candidate. Bauer, the pint-sized right winger, a shifty, hustling stickhandler, won the Byng three times in the seven years that followed.

As dynamic as this trio was, it was actually wiry centreman Bill Cowley, a master stickhandler and playmaker, who led all Bruin scorers. His superb passing helped rookie left winger Roy Conacher lead the league in goal scoring, and also fed Mel Hill, another rookie, on the right side. Ray Getliffe, Gord Pettinger, Dit Clapper, Charlie Sands, and, in his final campaign, old Cooney Weiland,

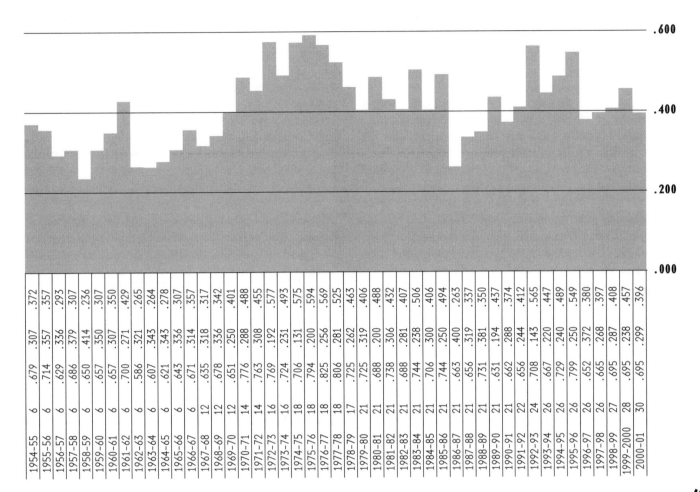

Season				GP
1954-55	.372	.307	.679	6
1955-56	.357	.357	.714	6
1956-57	.293	.336	.629	6
1957-58	.307	.379	.686	6
1958-59	.236	.414	.650	6
1959-60	.307	.350	.657	6
1960-61	.350	.307	.657	6
1961-62	.429	.271	.700	6
1962-63	.265	.321	.586	6
1963-64	.264	.343	.607	6
1964-65	.278	.343	.621	6
1965-66	.307	.336	.643	6
1966-67	.357	.314	.671	6
1967-68	.317	.318	.635	12
1968-69	.342	.336	.678	12
1969-70	.401	.250	.651	12
1970-71	.488	.288	.776	14
1971-72	.455	.308	.763	14
1972-73	.577	.192	.769	16
1973-74	.493	.231	.724	16
1974-75	.575	.131	.706	18
1975-76	.594	.200	.794	18
1976-77	.569	.256	.825	18
1977-78	.525	.281	.806	18
1978-79	.463	.262	.725	17
1979-80	.406	.319	.725	21
1980-81	.488	.200	.688	21
1981-82	.432	.306	.738	21
1982-83	.407	.281	.688	21
1983-84	.506	.238	.744	21
1984-85	.406	.300	.706	21
1985-86	.494	.250	.744	21
1986-87	.263	.400	.663	21
1987-88	.337	.319	.656	21
1988-89	.350	.381	.731	21
1989-90	.437	.194	.631	21
1990-91	.374	.288	.662	21
1991-92	.412	.244	.656	22
1992-93	.565	.143	.708	24
1993-94	.447	.220	.667	26
1994-95	.489	.240	.729	26
1995-96	.549	.250	.799	26
1996-97	.380	.372	.652	26
1997-98	.397	.268	.665	26
1998-99	.408	.287	.695	27
1999-2000	.457	.238	.695	28
2000-01	.396	.299	.695	30

provided solid depth at forward, and Boston led the NHL in scoring.

Boston also led the league in defence, and by a wide margin, thanks to forwards who backchecked as well they scored, a remarkable group of veteran rearguards, and superb goaltending. The blueline corps took their cue from Eddie Shore, in the penultimate season of his legendary career. Shore paired with Dit Clapper, who moved back to defence during the course of this season after a decade as a star forward. That duo tutored three less ancient vets, Bill Hollett, Jack Crawford, and Jack Portland. Stay-at-home types by nature, Hollett, who became known as "Flash" and developed into the top-scoring defenceman of the 1940s, and Crawford, a massive, easy-going sort who was one of the first NHLers to wear a helmet, learned to rush the puck from Shore and Clapper. Portland rarely ventured from his own zone but was a reliable presence there. Much of this line-up had been present the previous season, when Bruins finished an impressive first overall but fell to Toronto in the best-of-five opening round of the playoffs.

Early in the '38–39 season, coach and manager Art Ross dealt away Boston's great but aging goaltender, Tiny Thompson, and gambled on rookie netminder Frank Brimsek, a native of Eveleth, Minnesota, who would become the NHL's first American born-and-bred superstar. Brimsek, Shore and Clapper, Cowley, Weiland, and all three members of the Kraut Line would end up in the Hall of Fame.

Boston opened the 1939 playoffs against second-place Rangers and took a three-games-to-none lead with a pair of overtime victories, both thanks to goals by Hill. New York, however, despite the absence of their fine netminder Dave Kerr, fought back to tie the series and send it to a seventh game. Hill once more came through in overtime, also winning for himself the sobriquet "Sudden Death." Bruins had less trouble in the best-of-seven Final, revenging themselves on third-place Toronto and dispatching Leafs in five games.

The Spread of Competition

Hey! Stay awake! We're bringing history alive! Now then . . . A number of themes recur in recounting the stories of the amazing seasons these teams put together. One that jumps out at you is that only 13 of the 20 best modern teams (and 15 of the 23 best all-time) were able to sustain that regular-season excellence into Stanley Cup play and come home with the Venerable Bauble. Another, which is a little less obvious, is that almost all of these teams come from the NHL and its linear antecedents, not from its rival major leagues. A third point is that almost all these teams had their sensational year in a season of league-wide turmoil, either due to expansion or some other destabilizing effect on talent and scoring levels. The pre–World War I Senators, Wanderers, Bulldogs, and PCHA Vancouver Millionaires, all from the age of organizational chaos and radical rules adjustments; the 1929–30 Bruins from the year the old offsides rules were thrown out; the Canadiens of the World War II era, when talent levels fell and scoring skyrocketed; the Canadiens and Flyers of the 1970s, when NHL expansion and the WHA had diluted the major-league talent pool; the Oilers and Islanders of the early 1980s, when expansion-dulled defence had yet to come to grips with Euro-style offence and scoring again went through the roof . . . those are the teams that make the list, and those are the seasons in which they played. You don't see many teams here from the fairly stable 1930s, nor from the two steady post-war decades of the Original Six.

It's telling that every one of the spectacularly successful campaigns produced by these teams occurred during a season or an era when some substantial upheaval spawned competitive imbalance. To give you a bit more context for the facts we're about to present, let us first tell you that in the 93 seasons of ECHA-NHA-NHL play, the worst team in the league in 47 of those years has had a winning percentage below .300, and in 46 of those years has been at .300 or better. The .300 mark, then, represents an astonishingly reliable and convenient benchmark for futility; a .300 club is a typical, routine cellar-dweller, and while that may be one sorry team – a 49-point side in today's 82-game season – they're not *historically* godawful. In only 11 of those 93 seasons, however, has hockey had to wince and hold its nose as a team crawled through the year with a winning percentage, if we can dignify it by calling it that, below .200; there's your standard for monumental ineptitude.

Now then, with that in mind, consider: 16 of the 20 best records of the modern era (19 of the 23 best ever) were accomplished in a year in which at least one other team played worse than .300 hockey; 12 of the 20 best modern teams (15 of 23 all-time) played in a league with at least one team that played at a .250 clip or below; six of the 20 (or 9 of the 23) reached the heights while another team

was playing out an all-time stinker of a year at a .200 pace or worse.

The inescapable fact is that for every good season there has to be a fairly poor one, and for every astonishingly great season there's usually an *appallingly* bad one. In 1929–30, the year the Bruins went 38-5-1, the Pittsburgh Pirates – the NHL club, not the baseball team – went 5-36-3, a horrendous .148 pace. When the Habs went 38-5-7 in 1943–44, the Rangers went 6-39-5 – that's a .170 club. Granted, the great teams on the list didn't run up their shining season records by playing utterly hapless teams exclusively, or even mostly. This isn't meant to take too much, if anything, away from what those admirable teams achieved. But the distance from first place to last place isn't a constant, and the size of that distance says a lot about the health of the league. We call that distance the spread of competition – the best winning percentage that season minus the worst gives you the spread – and the fluctuations in it over the years are worth looking at. A well-run operation, deep in talent, shouldn't have one or two talent-gorged teams running away from the rest of the pack, nor should it have flimsy, attenuated sides comporting themselves as non-competitive laughingstocks. The closer the spread of competition, and the better the average last-place team, the more highly that speaks to the league-wide quality of hockey. The wider the chasm between first and last place, and the more inept the average tail-ender, the more it says to condemn the quality of hockey in that season or that era. So let's have a look.

Spread of Competition Through History

AGE/LEAGUE	AVG BEST	AVG WORST	AVG SPREAD
Disorder (1908–09 to 1916–17)	.745	.280	.465
Contentiousness (1917–18 to 1919–30)	.683	.265	.418
PCHA/WCHL/WHL (1911–12 to 1925–26)	.626	.360	.266
Equilibrium (1930–31 to 1939–40)	.657	.311	.346
Military Leave (1940–41 to 1944–45)	.713	.287	.426
Stasis (1945–46 to 1966–67)	.653	.336	.317
Expansion (1967–68 to 1979–80)	.737	.259	.478
WHA (1972–73 to 1978–79)	.643	.348	.295
Air Hockey (1980–81 to 1985–86)	.718	.262	.456
Precarious Balance (1986–87 to 1991–92)	.666	.304	.362
Miserable Greed (1992–93 to 2000–01)	.701	.257	.444

There ya go. Hockey's ancient Age of Disorder produced the first-place teams with the highest average winning percentage and, more important, a gulf between the best and worst teams exceeded in size only by the years of the Age of Expansion – which produced first-place teams with the second-best average winning percentage. By contrast, the PCHA and WHA were paragons of balance and parity. In NHL history, it's the Age of Stasis – the Original Six era – that

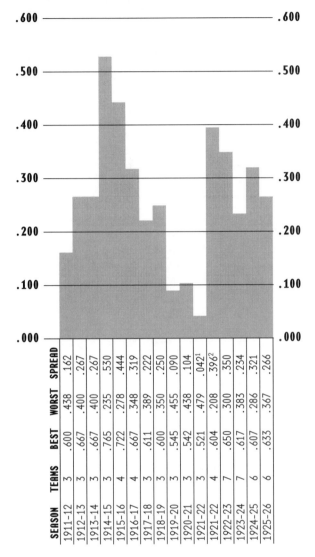

SEASON	TEAMS	BEST	WORST	SPREAD
1911–12	3	.600	.438	.162
1912–13	3	.667	.400	.267
1913–14	3	.667	.400	.267
1914–15	3	.765	.235	.530
1915–16	4	.722	.278	.444
1916–17	4	.667	.348	.319
1917–18	3	.611	.389	.222
1918–19	3	.600	.350	.250
1919–20	3	.545	.455	.090
1920–21	3	.542	.438	.104
1921–22	3	.521	.479	.042[1]
1921–22	4	.604	.208	.396[2]
1922–23	7	.650	.300	.350
1923–24	7	.617	.383	.234
1924–25	6	.607	.286	.321
1925–26	6	.633	.367	.266

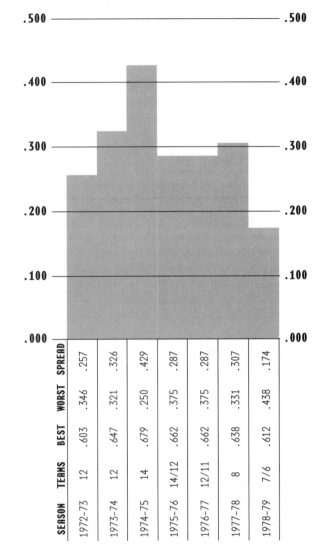

SEASON	TEAMS	BEST	WORST	SPREAD
1972–73	12	.603	.346	.257
1973–74	12	.647	.321	.326
1974–75	14	.679	.250	.429
1975–76	14/12	.662	.375	.287
1976–77	12/11	.662	.375	.287
1977–78	8	.638	.331	.307
1978–79	7/6	.612	.438	.174

1 PCHA only.
2 WCHL only.
The PCHA was founded in 1911 and played as a separate league through the 1921–22 season. The WCHL was founded in 1921 and played as a separate league for the 1921–22 season only. The two leagues remained distinct entities while playing a heavily interlocking schedule in the 1922–23, '23–24, and '24–25 seasons, and their statistics from those three seasons are combined here. In 1925 the PCHA was entirely absorbed by the renamed WHL.

shows the smallest average gap between first and last, and the best average record for last-place teams, a testament to the tight competition and high level of play that make those years so beloved to, and so badly missed by, the fans that watched the NHL over those 22 seasons. The consistent quality of that insular version of the league militated against even the best teams of that era reaching the list of all-time best records. Even the worst teams were close enough to the best, with regard to skill, that no team could run roughshod over the rest and run away from them in the standings. In fact, during those 22 years, only three teams finished with

a winning percentage higher than .700 or lower than .300.

On the other hand, here's a frightening figure from this synopsis of the table: today's Age of Miserable Greed is producing an average gap between first and last that rivals the figures from the Ages of Disorder, Expansion, and Air Hockey – which is bad enough – but worse, it's turning out the worst average last-place teams in the history of hockey. The gap between first and last isn't so large because of great teams atop the standings; it's because of horrendously godawful teams at the bottom of the standings. Make no mistake what a damning indictment this little stat is of the sad, depleted quality of the NHL today.

By contrast, the totals also show how competitive the PCHA and WCHL were – and, for that matter, the WHA. During its heyday, there were rumours that the tiny three- and four-team PCHA was having its rosters gerrymandered by the league office in order to keep the teams in such close

Teams

33

competitive balance, and thereby maintain a high level of fan interest all through the season. League president Frank Patrick offered a huge cash sum to anyone who could prove the charges, but no one was ever able to claim it. Additionally, while the NHL and the NHL-dominated media derided the WHA as a chaotic, bush-league affair – and frequent franchise moves and failures certainly aggravated that impression – the spread of competition there and the credible performances of even its worst teams were better than anything in the entire history of the NHL.

Devastation Scale

Another thing common to the teams with the best records ever is that they led their league, or were well up among the leaders, in both offence and defence. It's only common sense, again, really; you don't win as consistently as those teams did by playing a one-dimensional game. It is possible, of course, to win every game by 3-2 or 4-3, although living on the edge like that every night would probably necessitate the team hiring an ulcer specialist by the end of the season. But were the winningest teams of all time the teams that squeaked through in the tight ones night after night, or were they teams that routinely blew away the opposition and had their next opponent shaking in their skates? Well, it's easy enough to figure out which of history's teams crushed everything in their path; all we need to do is compare the ratio of the number of goals they scored to the number they allowed (goals-for divided by goals-against).

We're going to do that now, and after we weigh these juggernauts on what we call the Devastation Scale, we'll see how many of them are also among the sides with the best winning percentages. Again, our 16-game minimum is in effect, which again excludes three early clubs: the best of them, by this measure, were the 1909–10 Montreal Wanderers of the NHA, who went 11-1-0, outscoring their opponents 91-41 along the way to the Cup. Their rating on the Devastation Scale is 2.22, which would put them third all-time. The ECHA Ottawa team that ran up a 10-2-0 record in 1908–09 and were awarded the Cup outscored the opposition 117-63, a 1.86 Devastation mark. And Renfrew Millionaires went a surprisingly unremarkable 8-3-1 in the 1909–10 NHA season despite crushing opponents 96-54 on the year, good for a 1.78 rating. Even with a loaded line-up featuring Lester and Frank Patrick, Cyclone Taylor, Bobby Rowe, Herb Jordan, and goaltender Bert Lindsay, Renfrew started out 3-2-1, scoring 33 and allowing 25, before buying Newsy Lalonde from cellar-dwelling Canadiens. Millionaires won five of their last six, including season-ending blowouts against a hungover Ottawa side (17-2) and also-rans Cobalt (15-4). Ouch. That's why we don't include those really short seasons on the "official" lists.

Now here are the teams that played enough games to wreak a wider swath of devastation:

Devastation Scale
(minimum 16-game schedule)

RANK	TEAM	LEAGUE	SEASON	W-L-T	GF	GA	DR
1	Montreal Can	NHL	'27–28	26-11-7	116	48	2.42
2	Montreal Can	NHL	'76–77*	60-8-12	387	171	2.26
3	Montreal Can	NHL	'43–44*	38-5-7	234	109	2.15
4	Boston	NHL	'38–39*	36-10-2	156	76	2.05
5	Montreal Can	NHL	'77–78*	59-10-11	359	183	1.96
6	Montreal Can	NHL	'75–76*	58-11-11	337	174	1.94
7	Boston	NHL	'70–71	57-14-7	399	207	1.93
8	Ottawa	NHL	'19–20*	19-5-0	121	64	1.89
9	Ottawa	NHA	'16–17	15-5-0	119	63	1.89
10	Montreal Can	NHL	'44–45	38-8-4	228	121	1.88
11	Ottawa	NHL	'25–26	24-8-4	77	42	1.83
12	Boston	NHL	'29–30	38-5-1	179	98	1.83
13	Detroit	NHL	'95–96	62-13-7	325	181	1.80
14	Montreal Can	NHL	'72–73*	52-10-16	329	184	1.79
15	Ottawa	NHA	'10–11*	13-3-0	122	69	1.77
16	New York Ran	NHL	'39–40*	27-11-10	136	77	1.77
17	Boston	NHL	'39–40	31-12-5	170	98	1.74
18	Boston	NHL	'28–29*	26-13-5	89	52	1.71
19	Detroit	NHL	'50–51	44-13-13	236	139	1.70
20	Montreal Can	NHL	'55–56*	45-15-10	222	131	1.70

* Won Stanley Cup GF: Goals for GA: Goals against DR: Devastation Rating

Not surprisingly, the heavyweights on the Devastation Scale all but recapitulate the list of teams with the best-ever single-season winning percentages. Thirteen of history's 15 most devastating are on the list of all-time best winning percentages: the great Canadiens teams of the 1970s, the renascent Habs of the war years, the astonishing Bruin sides that opened and closed the 1930s, the original Senators from the years preceding and following the birth of the NHL – Montreal, Boston, and Ottawa all but own both lists. Here, though, let's look at three superlative teams we haven't yet discussed.

1927–28 Montreal Canadiens

Bestriding the entire list of Devastation Scale behemoths are the Flying Frenchmen of the 1920s. The 1927–28 Canadiens featured yet another Hall of Fame line-up: goaltender George Hainsworth, defencemen Sylvio Mantha and Herb Gardiner, and forwards Howie Morenz and Aurel Joliat all won immortalization. Art Gagne, who'd starred for Edmonton in the WCHL, Pit Lepine, Wildor Larochelle, Leo Gaudreault, and Gizzy Hart were the additional forwards, and Albert Leduc the third defenceman.

Hainsworth, the doughy-faced little netminding legend, was beaten only 48 times in 44 games this season, which is pretty impressive even in light of the fact teams were averaging well under two goals a game. Protecting him were the 36-year-old Gardiner; the tough, steady Mantha, in the midst of a fine 13-year tenure on the Hab blue line; and the stocky Leduc, who earned the nickname "Battleship" as much for his less-than-graceful skating as for his enthusiastically physical play.

Gaudreault and Hart were spare parts here up front, but Larochelle, the elfin-faced youngster of the team, would be a regular contributor on the wing in Montreal for more than 10 years, and Lepine, lanky and prematurely grey, would play his entire 13-year career with the Habs, eventually becoming their top centre and still later Canadiens coach. The combative little Gagne mopped up on right wing for his linemates, two of the most dynamic figures ever to skate on a major-league rink.

The tiny, irascible Joliat, "The Little Giant," just 5'6" and 135 pounds, was strong for his size and more than willing to mix it up with any player who got in his way; one often-documented eccentricity was his attachment to the black, short-peaked baseball cap he wore during games – a sartorial affectation sported by several players of the era – and his insistence on retrieving it, after an opponent had knocked it off his head, before rejoining the action. That probably didn't happen too often, as Joliat was one of the quickest, most agile skaters in the game, an outstanding stickhandler and passer as well as a top-flight goal scorer. Joliat played 16 years, all for Canadiens, eventually winning the Hart, and retiring after he equalled the career goal total of his linemate and friend Morenz. During this era, the swarthy, balding Morenz was hockey's most spectacular performer and most flamboyant personality. A sensational speedster, Morenz was also an aggressive banger, although a fairly small specimen himself. The 1927–28 campaign would mark the first of two NHL scoring titles and three Hart Trophy seasons for him.

The Canadiens this year would lose only once in their first 22 games, including an 18-game unbeaten streak. Lepine's value to the team is suggested by the fact that after he went down with a broken collarbone, the Habs slumped badly, winning just two of their next twelve. But they finished with a flourish, winning seven of their last ten games and winding up solidly atop the NHL standings. In the playoffs, however, they faced runners-up and arch-rival Montreal Maroons in a two-game total-goals series. Habs took a 2-0 lead in the frenetically paced, hard-hitting opener, but got in penalty trouble and Maroons tied the game at 2-2; both Hainsworth and Maroons netminder Clint Benedict were spectacular. The return match was a tough but more cautious affair. Benedict, who shut the door on Morenz and Joliat in both games, outduelled Hainsworth, and Canadiens fell 1-0 in overtime, bringing their year to a sudden and unexpected end.

1955–56 Montreal Canadiens
The first in a string of five consecutive Cup champion Montreal clubs, 1955–56 Canadiens were led by the tall, fiery, elegant centreman Jean Beliveau, flanked by fire-at-will Bernie "Boom-Boom" Geoffrion and tough-checking Bert Olmstead. Rocket Richard was skating with his little brother, Henri – "the Pocket Rocket" – and skilful, versatile Dickie Moore. Claude Provost, Kenny Mosdell, Donnie Marshall, and Floyd Curry also featured prominently among the forwards. Smooth, unflappable all-time great Doug Harvey was the star on defence, ably supported by Butch Bouchard, Tom Johnson, Jean-Guy Talbot, and Dollard St. Laurent, while the urbane immortal, Jacques Plante, manned the nets. Beliveau won his only scoring title this season and the first of his two Hart Trophies, while the Rocket, Olmstead, and Geoffrion wound up among the top seven NHL scorers for '55–56; the Canadiens won the Cup after shrugging aside Rangers and Red Wings in five games apiece; and 10 of these players – Beliveau, Geoffrion, Olmstead, Moore, both Richards, Harvey, Bouchard, Johnson, and Plante – would win election to the Hall of Fame.

1939–40 New York Rangers
The New York Rangers make the grade here, and since it's kind of a rarity for them to show up on any "all-time best" list, we'll give them their due. This was a terrific defensive side up and down the line-up, no surprise considering the legendary defenceman Lester Patrick was the manager and the great defensive forward Frank Boucher, the coach. Veteran goalie Dave Kerr was between the pipes; left underrated by history, Kerr played every minute in the Ranger nets between 1936 and 1941 and was a key component this season. A rugged quartet patrolled the blue line: strong, aggressive Ranger captain Art Coulter; big, mobile Ott Heller, in the midst of a 15-year Ranger career; tough, massive Babe Pratt; and Lester Patrick's younger son, Muzz, a pro prizefighter and cycling champion when not playing hockey. All four played it physical, and while all four played a conservative, position-conscious style, they were all outstanding pinpoint passers capable of the occasional dramatic rush up ice.

Bryan Hextall, the swift, solid right winger, led the NHL with 24 goals, Phil Watson was his centreman, and Dutch Hiller, on the left wing, completed the Rangers' top line. Lean, young, grey-haired Neil Colville centred the second line, flanked by his brother Mac and Alex Shibicky. Squeaky-clean Clint Smith was the pivot for a potent third line, with Lester's older son, Lynn, on one side and rookie-of-the-year Kilby MacDonald on the other. Alf Pike added even more depth at centre.

Rangers set a new NHL record with a 19-game unbeaten streak during the season; this club, by far the league's best on defence, finished second in the standings, just three points out of first in a race that went down to the final night of the season, while Boston, by far the league's best on offence, wound up first – and, in a bit of a statistical curiosity, a hair's breadth ahead of New York on this very same list as well. The two teams met in the best-of-seven opening round of the playoffs, and Kerr, who'd led the league with eight shutouts during the regular season, blanked the Bruins three times as Rangers won the series in six games. New York faced Toronto in the Final, and took a two-games-to-none lead on Madison Square Garden ice. With the circus taking over the Garden, the remainder of the series was played in Toronto. Leafs evened the series at two games a side, but Rangers won games five and six in overtime to take the Cup home for the first time in seven years – and the last time for the next 54.

Somewhat oddly, the teams that make the numbers fly on the Devastation Scale were even a bit less successful at translating their powerhouse regular-season performances into Stanley Cup mastery than were the teams on the list of winningest regular-season sides. Thirteen of the top 20 most consistent winners wound up hugging the Auld Mug; only 11 of history's 20 most devastating were able to embrace it.

One other telling fact: the '95–96 Red Wings, who appear in 13th place on this list and bumped the '78–79 New York Islanders off the bottom of the chart, are the only new team on *either* the best winning-percentage list *or* the Devastation chart since we last compiled them. In other words, in the last 15 years, only *one team* has had a season of historic magnitude in its greatness. Ominous.

If you insist on inferring the identity of the Best Team Ever from the numbers we've presented so far, you could make a good case at this point for the Habs of 1976–77 and of 1943–44, each of whom hold second spot on one list and third on the other, both of whom followed up their sensational year with a nearly as sensational year that likewise rated highly on both lists, and both of whom carried their superb regular-season play right on into the playoffs and on to the Stanley Cup. Among the many teams that appear on both lists, no other rates so high against all three standards. We're reluctant to claim there's *any* definitive answer to the question – but forced to choose between these two editions of Les Canadiens, we'd lean toward the '70s team. That's probably because we actually saw them and never saw the '40s Habs, but also because it's difficult for us to take a lot of the hockey of the war era seriously. On the other hand, had we been alive in the '40s, it probably would have been difficult for us to take an NHL of Cleveland Barons and Colorado Rockies seriously, either.

Team Scoring Dominance

There's another measure of team achievement to look at, less important than the bottom line of winning, less impressive than thorough domination at both ends of the rink, but in these days of league-wide goal-scoring poverty,

good to look back on: simply, team scoring. So we'll turn our attention for the moment solely to one end of the ice and figure out which teams stand out historically on the offensive side of the ledger. We call this stat Team Scoring Dominance.

If you've been following along, you'll realize that you can't just say this team or that was history's best scoring club because they scored the most goals in a season. No, what you have to do, of course, is compare a team's goals-per-game average to the league-wide goals-per-game average. The team whose goal-scoring average exceeds, by the largest ratio, that of the average team in its league that season, that – *that* – is the all-time scoring dreadnought. We need to make one further adjustment: we have to remove the team from the league-wide average, or else it would in effect undermine its own statistical excellence. So what we're *really* comparing is a team's goal-scoring success to the average goal scoring success of all the other teams – and *not* comparing it to all goal-scoring *including* the team's own. That formula works this way:

$$100 \times \frac{\text{Team goals-per-game average}}{\text{Goals-per-game average of all other teams}} - 100 = \text{Team Scoring Dominance}$$

Readers of the original *Compendium* may notice some small disparities (and one large one) between the chart in the first edition and the chart below. That, as an ironic complement to some of the score-first-and-ask-questions-later clubs on the Team Scoring list, is due to our diligent backchecking, which has corrected some erroneous overtime figures from the first time around and adjusted the numbers accordingly. Again, our 16-game standard applies. *Duck!* They're shooting!

Team Scoring Dominance
(minimum 16-game schedule)

RANK	TEAM	LEAGUE	SEASON	GP	GF	GPG	OTGPG	TSD
1	Montreal Wan	NHA	'14–15	19	127	6.50	3.59	81.17
2	Boston	NHL	'70–71	78	399	5.12	2.97	72.33
3	Ottawa	NHA	'10–11*	16	122	7.62	4.61	65.29
4	Toronto	NHL	'33–34	48	174	3.48	2.16	61.09
5	Boston	NHL	'39–40	48	170	3.47	2.25	54.43
6	Vancouver	PCHA	'14–15*	17	115	6.62	4.29	54.15
7	Montreal Can	NHL	'76–77*	80	387	4.84	3.23	49.66
8	Boston	NHL	'28–29*	44	89	1.98	1.34	47.83
9	Boston	NHL	'29–30	44	179	3.99	2.72	46.67
10	Montreal Can	NHL	'27–28	44	116	2.55	1.76	45.24
11	Edmonton	NHL	'83–84*	80	446	5.53	3.82	44.81
12	Pittsburgh	NHL	'95–96	82	362	4.39	3.05	43.86
13	Boston	NHL	'73–74	78	349	4.47	3.11	43.82
14	Boston	NHL	'71–72*	78	330	4.23	2.98	42.15
15	Detroit	NHL	'52–53	70	222	3.17	2.24	41.58

RANK	TEAM	LEAGUE	SEASON	GP	GF	GPG	OTGPG	TSD
16	Boston	NHL	'30–31	44	143	3.14	2.22	41.39
17	Toronto	NHL	'28–29	44	85	1.89	1.35	40.16
18	Edmonton	NHL	'82–83	80	424	5.30	3.79	39.73
19	Montreal Can	NHL	'74–75	80	374	4.68	3.35	39.49
20	Montreal Can	NHL	'77–78*	80	359	4.49	3.23	39.08

* Won Stanley Cup GP: Games played GF: Goals for GpG: Goals per game (including overtime) OTGpG: Other teams' goals per game (including overtime) TSD: Team Scoring Dominance

1914–15 Montreal Wanderers

We're as shocked as you are, and plenty embarrassed, to see the 1914–15 Montreal Wanderers perched atop this list. We had them rated second-best of all time when we first published this list years ago, and it's not like those guys went out for a twirl on the ice and scored some more goals anytime in the last few years. No, it was our mistake, and we concede the error. Amid ceiling-high piles of books, notes, and stat sheets, we overlooked the fact that Wanderers actually played one less game in that long-ago season than the schedule called for. Toronto Shamrocks asked Wanderers for a postponement of their mid-season tilt because two of their best players, George and Howard McNamara, were attending their father's funeral, but Wanderers refused, gaining a win by forfeit. Nice guys, huh? The unplayed game also means Wanderers scored their 127 goals not in 20 games plus overtime, but in just 19 plus overtime, boosting their goals-per-game average and vaulting them to the top of the list.

More popularly known as Redbands, for their distinctive sweaters, the Wanderers could boast three eventual Hall of Famers: hard-shooting Dr. Gordon Roberts on left wing, sharpshooting little Harry Hyland at centre and right wing, and the brutal if skilful Sprague Cleghorn at point. Sprague's brother, stickhandling wiz Odie Cleghorn, took the right wing when veteran star Don Smith wasn't at centre; Brownie Baker, in his only big year, added production at forward, and the always underrated Goldie Prodgers had cover point. Their weak spot may have been between the pipes; this was Charlie McCarthy's only major-league season, and we're guessing he quit hockey to pursue a career in radio and movies with Edgar Bergen. Must have been quite a sight to see the little fellow with the top hat and monocle manning the crease.

Despite their scoring prowess, Montreal wound up tied atop the NHA standings with Ottawa Senators, and a two-game total-goals playoff was required to determine the league champ. Ottawa, with Punch Broadbent, Jack Darragh, and Eddie Gerard up front, relied on the defence pair of Art Ross and Horace Merrill, and Clint Benedict's great work in the nets, and whitewashed Redbands 4-0 in the opener. Wanderers managed a bootless 1-0 win in the second game, and it was Ottawa that travelled west to face PCHA champion Vancouver Millionaires for the Cup.

1914–15 Vancouver Millionaires

Vancouver, who showed up with their 13-4-0 record on our all-time winners list, opened their year with six straight wins and closed it out the same way. Like most of the better teams of this era, they were loaded with star players who went on to the Hall of Fame, but this was an astoundingly stellar cast by the standard of any age. Their biggest weapon was the sensational young centre/rover Mickey MacKay, a magical stickhandler and sublime playmaker. He'd been called up from the Boundary League, an early developmental league – the farm system being another Patrick brothers innovation – with teams in mining-boom towns in southern British Columbia. Just 20, the rookie MacKay proceeded to lead the coast league in goals by a wide margin – 33 in his 17 games – and would be a superstar in Vancouver for years to come. Also on this Hall of Famer–packed side were the legendary Cyclone Taylor at rover and right wing; the brilliant Frank Nighbor on left wing; another young star, Barney Stanley, on right wing; manager and league president Frank Patrick, with Si Griffis, on defence; and Hugh Lehman in goal. Defenceman Lloyd Cook and winger Ken Mallen were stars in their own right and major contributors to this amazing collection of talent.

Vancouver racked up double-digit scores in each of their last four games, which should have sent a message east, but apparently the telegraph lines were down. Playing seven-man hockey in the first and third games of the best-of-five series and six-man hockey in the second game, Vancouver drubbed Senators 6–2 in the opener, routed them 8–3 two nights later, and blew them off the ice to the tune of 12–3 to close out the series and bring the Cup to the West Coast for the first time.

1933–34 Toronto Maple Leafs

Fourth on the Team Scoring Dominance list are the 1933–34 Maple Leafs, and like several of the teams keeping them company on the chart, they had an all-but-unstoppable top line with a nifty nickname – the Kid Line, so named because they were all pretty raw youngsters when coach Conn Smythe first put them together in the 1929–30 season. This was in their fifth and final full year as a combination, and although they had been one of the NHL's top troikas all along, it would be one of their best. Charlie Conacher, the Big Bomber, was a cannonball on the right wing; this was the third of five seasons in which he led the NHL in goal scoring, and the first of his two consecutive scoring titles. Harvey "Busher" Jackson, rambunctious on the ice and off, was at left wing, and finished seventh in the NHL scoring parade, earning the second of four first-team All-Star nods he would receive in his career. They were centred by the incomparably smooth passer Joe Primeau, the old man of the line at 28, who led the league in assists and wound up second in points.

The amazing little rearguard, King Clancy, was the Leafs' best offensive threat on the blue line, where he teamed with big, aggressive Red Horner. Hap Day and Alex Levinsky were the other defence pairing, and Andy Blair, Bill Thoms, Hec Kilrea, Baldy Cotton, Buzz Boll, Ken Doraty, and Charlie Sands provided solid depth at forward.

This was the season during which Toronto lost the services of another great forward, Ace Bailey, to a career-ending head injury courtesy of Eddie Shore. With Bailey in the line-up for the first dozen games of the season, Leafs were good for 3.70 goals per game. Bailey was hurt in game 13, and without him, over the last 35 games, Leafs averaged 3.39.

Toronto also lost Clancy to injury for two games of their best-of-five playoff series with Detroit, but with their imposing line-up, including George Hainsworth in goal, Leafs were favoured. However, they fell behind two games to none, tied the series at two, then lost the deciding game 3-2 – and as has happened so often before and since on the road to the Cup, another first-place campaign went for nought.

1995–96 Pittsburgh Penguins

The scoring exploits of the 1995–96 Pittsburgh Penguins, we're as startled as you are to realize, were of historic stature, virtually the equal of the very best of the 1980s Oilers, but receiving not a fraction of the acclaim. All the notice went to the spectacular individual accomplishments of Mario Lemieux and Jaromir Jagr, who were one and two in the NHL, respectively, in goals and points. Ronnie Francis also received his due as he tied Lemieux for the league lead in assists, and Sergei Zubov was their best on the blue line, seventh in scoring among NHL defencemen. Forwards Petr Nedved and Tomas Sandstrom also contributed big points to the Flightless Birds' attack – but the quartet of Lemieux, Jagr, Francis, and Zubov registered nearly as many points as the other 32 players who wore the Penguin sweater that season combined. And yet – what other fate would you expect? Pittsburgh skated past the Capitals and Rangers with little difficulty in the first two rounds of the playoffs, but were choked off in the semi-final by the defensive tactics of the Florida Panthers.

The real story running through this list of history's most overwhelming offensive clubs, however, is that of the Boston Bruins, who show up here again and again, just as they scored again and again, through several different eras. Powering in at second of all time are those infuriating 1970–71 Bruins, which should come as little surprise to anyone who saw them, nightly, filling opposition nets with rubber as if they were shovelling coal into a furnace. The Bruins are here in force: not only the Orr-Espo team of 1970–71, *and* of the following season, *and* of 1973–74, but also the Clapper-Weiland team of 1929–30, *and* of the preceding season, *and* of the 1930–31 season that followed, and again the Kraut Line team of 1939–40 as well – making an enormously impressive seven appearances on the list of history's top 20 goal-scoring clubs. If we extended this list just a couple more places, the Bruins would fill those spots too – the 1968–69 Orr-Espo Bruins and the Cup-winning Kraut Line Bruins of 1940–41 just miss the cut-off, but rank as the 21st- and 22nd-best scoring teams ever.

In fact, we see a lot of familiar faces here now: the great Canadiens dynasty of the late '70s shows up here three times – the '74–75, '76–77, and '77–78 editions – and the 1927–28 Habs of Morenz and Joliat also rate a place, making four for Montreal. Along with Edmonton's two berths, you'll also recognize the 1910–11 Ottawas with Walsh, Kerr, Ridpath, and Darragh, and those Production Line Red Wings of the early '50s, an extraordinary accomplishment for any team from the Age of Stasis.

What? we hear some of the younger fans out there gasp: how can the 1980s Oilers – Gretzky, Coffey, Kurri, and their pinball-machine scoring totals – not be atop the list? And by a whopping margin, to boot! Well, kids, it's like this: their monster scoring totals, their hundreds and hundreds of goals, *weren't all that big a deal.* Sure, Gretzky was fantastic; sure, they scored goals by the gross; sure, they often looked pretty doing it; and sure enough, two editions of those Edmonton clubs – the '83–84 team and that of '82–83 – are on the list, and another – the '85–86 Oilers – just misses the top 20. But the simple fact is that *every* team was scoring great gobs of goals in those years. Goals were cheaper than jellybeans. Goals came faster and more frenetically than snowflakes in a prairie blizzard. Goals were as common and frequent as overworked metaphors in anything we ourselves write.

None of which is to dismiss the Oilers; two of the top twenty offensive clubs in history is quite an achievement. But they did not *transcend* their era to the same degree that the '14–15 Wanderers or the '70–71 Bruins did. It's as if Edmonton ran a sub-four-minute mile, on a pristine track, with a strong tailwind, while Boston ran a mile in just over four minutes, but ran the whole distance in knee-deep water, carrying a bowling ball. The story of the '80s Oilers, and the main reason they're on the list at all, is really so much more about Gretzky than it is about anything else.

It's telling that the 1995–96 Penguins are the only team of the past 16 years to make this list. It's popular to put the blame for the NHL scoring drought of the last several years on the widespread use of obsessively defensive strategies, but there are so many more – and more important – reasons for that. And remember, this list isn't concerned with raw goal totals, but with which teams have transcended their era, regardless of how wide-open or how claustrophobic the league-wide scoring levels. Still, we're compelled to observe that the overwhelming majority of, if not all, NHL teams are now incapable of winning with the "firewagon" brand of hockey many of us remember being displayed by the Canadiens, Bruins, Oilers, or others among history's best teams. There's just not enough goal-scoring talent for that on any one team anymore, often not even on some teams' best line, in a league so damnably diluted by hockey's great evil of the '90s, short-sighted, greed-driven, rampant overexpansion. When you simply can't score, concentrating on defence is your only hope for winning consistently, and thus begins the vicious circle. Shut down six or 10 teams, though, fold the best talent on those teams back into the teams that remain, and we'd see a variety of styles and strategies and a healthy seven goals a game. Yep, and we'll win the lottery this weekend too.

One final point: only 13 of the 20 teams with the best winning percentages carried their regular-season excellence on to the Stanley Cup; just 11 of the 20 teams who won their games by the largest average margin – still a majority – were sufficiently devastating to claim the Venerable Bauble; but a mere seven of history's 20 greatest offensive sides could pump in enough goals to earn the Grail. It's a small sample in statistical terms, but it hints that pure offence, no matter how overpowering, means a lot less than the ability to blow teams out of the rink by excelling at both ends of the ice – which in turn isn't quite as important as being able to find a way to win the close ones as well as being able to stage the occasional blow-out.

Team Degeneration

Every story has an ending; the statistics immortalize what teams and their players achieved on the ice, but no team keeps the Cup forever, no one team leads the league every season. In the endless immensity of space, not even the stars are eternal; so it is in hockey. Great players must eventually surrender to age and injury, and their teams must step down from their plinth of glory. For some teams, it's not too deep a descent; they remain competitive and return quickly to a position of power. For others, however, the descent is steep, sudden, and dizzying, a terrifying fall from respectability. Well, all right then; we've had enough for a while of raving about the greatest. Let's turn the mood a little darker and talk about teams that went bad faster than the cold cuts you forgot to put away in the fridge.

Every season is a fresh start, a new journey for you and your team. It always reminds us of the launching of a cruise ship – maybe because we met on one. No, not really. We met back in the '60s when we were both playing for the Saginaw Gears in the "I." Anyway, whether you're among the revellers onboard ship, or just standing on the dock, waving a cheery *bon voyage* amid the confetti and streamers, there's a mood of celebration, and every confidence that good times are just ahead. Of course, everyone who watched the Titanic sail out of Southampton thought it could go all the way, too – and now, thanks to the smash-hit film, we know that it was a horrendous script and terrible acting that sank the great ship.

Largest Single-Season Declines in Winning Percentage
(All-Time)

	TEAM	LEAGUE	SEASON	W-L-T	PCT		SEASON	W-L-T	PCT	DECLINE IN PCT PTS
1	Montreal Wan	NHA	1909–10*	11-1-0	.917	->	1910-11	7-9-0	.438	-479
2	Victoria	PCHA	1913–14	10-5-0	.667	->	1914-15	4-13-0	.235	-431
3	Montreal Can	NHA	1913–14	13-7-0	.650	->	1914-15	6-14-0	.300	-350
4	Portland	PCHA	1915–16	13-5-0	.722	->	1916-17	9-15-0	.375	-347
5	Ottawa	NHA/L	1916–17	15-5-0	.750	->	1917-18	9-13-0	.409	-341
6	New York Ran	NHL	1941–42	29-17-2	.625	->	1942-43	11-31-8	.300	-325
7	Regina	WCHL	1923–24	17-11-2	.600	->	1924-25	8-20-0	.286	-314
8	Toronto	NHL	1917–18*	13-9-0**	.591	->	1918-19	5-13-0	.278	-313
9	Ottawa	NHA	1910–11*	13-3-0	.812	->	1911-12	9-9-0	.500	-312
10	Ottawa	NHL	1929–30	21-15-8	.568	->	1930-31	10-30-4	.273	-295
11	Montreal Wan	NHA	1914–15	14-6-0**	.700	->	1915-16	10-14-0	.417	-283
12	Montreal Can	NHL	1924–25	17-11-2	.600	->	1925-26	11-24-1	.319	-281
13	Chicago	NHL	1926–27	19-22-3	.466	->	1927-28	7-34-3	.193	-273
14	Detroit	NHL	1969–70	40-21-5	.625	->	1970-71	22-45-11	.353	-272
15	Chicago	NHL	1952–53	27-28-15	.493	->	1953-54	12-51-7	.221	-272
16	Boston	NHL	1930–31	28-10-6	.705	->	1931-32	15-21-12	.438	-267
17	Vancouver	PCHA	1914–15*	13-4-0	.765	->	1915-16	9-9-0	.500	-265
18	Ham/NY Amer	NHL	1924–25	19-10-1	.650	->	1925-26	12-20-4	.389	-261
19	Toronto	NHL	1924–25	19-11-0	.633	->	1925-26	12-21-3	.375	-258
20	Toronto	NHA	1913–14*	13-7-0	.650	->	1914-15	8-12-0	.400	-250

* Won Stanley Cup.
** Includes one victory in forfeited unplayed game.

In hockey, though, when a team takes an unanticipated nosedive in the standings, explanations for the sinking traditionally fall back on assumptions of almost superstitious vagueness – "the fire's missing," or "they've lost the chemistry," or "they couldn't summon up the magic" . . . yarr, the ship was jinxed! 'Twas a kraken what took 'er down! At year's end, the post-mortem usually still yields more in the way of guesswork and excuses than useful explanations. A little statistical analysis, though, provides some clearer insight into what suddenly makes good teams go bad, and bad teams get radically worse. In this case, we take a team's winning percentage and subtract from it the poorer record from the following year to arrive at a percentage point decline.

First, let's take a look at the beadroll of the 20 most precipitous single-season declines in the history of major-league hockey.

As you can see, 14 of these 20 notorious wrecks played seasons ranging in length from 12 to 36 games, and that's too small a sample from which to safely draw any conclusions. By today's standards, 1-9-0, or 4-13-0, are troubling, but may be just a brief slump in what might be a good year overall. The short seasons of hockey's early era, however, made every game critically important, a marvellous contrast to the 1,230 regular-season games we're forced to sit

through today before we even get to the playoffs. But given those compact schedules and the short rosters teams used before the 1930s, the loss of one key player to injury or illness for just a couple of weeks – or a player's last-minute departure, jumping to another team in a rival league – or a contract hold-out, or a dressing room snit for that matter – could sink his team's whole season. And the loss of a key performer is just what happened to most of the teams here. While short seasons are every bit as valid as long ones for many statistical comparisons, they don't suit our purposes for this examination. In a hockey season that now sprawls from September until late June, fans are relieved when they hear an injury will sideline their team's star for "only" three weeks – and besides, the team has 30 or 40 guys in the system who can at least fill in.

What we need are longer seasons to examine, to see whether something less simple, less obvious, undermined the year for teams that had expected so much better. Luckily for us, the 1926–27 season provides a convenient cut-off point. That year, after the Western Hockey League folded, the NHL added its players, created three new franchises, and went to a 44-game schedule, 8 games longer than the previous year's slate and 14 games longer than that of 1924–25. No other league up to that time had ever played more than

Largest Single-Season Declines in Winning Percentage
(minimum 44-game schedule)

	TEAM	LEAGUE	SEASON	W-L-T	PCT		SEASON	W-L-T	PCT	DECLINE IN PCT PTS
1	New York Ran	NHL	1941–42	29-17-2	.625	->	1942–43	11-31-8	.300	−325
2	Ottawa	NHL	1929–30	21-15-8	.568	->	1930–31	10-30-4	.273	−295
3	Chicago	NHL	1926–27	19-22-3	.466	->	1927–28	7-34-3	.193	−273
4	Detroit	NHL	1969–70	40-21-5	.625	->	1970–71	22-45-11	.353	−272
5	Chicago	NHL	1952–53	27-28-15	.493	->	1953–54	12-51-7	.221	−272
6	Boston	NHL	1930–31	28-10-6	.705	->	1931–32	15-21-12	.438	−267
7	Detroit	NHL	1936–37*	25-14-9	.615	->	1937–38	12-25-11	.365	−250
8	Montreal Mar	NHL	1936–37	22-17-9	.552	->	1937–38	12-30-6	.312	−240
9	Toronto	WHA	1974–75	43-33-2	.564	->	1975–76	24-52-5	.327	−237
10	Winnipeg	NHL	1984–85	43-27-10	.600	->	1985–86	26-47-7	.369	−231
11	Pittsburgh Pir	NHL	1927–28	19-17-8	.523	->	1928–29	9-27-8	.295	−228
12	Detroit	NHL	1995–96	62-13-7	.799	->	1996–97*	38-26-18	.573	−226
13	Los Angeles	NHL	1980–81	43-24-13	.619	->	1981–82	24-41-15	.394	−225
14	Montreal Can	NHL	1946–47	34-16-10	.650	->	1947–48	20-29-11	.425	−225
15	Chicago	NHL	1982–83	47-23-10	.650	->	1983–84	30-42-8	.425	−225
16	St. Louis Blu	NHL	1980–81	45-18-17	.669	->	1981–82	32-40-8	.450	−219
17	New York Ran	NHL	1983–84	42-29-9	.581	->	1984–85	26-44-10	.388	−193
18	Los Angeles	WHA	1972–73	37-35-6	.513	->	1973–74	25-53-0	.321	−192
19	Pittsburgh Pen	NHL	1981–82	31-36-13	.469	->	1982–83	18-53-9	.281	−188
20	Quebec Nor	NHL	1988–89	27-46-7	.381	->	1989–90	12-61-7	.194	−188
21	New York Ran	NHL	1991–92	50-25-5	.656	->	1992–93	34-39-11	.470	−186
22	Boston	NHL	1995–96	40-31-11	.555	->	1996–97	26-47-9	.372	−183
23	Tampa Bay	NHL	1996–97	32-40-10	.451	->	1997–98	17-55-10	.268	−183
24	Winnipeg	NHL	1992–93	40-37-7	.518	->	1993–94	24-51-9	.339	−179
25	New York Ran	NHL	1993–94*	52-24-8	.667	->	1994–95	22-23-3	.490	−177

* Won Stanley Cup.

Teams

40

a 30-game schedule. Using the 44-game schedule as our minimum, then, here are the largest one-season drop-offs of the modern era. We're extending the list to 25 places because several recent teams came close to, but just missed, qualifying among the 20 most badly decayed.

What happened to these teams? They might have split up or they might have capsized. They may have broke deep and took water. Nope, that's not it; as we'll see, one factor – a drop-off on defence – scuttled almost every club on this list.

Let's examine the wartime Rangers, whose rusting hulk rests in the silt at the very bottom of this Bermuda Triangle of sunken teams. As we've already explained, World War II took a tremendous toll on hockey; the war hit New York harder than it did any other club. Stanley Cup champions in 1940, a first-place team with a .625 winning percentage in 1941–42, the 1942–43 Rangers were without their entire number two line of the Colville brothers and Shibicky; two of their best defencemen, Art Coulter and Bill Juzda; and most damaging of all, their fine goaltender, Sugar Jim Henry, all of whom had joined the military. On top of that, New York had, at the start of the season, traded another eventual Hall of Fame defenceman, Babe Pratt, to Toronto, for promising rookie rearguard Dudley "Red" Garrett, who later that year died serving with the Royal Canadian Navy when his ship was torpedoed off the coast of Newfoundland. The first-place Rangers plunged to last in the NHL. By the next season, New York was struggling so badly the team requested – but was denied – a leave of absence from the league.

The crucial factor here is that the men unavailable to the Rangers were primarily defensive players. The Rangers still had their top scoring line of Phil Watson, Bryan Hextall, and Lynn Patrick, and the drop in the team's offensive output was noticeable but not crippling. The loss of their goaltender, their entire checking line, and their top three defencemen, however, proved devastating.

Ottawa, the second team on the list, paid the price for performing the biggest favour ever to benefit the Toronto Maple Leafs: trading them King Clancy. What were they thinking? The Senators had already sold off aging greats such as Frank Nighbor, Cy Denneny, Punch Broadbent, and Buck Boucher, but Clancy was in his very prime and was all that was holding the team together. The leprechaun-sized Hall of Fame defenceman, one of the very best ever to play the game, had ranked second in scoring among NHL blue-liners in 1929–30, but he brought even more to his own zone than he did to the attack. Ottawa's offence dulled a bit without Clancy's puck-rushing abilities, but without his defensive skills, Ottawa's goals-against mushroomed.

A pattern is quickly forming. One team lost half a roster, the other just one key figure, but in each case it was their defence that buckled and gave way, and caused them to sink in the standings.

To see how often defensive woes are the stumbling block resulting in a team's plunge in the standings, we've charted the offensive production and defensive record for each of the teams on the list of worst single-season declines. Because of the fluctuations in length of season and league-wide scoring levels, of course, raw numbers, again, can't provide a clear picture. To put these teams on a consistent scale, we've converted each club's numbers to a percentage by which their offence and defence were better or worse than the league average for their season of decline and for the one that preceded it.

Whether goals-for or goals-against, a figure better than the league average gets a plus, and a figure worse than the league average is prefaced with a minus. For example, the 29-17-2 Rangers of 1941–42 scored a league-high 177 goals that year, or, with overtime figured in, 3.59 goals per game – 18.5% better than the NHL average of about 3.03, as you'll see under the column headed "% +/– GF/gp." They allowed 143 goals, or 2.90 per game – 4.3% better than that league-wide average of 3.03, and shown in the adjacent column, headed "% +/– GA/gp." The 11-31-8 skeleton crew of 1942–43, however, scored 161 times – 3.20 goals per game, 11.1% less than that season's NHL average of roughly 3.60, and surrendered a league high 253 goals – 5.03 per game, or 39.7% worse than the NHL average.

The last two columns display the difference between the percentages in those two seasons. New York, 18.5% better on offence than the NHL as a whole in 1941–42, and 11.1% worse in 1942–43, drop 29.6 percentage points from their first-place campaign to their basement finish the next year. Better on defence than the league average by 4.3% in 1941–42 and worse by 39.7% in 1942–43, their fall is represented by a difference of – add 'em up – 44.0 percentage points.

Every single team on the list fell off both in scoring goals and in preventing them, but twice as many – 16 out of the 24 teams here – show a more severe decline on defence than on offence. And the average amount of decline on defence is significantly larger than that on offence. Obviously, a major drop-off in a team's ability to either score goals or prevent them hinders a team's ability to compete, and a decline in both pretty much guarantees serious trouble. But it seems safe to conclude that when a team really goes sour in its own end – when a team loses one or more vital defensive players through trade, injury, or what have you and doesn't address that loss – it's time to don your Mae West and lower the lifeboats.

Such was the case with the '43 Rangers and the '31 Sens – and the 1970–71 Detroit Red Wings are another case in point. The Dead Things show the most abrupt one-season downturn of any team since the advent of the centre red line and in any season of 60 games or more. They too were paying the price for mishandling their defence. Carl Brewer, by far Detroit's best blueliner, retired, and former Calder- and

	TEAM	LEAGUE	SEASON	% +/– GF/GP	% +/– GA/GP		SEASON	% +/– GF/GP	% +/– GA/GP	DIF % GF/GP	DIF % GA/GP
1	New York Ran	NHL	1941–42	+18.5	+4.3	->	1942–43	–11.1	–39.7	–29.6	–44.0
2	Ottawa	NHL	1929–30	+4.6	+10.5	->	1930–31	–12.9	–35.9	–17.5	–46.4
3	Chicago	NHL	1926–27	+29.8	–30.9	->	1927–28	–16.6	–64.2	–46.5	–33.4
4	Detroit	NHL	1969–70	+11.4	+9.9	->	1970–71	–14.2	–26.5	–25.6	–36.3
5	Chicago	NHL	1952–53	+0.8	–4.4	->	1953–54	–20.9	–43.9	–21.7	–39.5
6	Boston	NHL	1930–31	+35.9	+14.5	->	1931–32	+0.7	–3.4	–35.2	–17.9
7	Detroit	NHL	1936–37*	+8.5	+13.6	->	1937–38	–18.5	–9.5	–27.0	–23.1
8	Montreal Mar	NHL	1936–37	+6.1	+7.4	->	1937–38	–16.6	–23.0	–22.7	–30.4
9	Toronto	WHA	1974–75	+21.8	+6.1	->	1975–76	+10.8	–31.6	–11.0	–37.7
10	Winnipeg	NHL	1984–85	+15.0	–6.6	->	1985–86	–6.9	–17.4	–21.9	–10.9
11	Pittsburgh Pir	NHL	1927–28	–20.0	+9.2	->	1928–29	–29.2	–23.1	–9.2	–32.3
12	Detroit	NHL	1995–96	+26.8	+29.4	->	1996–97*	+4.9	+18.3	–21.9	–11.1
13	Los Angeles	NHL	1980–81	+9.6	+5.7	->	1981–82	–2.2	–15.0	–11.8	–20.7
14	Montreal Can	NHL	1946–47	–0.4	+27.2	->	1947–48	–16.3	+3.8	–15.9	–23.4
15	Chicago	NHL	1982–83	+9.3	+13.3	->	1983–84	–12.0	+1.2	–21.3	–12.1
16	St. Louis Blu	NHL	1980–81	+14.5	+8.6	->	1981–82	–1.9	–8.7	–16.4	–17.3
17	New York Ran	NHL	1983–84	–0.7	+7.9	->	1984–85	–5.3	–10.8	–4.6	–18.7
18	Los Angeles	WHA	1972–73	–7.4	+10.6	->	1973–74	–15.0	–20.6	–7.6	–31.2
19	Pittsburgh Pen	NHL	1981–82	–3.4	–5.0	->	1982–83	–16.9	–27.4	–13.5	–22.4
20	Quebec Nor	NHL	1988–89	–10.8	–14.7	->	1989–90	–18.2	–38.7	–7.4	–24.0
21	New York Ran	NHL	1991–92	+16.0	+11.1	->	1992–93	–0.5	–0.8	–16.5	–11.9
22	Boston	NHL	1995–96	+9.3	–4.3	->	1996–97	–2.0	–25.7	–11.3	–21.4
23	Tampa Bay	NHL	1996–97	–9.2	–3.2	->	1997–98	–29.9	–24.8	–20.7	–21.6
24	Winnipeg	NHL	1992–93	+5.9	–5.2	->	1993–94	–10.9	–26.5	–16.8	–21.3
25	New York Ran	NHL	1993–94*	+10.2	+14.9	->	1994–95	–2.4	+5.9	–12.6	–9.0

% +/– GF/gp   Percentage by which team's goals-per-game average is better or worse than goals-per-game average of all teams that season
% +/– GA/gp   Percentage by which team's goals-against-per-game average is better or worse than goals-against-per-game average of all teams that season
dif % GF/gp   Percentage points by which team's % +/– GF/gp figure in season of decline differs from figure of previous season
dif % GA/gp   Percentage points by which team's % +/– GA/gp figure in season of decline differs from figure of previous season

*   Won Stanley Cup.

Average rate of change in goals for: –18.6%
Average rate of change in goals against: –24.7%

Conn Smythe Trophy–winning goalie Roger Crozier was traded to Buffalo. Detroit's only answer to Brewer's absence was to experiment with 42-year-old Gordie Howe on defence, if you can believe it. And although Roy Edwards and Jimmy Rutherford were capable netminders, they weren't close to Crozier's level. He'd been dealt to Buffalo for young winger Tom Webster, who would actually go on to lead the Wings in scoring that year but was definitely no student of backchecking. Only California Golden Seals gave up more goals that year than did the Red Wings, who finished dead last, behind first-year expansion clubs Buffalo and Vancouver.

Similar forces were at play for the 1928–29 Pittsburgh Pirates. Icing essentially the same cast that, as the Pittsburgh Yellow Jackets, had won the final championship of the U.S. Amateur Hockey Association, Pirates were a competitive side their first three years in the NHL. But the cash-strapped club let their tiny, brilliant netminder, Roy Worters, go to the last-place New York Americans. With Worters, league MVP in 1928–29, the Amerks immediately sprang into Stanley Cup contention. Without Worters, Pittsburgh floundered, plunging 32.3% on defence and ending up in last place, with worse yet to come.

The '36–37 Maroons had Lionel Conacher, still a force on the blueline in his final season; with him absent in '37–38, Maroons faded to a sickly shade of mauve. As for the Canadiens, they traded little two-way centre Buddy O'Connor to Rangers in 1947, then lost top-notch checking forward Kenny Mosdell for most of the season with a broken arm, and missed the playoffs for the only time in Irvin's 15 years at the helm. Sometimes the reason for the defensive collapse is easy to pinpoint, sometimes it's more subtle. But whatever the cause, it's the failure of that defensive integrity that doomed most of these clubs.

Detroit appear twice more on this list, and both versions of the team offer interesting exceptions to the absent-defensive-star rule. The 1936–37 edition of the Red Wings were a dreadnought, leading the NHL in offence and defence en route to the best record in the league and a second straight Stanley Cup. More seemed in store as Detroit headed into 1937–38 with a virtually identical cast. But it had been a last kick at the can for many of Detroit's best players, particularly their great little forward line of Larry Aurie, Marty Barry, and Herbie Lewis. All of them barely 30, they seemed to age overnight. The Red Wings faded badly at both ends of the ice, followed their Cup triumph with a last-place finish, and all three were gone from the NHL within two years.

The 1996–97 Red Wings went the opposite way. Among the league's regular-season elite since 1991–92, winners of three straight division titles, and posting the NHL's best record for two years in a row, the Wings nonetheless fell consistently short in the playoffs. In 1996–97 they seemed finally to have learned the painful lesson that regular-season success is no guarantee of playoff glory. With a roster identical to the previous year's, but for the one significant acquisition of grinding goal-scorer Brendan Shanahan, the Red Wings paced themselves for a playoff run. There was plenty of cushion for a fall – Detroit's almost .800 pace in 1995–96 was the eighth-best in major-league hockey since 1911–12 – and importantly, their decline on defence was the third-smallest on this list. Having left something in the tank this time for the playoff drive, Red Wings finally kissed the Cup in 1996–97 – the only team on the list that stooped to conquer.

The All-Time Worst Single Seasons

We've been intoxicated by the view from Mount Olympus, where the best teams in history dwell; now we've started to lose our buzz strolling through the blighted neighbourhood of history's most deteriorated teams. Time now for a thoroughly sobering experience, as we stop to scour the stinking dumpster where the worst teams in history rot away. Put on your gas masks and rubber gloves, kids! We're going in!

Worst 20 Regular-Season Records
(minimum 16-game schedule)

RANK	TEAM	LEAGUE	SEASON	W-L-T	PTS	PCT
1	Washington	NHL	'74–75	8-67-5	21	.131
2	Philadelphia Q	NHL	'30–31	4-36-4	12	.136
3	Ottawa	NHL	'92–93	10-70-4	24	.143
4	San Jose	NHL	'92–93	11-71-2	24	.143
5	Pittsburgh Pir	NHL	'29–30	5-36-3	13	.148
6	Quebec Bul	NHL	'19–20	4-20-0	8	.167

RANK	TEAM	LEAGUE	SEASON	W-L-T	PTS	PCT
7	New York Ran	NHL	'43–44	6-39-5	17	.170
8	New York Isl	NHL	'72–73	12-60-6	30	.192
9	Chicago	NHL	'27–28	7-34-3	17	.193
10	Quebec Nor	NHL	'89–90	12-61-7	31	.194
11	Winnipeg	NHL	'80–81	9-57-14	32	.200
12	Washington	NHL	'75–76	11-59-10	32	.200
13	Boston	NHL	'24–25	6-24-0	12	.200
14	Toronto On/Sh	NHA	'14–15	4-16-0	8	.200
15	Saskatoon/MJaw	WCHL	'21–22	5-19-0	10	.208
16	Atlanta Thr	NHL	'99–00	14-61-7	35#	.213
17	Ottawa	NHL	'93–94	14-61-9	37	.220
18	Chicago	NHL	'53–54	12-51-7	31	.221
19	Kansas City	NHL	'75–76	12-56-12	36	.225
20	California	NHL	'73–74	13-55-10	36	.231
21	Victoria	PCHA	'14–15	4-13-0	8	.235
22	Pittsburgh Pen	NHL	'83–84	16-58-6	38	.238
23	Ottawa	NHL	'94–95	9-34-5	23	.240
24	San Jose	NHL	'91–92	17-58-5	39	.244
25t	Ottawa	NHL	'95–96	18-59-5	41	.250

Credited with 39 points in official NHL standings (.238) because four losses came in overtime.
t Tied with eight other teams with .250 winning percentage.

Eeuuuw! There's stuff *wriggling* in there! You go ahead and notify the Centers for Disease Control, while we have this beamed up to the cargo bay and placed in a containment field. After we've all washed our hands thoroughly and burned our clothes, we can observe a genuinely horrifying phenomenon.

How do go we about dissecting the corpses of history's worst ever? First, let's note that three pre-NHL teams also had winning percentages, if we can use that expression in connection with these clubs, of .250 or worse; having played seasons of less than 16 games, they don't appear on the list. The worst of them were Montreal Shamrocks of the ECHA, who went 2-10-0 (.167) in 1908–09. Beginning as Montreal Crystals, one of the original teams in the AHA, present at the very conception of the Stanley Cup in 1893, Shams won the Cup 1899 and 1900, led by their great star Harry Trihey. But those were the only years in which they put up a winning record; before and after, Shamrocks were resolutely horrible throughout their 18-year existence. Their combined record in the AHA, CAHL, ECAHA, ECHA, and NHA was 46-112-1. The other two Mesozoic fossils are *Les Canadiens* of 1909–10, who in their maiden season also went 2-10-0, and Quebec Bulldogs of 1908–09, who went 3-9-0 (.250).

As for the more modern punching bags dangling from our list, Washington still hangs lowest of all.

The 1974–75 Caps remain the worst team ever to embarrass a modern major-league rink. Their roster, culled from the dross of an NHL that had clearly thinned itself to transparency in its war of expansion against the WHA, was utterly starless, in ironic contrast to their star-spangled uniforms. Their top man was 34-year-old Tommy Williams, a star of the 1960 gold-medal-winning U.S. Olympic hockey team who was nearing the end of his long journeyman career in the NHL and WHA, and who led the team with 22 goals in a year when 50-goal seasons were becoming routine. Former Maple Leaf Denis Dupere actually potted 20 goals in 53 games for Washington and, apparently as a reward, was traded to a real team – St. Louis. Dave Kryskow (24 points in 51 games) and Mike Bloom (26 in 67) got similar reprieves, leaving mid-season acquisitions Ron Lalonde, Garnet "Ace" Bailey, and Stan Gilbertson to pick up the slack. No matter how thin the pool of available talent for the expansion draft, many of the Caps' early woes can be attributed to scouting blunders and to letting a misguided PR agenda influence their choices.

Other nostalgia-inducing names here for over-40 fans of comedy on ice are Mike Marson, Steve Atkinson, Pete Laframboise, Greg Joly, Jim Hrycuik, Bob Gryp, Bill Lesuk, and Nelson Pyatt. Penguin farmhand Yvon Labre emerged as the Caps' best defenceman and the team's policeman as well. Also manning the turnstiles at the Washington blue line was Bill Mikkelson, who remains saddled with the all-time raw minus record of -82, and ancient Bruin, Black Hawk, and North Star veteran Doug Mohns, who was listed as being 42 but who we always suspected was at least well into his late 60s at this point, since he'd played in Boston with the Kraut Line boys, who had played against Ranger great Frank Boucher, who had played against Joe Malone.

Heroic just for standing steadfast in the crease behind this motley crew were Ron Low and Michel Belhumeur. They themselves rarely transcended, but facing an average of almost 40 shots a night, they'd have had every excuse to retreat to the dressing room still flailing wildly at imaginary pucks, like the shell-shocked goalie of *Slapshot*'s Charlestown Chiefs. Belhumeur saw action in 35 games that season without once receiving credit for a win, but years later still valorously declined to criticize a single teammate.

The Crappies, as they were widely known, also set several NHL records as a team: at least 10 of them, all for futility – lowest winning percentage, .131; most goals allowed in a season, 446; most scoring points against in one game, 40; and seven more, like season benchmarks for most losses, most road losses, longest losing streak, longest home losing streak, fewest road wins, longest road winless streak, and longest road losing streak, all of which we declared in the original *Compendium* would stand forever and ever. Hmmph. Never say never.

Also visible in the wreckage here are the 1975–76 Kansas City Scouts, Washington's expansion sisters. While the Caps were historically awful for another season and resolutely bad for the first 8 years of their existence, they eventually came around and have actually been a consistently good team for almost 20 years now. The Scouts would have longer to wait; an impotent .256 team in their first season, they got worse in their sophomore campaign and left town for Denver, where, as the Colorado Rockies, they were nearly as bad for six more years. And so they again rode out of town on a wave of indifference, settling in a swamp in New Jersey, and stank away there for yet another five years, unnoticed amid the toxic dumps. It would be *14 years* before the Devils-né-Rockies-né-Scouts actually had a winning season.

You'll also spot those war-ravaged New York Rangers here – who, one infamous January night in Detroit, were tortured 15-0, still the NHL standard for humiliation – as well as the 1972–73 New York Islanders, in their first year in the league; the 1924–25 Bruins, in *their* first year in the league; the 1927–28 Black Hawks, in their second year; the 1914–15 Toronto Ontarios, who either had very short memories or a sardonic sense of humour when they tried to change their luck by renaming themselves the Shamrocks; and the 1980–81 Winnipeg Jets, still shivering after being denuded of almost all their great WHA talent the year before, as a sort of hazing ritual for joining the NHL fraternity.

But enough of this detritus. The more urgent story can be divined from the entrails of fresher roadkill. There was room for debate 10 years ago as to whether 21 teams were already too many for the NHL; there was no question that 21 was the upper limit and that there wasn't enough talent available to sustain anything more than that. Ignoring the obvious, dismissing any consideration for the quality of play, and transfixed solely by the silvery glint of expansion fees, the NHL barged ahead and expanded anyway. And expanded again. And expanded *again*. A helplessly over-inflated balloon, a grotesquely engorged tick; these are the images conjured by the horizonless rabble of the NHL today, which has simply proven correct everyone who knew Back When that 21 teams were more than enough.

San Jose showed up with their fanged cartoon crest in 1991–92 and immediately took a pratfall into the modern Worst 20 list; a year later they were shoved out of the bottom 20 by the 1992–93 version of the same club, *and* by *another* expansion team, the new Ottawa Senators. They each came within a single defeat of actually out-inepting the '75 Capitals as the Worst in History. To their credit, the Sens improved on their record of the previous season for six straight years; to their embarrassment, their maiden outing was still *so* horrendous that three successive *improvements* are still among the two-dozen worst campaigns in modern hockey history.

We're a little surprised that Ottawa's expansion sisters, the Tampa Bay Lightning, haven't made the list. With the Sharks and the Sens having achieved respectability, the Lightweights seem worse by comparison, having squeaked over the .500 mark and into the playoffs just once in their eight years, and playing .300 hockey over the last three seasons. But the first-year Atlanta Thrashers are here, no matter that the NHL would award them points for losing in overtime. We refuse to play along. You do not get points for a loss, not as long as we're around. Not that it matters a whole heck of a lot; give them their cheat-points, and they were still a .238 side.

Bear in mind that 15 years ago, we spent a fair amount of space ripping the NHL for its rapacious, wrong-headed overexpansion of the 1970s and produced as Exhibits A through D the '73 Islanders, '75 Scouts, and the Capitals of both '75 and '76 to support our argument. The crimes of the '70s must be reduced to misdemeanour status in view of the atrocities the Bettman regime has produced. Fully four *new* teams in less than a decade have tumbled into this black hole of badness, and as we extend the list just slightly, we find *seven* recent clubs are among the worst 25 in history. That's right, *more than a quarter of the worst 25 teams in the entire modern history of hockey* have hit the ice – face-first, presumably – in just *the last eight seasons. Egad.* Seriously – think about that for a minute.

It speaks volumes about the state of the NHL. Like the sound of a shot thudding against the boards in an empty rink, the problems that have plagued the NHL over the last several seasons will continue to echo through upcoming campaigns. Rampant, wrong-headed, talent-diluting expansion . . . increasingly blatant clutch-and-grab tactics and a universal, stifling emphasis on defence . . . the abandonment of cozy, legendary old arenas for gigantic, sterile mega-stadiums . . . the jilting of loyal, knowledgeable fans in the game's traditional northern centres for the antic pursuit of theoretical fans in the hockey wasteland of the American Sun Belt . . . In the States, all these things, and more, have returned the game to the marginality from which it emerged during its brief efflorescence as the "hot" sport of the mid-'90s. Attendance dwindled, TV ratings plummeted, and word has begun filtering out of business offices that merchandising and licensing fees are also dropping like a stone. That's what the NHL gets when it assembles a tedious parade of some of the worst major-league teams ever to lace up skates, serves up a steady diet of Phoenix Coyotes vs. Carolina Hurricanes, allows the Stanley Cup playoffs to meander lazily into mid-June, and permits the league to bloat to a ghastly 30 teams, populated by far too many nondescript types who, in any other era, would be playing in the Central Hockey League – so that a marginal forward can join your team and seem like a Meaningful New Addition, and clubs can run up a halfway decent record with – quick! name the starting six on any .500 team last season! – exactly nobody of note on the roster.

Fine, you might be saying there in Canada, the devil with U.S.-based teams and the NHL for that matter; we've got junior hockey a stone's throw away, ten times the thrills for a fraction of the price. Fair enough, and more power to ya – but you've got to admit it's a sad commentary, when the NHL should be the very highest expression of the game, the world's best players and the world's best teams playing the best quality of hockey imaginable. The NHL is the steward of a rich, living history spanning over a century, stories of greatness and pathos and courage, from Walsh and Ridpath, Lalonde and Taylor, Morenz and Joliat, to the Kid Line, the Kraut Line, the Production Line, the Punch Line, to the Rocket and Mr. Hockey and the Flower and the Kid and *Le Magnifique.* To see that history squandered on a tasteless, couldn't-care-less rabble of Tampa Bays and Carolinas, and to see that legacy of brilliant play devolve into an expansion-diluted puddle – that deserves the outrage of every hockey fan, not a phlegmatic shrug of their shoulders.

We were also surprised that Nashville, Columbus, and the Minnesota . . . the Minnesota . . . sorry, we still can't bring ourselves to say it . . . the new Minnesota club – there, that'll do – didn't make this list. We shouldn't have been. Just as the pattern of scoring levels being consistently inflated by expansion reversed, when overexpansion finally diluted goal-scoring talent just as it had first diluted defensive skill, the pattern of shamefully noncompetitive teams being produced by expansion also reversed, when overexpansion continued to produce grossly inept clubs but introduced them into a nightmarishly diluted league filled with other grossly inept clubs. Most of the teams on the list of history's worst were fledgling franchises, entering a relatively stable league populated by a few powerhouses and by reasonably solid teams throughout. By the end of the '90s, though, while the NHL was churning out new teams that made the Scouts' roster look imposing, those new teams were playing against half a dozen clubs that a year or two earlier had themselves just made the list of history's worst, and two dozen other teams enfeebled by a decade of expansion plunder. In retrospect, the latest additions to the NHL rabble *couldn't* fail to the same extent as their predecessors; the newest teams' opponents were now too weak. The test for them had been dumbed down, graded on a curve. Naturally, the NHL declared the new clubs' escape from utter humiliation in the standings to be evidence of the great success of continued expansion. This is what Hall of Fame legend Ted Lindsay told Cam Cole of the *National Post* in February 2000:

> I'm lucky because I watch a pretty good hockey team in Detroit. But let me tell you: I watch some of the stupidest hockey players come into Joe Louis Arena on some of these teams – well, every team. A team has one or two good hockey players and the rest of them ought to get down on their knees every night and thank the Lord that there's 28 teams, because a lot of them would have never got out of their hometown.

As for those Washington futility marks we thought couldn't be outdone? The Caps' 67 losses were exceeded by *both* the

Sharks and Sens in 1992–93, with 71 and 70, respectively. The Fish that season, who were boned and filleted one night in Calgary by a 13-1 score, also tied the Caps' NHL mark of 17 consecutive losses – while Ottawa went the Caps one worse with 40 road losses, and a 38-game road winless streak, which was also a record 38-game road losing streak. They also tied other Capitals' NHL marks with their single road win and an 11-game winless streak at home. Any excuses? Always close but never a cigar? A period late and a goal short? Or were these teams the pushovers and laughingstocks you might suspect? Easy enough to find out. Coach Terry Crisp, after his Lightning one night were drubbed 10-0, observed, "The only difference between this and Custer's Last Stand was Custer didn't have to look at the tape afterwards."

Devastated Scale

We don't have the videotape, but we do have the Devastation Scale: we'll just set these teams up on the opposite side of the same scale we used before and see how they weigh in. We call it the Devastated Scale when we use it this way. Who got bowled over, blown out, and disembowelled? Pile the limbs up here and let's find out.

RANK	TEAM	LEAGUE	SEASON	W–L–T	GF	GA	DR
	Devastated Scale (minimum 16-game schedule)						
1	Chicago	NHL	'28–29	7-29-8	33	85	2.58
2	Washington	NHL	'74–75	8-67-5	181	446	2.46
3	Boston	NHL	'24–25	6-24-0	49	119	2.43
4	Philadelphia Q	NHL	'30–31	4-36-4	76	184	2.42
5	Saskatoon/MJaw	WCHL	'21–22	5-19-0	67	137	2.04
6	New York Isl	NHL	'72–73	12-60-6	170	347	2.04
7	New York Ame	NHL	'27–28	11-27-6	63	128	2.03
8	Ottawa	NHL	'93–94	14-61-9	201	397	1.98
9	Chicago	NHL	'27–28	7-34-3	68	134	1.97
10	Ottawa	NHL	'92–93	10-70-4	202	395	1.96
11	Quebec Bul	NHL	'19–20	4-20-0	91	177	1.94
12	Toronto Ont	NHA	'13–14	4-16-0	61	118	1.93
13	New York Ran	NHL	'43–44	6-39-5	162	310	1.91
14	San Jose	NHL	'92–93	11-71-2	218	414	1.90
15	New York Ame	NHL	'40–41	8-29-11	99	186	1.88
16	Montreal Can	NHL	'39–40	10-33-5	90	167	1.86
17	Kansas City	NHL	'75–76	12-56-12	190	351	1.85
18	Atlanta	NHL	'99–00	14-61-7	170	313	1.84
19	Victoria	PCHA	'18–19	7-13-0	44	81	1.84
20	Chicago	NHL	'53–54	12-51-7	133	242	1.82

GF: Goals for
GA: Goals against
DR: Devastated Rating

Is anyone surprised to once again see most of the same Remedial Hockey drop-outs? The '75 Craps are still the most severely beaten side of the last 70 years; the Quakers collapse,

boneless, into fourth; the wartime Ranger cadaver won't go away; the poorly bound first editions of both the Bruins and Islanders remain bad reading. The 1922 Western League team that shows up on both the Worst and Devastated lists are the Saskatoon Sheiks, with whom the great Bill Cook began his career. After disappointing the fans there with a 4-10-0 start, the team moved to Moose Jaw and played even worse. The club returned to Saskatoon the following season and, renaming themselves the Crescents, would improve under the guidance of player/coach Newsy Lalonde.

Ground into a pulp at the very top of this inverted list, which is to say at the very bottom of history's discard pile, are the third-year Chicago Black Hawks, who in 44 games timidly dribbled a grand total of 33 pucks across their opponents' goal line. By any statistical measure this was the most punchless, powerless offensive side in modern hockey history, if not of all time, possibly including our old rec-league club. Look, just for the record – for any of you who don't understand the fans' privilege and pleasure in ridiculing a really bad team – we readily acknowledge that the worst player on the worst professional team ever, on his worst day, could skate circles around either one of us. There. Satisfied? Now back to the ridicule.

What common factor links all these teams? Well, they couldn't score, and they couldn't keep the other team from scoring. What did you expect? It ain't rocket science. But there is one other thing: most of them have ridiculous uniforms. The Capitals debuted with their star-spangled red-white-and-blue sweaters and *white pants*. The star-studded motif was reminiscent of the sweaters of the New York Americans, and if the Caps were looking for a winning tradition this was not the model to follow. You'll see the gaudily attired '27–28 Amerks here as history's seventh-most devastated team and the '40–41 version at 15th.

Washington revived New York's stellar festooning, and as a crest, spelled out "Capitals" across their chests – in lower-case letters. With the "t" morphed into a little stylized hockey stick. The white pants experiment was soon abandoned; it was immediately noticeable that the white fabric became translucent wherever it got wet, allowing the brown interior padding to show through and creating a sight almost as embarrassing as the Capitals' actual performances. Although a routinely good side now, Washington changed their colours and style a couple of years ago and now sport what appears to be the speed-lined eagle logo of the U.S. Postal Service on their sweaters.

Ottawa's uniforms really aren't all that bad in comparison to many new designs, even if they're done-to-death basic black, but we have yet to hear a convincing explanation as to why they depict *not* a senator, but a *centurion*, in their crest. San Jose's hockey-stick-chomping shark logo quickly became one of the hottest-selling bits of sports merchandise in history – which, as far as we're concerned, only proves once again that no one ever went broke underestimating the intelligence of the American public. Worse, fanged carnivores suddenly became *de rigueur* throughout hockey.

There are the California Golden Seals, who actually wore white skates one season, and whose crest had a big "C" enclosing a sort of cubist seal holding a little hockey stick. There are the Islanders, whose crest has a map of Long Island with the letters "NY" superimposed, and the "Y" bent into a stylized hockey stick. And the Winnipeg Jets, who had the word "JETS" enclosed in a circle, with the "J" turned into a stylized hockey stick. In an uncharacteristically lenient mood, we can find little to complain about with the Thrashers name, or overly busy uniforms, or crest. Although – why does the bird have to be gripping *a little hockey stick*? Maybe all these teams have a little hockey stick in their crests because, if it wasn't there, you couldn't be certain what game it was they were futilely attempting to play. We're tempted to do a rant on the current proliferation of inverted triangles in hockey logos, but, alas, we have more stats to attend to.

Team Regeneration

Open your eyes now, if you've kept them covered during our stroll through the dismal, terrifying Cemetery of Clowns. Here's our final study of team performance, and it's much more upbeat. The list of hockey's most suddenly degenerated teams and history's worst ever should serve as a sort of memento mori for bandwagon fans of the Dallas Stars, Colorado Avalanche, even the Detroit Red Wings and other teams who've been riding high the last few seasons. But take heart, you who are fans of teams that seem to be forever chained to a dank wall in the basement: there's always hope – which is an amazing thing to hear us say, since we're from Buffalo, where disaster on the threshold of glory is a recurring theme, and the utter crushing of hope and imagination is a way of life. Still, it's true – as suddenly as one team may slip on the Great Banana Peel of injury, age, or bad trades and tumble from the heights, another may hit some springboard and vault upward from the depths. Here's a cheer-inducing roll call of the teams that have done that most dramatically. We'll apply the 44-game standard we used for hockey's most deteriorated and see what we can see.

One quick yarn before we go there, because there's a fascinating story to be wrested from the best one-season improvements before 1931–32, as well. The Canadiens of 1915–16 show the biggest one-season turnaround in history – from 6-14-0 to 16-7-1, +.388 – as the result of wholesale

Largest Single-Season Increases in Winning Percentage
(minimum 44-game schedule)

	TEAM	LEAGUE	SEASON	W-L-T	PCT		SEASON	W-L-T	PCT	IMPROVEMENT IN PCT PTS
1	San Jose	NHL	1992–93	11-71-2	.143	->	1993–94	33-35-16	.488	+345
2	Montreal Can	NHL	1942–43	19-19-12	.500	->	1943–44*	38-5-7	.830	+330
3	Winnipeg	NHL	1980–81	9-57-14	.200	->	1981–82	33-33-14	.500	+300
4	Quebec Nor	NHL	1991–92	20-48-12	.325	->	1992–93	47-27-10	.619	+294
5	Chicago	NHL	1928–29	7-29-8	.250	->	1929–30	21-18-5	.534	+284
6	Boston	NHL	1966–67	17-43-10	.314	->	1967–68	37-27-10	.568	+254
7	New York Ame	NHL	1927–28	11-27-6	.318	->	1928–29	19-13-12	.568	+250
8	Detroit	NHL	1985–86	17-57-6	.250	->	1986–87	34-36-10	.488	+238
9	Buffalo	NHL	1971–72	16-43-19	.327	->	1972–73	37-27-14	.564	+237
10	Dallas	NHL	1995–96	26-42-14	.402	->	1996–97	48-26-8	.634	+232
11	Detroit	NHL	1976–77	16-55-9	.256	->	1977–78	32-34-14	.488	+231
12	Edmonton	NHL	1980–81	29-35-16	.462	->	1981–82	48-17-15	.694	+231
13	Boston	NHL	1928–29*	26-13-5	.648	->	1929–30	38-5-1	.875	+227
14	Indianapolis	WHA	1974–75	18-57-3	.250	->	1975–76	35-39-6	.475	+225
15	Quebec Nor	NHL	1993–94	34-42-8	.452	->	1994–95	30-13-5	.677	+225
16	Ottawa	NHL	1995–96	18-59-5	.250	->	1996–97	31-36-15	.470	+220
17	Buffalo	NHL	1973–74	32-34-12	.487	->	1974–75	49-16-15	.706	+219
18	Montreal Can	NHL	1935–36	11-26-11	.344	->	1936–37	24-18-6	.562	+219
19	Chicago	NHL	1938–39	12-28-8	.333	->	1939–40	23-19-6	.542	+209
T20	St. Louis Blu	NHL	1978–79	18-50-12	.300	->	1979–80	34-34-12	.500	+200
T20	Chicago	NHL	1981–82	30-38-12	.450	->	1982–83	47-23-10	.650	+200

* Won Stanley Cup.

Bonus points for losses in overtime not included in teams' winning percentages; thus, Washington's improvement from 31-45-6 in 1998–99 to 44-26-12 in 1999–2000 represents an increase of .195, not .207 as suggested by bonus points for OT losses.

personnel changes. Newsy Lalonde and Skinner Poulin returned, Amos Arbour came on board, and Goldie Prodgers, Howard McNamara, and Bert Corbeau took charge on defence. Prodgers, who would play with eight separate teams in his 14-year major-league career, set the tone for the campaign, scoring both Montreal goals in a 2-1 win over Toronto in the season opener. Montreal's goals-against total, not a bad figure even in the chaotic year previous, improved slightly, but the capable defence trio sprang the offence loose, upping the team output by 60%. PCHA champion Portland travelled to Montreal to vie for the Cup, and in a ding-dong best-of-five series, Canadiens closed out the season much as they began it, edging the westerners 2-1 in Game 5 as Prodgers scored the winning goal.

The second-best one-year remodelling job ever was done by that fantastic Vancouver club of 1914–15; third-best, with a +.350, are Montreal Wanderers of that same season, who you'll recall as the most outstanding offensive side in history. Hyland, Roberts, and the Cleghorn brothers were on both the 7-13 club of 1913–14 and the 14-6 club of '14–15. The only changes were in goal, where the questionable McCarthy replaced an ineffective platoon, and on defence, where Montreal added . . . hmm . . . Goldie Prodgers. Wanderers improved 25% on offence and cut their goals against by a full third.

Quebec Bulldogs of 1911–12 would rank 8th on an all-time list of one-season turnarounds, with a gain of .306. Again, the 10-8 team was nearly identical to the 4-12 side of the preceding year, despite the transition from seven-man to six-man hockey; the one significant roster change was the addition of . . . huh! Goldie Prodgers. The Bulldog offence improved 25%, their goals against fell by almost 20%, and Quebec claimed the Cup. Prodgers's arrival co-incided with three of the eight greatest single-season team improvements in hockey history, and in fact, if you follow his peripatetic career closely, every single team he joined – and that's eight different franchises – immediately showed significant improvement on defence with him in the line-up. It's odd that a guy who seems to have had such a consistently positive impact – and the big, rugged, red-headed rushing defender was hardly easy to miss on the ice – has been all but forgotten when most of the regular performers from his era were welcomed into the Hall of Fame. Prodgers did go into coaching after he retired as a player, although never in the NHL, and it would be interesting to learn how well he did in that endeavour. Regardless, his playing career deserves more recognition than it's gotten.

Boing! Well! You do have to hand it to those third-year Sharks, who surged from being the fourth-losingest club in history and the 14th-most devastated team of modern times all the way up to, well, all the way to almost-not-a-loser. There were several changes, of course, most notably the acquisition of the two remaining members of Central Army's and the Soviet National Team's great KLM line,

34-year-old Igor Larionov and 35-year-old Sergei Makarov. The duo brought skill and intelligence to the Shark attack and led the team's plus/minus charts, although every club in the 26-team league except Florida, Tampa, and Anaheim had better point producers. Young Ozolinsh really blossomed on the blue line, and new rearguard Jeff Norton had a fine year as well, while Irbe took the crease in 74 of San Jose's 84 games, but these weren't anybody's first-team All-Stars either. New no-nonsense coach Kevin Constantine had to have been a major factor. Squeezing into the playoffs, San Jose upended Western Conference leaders Detroit, who had posted the fourth-best record in the NHL, in seven games, and took Western runners-up Toronto, the team with the league's fifth-best record, to the limit before succumbing.

The '43–44 Habs rank second among most improved teams on this modern list, and that's worth noting again because they're the only team on the modern list to have carried that momentum all the way to the Stanley Cup. Six of the teams on the all-time list improved themselves enough to include the ultimate prize, but these wartime Canadiens are the only club to achieve the feat since 1926. So while there's always hope your team might shake itself out of a regular-season coma, don't expect them to jump out of bed and jog right up to the Cup besides. Too much too soon. Lord Stanley, it seems, doesn't care much for *arrivistes*. The 1993–94 Rangers rank 22nd on the modern list and they did indeed earn the Cup that year, but they also had a pedigree of playoff suffering that qualified them for success this time around.

Similar to the war-era Habs, crucial personnel changes on both offence and defence propelled Buffalo, the ninth team here, into contention, and the rapid ascent of the Sabres in 1972–73 made Buffalo positively giddy. The third-year Sabres' new defence pair of 43-year-old hard-rock Tim Horton and 20-year-old roughhouse Jim Schoenfeld cut nearly a goal a game from what the club had allowed in its second season. They were aided by the defensive genius of checking line forwards and penalty killers Craig Ramsay, the sophomore winger, and Don Luce, the veteran centre. This was also the first full year together for Buffalo's dazzling young forward line – the swift, high-scoring French Connection of centre Gil Perreault and wingers Richard Martin and Rene Robert. Thank you, Sabres! The regional enthusiasm and affection for this Buffalo team may have been exceeded only by the civic support shown the Jets in their final year in Winnipeg. Sadly, hockey – having earned, like most other sports, every bit of the fans' cynicism in recent years – is unlikely to see a repeat of those sort of genuinely guileless outpourings of emotion. Buffalo's second showing on the list, incidentally, at 17th, was really a Stanley Cup Final-bound correction to the intervening, tragically anomalous 1973–74 campaign, in which Perreault broke his leg in game action and Horton was killed in a car wreck.

The number three team here, the 1981–82 Winnipeg Jets, actually did have one phenomenal impact player instrumental in their sudden vault to competitive status: 18-year-old rookie Dale Hawerchuk, whose 45 goals, 58 assists, and 103 points were almost exactly half as much as the figures Gretzky posted for Edmonton that year, but were an order of magnitude better than what Winnipeg had the year before. The Jets also had a new coach, Tom Watt, and added a potent young sniper on the wing, Paul MacLean. Underappreciated Eddie Staniowski took over in goal for the previous season's cavalcade of less able netminders; Serge Savard, one of the Canadiens' Big Three in the '70s, finished up here as a sort of mentor on defence. Winnipeg added 73 goals to their attack and sliced their goals against by 68.

The sixth team here, Boston, likewise fuel-injected their offence to blast off in the standings. The Bruins' 1967 trade that landed them Esposito, Stanfield, and Hodge was the catalyst for their turnaround, more so than the presence of Orr, brilliant even as a rookie in '66–67 but injured for much of '67–68 and yet to achieve his full powers.

It was one vital defensive player that made the difference for the seventh-most improved modern team. The 1928–29 Americans were the counterpoint to the catastrophically worsened Pittsburgh Pirates. Billy Burch and Normie Himes were the Amerks' best forwards both years, and Lionel Conacher, Bullet Joe Simpson, and Leo Reise their top three defencemen, but New York's acquisition of the great little netminder Roy Worters from the Ice Bucs effectively reversed the positions of the two teams.

Coaches and broadcasters like to talk about "chemistry," that combination of elements and attitude that make a team a winner. Chemistry, however, is an exact science; mix a specific amount of this known substance with an exact amount of that known compound and you get a perfectly predictable result. Hockey don't work that way, of course; the cliché should really refer to "alchemy," the mediaeval pseudo-science that attempts to combine matter, mysticism, guesswork, and faith in order to yield something miraculous. Case in point, the '92–93 Quebec Nordiques, who, with the same coach as the previous year and almost all the same players in the lead roles, transmuted base metal into gold. Cutting a mere 18 goals from their goals-against mark but adding nearly 100 to their attack, Les Nords doubled their point total, from 52 to 104. Mobile, under-rated Steve Duchesne joined the Quebec defence corps, but mainly it looked like the Nords, to a man, from stars like Joe Sakic and Mats Sundin, to fine second-liners like Owen Nolan, Mike Ricci, and Scott Young, to the 20th or 25th guy

on the roster, simply picked up their game by one or more notches – in many cases, just maturing with a year or three of NHL play under their belts. Coach Pierre Page oversaw the upgrade. Alas, Quebec fell in six games in the opening round of the playoffs to provincial arch-rival and eventual Cup champion Montreal.

The NHL's unshackling of offence for the 1929–30 season was a tonic for the abysmally punchless Black Hawks. Massive rearguard Taffy Abel strengthened the defence, and good young players who had been with the impotent 1928–29 club began to blossom – most notably their wiry young stickhandling wizard on left wing, Johnny Gottselig. Gottselig played his entire 16-year career in Chicago, a star for many of those years, and afterward the Hawks' coach.

Detroit had several factors working in their favour in 1986–87: Steve Yzerman, absent with injuries for a chunk of the stinker '85–86 campaign, returned to lead the club; playmaking centre Adam Oates, a rookie part-timer in '85–86, grew into a full-time role in '86–87; Darren Veitch and Dave Lewis were obtained in trades and made a world of difference on the Red Wing blue line; rookie Shawn Burr sparkled as a defensive forward; and Glen Hanlon arrived from the Rangers to provide great netminding. The overriding factor may well have been new coach Jacques Demers – who had worked similar magic at Indianapolis in the WHA in 1975–76. The acquisition of the fine fireplug defenceman Whitey Stapleton and the promotion of goalie Michel Dion were key to the Racers' acceleration through the WHA standings, and it's true that fully 16 of the 21 teams on this list had also installed a new coach at the start of their year of renascence. Besides Demers, Constantine, and Watt, the new bench bosses were, in order, Tom Shaughnessy, Chicago 1929 (replaced in mid-season by Bill Tobin); Harry Sinden, Boston 1967; Tommy Gorman, Americans 1928; Ken Hitchcock, Dallas 1996; Bobby Kromm, Detroit 1977; Art Ross, Boston 1929; Marc Crawford, Quebec 1994; Jacques Martin, Ottawa 1996; Floyd Smith, Buffalo 1974; Cecil Hart, Canadiens 1936; Paul Thompson, Chicago 1939; and Orval Tessier, Chicago 1982. The fact remains that Demers is the only coach to have produced, upon his arrival, *two* of the twenty biggest one-season improvements in major-league hockey history.

So is it the coach, or is it the players? We don't have any definitive answers on that broad question. But we have plenty of definitive answers to some specific questions about the accomplishments of individual players, and we're going to address those next.

3.
Players

Phantom Joe Malone's still-famous 44 goals in 20 games in 1917–18 made him the NHL's first scoring leader. For 27 years Malone's 44-goal season remained the gold standard in hockey, until Rocket Richard became the first man to hit for 50 in a season. It took another 16 years before Boom-Boom Geoffrion matched Richard, and 19 before Bobby Hull *broke* the Rocket's mark. Fifty's been the magic figure ever since, even though it's been matched or exceeded 153 times in the last 26 years. Still, after more than 80 years, Malone's 44 in 20 is cited anytime somebody has a big goal-scoring year, because Malone did it in so few games – and the fact he did do it in so few games is mind-boggling to writers and broadcasters with no idea how different conditions were back then.

This is where they get into trouble. They try to compare Malone's mark to what somebody did this season, or last, and suggest that if he'd played a modern schedule four times as long – 80 games instead of 20 – he'd have scored four times as many goals – 176 instead of 44. Or, with the vague knowledge that scoring was somehow, to some unknown extent, higher back in Joe's day, they suggest that 176 goals may not be exactly right, because you have to consider, um, er . . . we'll be right back after this commercial break!

Well, they're right, and they're wrong. Listen to us; we're *always* right. If Malone had played 80 games in 1917–18 –

yeah, we know the NHL plays 82, but let's keep the figures round for convenience's sake – he may well have scored 176 goals. Just as Marty Walsh may well have scored 250 if he'd played 80 games instead of just 12 when he scored 38 times in 1908–09. There's nothing wrong with your arithmetic if you just want to pro-rate figures from one particular season. But it's pointless, eh? Pro-rated figures have no direct, easy relationship to a modern 80-game season, where Paul Kariya's 33 goals in 66 games in 2000–01 become 40 in 80 games – nor for that matter any relevance to similarly pro-rated figures from the 1918–19 season, where Newsy Lalonde's total that year translates into 108 goals over 80 games, or from the 1944–45 season, where the Rocket's 50 become 80 over 80 games.

That, most emphatically, is not to say Malone's season, or Lalonde's, or Richard's, isn't relevant to today's hockey and to Kariya's season. It's meant only to point out that pro-rating figures on that goals-per-game basis is valid only if you assume that the conditions under which Malone scored 44 goals in 20 games, or Lalonde 23 in 17, or Richard 50 in 50, or Pavel Bure 58 in 74, continue to be in effect for an 80-game season. As we've already seen in earlier chapters, conditions have varied far too widely over the history of the game to give any validity to comparing simple pro-rated stats from any one season to simple pro-rated stats from any other. The rules, the style of play, the level of competition – they all combine to establish a set of conditions that enhance or suppress goal scoring.

Just as environments and ecosystems vary from one continent to another, just as gravity and atmosphere vary from one planet to another, scoring conditions vary from one season to another. You couldn't expect to see parrots and monkeys that gambol through lush jungle plant growth flourishing on the cold, windy slopes of the northern Rockies, nor polar bears lumbering through a tropical rain forest; the environment is all wrong for that to happen. You couldn't expect to see an astronaut who can bound effortlessly 20 feet at a time in the light gravity of the moon be able to do that back on Earth; the gravity prevents its happening.

And just like that, you can't expect a player in a league and a season that produces an average of 4 or 5 goals per game to put up numbers at the same rate as a guy who played in a league and a season that produces 8 or 10 goals per game. So the next hurdle we have to clear in comparing goal-scoring performances is factoring in any given season's goals-per-game average.

The goals-per-game average in the NHL's inaugural season, 1917–18 – the year Malone scored his 44 in 20 games – was nearly 10 goals per game, 9.93, to be exact. Just seven years later, in 1924–25, the NHL per-game average had plunged to just less than half of that, 4.94 goals per game. Babe Dye was the league leader in goals that season, with 38 in 29 games. So let's compare: in a 10-goals-a-game year, Malone averaged 2.20 goals per game, or 176 in 80 games; in a 5-goals-a-game year, Dye averaged 1.31 per game, or 105 goals in 80 games. So what do we do now, just roughly double Dye's 1924–25 pro-rated total to put it on the same basis as Malone's 1917–18 total: Malone, 176, Dye, 210? Or, to the same end and with the same practical result, cut Malone's total in half to put it on the same basis as Dye's: Malone, 88, Dye, 105? Well, ah, yes – and no.

This goals-per-game hurdle trips up so many who want to make season-to-season comparisons. They make the quantum leap to the realization of what an enormous factor scoring conditions are in comparing individual scoring feats from different seasons, then tumble to the ground thinking the race is done. Get up already! There are more hurdles ahead.

Let's look at the 1923–24 NHL campaign, which produced 5.31 goals per game, very similar to the 2000–01 NHL average of 5.44, and even closer to the 1956–57 average of 5.38. Cy Denneny led the NHL with 22 goals in 21 games in '23–24, Gordie Howe led the league with 44 in 70 games in '56–57, and Kariya's 33 in 66 was among the better marks in 2000–01. Just for argument's sake, let's say the scoring conditions – the scoring "environments" – were equivalent, no matter that in Denneny's day offence was hindered by the prohibition against forward passing, in Howe's day by a consistently high level of competition, and today by the tyranny of clutch-and-grab tactics and a league overwhelmingly populated by minor-league-quality goal-scoring talent. Regardless of the reasons for the generally low levels of scoring, that level is similar in each season – again, for this little exercise, let's say it's equal. So is it fair to say that playing 80 games apiece, Denneny's 1.05 goals-a-game performance was worth 84 goals, Howe's 0.63 goals-a-game year was worth 50, and Kariya's 0.50 season worth 40? In a word, no.

Denneny, like Malone and Lalonde, played in an era in which players were on the ice the majority of the time – sometimes, literally all game long. There were only one or two spare players on a team, and substitutions were rare, often nonexistent. The entirety of a team's scoring, therefore, obviously fell pretty much to its starting five skaters (or six, in seven-man hockey). While this dictated a somewhat slower pace than the modern game, it also means Denneny, Malone, Lalonde, and their contemporaries had twice as much ice time, and twice as many opportunities per game to score, as did Howe, in the three-line days of the 1950s – and two to three times the ice time, and two to three times as many scoring opportunities, as did Kariya in the four-line game of today. So ice time's another element that needs to be taken into account, and equalized, before we can put Malone and Denneny, and Howe and Richard, and Gretzky and Kariya and Lemieux, all on the same scale.

The All-Time Scoring Leaders

Before we dive right in and try to identify the greatest scorers in the history of hockey, let's take a slow walk around the whole subject of individual scoring and come at it from a wider perspective. Even the youngest or newest fans know Gretzky is hockey's all-time scoring leader. If they examine any current list of the game's all-time leaders in goals, assists, or points, though, they'd have no idea that hockey was even played before World War II. In fact, Gordie Howe, Maurice Richard, and Red Kelly are the only players among the top 100 on any of those lists to have played any part of their careers before the 1950s, and only 17 "Top-100" players performed before the 1960s. This might lead some newcomer to the ghastly assumption that all the game's greatest scorers have played in only the last 50 years, or 40, or 20, and that no one who came before them rates among history's best. Fie upon it! Let's crack open the old photo album. We'll show you a thing or two.

One thing obscuring the giants who skated in the early days of the NHL is that few reference sources augment their totals with the scoring they did in the NHL's major-league predecessors and rivals. Let's just see, though, who dominated major-league scoring – NHL and otherwise – between the inception of the pro game in 1908 and the end of the NHL's western competition in 1926. This first list reveals the scoring leaders – with their league totals combined – in all of major-league pro hockey from those years. The years in which they played are shown in parentheses. If a player's career continued beyond 1925–26, it's indicated by an arrow (>). All-time leading totals for games played, goals, assists, and points are noted with an asterisk when they appear.

One grain of salt, though, with which to take the stories accompanying these lists and all the charts to follow: we'll be making frequent mention, again, that many of the players listed are enshrined in the Hall of Fame. Be aware that 218 players have been inducted into the Hall, and that 99 of them played all or part of their careers before 1925–26. Considering the small fraction of all major-league players, ever, represented by the few guys who played on the short rosters in the small leagues up to 1926, you'd have to say they're overrepresented, and guess that there was a little friendly cronyism at work in the nominations and voting. That's not to say there's any bums in there, but the Hall is supposed to immortalize the great, not the merely very good. On the other hand, it's safe to say that those HOF inductees who rank high or show up repeatedly on our charts certainly belong in the Hall, which is something you definitely can't say about a lot of the guys inducted in the "Builders" category. Bill Wirtz? P. D. Ross? Jim Norris? *Harold Ballard?* C'mon. Don't get us started. On to the players.

Top 20 Scorers, 1909–1926				
	GP	G	A	P
1 Newsy Lalonde ('10–26 >)	296	362*	81	443*
2 Joe Malone ('09–24)	273	343	58	401
3 Cy Denneny ('15–26 >)	259	258	82	340
4 Frank Nighbor ('13–26 >)	287	238	96	334
5 Frank Foyston ('13–26 >)	297	223	72	295
6 Cyclone Taylor ('09–23)	169	189	104*	293
7 Mickey MacKay ('15–26 >)	247	198	92	290
8 Didier Pitre ('10–23)	271	233	52	285
9 Tom Dunderdale ('10–24)	279	223	61	284
10 Odie Cleghorn ('11–26 >)	296	229	53	282
11 Eddie Oatman ('11–26)	302	178	98	276
12 Harry Cameron ('13–26)	315	173	91	264
13 Bernie Morris ('15–25)	217	176	85	261
14 Jack Darragh ('11–24)	253	191	62	253
15 Smokey Harris ('12–25)	272	158	93	251
16 Corb Denneny ('15–26 >)	263	178	70	248
17 Cully Wilson ('13–26 >)	304	179	69	248
18 Gordon Roberts ('10–20)	170	203	41	244
19 Duke Keats ('16–26 >)	174	154	76	230
20 Babe Dye ('20–26 >)	172	176	39	215

Newsy Lalonde headlines this early edition of the game's top scorers, followed by Malone, Cy Denneny, and a dozen other Hall of Fame inductees among the top 20 (only Cleghorn, Oatman, Harris, Wilson, and Corb Denneny were never enshrined). Five of them had averaged better

than a goal a game over their careers to this point – in order of per-game productivity, Malone, Lalonde, Roberts, Taylor, and Dye. They almost had to, in order to make the list; as you can see, the goal totals for every player here dwarf their assist totals. Of course, that's not because they were horrendous puckhogs; some of the finest passers and play-makers ever to handle a puck are among this group. It's because most of the leagues in which they played simply never recorded assists, and once the tabulation began, the official definition of what constituted an assist was so rigorous, and official scorekeeping often so cursory, that assists were awarded on only a tiny fraction of goals scored.

In fact, the NHL's forerunner, the NHA, kept no record whatsoever of assists, nor, in its first year of operation, did the NHL itself. Nor were assists part of the official record in the PCHA's early days, nor anywhere available, despite their compilation, for most seasons of PCHA and WHL play. Furthermore, since the original *Compendium* first appeared, we learned that significant numbers of NHL scoresheets from the league's early years are, to this day, missing entirely (they *might* be somewhere in the NHL's Montreal offices), many more do not indicate any assists even from those seasons in which assists were to be part of the official record (no assists, for instance, were *ever* recorded for any NHL games played in Hamilton), and plenty of others were either so hard to read or so carelessly interpreted by NHL statisticians of the day that those early NHL figures must now be regarded as wholly unreliable.

The task of locating, exhuming, and transcribing sometimes conflicting lists of PCHA scoring leaders from old microfilm of ancient newspapers from Vancouver, Victoria, Winnipeg, Edmonton, Calgary, and Regina was one of the most fascinating, if tediously labour-intensive, not to mention myopia-inducing, chores we undertook in compiling the first *Compendium*. Number-cruncher extraordinaire Bob Duff, the man most responsible for the great research in Stan and Shirley Fischler's 1983 *The Hockey Encyclopedia* – until *Total Hockey*, far and away the best of any hockey encyclopaedia previously published – handled an even more daunting chore to fill in the gaping holes in the record the NHL had always presented as complete and official. Like the sainted Charles Coleman before him, Duff went through the first eight years of NHL games, scoresheet by scoresheet and news report by news report, to compile a far more thorough and accurate record of early NHL scoring than had ever before been assembled. Ernie Fitzsimmons and his associates in the Society for International Hockey Research have performed equally painstaking labour to exhume records from the NHA, the PCHA, WCHL, and WHL, as well as reams of reports and statistics from the International Pro League, from other early rivals for major-league status, and from senior, amateur, and semi-pro leagues from earlier in the 20th century. Thanks to the work of Duff, Fitzsimmons, and our colleagues at *Total Hockey* – Dan Diamond, Ralph

Dinger, James Duplacey, and the entire staff – following in the dusty footprints we left in the game's buried archives more than 15 years ago, we – and all hockey fans – have access to a far more nearly complete and accurate record of the pro game's early era.

It does mean, of course, that a lot of the figures here have been adjusted from those we presented confidently in earlier editions of the *Compendium*. Assists and recredited goals, unearthed by Duff's archaeological digs as well as Fitzsimmons's findings, locating assists for the NHA and PCHA, have likewise resulted in some reshuffling in our rankings of players who performed prior to the formation of the NHL. Harry Cameron and Eddie Oatman, notably, get a big boost up the career scoring ladder here with the addition of their assists.

One last point about the 1909–1926 list. Cameron is the only man here to have played his entire career on defence – and he, Bill Gadsby, Bobby Orr, Ray Bourque, and Paul Coffey are the only rearguards you'll find in any of the snapshots to follow. Cameron is third in games played at this point, behind Canadiens mainstay Louis Berlinquette (322) and goalie Harry "Hap" Holmes (324). The rapid ascent of Babe Dye, the only man here whose career doesn't predate the NHL, speaks highly for his deadly skills as a sniper, but also augurs badly for the fate of the other immortals here on subsequent lists.

which assists were awarded – or more to the point, not awarded – in their day jumps right out at you, with their shy little double-digit career totals in that column, compared to the totals for more recent players here who received less grudging credit for their playmaking. And the fact that most of the new immortals here, with careers of similar length to those of the ancient greats, have played roughly twice as many games, reflects the disparity in the length of schedules. Lalonde has already been overtaken five times in career points, even though he remains the all-time *goal-scoring* leader by a goodly margin. Only Malone, Cy Denneny, Frank Nighbor, and Mickey MacKay accompany him from 1926 onto the 1940 list.

The new NHL leaders at this point are Ol' Poison, Nels Stewart, the big, tough, durable, hard-shooting centreman of the Montreal Maroons, Boston Bruins, and New York Americans, followed by Bill Cook, the rugged Ranger sniper. Again, recent revisions to decades-old statistics result in some reordering; here it's Nighbor who's helped most. Frank Boucher, the smooth, clean, two-way centre for the Cook brothers, holds down third place; he'd pass Bill during a brief comeback as player/coach in 1943–44. Bun Cook is here too, completing one of several pairs and trios of long-time linemates on this chart: the great Canadien duo of Howie Morenz and Aurel Joliat is close behind; Canadian Olympic star Hooley Smith teamed with Stewart on three separate clubs, and lined up alongside Nighbor in Ottawa; Nighbor spent even more time centring Cy Denneny there. Toronto's Kid Line wingers Conacher and Jackson stand adjacent; Chicago has Johnny Gottselig and Paul Thompson; and Boston can boast two sets of linemates – Marty Barry and Harry Oliver, as well as Dit Clapper and Cooney Weiland. Small world, eh? Indeed, it was.

Among the 20 players here, every one of them but Gottselig and Thompson were admitted to the Hall of Fame. Yet, due to even longer schedules as well as the scoring inflation of the war era, more than half the great players on this list will have been replaced barely 10 years down the road.

Top 20 Scorers, 1909–1940

		GP	G	A	P
1	Nels Stewart ('25–40)	650	324	191	515*
2	Bill Cook ('22–37)	591	317	191	508
3	Frank Boucher ('22–38 >)	655	213	286*	499
4	Howie Morenz ('24–37)	550	270	197	467
5	Aurel Joliat ('23–38)	654	270	190	460
6	Newsy Lalonde ('10–27)	297	362*	81	443
7	Hooley Smith ('25–40 >)	674*	198	208	406
8	Joe Malone ('09–24)	273	343	58	401
9	Marty Barry ('28–40)	509	195	192	387
10	Charlie Conacher ('30–40 >)	413	218	157	375
11	Busher Jackson ('30–40 >)	475	198	173	371
12	Cy Denneny ('15–29)	368	279	90	369
13	Frank Nighbor ('13–30)	438	255	111	366
14	Mickey MacKay ('15–30)	394	242	111	353
15	Dit Clapper ('28–40 >)	583	196	156	352
16	Harry Oliver ('22–37)	593	217	133	350
17	Bun Cook ('25–37)	531	183	152	335
18	Johnny Gottselig ('29–40 >)	528	165	170	335
19	Cooney Weiland ('29–39)	509	173	160	333
20	Paul Thompson ('27–39)	582	153	179	332

That's the list of major-league hockey's all-time top scorers through 1940. The almost complete disappearance here, after just 14 years, of the men on the initial list is sad, but the two main reasons for that are obvious. The way in

Top 20 Scorers, 1909–1951

		GP	G	A	P
1	Bill Cowley ('35–47)	549	195	353*	548*
2	Syd Howe ('30–46)	698	237	291	528
3	Toe Blake ('33–48)	577	235	292	527
4	Doug Bentley ('41–51 >)	538	215	311	526
5	Nels Stewart ('25–40)	650	324	191	515
6	Frank Boucher ('22–38, '44)	670	217	296	513
7	Bill Cook ('22–37)	591	317	191	508
8	Elmer Lach ('41–51 >)	493	179	313	492
9	Maurice Richard ('43–51 >)	469	292	187	479
10	Busher Jackson ('30–44)	633	241	234	475
11	Dit Clapper ('28–47)	833*	228	246	474
12	Howie Morenz ('24–37)	550	270	197	467

		GP	G	A	P
13	Aurel Joliat ('23–38)	654	270	190	460
14	Max Bentley ('41–51 >)	484	194	254	448
15	Milt Schmidt ('37–51 >)	554	179	268	447
16	Newsy Lalonde ('10–27)	297	362*	81	443
17	Syl Apps Sr. ('37–48)	423	201	231	432
18	Lorne Carr ('34–46)	580	204	222	426
19	Roy Conacher ('39–51 >)	478	223	199	422
20	Hooley Smith ('25–41)	715	200	215	415

By the end of the 1950–51 season, the boil-over of wartime scoring had simmered down, but during those years Stewart had in turn been passed by four players. At this point the great Bruin pivot Bill Cowley is the all-time scoring leader, having dethroned Syd Howe, who briefly held the title himself. The accomplishments of Lalonde, Stewart, Boucher, Cook, Clapper, Jackson, Morenz, Joliat, and Smith continue to shine through here, but every other player from the 1940 list has been superseded, and, but for Lalonde, no one who answered the roll call in 1926 is any longer present. It's vital to note, however, that Lalonde is *still* the all-time goal-scoring master here, and Malone still stands second, although the handful of assists allotted them has by now dropped Malone off the points leader board. Lalonde's antediluvian career mark of 362 goals wouldn't be exceeded until Rocket Richard equalled and passed it during the 1954–55 season. By the way, the only guy on the 1909–1951 list not in the Hall of Fame is Lorne Carr, the clean, steady wingman for Americans and Leafs, whose inclusion in the distinguished company of this list suggests how underrated he's been left by time.

Top 20 Scorers, 1909–1967

		GP	G	A	P
1	Gordie Howe ('47–67 >)	1398*	649*	852*	1501*
2	Maurice Richard ('43–60)	978	544	421	965
3	Jean Beliveau ('51–67 >)	864	399	545	944
4	Andy Bathgate ('53–67 >)	919	314	556	870
5	Alex Delvecchio ('51–67 >)	1090	328	536	864
6	Ted Lindsay ('45–60,'65)	1068	379	472	851
7	Red Kelly ('48–67)	1316	281	542	823
8	Bernie Geoffrion ('51–67 >)	824	388	413	801
9	Bobby Hull ('58–67 >)	674	370	345	715
10	Henri Richard ('56–67 >)	764	264	446	710
11	Norm Ullman ('56–67 >)	817	294	409	703
12	Elmer Lach ('41–54)	664	215	408	623
13	Bert Olmstead ('49–62)	848	181	421	602
14	Dickie Moore ('52–67 >)	692	256	344	600
15	George Armstrong ('50–67 >)	964	252	347	599
16	Dean Prentice ('53–67 >)	923	265	323	588
17	Stan Mikita ('59–67 >)	549	215	369	584
18	Milt Schmidt ('37–55)	778	229	346	575
19	Johnny Bucyk ('56–67 >)	755	227	346	573
20	Bill Gadsby ('47–66)	1248	130	437	567

That's the way the all-time scoring leaders stood at the close of the Original Six era and the dawn of expansion. During the changeless years of the Original Six, the names on the list have nonetheless changed almost completely over the 17 seasons since the previous set of standings; only the Rocket, Elmer Lach, and Milt Schmidt survive the turnover. That's due partly to the introduction of the 70-game schedule in 1949–50, and partly to the durability of the players who now appear here. The gulf between Howe and the rest of the pack is awe-inspiring, testimony to his domination of the game during these years – and perhaps eye-opening to even middle-aged fans who saw him play only late in his jaw-dropping 34-year major-league career and appear as a soft-spoken, grandfatherly TV presence after his retirement. His numbers are even more breathtaking when you realize every single guy left in his wake on this list is a member of the Hall of Fame, with the exception of Dean Prentice. Not seen here is Leaf great Teeder Kennedy, whose career straddles the era of this and the preceding list, and who ranked well up here before he retired in 1957. Two other names not present, of course, are those of Lalonde and Malone, who still rank seventh and eighth, respectively, in all-time goal scoring at this juncture, more than 40 years after their last major-league appearances.

Top 20 Scorers, 1909–1979

		GP	G	A	P
1	Gordie Howe ('47–71, '74–79 >)	2026*	945*	1331*	2276*
2	Bobby Hull ('58–79 >)	1447	907	884	1791
3	Phil Esposito ('64–79 >)	1161	676	816	1492
4	Stan Mikita ('59–79 >)	1377	539	921	1460
5	Johnny Bucyk ('56–78)	1540	556	813	1369
6	Norm Ullman ('56–77)	1554	537	822	1359
7	Frank Mahovlich ('57–78)	1418	622	713	1335
8	Alex Delvecchio ('51–74)	1549	456	825	1281
9	Jean Beliveau ('51–71)	1125	507	712	1219
10	Jean Ratelle ('61–79 >)	1167	452	705	1157
11	Dave Keon ('61–79 >)	1363	467	682	1149
12	Henri Richard ('56–75)	1256	358	688	1046
13	Rod Gilbert ('61–78)	1065	406	615	1021
14	Andy Bathgate ('53–75)	1080	350	630	980
15	Andre Lacroix ('68–79 >)	847	327	652	979
16	Maurice Richard ('43–60)	978	544	421	965
17	Bobby Orr ('67–79)	657	270	645	915
18	Ralph Backstrom ('57–77)	1336	378	514	892
19	Johnny McKenzie ('59–79)	1168	369	518	887
20	Bobby Clarke ('70–79 >)	773	270	598	868

This is the all-time scoring parade following the WHA's final surrender in 1979. (Once again, career totals listed here reflect all major-league scoring. Points compiled in the WHA are included.) Twelve years after the previous list, dozens of NHL expansion teams and new teams in the rival WHA later, thousands of games and goals, and what's changed most on this list is the numbers, not the names. The dilution of talent and the inflated scoring that NHL expansion and the WHA wrought also allowed many of the stars on the last pre-expansion list to extend their careers to unprecedented lengths and keep adding to their already sky-high career scoring totals. Esposito and Mahovlich are the only new names here among the top nine. It's true that many of the players on this roll call of hockey's all-time leading scorers had registered many of their points in WHA action, but even if all those WHA totals were taken away, only Lacroix, Backstrom, and McKenzie – not surprisingly, the only three guys here not admitted to the Hall of Fame – would fail to qualify for a spot. Their places would be taken by Yvon Cournoyer, Dean Prentice, and Ted Lindsay.

One other vantage point before we head farther down the trail: when the Original Six era closed, Gordie Howe was the only man after 60 years of major-league hockey to have amassed a thousand points. As the 1980s began, only 13 men in more than 70 years of major-league play had cracked the thousand-point barrier. By the start of the 2001–02 season, more than 60 players will have joined the 1,000 club. Once more, here's a testament to how the enormous length of the modern schedule and evolutionary changes to statistical criteria make raw totals wholly unsuitable as a basis for cross-era comparisons.

Top 20 Scorers, 1909–2001

		GP	G	A	P
1	Wayne Gretzky ('79–99)	1567	940	2027*	2967*
2	Gordie Howe ('47–71, '74–80)	2106*	960*	1357	2317
3	Mark Messier ('79–01 >)	1613	652	1140	1792
4	Bobby Hull ('58–80)	1447	907	884	1791
5	Marcel Dionne ('72–89)	1348	731	1040	1771
6	Ron Francis ('82–01 >)	1489	487	1137	1624
7	Steve Yzerman ('84–01 >)	1310	645	969	1614
8	Phil Esposito ('64–81)	1282	717	873	1590
9	Ray Bourque ('80–01 >)	1612	410	1169	1579
10	Mario Lemieux ('85–97, '01 >)	788	648	922	1570
11	Paul Coffey ('81–01 >)	1409	396	1135	1531
12	Stan Mikita ('59–80)	1394	541	926	1467
13	Bryan Trottier ('76–94)	1279	524	901	1425
14	Dale Hawerchuk ('82–97)	1188	518	891	1409
15	Jari Kurri ('81–98)	1251	601	797	1398
16	Mike Gartner ('80–98)	1510	735	752	1387
17	Johnny Bucyk ('56–78)	1540	556	813	1369
18	Norm Ullman ('56–77)	1554	537	822	1359
19	Guy Lafleur ('72–85, '89–91)	1126	560	793	1353
20	Doug Gilmour ('84–01 >)	1342	429	914	1343

Even with all their WHA scoring subtracted, Gretzky and Howe would still easily top this list. Bobby Hull, Norm Ullman, and Mike Gartner, however, would fall off the chart if it listed only NHL scoring, moving Denis Savard (1,338), Gil Perreault (1,326) – who in the mid-1980s ranked well up among the top 10 of all time – and Alex Delvecchio (1,281) into the final berths on the top 20. Mark Messier is the only other player here credited with WHA points; without those Messier would drop only one rung on the ladder. Frank Mahovlich (1,103 NHL, 232 WHA) is the only other man besides these to have scored more than 1,300 major-league points.

That was a lovely stroll down Memory Lane, wasn't it? But what's the real point of that exercise, you ask. Well, for one thing, it's always rewarding to be able to mention the game's ancient and all-but-forgotten immortals in the same discussion as the modern superstars. Mainly, though, it illustrates how the changing nature of the game – notably the lack of statistical reward in the assist column for pre-war players, and particularly the immense number of games played in more modern seasons – serves to bury the stars of an earlier era unjustly. How much more fair and telling it would be to look not at today's list of hockey's all-time top 20 scorers, completely populated as it is by players who competed no longer ago than 1977, but instead to skim the top three or four players off the top of each of these era-by-era lists, *la crème de la crème de la crème*, and regard that with the reverence due the men who dominated scoring throughout their own long brilliant day, regardless of how record-keeping and league schedules have enhanced or suppressed their feats: Lalonde and Malone deserve to stand alongside Gretzky and Howe, and with them Richard, Boucher, Esposito, Cook, Hull, Morenz, Beliveau, Dionne, Denneny, Stewart, Blake, Bathgate, Bentley, Cowley, Mikita, and Syd Howe.

Still, there's more sentimentality than statistical rigour in concluding that the above group of 20 all-time greats are the most magnificent offensive forces ever to lace up skates. And it leaves acres of room for argument. Longevity is one thing all those players had in common, which raises the question: how much of a factor should that be in assessing the best of all time? Durability is certainly admirable, but the careers of Mario Lemieux, Marty Walsh, and other brilliant stars weren't interrupted or ended by a hangnail, exactly. Should their careers, so grimly curtailed, earn less recognition than those of guys who were a little less productive, a bit less dangerous, on a per-game basis but who kept piling up points as their careers went on for more seasons than "Man Alive"? For now, we'll leave that imponderable debate to the rest of you fans. The total value of a player – goal scoring, playmaking, defensive skill, ability in the clutch, and anything else you want to throw in there – over the course of an entire career is in a sense the Holy Grail of hockey statistics, and that's a quest we're not willing to undertake at this point. At least, not without first getting a seven-figure grant from the Ford Foundation. What we *can* do, though, is try to determine who had the best single season by the measure of those separate criteria, and we're going to start doing that now.

Presence

This may seem to be a left-turn, trivial sort of study, but there's method to our madness. Bear with us. We first cooked up this stat years ago while watching Gil Perreault, late in his career, saddled with wingmen like Ric Seiling and Steve Patrick, skating for the wreckage Scotty Bowman had made of the mid-'80s Sabres. Still dazzlingly creative, Perreault, game after game, created vast swaths of open ice for teammates who without fail declined to enter it, or got himself open for passes that never came, or put the puck on the tape for a linemate who consistently fired wide, or high, or flubbed it into the goalie's midsection, or fanned entirely. Ten years later, Gretzky, still astonishingly creative, wound up doing the same brilliant things with the same frustrating results for the decadent post-Stanley Cup Rangers.

Perreault and Gretzky nonetheless were their team's best point-producers, and, needless to say, many another offensive force has had to carry a team otherwise sorely lacking in firepower. The NHL's bravura solo act for the last two years has been the Pavel Bure Show in Florida. Even a superb sniper gets fewer chances, fewer goals, without decent linemates to set him up; even an expert playmaker gets less return, fewer assists, without teammates who can put away his passes. Worse for the guy who alone on his team has real offensive skills, he gets all the attention from the other team's checking. That's obvious, and the equally obvious corollary, of course, is that any player's point totals are boosted by playing with skilful passers and goal-scoring marksmen. The great scoring lines through history – the Kid Line of Primeau, Conacher, and Jackson; the Punch Line of Blake, Lach, and Richard; the Production Line of Abel, Lindsay, and Howe; the Kraut Line, the Dynamite Line, the Triple Crown Line, the GAG Line, the French Connection, and more – none of them achieved what they did with one outstanding player skating with a couple of stiffs. More recently, dynamic duos such as Gretzky and Jari Kurri, Lemieux and Jaromir Jagr, Brett Hull and Adam Oates, and Eric Lindros and John LeClair, among others, have fed off each other with spectacular success. Each guy's sensational abilities lift the production of the other. What we got to wondering, though, was who really did the most with the *least* amount of help. As it turned out, the answer's not so easy to come by.

One huge difficulty is posed by the widely varying rate at which assists were doled out before the 1950s. That rate has been pretty consistent for more than 40 years, but we're trying to look at 93 years of major-league hockey, and prior to the '50s, we run into a nearly insurmountable problem with assists for the purposes of this exercise. Take our word for it. It involves a graph with parabolas and solving pi to the last decimal place or something. So we'll confine our study to goal scoring, not playmaking or point production, and playmakers like Perreault and Gretzky will just have to wait until someone can feed their numbers into Univac. We

call the stat we've concocted "Presence," since what we're measuring is how much a player's presence, in fact, contributed to his team's overall goal total. Here's how we go about it:

$$\frac{\dfrac{\text{Player's goals}}{\text{per game}} \times \text{scheduled games}}{\text{Team's goal total} - \text{player's goal total}} = \frac{\text{Presence in}}{\text{goal scoring}}$$

We pro-rate a player's goal production to the full season so he's not penalized for what he was unable to add when he was out of the line-up; we want to know what he meant to the team when he was actually there. And we subtract his raw goal total from the team total so that he isn't competing against himself; we want to know what the rest of the team did without him. So, for example, in the 82-game schedule of 1996–97, Jagr played only 63 times but still racked up 47 goals, an average of .746 goals per game. His Penguins scored 285 goals. Plug in the numbers and it looks like this:

$$\frac{.746 \times 82}{285 - 47} = \frac{61.17}{238} = .257$$

Jagr's Presence figure was .257, which tells us that when he was in the Pittsburgh line-up, he accounted for better than a quarter as many goals as the entire rest of the Penguins combined. That's an extremely impressive figure, as you'll realize after you get a look at the tables below, but it's not close to the best ever. In fact, nothing anyone has done anywhere in the last 70 years even begins to approach the best ever. Check this out.

The chart on p. 58 is another charming tintype from a bygone era, but even we'll admit that, except as a historical artifact, the chart above isn't really relevant to today's hockey. What it gives us is a picture of some great players (and at least one not-so-great one) who often single-handedly carried the whole load for otherwise punchless teams – 30-goal-man Didier Pitre's runner-up on the '15 Habs was somebody named Harry Scott, with 8 – but who, often as not, were simply the best goal scorers on teams fairly capable of scoring anyway. They show up here because teams of that era relied so heavily on their top line to do all the scoring – not because there wasn't a second line that could score, but because *there wasn't a second line*. These were the days of eight- and nine-man rosters, and the big scorers were out on the ice the vast majority of the game. (As the camera slowly zooms in to a tight close-up of the list, the music swells, and the screen cuts to black, you know that's a plot point.) Most of the stars of those days have Presence figures well over .300, frequently over .400, year after year during their careers. Those tiny rosters skew the Presence numbers. Joe Malone and Tommy Smith, teammates on the 1913 Stanley Cup champion Quebec Bulldogs, both appear

	PLAYER, TEAM	LEAGUE	SEASON	SCHED	GP	G	TEAM GF	PRESENCE
1	Pitre, Mtr C	NHA	'14–15	20	20	30	65	.857
2	Pitre, Mtr C	NHA	'11–12	18	18	27	59	.844
3	F Taylor, Van	PCHA	'17–18	18	18	32	70	.842
4	Dunderdale, Vic C	PCHA	'19–20	22	22	26	57	.839
5	J MacDonald, Tor On	NHA	'13–14	20	20	27	61	.794
6	Foyston, Sea	PCHA	'19–20	22	22	26	59	.788
7	Dye, Tor	NHL	'24–25	30	29	38	90	.756
8	Jo Malone, Qbc B	NHL	'19–20	24	24	39	91	.750
9	Jo Malone, Qbc B	NHA	'16–17	20a	19	41	97	.732
10	E Lalonde, Mtr C/Renf	NHA	'09–10	12	11	38	b	.725
11	Frederickson, Vic C	PCHA	'22–23	30	30	39	94	.709
12	T Smith, Qbc B/Tor OS	NHA	'14–15	20a	19	40	c	.683
13	Jo Malone, Mtr C	NHL	'17–18	22	20	44	115	.682
14	Ripley, Chi	NHL	'28–29	44	34	11	33	.647
15	Jo Malone, Qbc B	NHA	'12–13	20	20	43	112	.623
16	Cy Denneny, Otw	NHL	'17–18	22	20	36	102	.600
17	N Stewart, Mtr M	NHL	'25–26	36	36	34	91	.596
18	T Smith, Qbc B	NHA	'12–13	20	18	39	112	.594
19	H Jordan, Qbc B	ECHA	'08–09	12	12	29	78	.592
20	A Joliat, Mtr C	NHL	'24–25	30	24	29	93	.566

a League schedule 20 games, but Quebec and Toronto played only 19.
b Lalonde scored 16 goals in 6 games for Montreal, which totalled 59 goals, and 22 goals in 5 games for Renfrew, which totalled 96 goals.
c Smith scored 17 goals in 10 games for Quebec, which totalled 76 goals, and 23 goals in 9 games for Toronto, which totalled 85 goals.

on this list with their totals from that same season; they combined for 82 of Quebec's 112 goals. Malone shows up four times here, in fact; Smith, Pitre, and Cy Denneny each appear twice.

You hardly ever hear Didier Pitre's name mentioned today, but since he occupies the top two spots on this list, we'll pause to tell you just a little about his Hall of Fame career: he started out as a defence player for Montreal Nationals in the FAHL, but found his game when he went out to the IPL and switched to rover for the American Soo. He promptly led that league in scoring; after it folded in '07, he played senior hockey in Edmonton and eventually found his way back east, where Jack Laviolette signed him for the brand-new Canadiens in 1909. Playing first on defence, then on right wing, the husky Valleyfield native bedevilled NHA goalies for four straight years with a long sweep of the puck and a hard snap of the wrists. His wicked shot earned him the nickname "Cannonball." In a rare interleague trade in 1913, Pitre was sent to Vancouver of the PCHA in exchange for Newsy Lalonde, but he rejoined the Flying Frenchmen the next season – the season that tops this chart – and the following year combined with Lalonde and Laviolette to lead Canadiens to the Stanley Cup. Pitre remained with Montreal the rest of his career, which lasted until he was 38.

The guy you've never heard of at all, sitting at 14th on the list, is Vic Ripley, a tricky little forward who debuted in the NHL with the Chicago Black Hawk team that we earlier derided as the most offensively helpless club in the history of major-league hockey. All due respect to Ripley and his 11 goals, his inclusion among the giants here points out a vulnerability in the Presence stat itself, in that a merely adequate scorer on a truly feeble team can qualify for the list. Nonetheless, this stat has proven to be one of the more popular we've created, and we know you want to see who, among more modern players, has done well by it. Having established the early 1930s – when the rules, rosters, and strategies of hockey began to most noticeably resemble those of today's game – as the true dawn of hockey's modern era, let's take a look at the best Presence figures since 1931–32.

The chart on p. 59 is the list to go to for go-to guys, and nobody got up and went better than the Russian Rocket. Pavel Bure's astounding one-man show in Florida in 2000–01 was the most dazzling solo performance, by miles, in more than 70 years. The Worst Trade Vancouver Ever Made (Part II) outdid his own amazing 1999–2000 campaign – now eighth on this chart – and last year racked up more goals than the next *five* Panther goal scorers combined. *Nyevyeroyatnii!* And yet commentators ripped him for "selfish" play. Oy. If they weren't all crippled with a case of cliché reaction, they might have looked closer and noticed that Bure scored five of his goals short-handed, and nearly *led* the group of pylons standing in for NHL players

	PLAYER, TEAM	LEAGUE	SEASON	SCHED	GP	G	TEAM GF	PRESENCE
1	P Bure, Fla	NHL	'00–01	82	82	59	200	.418
2	B Hull, StL B	NHL	'90–91	80	78	86	310	.394
3	Selanne, Ana	NHL	'97–98	82	73	52	205	.382
4	B Hull, StL B	NHL	'91–92	80	73	70	279	.367
5	Rea Cloutier, Qbc N	WHA	'78–79	80	77	75	288	.366
6	C Neely, Bos	NHL	'93–94	84	49	50	289	.359
7	Bondra, Was	NHL	'95–96	82	67	52	234	.350
8	P Bure, Fla	NHL	'99–00	82	74	58	244	.346
9	M Richard, Mtr C	NHL	'50–51	70	65	42	173	.345
10	M Lemieux, Pit Pe	NHL	'88–89	80	76	85	347	.342
11	Bondra, Was	NHL	'94–95	48	47	34	136	.340
12	W Cook, NYR	NHL	'31–32	48	48	34	134	.340
13	Bondra, Was	NHL	'97–98	82	76	52	219	.336
14	M Richard, Mtr C	NHL	'49–50	70	70	43	172	.333
15	M Lemieux, Pit Pe	NHL	'92–93	84	60	69	367	.324
16	L Goldsworthy, Mtr C	NHL	'34–35	48	33	20	110	.323
17	B Hull, StL B	NHL	'89–90	80	80	72	295	.323
18	M Barry, Bos	NHL	'33–34	48	48	27	111	.321
19	Mogilny, Buf	NHL	'92–93	84	77	76	335	.320
20	T Sloan, Tor	NHL	'55–56	70	70	37	153	.319
21	R Hull, Wpg	WHA	'74–75	78	78	77	322	.314
22	R Hull, Chi	NHL	'65–66	70	65	54	240	.313
23	M Richard, Mtr C	NHL	'46–47	60	60	45	189	.312
24	Selanne, Wpg	NHL	'92–93	84	84	76	322	.309
25	C Conacher, Tor	NHL	'31–32	48	44	34	155	.307

there in plus/minus. *Pretchudlevii!* Bure played far more minutes per game (almost 27) and took far more shots (384) than any other forward in the NHL, skating for a team riddled with injuries, yes, but also – repulsively typical of Bettman-era bottom-feeders – so lacking in depth and offensive punch that, but for Bure, the 2000–01 Panthers might well have established a new nadir for ineptitude on the level of the '75 Caps or the early '90s Sens and Sharks. Joe Sakic, Jaromir Jagr, Sean Burke – each of them had a superb season, no argument, but Bure got strong consideration for our vote for the Hart in 2001, and not just because we'd like a date with his mum. Hubba hubba.

Until Bure, the Golden Brett's 1990–91 campaign for St. Louis had topped this chart for 10 years. The hippy-dippy goal scorer now ranks second, and his seasons immediately following and preceding that one are the 4th- and 17th- best of the modern era by this measure. Teemu Selanne, the gentlemanly Finn, earns the third spot and the 24th; Bure's unbelievable year knocks Selanne's '98–99 season off the bottom of the leader board. Peter Bondra and Rocket Richard carried enough of the goal-scoring weight for their teams to make the list three times; Mario Lemieux and Bobby Hull are the only others to appear here more than once.

If you're looking for the players who fit the profile of the "lone wolf" – the guys who ripped in the goals while the rest of the pack was figuring out which end of the stick to

hold – Bure, Selanne, and Lemieux are three recent candidates. Mario did it all for the Pens in '89, ringing up 76 goals while dishing off so well he helped minor-league marksman Rob Brown to a career-high 49-goal year. By 1992–93, Lemieux had a far better supporting cast, but his 60 goals were still far enough superior to the rest that he qualifies here again. As for Bure, the Russian Rocket was orders of magnitude brighter than any other star in the Florida sky in 1999–2000 as well. Despite missing eight games, his 58 goals were fully twice that of Panther runner-up Ray Whitney, and this outing knocked Bure's own 60-goal season for Vancouver in '93–94 out of the top 25. Selanne's performances, though, were nearly as astonishing. As a rookie in Winnipeg in '92–93, he scored more goals than any other Jet had points, and nearly as many points as the next two Jet forwards combined. But in Anaheim in '97–98, without the assistance of the injured Paul Kariya, Selanne's point production equalled the combined total of his two next-most productive teammates, and he fired home more than three times as many goals as any other Duck.

Relatively obscure Leroy Goldsworthy is the other "lone wolf" here. The looming journeyman, a Minnesota native, had a career year for the mediocre Canadiens of '34–35. The rest, however, had significant help as they took charge of goal-scoring duties for their teams. Real "Buddy" Cloutier lined up with WHA stars Marc Tardif and Serge Bernier for

Players

59

an exciting, freewheeling Nordiques team. Richard, of course, was the ferocious triggerman set up by the expert passing of Buddy O'Connor, Toe Blake, and Elmer Lach. Bobby Hull, the Golden Jet, was fuelled by the passing of Stan Mikita and Phil Esposito in Chicago, and, a decade later, by artful Euro-linemates Ulf Nilsson and Anders Hedberg in Winnipeg. Bill Cook, of course, was the big shooter for Rangers on a line with brother Bun on left wing and Frank Boucher at centre. Marty Barry had Harry Oliver on his wing, and behind him a second line centred by Nels Stewart wearing down Boston opponents. Alex Mogilny's great year in Buffalo was ignited by Pat LaFontaine's spectacular work at centre. Tough little Tod Sloan had a career year on the Maple Leaf checking line with stalwarts George Armstrong and Dickie Duff. Charlie Conacher was the heavy artillery on Toronto's legendary Kid Line.

There's one name you won't see here but who's nonetheless present in spirit. It's no coincidence that Brett Hull, Cam Neely, and Peter Bondra, outstanding goal scorers though each of them is in his own right, all make appearances here with the same dispenser of seeing-eye passes centring for all of them – Adam Oates. Hull and Oates were chart-toppers for two and a half of the three seasons Hull makes this list; another sweet passer, Craig Janney, fed Hull later in his third year here. Oates moved over to Boston and helped Neely turn on the red light with historic frequency in '93–94. Bondra had Michal Pivonka as a playmaking pivot for his first two appearances on the Presence chart, but Oates, now in Washington, sent Peter the Great onto the list for a third time.

Something worth noticing about this chart is that 8 of the 10 seasons listed – 14 of the top 25 – have occurred since 1988–89, and something worth knowing is that when this chart was compiled in the late '80s, players from the preceding six decades were pretty evenly represented among the top 15. The proliferation of big Presence figures by players of the last 10 or 12 years is another indication of a sea change in the nature of NHL hockey in the '90s, and not a change for the better. Although they're classic goal scorers by any standard, one major reason so many current players are taking over the Presence list is not that they're miles better than other excellent teammates, but that they're light years better than the weak, marginal talent left to them as teammates by overexpansion.

Quality of Victory

There are better ways to identify great single-season performances, though, so let's look through some different lenses. Instead of gazing inward at how much better one player was than the rest of his teammates, let's take a wider view and see how much better one player was than everybody else in his league. We don't promise a definitive answer from this next stat alone, but it's proven an easy, accurate rule of thumb for spotting truly great individual seasons. We call it "Quality of Victory," and what it measures is the distance between any year's leader in goals, assists, and points and his runner-up. So, for instance, were Malone and his 44 goals, or Richard and his 50, or Gretzky and his 92, as fantastic as they seem when seen out of context? Were they miles ahead of what anyone else did that season? Or were half a dozen other guys right on their heels in a year of wide-open hockey when goals came easily to everyone? Here's the formula for this simple calculation:

$$100 \times \left(\frac{\text{Leader's goals per game}}{\text{Runner-up's goals per game}} \right) - 100 = \text{Quality of Victory}$$

Spotlight, please . . .

Players

60

Quality of Victory, Goals, 1909–2001							
PLAYER, TEAM		LEAGUE	SEASON	GP	G	G/GP	Q OF V
1 Leader	R Hull, Chi	NHL	'65–66	65	54	.831	76.44
Runner-up	F Mahovlich, Tor			68	32	.471	
2 Leader	JJ Adams, Van	PCHA	'21–22	24	26	1.083	62.50
Runners-up	Foyston, Sea			24	16	.667	
	Jm Riley, Sea			24	16	.667	
3 Leader	F Taylor, Van	PCHA	'17–18	18	32	1.778	60.00
Runners-up	Go Roberts, Sea			18	20	1.111	
	B Morris, Sea			18	20	1.111	
4 Leader	Dunderdale, Vic A	PCHA	'12–13	15	24	1.600	60.00
Runners-up	F Harris, Van			14	14	1.000	
	C Kendall, Van			14	14	1.000	
5 Leader	R Hull, Chi	NHL	'66–67	66	52	.788	57.58
Runner-up	Mikita, Chi			70	35	.500	
6 Leader	M Richard, Mtr C	NHL	'44–45	50	50	1.000	56.25
Runner-up	H Cain, Bos			50	32	.640	

		PLAYER, TEAM	LEAGUE	SEASON	GP	G	G/GP	Q OF V
7	Leader	G Howe, Det	NHL	'52–53	70	49	.700	53.12
	Runner-up	T Lindsay, Det			70	32	.457	
8	Leader	R Hull, Chi	NHL	'61–62	70	50	.714	51.52
	Runners-up	G Howe, Det			70	33	.471	
		F Mahovlich, Tor			70	33	.471	
		Provost, Mtr C			70	33	.471	
9	Leader	G Howe, Det	NHL	'51–52	70	47	.671	49.95
	Runner-up	B Geoffrion, Mtr C			67	30	.448	
10	Leader	B Hull, StL B	NHL	'90–91	78	86	1.102	49.17
	Runner-up	C Neely, Bos			69	51	.739	
11	Leader	P Esposito, Bos	NHL	'70–71	78	76	.974	49.02
	Runner-up	Bucyk, Bos			78	51	.654	
12	Leader	C Conacher, Tor	NHL	'34–35	47	36	.766	46.23
	Runner-up	Hv Jackson, Tor			42	22	.524	
13	Leader	M Richard, Mtr C	NHL	'46–47	60	45	.750	45.00
	Runner-up	Bauer, Bos			58	30	.517	
14	Leader	W Gretzky, Edm	NHL	'83–84	74	87	1.176	44.70
	Runner-up	Kurri, Edm			64	52	.812	
15	Leader	W Gretzky, Edm	NHL	'81–82	80	92	1.150	43.75
	Runner-up	Bossy, NYI			80	64	.800	
16	Leader	T Smith, Tor OS–Qbc B	NHA	'14–15	19	40	2.105	37.93
	Runner-up	Go Roberts, Mtr W			19	29	1.526	
17	Leader	C Conacher, Tor	NHL	'33–34	42	32	.762	35.45
	Runner-up	M Barry, Bos			48	27	.562	
18	Leader	Du MacKay, Van	PCHA	'14–15	17	33	1.941	35.04
	Runner-up	F Taylor, Van			16	23	1.438	
19	Leader	E Lalonde, Mtr C/Renf	NHA	'09–10	11	38	3.455	33.72
	Runner-up	E Russell, Mtr W			12	31	2.583	
20	Leader	M Walsh, Otw	ECHA	'08–09	12	38	3.167	31.03
	Runner-up	H Jordan, Qbc B			12	29	2.417	

It's Hull the Elder who tops this chart, and dominates it, really, with three of the seven biggest goal-scoring runaways in hockey history. An absolutely terrifying gunner with his cannon shot, blazing speed, toughness, and '60s he-man good looks, the Golden Jet was hockey's most exciting player in his heyday, and his victories in this category remind us how much substance there was to all the flash. He scored big, loud, overpowering goals with record-breaking prolifigacy, a fact unfairly and too often forgotten amid the raw totals later run up by Phil Esposito, Gretzky, and Lemieux.

Jack Adams comes in second; he starred for both Vancouver in the coast league and Toronto in the NHL, but is better remembered for his 35 years as the arrogant, hard-bitten general manager and coach of the Red Wings. Just deserts. Hull's son Brett arrives here as well, in the 10th spot.

The others here are the fabled Cyclone Taylor; PCHA number two all-time scorer Tom Dunderdale; goal-scoring machine Phil Esposito; pint-sized scoring whiz Tommy Smith; Mickey MacKay, the PCHA's gentlemanly superstar; Joe Malone and Newsy Lalonde, together again; and the brilliant, tragic Marty Walsh. With the exception of the still active Hull the Younger, every single player here is a member of the Hall of Fame. Mario Lemieux's '95–96 goalscoring cakewalk falls just short of the chart.

Two of the great seasons to which we alluded earlier – the Rocket's 50 in 50, and Gretzky's 92-goal year – do indeed both qualify, as does the mark Gretzky broke, Esposito's magnificent 76-goal campaign from 1970–71. But Malone's watershed 44 in 20 in the NHL's inaugural season, trailed closely by Cy Denneny's 36 goals in 20 games that year, gets a Q of V mark of 22.22. Brett Hull's '90–91 season knocked Espo's '73–74 victory out of the final berth here, leaving Bobby Hull, Maurice Richard, Gordie Howe, Charlie Conacher, and Wayne Gretzky as the only men to have led their league twice in goalscoring by these historic distances.

Quality of Victory allows us at long last to rate the playmakers as well as the goal scorers, so let's put the season-by-season assist leaders under the scope now and find out who dished off with unparalleled success. The equation's the same, except that we're plugging in assists instead of goals:

$$100 \times \left(\frac{\text{Leader's assists per game}}{\text{Runner-up's assists per game}} \right) - 100 = \begin{array}{l} \text{Quality of} \\ \text{Victory} \end{array}$$

Because of the extremely chary allotment of assists in the game's early days – even with those numbers enhanced by the work of modern historians – we're also applying the 16-game minimum here. Wouldn't want to have a historic victory of four assists to three, now, would we.

Well, well, well. It's the Ancients who top the chart with some mind-boggling numbers, but after them, Wayne Gretzky almost owns this list, outdistancing his rival set-up men by the three widest margins of the modern era, and showing up seven times among the top 20 – eight among

		PLAYER, TEAM	LEAGUE	SEASON	GP	A	A/GP	Q OF V
Quality of Victory, Assists, 1909–2001								
1	Leader	F Taylor, Van	PCHA	'14–15	16	22	1.375	112.50
	Runner-up	Du MacKay, Van			17	11	.647	
2	Leader	Keats, Edm	WCHL	'21–22	25	24	.960	100.00
	Runner-up	J Simpson, Edm			25	12	.480	
3	Leader	W Gretzky, Edm	NHL	'85–86	80	163	2.038	73.08
	Runner-up	M Lemieux, Pit Pe			79	93	1.178	
4	Leader	W Gretzky, Edm	NHL	'86–87	79	121	1.532	65.93
	Runner-up	R Bourque, Bos			78	72	.923	
5	Leader	W Gretzky, Edm	NHL	'84–85	80	135	1.688	60.71
	Runner-up	Coffey, Edm			80	84	1.050	
6	Leader	Cowley, Bos	NHL	'40–41	46	45	.978	56.52
	Runner-up	P Watson, NYR			40	25	.625	
7	Leader	R Orr, Bos	NHL	'69–70	76	87	1.145	55.36
	Runner-up	P Esposito, Bos			76	56	.737	
8	Leader	T Lindsay, Det	NHL	'49–50	69	55	.797	54.59
	Runner-up	D Bentley, Chi			64	33	.516	
9	Leader	Pitre, Mtr C	NHA	'15–16	24	15	.625	50.00
	Runner-up	Jo Malone, Qbc B			24	10	.417	
10	Leader	W Gretzky, Edm	NHL	'83–84	74	118	1.595	48.33
	Runner-up	Coffey, Edm			80	86	1.075	
11	Leader	W Gretzky, Edm	NHL	'82–83	80	125	1.562	43.48
	Runner-up	D Savard, Chi			78	85	1.162	
12	Leader	Cowley, Bos	NHL	'38–39	34	34	1.000	42.42
	Runner-up	Haynes, Mtr C			47	33	.702	
13	Leader	J Darragh, Otw	NHL	'20–21	24	15	.625	38.89
	Runner-up	Jo Malone, Ham			20	9	.450	
14	Leader	J Primeau, Tor	NHL	'30–31	38	32	.842	37.23
	Runner-up	F Boucher, NYR			44	27	.614	
15	Leader	F Taylor, Van	PCHA	'13–14	16	15	.938	36.36
	Runner-up	Alb Kerr, Vic			16	11	.688	
16	Leader	A Gagne, Edm	WCHL	'22–23	29	21	.724	35.78
	Runners-up	W Cook, Ssk	WCHL		30	16	.533	
		Frederickson, Vic C	PCHA*		30	16	.533	
17	Leader	R Orr, Bos	NHL	'70–71	78	102	1.308	34.21
	Runner-up	P Esposito, Bos			78	76	.974	
18	Leader	W Gretzky, Edm	NHL	'87–88	64	109	1.703	33.82
	Runner-up	M Lemieux, Pit Pe			77	98	1.273	
19	Leader	W Gretzky, Edm	NHL	'80–81	80	109	1.362	32.93
	Runner-up	K Nilsson, Clg			80	82	1.025	
20	Leader	Lach, Mtr C	NHL	'44–45	50	54	1.080	32.30
	Runner-up	Cowley, Bos			49	40	.816	

* WCHL and PCHA played interlocking schedule, effectively operating as one league.

the top 35, in fact, if we'd extended the chart by a few more berths and included his 1981–82 runaway over Peter Stastny. Cyclone Taylor and two great Bruins – Bill Cowley, the silky smooth centreman for Roy Conacher and Mel Hill, and Bobby Orr, the Pride of Parry Sound – are the only other guys to reach the list twice.

Readers of the earlier editions of the *Compendium* – who meet annually in a phone booth near Bloor and Spadina – will notice significant changes to the entries here since the chart last appeared, and not because anyone other than Gretzky, in '88, and Lemieux, in '93, threw passes around with godlike elegance. Armed with the evidence of newly retranscribed raw statistics, we see it's actually the storied whirlwind of the PCHA, Cyclone Taylor, who tops the entire chart with what must have been a supernatural performance, more than doubling the assist rate of Mickey MacKay, his teammate on that incredible Vancouver team and a great playmaker in his own right. The year before, Taylor out-distributed Dubbie Kerr to earn the 15th slot. And two years later, despite missing half the season with appendicitis, Taylor nearly tied fellow Vancouver star Barney Stanley for the league lead in assists, which would've been a 74.24 Q of V mark if we gave credit for partial work. Also doubling his runner-up's total is Duke Keats, the WCHL's pre-eminent

superstar through all five years of its existence. A little farther down the list, Didier Pitre gets his recognition, 85 years later, for his best season in the helper column. More than 80 years after he outdid Joe Malone, the distinguished Senator Jack Darragh finally gets his due. And almost 80 years after the fact, western leaguer Art Gagne is recognized for outdealing Bill Cook. Rambunctious tough-guy, fine goal scorer, dogged checker, and heroic labour activist Ted Lindsay gives evidence of his all-around skills with an appearance on this chart, busy grinding in the corners for Gordie Howe long before their falling out.

The more accurate numbers, however, also mean that Corb Denneny's high ranking from 1920 vanishes from the previous edition of this list, and they lock out Lemieux's inspirational '92–93 performance ahead of Adam Oates. Also gone is PCHA star Eddie Oatman's 1920 playmaking victory; while we were away, not only did Oatman lose credit for an assist, but his runner-up that year, PCHA lifer Fred "Smokey" Harris, became "Tom" Smokey Harris. Now that bears looking into.

But it's time now to apply the Quality of Victory template to the overall scoring leaders through history. Same formula again, but now points instead of goals or assists. Brace yourselves!

Quality of Victory, Points, 1909–2001

		PLAYER, TEAM		LEAGUE	SEASON	GP	P	P/GP	Q OF V
1	Leader	Keats, Edm		WCHL	'21–22	25	55	2.200	60.00
	Runner-up	E Arbour, Edm				24	33	1.375	
2	Leader	W Gretzky, Edm		NHL	'83–84	74	205	2.770	56.90
	Runner-up	Kurri, Edm				64	113	1.766	
3	Leader	M Lemieux, Pit Pe		NHL	'92–93	60	160	2.667	51.35
	Runner-up	LaFontaine, Buf				84	148	1.762	
4	Leader	W Gretzky, Edm		NHL	'85–86	80	215	2.688	50.58
	Runner-up	M Lemieux, Pit Pe				79	141	1.785	
5	Leader	W Gretzky, Edm		NHL	'82–83	80	196	2.450	48.19
	Runner-up	P Stastny, Qbc N				75	124	1.653	
6	Leader	W Gretzky, Edm		NHL	'81–82	80	212	2.650	44.22
	Runner-up	Bossy, NYI				80	147	1.838	
7	Leader	W Gretzky, Edm		NHL	'84–85	80	208	2.600	40.59
	Runner-up	Kurri, Edm				73	135	1.849	
8	Leader	W Gretzky, Edm		NHL	'86–87	79	183	2.316	36.39
	Runner-up	M Lemieux, Pit Pe				63	107	1.698	
9	Leader	Dunderdale, Vic A		PCHA	'12–13	15	29	1.933	35.33
	Runners-up	F Harris, Van				14	20	1.429	
		C Kendall, Van				14	20	1.429	
10	Leader	F Taylor, Van		PCHA	'17–18	18	43	2.389	34.38
	Runner-up	B Morris, Sea				18	32	1.778	
11	Leader	H Morenz, Mtr C		NHL	'27–28	43	51	1.186	33.91
	Runner-up	A Joliat, Mtr C				44	39	.886	
12	Leader	G Howe, Det		NHL	'52–53	70	95	1.357	33.80
	Runner-up	T Lindsay, Det				70	71	1.014	

	PLAYER, TEAM		LEAGUE	SEASON	GP	P	P/GP	Q OF V
13	Leader	E Lalonde, Mtr C/Renf	ECHA	'09–10	11	38*	3.455	33.72*
	Runner-up	E Russell, Mtr W			12	31*	2.583	
14	Leader	M Walsh, Otw	ECHA	'08–09	12	38*	3.167	31.03*
	Runner-up	H Jordan, Qbc B			12	29*	2.417	
15	Leader	Dye, Tor	NHL	'22–23	22	37	1.682	30.20
	Runner-up	Cy Denneny, Otw			24	31	1.292	
16	Leader	R Hull, Chi	NHL	'65–66	65	97	1.492	29.85
	Runner-up	Beliveau, Mtr C			67	77	1.149	
17	Leader	T Smith, Tor OS–Qbc B	NHA	'14–15	19	44	2.316	29.41
	Runner-up	Go Roberts, Mtr W			19	34	1.789	
18	Leader	M Lemieux, Pit Pe	NHL	'95–96	70	161	2.300	26.58
	Runner-up	Jagr, Pit Pe			82	149	1.817	
19	Leader	Cowley, Bos	NHL	'38–39	34	42	1.235	26.16
	Runner-up	H Blake, Mtr C			48	47	.979	
20	Leader	F Taylor, Van	PCHA	'13–14	16	39	2.438	25.81
	Runner-up	Alb Kerr, Vic A			16	31	1.938	

* Point total includes only goals; assists not credited this season.

Wow. It wasn't like we didn't all know Gretzky was pretty good, but his virtual monopoly of this category's upper reaches is stunning even by Gretzky's impossible standards. Six of the eight largest-ever routs of the competition, including the second-biggest runaway of all time – and again, a 21st slot here would accommodate Wonder Wayne's 1981 sprint past Marcel Dionne – provide some tangible statistical evidence for those who have proclaimed him the greatest offensive force in the history of the game. Luddites who would dig in to defend that title for Gordie Howe, and radicals who would instead bestow it upon Mario Lemieux, will find ammunition here as well: Mario's miraculous back-from-Hodgkin's-disease season of 1992–93 is the third-best ever by this measure, his '96 campaign 18th. Gordo's dreadnought style left all rivals floundering in his wake twice in the early '50s, his '53 effort coming in 12th and '52 just a shade short of registering here. Flamboyant Vancouver legend Cyclone Taylor is the only other player to have so outdistanced every other player in his league twice.

And yet, atop the list with most yawning chasm between himself and the competition ever recorded, it's Gordon "Duke" Keats of the WCHL Edmonton Eskimos. Keats's goal, assist, and point totals in this, the western league's maiden season, would not be equalled in the loop's five-year existence. Tom Dunderdale, Howie Morenz, Newsy Lalonde, Marty Walsh, Babe Dye, Bobby Hull, Tommy Smith, and Bill Cowley – all inarguably among the best ever to lace up skates – complete the list of guys who stood head and shoulders, and kneepads, above everyone else in a major-league season. Nearly as impressive are the runners-up in each of these entries. The "also-rans" are a roll call of Hall of Famers – Lemieux himself twice, Jari Kurri, Peter Stastny, Mike Bossy, Aurel Joliat, Ted Lindsay, Ernie Russell, Cy Denneny, Jean Beliveau, Gordon Roberts, Toe Blake – and future Hall of Famers – Jaromir Jagr, Pat LaFontaine. It's mind-blowing to think how the winners in Quality of Victory were able to leave stars like those eating their dust.

Even though Q of V shows only how well the top scorer in a given season did compared to the second-best scorer, it has shown itself to be a reliable, if rough, barometer of transcendent performances. But why take our word for it? We've only spent years and sacrificed our personal lives and professional careers to devise and compile these stats. A lot you care! But don't give us a second thought. Here, go on and take a look at this next stat, revealing who shone brightest compared to their entire league, while we just go quietly back down to the cellar with our cold bowl of gruel and a crateful of old scoresheets.

Individual Scoring Dominance

This little number is called "Individual Scoring Dominance." You may have seen some scaled-down version of the Presence stat presented under this name recently in the literary lobotomy ward known as *The Hockey News*, where we debuted it in the early '80s. You know, *The Hockey News*, the magazine that never met a Gary Bettman idea it didn't like, and bravely stood on the cutting edge of hockey analysis by venturing, as far back as the spring of 2001, that save percentage just *might* possibly be a better indicator of goalie performance than goals-against average or won-lost-tied record. Anyway, that's all water under a dead horse, as THN might say.

What Individual Scoring Dominance measures is a player's scoring rate compared to the league scoring rate. Ferinstance, if a player averages a goal per game, and the average team in the league averages three goals per game, that player's ISD would be one-third, or .333. Not exactly theoretical astrophysics, and here's the formula:

$$\frac{\text{Player's goals-per-game average}}{\text{League-wide team goals-per-game average}} = \text{Individual Scoring Dominance}$$

We're going to have to split the results again, at the same, only slightly arbitrary, juncture of the 1931–32 season. That's because, as with Presence, the small rosters and game-length shifts for pre-1930s players give those players ISD figures consistently far higher than those of more modern skaters. Remember, though, there's really no sharply inscribed line separating some distinct "Early Era" from some clearly defined "Modern Era." It's just a convenience, a conceit, artificially imposed on a game that's evolved in small fits and starts but, in the long view, gradually. The demarcation between everything up to 1930–31 and everything from 1931–32 on simply reflects the point at which those changes are most apparent, if not necessarily most dramatic. As a result, some late '20s players suffer a bit here, statistically speaking, and some early '30s players have a slight statistical advantage. Be that as it may, we forge ahead.

Individual Scoring Dominance, Goals, 1909–1931

	PLAYER, TEAM	LEAGUE	SEASON	GP	G	GPG	AVG TEAM GPG	GOAL ISD
1	E Lalonde, Mtr C /Renf	NHA	'09–10	11	38	3.45	6.40	.540
2	Dye, Tor	NHL	'24–25	29	38	1.31	2.47	.530
3	T Smith, Qbc B /Tor OS	NHA	'14–15	19	40	2.10	4.06	.518
4	F Taylor, Van	PCHA	'17–18	18	32	1.78	3.45	.515
5	T Smith, Qbc B	NHA	'12–13	18	39	2.17	4.29	.505
6	Jo Malone, Qbc B	NHA	'12–13	20	43	2.15	4.29	.501
7	A Joliat, Mtr C	NHL	'24–25	24	29	1.21	2.47	.489
8	T Smith, Qbc B	NHA	'13–14	20	39	1.95	4.21	.463
9	M Walsh, Otw	ECHA	'08–09	12	38	3.17	6.90	.459
10	Keats, Edm	WCHL	'21–22	25	31	1.24	2.76	.449

Newsy Lalonde's amazing little season, split between the Canadiens and Renfrew, tops the list. Lalonde's quick temper is almost as legendary as his scoring prowess, but you have to wonder how often he actually instigated the many scraps he got into. He picked up 16 of his goals this year in six games for Montreal, then went completely wild after he was sold to Millionaires, ripping home 22 goals in

just five games. Seeing how well he's done in the other tables we've presented, goading the fiery Cornwall native into a fight may have been the only way to stop him from scoring.

Babe Dye, Cyclone Taylor, Joe Malone, Aurel Joliat, Marty Walsh, and Duke Keats all reiterate their greatness with an appearance here, but tiny Tommy Smith stands like a giant among them with three separate seasons of superlative marksmanship. Smith also had 40 goals in 13 games for Brantford of the Trolley League in '09–10, and in 1911–12 racked up an amazing 53 goals in 18 games for Moncton of the Maritime League, which challenged for the Stanley Cup. He scored nine goals in one game against Wanderers in 1913–14, tying Lalonde's NHA record, and had four five-goal games and a six-goal outing in NHA action. Considering how often he's shown up already on our other lists, and considering that just about every other star player of his era was voted into the Hall of Fame by 1950, we'd like to know just who he pissed off and what he did that kept him waiting 25 years longer than his contemporaries before he was quietly, and posthumously, ushered in.

Individual Scoring Dominance, Goals, 1932–2001

	PLAYER, TEAM	LEAGUE	SEASON	GP	G	GPG	AVG TEAM GPG	GOAL ISD
1	C Conacher, Tor	NHL	'33–34	42	32	.76	2.30	.331
2	C Conacher, Tor	NHL	'31–32	44	34	.77	2.38	.324
3	B Hull, StL B	NHL	'90–91	78	86	1.10	3.41	.323
4	M Lemieux, Pit Pe	NHL	'92–93	60	69	1.15	3.59	.320
5	M Lemieux, Pit Pe	NHL	'95–96	70	69	.99	3.10	.318
6	C Conacher, Tor	NHL	'34–35	47	36	.77	2.44	.314
7	P Esposito, Bos	NHL	'70–71	78	76	.97	3.12	.312
8	M Lemieux, Pit Pe	NHL	'88–89	76	85	1.12	3.70	.303
9	W Gretzky, Edm	NHL	'83–84	74	87	1.18	3.90	.301
10	W Cook, NYR	NHL	'31–32	48	34	.71	2.38	.297
11	G Howe, Det	NHL	'52–53	70	49	.70	2.40	.292
12	P Bure, Fla	NHL	'99–00	74	58	.78	2.70	.290
13	W Gretzky, Edm	NHL	'81–82	80	92	1.15	4.01	.287
14	P Esposito, Bos	NHL	'71–72	76	66	.87	3.07	.283
15	B Hull, StL B	NHL	'91–92	73	70	.96	3.43	.279
16	C Neely, Bos	NHL	'93–94	56*	50	.89	3.20	.279
17	R Hull, Chi	NHL	'68–69	74	58	.78	2.84	.275
18	Mogilny, Buf	NHL	'92–93	77	76	.99	3.59	.275
19	Selanne, Ana	NHL	'97–98	73	52	.71	2.60	.274
20	R Hull, Chi	NHL	'65–66	65	54	.83	3.04	.273
21	P Esposito, Bos	NHL	'73–74	78	68	.87	3.20	.273
22	M Richard, Mtr C	NHL	'44–45	50	50	1.00	3.68	.272
23	W Cook, NYR	NHL	'32–33	48	28	.58	2.20	.266
24	G Howe, Det	NHL	'55–56	70	47	.67	2.53	.265
25	P Bure, Fla	NHL	'00–01	82	59	.72	2.72	.265

*	Neely scored 50 goals in 49 games (1.02 GPG), but has seven scoreless games added to his record here in order to have enough games played to qualify.

It's Conacher, the intimidating right winger on the Kid Line, who's king of the hill on this later edition of the chart, owning the top two spots and three of the top six. A product of the Toronto slums who lost a kidney as a youngster, Conacher developed into a huge, strong physical specimen with a howitzer shot, becoming an NHL All-Star five times and twice the league's scoring champ. His contemporary, Frank Boucher, described Conacher in Tim Moriarty's *Hockey's Hall of Fame*: "Charlie was big all right, but he was one of the cleanest players around. He never went out of his way to hurt anybody. He could have, of course. My God, he was big enough to murder most players. The thing I remember most about Charlie was his wrist shot. It was frightening. In later years they talked about Boom Boom Geoffrion's shot and Bobby Hull's shot, but Charlie Conacher's was every bit as good."

Another star of the day, Leaf teammate Baldy Cotton, whom Conacher once held suspended out a seventh-floor hotel window to resolve a disagreement, recalled that the Big Bomber often used his renowned firepower as a decoy and could finish a play with surprising finesse. "Charlie would use a shoulder or head fake, get the goaltender moving the wrong way, and then beat him cleanly. It was something to watch him mesmerize the goalies."

Boucher's own linemate, Ranger marksman Bill Cook, makes the grade here too, but as we warned, early '30s players have a bit of an advantage on this scale, getting loads of ice time with short rosters and little scoring beyond the top forward line. So, for that matter, do star players of the '90s, who find a lot of guys on three more lines behind them, but just as little scoring support in the depth-depleted post-post-expansion era – like Pavel Bure, whose 2000–01 campaign knocked Bobby Hull's 52-goal effort of 1966–67 off the end of the chart. Still, two of the modern game's most outspoken critics – young Hull, the Golden Brett, and especially Mario Lemieux, the only other player to appear three times in the modern top 10 – certainly deserve all the respect their appearances here merit, as well as every other accolade ever thrown their way, but the achievements of Gretzky, Phil Esposito, and, particularly, Gordie Howe may actually be the most impressive on the ISD scale.

Another fantastic performance of quite recent vintage makes the table under special circumstances. We apply the "Sweeney Schriner rule" to some of these lists: Schriner, a Hall of Fame star and two-time NHL scoring champ for the 1930s Americans and 1940s Leafs, was having an amazing year in 1944–45 – 22 goals in just 26 games – but was sidelined for almost half the schedule with a leg injury. Our guideline here is that a player must appear in two-thirds of his team's games to qualify. That puts a bit of a damper on Boston's Cam Neely, who was on a phenomenal tear in '93–94 before suffering a relapse of what turned out to be a career-ending leg injury of his own. Neely ripped in 50

goals in 49 games, but in order to get him on board here, we've had to add seven phantom, and goalless, games to his record. The Worst Trade Vancouver Ever Made (Part I) still qualifies here, even with that statistical handicap.

We can use ISD to measure playmaking as well as goal scoring. Just watch.

$$\frac{\text{Player's assists-per-game average}}{\text{League-wide team assists-per-game average}} = \text{Individual Scoring Dominance}$$

Individual Scoring Dominance, Assists, 1909–1931								
PLAYER, TEAM	LEAGUE	SEASON	GP	A	A/GP	AVG TEAM ASSIST A/GP	ISD
1 F Taylor, Van	PCHA	'14–15	16	22	1.38	2.21	.623
2 Keats, Edm	WCHL	'21–22	25	24	.96	1.76	.546
3 R Irvin, Chi	NHL	'26–27	43	18	.42	0.90	.468
4 H Morenz, Mtr C	NHL	'27–28	43	18	.42	0.91	.459
5 F Boucher, NYR	NHL	'28–29	44	16	.36	0.83	.436
6 A Blair, Tor	NHL	'28–29	44	15	.34	0.83	.408
7 Co Denneny, Ssk	WHL	'25–26	30	16	.53	1.33	.402
8 J Primeau, Tor	NHL	'30–31	38	32	.84	2.14	.394
9 Gerard, Otw	NHA	'16–17	19	16	.84	2.18	.386
10 W Cook, Ssk	WCHL	'23–24	30	14	.47	1.21[a]	.386

a The WCHL and PCHA played an interlocking schedule in 1923–24; the average team assists per game figure is the combined average for all WCHL and PCHA games that season.

Once again, archaeology reveals the truth at the root of myth. Due to new revisions in the records of assists from these years, no category has undergone more reshuffling of its original results than this one, and here it's the legend of Frederick Wellington "Cyclone" Taylor, regarded by many in his day as the greatest player in hockey and certainly known to all as the flashiest, that's substantiated by the exposition of his numbers. The Listowel, Ontario, native started with Ottawa in the ECHA, then Renfrew in the NHA, but headed west in 1912 and starred in Vancouver for the next nine years. He tops the list playing with that staggering collection of talent – MacKay, Nighbor, Si Griffis, Lloyd Cook, Frank Patrick, Hughie Lehman in goal – that won the Cup in 1915.

In second: behold! His Royal Highness, Gordon, Duke of Keats, who finally gets his due for his sensational work in the WCHL's maiden season. Montreal-born but North Bay–bred, Keats began his major-league career centring the Denneny brothers for the NHA Toronto Blueshirts – a pre-potent combination. The team was shut down midway through the following season, and he lost the next two years to military service with the 228th Battalion in the Great War. He returned to star spectacularly for two years in amateur hockey in Edmonton, then turned pro again and dominated the new western circuit for five straight years. Keats was well over 30 and past his prime when he came over to the NHL, playing his last few years for Boston, Detroit, and Chicago, and that, and the previous blanks in his statistical record, have left him a bit anonymous among the more celebrated greats of his era. But this is the fifth of our lists on which he's appeared, and just maybe we should all hold this Hall of Famer in higher esteem.

In third: hey, it's Dick Irvin! It's nice to see Irvin – for years a superstar in the Manitoba Senior League and the WCHL, later an outstanding coach through 26 NHL seasons, and the father of long-time genial "Hockey Night in Canada" host-turned-author Dick Irvin, Jr. – show up with his late-career performance as captain of the first-year Black Hawks. The previous year, with Portland, Irvin Sr. tied with Bill Cook for the final western league goal-scoring crown, and lost this season's NHL scoring title to Cook by a single point.

Howie Morenz snags fourth place; you'll usually hear him referred to as "the Babe Ruth of Hockey." That's not all that accurate, but we'll let it slide inasmuch as they were both arguably the best, most exciting, most flamboyant players in their respective games during the so-called Golden Age of Sport. What annoys us is that you never hear Ruth referred to as "the Howie Morenz of baseball." How about that, huh? How about hockey, and hockey fans, not invariably using other sports – American sports at that – as their touchstone for context? Let's call Michael Jordan "the Wayne Gretzky of basketball" instead of the other way around. Actually, Jordan would be more like "the Howie Morenz of basketball," but you get the point. Apply it to everything. Earl Anthony could be the Gordie Howe of bowling. Celine Dion could be the Harold Snepsts of pop music. We might be the Nick Libett and Tim Ecclestone of sports writing.

Frank Boucher, seven-time winner and eventual owner of the Lady Byng Trophy, is even more impressive than his lone appearance here suggests; he actually has three seasons among the top dozen, confirming his reputation as one of the greatest playmakers ever to feather a pass. Somewhat of a surprise here is Andy Blair, in '29 a rookie centreman from the University of Manitoba, an unusually tall player for his day, who would be a reliable regular for Leafs through the 1930s and was the first NHLer to sport a moustache. Also surprising is Bill Cook, the ceaselessly prolific goal scorer. Two other early worthies earn their way on board: all-time Senator great Eddie Gerard, here the left winger on a line with Frank Nighbor and Jack Darragh, and Cy's little brother Corb Denneny, demonstrating in this WHL stint how expertly he could dig and dish off. No surprise at all is passer nonpareil Joe Primeau. On to the modern list.

Individual Scoring Dominance, Assists, 1932–2001

	PLAYER, TEAM	LEAGUE	SEASON	GP	A	A/GP	AVG TEAM ASSIST A/GP	ISD
1	J Primeau, Tor	NHL	'31–32	46	37	0.80	2.49	.323
2	W Gretzky, Edm	NHL	'85–86	80	163	2.04	6.50	.314
3	Re Smith, Mtr M	NHL	'31–32	43	33	0.77	2.49	.308
4	W Gretzky, Edm	NHL	'87–88	64	109	1.70	6.10	.279
5	J Primeau, Tor	NHL	'33–34	45	32	0.71	2.61	.273
6	W Gretzky, LA	NHL	'90–91	78	122	1.56	5.72	.273
7	W Gretzky, Edm	NHL	'84–85	80	135	1.69	6.28	.269
8	Cowley, Bos	NHL	'38–39	34	34	1.00	3.79	.264
9	Oates, StL B	NHL	'90–91	61	90	1.48	5.72	.258
10	R Orr, Bos	NHL	'70–71	78	102	1.31	5.10	.256
11	Cowley, Bos	NHL	'40–41	46	45	0.98	3.84	.255
12	W Gretzky, Edm	NHL	'86–87	79	121	1.53	6.00	.255
13	M Lemieux, Pit Pe	NHL	'95–96	70	92	1.31	5.17	.254
14	M Lemieux, Pit Pe	NHL	'92–93	60	91	1.52	6.04	.251
15	W Gretzky, Edm	NHL	'83–84	74	118	1.59	6.42	.248
16	Lach, Mtr C	NHL	'44–45	50	54	1.08	4.40	.245
17	W Gretzky, Edm	NHL	'82–83	80	125	1.56	6.37	.245
18	R Orr, Bos	NHL	'69–70	76	87	1.14	4.69	.244
19	M Lemieux, Pit Pe	NHL	'88–89	76	114	1.50	6.18	.242
20	F Boucher, NYR	NHL	'33–34	48	30	0.62	2.61	.240
21	W Gretzky, Edm	NHL	'88–89	78	114	1.46	6.18	.236
22	M Lemieux, Pit Pe	NHL	'91–92	64	87	1.36	5.77	.235
23	Jagr, Pit Pe	NHL	'98–99	81	83	1.02	4.37	.234
24	R Orr, Bos	NHL	'73–74	74	90	1.22	5.19	.234
25	R Francis, Pit Pe	NHL	'95–96	77	92	1.19	5.17	.231

Seventy years later, Joe Primeau still shines as one of smoothest, pinpoint, thread-the-needle passers ever to grace the rink. His numbers are also boosted a bit by that early '30s syndrome, though, and after Joe, the list belongs to Gretzky. "Some guys play hockey," said sports writer Lowell Cohn. "Gretzky plays 40-mph chess." Wonder Wayne holds seven slots here, including one of his years in LA. Hooley Smith takes third place. Bill Cowley appears again; it was said Cowley made more wings than Boeing Aircraft, and two campaigns by the ethereal Bruin sandwich the year Adam Oates spent feeding Brett Hull until Hull burst the top of the Goalscoring Presence chart. Here too is Bobby Orr, and it's great to see the dazzlingly inventive and dynamic defenceman reassert the record-obliterating production that already appeared in the Q of V list. As a blue-liner, Orr's talent for offence, phenomenal though it was, is inevitably overshadowed by the output of forwards on these lists, but if we put together separate lists for defence-men, Orr would occupy almost as many slots on them as he played seasons, and Harry Cameron, Bullet Joe Simpson, Sprague Cleghorn, Buck Boucher, King Clancy, Eddie Shore, Flash Hollett, Red Kelly, Doug Harvey, Pierre Pilote,

Brad Park, Denis Potvin, Paul Coffey, Ray Bourque, Al MacInnis, Sergei Gonchar, Brian Leetch, and every other defenceman, ever, would have to take a back seat to him. Mario's generosity is displayed four times on the lower half of the table; one of those occasions is reciprocated by teammate Ron Francis, who's been called "underrated" for so long it's now legally his first name.

You're probably expecting the Individual Scoring Dominance table for Points to come up next. We're reluctant to give it to you. It seems like it should be a simple matter to add the ISD figure for goals and the ISD figure for assists and get the ISD figure for points, but it don't work like that. It's a bit like putting pine cones and apples in a blender and expecting to get pineapple juice. Oh, we could plough ahead and do it, but it would artificially favour goal scorers over playmakers in one era, and playmakers over goal scorers in another. What we do instead is apply a sensible, reasoned constant to one part of the equation, to boost one set of variables and damp the other, in an effort to even everything out.

Player's ISD for Goals + 1⅓ (Player's ISD for Assists) = Player's ISD for Points

It feels kind of arbitrary and manipulative. It feels like the fuzzy math you keep hearing U.S. Republicans whine about every time an indisputable fact confronts them. But if we don't come across with it here, you'd be left feeling we were just leading you on, wouldn't you? So have it your way. Here it is. *Caveat emptor.*

Individual Scoring Dominance, Points, 1909–1931

	PLAYER, TEAM	LEAGUE	SEASON	GOAL ISD	1⅓xA ISD	POINT ISD
1	Keats, Edm	WCHL	'21–22	.449	.728	1.177
2	F Taylor, Van	PCHA	'14–15	.285	.831	1.116
3	H Morenz, Mtr C	NHL	'27–28	.418	.612	1.030
4	A Gagne, Edm	WCHL	'22–23	.235	.734	.969
5	Frederickson, Vic C	PCHA	'22–23	.402	.541	.943
6	F Taylor, Van	PCHA	'18–19	.395	.526	.921
7	A Joliat, Mtr C	NHL	'24–25	.489	.413	.902
8	F Taylor, Van	PCHA	'17–18	.515	.381	.896
9	Pitre, MtrC	NHA	'15–16	.265	.620	.886
10	Cy Denneny, Otw	NHL	'24–25	.390	.483	.873

Individual Scoring Dominance, Points, 1932–2001

	PLAYER, TEAM	LEAGUE	SEASON	GOAL ISD	1⅓xA ISD	POINT ISD
1	M Lemieux, Pit Pe	NHL	'92–93	.320	.335	.655
2	W Gretzky, Edm	NHL	'83–84	.300	.331	.631
3	M Lemieux, Pit Pe	NHL	'88–89	.303	.324	.627
4	W Gretzky, Edm	NHL	'84–85	.236	.359	.595
5	W Gretzky, Edm	NHL	'85–86	.168	.419	.587
6	C Conacher, Tor	NHL	'33–34	.331	.244	.575
7	P Esposito, Bos	NHL	'70–71	.312	.255	.567
8	W Gretzky, Edm	NHL	'82–83	.230	.327	.557
9	W Gretzky, Edm	NHL	'86–87	.216	.340	.556
10	J Primeau, Tor	NHL	'31–32	.119	.431	.550

The results are no surprise, really; only that rarest of players, one who combines the talents of both a big goal scorer and an excellent playmaker, could hope to rank high on this list. Among the Ancients, Taylor, Keats, Morenz, Frederickson, and Joliat certainly leap to mind among those who fit the description, and the results speak well, too, for the all-around skills of Denneny and Pitre, Hall of Famers all, and for those of all-but-forgotten Art Gagne. Three separate showings on this list, though, suggest Taylor's name ought to carry more weight in any best-of-all-time debate. Among the Moderns, well, just look – Lemieux! Gretzky! Lemieux! Gretzky! Sounds like another argument at our corner tavern. By the ISD yardstick, Mario's sensational '92–93 season was the greatest of the modern era, all the more miraculous for having been interrupted for radiation treatments for Hodgkin's. Anti-Lemieuxvian forces who complained that the k. d. lang lookalike won the Hart Trophy only on sentiment and sympathy should hang their heads in shame. Let it be noted, however, that it's the Brantford Biped, Gretzky, who occupies fully half the floors of this high-rise.

The Individual Scoring Dominance statistical category for points still troubles us, though. We could try jiggering the stats from each and every year, using some sort of slide-rule function to micromanage the numbers incrementally, but that would defeat the purpose of what we're doing, which is to devise stats that measure player performance as accurately as possible, yet simply enough that You Can Do It at Home and we don't scare off anybody who flunked high school algebra like one of *us* did. The results we got with ISD for Points *feel* right – they show us pretty much who we'd expect to see showing up – but good stats, like all good science, aren't about manipulating numbers into saying what you want to hear, but rather about setting up a completely impartial standard, plugging in the raw data, and acknowledging the truth they reveal. So we're moving on to a new category. And this is the biggie. This is where we apply all the lessons we've learned and the information we've extracted from the stats we've already shown you.

Ideal Scoring

We've toured the halls of the all-time scoring leaders, and seen the portraits of Newsy Lalonde, Gordie Howe, and Wayne Gretzky prominent among the gallery of the immortals – and realized how much the ever-lengthening schedules and the more generous awarding of assists in more modern seasons have elevated the achievements of very good modern players at the expense of the greatest players of bygone eras. We've examined Presence, and seen how much Joe Malone, Didier Pitre, Pavel Bure, and Brett Hull meant to their teams – and realized how much the increasing size of rosters and decreasing amounts of ice time have affected the proportion of scoring through the years. We've inspected Quality of Victory, and seen how Cyclone Taylor, Gordie Howe, Bobby Hull, and Gretzky blew away the competition – and begun to see a concordance between the same several players who rate well by several different standards. And we've studied Individual Scoring Dominance, and seen Tommy Smith, Charlie Conacher, Frank Boucher, Mario Lemieux, and Gretzky again, reigning over their leagues season after season – and been reminded how changes in scorekeeping and record-keeping again weigh against the Old Ones and benefit more recent stars.

We stand by all those stats – they all do what they set out to do – but we'll be the first to admit that none of them give us the whole picture. They provide valid, additional perspectives on which players excelled – and the fact that the stats tend to substantiate one another, revealing many of the same guys grading out well by separate measures, gives them credence. But they have to be divided into eras, which is annoying; they read out with an unfamiliar percentage instead of in more embraceable terms of real goals, assists, and points, which is unwieldy; they don't directly factor in ice time, which we've demonstrated is an enormous consideration; and they rate players by the standard of their own season – not against a constant historical standard, a computation devoutly to be wished. By now you should be able to see what's coming. If we want to identify the greatest single-season scoring performances of all time, what we need is something that takes into account the length of the schedule, the league-wide level of scoring, the rate at which assists were awarded, and ice time for the players we're rating.

That last variable, so very necessary to a fair rating, is a bit problematic. Ice time has been recorded officially in only the last couple of seasons. But if you bear with us, there's an extremely good indicator of ice time to be derived from one of the previous stats. It's in Presence, the one we led off with, and it's about the only reason we keep it around. Presence clearly reflected what was, in hockey's early years, the overwhelming proportion of a team's scoring done by its first-line players, who we know received an overwhelming proportion of the ice time. And we saw how that proportion fell, as hockey changed from the six-starters-and-maybe-two-substitutes system of its adolescence into the 12- and 14-man roster, two-line/three-line days of the 1920s and '30s, and continued to drop well into the modern era as teams began to dress 20 players and roll four lines through

every game. That's all indisputable. You can find plenty of citations describing how long the starters of long ago stayed on the ice: Joe Malone remembered playing 50 minutes or more on many nights, for example; Frank Nighbor is documented to have once played six straight games without taking a seat on the bench, which was only slightly remarkable for first-liners in those days; King Clancy, Paul Thompson, and Murray Murdoch, among others, have told us how they and players of their era nightly logged twice the ice time of today's 15- and 20-minute front-line players.

We have to perform a few mathematical contortions to wrest an ice-time figure from Presence. We're going to take the Presence figures of the first-line players – which we know correspond to actual ice time – compensate for the scoring, or lack of scoring, by the back-ups, and then, through the magic of basic arithmetic, arrive at a number that we can read as actual minutes played. You can try this at home, but only under the direct supervision of a professional accountant. Here's what we do, and why:

a. Average the Goal Scoring Presence figures of each team's goal-scoring leader in a given season, and express it as a straight percentage (e.g., the average Presence figure for the six team leaders in 1949–50 was .20217, or 20.217%); we have to use goal scoring because of the paucity, and sometimes complete absence, of assists in the early years.
b. Multiply that percentage by 6 (e.g., 6 × 20.217 = 121.302); this figure stands for all first-line players' Presence.
c. Subtract the average Presence figure from 100 (e.g., 100 – 20.217 = 79.783); this serves as a reciprocal figure standing for the scoring done by the subs and second-, third-, and fourth-liners while the starters are on the bench.
d. Add the product of step b to the difference from step c (e.g., 121.302 + 79.783 = 201.085); this figure stands for all the scoring done and prevents a lack of production by depth players from overinflating the starters' Presence.
e. Divide the result of step d by 6 (e.g., 201.085 / 6 = 33.514); this translates Presence into an approximation of real ice time in terms of minutes.

What we're seeing in the result of that bit of sleight of hand is an average of 33.5 minutes of ice time per game for the top scorers of 1949–50. We know it's not exact; we'll never know the true figure for sure. But is it a fair estimate? Lloyd Percival's 1960 classic *The Hockey Handbook* revealed some of the results of the 1949–50 Sports College Hockey Survey. The Sports College was a Canadian public service organization dedicated to raising standards of health, fitness, and athletic efficiency, and the observations it made and tests it ran on NHL players yielded the first hockey stats that go beyond goals, assists, penalty minutes, and goals-against average. They formed much of the basis of Percival's book, and among their findings in their very brief survey of ice time for '49–50 were these:

PLAYER, TEAM	MINUTES PLAYED
Ken Reardon, Mont C	28
Bill Mosienko, Chi	23
Ted Lindsay, Det	22
Roy Conacher, Chi	20
Ted Kennedy, Tor	19
Milt Schmidt, Bos	17

That's an average of 21.5 minutes for those six players, so even allowing for the imprecision of the Sports College's small statistical sample – it's mentioned that Kennedy was playing through some injuries while he was under scrutiny and his ice time here was well below his usual – our Presence-derived number looks too high by about half. What about some other seasons? Our formula produces a number slightly higher than 60 minutes for many of the seasons prior to World War I, and in the high 50-minute range for most of the 1920s. We know from reliable anecdotal evidence that figure could occasionally be on the money, but on average was actually closer to, again, about two-thirds that mark. As for recent seasons, our derived figure is again in the low 30s, and now we have actual ice time officially charted, showing that top-line scorers are on the ice a little over 20 minutes per game – once more, about two-thirds the number we calculated. It looks pretty consistent. So we'll make one final adjustment to our calculations: we'll use two-thirds the number we wound up with and have that stand for actual minutes played. Now don't get all huffy thinking we're claiming this number is unassailably precise. It's an estimate, that's all, an approximation – but it's vital that we have ice time as a component in any formula that purports to put all scoring on the same scale, or else every one of those pre-1930s players will show up with 200 pro-rated goals a year, and great as many of them were, that's just silly. You have to take into account that they were out on the ice most of the game, that they were responsible for almost all their teams' scoring, and that they were given the opportunity, or the burden, of doing just that. To leave that element out of the formula would be to ignore one of the most essential and influential factors in the changing way hockey's been played. Here's what we get, year by year, as estimated ice time for front-line players in all major-league seasons:

Estimated Ice Time, 1909–2001

LEAGUE	SEASON	ESTIMATED ICE TIME (IN MINUTES)	LEAGUE	SEASON	ESTIMATED ICE TIME (IN MINUTES)
ECHA	'08–09	37:20			
NHA	'09–10	39:20			
	'10–11	36:00			
	'11–12	41:20	PCHA	'11–12	34:40
	'12–13	36:40		'12–13	30:40
	'13–14	40:00		'13–14	33:20
	'14–15	38:00		'14–15	31:20
	'15–16	34:40		'15–16	33:20
	'16–17	37:20		'16–17	34:40
NHL	'17–18	40:00		'17–18	40:00
	'18–19	28:40		'18–19	36:00
	'19–20	34:40		'19–20	45:20
	'20–21	39:20		'20–21	34:40
	'21–22	33:20		'21–22	32:40
			WCHL	'21–22	31:20
	'22–23	33:20	PCHA/WCHL	'22–23	35:20
	'23–24	35:20		'23–24	30:00
	'24–25	40:40		'24–25	29:20
	'25–26	34:40	WHL	'25–26	32:40
	'26–27	28:00			
	'27–28	30:40			
	'28–29	29:20			
	'29–30	27:20			
	'30–31	28:00			
	'31–32	24:40			
	'32–33	24:00			
	'33–34	24:40			
	'34–35	24:00			
	'35–36	22:40			
	'36–37	23:20			
	'37–38	22:00			
	'38–39	22:40			
	'39–40	22:00			
	'40–41	22:00			
	'41–42	22:00			
	'42–43	22:00			
	'43–44	22:40			
	'44–45	22:40			
	'45–46	21:20			
	'46–47	22:40			
	'47–48	22:00			
	'48–49	20:40			
	'49–50	22:40			
	'50–51	22:40			
	'51–52	23:20			
	'52–53	23:20			
	'53–54	21:20			
	'54–55	22:40			
	'55–56	23:20			
	'56–57	22:40			
	'57–58	22:40			
	'58–59	23:20			
	'59–60	22:00			
	'60–61	22:40			
	'61–62	21:20			

LEAGUE	SEASON	ESTIMATED ICE TIME (IN MINUTES)	LEAGUE	SEASON	ESTIMATED ICE TIME (IN MINUTES)
	'62–63	22:00			
	'63–64	20:40			
	'64–65	22:00			
	'65–66	22:00			
	'66–67	20:40			
	'67–68	21:20			
	'68–69	22:00			
	'69–70	21:20			
	'70–71	20:40			
	'71–72	22:40			
	'72–73	21:20	WHA	'72–73	22:00
	'73–74	22:00		'73–74	21:20
	'74–75	21:20		'74–75	22:00
	'75–76	20:40		'75–76	20:40
	'76–77	20:40		'76–77	22:00
	'77–78	21:20		'77–78	21:20
	'78–79	20:40		'78–79	23:20
	'79–80	21:20			
	'80–81	20:40			
	'81–82	21:20			
	'82–83	21:20			
	'83–84	20:40			
	'84–85	20:40			
	'85–86	20:40			
	'86–87	21:20			
	'87–88	22:00			
	'88–89	21:20			
	'89–90	22:00			
	'90–91	22:00			
	'91–92	21:20			
	'92–93	22:00			
	'93–94	22:00			
	'94–95	22:00			
	'95–96	22:40			
	'96–97	22:20			
	'97–98	22:20			
	'98–99	22:20			
	'99–00	22:00			
	'00–01	22:20			

That's one variable down. Next up is the fluctuation in league-wide rates of goal scoring over the years. When Marty Walsh and Newsy Lalonde and Joe Malone were averaging two and three goals a game in the ECHA and the NHA and the first seasons of the NHL, it was possible because – well, because they were immensely talented players, of course – but also because the type of hockey being played, the scoring environment, was conducive to 8, 10, 12 or more goals a game. When Ace Bailey and Nels Stewart were the NHL's only 20-goal scorers over a 44-game schedule in 1928–29, it was because the rules and style of that season

were conducive to fewer than three goals being scored on any night. Those are the extremes, but in just the same way, the eight-goals-a-game hockey in the war-depleted 1940s or in the 1980s' Age of Air Hockey enabled players to do far more scoring than did the five-goals-a-game hockey of the Original Six days in the 1950s or does the expansion-diluted NHL of today. We have to put all scoring on a consistent scale, so the relatively easy-to-come-by goals of those wide-open seasons and the rare-as-hen's-teeth goals of those more costive years, don't misrepresent a player's real achievement. Which standard do we apply? This one: 6.45 goals per game. That figure should ring a bell: it's the average goals-per-game figure for all seasons of play in the ECHA-NHA-NHL continuum, which we indicated in that big nasty table back in Chapter One. We can think of a hypothetical year featuring an average of 6.45 goals per game as a sort of "ideal season." We can, and we will.

Pavel Bure led the NHL in goal scoring in 2000–01 with 59 in 82 games. The clutch-and-grab-congested, bush-league-plodder-infested NHL, though, saw an average of only 5.44 goals scored per game, well below the historical average. How would we expect Bure to have done in a season of more traditionally typical action? Let's pro-rate his scoring accordingly:

$$\frac{\text{Bure's goals} = 59}{\text{League-wide average GPG} = 5.44} = \frac{?}{6.45}$$

? = 70 = Bure's projected goal total in an "ideal season"

Bure's impressive 2000–01 total goes even higher when put on the scale of the historical average. On the other side of the scale, Blaine Stoughton scored 56 goals for the Hartford Whalers in 1979–80, when the NHL averaged 7.03 goals per game. In the "ideal" season of 6.45 goals per game, Stoughton would be expected to score a little less, and by this formula, that number would be 51.4. It's just the same as adjusting financial figures for inflation and depression. The same job, the same amount of work, that earned a worker $10 an hour 30 years ago earns him maybe $25 an hour today. Just as a goal was worth more in 1928–29 or 30 years ago than it was in 1979–80, Bailey and Stewart had to play just as well to lead the league and get "paid" with 21 or 22 goals as Stoughton did to lead the league and get paid with 56.

Stoughton was actually one of three players to score 56 goals back in '79–80; Danny Gare and Charlie Simmer both hit for that many as well. Stoughton played all 80 games that year, but Gare missed four games that season and Simmer did it in only 64. It's safe to assume Gare, and certainly Simmer, would have added to their totals had they played the whole year, just as it's easy to conclude everyone from Joe Malone to Nels Stewart to Rocket Richard and Gordie Howe would have scored more had their 12-game or 48-

game or 60-game seasons run for 82 games as the schedule does today. So we have to put scoring on a per-game basis. Ah! But a game for Malone meant upwards of 35 or 40 minutes of goal-scoring opportunity a night, for Simmer or Bure only 21 or 22. We'll go one step further: we'll put scoring on a per-minute basis. Let's see how Simmer fared. Multiply his 64 games by the 1979–80 standard of 21⅓ minutes of ice time per game, and we get 1,365⅓ minutes. Divide his 56 goals by his total estimated playing time –

$$\frac{56 \text{ goals}}{1365.33 \text{ minutes}} = .041016 \text{ goals per minute}$$

and we see he scored .041016 goals per minute in 1979–80. To put this on the "ideal" scale, we'll use that goals-per-minute figure instead of his raw total.

$$\frac{\text{Simmer's goals per minute} = .041016}{\text{League-wide goals per game} = 7.03} = \frac{?}{6.45}$$

$$? = .037632$$

Simmer's goal-per-minute average would have been .037632 in an "ideal" season, which we can now convert into a raw total for an 80-game season. We can't just multiply it by 4,800, though – 80 games times 60 minutes; that would yield a figure representing what Simmer would have done had he played the entirety of every game. We'd like a round number here, and although 20 minutes seems just a hair low, it's pretty realistic by today's standard. Some workhorse defencemen such as Chris Pronger and Brian Leetch

may regularly see 30 minutes and more a night, but the actual real-time average for the top scorer on all 30 teams in 2000–01 was 20 minutes, 17 seconds per game. So let's go with 20. It really doesn't matter what number we choose, as long as it's the same for everybody. So now, let's multiply that goals-per-minute figure by 1600:

.037632 goals per minute $\times$ 1600 minutes
= 60.21 goals

and we calculate Simmer's 56 goals in 1979–80 were worth 60.2 in an "ideal" year – fine production by the King winger even if scoring *was* slightly inflated that year.

If you're still not quite grasping the concept of an "ideal" year, think of it in terms of putting all scoring in the context of the 1993–94 season. That was about the last time we saw pretty good hockey on a consistent basis in the NHL. The league's 26 teams averaged 6.40 goals a game that year, very close to the all-time average, and Bure was the league's top goal-getter with 60. For you more veteran fans, think back to 1973–74, when the 16-team NHL averaged 6.39 goals a game, and Espo led the league with 61 goals. Our Ideal Season resembles those years.

Now then, having looked at every big goal-scoring performance, and lots of medium-sized ones, in the entire history of major-league professional hockey – after which we collapsed to the floor in the foetal position, mumbling incoherently, our pocket calculators sparking and smouldering nearby – we can reveal the best of them, all adjusted to compensate for the wide variations in ice time, length of schedule, and league-wide scoring levels. Behold:

Single-Season Ideal Goals

	PLAYER, TEAM	LEAGUE	SEASON	GP	G	G/GP	EST MIN/GP	LEAGUE G/GP	IDEAL GOALS
1	P Esposito, Bos	NHL	'70–71	78	76	.974	20:40	6.24	77.9
2	B Hull, StL B	NHL	'90–91	78	86	1.116	22:00	6.82	75.9
3	W Gretzky, Edm	NHL	'83–84	74	87	1.176	20:40	7.85	75.2
4	M Lemieux, Pit Pe	NHL	'92–93	60	69	1.150	22:00	7.18	75.2
5	M Lemieux, Pit Pe	NHL	'88–89	76	85	1.118	21:20	7.39	73.2
6	W Cook, NYR	NHL	'26–27	44	33	.750	28:00	3.80	72.7
7	M Lemieux, Pit Pe	NHL	'95–96	70	69	.986	22:40	6.20	72.3
8	T Smith, Qbc B	NHA	'12–13	18	39	2.167	36:40	8.58	71.1
9	E Lalonde, Mtr C/Renf	NHA	'09–10	11	38	3.454	39:20	12.79	70.9
10	Jo Malone, Qbc B	NHA	'12–13	20	43	2.150	36:40	8.58	70.6
11	H Morenz, Mtr C	NHL	'27–28	43	33	.767	30:40	3.67	70.4
12	T Smith, Qbc B/Tor OS	NHA	'14–15	19	40	2.053	38:00	8.12	70.4
13	W Gretzky, Edm	NHL	'81–82	80	92	1.150	21:20	8.02	69.3
14	C Conacher, Tor	NHL	'33–34	42	32	.762	24:40	4.61	69.1
15	P Bure, Fla	NHL	'99–00	74	58	.784	22:00	5.41	67.9
16	C Conacher, Tor	NHL	'31–32	44	34	.730	24:40	4.77	67.8
17	B Hull, StL B	NHL	'91–92	73	70	.959	21:20	6.86	67.6
18	C Conacher, Tor	NHL	'34–35	47	36	.766	24:00	4.87	67.6

PLAYER, TEAM	LEAGUE	SEASON	GP	G	G/GP	EST MIN/GP	LEAGUE G/GP	IDEAL GOALS
19 Dye, Tor	NHL	'24–25	29	38	1.310	40:40	4.94	67.2
20 C Conacher, Tor	NHL	'30–31	37	31	.838	28:00	4.63	66.7
21 F Taylor, Van	PCHA	'17–18	18	32	1.778	40:00	6.90	66.4
22 A Hedberg, Wpg	WHA	'76–77	68	70	1.029	22:00	7.27	66.4
23 R Hull, Chi	NHL	'66–67	66	52	.788	20:40	5.96	66.0
24 C Neely, Bos*	NHL	'93–94	56	50	.893	22:00	6.40	65.5
25 Weiland, Bos	NHL	'29–30	44	43	.977	27:20	5.69	64.8
26 G Howe, Det	NHL	'52–53	70	49	.700	23:20	4.79	64.6
27 R Hull, Chi	NHL	'68–69	74	58	.784	22:00	5.69	64.6
28 P Esposito, Bos	NHL	'71–72	76	66	.868	22:40	6.13	64.5
29 Mogilny, Buf	NHL	'92–93	77	76	.987	22:00	7.18	64.5
30 M Walsh, Otw	NHA	'10–11	16	37	2.312	36:00	10.33	64.2
31 R Hull, Chi	NHL	'65–66	65	54	.831	22:00	6.08	64.1
32 P Esposito, Bos	NHL	'73–74	78	68	.872	22:00	6.39	64.0
33 M Walsh, Otw	ECHA	'08–09	12	38	3.167	37:20	13.80	63.4
34 R Hull, Wpg	WHA	'74–75	78	77	.987	22:00	7.30	63.4
35 Selanne, Ana	NHL	'97–98	73	52	.712	22:20	5.20	63.3
36 Du MacKay, Van	PCHA	'14–15	17	33	1.941	31:20	10.09	63.3
37 Kurri, Edm	NHL	'84–85	73	71	.973	20:40	7.68	63.3
38 N Stewart, Mtr M	NHL	'25–26	36	34	.944	34:40	4.45	63.2
39 I Bailey, Tor	NHL	'28–29	44	22	.500	29:20	2.80	62.8
40 W Cook, Ssk	WHL	'25–26	30	31	1.033	32:40	5.20	62.8
40 R Irvin, Por	WHL	'25–26	30	31	1.033	32:40	5.20	62.8
42 W Cook, NYR	NHL	'31–32	48	34	.708	24:40	4.77	62.2
43 A Joliat, Mtr C	NHL	'24–25	24	29	1.208	40:40	4.94	62.0
44 JJ Adams, Van	PCHA	'21–22	24	26	1.083	32:40	5.45	61.9
45 M Richard, Mtr C	NHL	'44–45	50	50	1.000	22:40	7.35	61.9
46 Clapper, Bos	NHL	'29–30	44	41	.932	27:20	5.69	61.8
47 Bossy, NYI	NHL	'78–79	80	69	.862	20:40	7.00	61.6
48 P Bure, Fla	NHL	'00–01	82	59	.720	22:20	5.44	61.1
49 Bondra, Was	NHL	'97–98	76	52	.684	22:20	5.20	60.8
50 H Morenz, Mtr C	NHL	'29–30	44	40	.909	27:20	5.69	60.3
51 Simmer, LA	NHL	'79–80	64	56	.875	21:20	7.03	60.2
52 Jagr, Pit Pe	NHL	'96–97	63	47	.746	22:20	5.75	60.0
53 T Smith, Qbc B	NHA	'13–14	20	39	1.950	40:00	8.42	59.7
54 M Tardif, Qbc	WHA	'75–76	81	71	.876	20:40	7.36	59.5
55 W Gretzky, Edm	NHL	'84–85	80	73	.912	20:40	7.68	59.4
56 E Lalonde, MtrC	NHL	'18–19	17	23	1.353	28:40	8.22	59.3
57 B Geoffrion, Mtr C	NHL	'60–61	64	50	.781	22:40	6.00	59.2
58 Rea Cloutier, Qbc N	WHA	'78–79	77	75	.974	23:20	7.28	59.2
59 Selanne, Wpg	NHL	'92–93	84	76	.905	22:00	7.18	59.1
60 Frederickson, Vic	PCHA	'22–23	30	39	1.367	35:20	6.46	58.8
61 Beliveau, Mtr C	NHL	'55–56	70	47	.671	23:20	5.07	58.6
62 A Joliat, Mtr C	NHL	'27–28	44	28	.636	30:40	5.49	58.4
t63 Jo Malone, Qbc B	NHA	'16–17	19	41	2.158	37:20	10.24	58.2
t63 Nighbor, Otw	NHA	'16–17	19	41	2.158	37:20	10.24	58.2
65 Keats, Edm	WCHL	'21–22	25	31	1.240	31:20	7.02	58.2
66 M Lemieux, Pit Pe	NHL	'87–88	77	70	.909	22:00	7.33	58.1
67 B Hull, StL B	NHL	'89–90	80	72	.900	22:00	7.28	58.0
68 Nicholls, LA	NHL	'88–89	79	70	.886	21:20	7.39	58.0
69 Dunderdale, Vic A	PCHA	'12–13	15	24	1.600	30:40	9.30	57.9

	PLAYER, TEAM	LEAGUE	SEASON	GP	G	G/GP	EST MIN/GP	LEAGUE G/GP	IDEAL GOALS
70	P Bure, Van	NHL	'93–94	76	60	.789	22:00	6.40	57.9
71	Jagr, Pit Pe	NHL	'99–00	63	42	.667	22:00	5.41	57.8
72	Bondra, Was	NHL	'94–95	47	34	.723	22:00	5.90	57.5
73	R Hull, Chi	NHL	'61–62	70	50	.714	21:20	6.02	57.4
74	G Howe, Det	NHL	'51–52	70	47	.671	23:20	5.19	57.2
t75	Jo Malone, Mtr C	NHL	'17–18	20	44	2.200	40:00	9.93	57.2
t75	M Lemieux, Pit Pe	NHL	'86–87	63	54	.857	21:20	7.25	57.2

* Neely scored 50 goals in 49 games (1.02 G/GP), but has seven scoreless games added to his record here in order to have enough games played to qualify.

It's Espo who still reigns supreme after 30 years with the greatest goal-scoring performance ever. He did it with a record-smashing 1970–71 season, for that juggernaut Bruin side that ranks as the most awesome scoring machine of the modern era and the second-best of all time. We remember following Espo's relentless progress through that season as he rammed home goal after goal, night after night, with the same inevitability that younger fans may recall being exhibited by Gretzky or Brett Hull. Espo capped his year with a hat trick, in a matinee game against Minnesota and Gump Worsley, on the final day of the season. Boston Garden erupted in adoration with Espo's third of the afternoon and carpeted the ice with hats. Worsley, not pleased, skated from his crease during the delay and ceremoniously stomped his skate into a nice fedora that had landed closest to him. Big number 7 got enormous assistance all year from his excellent supporting cast – particularly the play-making genius of Bobby Orr, which is why he doesn't get much juice on the Quality of Victory chart – but make no mistake, this was a leviathan effort. Jesus saves – but Espo scores on the rebound!

Four more recent campaigns follow with more than 70 Ideal Goals each. Hull the Younger's '90–91 season for St. Louis was the second of three straight years he led the NHL in goals, each of them with 70 or more actual goals. Gretzky's '83–84 season got far less fanfare than his record-setting 92-goal outing two years earlier, but his five fewer goals here came in six fewer games and in a slightly lower-scoring year league-wide. Gretzky's law: "100% of all shots not taken don't go in." Taken in a metaphorical sense, that's a fine philosophy with which to approach life as well.

Lemieux takes charge in the fourth and fifth spots, and again it's that storybook '92–93 season leading the way. Mario, Lord of the Iron City Sphenisciforms, also claims the seventh-best goal-scoring performance ever. Only he, the Wayner, and Tommy Smith have more than one season among the top 15. Ranger Bill Cook guns his way into the sixth spot. Cup champion Quebec teammates Smith and Joe Malone win the eighth and tenth slots; Newsy Lalonde's goal-scoring frenzy of 1914–15 ranks ninth. It's like a party where everyone you invited showed up! Right behind them

are Howie Morenz, Charlie Conacher, Pavel Bure, Babe Dye, Bobby Hull, Cyclone Taylor – all the guys who've lit the lamp with the best goal-scoring seasons by the other measures we've applied.

We've carried this list out to a tie for the 75th berth, because Ideal Goals are the ultimate test for goal scoring and because of the inevitable questions about some famous goal-scoring feat that doesn't qualify for a shorter list. Despite its size, it's still an exclusive society. Among all the thousands of single-season goal-scoring performances over nearly a century of major-league hockey, these are the very best, and the 43 players who make the list are a true elite. Lemieux and Bobby Hull each appear here with five separate seasons of goal-scoring greatness. Charlie Conacher rings in with four superb seasons, all among the top 20. Espo, Gretz, Tommy Smith, Bill Cook, Joe Malone, Pavel Bure, and Brett Hull each make the honour roll three times. Lalonde, Morenz, Gordie Howe, Marty Walsh, Teemu Selanne, Aurel Joliat, Peter Bondra, and Jaromir Jagr all make two appearances on the list. Sweeney Schriner (52.4 Ideal Goals in '44–45) misses out here, but even with the Schriner Rule imposed, Cam Neely's astounding '93–94 effort (74.8 Ideal Goals without the handicap) still nearly cracks the top 20 for Ideal Goals. The active players here are Brett Hull, Alexander Mogilny, Lemieux, Bure, Selanne, Bondra, and Jagr; Neely, Anders Hedberg, Charlie Simmer, and the active players other than Lemieux are the only men here not in the Hall of Fame.

We'll look for Ideal Assists now, but we have to provide you with another reference table before we start our search. Just as Ideal Goals are determined by each season's goals-per-game average, so Ideal Assists are determined by each season's assists per game, which as you might well imagine varies even more widely than does the goal figure. Not only does the number of goals on which assists might be credited fluctuate, but the rules defining what qualifies as an assist, and how many may be awarded on each goal, have changed over the years as well. In spite of the herculean efforts of hockey historians and researchers, recently uncovering boxloads of assists not previously part of the official record, the fact remains that helpers were handed out with an eye-dropper in the game's early days, when they were awarded at all, and no matter how much that boosts the value of each assist for the purposes of this chart, there usually just isn't enough raw material, so to speak, to enable many of the playmaking stars from hockey's early days to qualify for the Ideal Assist chart. First, here's what you need to know:

Assists by Season, 1908–09 to 2000–01

LEAGUE	SEASON	GOALS	ASSISTS	APG	LEAGUE	SEASON	GOALS	ASSISTS	APG
ECHA	1908–09	333	–	–					
NHAa	1909–10	543	–	–					
	1910–11	417	–	–					
	1911–12	334	–	–	PCHA	'11–12a	261	–	–
	1912–13	520	–	–		'12–13b	219	89	3.78
	1913–14	517	278	4.53		'13–14b	231	117	4.88
	1914–15	492	171	2.81		'14–15b	270	118	4.41
	1915–16	460	164	2.69		'15–16b	288	163	4.51
	1916–17	536	228	4.36		'16–17b	459	262	5.50
NHL	1917–18a	342	142	4.12		'17–18b	200	124	4.28
	1918–19b	224	115	4.22		'18–19b	182	103	3.29
	1919–20b	460	212	4.39		'19–20b	191	95	2.87
	1920–21b	406	179	3.74		'20–21b	235	140	3.70
	1921–22b	380	218	4.44		'21–22b	203	105	2.86
					WCHL	'21–22b	353	177	3.52
	1922–23b	313	206	4.25	PCHA/WCHL	'22–23	697	284	2.63
	1923–24b	255	126	2.62		'23–24	575	261	2.42
	1924–25	450	269	2.96	WCHL	'24–25	552	278	3.28
	1925–26	581	305	2.33	WHL	'25–26	474	248	2.67
	1926–27	879	414	1.79					
	1927–28	836	416	1.82					
	1928–29	642	382	1.67					
	1929–30	1301	1079	4.72					
	1930–31	1054	975	4.28					
	1931–32	957	1000	4.98					
	1932–33	983	1186	5.30					
	1933–34	1041	1178	5.21					
	1934–35	1087	1420	6.37					
	1935–36	831	1163	5.81					
	1936–37	946	1188	5.97					
	1937–38	972	1365	6.85					
	1938–39	851	1316	7.59					
	1939–40	838	1228	7.10					
	1940–41	900	1348	7.67					
	1941–42	1047	1613	9.33					
	1942–43	1083	1647	10.94					
	1943–44	1225	1748	11.65					
	1944–45	1103	1321	8.81					
	1945–46	1003	1138	7.59					
	1946–47	1138	1479	8.22					
	1947–48	1054	1444	8.02					
	1948–49	978	1232	6.84					
	1949–50	1148	1665	7.93					
	1950–51	1139	1638	7.80					
	1951–52	1090	1630	7.76					
	1952–53	1006	1513	7.20					
	1953–54	1009	1556	7.41					
	1954–55	1059	1652	7.87					

LEAGUE	SEASON	GOALS	ASSISTS	APG	LEAGUE	SEASON	GOALS	ASSISTS	APG
	1955–56	1064	1692	8.06					
	1956–57	1130	1821	8.67					
	1957–58	1175	1943	9.25					
	1958–59	1212	1987	9.46					
	1959–60	1238	2061	9.81					
	1960–61	1261	2080	9.90					
	1961–62	1264	2090	9.95					
	1962–63	1249	2024	9.64					
	1963–64	1166	1915	9.12					
	1964–65	1208	1960	9.33					
	1965–66	1277	2114	10.07					
	1966–67	1252	2054	9.78					
	1967–68	2476	4018	9.05					
	1968–69	2718	4477	9.82					
	1969–70	2649	4276	9.38					
	1970–71	3409	5571	10.20					
	1971–72	3348	5404	9.90					
	1972–73	4088	6716	10.76	WHA	'72–73	3343	5482	11.55
	1973–74	3989	6483	10.39		'73–74	3405	5609	11.83
	1974–75	4932	8026	11.15		'74–75	4032	6587	11.93
	1975–76	4913	8025	11.15		'75–76	3975	6508	12.05
	1976–77	4783	7787	10.82		'76–77	3429	5711	12.11
	1977–78	4747	7745	10.76		'77–78	2446	4256	13.13
	1978–79	4757	7821	11.50		'78–79	1912	3126	11.90
	1979–80	5902	9593	11.42					
	1980–81	6457	10532	12.54					
	1981–82	6741	11173	13.30					
	1982–83	6493	10703	12.74					
	1983–84	6626	10904	12.84					
	1984–85	6530	10690	12.57					
	1985–86	6668	11027	12.99					
	1986–87	6165	10196	11.99					
	1987–88	6237	10375	12.20					
	1988–89	6286	10506	12.36					
	1989–90	6189	10346	12.16					
	1990–91	5805	9739	11.44					
	1991–92	6123	10299	11.54					
	1992–93	7311	12314	12.09					
	1993–94	7081	11809	10.67					
	1994–95	3727	6209	9.83					
	1995–96	6701	11166	10.34					
	1996–97	6216	10295	9.52					
	1997–98	5624	9349	8.64					
	1998–99	5830	9822	8.75					
	1999–00	6306	10647	9.14					
	2000–01	6782	11504	9.22					

a Assists not recorded as part of league's official record; figures shown indicate assists as tabulated by modern researchers.
b Assists recorded as part of league's official record, but not recorded consistently or reliably; figures shown indicate assists as retabulated by modern researchers.

And now, armed with that information, we can assess history's outstanding playmakers on the basis of Ideal Assists. The formula is basically the same as that for Ideal Goals:

$$\frac{\text{player's assists per minute}}{\text{league-wide assists per game}} = \frac{?}{8.49 \times 1600 \text{ minutes}}$$

? = Ideal Assists

Because of the exceedingly meagre number of assists handed out in the pro game's early days, we use the average number of assists per game since the beginning of the NHL – 8.49 – as the constant here in order to obtain a more familiar-looking result for each player. Again, what's important is just that that number's the same for everybody; nobody, regardless of the era in which they played, is unfairly helped or disadvantaged by which number we use. Umm, except... except that we also make one further adjustment. Sorry. We just have to. It applies only to seasons prior to that pivotal 1931–32 campaign. That was the year the assist was redefined in more modern terms, and the first year such a definition was made official. It's not by coincidence that '31–32 was also the first season in major-league hockey in which more than one assist, on average, was awarded on each goal. The rarity of assists in the years preceding that mean that, even with everything we've accounted for and applied in this formula, elementary algebra inflates the assist totals of pre-1932 players out of all reasonable proportion. For example, Frank Boucher would have his 16

assists in 44 games in 1928–29 translated into 100.8 Ideal Assists. Raffles was a great passer in his day, no question, but it's an extreme leap of mathematical extrapolation to say his 16 helpers were actually worth more than a hundred. So for seasons up to and including 1930–31, when less than one assist was handed out per goal, we're going to adjust the Ideal Assist figure by multiplying it by the pertinent season's assists-per-goal average. In 1928–29 that average was .595, which gives Boucher 60 Ideal Assists, a safer and more reasonable translation of his 16 assists than 100.8. We do this not out of prejudice against the Old Ones; we'd love to see their great abilities and achievements recognized alongside those of today's superstars, as they deserve to be. But it's just plain wrong to turn one assist into six or ten. If they were still around, they'd be advised to direct their anger not toward us, but toward the rules committees of their day that thought only the goal scorer created the goals. As a teaser, we'll tell you that only one pre-1930s player, in fact, transcended the grudging allotment of assists in his day and arrived on the Ideal Assists chart – which means only a handful of the most

Single-Season Ideal Assists

	PLAYER, TEAM	LEAGUE	SEASON	GP	A	A/GP	EST MIN/GP	LEAGUE A/GP	IDEAL ASSISTS
1	W Gretzky, Edm	NHL	'85–86	80	163	2.038	20:40	12.99	103.1
2	J Primeau, Tor	NHL	'31–32	46	37	.804	24:40	4.98	88.9
3	J Primeau, Tor	NHL	'30–31	38	32	.842	28:00	4.28	88.2
4	W Gretzky, Edm	NHL	'84–85	80	135	1.688	20:40	12.57	88.2
5	W Gretzky, Edm	NHL	'87–88	64	109	1.703	22:00	12.20	86.2
6	Re Smith, Mtr M	NHL	'31–32	43	33	.767	24:40	4.98	84.9
7	W Gretzky, LA	NHL	'90–91	78	122	1.564	22:00	11.44	84.4
8	R Orr, Bos	NHL	'70–71	78	102	1.308	20:40	10.20	84.3
9	W Gretzky, Edm	NHL	'83–84	74	118	1.595	20:40	12.84	81.6
10	W Gretzky, Edm	NHL	'86–87	79	121	1.532	21:20	11.99	81.3
11	Oates, StL B	NHL	'90–91	61	90	1.475	22:00	11.44	79.6
12	Cowley, Bos	NHL	'38–39	34	34	1.000	22:40	7.59	79.0
13	Cowley, Bos	NHL	'40–41	46	45	.978	22:00	7.67	78.7
14	W Gretzky, Edm	NHL	'82–83	80	125	1.562	21;20	12.74	78.1
15	R Orr, Bos	NHL	'69–70	76	87	1.145	21:20	9.38	77.7
16	M Lemieux, Pit Pe	NHL	'92–93	60	91	1.517	22:00	12.09	77.5
17	M Lemieux, Pit Pe	NHL	'88–89	76	114	1.500	21:20	12.36	77.3
18	F Taylor, Van	PCHA	'14–15	16	22	1.375	31:20	4.41	77.0
19	M Lemieux, Pit Pe	NHL	'95–96	70	92	1.314	22:40	10.34	76.2
20	W Gretzky, LA	NHL	'88–89	78	114	1.462	21:20	12.36	75.3
21	J Primeau, Tor	NHL	'33–34	45	32	.711	24:40	5.21	75.1
22	M Lemieux, Pit Pe	NHL	'91–92	64	87	1.359	21:20	11.55	74.9
23	F Boucher, NYR	NHL	'29–30	42	36	.857	27:20	4.72	74.8
24	Lach, Mtr C	NHL	'44–45	50	54	1.080	22:40	8.81	73.5
25	R Orr, Bos	NHL	'73–74	74	90	1.216	22:00	10.39	72.3
26	W Gretzky, Edm	NHL	'81–82	80	120	1.500	21:20	13.30	71.8
27	W Gretzky, Edm	NHL	'80–81	80	109	1.362	20:40	12.54	71.4
28	Jagr, Pit Pe	NHL	'98–99	81	83	1.025	22:20	8.75	71.3
29	D Bentley, Chi	NHL	'48–49	58	43	.741	20:40	6.84	71.2
30	W Gretzky, LA	NHL	'89–90	73	102	1.397	22:00	12.16	70.9

PLAYER, TEAM	LEAGUE	SEASON	GP	A	A/GP	EST MIN/GP	LEAGUE A/GP	IDEAL ASSISTS
31 An LaCroix, SD	WHA	'74–75	78	106	1.359	22:00	11.93	70.3
32 R Francis, Pit Pe	NHL	'95–96	77	92	1.195	22:40	10.34	69.3
33 R Clarke, Phi F	NHL	'75–76	76	89	1.171	20:40	11.15	69.1
34 R Francis, Pit Pe	NHL	'94–95	44	48	1.091	22:00	9.83	68.5
35 R Orr, Bos	NHL	'72–73	63	72	1.143	21:20	10.76	67.6
36 R Conacher, Chi	NHL	'48–49	60	42	.700	20:40	6.84	67.2
37 M Lemieux, Pit Pe	NHL	'89–90	59	78	1.322	22:00	12.16	67.1
38 W Gretzky, LA	NHL	'91–92	74	90	1.216	21:20	11.55	67.0
39 F Boucher, NYR	NHL	'33–34	48	30	.625	24:40	5.21	66.1
40 W Gretzky, LA	NHL	'93–94	81	92	1.136	22:00	10.67	65.7
41 B Trottier, NYI	NHL	'78–79	76	87	1.145	20:40	11.50	65.4
42 P Esposito, Bos	NHL	'68–69	74	77	1.041	22:00	9.82	65.4
43 Forsberg, Col A	NHL	'97–98	72	66	.917	22:20	8.64	64.6
44 M Lemieux, Pit Pe	NHL	'87–88	77	98	1.273	22:00	12.20	64.4
45 Gainor, Bos	NHL	'29–30	42	31	.738	27:20	4.72	64.4
46 F Boucher, NYR	NHL	'30–31	44	27	.614	28:00	4.28	64.3
47 A Chapman, NYA	NHL	'34–35	47	34	.723	24:00	6.37	64.3
48 R Orr, Bos	NHL	'71–72	76	80	1.053	22:40	9.90	63.7
49 F Boucher, NYR	NHL	'32–33	47	28	.596	24:00	5.30	63.6
t50 R Clarke, Phi F	NHL	'74–75	80	89	1.112	21:20	11.15	63.5
t50 R Orr, Bos	NHL	'74–75	80	89	1.112	21:20	11.15	63.5
52 Mosienko, Chi	NHL	'45–46	40	30	.750	21:20	7.59	62.9
53 P Esposito, Bos	NHL	'70–71	78	76	.974	20:40	10.20	62.8
54 U Nilsson, Wpg	WHA	'74–75	78	94	1.205	22:00	11.93	62.4
55 H Morenz, Mtr C	NHL	'30–31	39	23	.742	28:00	4.28	61.8
56 Jagr, Pit Pe	NHL	'95–96	82	87	1.061	22:40	10.34	61.5
57 A Chapman, NYA	NHL	'35–36	47	28	.596	22:40	5.81	61.4
58 Coffey, Det	NHL	'94–95	45	44	.978	22:00	9.83	61.4
59 Jagr, Pit Pe	NHL	'97–98	77	67	.870	22:20	8.64	61.3
60 U Nilsson, Wpg	WHA	'76–77	71	85	1.197	22:00	12.11	61.0
61 Lafleur, Mtr C	NHL	'76–77	80	80	1.000	20:40	10.82	60.8
62 Forsberg, Col A	NHL	'95–96	82	86	1.049	22:40	10.34	60.8
63 W Gretzky, Edm	NHL	'79–80	79	86	1.089	21:20	11.42	60.7
64 Ratelle, NYR	NHL	'71–72	63	63	1.000	22:40	9.90	60.5
65 M Lemieux, Pit Pe	NHL	'96–97	76	72	.947	22:20	9.52	60.5
66 T Lindsay, Det	NHL	'49–50	69	55	.797	22:40	7.93	60.2
67 Oates, Bos	NHL	'93–94	77	80	1.039	22:00	10.67	60.1
68 F Boucher, NYR	NHL	'28–29	44	16	.364	29:20	1.67	60.0
69 Forsberg, Col A	NHL	'98–99	78	67	.859	22:20	8.75	59.7
70 J Sakic, Col A	NHL	'99–00	60	53	.883	22:00	9.14	59.7
71 M Lemieux, Pit Pe	NHL	'85–86	79	93	1.177	20:40	12.99	59.6
72 Mikita, Chi	NHL	'66–67	70	62	.886	20:40	9.78	59.5
t73 W Cook, NYR	NHL	'29–30	44	30	.682	27:20	4.72	59.5
t73 Weiland, Bos	NHL	'29–30	44	30	.682	27:20	4.72	59.5
75 Keats, Edm	WCHL	'21–22	25	24	.960	31:20	3.52	59.3

phenomenal pre-1930s performances will show up on the Ideal Points chart as well. Before we go there, then, let's salute the Ancient Greats, who made their last thrilling stand here measured solely by their goal scoring.

Gretzky. Number 99 in your program, number 1 in Ideal Assists. Three seasons among history's top 5. Six seasons among the top 10. Thirteen seasons among the 40 best ever. Need we say more? We'll just add that Gretzky's 1985–86 campaign, with his record 163 helpers, is the only two-assist-a-game season ever. Still showing the second- and third-best results ever by this measure, Joe Primeau, with his dazzling distribution as the Kid Line pivot over the 1931 and '32 seasons, certifies his standing among history's most brilliant playmakers – yet consider the gap between Gretzky's all-time best and Primeau's. Hooley Smith's fine work with Nels Stewart and Babe Siebert on the Maroons' 3-S Line is something of a surprise at sixth. Not surprising, yet still amazing, is defenceman Bobby Orr's presence in eighth, the best of his six appearances here, all among the top 50, for the Bruin playmaking genius. Adam Oates's year in St. Louis in the company of Brett Hull ranks 11th; his season in Boston with Cam Neely also makes the grade, farther down the chart. Magical Bruin Bill Cowley sets himself up twice in a row at 12th and 13th. Mario Lemieux bunches three seasons here at 16th, 17th, and 19th. Cyclone Taylor, incredibly, is right up there in 18th; Duke Keats is the only other true Ancient to qualify for a spot.

Gretzky has 14 seasons here altogether; Mario Lemieux is next with eight appearances, followed by Orr with six, and Frank Boucher with five excellent years. Primeau and two of today's superstars, Jaromir Jagr and Peter Forsberg, have three seasons apiece on the chart. Here twice each are Bill Cowley, Ron Francis, Bobby Clarke, hooking, slashing, tackling, and digging in the corners, and Phil Esposito, reminding us he could move the puck around with aplomb when he wasn't banging it home from the crease.

Only 36 players account for the 75 places on this chart. Of especial interest among them: Elmer Lach, helping the Rocket to his 50-goal year; 1949 Black Hawk teammates Doug Bentley and Roy Conacher; their linemate that season, Bill Mosienko, but here from his year with both Bentley brothers on Chicago's great little Pony Line; Andre Lacroix, the WHA's all-time top set-up man; Bryan Trottier, feeding scoring ace Mike Bossy; Dutch Gainor, in the one big season of his career, skating with Cooney Weiland, also here, from the Bruin team that lost only 5 of 44 games; Ulf Nilsson, the artistic centre in Winnipeg for Bobby Hull and Anders Hedberg, one of the great lines not just in the WHA but of the entire modern era; Howie Morenz, centring his pal Joliat; Ted Lindsay, working with Howe; and Stan Mikita, feeding Bobby Hull. Worth a closer look are two players left underrated by the passage of time: Art Chapman, the now all-but-forgotten centreman for Sweeney Schriner and Lorne Carr for many years on the New York Americans, and Jean Ratelle, a consistently fine player for many years whose extraordinary, injury-shortened 1972 season went all but unrecognized even then. Ratelle ranks 25th on the all-time major-league scoring list, having averaged nearly a point a game, and in 21 NHL seasons never once lowered himself to get into a fight.

Now it's time to gather up our data, put them all together and make them spell "M-o-t-h-r-a." It's the ultimate test, the list of the best individual seasons in history ranked by Ideal Points. Strap yourselves in. This is what you spent your money to see.

Single-Season Ideal Points

	PLAYER, TEAM	LEAGUE	SEASON	GP	PTS	EST MIN/GP	LEAGUE PTS/GP	IDEAL G	IDEAL A	IDEAL POINTS
1	W Gretzky, Edm	NHL	'83–84	74	205	20:40	20.65	75.2	81.6	156.8
2	M Lemieux, Pit Pe	NHL	'92–93	60	160	22:00	19.26	75.2	77.5	152.7
3	M Lemieux, Pit Pe	NHL	'88–89	76	199	21:20	19.75	73.2	77.3	150.5
4	M Lemieux, Pit Pe	NHL	'95–96	70	161	22:40	16.54	72.3	76.2	148.5
5	W Gretzky, Edm	NHL	'84–85	80	208	20:40	20.24	59.4	88.2	147.6
6	W Gretzky, Edm	NHL	'85–86	80	215	20:40	20.85	41.3	103.1	142.4
7	W Gretzky, Edm	NHL	'81–82	80	212	21:20	21.33	69.3	71.8	141.1
8	P Esposito, Bos	NHL	'70–71	78	152	20:40	16.45	77.9	62.8	140.7
9	W Gretzky, Edm	NHL	'86–87	79	183	21:20	19.24	52.4	81.3	133.7
10	W Gretzky, Edm	NHL	'82–83	80	196	21:20	20.47	55.5	78.1	133.6
11	W Gretzky, Edm	NHL	'87–88	64	149	22:00	19.54	40.0	86.2	126.2
12	Weiland, Bos	NHL	'29–30	44	73	27:20	10.42	64.8	59.5	124.3
13	M Lemieux, Pit Pe	NHL	'91–92	64	131	21:20	18.41	48.4	74.9	123.3
14	P Esposito, Bos	NHL	'73–74	78	145	22:00	16.78	64.0	58.7	122.7
15	M Lemieux, Pit Pe	NHL	'87–88	77	168	22:00	19.54	58.1	64.4	122.5
16	R Orr, Bos	NHL	'70–71	78	139	20:40	16.45	37.9	84.3	122.2
17	H Morenz, Mtr C	NHL	'27–28	43	51	30:40	5.59	70.4	50.6	121.0
18	W Gretzky, LA	NHL	'88–89	78	168	21:20	19.75	45.3	75.3	120.6
19	W Gretzky, LA	NHL	'90–91	78	163	22:00	18.26	36.2	84.4	120.5
20	P Esposito, Bos	NHL	'68–69	74	126	22:00	15.51	54.6	65.4	120.0
21	Jagr, Pit Pe	NHL	'98–99	81	127	22:20	13.94	48.5	71.2	119.6
22	C Conacher, Tor	NHL	'33–34	42	52	24:40	9.82	69.1	50.3	119.4
23	H Morenz, Mtr C	NHL	'30–31	39	51	28:00	8.91	57.2	61.8	119.0

PLAYER, TEAM	LEAGUE	SEASON	GP	PTS	EST MIN/GP	LEAGUE PTS/GP	IDEAL G	IDEAL A	IDEAL POINTS
24 P Esposito, Bos	NHL	'71–72	76	133	22:40	16.03	64.5	53.4	117.9
25 G Howe, Det	NHL	'52–53	70	95	23:20	12.00	64.6	53.1	117.7
26 Keats, Edm	WCHL	'21–22	25	55	31:20	10.54	58.2	59.3	117.5
27 Jagr, Pit Pe	NHL	'95–96	82	149	22:40	16.54	55.5	61.5	117.0
28 M Lemieux, Pit Pe	NHL	'89–90	59	123	22:00	19.44	49.2	67.1	116.3
29 W Gretzky, Edm	NHL	'80–81	80	164	20:40	20.22	44.7	71.4	116.0
30 F Boucher, NYR	NHL	'29–30	42	62	27:20	10.42	41.0	74.8	115.8
31 Jagr, Pit Pe	NHL	'99–00	63	96	22:00	14.55	57.8	57.9	115.7
32 Ratelle, NYR	NHL	'71–72	63	109	22:40	16.03	54.2	60.5	114.7
33 R Orr, Bos	NHL	'69–70	76	120	21:20	15.19	36.2	77.7	113.8
34 J Primeau, Tor	NHL	'31–32	46	50	24:40	9.75	24.8	88.9	113.7
35 Lafleur, Mtr C	NHL	'76–77	80	136	20:40	17.46	52.6	60.8	113.4
36 M Lemieux, Pit Pe	NHL	'96–97	76	122	22:20	15.27	52.9	60.5	113.4
37 Cowley, Bos	NHL	'40–41	46	62	22:00	12.80	33.8	78.7	112.5
38 Yzerman, Det	NHL	'88–89	79	155	21:20	19.75	53.8	58.7	112.5
39 A Hedberg, Wpg	WHA	'76–77	68	131	22:00	19.38	66.4	45.7	112.1
40 Selanne, Ana	NHL	'98–99	75	107	22:20	13.94	55.8	55.6	111.4
41 M Tardif, Qbc	WHA	'75–76	81	148	20:40	19.40	59.5	51.9	111.4
42 Lafleur, Mtr C	NHL	'77–78	78	132	21:20	17.35	56.4	54.6	111.0
43 Jagr, Pit Pe	NHL	'00–01	81	121	22:20	14.66	54.6	56.2	110.7
44 Nicholls, LA	NHL	'88–89	79	150	21:20	19.75	58.0	52.2	110.2
45 B Trottier, NYI	NHL	'78–79	76	134	20:40	18.50	44.1	65.4	109.5
46 Kurri, Edm	NHL	'84–85	73	135	20:40	20.24	63.3	45.8	109.1
47 P Esposito, Bos	NHL	'72–73	78	130	21:20	17.31	52.1	56.9	109.0
48 Hv Jackson, Tor	NHL	'31–32	48	53	24:40	9.75	51.2	57.6	108.8
49 M Tardif, Qbc	WHA	'77–78	78	154	21:20	20.67	53.4	55.4	108.7
50 Jagr, Pit Pe	NHL	'96–97	63	95	22:20	15.27	60.0	48.7	108.6
51 Oates, StL B	NHL	'90–91	61	115	22:00	18.26	28.2	79.6	107.8
52 D Bentley, Chi	NHL	'48–49	58	66	20:40	12.28	36.4	71.2	107.6
53 J Sakic, Col A	NHL	'00–01	82	118	22:20	14.66	56.0	51.5	107.4
54 Lafleur, Mtr C	NHL	'74–75	70	119	21:20	18.00	53.5	53.9	107.3
55 C Conacher, Tor	NHL	'34–35	47	57	24:00	11.24	67.6	39.7	107.3
56 J Primeau, Tor	NHL	'30–31	38	41	28:00	8.91	18.9	88.2	107.1
57 R Conacher, Chi	NHL	'48–49	60	68	20:40	12.28	39.8	67.2	107.1
58 B Hull, StL B	NHL	'90–91	78	131	22:00	18.26	75.9	31.1	107.0
59 R Hull, Wpg	WHA	'74–75	78	142	22:00	19.24	63.4	43.1	106.5
60 G Howe, Det	NHL	'53–54	70	81	21:20	12.21	47.5	58.9	106.4
61 Rea Cloutier, Qbc	WHA	'76–77	76	141	22:00	19.38	56.0	50.3	106.3
62 W Gretzky, LA	NHL	'89–90	73	142	22:00	19.44	35.3	70.9	106.3
63 R Hull, Chi	NHL	'68–69	74	107	22:00	15.51	64.6	41.6	106.2
64 E Lindros, Phi F	NHL	'94–95	46	70	22:00	15.74	50.1	56.0	106.1
65 W Cook, NYR	NHL	'32–33	48	50	24:00	9.69	57.1	48.9	106.0
66 J Bucyk, Bos	NHL	'70–71	78	116	20:40	16.45	52.3	53.7	106.0
67 F Taylor, Van	PCHA	'14–15	16	45	31:20	14.50	46.9	59.1	106.0
68 Lach, Mtr C	NHL	'44–45	50	80	22:40	16.16	32.2	73.5	105.7
69 W Gretzky, Edm	NHL	'79–80	79	137	21:20	18.45	44.4	60.7	105.1
70 Cowley, Bos	NHL	'43–44	36	71	22:40	19.82	46.5	58.6	105.0
71 R Hull, Chi	NHL	'65–66	65	97	22:00	16.15	64.1	40.6	104.7
72 M Dionne, LA	NHL	'79–80	80	137	21:20	18.45	45.6	58.5	104.2
73 R Orr, Bos	NHL	'74–75	80	135	21:20	18.00	40.6	63.5	104.1
74 An Lacroix, SD	WHA	'74–75	78	147	22:00	19.24	33.8	70.3	104.1
75 R Orr, Bos	NHL	'73–74	74	122	22:00	16.78	31.7	72.3	104.0

PLAYER, TEAM	LEAGUE	SEASON	GP	PTS	EST MIN/GP	LEAGUE PTS/GP	IDEAL G	IDEAL A	IDEAL POINTS
76 M Dionne, LA	NHL	'78–79	80	130	20:40	18.50	52.6	50.7	103.4
77 J Primeau, Tor	NHL	'33–34	45	46	24:40	9.82	28.2	75.1	103.4
78 W Cook, NYR	NHL	'29–30	44	59	27:20	10.42	43.7	59.5	103.2
79 Lafleur, Mtr C	NHL	'79–80	74	125	21:20	18.45	46.5	56.5	103.0
80 B Trottier, NYI	NHL	'77–78	77	123	21:20	17.35	43.8	59.2	103.0
81 C Conacher, Tor	NHL	'31–32	44	48	24:40	9.75	67.8	35.2	103.0
82 Jagr, Pit Pe	NHL	'94–95	48	70	22:00	15.74	53.0	49.7	102.7
83 J Sakic, Col A	NHL	'98–99	73	96	22:20	13.94	50.0	52.4	102.4
84 LaFontaine, Buf	NHL	'91–92	57	93	21:20	18.41	56.9	45.5	102.3
85 Bossy, NYI	NHL	'78–79	80	126	20:40	18.50	61.6	40.	102.3
86 P Esposito, Bos	NHL	'74–75	79	127	21:20	18.00	54.5	47.7	102.2
87 M Dionne, LA	NHL	'76–77	80	122	20:40	17.46	49.8	52.4	102.2
88 P Kariya, Ana	NHL	'96–97	69	99	22:20	15.27	51.2	50.9	102.2
89 Lafleur, Mtr C	NHL	'75–76	80	125	20:40	17.97	51.2	50.9	102.1
90 E Lindros, Phi F	NHL	'98–99	71	93	22:20	13.94	50.1	51.9	102.0
91 M Lemieux, Pit Pe	NHL	'86–87	63	107	21:20	19.24	57.2	44.7	101.9
92 B Geoffrion, Mtr C	NHL	'60–61	64	95	22:40	15.91	59.2	42.5	101.8
93 Jagr, Pit Pe	NHL	'97–98	77	102	22:20	13.83	40.4	61.3	101.7
94 R Orr, Bos	NHL	'72–73	63	101	21:20	17.31	34.0	67.6	101.6
95 Mikita, Chi	NHL	'63–64	70	89	20:40	14.67	50.1	51.5	101.6
96 H Morenz, Mtr C	NHL	'31–32	48	49	24:40	9.75	43.9	57.6	101.5
97 Clapper, Bos	NHL	'29–30	44	61	27:20	10.42	61.8	39.7	101.4
98 Lafleur, Mtr C	NHL	'78–79	80	129	20:40	18.50	46.4	55.0	101.4
99 Mikita, Chi	NHL	'66–67	70	97	20:40	15.74	41.9	59.5	101.4
100 M Bentley, Chi	NHL	'45–46	47	61	21:20	14.27	47.7	53.6	101.3

Wow. Wow. It's quite a contest. But with every last thing fully accounted for, the fairest possible assessment strongly suggests Gretzky is still Da Man. Only Mario Lemieux seriously rivals him in offensive production. But Gretzky's incredible consistency must earn him the nod here.

Graceful, wiry, boyishly handsome, and squeaky clean, Gretzky was a revelation, his startling creativity a refreshing tonic to the mayhem of the mid- and late '70s. He was an immediate sensation on and off the ice, his popularity skyrocketing right along with his point totals. He was not without his critics; a few hidebound Original Six nostalgists scoffed at his slight build and lack of physical play, suggesting he'd have struggled to make the third line in the Good Old Days – conveniently forgetting small, clean, creative players such as Bill Cowley, Frank Boucher, Lorne Carr, Cooney Weiland, Art Chapman, Johnny Gottselig, Buddy O'Connor, the Bentley brothers, and dozens of others who were among the brightest stars of that bygone era. When we updated this list after the 1987–88 season, Gretzky owned eight of the top nine places here, and whatever doubt any Original Six apologists had about him being the greatest offensive player of all time should have been erased. Yet with his career, well, on the wane in his final seasons in New York, presumably pre-adolescent Gretzky-haters crawled out of the Internet woodwork, posting gigabytes of toxic piffle on alt-dot newsgroups dismissing the Wayner as a "fraud" who was "made" by his "great wingers" (presumably wingers such as B. J. MacDonald or Glenn Anderson or Tomas Sandstrom). Reading these adenoidal mewlings left our jaws hanging like the "Springtime for Hitler" audience in *The Producers*. Take away every assist Gretzky earned setting up his best winger – usually Jari Kurri – in the '80s, and the Great One still leads the NHL in scoring season after season through that decade. Take away every goal Gretzky himself scored in several seasons, and he still could have won the scoring title on his playmaking alone. His production was unprecedented; until he achieved them, his numbers were unimaginable. He rose far above the debased Age of Air Hockey in which he flourished, a creature with the power of flight among earthbound beasts. Gretzky would have dominated regardless of the age in which he played. No other player had ever mastered the dual skills of both goal scoring and playmaking at such a level.

Until, that is, the arrival of Mario Lemieux. Gretzky's '83–84 performance is the greatest offensive season of all time, and he can claim an incredible seven of the eleven best ever – but the Emperor Penguin has already earned himself the second, third, and fourth positions behind Gretzky on the Ideal Points list, and with Lemieux's astonishing return from three years of self-imposed exile, the Assault on the Wayne is again underway. It's a two-pronged attack, being fought both in the record books and among the fans and media. Who is the best? Lemieux is a Brobdingnagian talent, no question, the only player to rival Gretzky on this ultimate list, his revenant performance last season a brilliant one. But even if his chronic back troubles allow him to play on, he is 36 after all, 250 goals and 1,300 points behind Gretzky on the all-time scoresheet, and time is running out on him to surpass Gretzky's best.

Gretzky's domination of the all-time Ideal Points list – ten – ten! – of the 30 best seasons in the entire history of hockey – is still so strong it makes everyone else on the list look small. But consider – these are the 100 best performances out of thousands upon thousands of individual single-season performances acted out over 93 years of major-league hockey. Gretzky has put in an awe-inspiring total of 12 appearances here, altogether, nine of them with the Oilers and three more with the Kings.

Lemieux appears eight times, seven of them among the top 36. The magnitude of le Magnifique's best seasons is underscored by the realization that seven other campaigns of historic stature have occurred in his very shadow. Somewhat surprisingly, Jaromir Jagr – "Mario Jr." – has also cracked the list seven times, topped by his '98–99 campaign in the 21st spot; last season's effort earned him the 43rd spot on this list. We heard precious little mention of the fact that the dazzling Jagr, with his 2000–01 Ross Trophy performance, became the only man in history besides Gordie Howe, Phil Esposito, and Gretzky to win his league's scoring title four years in a row. Hab superstar Guy Lafleur, le Démon Blond, is next with six seasons of excellence. Close behind are the Alpha and Omega of the '60s–'70s Bruins, Esposito and Orr, with five showings apiece on the list; all of Espo's are among the top 50, while Orr's genius is reflected in the

fact he's the only defenceman to appear here even once.

Another Canadien great – Howie Morenz, l'Homme Éclair – and two Leaf legends – Charlie Conacher, the Big Bomber, and his centreman, Gentleman Joe Primeau, are here three times each, as are Bobby Hull, the Golden Jet – here twice with the Black Hawks and once with the WHA Jets – and Marcel Dionne, the Little Beaver, here each time with the L.A. Kings. Seven more greats register twice each among history's hundred best: Bill Cook, war veteran and scoring champ of two leagues; Bruin Bill Cowley, the finest passer of his day; Mr. Hockey himself, Gordie Howe; Stan Mikita, four times the NHL scoring champ during his 22-year career, all of it with Chicago; Marc Tardif, a sensational performer for the WHA Nordiques; the Flyers' oft-concussed Gargantua, Eric Lindros; and Joe Sakic, the pride of Burnaby, B.C.

All three members of the Kid Line – Conacher, Primeau, and Busher Jackson – make the list, something no other line has accomplished. Brothers Charlie and Roy Conacher, and Doug and Max Bentley, all have seasons here, as do father Bobby Hull and son Brett. In all, only 44 different men have produced the top 100 scoring seasons in history; nine of them are still active, while 29 of them are members of the Hall of Fame.

That concludes our museum tour. The gift shoppe is on your right.

2000–01 Season

We hope you found our stroll through 93 years and 116 seasons of major-league history entertaining as well as illuminating. With that fresh perspective, let's check on how last season's leaders fared on the scales of history.

Individual Presence in Team Goal Scoring, 2000–01

PLAYER, TEAM	LEAGUE	SEASON	SCHED	GP	G	TEAM GF	PRESENCE
1 P Bure, Fla	NHL	'00–01	82	82	59	200	.418
2 P Kariya, Ana	NHL	'00–01	82	66	33	188	.265
3 J Sakic, Col	NHL	'00–01	82	82	54	270	.250

Quality of Victory, Goals, 2000–01

PLAYER, TEAM		LEAGUE	SEASON	GP	G	G/GP	Q OF V
Leader	P Bure, Fla	NHL	'00–01	82	59	.720	9.25
Runner-up	J Sakic, Col			82	54	.659	

Quality of Victory, Assists, 2000–01

PLAYER, TEAM		LEAGUE	SEASON	GP	A	A/GP	Q OF V
Co-leader	Jagr, Pit	NHL	'00–01	81	69	.852	0.00
Co-leader	Oates, Was			81	69	.852	

Quality of Victory, Points, 2000–01

PLAYER, TEAM		LEAGUE	SEASON	GP	P	P/GP	Q OF V
Leader	Jagr, Pit	NHL	'00–01	81	121	1.494	3.81
Runner-up	J Sakic, Col			82	118	1.439	

Individual Scoring Dominance, Goals, 2000–01

	PLAYER, TEAM	LEAGUE	SEASON	GP	G	G/GP	AVG TEAM G/GP	GOAL ISD
1	P Bure, Fla	NHL	'00–01	82	59	.72	2.72	.265
2	J Sakic, Col	NHL	'00–01	82	54	.66	2.72	.242
3	Jagr, Pit	NHL	'00–01	81	52	.64	2.72	.236

Individual Scoring Dominance, Assists, 2000–01

	PLAYER, TEAM	LEAGUE	SEASON	GP	A	A/GP	AVG TEAM A/GP	ASSIST ISD
1	Jagr, Pit	NHL	'00–01	81	69	.85	4.61	.185
1	Oates, Was	NHL	'00–01	81	69	.85	4.61	.185
3	Forsberg, Col	NHL	'00–01	73	62	.85	4.61	.184

Individual Scoring Dominance, Points, 2000–01

	PLAYER, TEAM	LEAGUE	SEASON	GOAL ISD	$1\frac{1}{3}$XA ISD	POINT ISD
1	Jagr, Pit	NHL	'00–01	.236	.246	.482
2	J Sakic, Col	NHL	'00–01	.242	.226	.468
3	Palffy, LA	NHL	'00–01	.192	.202	.394

Single-Season Ideal Goals, 2000–01

	PLAYER, TEAM	LEAGUE	SEASON	GP	G	G/GP	MIN/GP	LEAGUE G/GP	IDEAL GOALS
1	P Bure, Fla	NHL	'00–01	82	59	.720	22:20	5.44	61.2
2	J Sakic, Col	NHL	'00–01	82	54	.658	22:20	5.44	55.9
3	Jagr, Pit	NHL	'00–01	81	52	.642	22:20	5.44	54.6

Single-Season Ideal Assists, 2000–01

	PLAYER, TEAM	LEAGUE	SEASON	GP	A	A/GP	EST MIN/GP	LEAGUE A/GP	IDEAL ASSISTS
1	Jagr, Pit	NHL	'00–01	81	69	0.85	22:20	9.22	56.2
2	Oates, Was	NHL	'00–01	81	69	0.85	22:20	9.22	56.2
3	Forsberg, Col	NHL	'00–01	73	62	0.85	22:20	9.22	56.0

Single-Season Ideal Points, 2000–01

	PLAYER, TEAM	LEAGUE	SEASON	GP	PTS	EST MIN/GP	LEAGUE PTS/GP	IDEAL G	IDEAL A	IDEAL POINTS
1	Jagr, Pit	NHL	'00–01	81	121	22:20	14.66	54.6	56.2	110.7
2	J Sakic, Col	NHL	'00–01	82	118	22:20	14.66	56.0	51.5	107.4
3	Kovalev, Pit	NHL	'00–01	79	95	22:20	14.66	47.3	42.6	89.9

And that's the most recent season's scoring in review. Some questions remain unanswered, however. We're about to address a few of them, but we're limited by the unavailability of some raw data. Hockey's come a long way in the right direction with the volume of things it now tabulates, and one of the few things the NHL can point to with justifiable pride is the work done by the people in its statistical and media service departments. Believe it or nuts, though, after everything we've said so far, we're not so sure everything's worth keeping track of. Those "giveaway," "takeaway," and "hit" categories don't seem to tell us much, and we've never liked "shooting percentage" even though that one's been around forever. Shooting percentage – goals as a percentage of a skater's shots on goal – says more about the goaltending the shooter's facing than it does about the accuracy of his shot. Wouldn't shots on goal as a percentage of shots taken be a much more useful figure? On the other side of the same coin, we've longed for years to see an accounting of shots blocked by defencemen. Perhaps some day soon. For now, we do have enough data to discuss just a few more items. Like even-strength scoring, for instance.

Even-Strength Scoring

It's a given that it's easier to score with a man advantage than at even strength. It's also a given that to be successful, you have to take advantage of the opportunities presented you. If you squander those opportunities in real life, you might wind up a hockey writer or something. If you squander your opportunities in a game, you usually lose. That's why coaches make having an effective power play a priority. Fifteen years ago they were absolutely obsessed with it, though, which was pretty stupid, and we said so at the time. Then, as now, the majority of a hockey game is played with both sides even. It makes a lot more sense to concentrate on outplaying and outscoring the other team at even strength than it does to blow off the situation in which most of the game is played and instead focus on the little bit of time you might be a man up. In the Air Hockey of the '80s, so many goals were being scored with both sides even that power-play scoring, rather than being paramount as every coach and commentator seemed to think, was actually an almost negligible factor. We did a study on it at the time, removing every power-play goal from every game played in some mid-'80s season, and found that only a handful of teams saw any noticeable effect on their won-lost-tied record, and that there was little correlation between power-play success and winning percentage. How well teams performed at even strength was the overwhelming determinant of their position in the standings.

Things change. With goals harder to come by now than at any time in more than 40 years, maybe a potent power play – and reliable penalty killing, which got puzzlingly little corollary attention in the '80s – have a lot more to do with a team's overall success these days than they did 15 years ago, eh? Indeed, there was a much closer correspondence between teams' success rates with the man advantage and their rank in the standings in 2000–01 than there was in the mid- and late '80s. But left undemonstrated amid the ubiquitous tables ranking "special teams" units – a football term, for crying out loud; when will hockey return to developing its own language? – is the even closer correspondence between winning percentage and effectiveness at even strength. So just take a gander at this. It's a ranking of all NHL teams by their proficiency in scoring at even strength in 2000–01, with their point total in the final standings for comparison.

Team Even-Strength Scoring For and Against, 2000–01

TEAM	ESGF	ESGA	DIFF	PTS
New Jersey	215	140	+75	111
Colorado	179	122	+57	118
Ottawa	193	151	+42	109
Dallas	162	131	+31	106
St. Louis	162	131	+31	103
Philadelphia	174	143	+31	100
Pittsburgh	198	167	+31	96
San Jose	152	121	+31	95
Toronto	173	143	+30	90
Detroit	158	140	+18	111

TEAM	ESGF	ESGA	DIFF	PTS
Los Angeles	167	150	+17	92
Edmonton	171	156	+15	93
Buffalo	152	139	+13	98
Washington	152	142	+10	96
Phoenix	148	142	+6	90
Vancouver	156	153	+3	90
Nashville	128	147	−19	80
Calgary	129	149	−20	73
Minnesota	119	139	−20	68
Boston	155	177	−22	88
New York Ran	169	192	−23	72
Florida	146	169	−23	66
Columbus	131	155	−24	71
Chicago	154	182	−28	71
Carolina	134	164	−30	88
Montreal	133	169	−36	70
Atlanta	148	191	−43	60
Anaheim	116	161	−45	66
New York Isl	125	175	−50	52
Tampa Bay	139	197	−58	59

Call us easily impressed, but we'd say that proves an overwhelmingly convincing relationship between even-strength ability and winning. Only three teams out of thirty – Detroit, Carolina, and Boston – achieved a significantly better record than their even-strength performance justified. In the case of the Red Wings and Hurricanes, their excellence on the power play and in killing penalties made up for their shortcomings with both sides even; how Boston managed to overcome their weak numbers in all categories is a mystery we'll leave to Russ Conway. The point is, there's a nearly direct correspondence in almost every case, team by team, between even-strength success and success in the standings. Which leads to the question, which players contributed the most scoring at even strength, and thereby really did the most to help their teams? You can find a list of the top power-play scorers almost anywhere every season, but here's something you don't see often: the top even-strength scorers in the NHL. We've added columns for total points, short-handed points, and power-play points to give you the complete picture.

Even-Strength Scoring Leaders, 2000–01

	PLAYER, TEAM	GP	P	ESG	ESA	ESP	SHP	PPP
1	Jaromir Jagr, Pit	81	121	37	41	78	2	41
2	Joe Sakic, Col	82	118	32	34	66	6	46
3	Patrik Elias, NJ	82	96	29	35	64	3	29
4	Pavel Bure, Fla	82	92	35	24	59	5	28
5	Alex Tanguay, Col	82	77	19	39	58	1	18
6	Bill Guerin, Edm-Bos	85	85	28	28	56	1	28
7	Sergei Samsonov, Bos	82	75	26	30	56	1	18
8	Alexei Yashin, Otw	82	88	25	31	56	2	30
9	Petr Nedved, NYR	79	78	22	34	56	1	21

PLAYER, TEAM	GP	P	ESG	ESA	ESP	SHP	PPP
10 Mike Modano, Dal	81	84	22	34	56	3	25
11 Alexei Kovalev, Pit	79	95	30	25	55	3	37
12 Robert Lang, Pit	82	80	22	33	55	0	25
13 Alexander Mogilny, NJ	75	83	31	23	54	0	29
14 Petr Sykora, NJ	73	81	24	30	54	3	24
15 Shawn McEachern, Otw	82	72	23	30	53	0	19
16 Martin Straka, Pit	82	95	19	34	53	2	40
17 Mark Recchi, Phi	69	77	19	32	51	2	24
18 Pierre Turgeon, StL	79	82	19	32	51	0	31
19 Mats Sundin, Tor	82	74	19	32	51	1	22
20 Radek Dvorak, NYR	82	67	24	26	50	4	13
21 Keith Primeau, Phi	71	73	23	27	50	1	22
22 Jeremy Roenick, Phx	80	76	17	33	50	0	26
23 Doug Weight, Edm	82	90	17	33	50	0	40
24 Milan Hejduk, Col	80	79	28	21	49	3	27
25 Steve Sullivan, Chi	81	75	20	29	49	10	16

The list of last year's even-strength scoring leaders, alas, doesn't offer many surprises, like we had on occasion through the 1980s. Then, it seemed, there was always a player or three among the even-strength scoring leaders who wasn't also among the top point producers overall. As you can see, though, the even-strength list for 2000–01 bears a marked resemblance to the league's scoring parade; every big point-producer at even strength added 20, 30, 40-odd power-play points to his overall total. Obviously, these guys earned plenty of time on the power-play unit with which to boost their numbers.

This always gets us wondering about who produced the most scoring without the benefit of service on the power play. Here we've charted the guys who registered the smallest proportion of their points in man-advantage situations and still rolled up at least 32 points last season. Just in case they've had opportunity on the power-play unit but consistently failed to cash in, we've included their actual average time on ice per game, and their actual average power-play time on ice per game, as tracked by the league itself.

Power Play Be Damned — 32 or More Points, Less Than 20% on PP

					AVG TOI/GP	AVG PPTOI/GP
	GP	P	PPP	PCT	MIN:SEC	MIN:SEC
1 John Madden, NJ	80	38	0	0.0	15:16	00:10
2 Shjon Podein, Col	82	32	0	0.0	14:23	00:26
3 Magnus Arvedson, Otw	51	33	1	3.0	16:00	00:29
4 Greg Johnson, Nas	82	32	1	3.1	17:49	00:29
5 Rob Zamuner, Otw	79	37	2	5.4	14:46	00:47
6 Mike Grier, Edm	74	36	2	5.6	16:44	00:43
7 Stephane Matteau, SJ	80	32	2	6.2	10:54	00:16
8 Craig Conroy, StL-Clg	83	32	3	9.4	14:43	00:38

					AVG TOI/GP	AVG PPTOI/GP
	GP	P	PPP	PCT	MIN:SEC	MIN:SEC
9 Todd Marchant, Edm	71	39	4	10.3	17:53	01:09
9 Glen Murray, LA	64	39	4	10.3	17:55	02:25
11 Darcy Tucker, Tor	82	37	4	10.8	16:09	01:02
12 Rem Murray, Edm	82	36	4	11.1	15:20	01:03
12 Steven Reinprecht, LA-Col	80	36	4	11.1	13:26	01:18
14 Curtis Brown, Buf	70	32	4	12.5	16:34	00:53
14 Chad Kilger, Edm-Mtr	77	32	4	12.5	13:30	01:03
14 Marco Sturm, SJ	81	32	4	12.5	15:53	01:40
17 Ruslan Fedotenko, Phi	74	36	5	13.9	14:37	01:44
18 Claude Lapointe, NYI	80	32	5	15.6	18:40	00:39
19 Marcus Nilson, Fla	78	36	6	16.7	15:46	02:10
20 Sergei Brylin, NJ	75	52	9	17.3	15:15	01:16
21 Martin St. Louis, TB	78	40	7	17.5	14:56	01:14
22 Richard Zednik, Was-Mtr	74	44	8	18.2	15:46	02:00
23 Andrei Nikolishin, Was	81	38	7	18.4	15:32	01:14
24 Jan Hrdina, Pit	78	43	8	18.6	15:43	00:54
25 Kevin Stevens, Phi-Pit	55	32	6	18.8	15:57	02:58
26 Jeff Halpern, Was	80	42	8	19.0	16:07	01:46
27 Radek Dvorak, NYR	82	67	13	19.4	19:04	03:05

John Madden. One of our favourites. What a hoss. All in all, that's a pretty good collection of penalty killers and checking-line forwards. In a similar vein, here are the brave souls who turned adversity to their advantage and led the NHL in short-handed scoring last season.

Short-handed Scoring Leaders, 2000–01

	PLAYER, TEAM	GP	P	ESP	SHG	SHA	SHP
1	Steve Sullivan, Chi	81	75	49	8	2	10
2	Theo Fleury, NYR	62	74	34	7	2	9
3	Wes Walz, Min	82	30	20	7	2	9
4	Todd Marchant, Edm	71	39	28	4	3	7
5	Mike Eastwood, StL	77	23	15	2	5	7
6	Mike Grier, Edm	74	36	28	3	3	6
7	Mark Messier, NYR	82	67	32	3	3	6
8	Joe Sakic, Col	82	118	66	3	3	6
9	Peter Forsberg, Col	73	89	47	2	4	6
10	Nine players tied with						5

How can ya not like a short-handed goal? Unless it's scored against your team, of course. It kind of ties in to that whole concept of Canadian machismo that permeates hockey, too, which is all well and good if you're talking about overcoming overwhelming odds and playing through pain and sacrificing for the team and keeping your wits about you under pressure and what-not, but tends to get a little sickening when it lapses into overworked tripe about "superior force of will" and "doing anything to win" and all that crypto-fascist malarkey that winds up saying Might Makes Right.

Clutch Scoring

Nobody likes a mindless bully, and those "power-ranking" charts that pop up like dandelions, rating "power forwards" – egads, a *basketball* term, no less – by combining their point totals and one-tenth or one-half their penalty minute totals to produce a number reflecting some sort of "intimidation factor," just make us roll our eyes. And how many of those penalty minutes turned into power-play goals for the other team? Instead, here's our own response to that stuff, which you might think of as a sort of "pure skill" ranking, or "Clean Play Points." With a rough rule of thumb based on the fact that opponents score on about one of five power-play opportunities, we can project that every 10 minutes in penalties results in a goal-against. Of course, that penalty that yields the goal doesn't last the full two minutes, so we'll ratchet it down a notch. We've rated these scoring artists by subtracting one-eighth of their penalty minute total from their point total. Yeah, yeah, we know all about coincidental minors and short-handed goals and the rest. But at least we're not whipping up some completely arbitrary number like those "intimidation" rankings. Check it out:

Clean Play Points, 2000–01

	PLAYER, TEAM	PTS	PIM	CPP
1	Jaromir Jagr, Pit	121	42	115.8
2	Joe Sakic, Col	118	30	114.2
3	Patrik Elias, NJ	96	45	90.4
4	Martin Straka, Pit	95	38	90.2
5	Zigmund Palffy, LA	89	20	86.5
6	Pavel Bure, Fla	92	58	84.8
7	Jason Allison, Bos	95	85	84.4
8	Alexei Yashin, Otw	88	30	84.2
9	Alexei Kovalev, Pit	95	96	83.0
10	Peter Forsberg, Col	89	54	82.2
11	Luc Robitaille, LA	88	66	79.8
12	Doug Weight, Edm	90	91	78.6
13	Adam Oates, Was	82	28	78.5
14	Alexander Mogilny, NJ	83	43	77.6
15	Mike Modano, Dal	84	52	77.5
16	Pierre Turgeon, StL	82	37	77.4
17	Petr Sykora, NJ	81	32	77.0
18	Brett Hull, Dal	79	18	76.8
19	Robert Lang, Pit	80	28	76.5
20	Brian Leetch, NYR	79	34	74.8
21	Milan Hejduk, Col	79	36	74.5
22	Mario Lemieux, Pit	76	18	73.8
23	Peter Bondra, Was	81	60	73.5
24	Mark Recchi, Phi	77	33	72.9
25	Sergei Samsonov, Bos	75	18	72.8

Hmm . . . that wasn't as satisfying as we'd hoped. A closely bunched scoring race without much variety in their penalty-minute totals means we don't see the kind of reshuffling in last year's scoring parade that we saw a few years ago, when Lady Byng candidates like Paul Kariya and Teemu Selanne were contending with roughhousers like Cam Neely and Brendan Shanahan on the NHL points leader board. But now here's something you'll *really* like. It's a *Hockey Compendium* exclusive. That's too bad in a way, because every season, it's the biggest pain-in-the-ass stat we have to compile by hand, game by game and goal by goal. But it's worth it.

We mentioned some official stats we don't care much for; "game-winning goals" and "game-tying goals" are a couple more. These two antiquated numbers harken back to the days of Morenz and Shore, when every game wound up 2-1 or 1-0, and the game-winning goal was a pretty dramatic event and actually meant something. On second thought, that sounds like the last three or four years in the NHL. But never mind! The point is that in the intervening years and eras of much larger scores, the game-winning or game-tying goal became an accident of later circumstance that you had to stop to locate on the scoresheet. There's not much pressure or drama involved in the goal that puts a team ahead 4-0 in an 8-3 win, but that's the one that goes down as the game-winner. That's not what a game-winning or game-tying goal is supposed to be about, is it? When you hear those phrases, don't you picture some highlight-reel effort in the final seconds to even the score or put a team ahead?

We can't vouch for highlight-reel quality, but we can say with certainty that every goal that actually affects the lead in a game has a lot more to do with a team's success over the course of a season, and about which skaters actually produce in the clutch, than do "game-winning goals" as traditionally tabulated. So we keep track of 'em, every stinkin' goal and every last assist tallied by every one of the 12,000 guys that play in every one of the 6,600 games on the NHL schedule each year, and we count up every one of 'em that ties the score or puts a team ahead at any point in any of those games. We call them "Crucial Points." Those figures are significant: it only takes a moment's reflection to realize that the difference between the total number of times a team ties the score or takes a lead, and the number of times its opponents tie the score or take a lead, will perfectly indicate the team's winning percentage. And therefore, a guy who can deliver consistently in those situations, by setting up or bagging a goal that draws his team even or puts it ahead, is a lot more valuable than a guy who does plenty of scoring when the outcome's pretty well decided one way or the other but dries up when the score's tied or his team's down by a goal.

Crucial Scoring Leaders, 2000–01

	PLAYER, TEAM	GP	P	LGG	LGA	STG	STA	CruP
1	Joe Sakic, Col	82	118	25	20	9	14	68
2	Jaromir Jagr, Pit	81	121	13	24	11	14	62

	PLAYER, TEAM	GP	P	LGG	LGA	STG	STA	CruP
3	Martin Straka, Pit	82	95	9	18	7	22	56
4	Patrik Elias, NJ	82	96	16	20	7	10	53
5	Alexei Kovalev, Pit	79	95	15	15	9	12	51
6	Pavel Bure, Fla	82	92	18	11	15	6	50
6	Doug Weight, Edm	82	90	5	21	9	15	50
8	Alexei Yashin, Otw	82	88	17	16	9	7	49
9	Peter Forsberg, Col	73	89	8	24	6	10	48
9	Milan Hejduk, Col	80	79	18	13	6	11	48
9	Mike Modano, Dal	81	84	13	16	8	11	48
12	Donald Audette, Atl-Buf	76	79	14	18	7	8	47
12	Bill Guerin, Edm-Bos	85	85	14	19	6	8	47
12	Robert Lang, Pit	82	80	7	18	11	11	47
12	Zigmund Palffy, LA	73	89	16	19	3	9	47
16	Jason Allison, Bos	82	95	13	22	4	7	46
16	Brendan Shanahan, Det	81	76	15	14	2	15	46
18	Alex Tanguay, Col	82	77	8	22	8	7	45
19	Peter Bondra, Was	82	81	16	8	10	10	44
19	Sergei Fedorov, Det	75	69	13	15	8	8	44
19	Ray Ferraro, Atl	81	76	11	16	6	11	44
19	Adam Oates, Was	81	82	2	23	4	15	44
19	Mats Sundin, Tor	82	74	13	18	3	10	44
19	Keith Tkachuk, Phx-StL	76	79	15	17	6	6	44
25	Mario Lemieux, Pit	43	76	13	14	8	8	43

	PLAYER, TEAM	GP	P	LGG	LGA	STG	STA	CritP
4	Doug Weight, Edm	82	90	0	5	6	3	14
7	Pierre Turgeon, StL	79	82	2	4	3	4	13
8	Patrik Elias, NJ	82	96	2	1	4	5	12
8	Alexei Kovalev, Pit	79	95	2	4	4	2	12
8	Mike Modano, Dal	81	84	5	4	1	2	12
11	Marian Hossa, Otw	81	75	5	4	2	0	11
11	Robert Lang, Pit	82	80	1	3	4	3	11
11	Brendan Shanahan, Det	81	76	1	5	1	4	11
11	Alexei Yashin, Otw	82	88	2	4	2	3	11
15	Chris Drury, Col	71	65	2	3	3	2	10
15	Jonas Hoglund, Tor	82	49	3	2	3	2	10
15	Tomas Holmstrom, Det	73	40	2	3	2	3	10
15	Mario Lemieux, Pit	43	76	3	4	1	2	10
15	Keith Primeau, Phi	71	73	2	3	2	3	10
15	Ryan Smyth, Edm	82	70	2	3	2	3	10

That's why Jagr gets paid the big bucks. And there's Mats Sundin not far behind, which is pretty good for a guy who gets an absurd amount of flak for supposedly being "soft."

Plus/Minus

We've applied every yardstick and measuring tape we have at hand, put every season on every scale we could find, examined every player under infrared and ultraviolet light, poked, prodded, X-rayed, and resonance-imaged them from every angle, and now you can argue your opinion with some solid evidence at your command. And you will have to argue them, still, because after all of those examinations, all we've analyzed is pure offence. And of course there's a lot more to the game than that. Unless you're the '84 Oilers or the '92 Penguins.

You'll still get a hassle from old-timers who'll decry the rankings we've presented as horseshit because Gordie Howe didn't top every list and "It don't matter how many points yer Bobby Orr scored, he did it cuz he didn't play defence worth a damn and Eddie Shore wuz the best ever on the blue line." Actually, they'd be raising a good point, even though they'd be wrong in their conclusions.

How much a skater contributes to the other side of the ledger, to defence, was long a mystifying matter that was finally judged solely on subjective observation. Emile Francis often got credit for devising plus/minus, the system that earns a player a plus for every even-strength or short-handed goal his team scores while he's on the ice and a minus for every even-strength or short-handed goal the opposition scores while he's out there. But well before Francis employed it in the 1960s, it was already in use by the Canadiens in the '50s. Would that we still had those figures.

Allan Roth, later the long-time stats and information chief for baseball's Los Angeles Dodgers, started out in the Canadiens PR department and helped keep track of plus/minus for the club while he was there. We found this out

Sakic. He's terrific. All these guys produced well and nobly in the clutch. But that chart didn't exactly lift us all out of our seats as we might have anticipated. Nobody there, really, you wouldn't expect to see contributing most of their team's Crucial Scoring. So let's apply some added pressure to those figures. We're going to look at Crucial Scoring done only in the third period of the 2000–01 season's games. Every time the score's close going into the third, you'll inevitably hear, near the end of the second intermission broadcast, that one of the teams involved is something like 31-2-4 when leading after two, and the other is around 3-29-3 when trailing after two. Makes one sound like a power-house and the other like a doormat. Well, you hear those figures constantly because those are pretty much the record for every team in the league. Third-period comebacks are a real rarity league-wide, especially in the midst of a scoring drought. A goal that ties the score or puts a team ahead in the third, then, really is something special. To emphasize the adrenaline-saturated nature of scoring in that situation, we call this subset of Crucial Scoring "Critical Scoring." Hold onto your hats.

Critical Scoring Leaders, 2000–01								
	PLAYER, TEAM	GP	P	LGG	LGA	STG	STA	CritP
1	Jaromir Jagr, Pit	81	121	7	7	5	3	22
2	Bill Guerin, Edm-Bos	85	85	6	4	2	5	17
3	Mats Sundin, Tor	82	74	4	6	1	4	15
4	Jason Allison, Bos	82	95	4	5	1	4	14
4	Sergei Fedorov, Det	75	69	5	2	4	3	14

several years ago after following a series of leads that took more turns and went through more characters than an episode of "The Rockford Files." At last we got hold of Roth, retired in southern California, and he was pretty sure he must still have those old plus/minus sheets lying around somewhere! It was like finding an old prospector who claimed he had the map to the Lost Dutchman Mine. What treasure trove of long-lost statistics would reveal themselves? The Rocket – Plus Powerhouse, or Minus Monster? Ah . . . alas. Weeks later, Roth told us he'd searched, but, unable to locate anything, he concluded he must have just thrown them out along with a lot of other stuff that got ruined when his garage was flooded a few years earlier. Such is the care afforded the annals and artifacts of our game's legacy. Not quite as bad as the atrocity committed in 2000 by hockey card entrepreneur Brian Price, when he bought the only set of pads the sainted Georges Vezina ever wore and gleefully ran them through a shredder as a promotional gimmick, but a sad loss for hockey by any standard.

Now plus/minus numbers are part of the standard stats package and are available for every player since expansion began. Fans know it, if it's true that they don't exactly love it. What does it matter? some of them will ask, contending that plus/minus is a bogus stat that is so deceptive it tells us exactly nothing. We still run into a few vociferous fans who think that way. Curiously, they always seem to raise this argument when defending some favourite player of theirs who is clueless in his own zone and whom the latest plus/minus numbers have just revealed to be clueless in his own zone, or when getting some barbed comments from teammates exasperated by the plus/minus naysayer's own inept, lackadaisical backchecking for their rec-league team.

Yet they have a point, too, even if their conclusions are wrong as well. Their inarticulate contention is that plus/minus is somehow, in some way, unfair. We would argue, as would most fans, that it is eminently fair, if, *if*, you know how to read it. You can't automatically conclude a +40 mark is better than a +20 mark any more than you can assume a 40-goal season is better than a 20-goal season. Right? You need more information. You gotta have context. Maybe the +40 guy amassed his figure playing for a dreadnought club that blew every other team off the rink, a team on which every player was +30, +40, +50, while the +20 guy played for a miserable team that was frequently routed, a team on which every other player was well into minus. No matter how clever and diligent a player is, if he's surrounded by lazy, irresponsible teammates on a lousy club, he's going to have his plus/minus figure dragged down by the incompetence of the other guys he's skating with. Conversely, even offence-minded danglers or witless lugs who couldn't find their way back into their own end with a roadmap and a brace of bloodhounds will have their plus/minus numbers boosted if they're playing on a top-flight side with bright, hard-working teammates who cover for their screw-ups and

produce bushels of goals. It would indeed be unfair to compare their numbers straight up, and you should know that all raw plus/minus says is something about how a player performed relative to his own teammates.

Well, we'll fix that. We're going to make a little adjustment that puts the plus/minus figures of every player, no matter how good or bad his team, on the same scale, so that we can make those comparisons. It's simple enough to do, and it works like this: we put every player's plus/minus rating on a zero scale by adjusting for the average plus/minus mark of each team. Plusses and minuses aren't credited on power-play goals, so leave those aside; just subtract the total of all even-strength and short-handed goals scored against a team from the total of all even-strength and short-handed goals scored by that team. There are usually five players aside on the ice when even-strength goals are scored – four-on-four goals and shorties make up only a tiny percentage of the non-power-play total – so divide the result of the team total by five to get the average player's plus/minus figure. Then subtract that average from the real player's raw plus/minus figure to get his Adjusted +/– mark and see how much better or worse he did than the guys he skated with.

Team ESG + SHG	Player raw +/–
– Opponent ESG + SHG	– Team Adjusted +/–
Team Adjusted +/–	Player Adjusted +/–

We've already peeked at the results for 2000–01, and we can tell you the extremes of Adjusted Plus and Adjusted Minus were pretty modest in a historical sense. The highest raw plus mark ever recorded, Bobby Orr's +124 for the 1970–71 season, translated to an Adjusted Plus record of +91.0. Orr produced Adjusted Plus numbers that were among the NHL's very best every year he played, *averaging* an incredible Adjusted +50.5 over his last seven seasons. Stars of the 1970s and '80s such as Larry Robinson, Wayne Gretzky, and Guy Lafleur were, in their primes, regularly among the league leaders as well, with Adjusted Plus marks that often reached the +50, +60 range. Oiler stars Gretzky, Jari Kurri, and, astonishingly, Paul Coffey, Canadien greats Robinson, Lafleur, Jacques Lemaire, Serge Savard, Guy Lapointe, and Jacques Laperriere, Flyers Bobby Clarke and Brian Propp, Dave Taylor and Charlie Simmer of the Kings, and Islanders Bryan Trottier, Mike Bossy, and Denis Potvin were among the best in this category throughout most of their careers. So were smart, clean, tenacious checking forwards Craig Ramsay and Don Luce of Buffalo, and reliable, underrated defencemen Bill Hajt, Bill White, Keith Magnuson, and Rod Seiling.

Even with our treatment of the raw figures, it would do you well to think about the Adjusted numbers in some context as well. Riding shotgun with a Gretzky or an Orr, for example, was a season-long gift of plus. Gretzky's wingers and Orr's defence mates invariably soared into the stratosphere of plus, only to settle back into the middle of the pack or lower once the combination was broken up and Gretzky's and Orr's aura of plus embraced a new winger or blue-line partner. Some guys create plus, others just stand around and gather it up. On the other hand, there's an effect we call the Phil Russell Syndrome, named for the pretty decent journeyman defenceman of the '70s and '80s. Russell often seemed to wind up with defensively challenged teams where he was counted on to stabilize things in their end of the rink. There's only so much one man can do! Getting great gobs of ice time as a poor team's best player, Russell and his kind – Doug Wilson of the expansion Sharks is a more recent example – wind up with a disproportionate number of minuses as their teammates screw up beyond the good player's ability to cover up for them. Some guys create minus, others are merely afflicted by it.

With that small caution delivered, let's see now who shone brightest, and who wore the darkest tarnish, with regard to two-way play last year.

Adjusted Plus/Minus Plus Leaders, 2000–01

PLAYER, POS, TEAM	ADJ +/-
Joe Sakic, c, Col	+33.6
Patrik Elias, lw, NJ	+29.4
Scott Stevens, d, NJ	+24.4
Alex Tanguay, lw, Col	+23.6
Brad Lukowich, d, Dal	+21.8
Milan Hejduk, rw, Col	+20.6
Petr Sykora, rw, NJ	+20.4
Brian Rafalski, d, NJ	+20.4
Mike Modano, c, Dal	+19.8
Radek Bonk, c, Otw	+17.6
Simon Gagne, lw, Phi	+17.4
Zigmund Palffy, rw, LA	+17.0
Luke Richardson, d, Phi	+16.4
Colin White, d, NJ	+16.4
Sergei Zubov, d, Dal	+15.8
Karl Dykhuis, d, Mtr	+15.8
Chris Therien, d, Phi	+15.4
Al MacInnis, d, StL	+15.2
Jason Strudwick, d, Van	+15.2
Jozef Stumpel, c, LA	+15.0

Adjusted Plus/Minus Minus Leaders, 2000–01

PLAYER, POS, TEAM	ADJ +/-
Patrice Brisebois, d, Mtr	−24.2
Mark Messier, c, NYR	−21.2
Corey Sarich, d, TB	−21.0
Vincent Lecavalier, c, TB	−21.0
David Harlock, d, Atl	−19.6
Todd Bertuzzi, lw, Van	−18.8
Nelson Emerson, rw, LA	−18.0
Andrei Nazarov, rw, Ana-Bos	−17.6
Ladislav Kohn, rw, Ana-Atl	−17.4
Tony Amonte, rw, Chi	−17.0
Sandis Ozolinsh, d, Car	−17.0
Mattias Ohlund, d, Van	−16.8
Scott Gomez, c, NJ	−16.6
Olli Jokinen, c, Fla	−16.4
Wayne Primeau, c, TB-Pit	−16.4
Tomas Holmstrom, lw, Det	−16.2
Mark Parrish, rw, NYI	−16.0
Zdeno Chara, d, NYI	−16.0
Valeri Bure, rw, Clg	−15.4
Bob Corkum, c, Ana-NJ	−15.2

Holy crow, here's Sakic leading this category too. Fair enough, then. Give him the Hart. It's no shock to see players from Colorado, New Jersey, and Dallas showing up with nifty Adjusted plus marks; they're not high in plus because they play for excellent teams, their teams are excellent because they're loaded with fine two-way players. It's nice to see some throwback, stay-at-home defencemen such as Luke Richardson and young Jason Strudwick posting fine Adjusted Plus marks, and Karl Dykhuis was an unappreciated gem on the Montreal blue line in 2000–01.

We've looked at the entirety of the game's major-league history. We've looked at the 2000–01 season. Have we settled once and for all the argument over which player was better than another, or who was the best of all time? Of course not. As we've pointed out, our discussions have been concerned mainly with offensive production; even in that context, we're limited by the sketchiness of the statistical record in the early days of hockey. And hockey, unlike other sports, is full of not only fans but media people who flatly deny anything in hockey can be measured by an analytical look at the numbers. And so they'll continue to argue – in a vacuum. We're here to shed light, not heat, on the debate. The biggest fallacies in hockey are not that Player X was better than Player Y, but that all seasons are equal, that all numbers are equal, and that the game defies statistical analysis. If hockey so far has remained resistant to a magic mirror that would perfectly reflect the total value of a player on offence, on defence, and in the clutch, in a historical context, we'd like to think we have at least a multifaceted lens, allowing us to see enough separate flashes of excellence to put together an answer to questions too long debated in the dark.

4.

Goaltending

We're going to depart for once from our penchant for beating around the bush and tell you right off the draw that in this chapter we will show you that Dominik Hasek is the best goaltender in the recorded history of NHL netminding.

There it is, complete with dramatic paragraph break. Hasek, by now recognized pretty much universally as "the world's best goalie," is in fact more than just the world's best goalie. He seems to be the best goalie that ever was, or, more accurately, he has compiled what is by far the best statistical performance in all the years for which we have detailed and comprehensive goalkeeping stats. More on those stats in a bit, but first, back to Hasek himself.

Most hockey fans, we're sure, are aware of the knock that used to exist against the Dominator: "Sure he's good, but what has he won?" It's a ridiculous old saw used at one time or another against practically every great player who has ever laced up his skates. No matter how incredible, creative, successful that player has been, he is nothing until he has won the Stanley Cup. In fact, he's less than nothing; he's not to be counted on when the chips are down, useless when everything is on the line, lacking in character, gutless, slinking, craven. How many tremendous players have had to endure these insinuations? Gil Perreault, Marcel Dionne, and Mike Gartner spring to mind first; no less insightful an observer than Ken Dryden made the accusation against Perreault and Dionne in *The Game*, though not quite in so many words:

> The attitude of a team depends so much on its best player. A coach and a manager can be neutralized; a best player has followers, and must be a leader. He must have the character and personality to match his skills. It's why the Flyers won and the Sabres didn't; why the Kings and Blues never went far.

The idea was that Guy Lafleur and Bobby Clarke had won Stanley Cup titles while Perreault and Dionne hadn't because Lafleur and Clarke possessed some ineffable quality of leadership that the other two lacked. Mind you, we'd argue that what Lafleur possessed, and what Perreault didn't, was 19 teammates who together with regard to talent constituted one of the best hockey teams of all time, but never mind. In North American hockey, with its rock-ribbed Calvinist belief in hard work, sacrifice, and grim determination to the exclusion of creativity, self-expression, and joy, the only thing that counts is getting to heaven as the end reward. Thus, you are nothing if you haven't won the Cup.

91

Think of how Mario Lemieux and Brett Hull were perceived until they each won their first Stanley Cup: selfish, spoiled choke artists who couldn't get it done when the Auld Mug was on the line, one a sulking diva, the other a blabbermouth prima donna. In reality, of course, they were both great, always great, and always going to be great whether they won the Cup during their careers or not. The same goes for Darryl Sittler, Bill Gadsby, Jean Ratelle, Borje Salming, and any number of other truly superb players of hard work and high character. And the same goes for Dominik Hasek. The real point is that no matter how fantastic a pro hockey player you are, there's no way you're ever going to win the Stanley Cup unless you play for what is at least a very good team. Ask Ray Bourque.

In 1998 Hasek was the goaltender for the Czech Olympic Team, which won the gold medal at Nagano. That, fortunately for him, has absolved him somewhat in the eyes of those who believe you're nothing till you've won a major championship. The irony, though, is that while Hasek was the most important factor in getting the Czech Republic past Canada in that memorable tournament, he was not the reason the Czechs beat Russia in the gold medal game. It was their success at playing a boring, close-checking, trapping NHL-style game that smothered the Russians' speed-demon skaters in the 1-0 finale, a game that featured a grand total of 41 shots on goal by both teams. But that is neither here nor there. Hasek's richly deserved gold medal – his save percentage in the six-game Olympic tournament was .963 – finally lifted the burden of achievement from his shoulders. He had won his championship, and now everyone could call him the world's best goalie without reservation.

Or so you'd think. We still run into people who gainsay the towering majesty of Hasek's career with the very words "What has he won?" Come *on*. Consider the team he has played for in recent seasons. Would the Buffalo Sabres have had even a fraction of the success they enjoyed in the late '90s with anyone besides Hasek in the nets? Can you possibly conceive of the Sabres, a team of courageous pluggers, yes, but also one of negligible talent, reaching the semifinals in '98 and the Cup Final in '99 without him working miracles night after night? They barely made the playoffs in 1999–2000, and only then because Hasek returned from injury late in the season to backstop them to a strong stretch run that got them into the eighth and final spot. Look at the Sabres' line-up during Hasek's tenure. Except for two years when Pat LaFontaine was healthy, they have been without a high-scoring forward, and their best defenceman during any of his years would have been hard pressed to make even the second blue-line pairing on any good team in the league. They're a low-payroll club built on grit, surely, but mainly on the knowledge that any mistake they make – and they make plenty – will be covered up for by Hasek. When you look at the shots-against figures that appear in the latter half of this chapter, you'll see that in this decade the Sabres have consistently left him to face the highest volumes of shots anyone has had to contend with. Yet despite all that, he has remained virtually unbeatable.

In fact, as John LeClair showed in the Flyers' first-round defeat of Buffalo in 2000, the only sure way to beat the Dominator is to drill the puck through a hole in the side of the net and hope no one notices that it shouldn't have been a goal. Remember Hasek's priceless reaction to that shot, a blast to the short side? He thought he had it covered, which of course he did, then he looked over his left shoulder to find where the puck had come to rest, presumably behind the net or against the end boards, looked back out in front, then looked into the net again – *boing!* – and saw the disk sitting inside the cage: a classic double-take. We've never seen a goalie react to a goal that way. It speaks volumes about Hasek's innate technical grasp of his position. He *knew* he had the angle covered, he *knew* the puck was going wide of the net, even if only six inches wide, he *knew* the puck hadn't touched him, he *knew* it wasn't a goal. Yet there was the puck, in the net, and it was utterly baffling to him. It was only several minutes later, after the television producers had looked at the play in super-slow motion, that word started leaking out that the puck had entered through a hole in the side mesh. Hasek should have trusted his instincts and said something at the time of the goal, but can you blame him for not doing so? How many times have you seen a puck go *through* the net in a pro game?

So this whole notion that Hasek is not really a great goalie because he hasn't won the Stanley Cup is complete rubbish. Hey, we're not so sure he *hasn't* won a Cup. . . . More on that later in this chapter.

Goalie Perseverance

All right, it's time we got down to the goaltending stats. To explain our methodology, we're going to adapt something we wrote in the original *Compendium* and, with substantial alterations and updatings, present parts of it here. What we said in the mid-'80s remains true today, so this is how we figure it all out.

The statistical method hockey has used since the very beginning of the game for determining who is a good goalie and who is a bad one is all wrong. Goals-against averages they're called, and as we all know, you figure out a goalie's GAA by taking the number of goals he allows and dividing it by the number of minutes he plays, then multiplying that figure by 60; in essence, you're dividing his goals-allowed figure by the number of games he played. This is patently ridiculous, and it doesn't take a genius to show why. That's where we come in.

Let's say you're a goalie and each night your team allow the opposition to pelt you with 50 shots. You stop 46 of them every game, which is really quite an accomplishment. You have a lot to be proud of. Okay, now another goalie on another team faces only 20 shots each night, and he stops 17 or 18 per game. Pretty good, but no great shakes either. All right, now the statistics come out, and your goals-against average is 4.00; this other guy's is 2.50. Immediately, all the fans and TV announcers and sports writers are saying that the other guy's really great, but you're having an "off year." An off year?! Hold on, you say, I've been great! Every night I'm stopping an unrelenting barrage of frozen vulcanized rubber! I'm like the 300 Spartans at Thermopylae, that unnamed Viking at Stamford Bridge! Tough shit, says everyone else. You're allowing four goals a game, and this other guy's allowing only two and a half. He's better than you are. Stop being such a whiner.

You look for something to back up your case. All you need are the shot totals, but no one's paying any attention to them. Instead, your detractors go for the jugular. What's your won-lost record? they ask, a malevolent twinkle in their eyes. Well, it's 15-30-10, you answer, but that's because the other teams get so many shots on me, and since the play is always in our end we never get more than three goals against our opponents. Aha! shout your inquisitors. You're a *loser*. This other guy's won-lost record is 30-15-10. Yeah, you protest, but he's got so little to do. His defencemen stop every opposition thrust before it even reaches him. Play is always in the other end. The learned ones aren't impressed. He's a *winner*, they say. *The numbers prove it.*

What completes this Kafkaesque picture is the knowledge that years from now, the only statistics in the record books will be your goals-against average and your won-lost-tied record, and neither one looks that good. Twenty years from now, Stan Fischler will see these stats and make up some kind of derogatory nickname, like "The Human Sieve" or "He Who Walks Like a Man but Plays Goal Like Facial Tissue." Everyone will think you were a bumbling oaf and you'll be humiliated all over again, which is the goalie's lot anyway. You may think this far-fetched, but are you really certain that Howie "Holes" Lockhart and Steve "The Puck Goes Inski" Buzinski were bad goalers? Maybe their teammates left them to the mercy of the opposition. Maybe they never had a prayer. Until their shots-against totals and save percentages are exhumed from old newspaper summaries or official game reports, we'll never know for sure.

Even goalies whom everyone knows are good are victims of airheaded pronouncements based on faulty statistical data. For instance, during the 1985–86 All-Star game, and we admit this is going back a bit, the usually perceptive John Davidson was talking about Grant Fuhr. Davidson said that Fuhr was an excellent goaltender, then he apparently looked at his stat sheet to back up his statement with some cold, hard, indisputable numbers. He paused for a moment, then said something like, "Well, his goals-against average is up around four and a half, so actually he's not having a very good year." Not having a very good year! His Edmonton teammates were constantly down in the other end, gleefully

attending to their ever-bulging scoring totals, paying no mind to playing in their own end. Fuhr and his netmate at the time, Andy Moog, had to face breakaway after breakaway because of this. The Oilers would still win, by scores of 7-4 and 8-5, but it was often because Fuhr and Moog turned aside most of the 35 to 40 shots per game they were forced to handle. Davidson, a former goaler himself, should have known better than to go by Fuhr's GAA.

If GAA were in any way an accurate measure of goaltending performance, it'd be easy to figure out who the best goalies of all time are. But it is not. So we have to ask ourselves, What does a goalie do? He *stops shots*. What statistic measures the stopping of shots? Save percentage. The NHL started keeping track of save percentages at the start of the '82–83 season (even though newspapers were publishing shot and save totals in game summaries at least 30 years earlier), which is now so long ago that the last goaler who played in the pre-save-percentage era, Grant Fuhr, retired after the 1999–2000 season. (Fuhr, incidentally, debuted in the NHL in '81–82.) Now with Fuhr gone and the shots-and-saves records of all active goalies intact and recorded, you'd think the league would keep close tabs on things like career save percentage and career shot totals. But beyond minting yet another corporate-sponsored trophy for the goalie with the year's best save percentage, the NHL doesn't pay much attention to the statistic, and we're not convinced that the GMs who vote the Vezina or the writers who make the post-season All-Star selections do either. Even if they do, what you usually hear or see when announcers or writers discuss goalies is goals-against averages, or more ridiculous still, won-lost records, as if it's somehow the goalie's fault that he didn't score a couple of goals himself when his teammates failed to do anything at the other end.

Now that we have save totals, we can measure what a goalie really does: stop shots. We could just use save percentages as our means of measuring goalkeepers, but that doesn't quite work. Why? Let's say you've got two goalers, each of them with a .900 save percentage. Goaler X faces 20 shots per game, while Goaler Y faces 40 per game. Who's done better? According to save percentage alone, they're equal. But considering that Goaler Y is facing a far greater number of shots per game, isn't it really fair to say he did better? Goaler Y, after all, had a lot more work to do, a lot more chances to be beaten. Think about it: what would be harder in a game – stopping 9 out of 10, or stopping 54 out of 60? You don't have to be Lorne Chabot to know that the second scenario is the more difficult one. The more shots you face in a game, the greater the likelihood that those shots include more rebounds, breakaways, screened drives – in short, that there is a higher degree of difficulty. If you face 10 shots a game, it means the puck comes at you just once every six minutes. If you face 60 shots a game, pucks are coming your way once every minute. The more shots you face, and the faster they come, the less likely the chance that you have the time to get set for each shot, to be in position for each shot, to *see* each shot. Your workload is much more taxing, and so, like Lucille Ball scrambling to keep pace when the assembly line at the chocolate factory speeds up, it's more likely that you'll screw up. More of those chocolates will get by you than when the conveyor belt was moving at a nice, slow, steady pace.

Save percentage is a good start, but by itself it's not sufficient. It measures success, but it doesn't measure workload, and since workload plays such an essential role in determining success, we need a stat that combines both factors. Only then can there be an accurate barometer for goaltending skill. And hey, whaddaya know: we have that stat. We call it the perseverance index, because it measures how well a goalie perseveres under fire. We came up with it 20 years ago, and it has served us well ever since. Here's how it works, using a hypothetical goalie as our guinea pig.

First, we look at his shots and saves record. Our hypothetical goalie stopped 588 out the 658 shots he faced while he was in the nets. You divide the first number by the second, and voila! you find that his save percentage is .894.

Our next step is to measure accurately his workload, that is, the number of shots he faces per game. Let's say our hypothetical netminder had to handle those 658 shots over 1,257 minutes of play. First, you divide 658 by 1,257, and you find that he faced .523 shots per minute. Once you multiply that by the 60 minutes of a regulation game, you've figured out that he faced 31.4 shots per game.

Now comes the tricky part, where we combine the save percentage and workload figures. We tried several combinations when we were first devising this stat, and we chose this one because it seemed the most satisfying, accurate, and symmetrical. It is based on our best perceptions, and in that sense it is subjective to some degree. But in two decades of using the perseverance statistic, it has always yielded a fair result, game by game, season by season, and we believe in it wholeheartedly. Our eyes are misting up, but we must go on.

We take our goalie's save percentage of .894 and multiply it by 600. The answer is 536. Now we add to it his shots-per-game average of 31.4, which gives us a figure of just under 568.

Finally, to put the whole thing onto an easy-to-comprehend scale of 1000, we divide 568 by six-tenths (.6). And we get 946, and that's our hypothetical goalie's perseverance rating.

Here's the whole process presented in algebraic form, which we know you'll love.

TO FIND SAVE PERCENTAGE:
saves divided by *total shots faced* = save percentage

TO FIND SHOTS PER GAME:
total shots faced divided by *minutes played*

= shots per minute
shots per minute $\times$ 60 = shots per game

TO FIND PERSEVERANCE RATING:
(*save percentage* $\times$ 600) + *shots per game* = z
z divided by .6 = perseverance rating

There you have it. In a nutshell, you can think of a goalie's perseverance rating as being six parts save percentage and one part shots against. And you can also think of a perseverance mark of 1000 as being perfection, although it is also possible to earn a rating of more than 1000. It's fairly common in a single game (a shutout is automatically worth more than 1000), but over the course of a season a goalie would have to be so flawless as to defy belief. For example, you'd get a 1000 rating if you recorded a save percentage of .930 while facing an average of 42 shots per game. Algebraically, it looks like this:

.930 $\times$ 600 = 558
558 + 42 = 600
600 divided by .6 = 1000

You'd also get a 1000 rating should you face 48 shots per game and stop 92% of them. Or if you face 30 shots per game and record a save percentage of .950. On the other hand, if you face 30 shots per game but stop only 80% of them, you'd get a perseverance rating of 850, which would mark you as a bad goalie. As we examine the stats of goalies through the years, we'll see that in certain eras perseverance figures will be higher than in others. This is a reflection of fluctuations in save percentage and shot averages from era to era, and it's fascinating to follow. Right now, we're living in an era of low shot totals and high save percentages, which means a lot of shutouts and 2-1 games. Fifteen years ago, shot totals were moderate, but save percentages were low, hence the 8-6 games of the '80s. Thirty years ago, shot totals were high, but save percentages were high, too, which translated to a lot of 4-2 results. *Plus ça change, plus . . . ça change.*

There are mitigating circumstances, of course. For instance, a goalie on a team whose defencemen are unable to clear rebounds will suffer statistically. Let's say there's a scramble in the slot and the goalie makes four incredible stops, one after another, but his defence is still unable to clear the rebound, and the fifth shot goes in. It's not the goalie's fault (assuming the rebounds were not his fault, and let's assume that for this case), but his save percentage for this sequence is only .800. If this happens a lot over the course of a season, the goalie's low save percentage will unjustly make him look bad, and since the perseverance statistic is heavily dependent on save percentage, his perseverance rating will be unjustly low. But that's the way it is in hockey – everything's interdependent, everything happens lightning-fast, and no one thrives unless his teammates help him thrive. This isn't baseball, where the action stops for a few seconds so everyone can total up the neat little percentages. It's hockey, so quit complaining, take your stitches, and get the hell back out on the ice.

Fifteen years ago, after the original *Compendium* came out, we got a package from a reader in Regina, Saskatchewan, named Edward Yuen. Inside was a stack of papers, upon which were laid out dozens of tiny handwritten charts. Those charts, Yuen explained in a long, well-written letter that concisely explained some very involved concepts, were the fruits of many months of labour. They were nothing less than the complete shots-and-saves records for every goalie, in every NHL regular-season game, from 1954–55 through 1966–67, as well as those for three seasons in the '70s. Yuen had reconstructed this information by going through newspaper accounts day by day, and then checking them against the accounts in other newspapers. All of this he did on library microfilm and microfiche machines.

This heroic amateur historian had read a long and pointless story we told in the first *Compendium* (although mind you, almost all the stories in there were long and pointless) about spending several days in the library, trying to reconstruct the goaltending stats for the '81–82 season, the year that preceded the NHL's official recording of shot and save totals. We published those figures – with the caveat that they should not be regarded as official, of course – and this seems to have struck a chord with Yuen when he read the book. However, once we got a look at just how thorough and diligent Yuen was, far more thorough and diligent than we had been, we came to the conclusion that our '81–82 stats couldn't be trusted. That's why *our* '81–82 stats don't appear in this version of the *Compendium*, not that thousands of people are going to miss them anyway. (We must also mention that we no longer carry our perseverance ratings out to two decimal places; we learned the concept of significant digits after we wrote that first book. We also use save percentage rather than the unfamiliar "efficiency" we formerly used, so where in the past we said a goalie had a 90.26 efficiency, we now conform to common parlance and say he had a .903 save percentage.)

The completeness of Yuen's research method deserves description, both as a tribute to him and to bolster your confidence in the accuracy of the figures he compiled. Holed up in the Regina Public Library, he checked shot and save totals as published in these four newspapers, which he listed in order of dependability: *The Winnipeg Free Press*, *Le Devoir* of Montreal, *The New York Times*, and *The Globe and Mail* of Toronto. In addition to their own accounts for games, these papers printed Canadian Press and Associated Press game summaries featuring shot totals; furthermore, the *Free Press* and *Le Devoir* printed weekly shot-and-save stats compiled by the CP for a few years in the '50s. Yuen then went through each season four

times, paper by paper, then buttressed the information he gathered through NHL Guides and *The Hockey News*. He found that some discrepancies remained among the various sources, perhaps as much as 5% in some cases. But we are confident that it would be highly difficult to check the published figures more closely than he did. The only conceivable improvement would be to have the league make available its official game reports, assuming those reports contain shot-and-save totals, which they very well may not.

Yuen's studies left us with these red-letter dates in newspaper-agate history, which will be of great interest to anyone else who wants to undertake this deep level of research. OCTOBER 1952: *Winnipeg Free Press* starts printing shot totals for every NHL game, though on an inconsistent basis for the first several years. DECEMBER 20, 1952: *New York Times* starts printing shot totals for every NHL game. 1956–57 SEASON: Canadian Press issues weekly shot-and-save totals, though papers did not have room to print them every week. CP continued issuing totals until mid-season, '58–59. In the early '60s, CP issues a monthly total for October only. 1963–64 SEASON: NHL begins officially recording empty-net goals. 1967–68 SEASON: Vince DeMarco, a fan in New York City, starts compiling shot-and-save totals, which he terms "goaltender fielding percentages." 1974–75 SEASON: DeMarco sends monthly totals in newsletters to paying subscribers. 1982–83 SEASON: NHL finally records shots and saves, makes save percentage an official statistic. 1990–91 SEASON: NHL stops crediting *shots* into an empty net against the goalie who was pulled. Finally, all shot-and-save statistics released by the league are completely accurate.

This would be a good place to note that both Yuen and we have taken care to exclude empty-net goals from the goalie records, something the league did not start doing until the early '80s. Whenever possible, therefore, our save percentage and perseverance figures for any particular netminder are unsullied by shots taken and goals scored when that netminder was sitting on the bench.

Yuen, like Charles Coleman before him, is a true blessing for hockey fans everywhere. But unlike Coleman, who had the help and sponsorship of the NHL in assembling and writing *The Trail of the Stanley Cup*, Yuen did it all by himself. He entrusted his findings to us, and here they are now, a treasure trove unearthed by one man, Edward Yuen.

We'll go year by year, and in the chart that covers each year's goaltenders, we define a "regular goalie" as one who plays at least one-third of the season. An asterisk (*) denotes a rookie, a dagger (†) denotes a league-best figure among regulars in a category, and a double-dagger (‡) a league-worst figure.

1954–55

Yuen's records begin with 1954–55, the seventh consecutive year of an incredible run in which Detroit finished first in the six-team NHL. Perhaps this is one reason Terry Sawchuk is remembered by many as the best goalie who ever played. Doubtlessly, Sawchuk was a big reason why the Wings did so well for so long. He joined the team for a few games in '49–50, the second year of the Wings' seven-year skein, and took over as the lone netminder the following season. Since we came to hockey in '67–68, we only saw Sawchuk as the old guy minding the crease for the Los Angeles Kings, and later as the unlucky victim of that fatal front-yard fight or mock fight or whatever it was with Ron Stewart, but most people who saw him during the Red Wings' dynasty years in the early '50s say he was the greatest. We'll just have to take their word for it, until some other research hero like Yuen comes along and compiles the records from those years.

One other thing older folks say is that Gump Worsley and Harry Lumley were very good goalies, though not quite the equal of Sawchuk. Well, going by what we see on the chart below, we'd have to differ. The statistics don't lie. They may fib a bit here and there, but outright lying? Doesn't happen. Seems that in '54–55 the Gumper and Apple Cheeks, as well as Jacques Plante, were every bit as good as Sawchuk, and in fact a tad better. Hmm. This particular season saw the Vezina Trophy, then awarded to the goalie with the lowest goals-against average, bestowed upon Sawchuk, with Lumley finishing second. Those of you old enough to remember know that back in the days when the Vezina was determined solely by GAA, the winning goalkeeper always, *always* looked abashed and, blushing a little, said that the Vezina is a team award, not an individual award, and of course he was absolutely right. These days, the Vezina is decided by a vote among the NHL's general managers, so it is an individual award. If it were to be awarded retroactively, we'd split our vote between Worsley and Lumley.

The plump and lovable Gumper earned his right to a share of our vote while facing a storm of frozen black rubber in the Ranger nets. Look at that shots-per-game figure: 35.6! Truly, the Rangers – to use the favourite term of New York hockey fans – sucked. Yet despite the barrage, Worsley turned aside more than 91% of the shots allowed by his fifth-place Blueshirt compadres.

Here's the thing: again, since we came to hockey in '67–68, we only know Worsley as the jolly old, roly-poly, bare-faced guy who, in the early '70s, shared the North Stars netminding chores with the spidery Cesare Maniago. In fact, our memories of Worsley are inextricably bound up with the swelling, ebbing, hectoring voice of Dan Kelly, calling the play on the CBS Sunday afternoon telecasts. *"Here's Saaah Marseille for the Blues! He caaaaantres it! Berenson shoots! Ooooooohhhhh, Worsley turns it aside!"* And so on, with vowels drawn out for several yards at a time during moments of tension, and the little round man in green standing in the Minnesota crease with crewcut and long sideburns improbably coexisting on his little round head, and we swear to god it always looked like he was chuckling at something. This is not the Lorne Worsley older Ranger fans see when they look back through the cigar-smoke haze that enveloped the upper reaches of the old Madison Square Garden. They remember a heroic figure, acrobatically turning back wave after wave of visiting attackers, and the acrobatic part made it all the more amazing, because Worsley was always on the zaftig side. Once, when asked what team gave him the most trouble, the Gumper replied, "The Rangers."

Harry Lumley, on the other hand, we never saw. He first came to the NHL for a couple of games with Detroit as a 17-year-old in '43–44, the manpower shortage of the war making him the youngest goalie ever to play in the big leagues, before or since. He played his last NHL season in '59–60, stuck around for another year in the minors, then retired. Lumley stood in the barrel for five of the NHL's six teams during his career, and it is his misfortune that the only one he didn't play for was Montreal. Hence, he has a place in the Hall of Fame, but few misty-eyed encomiums to his greatness, no bilingual laurels as a lion in winter, etc., etc. Here, though, we see him leading the league in save percentage with a whopping .929 figure behind Toronto's efficient defence, which in this season allowed just one more goal than Sawchuk's Red Wings. Hockey – it's a game of inches. Or centimetres, depending on where you're from.

We'll close our discussion by noting that the one honour that was voted upon in those days was, of course, not the Vezina, but selection to the post-season All-Star team, a task handled by the Professional Hockey Writers' Association. In '54–55 the first team All-Star spot was voted to Lumley. Okay, very good. The second team selection was . . . Terry Sawchuk. Hey, where's Worsley?

Other goalers of note on our list: Jacques Plante between the pipes in his first season as a starter and making quite a splash. And is that Johnny Bower lurking in the lower reaches of minutes played? He'd been the Rangers starter the year before, but now the job goes to Worsley. Bower and the Gumper – what a combo. And that young fella Glenn Hall looked pretty good in his two games. Wonder if he'll get a starting job someday?

	GOALER, TEAM	MINS	SAVES-SHOTS	SH/GP	SVPCT	PERSEV
1t	Worsley, NY	3900	2117-2312	35.6‡	.916	975
1t	H Lumley, Tor	4140	1745-1878	27.2	.929†	975
3	J Plante, Mtr	3120	1367-1476	28.4	.926	973
4	Sawchuk, Det	4080	1659-1791	26.3	.926	970
5	J Henry, Bos	1548	706-785	30.4	.899	950
6	Rollins, Chi	2640	1250-1399	31.8	.893‡	946
7	*J Henderson, Bos	2652	1011-1120	25.3†	.903	945

1954–55 (minimum 1400 minutes played)

Goaltending

GOALER, TEAM	MINS	SAVES-SHOTS	SH/GP	SVPCT	PERSEV
*H Bassen, Chi	1260	666-729	34.7	.914	971
*C Hodge, Mtr	820	343-374	27.4	.917	963

(1–465 minutes played)

GOALER, TEAM	MINS	SAVES-SHOTS	SH/GP	SVPCT	PERSEV
*Gl Hall, Det	120	59-61	30.5	.967	1018
*G Mayer, Tor	60	18-19	19.0	.947	979
Bower, NY	300	143-156	31.2	.917	969
*Frederick, Chi	300	148-170	34.0	.871	927
*Cl Evans, Mtr	200	84-96	28.8	.875	923
*Binette, Mtr	60	23-27	27.0	.852	897
All goalers	25200	11339-12393	29.5	.915	964

1955–56

All hail the Gumper! This year he gets bombarded even more mercilessly behind the Maginot Line that is the Rangers blue-line corps, to the tune of 36.3 shots faced per game, yet he holds off the Jerries heroically. Never have so many owed so much to so few, or in this case, to one. This year the Blueshirts finished third, four games above .500, and looking at the goalkeeping figures we'd have to say that Worsley is the man who deserves all the credit. The Rangers got bounced by the Habs in a five-game semi-final, so same old story. Poor Gump, it'll be nine more seasons before he's evacuated from the Dunkerque of New York hockey.

Worsley's perseverance rating of 982 is 10 points better than that of the runner-up, the suave if jumpy Jacques Plante, though in that era of flimsy equipment and bare faces every goalie was justifiably nervous, puking during face-offs, renditions of "God Save the Queen," and post-game interviews with Foster Hewitt. Worsley's margin of victory is large, but we shall see larger margins between the leader and the runner-up as the years pass.

Terry Sawchuk, now a Bruin, does well with a fifth-place side that missed out on the playoffs by a mere two points, but not that well; he rates as fifth-best among the league's six starters. After the Red Wings won the Stanley Cup the previous season, they dealt Sawchuk to Boston, a move that really shook his confidence. Being shipped out of Detroit in those days was regarded as a disaster, especially if it was to a cellar-dweller like Boston. But for Sawchuk it was even more disturbing, given the relatively fragile nature of his psyche, forged in part by the death of two of his brothers during childhood and characterized by bouts of brooding, intermittent rage, and alcohol addiction. "A moody man of exuberant peaks and mute hollows," Trent Frayne called him. The departure of Sawchuk didn't help the Red Wings, either; for the first time in eight years, they did not finish first, and their .543 winning percentage was their worst performance in 10 years. With Sawchuk gone, they also failed

to win the Cup, ending a stretch in which they lifted the Ultimate Prize four times in six seasons. Detroit did not win it again until 1997. The Curse of Mr. Shutout.

One more thing about Sawchuk's move to Boston. It dispossessed Long John Henderson of the B's starting job. The previous season, 1954–55, was Henderson's only year as an NHL starter. This season, 1955–56, was the only other one in which he appeared in a big-league game – and we mean that literally, because he appeared in only one game. Then it was back to the seniors and the minors whence he came, stopping pucks for Whitby Dunlops, Hull-Ottawa Canadiens, Cleveland Barons, Kingston Frontenacs, Oklahoma City Blazers, San Francisco Seals, Victoria Cougars, California Seals (of the WHL, not the NHL), and Hershey Bears – this on top of previous pre-Bruins sojourns with Hershey, Syracuse Warriors, Springfield Indians, and Pittsburgh Hornets. We encountered him at the end of the '60s, in the twilight of his career, when we were newbie hockey fans rooting for the Buffalo Bisons of the AHL, the team with the famous Pepsi bottle cap on their sweaters, only the script on the bottle cap read "Buffalo," not "Pepsi." Henderson was Hershey's goalie, the crest on their sweaters featured a Hershey bar being carried by a cute, beaming bear, and he was universally known not as John, but as Long John. That name made him seem very, very tall. In fact, he was 6'1" and weighed 175 pounds, which, looking back, would qualify as slim but not especially "long." But people were shorter in those days, and John Henderson will always be Long John Henderson.

That would've been a good place to end the section; you know, wistful, dramatic finish and all. But we can't leave this season without noting whom the writers picked as the post-season All-Stars. Ready? The first team All-Star: Jacques Plante. The second team All-Star: Glenn Hall. Hey, where's Worsley?

1955–56
(minimum 1400 minutes played)

	GOALER, TEAM	MINS	SAVES-SHOTS	SH/GP	SVPCT	PERSEV
1	Worsley, NY	4200	2343-2542	36.3‡	.922	982
2	J Plante, Mtr	3840	1551-1670	26.1†	.929†	972
3	Rollins, Chi	3480	1802-1974	34.0	.913	970
4	Gl Hall, Det	4200	1729-1876	26.8	.922	966
5	Sawchuk, Bos	4080	1847-2024	29.8	.913	962
6	H Lumley, Tor	3527	1495-1654	28.1	.904‡	951

(466–1399 minutes played)

GOALER, TEAM	MINS	SAVES-SHOTS	SH/GP	SVPCT	PERSEV
H Bassen, Chi	720	304-345	28.7	.881	929

(1–465 minutes played)

GOALER, TEAM	MINS	SAVES-SHOTS	SH/GP	SVPCT	PERSEV
*Rs Wilson, Tor	13	9-9	41.5	1.000	1069
*C Pronovost, Bos	60	31-31	31.0	1.000	1052
*Chadwick, Tor	300	126-129	25.8	.977	1020

GOALER, TEAM	MINS	SAVES-SHOTS	SH/GP	SVPCT	PERSEV
*R Perreault, Mtr	60	162-174	29.0	.931	979
J Henderson, Bos	60	28-32	32.0	.875	928
*G Mayer, Tor	360	122-140	23.3	.871	910
All goalers	25200	11549-12600	30.0	.917	967

1956–57

Funny how misleading memory can be, or more accurately, how misleading partial information can be. If you go by subjective opinion, your own or someone else's, your opinion is formed by seeing the player in question only a few times. The phenomenon can work in a number of ways. Remember when the Bruins' Steve Kasper was hailed as the best defensive forward in hockey? He'd held Gretzky scoreless a couple of times while the young Great One was tearing up the league and the record books, and so the 1982 Selke Award went to Kasper. No one, however, had bothered to look at Kasper's plus/minus mark. We did, and boy, were we surprised to find that his plus/minus mark *sucked*. Way, way down in minus. But everyone judged Kasper on the strength of three or four games, and formed – forgive us, Steve – an inaccurate opinion of him.

Nowadays, with 30 teams in the NHL – wait, what time is it? 4:30? Make that *34* teams in the NHL – there's no way on earth anyone can see all or even a majority of the players in the league. Some players exist only as rumours, others as complete ciphers, still others as those theoretical subatomic particles without any mass at all. Under these conditions, how can anyone judge how really good or bad a player is? You can't – you have to go by other people's opinions, which are probably based on having seen the guy maybe five times anyway. It's the same thing when looking back at those who played a generation or two or three before. Who was really great? Is it possible that maybe one or two of those touted as all-timers weren't altogether deserving of the accolade? Is it possible that some players lost in the mists of history were unjustly overlooked? Absolutely, but without statistics to help us judge their performances more objectively, we'll never know.

We find this very principle at work right here, right now, as we look at Glenn Hall's league-best performance of 1956–57, which just so happens to be the first full hockey season of both our lives. We remember Hall as the old guy manning the St. Louis Blues' nets, and he was great. We'd heard right from the start of our fandom that he was a goaltending legend in Detroit and mainly Chicago, but how great was he? We couldn't tell, because we'd never seen him in a Wings or Hawks uniform. We can now, thanks to Yuen's diligent work.

Here it is in black and white, Hall kicking out almost 93% of the shots he faced, outstripping the other giants of his era, Sawchuk, Worsley, Simmons (*Simmons?*), Plante, leading the Red Wings to a first-place finish they would not repeat for another nine years. The sports writers got it right this year, anointing Hall the first team All-Star, even if they made a somewhat baffling choice by putting Plante on the second team. Perhaps the most amazing thing about Hall's performance this season was that he accomplished it while giving the silent treatment to Jack Adams, the Red Wings GM who'd dealt away Terry Sawchuk because he thought Hall would be just as good or better; the Detroit supremo had criticized Hall after the Wings bombed out of the '56 Final. Adams was not an easy man to like, especially if you were one of his players, trying to get a decent contract out of the spiteful old chiseller.

Sawchuk, meanwhile, weighs in with an excellent season in Boston, helping to backstop the Broons to a third-place finish 10 games over the .500 mark. Or we should say *half* an excellent season, for this is the year Sawchuk came down with a bad case of mononucleosis. Boston were in first place at the halfway mark, but Sawchuk, exhausted and having already spent two weeks in hospital, announced that he was quitting. He went home to Detroit, where his doctor told reporters, "Mr. Sawchuk is on the verge of a complete nervous breakdown." This being the Eisenhower-Diefenbaker era, none of this went down well with the Boston writers. They questioned Sawchuk's commitment, noted that he had never wanted to be traded out of Detroit, and insinuated that he was dogging it. "Those Boston reporters," Sawchuk later said, "called me everything in the book, including a quitter. It was so bad I threatened to sue four newspapers for libel." Sawchuk sat out the rest of the season, and Boston called Don Simmons up from Eddie Shore's Springfield Indians for the second half, in which he performed ably.

1956–57
(minimum 1400 minutes played)

	GOALER, TEAM	MINS	SAVES-SHOTS	SH/GP	SVPCT	PERSEV
1	Gl Hall, Det	4200	1971-2127	30.4	.927†	977
2	Sawchuk, Bos	2040	939-1020	30.0	.921	971
3	Worsley, NY	4080	2124-2341	34.4‡	.907	965
4	*D Simmons, Bos	1560	678-741	28.5	.915	962
5	J Plante, Mtr	3660	1395-1517	24.9†	.920	961
6	Rollins, Chi	4200	2031-2253	32.2	.901‡	955
7	*Chadwick, Tor	4200	1776-1962	28.0	.905	952

(466–1399 minutes played)

GOALER, TEAM	MINS	SAVES-SHOTS	SH/GP	SVPCT	PERSEV
*Defelice, Bos	600	240-270	27.0	.889	934
McNeil, Mtr	540	219-250	27.8	.876	922

(1–465 minutes played)

GOALER, TEAM	MINS	SAVES-SHOTS	SH/GP	SVPCT	PERSEV
Bower, NY	120	45-41	25.5	.882	925
All goalers	25200	11418-12532	29.8	.911	961

1957–58

The late '50s is the era of the man's man, when a two-fisted man takes no guff from anyone and if he does, he gives him a good punch in the nose, when a bread-winning man goes to work, day after day, without complaining, and provides those who depend on him with three squares a day and a roof over their heads. A man's man comes home after a hard day's work, lies back in his easy chair, turns on the TV, and watches *Gunsmoke* or *Wanted: Dead or Alive*, where he can see men from an earlier era, when men were men, shoot and kill all those who needed killin'. Leave the unnecessary talk to the wives playing mah-jongg on Tuesday nights, leave the tears and the complaining to the little kids. A man's man works hard and likes it.

Thus we come to the era of the 4,200-minute goaler, which is to say the netminder who plays every minute of every game of every season. Does he suffer nervous breakdowns from the relentless, dangerous work? Sure! Does he barf between periods from the angst and the fear, both of grievous personal injury and of the horrible responsibility of carrying a team's fortunes on his back? Of course! Does he live with the constant prospect of losing one of the six, count 'em, six, goaling jobs the NHL has to offer? You bet! Does he complain about it? Not on your life! Forty-two hundred minutes, and anyone who plays less, unless he has been maimed, is a sissy.

So here we see that three of the eight goalkeepers who played enough minutes to qualify as a regular played the full 4,200 minutes. But wait, those three guys finished as the last three goalies on the list! Hall, Sawchuk, and Toronto's obscure Ed Chadwick all patrolled the crease for the full monty, and while none of them were bad, all the part-timers finished ahead of them. We're tempted to draw the conclusion that playing every minute of every game hurts a goalie's performance, but in previous and subsequent years we see full-timers leading the league, so we'll draw none. But that man's-man trope had to be at work among the hockey writers, at that time hardly a group of convention-busting Beat poets, when they voted the first team All-Star spot to Glenn Hall, who was really only the sixth-best goaler in the league that year. The second-team slot went to Jacques Plante, which seems like the right choice. But hey, where's Worsley?

Nowhere on the All-Star teams, but the roly-poly goalie returns to his accustomed number-one spot on the perseverance scale. Thing is, he got injured and played a bit less than half the season. What is he, brittle or something? Come on, be a man, Gumper. Still, you've got to admit that anyone subjected to the nightly barrage the Rangers permit has got to get hurt at one time or another. Worsley was superb while he was in there – that 14-point victory in the perseverance column is enormous. The writers weren't impressed, though, as they never were with Worsley. That's why hockey remembers him today as a "colourful" player

rather than one of the very greatest ever. Sure, no one begrudges him his place in the Hall of Fame, but we think his stature needs to be upgraded quite a bit.

Taking over for Worsley this season is another man we remember fondly from the late '60s AHL, Marcel "the Straw Man" Paille. Sawchuk emerges from illness, seclusion, and the Bruins to return to Detroit, where Adams is happy to have him back, especially as it allows him to sell Hall and his cold shoulder to Chicago. But the Wings plummet to .500, and Hall gets the Black Hawks out of last place and into fifth, starting the steady rise that will see them emerge as a powerful team in the '60s.

A committee of Boston goalies, Simmons, Lumley, and some anonymous fill-ins, get the Hubmen into the playoffs. Here in the '50s, we already get to witness the practice, peculiar to the Bruins, of carting a couple of unknowns into the nets, leaving them there for a season, then dumping them no matter how well or poorly they do and hauling in a new set of unknowns for the next season. Recite with us now: Long John Henderson, Claude Pronovost, Norman Defelice, Claude Evans, Al Millar . . . John Adams, Marco Baron, John Blue, Blaine Lacher, Scott Bailey, Rob Tallas, and so on, right through into the new millennium.

1957–58 (minimum 1400 minutes played)						
	GOALER, TEAM	MINS	SAVES-SHOTS	SH/GP	SVPCT	PERSEV
1	Worsley, NY	2220	1117-1203	32.5	.929†	983
2t	J Plante, Mtr	3386	1411-1530	27.1†	.922	967
2t	H Lumley, Bos	1500	740-811	32.4	.912	967
4t	D Simmons, Bos	2228	1005-1097	29.5	.916	965
4t	Paille, NY	1980	1016-1118	33.9‡	.909	965
6	Gl Hall, Chi	4200	1990-2190	31.3	.909	961
7	Sawchuk, Det	4200	1992-2197	31.4	.907	959
8	Chadwick, Tor	4200	1913-2136	33.6	.896‡	952

(466-1399 minutes played)						
	GOALER, TEAM	MINS	SAVES-SHOTS	SH/GP	SVPCT	PERSEV
	*C Hodge, Mtr	720	322-353	29.4	.912	961

(1-465 minutes played)						
	GOALER, TEAM	MINS	SAVES-SHOTS	SH/GP	SVPCT	PERSEV
	*Rs Wilson, Bos	52	23-24	27.7	.958	1004
	*L Broderick, Mtr	60	20-22	22.0	.909	946
	*Cl Evans, Bos	60	31-35	35.0	.886	944
	*Millar, Bos	360	167-192	32.0	.870	923
	*Aiken, Mtr	34	12-18	31.8	.667	720
	All goalers	25200	11759-12926	30.8	.910	961

1958–59

Jacques Plante stakes his claim to greatness this season by winning his first perseverance crown, and by a fairly convincing margin too. In the '50s, Plante struck people as an oddball, what with his knitting and his "wandering" out of the crease, and as time went on people finally started recognizing these so-called oddball qualities not simply as the quirks of a highly talented player, but as the mark of an innovative mind, a man who added so much to how the position is played. Throughout his seemingly endless career, he turned in one astonishing performance after another, and if you don't think the two second-place finishes he already logged as a mere babe in pads qualify as astonishing, certainly his '58–59 record does. A huge .925 save percentage behind Montreal's stingy defence: unbeatable. Indeed, this is the fourth year of the Canadiens' five-year Stanley Cup run, a season in which the Habs allowed just 158 goals while the next closest defensive team, Toronto, allowed 201. We haven't said enough here, really, about how great the Canadiens were at this point, probably because we've been focusing on regular-season performance. But to make up for that, we'll point out that *les glorieux* finished first this season, as they had in two out of the previous three, and as they would for the next three seasons in a row. And who was the man in goal for these years? Jacques Plante. His rise coincides perfectly with the reign of the first Canadiens' dynasty.

We're happy to report that the hockey writers recognized Plante's remarkable season by naming him the first team All-Star goalie, but really, they'd have to have been pretty stupid to miss that one. In second, though, they chose Sawchuk, who looks to us to have been merely the sixth-best among seven regulars this season. The second-place finisher on the perseverance scale in '58–59 was . . . Johnny Bower! He of "Honky, the Christmas Goose," vaguely filled-out birth certificates, Wheat Chex commercials ("Mr. Bower is puck-shy, your honour!"), and countless jokes about arthritis, memory loss, dentures, and other signifiers of old age. Actually, those arthritis jokes were based on a very real case of arthritis Bower did have in his hands. It was so bad he was discharged from the army, during World War II, no less, because of it. "I used to think I'd never be able to hold a goal stick again," he once said. "When I was with the Leafs, I'd finish a game, and my stick hand would be locked right up like a claw. Some nights it was so stiff and sore, it'd take me an hour just to get it open and working."

Bower, though, like Worsley, was seen at the time as some kind of novelty act and has been seen that way ever since. A very good goaler, to be sure, a Hall of Famer, certainly, but great? Naah. Well, we don't know, maybe Bower was better than everyone thought. This particular year the China Wall was already 35 years old, if documents are to be believed, having spent 12 seasons with Cleveland Barons and Providence Reds of the American League and one with Vancouver Canucks of the Western League. The Leafs have called him in because they're souring on Eddie Chadwick,

an extremely wise move, which tells you this was a long time ago, because when was the last time you heard the phrase "extremely wise move" used in conjunction with the Maple Leafs?

In third place is the by now inevitable Worsley, and we see Glenn Hall, last of the full-time goalies, mired in last among the starters. Our man of the year, however, appears at the very bottom of the entire list, having stopped seven of nine shots during his 19 minutes of fame as a Ranger: Julian Klymkiw. He was the Red Wings' practice goalie and an assistant trainer, but back in the days before teams carried back-up goalies and the home team had to supply a substitute if the visiting number one went down, Klymkiw was pressed into service to finish an early-season contest after Worsley got hurt. He allowed his employers two goals in a game that finished 3-0, but fear not, the Rangers were already losing 1-0 when he came in. Julian Klymkiw – his entire NHL career lasted 19 minutes, but ever since we first saw it while flipping through a hockey encyclopaedia years ago, we've never forgotten his name.

1958–59
(minimum 1400 minutes played)

	GOALER, TEAM	MINS	SAVES-SHOTS	SH/GP	SVPCT	PERSEV
1	J Plante, Mtr	4000	1777-1921	28.8†	.925†	973
2	Bower, Tor	2340	1119-1226	31.4	.913	965
3	Worsley, NY	4001	1942-2141	32.1‡	.907	961
4	Chadwick, Tor	1860	858-950	30.6	.903	954
5	D Simmons, Bos	3480	1642-1825	31.5	.900	952
6	Sawchuk, Det	4020	1807-2009	30.0	.899	949
7	Gl Hall, Chi	4200	1821-2029	29.0	.897‡	946

(466–1399 minutes played)

GOALER, TEAM	MINS	SAVES-SHOTS	SH/GP	SVPCT	PERSEV
H Lumley, Bos	660	289-316	28.7	.915	962

(1–465 minutes played)

GOALER, TEAM	MINS	SAVES-SHOTS	SH/GP	SVPCT	PERSEV
*D Keenan, Bos	60	37-41	41.0	.902	971
*B Gamble, NY	120	60-66	33.0	.909	964
*R Perreault, Det	180	77-86	28.7	.895	943
C Hodge, Mtr	120	51-57	28.5	.895	942
Paille, NY	60	28-32	32.0	.875	928
*C Cyr, Mtr	20	6-7	21.0	.857	892
*C Pronovost, Mtr	60	26-33	33.0	.788	843
*Klymkiw, NY	19	7-9	28.4	.778	825
All goalers	25200	11547-12748	30.4	.906	956

1959–60
We are honoured to witness Johnny Bower's apotheosis, or at least his statistical apotheosis, because just about the only

thing you hear about him nowadays is how old he and all the other Leafs on the ice were when they won their last Stanley Cup in '67. Here, as a spry 36-year-old, he backstops Toronto to second place behind only implacable Montreal, the best regular-season finish a Hogtown sextet had managed in 10 years.

The rest of the list looks pretty familiar, with the exception of a poor season for Worsley. The writers picked Hall and Plante, respectively, as the first- and second-team All-Stars, which would have been smart choices if Johnny Bower didn't exist. This is the season, by the way, in which Plante got hit in the face by one of Andy Bathgate's wicked backhanders from 25 feet away, retreated to his dressing room covered in blood, took several stitches, and returned with his mask. He'd been wearing it in practice and drawing disdainful, snarky remarks from coach Toe Blake, but Plante had had enough – including 200 stitches in his face, a nose broken four times, two cheekbones fractured by shots in practice, and a fractured skull. As for the Bathgate shot, he said, "It nearly ripped my nose off." He put on the fibreglass mask, which he had made himself, the Canadiens won, and so was born another innovation wrought by Plante.

Now look down the list, past Pat Riggin's father Dennis, at the Ranger who played 240 minutes, Jack McCartan. You Canadians reading this book probably don't know who he is, eh? McCartan was the hero goalie of the U.S. Olympic team, which won the gold medal at Squaw Valley, California, this year. McCartan's heroics included a 39-save performance against Canada in a 2-1 quarter-final victory, limiting the Soviets to three goals in a 4-3 semi-final, and coasting past Czechoslovakia in the gold-medal game by 9-4. It was one of only two gold medals for the Amerks in Olympic play – both at home, we must add – and in each case the hero goalie had a quick shot at the NHL that didn't work out. In 1980 it was Jim Craig, and here it was McCartan. Craig played a total of 30 games with Atlanta, Boston, and Minnesota over three seasons. McCartan had just 12 games, all, unfortunately, with New York, over two seasons. Here in '59–60 he shows excellent form with his gigantic 999 perseverance mark during a four-game amateur tryout, and although he'd fall off the next season, that 999 is the harbinger of a long, distinguished career in the minors that would eventually carry McCartan all the way to the WHA.

Down a bit farther, at the very bottom of the list, is Joe Schaefer, who passed away as we were writing this book. If you look at Schaefer's record in *Total Hockey* (you can't miss it; it comes right after "Terry Sawchuk"), you'll see that he played one game for New Haven of the EHL in '56, two for Philadelphia in the EHL in '57, one for AHL Buffalo and one for EHL Philly in '58, one for EHL Johnstown in '59, one for New York in '60, and one for New York in '61. Schaefer was a statistician, practice goaler, penalty timekeeper, goal judge, and so on at Madison Square Garden, and he was the one who was called upon, once a year, it seems, to fill in when the starter went down in the building. We are indebted to Richard Goldstein of *The New York Times* sports desk for writing a very nice obit for Schaefer, from which we will now crib.

On February 17, 1960, Bobby Hull's skate blade ran over Gump Worsley's stick-hand glove and tore some tendons, so as Worsley was being taken to hospital, the game was delayed 23 minutes while the 5'8", 200-pound Schaefer suited up and was draped with what must have been a tent-like sweater, although with the Gumper on the team, maybe they had no trouble finding something that fitted. Schaefer entered the game one minute into the second period and with New York ahead, 1-0, but the Black Hawks came pouring in and wound up winning, 5-1. "Schaefer had little to offer except courage," wrote Joe Nichols in his game report in *The Times*.

1959–60
(minimum 1400 minutes played)

	GOALER, TEAM	MINS	SAVES-SHOTS	SH/GP	SVPCT	PERSEV
1	Bower, Tor	3960	2007-2185	33.1	.919†	974
2	Gl Hall, Chi	4200	2004-2184	31.2	.918	970
3	J Plante, Mtr	4140	1875-2050	29.7	.915	964
4	Sawchuk, Det	3480	1539-1695	29.2†	.908	957
5	D Simmons, Bos	1680	824-915	32.7	.901	955
6	H Lumley, Bos	2520	1245-1391	33.1‡	.895	950
7	Worsley, NY	2301	1125-1260	32.9	.893‡	948

(466–1399 minutes played)

GOALER, TEAM	MINS	SAVES-SHOTS	SH/GP	SVPCT	PERSEV
Rollins, NY	600	355-386	38.6	.920	984
*D Riggin, Det	540	221-252	28.0	.877	924
Paille, NY	1020	448-515	30.3	.870	920

(1–465 minutes played)

GOALER, TEAM	MINS	SAVES-SHOTS	SH/GP	SVPCT	PERSEV
*McCartan, NY	240	121-128	32.0	.945	999
*Boisvert, Det	180	73-81	27.0	.901	946
Chadwick, Tor	240	120-135	33.8	.889	945
C Hodge, Mtr	60	22-25	25.0	.880	922
*Schaefer, NY	39	17-22	33.8	.773	829
All goalers	25200	11996-13224	31.5	.907	960

1960–61
Johnny Bower wins the perseverance title for the second year in a row, nosing out Gump Worsley, and now we're getting the impression that the two clown princes of Original Six goalkeeping, the two "beloved" netminders, the two "characters," may just have been the two best goalies of the era, period. Look at Bower's superb save percentage,

approached only by Glenn Hall among the season's regulars. Look at Worsley's shots-faced figure, 37.3, and then tell us how on earth he was able to kick out more than 91% of that bombardment. Hall finishes a close third this season, but we're still blown away by what Bower and Worsley did here. Let's see who the writers picked for the All-Star team. First team All-Star: Johnny Bower. Bravo! Second team All-Star: Glenn Hall. Pretty good, but . . . hey, where's Worsley?

Let's get back to the China Wall for a moment. He got his first taste of the NHL, you'll remember, with the Rangers in '53–54 and '54–55. He came from the AHL's Cleveland Barons, and a lot of people have the mistaken impression that he was called up by New York from their farm club. But that's not how it worked. The Barons were an independent team, and a pretty strong one at that – so strong, in fact, that they issued a challenge for the Stanley Cup in 1952, but were refused. (In 1946, P. D. Ross, a Cup trustee whose job it was to judge challenges for what was the symbol of supremacy for all hockey, turned over full authority for Cup challenges to the NHL. The Stanley Cup, in other words, was no longer controlled by an independent authority that could, at least in theory, allow the champion of a sufficiently tough league to challenge the NHL champion. Ross, of course, is in the Hall of Fame. He'd be the first person we'd kick out of there.) The only way the Rangers could acquire Bower was by trade, so they gave up Emile "Cat" Francis and minor-leaguer Neil Strain to get him. The Barons got him back by trade, and the Leafs got him through waivers from Cleveland, just as if the Barons were a "real" team.

In those days, the AHL really was an excellent league. You've got to remember that the NHL, with its extremely limited universe of six teams, was a tiny, tiny circuit. Moreover, all power in the NHL was concentrated in three teams – Montreal, Detroit, and Toronto – with the other three basically there to make up the numbers. There's no question that while even the best of today's AHL teams are pretty terrible, the best AHL teams of the '50s and early '60s would have fit in quite well in the National League, maybe even snare a playoff spot. So if you look at the list of Bower's AHL achievements, you can see why the Rangers and later the Leafs went out of their way to get him: he was an AHL first-team All-Star five times and a second-teamer once (okay, we know All-Star selections are flawed, but cut us some slack here), and he even won the Les Cunningham Plaque three times as the AHL's most valuable player. Puck-shy, your honour? We think not.

Elsewhere we see Plante and Sawchuk having mediocre seasons, and there's Hank Bassen (Bob's father, for you Islander fans), and there's Joe Schaefer again, making his final pro hockey appearance. This time it's March 8, 1961, and Worsley has just been stretchered off after tearing his thigh muscle trying to stop a Bobby Hull shot. The game is only 13 minutes old, tied 1-1. On comes Schaefer again, and

this time he does better, turning aside, as you can see, 27 shots in a game the Rangers lose, but only by 4-3. The crowd of 8,515 gave him several ovations. Schaefer, we learn from the *Times* obit, earned $100 for his appearances in goal, a big improvement over the $10 per game he was paid for keeping the stats. He remained a Ranger statistician until 1986, then retired. His last performance was worth a very impressive 964 on the perseverance scale, a mark anyone would be proud to have.

1960–61
(minimum 1400 minutes played)

	GOALER, TEAM	MINS	SAVES-SHOTS	SH/GP	SVPCT	PERSEV
1	Bower, Tor	3480	1727-1872	32.3	.923†	976
2	Worsley, NY	3473	1970-2161	37.3‡	.912	974
3	Gl Hall, Chi	4200	2020-2196	31.4	.920	972
4	C Hodge, Mtr	1800	803-877	29.2	.916	964
5	J Plante, Mtr	2400	1081-1193	29.8	.906	956
6	Sawchuk, Det	2080	999-1111	32.0	.899	953
7	*B Gamble, Bos	3120	1585-1778	34.2	.891‡	948
8	H Bassen, Det	2120	860-958	27.1†	.898	943

(466–1399 minutes played)

GOALER, TEAM	MINS	SAVES-SHOTS	SH/GP	SVPCT	PERSEV
D Simmons, Bos	1080	531-589	32.7	.902	956

(1–465 minutes played)

GOALER, TEAM	MINS	SAVES-SHOTS	SH/GP	SVPCT	PERSEV
*Maniago, Tor	420	219-236	33.7	.928	984
*Gd McNamara, Tor	300	135-147	29.4	.918	967
*Schaefer, NY	47	27-30	38.3	.900	964
Paille, NY	240	137-153	38.2	.895	959
*McCartan, NY	440	203-238	32.5	.853	907
All goalers	25200	12297-13539	32.2	.908	962

1961–62

Another thing about a six-team league: it's the same guys, over and over and over again. We've written elsewhere about the monotony of the so-called golden age of the Original Six, and we think history confirms that it was an ingrown, hermetic, blinkered period that for all its intensity made Canadian hockey stagnant. Let's concentrate on the idea of how great this golden age was for the fan. Great, sure, for fans in Montreal, Toronto, and Detroit, which happen to have been the two Canadian teams and the American one on the border. These are the places where the histories of hockey are written and extolled, and we don't know about you, but it seems to us that nine out of ten histories of hockey are about the Montreal, Toronto, and Detroit teams of the '50s and '60s. The same ones, over and over again. If it's not "Looking Back on the Golden Years of the Leafs," it's "Looking Back on the Defencemen of the

Golden Years of the Leafs" or "Looking Back on the Right-Handed Left Wingers of the Golden Years of the Leafs" or "Looking Back on the Rink Attendants of the Golden Years of the Leafs."

If you were a fan in Boston, Chicago, or New York, on the other hand, the Original Six years must have sucked, and the surprisingly tiny attendance figures of the era in those cities support that contention. Just up above we mentioned the 8,500 on hand when Joe Schaefer went between the pipes, and some will remember that there were only 3,254 in the stands in New York when Chicago's Bill Mosienko scored his three goals in 21 seconds back in 1952. The Black Hawks, slogging through the motions in a sparsely peopled Chicago Stadium, were constantly on the brink of bankruptcy through the '50s. Who can blame the fans in those cities for not filling their buildings? Every year, it was *guaranteed* that your team would not win the Cup, that they would be thrashed by one of the Big Three. Imagine what it'd be like: from 1942 through 1969, a span of 28 seasons, the Canadiens, Red Wings, or Maple Leafs won the Stanley Cup 27 times. The only exception came in '61, when, by some incomprehensible fluke, the Black Hawks won it. So yeah, the Original Six was a fabulous, fabulous time, and we're kind of glad we didn't have to suffer through it.

All right, let's look at our winner for '61–62: Jacques Plante, logging the second perseverance victory of his career, beating out the cuddly tandem of Bower and Worsley, with Hall finishing a strong fourth and everyone else way back in the pack, including Sawchuk, at whom we're starting to look askance. The All-Stars as voted by the writers this season? First team, Plante; second team, Hall. We've said it before and we'll say it again: where's Worsley? To which we add: where's Bower? Well, at least Bower was consoled by winning the Stanley Cup with the Leafs this year.

This was the season Jacques Plante won not only the Vezina for a sixth time, but the Hart Trophy as well. He was only the fourth goalie ever to win the Hart, and only one has won it since, Dominik Hasek in '97 and '98.

Other goalers of interest making their debut here are Gerry Cheevers of Toronto; Dave Dryden of New York, Ken's older brother, of course, and later a fine guardian for Buffalo and WHA Edmonton; and Don Head, love that name, of Boston. This is Head's only NHL season. He came out of senior hockey and the Canadian Olympic team (he was on the other end of the ice when McCartan and the Amerks pulled off the quarter-final upset), and wound up his career with several years as a star in the Western League with Portland Buckaroos and Seattle Totems. We've seen pictures of Head with the Totems, so it'd have to be between '67–68 and '70–71, playing bare-faced. You can find them on the Web, but look out when you search for "Don Head" and "hockey" – you'll get a number of sites that talk about the need to "don head gear."

1961–62
(minimum 1400 minutes played)

	GOALER, TEAM	MINS	SAVES-SHOTS	SH/GP	SVPCT	PERSEV
1	J Plante, Mtr	4200	1978-2144	30.6	.923†	974
2t	Bower, Tor	3540	1675-1826	30.9	.917	969
2t	Worsley, NY	3530	1808-1981	33.7	.913	969
4	Gl Hall, Chi	4200	1941-2126	30.4	.913	964
5	H Bassen, Det	1620	689-764	28.3‡	.902	949
6	B Gamble, Bos	1680	883-1004	35.9†	.879	939
7	Sawchuk, Det	2580	1111-1252	29.1	.887	936
8	*D Head, Bos	2280	1146-1307	34.4	.877‡	934

(466–1399 minutes played)

GOALER, TEAM	MINS	SAVES-SHOTS	SH/GP	SVPCT	PERSEV
D Simmons, Tor	540	265-286	31.8	.927	980
Paille, NY	600	290-318	31.8	.912	965

(1–465 minutes played)

GOALER, TEAM	MINS	SAVES-SHOTS	SH/GP	SVPCT	PERSEV
*Cheevers, Tor	120	66-73	36.5	.904	965
*Olesevich, NY	30	17-19	38.0	.895	958
*D Dryden, NY	40	23-26	39.0	.885	950
Chadwick, Bos	240	127-149	37.2	.852	914
All goalers	25200	12019-13275	31.6	.906	958

1962–63

Here's Worsley on top of the heap again, for the fourth time since the start of Yuen's remarkable record of "golden age" goalkeeping, now confronted by a cataclysmic 38.2 shots per game as he guards the smouldering hulk, the broken ruins, the festering carcass that is the Ranger goal net. We wish we could have seen this performance; it must have been unbelievable. For while Worsley put himself in harm's way more than any other goaler this year, facing by far the most total shots *and* with the frozen disks tracering in at a greater frequency on him than on anyone else, the brave Gumper still managed to record the second-best save percentage in the league. All this, taken together, translates to a whopping 13-point victory in the perseverance department. The runners-up were Hall and Bower, and Sawchuk finished fourth.

Now let's see how hard you studied and how much you've absorbed up till now. Of these four men, Worsley, Hall, Bower, and Sawchuk, which two were elected to the NHL first and second All-Star teams? You guessed it. The first-team All-Star goalie as selected by the writers this season was Glenn Hall. The second team All-Star backstop was Terry Sawchuk.

If you got that question wrong, we're sorry, but you're an idiot. The writers were never going to recognize what Worsley and Bower did, even though they saw each of these guys 12, 13, 14 times a season. Surely they had to notice that

Worsley and Bower were standing on their heads. But no, they went with the safe picks, not that there's anything *wrong* with choosing Hall and Sawchuk this year. This is the season that Hall's consecutive-games streak ended, at 502. Halfway through the first period of the 503rd game, against Boston at Chicago Stadium, he bent over to adjust a strap on the new pair of leg pads he was wearing, and when he tried to straighten up, he couldn't; his back gave out. That was the end of the streak, for which the NHL credited Hall with 30,130 consecutive minutes of play, which is pretty amazing, even if in reality he had sometimes been pulled in the final minute for an extra attacker, which the league in those days didn't account for in minutes-played stats. Nevertheless, 30,130 straight minutes is a long time – nearly 21 consecutive days – and you can see how the writers would've wanted to give Hall something special to mark the achievement.

1962–63
(minimum 1400 minutes played)

	GOALER, TEAM	MINS	SAVES-SHOTS	SH/GP	SVPCT	PERSEV
1	Worsley, NY	3980	2317-2534	38.2‡	.914	978
2t	Gl Hall, Chi	3910	1792-1958	30.0	.915†	965
2t	Bower, Tor	2520	1163-1272	30.3	.914	965
4t	Sawchuk, Det	2775	1226-1343	29.0	.913	961
4t	J Plante, Mtr	3320	1440-1578	28.5	.913	961
6	*E Johnston, Bos	2880	1595-1788	37.2	.892‡	954
7	D Simmons, Tor	1680	636-706	25.2†	.901	943

(466–1399 minutes played)

GOALER, TEAM	MINS	SAVES-SHOTS	SH/GP	SVPCT	PERSEV
*R Perreault, Bos	1320	696-778	35.4	.895	954
H Bassen, Det	980	457-509	31.2	.898	950
*Maniago, Mtr	820	367-409	29.9	.897	947

(1–465 minutes played)

GOALER, TEAM	MINS	SAVES-SHOTS	SH/GP	SVPCT	PERSEV
*DeJordy, Chi	290	154-166	34.3	.928	985
*Wakely, Mtr	60	31-34	34.0	.912	968
Paille, NY	180	97-107	35.7	.907	966
*M Pelletier, NY	40	24-27	40.5	.889	956
*D Riggin, Det	445	194-216	29.1	.898	947
All goalers	25200	12189-13425	32.0	.908	961

1963–64

Bower stands atop the plinth of perseverance; now he's stopping better than 93% of the shots sent his way, so it's little wonder that he has returned to the apex. Nevertheless, Hall's .929 puts him close behind, the solid foundation that allows Hull, Mikita, and company the licence to freewheel. Those two led the league in scoring, and the Hawks, who scored more goals than any other team this year, finished second to Montreal by a single point. They also missed the Vezina by a mere two goals, just behind the Habs. But look at the shots per game Chicago allowed to get through to Hall: 32.6. Montreal's starter, Charlie Hodge, had to handle only 28.1 per game. No wonder Hall was always throwing up. You know, you can always get a laugh with a joke like that at the expense of Mr. Goalie and his nervousness, and we wonder if he ever rued the day the hockey scribes found out about how sick he often got. There's even a quote attributed to Hall that sounds like it was made up by some ink-stained wretch on deadline: "Playing goal is a winter of torture for me." Come on, *no one* talks that way.

Then again, maybe Hall really did say it like that, just as he is reported to have said, "I sometimes ask myself, what the hell am I doing here? But it's the only way I can support my family." What's hard for us to imagine now, in an era when every goalie wears lightweight armour that covers every square millimetre of his body, is the egregious nature of goaltending injuries back in the day when goalies had the flimsiest pads or no padding at all. Tendons were severed, pucks were fired into faces, muscles and ligaments shredded and torn. It's almost impossible to conceive of the psychic toll taken by forcing yourself to stick your naked face right in front of frozen pucks, slashing sticks, and slicing skate blades night after night: it was the most unnatural act in any team sport. It affected the way goalers played – in the '50s and '60s, they stood up at all costs, because to go down meant your head was *right there*, and you didn't want that; in fact, it was such a horrifying prospect that players often refrained from shooting if the goalie's face was near the ice and in the way (there's a famous picture of Gordie Howe holding off on a shot because Gump Worsley's face is right in front of Howe's stick). Today's goalies, by contrast, spend the entire game sprawled on the ice, bending over to put their paddle flat on the surface, spread-eagled with their heads sticking out into the goal mouth, even nodding hard-shot pucks out of the way as if they were soccer balls, as Dominik Hasek and Roman Cechmanek do, all because *pain is no longer a factor*. With today's padding, no shot hurts. In the past, every shot hurt.

Hence the expressions of job hatred, even to the point of self-loathing, among goalies of the past, as in Hall's confessions of misery or something Roger Crozier once said: "I've hated this game for longer than I can remember. I had hoped that I would never come back." Some goalers even embraced the physical horror of their job in a kind of Stockholm Syndrome. Terry Sawchuk kept a jar full of the bone chips that were annually removed from his arm and another containing his removed appendix, floating in formaldehyde, and when he got three stitches in his eyeball after taking a stick there, he is reported to have had some mirrors set up so that with his other eye he could watch the

Goaltending

operation, which supposedly involved having his stricken eyeball laid out upon his cheek. We find this last detail hard to believe, but it speaks to the horror of goaltending in the allegedly halcyon days of the Original Six. It's impossible to imagine today's goalies, shielded in a sensible cocoon of head-to-toe protection, saying the things the old goalies said or developing an accommodation with pain and mutilation as their predecessors did. Or, as Sawchuk once put it when asked what he did in the off-season, "I spend my summers in hospital."

Farther down the list, the results of a big trade: Jacques Plante has become a New York Ranger, and you know what *that* means. Yup, you got it – 37.6 shots per game. Plante had to be knitting a whole lot of toques this season. Gump Worsley, meanwhile, has become a Montreal Canadien, but he gets injured early on, so the number-one job goes to Hodge. Worsley, meanwhile, plays himself back into shape with Quebec Aces, where he is named to the AHL first All-Star team. Ed Johnston, who many years later would forge a career as a Pittsburgh Penguins executive, plays the whole season for Boston, and there's Sawchuk in his last season at Detroit. Six teams, six goalers, and they all did well this year, but the writers chose Glenn Hall and Charlie Hodge, respectively, as the first- and second-team All-Stars, and God only knows why.

1963–64
(minimum 1400 minutes played)

	GOALER, TEAM	MINS	SAVES-SHOTS	SH/GP	SVPCT	PERSEV
1	Bower, Tor	3009	1481-1587	31.6	.933†	986
2	Gl Hall, Chi	3860	1950-2098	32.6	.929	984
3	J Plante, NY	3900	2222-2442	37.6‡	.910‡	973
4	E Johnston, Bos	4200	2235-2446	34.9	.914	972
5	Sawchuk, Det	3140	1518-1656	31.6	.917	969
6	C Hodge, Mtr	3720	1605-1745	28.1†	.920	967

(466–1399 minutes played)

GOALER, TEAM	MINS	SAVES-SHOTS	SH/GP	SVPCT	PERSEV
*R Crozier, Det	900	458-509	33.9	.900	956
D Simmons, Tor	1191	503-566	28.5	.889	936

(1–465 minutes played)

GOALER, TEAM	MINS	SAVES-SHOTS	SH/GP	SVPCT	PERSEV
*DeJordy, Chi	340	185-204	36.0	.907	967
*Villemure, NY	300	161-179	35.8	.899	959
Worsley, Mtr	444	185-207	28.0	.894	940
H Bassen, Det	60	30-34	34.0	.882	939
*P Rupp, Det	60	26-30	30.0	.867	917
*H Gray, Det	40	26-31	46.5	.839	916
*Morissette, Mtr	36	12-16	26.7	.750	794
All goalers	25200	12597-13750	32.7	.916	971

1964–65

Bower wins his second perseverance title in a row and the fourth of his career, tying him with Worsley, and for the second year in a row, Bower and Hall finish a close one-two. It's another remarkable performance by the aged Leaf, but let's leave him for the moment and look at the minutes-played column. You'll see that most of the numbers here are in the 2,000s. Remember just a few years before, when it seemed like every other goalie was logging the maximum 4,200 minutes per season, and those who weren't were playing 4,000? It's no longer true here, and aptly so, for this is the first year in which teams could dress a spare goalie and take him with them everywhere they went. So among the regulars below, only one, rookie Roger Crozier of Detroit, played without relief. The other five teams developed goaltending tandems, as Punch Imlach did in running Toronto. Both Bower and Sawchuk thrived under this arrangement, or more accurately Sawchuk did, because Bower had been thriving all along. Just as impressive, if less famous, is Chicago's duo of Hall and Denis DeJordy, the latter a bright young star from the AHL. The other three teams that alternated netminders didn't enjoy quite the same success as the Leafs and Black Hawks, but clearly the nature of goaltending changes this year. You can call '64–65 the first season of modern goalkeeping. It was also Jacques Plante's last season for a while. He retired after this one, in which, as you can see, he stood up bravely to the ebon storm of rubber. He wouldn't come out of retirement until the '68–69 season, when he teamed with Hall to form St. Louis's unforgettable goaling duo.

Now let's return to Johnny Bower, né John Kizhkan, of Prince Albert, Saskatchewan. Since he joined the Maple Leafs in '58–59, his finishes on the perseverance list, season by season, read thus: second, first, first, second, third, first, first. Wow. Maybe *this* is the year he gets on the All-Star team? Sorry. The writers chose Roger Crozier for the first team, obviously because he was the only guy who played the tough, old-fashioned way – all the time – and because the Red Wings finished first. And they chose Charlie Hodge for the second team, probably for no other reason than that he played for Montreal.

One note about this particular season. Way back when we did the first *Hockey Compendium* in '86 and '87, we went through old newspapers and tried to reconstruct the '64–65 goaling stats. Our point then was to contrast the high save percentages of the six-team era with the low save percentages of the '80s, but we also wanted to see whether stats from long-past seasons could indeed be recompiled using newspaper accounts. We printed the results, and those of you who read the original *Compendium* – both of you – may remember them. Well, they're inaccurate. Please do not use them for research. Yuen did a far more thorough job than we did, providing back-ups and double-checks. What you see below is the accurate reconstruction of the goalie stats for '64–65. Behold:

1964–65
(minimum 1400 minutes played)

	GOALER, TEAM	MINS	SAVES-SHOTS	SH/GP	SVPCT	PERSEV
1	Bower, Tor	2040	984-1065	31.3	.924†	976
2	Gl Hall, Chi	2440	1169-1268	31.2	.922	974
3	*DeJordy, Chi	1760	838-912	31.1	.919	971
4	Sawchuk, Tor	2160	979-1071	29.7	.914	964
5	J Plante, NY	1938	1007-1116	34.6‡	.902	960
6	*R Crozier, Det	4167	1762-1930	27.8	.913	959
7	E Johnston, Bos	2820	1440-1603	34.1	.898	955
8	C Hodge, Mtr	3120	1288-1423	27.4†	.905	951
9	Paille, NY	2262	1113-1248	33.1	.892‡	947

(466–1399 minutes played)

GOALER, TEAM	MINS	SAVES-SHOTS	SH/GP	SVPCT	PERSEV
*Jk Norris, Bos	1380	749-834	36.3	.898	959
Worsley, Mtr	1080	485-535	29.7	.907	956

(1–465 minutes played)

GOALER, TEAM	MINS	SAVES-SHOTS	SH/GP	SVPCT	PERSEV
*Wetzel, Det	33	14-18	32.7	.778	832
All goalers	25200	11828-13023	31.0	.908	960

1965–66

One more reason to admire Edward Yuen: he's honest. He had a horrible time trying to compile this season, and in the end he had to estimate the totals for 11 of the 19 goalies who appeared. To his credit, he did not try to pass his estimates off as true and accurate stats. We present those estimates below in italic type. Anyone wishing to use their year's statistics for their own research or calculations will be curious to know how much of an estimate Yuen made here. Sometimes, confusion in reporting shot totals in newspaper accounts was caused by stunts like Imlach's on March 3 and April 2, 1966, when the Puncher, still marvelling at the year-and-a-half-old concept of having a substitute goalie to fool around with, alternated the Leaf netminders every five minutes. That messed with the numbers for Bower, Sawchuk, and Bruce Gamble. In other cases, unclear summaries, especially when goalers left games in the middle of a period, muddied the waters. That happened for the games of December 1 (Boston at Chicago), January 23 (Montreal at Chicago), January 27 (Chicago at Boston), January 29 (Boston at Toronto), February 19 (New York at Toronto), February 23 (Toronto at Chicago), and March 5 (Chicago at Toronto).

Well, whaddaya know? Bower wins even when we're estimating. And look how much he wins by – a huge margin over the perennial bridesmaid, Glenn Hall. Sawchuk has found new life in Toronto, Gump Worsley's back and looking awfully good in Montreal, where he's rewarded for his long suffering by winning the first Stanley Cup of his career, and a young Montreal native named Bernie Parent makes his NHL debut with the Bruins and gives a savoury foretaste of things to come. Eddie Giacomin has taken his place as New York's number one goalie – a position that will be his for the next 10 and a half years – although this year, Cesare Maniago was better. That happened a fair bit with Giacomin in the '70s: his long-time understudy Gilles Villemure was sometimes better, but Giacomin was always the main guy.

The '65–66 season is the 12th for which statistics have been unearthed and for which the perseverance rating can be applied. And with this third straight victory, the 41-year-old Bower has now captured five perseverance titles, one more than Worsley, three more than Plante.

And now our annual exercise of seeing who the Professional Hockey Writers' Association picked. First team: Glenn Hall. Second team . . . what?! Really?! Remember all those times we asked "Where's Worsley?" Well, here he is, chosen by the PHWA as the NHL second-team All-Star. The writers must have missed the Gumper, whose last few seasons have been marked by injury, demotion to Quebec, the number two spot in Montreal. Now he's a Cup-winner, and thus for the first time, an All-Star.

1965–66
(minimum 1400 minutes played)

	GOALER, TEAM	MINS	SAVES-SHOTS	SH/GP	SVPCT	PERSEV
1	Bower, Tor	1998	999-1074	32.3	.930†	984
2	Gl Hall, Chi	3747	1810-1974	31.6	.917	970
3	Sawchuk, Tor	1521	756-830	32.7	.911	965
4	Worsley, Mtr	2899	1244-1358	28.1†	.916	963
5	*B Parent, Bos	2083	1128-1256	36.2‡	.898	958
6	E Johnston, Bos	1744	923-1031	35.5	.895	954
7	Maniago, NY	1613	818-912	33.9	.897	953
8	R Crozier, Det	3734	1632-1805	29.0	.904	952
9	*Giacomin, NY	2096	970-1098	31.4	.883‡	936

(466–1399 minutes played)

GOALER, TEAM	MINS	SAVES-SHOTS	SH/GP	SVPCT	PERSEV
B Gamble, Tor	501	256-277	33.2	.924	979
C Hodge, Mtr	1320	535-591	26.9	.905	950
D Simmons, NY	491	204-241	29.5	.846	896

(1–465 minutes played)

GOALER, TEAM	MINS	SAVES-SHOTS	SH/GP	SVPCT	PERSEV
*Al Smith, Tor	62	33-35	33.9	.943	999
*G Gardner, Det	60	23-24	24.0	.958	998
*Ga Smith, Tor	118	60-67	34.1	.896	952
H Bassen, Det	406	160-177	26.2	.904	948

GOALER, TEAM	MINS	SAVES-SHOTS	SH/GP	SVPCT	PERSEV
*D Dryden, Chi	453	202-225	29.8	.898	947
*Cheevers, Bos	340	162-196	34.6	.827	884
*Ring, Bos	34	12-16	28.2	.750	797
All goalers	25200	11927-13187	31.4	.904	957

1966–67

And now for the season all you Toronto fans have been waiting for, 1966–67, the last before expansion, the last Stanley Cup for the Maple Leafs. How long will you have to wait until you win it again? As we write this, it's been 34 years. The Blackhawks have been waiting 40 years. The Red Wings had to wait 42 years, the Rangers, 54. In baseball, the Chicago Cubs and Boston Red Sox have been waiting much longer than that. There are plenty of soccer clubs around the world that have existed for more than a century and have yet to win a championship. Are we being cruel? Well, as Sabres fans we'd have no right to be; after all, our winless streak is at 31, even counting 1999. (Brett Hull was in the crease *illegally*. They should still be playing.) No, we're not being cruel, just trying to show that others have suffered, or are suffering, longer than you. Besides, the long wait will make it so much the sweeter when it comes. If the Buds do win the Cup, we'd like to be there for the celebration, which should be wild, at least by Toronto standards. Insert joke here. But seriously, we do hope the Leafs win the Cup soon. After the Sabres win it. Five times in a row.

We are genuinely happy to report that Terry Sawchuk was the top goaler on the perseverance scale for this very special season, and his antique pal Bower finished tied for third (though they both played barely enough to qualify). That's sort of a comedown for the China Wall, but look how close the top five goalies wound up. Anyway, what does it matter? Sawchuk and Bower will skate together forever in people's memories as the men between the pipes for the '67 Leafs.

One man who, we're sorry to say, will not be doing much skating in people's memories is Denis DeJordy. He's got the Chicago starting job now and will make Glenn Hall, our fourth-place finisher for the year, expendable in the coming expansion draft for the six new teams. Hall will be picked by the St. Louis Blues, retire, then be lured back when the Blues proffer a $45,000 contract, the highest salary ever paid a goalie. But things won't work out for DeJordy; he'll eventually be upstaged by Tony Esposito and wind up in L.A. and Detroit, mostly warming the bench.

Giacomin proves an able workhorse with the improving Rangers, who have made the playoffs for the first time in five years. Hodge cruises along unimpressively, and Rogie Vachon emerges from the primordial ooze, soon to replace him. You can look up and down the list and see all the goalers who'll go in the expansion draft: Sawchuk to Los Angeles, Hall to St. Louis, Hodge and Gary Smith to Oakland, Parent to Philadelphia, and Maniago to Minnesota. This table below feels like an inscription from the distant past, a story marked down moments before everything changes forever, like a map of the world drawn in 1491 or the last hieroglyphs in some Nile Valley tomb, silently bearing witness to the death of a 3,000-year-old religion.

Or maybe it just feels like a list of goalies, and you're wondering why Roger Crozier and George Gardner's stats are in italics. Once again the diligent Yuen could not tell a lie. There was one game out of this entire season that he could not be sure of: Detroit at Toronto on January 14. Crozier left the nets, replaced by Gardner, after 23 minutes 9 seconds, but how many shots they each faced that period cannot be determined from newspaper reports. Nevertheless, that means the true final totals for Crozier and Gardner, whatever they are, cannot be off by more than a handful of shots. Anyway, the hockey writers chose Giacomin and Hall, respectively, as the first- and second-team All-Stars, and we've given up being outraged about it. To tell you the truth, they're pretty good choices, but somebody explain to us why Hall is rated ahead of DeJordy here. Wait. We're not going to get upset about this.

And so we bid adieu to the so-called Original Six, and here too the uninterrupted run of Yuen's research ends. After going through 13 seasons' worth of goaltending statistics, we are surprised – but convinced – that Johnny Bower was the best goaler of this period. Just behind him, Gump Worsley. And close behind Worsley, Glenn Hall and Jacques Plante.

1966–67 (minimum 1400 minutes played)						
	GOALER, TEAM	MINS	SAVES-SHOTS	SH/GP	SVPCT	PERSEV
1	Sawchuk, Tor	1409	756-822	35.0‡	.920	978
2	DeJordy, Chi	2536	1235-1339	31.7	.922†	975
3t	Bower, Tor	1431	707-770	32.3	.918	972
3t	Gl Hall, Chi	1664	772-838	30.2	.921	972
5	Giacomin, NY	3981	1917-2090	31.5	.917	970
6	C Hodge, Mtr	2055	900-988	28.8†	.911	959
7	R Crozier, Det	3256	1553-1735	32.0	.895	948
8	E Johnston, Bos	1880	858-974	31.1	.881‡	933

(466–1399 minutes played)					
GOALER, TEAM	MINS	SAVES-SHOTS	SH/GP	SVPCT	PERSEV
B Gamble, Tor	1185	646-713	36.1	.906	966
*R Vachon, Mtr	1137	507-554	29.2	.915	964
Worsley, Mtr	888	421-468	31.6	.900	952
*Cheevers, Bos	1298	630-702	32.4	.897	952
*G Gardner, Det	560	292-328	35.1	.890	949
B Parent, Bos	1022	504-566	33.2	.890	946

GOALER, TEAM	MINS	SAVES-SHOTS	SH/GP	SVPCT	PERSEV
H Bassen, Det	384	202-224	35.0	.902	960
*Bauman, Mtr	120	52-57	28.5	.912	960
*Ga Smith, Tor	115	58-65	33.9	.892	949
*Al Smith, Tor	60	30-35	35.0	.857	915
Maniago, NY	219	88-102	27.9	.863	909
All goalers	25200	*12128-13370*	*31.8*	*.907*	*960*

1970–71

Yuen jumped ahead and reconstructed the goaltending stats for an expansion year, and we're thankful that he chose one of our favourites, 1970–71. We love it not only because it marks the debut of our team, Buffalo, but because it's the year of the most amazing regular-season performance ever recorded – that of Jacques Plante when he was with the Maple Leafs. Look at his numbers. That's the highest perseverance rating and largest margin of victory ever recorded. If you don't really buy our perseverance statistic, that's all right, look at Plante's save percentage – an unprecedented, unchallengeable .942 – while he was facing a pretty hefty 32.6 shots per game. It defies belief. We remember watching a lot of Plante that season on CBC and CTV, and he blew us away. At first, his performance was framed in the context of "isn't this remarkable coming from a 41-year-old man?" But as the season rolled on, we knew we were seeing something beyond remarkable, beyond amazing. We were seeing something possibly historic, only there was no way to measure what Plante was doing. We did know that the Leafs usually seemed to win when Plante was in the nets and were pretty bad when he wasn't. Looking at the records confirms this impression: Toronto were 24-11-4 with Plante, 13-22-4 without him. His goals-against average, which ended up leading the league, was 1.88; the rest of the Leaf goalies had a 3.39 mark. But those numbers merely hint at what he did that season. The perseverance numbers tell us just how jaw-droppingly astonishing Jacques Plante was.

Plante had retired after the '64–65 season, but in December of '65 he was called in to tend goal for the Canadian national team, made up mostly of junior players, against the Soviet national team in Montreal. Canada won, 2-1. He turned in his pads and stayed retired for three years, but decided to return for '68–69. He tried out for the California Seals, who naturally were ready to sign him, but his contract still belonged to New York, so Plante did not wind up a Seal, thank God. He hooked up with Glenn Hall in St. Louis instead, and together they made the Blues a decent team and carried them to the Cup Final twice (Hall had already helped get them there once before). A lot of people were amazed by Mario Lemieux's comeback in 2000–01, and rightly so. Everyone agreed it was the biggest and best comeback in hockey history, even team sports

history. We agree too, but we'd also argue that until Lemieux's comeback, Jacques Plante's return from three years of retirement was the best one ever.

Plante would play with the Leafs for one and a half more seasons after '70–71, plus a half season and playoffs with the Bruins. Before '73–74, he retired again – and came out of retirement again in '74–75, signed with the Edmonton Oilers of the WHA, and played 31 games. He was 46 years old, hair almost entirely grey, and he still looked fit, nimble, and debonair as always. Plante was born into a family of 11 children in Shawinigan Falls, so poor that a bottle of soda, he later said, was a once-a-year treat. He became self-sufficient, learning to knit and cook, and he supposedly knitted the sweater and toque he wore while guarding the nets for the amateur Montreal Royals. From these humble beginnings, he became a great goalie and a great goaltending coach. As time passes, the story of Plante's achievements is being shrunk down to his invention of the mask and little more. There was so much more to him, though: his self-reliance in life and between the pipes, his freedom of movement, his place as the first goalie to go behind the net to stop the puck, his brilliance as a teacher of goaltending, his tremendous comeback after three years' retirement, his agelessness as a player, and, most important of all, the fact that he was a brilliant goalkeeper at the beginning, in the middle, and at the end of his career. Jacques Plante spent his final years living in Switzerland, where he died in 1986 of stomach cancer. He was only 57.

Plante died young, and there's a lot of anecdotal evidence that as enormous a physical toll as playing goal took back in the days of bare faces and insubstantial protective equipment, the far greater toll was paid later, when the effects of the position's emotional strain set in. The pressure of having to stick your face in there, knowing that sooner or later bones in your cheeks and your nose and your brow will break, eyes will be struck and maybe lost, the skin and tendon and muscle of your hands or arms or legs will be slashed open by cold, dirty steel – and you knew that none of these things *may* happen, they *will* happen – is hard to imagine. Despite the torture of knowing what would happen to you, you had to perform all-out all the time, because to fail even for a short while meant you were out of a job, and a Canadian boy growing up in the '30s and '40s and '50s and training to be a hockey player didn't learn much else in the way of employable skills. The pressure must have been immeasurable.

Author Andrew Podnieks has pointed out that many, many goalies died young: Terry Sawchuk (who was 40 when he died), Turk Broda (58), George Hainsworth (55), Frank "Ulcers" McCool (55), Georges Vezina (38), Lorne Chabot (46), Alec Connell (57), Bill Durnan (57), Roy Worters (57), Bunny Larocque (40). The season after Bruce Gamble appeared on this year's list, he suffered chest pains during a game against Vancouver. When he went to hospital to have it checked out, doctors found that he had had a heart attack. Gamble, then 34, never played again. He died 10 years later.

Fortunately, goaltending is no longer the way it was. They're well-protected now, and they suffer the same injuries every other athlete suffers: pulled muscles, torn ligaments, the occasional broken bone, but shattered facial bones and severed tendons are no longer part of the bargain. The only pressure goalies confront now is of the manageable success-or-failure variety. The all-consuming fear is gone.

Our fondest memories from this year, needless to say, are provided by the Buffalo Sabres' first season. There's something very special about a team's first campaign, this is one thing fans of the Original Six miss out on and can never truly appreciate. You remember practically every game from that first season: the team's first goal, the first time they beat some big, bad opponent, a particular player's triumph against overwhelming odds, because every game is a battle against overwhelming odds.

Look at Joe Daley down there in 13th place on the 22-man list. Seems like nothing special, but we were watching on December 10, the night Daley, one of the last of the bare-faced goalers, did personal battle with the Bruins at Boston Garden. The B's were at the height of their majesty, the defending Cup-holders of Orr, Espo, Hodge, Bucyk, Cashman, and an offence the intimidating likes of which we have never seen before or since, including the Oilers of the '80s. The Sabres, of course, were terrible. Daley was incredible, stopping practically everything the Bruins were throwing at him; several times Esposito and his pals were certain they had goals and started to lift their sticks skyward, only to skate away in amazement, shaking their heads. That's not just a stock phrase; we actually remember Esposito repeatedly shaking his head, commiserating with his teammates, a look of total disbelief on his demonstrative face. After two periods of Daley's impossible performance, the game was tied, 2-2, but in the third period the dam finally burst: Boston scored six times and won, 8-2. They had taken 72 shots (to Buffalo's 28), Daley stopped 64 of them, and as he came off the ice the fans at the Boston Garden gave him a standing ovation and several of the Bruins came over to shake his hand. Daley went to Winnipeg in the WHA a couple of years later and provided Jets fans with seven seasons of happy memories.

Just ahead of Daley is Buffalo's main goaltending hero, Roger Crozier, still an exalted name in the Queen City of the Lakes. Buffalonians old enough to remember can see him in their mind's eye, acrobatically holding the Sabres' foes at bay and prompting the play-by-play man, Ted Darling, to exclaim in his perfect announcer's timbre, ". . . and oh *CROZIER! HOW DID HE STOP THAT ONE?!*" We could've sworn all up and down that Roger the Dodger would finish in the highest reaches of this perseverance list, right up there with Plante, but how our memories make our first loves more beautiful, more thrilling, more enchanting

than perhaps they actually were. Oh Crozier. His entire career was spent battling pancreatitis and stomach pain, and finally he died of prostate cancer at the age of 53. In our minds we'll always see the straps of his mask criss-crossed against the thinning hair and bald pate of his head, the wan smile on his tired accountant's face, the big number 1 on his back, making him seem yet smaller than he really was as he bounced around in the crease like a jack-in-the-box, covering for his teammates' errors. Oh Crozier. We miss you still.

Who else is here? Gerry Cheevers, whom we never thought much of, finishes way ahead of everyone except Plante. Indeed if Plante were not here, Cheevers would've run away with the perseverance laurels this year. We guess Cheesy really was a good goalie. Doug Favell and Bernie Parent provide a potent pairing in Philly, but the Flyers decide to go with Favell and deal Parent to Toronto for Bruce Gamble and Mike "Shaky" Walton. What were the Flyers thinking? Giacomin and Villemure here begin a five-year partnership that makes them one of the most effective and enduring tandems in NHL history. Glenn Hall soldiers on in St. Louis, with Ernie Wakely taking over for the departed Plante as his partner in pads. There's Les Binkley; we just like saying his name. And look down there among the fill-in goalies, at that young Cornell graduate named Ken Dryden. Called up from the Montreal Voyageurs of the AHL, Dryden played six of the last games of the season for the Canadiens, won them all while stopping almost 96% of the shots he faced, and went on to lead the Habs to the Stanley Cup in the most unlikely came-out-of-nowhere story in the annals of hockey, maybe any sport. And you could look it up, right there in the perseverance ratings.

1970–71
(minimum 1560 minutes played)

	GOALER, TEAM	MINS	SAVES-SHOTS	SH/GP	SVPCT	PERSEV
1	J Plante, Tor	2329	1192-1265	32.6	.942†	997
2	Cheevers, Bos	2400	1227-1336	33.4	.918	974
3t	Favell, Phi	2434	1164-1272	31.4	.915	967
3t	Villemure, NY	2039	893-971	28.6	.920	967
3t	A Esposito, Chi	3325	1447-1573	28.4	.920	967
3t	Giacomin, NY	2641	1113-1208	27.4†	.921	967
3t	Maniago, Min	2380	1144-1251	31.5	.914	967
3t	B Parent, Phi-Tor	2626	1266-1385	31.6	.914	967
9	R Vachon, Mtr	2676	1258-1376	30.9	.914	966
10	Gl Hall, StL	1761	772-843	28.7	.916	964
11t	E Johnston, Bos	2280	1015-1111	29.3	.914	962
11t	R Crozier, Buf	2198	1216-1351	36.9‡	.900	962
13	*Myre, Mtr	1677	824-911	32.6	.905	959
14	J Daley, Buf	2073	1121-1249	36.2	.898	958
15	Wakely, StL	2859	1246-1379	28.9	.904	952
16	B Gamble, Tor-Phi	1946	996-1116	34.4	.892	950
17	Binkley, Pit	1870	801-890	28.6	.900	948
18	R Edwards, Det	2104	1002-1121	32.0	.894	947
19t	Al Smith, Pit	2472	1133-1268	30.8	.894	945

GOALER, TEAM	MINS	SAVES-SHOTS	SH/GP	SVPCT	PERSEV
19t C Hodge, Van	1967	929-1041	31.8	.892	945
19t DeJordy, LA	3375	1698-1912	34.0	.888	945
22 Ga Smith, Clf	3975	1959-2215	33.4	.884	940
23 *Du Wilson, Van	1791	929-1057	35.4	.879‡	938

(520–1559 minutes played)

GOALER, TEAM	MINS	SAVES-SHOTS	SH/GP	SVPCT	PERSEV
G Gardner, Van	922	534-586	38.1	.911	975
G Desjardins, Chi	1217	535-584	28.8	.916	964
Worsley, Min	1369	599-656	28.8	.913	961
Jk Norris, LA	1305	680-765	35.2	.889	948
Gi Gilbert, Min	931	473-532	34.3	.889	946
Rutherford, Det	1498	664-758	30.4	.876	927

(1–519 minutes played)

GOALER, TEAM	MINS	SAVES-SHOTS	SH/GP	SVPCT	PERSEV
*K Dryden, Mtr	327	200-209	38.3	.957	1021
*Kn Brown, Chi	18	12-13	43.3	.923	995
*G Meloche, Chi	120	66-72	36.0	.917	977
*Plasse, StL	60	33-36	36.0	.917	977
D Dryden, Buf	409	195-218	32.0	.894	948
*G Gray, Det	380	196-226	35.7	.867	927
*Worthy, Clf	480	242-281	35.1	.861	920
*D McLeod, Det	698	348-408	35.1	.853	911
*Newton, Pit	281	101-117	25.0	.863	905
*Sneddon, Clf	225	96-117	31.2	.821	873
*McLachlan, Tor	25	11-15	36.0	.733	793
*P Hoganson, Pit	57	20-27	28.4	.741	788
All goalers	65520	30686-33963	31.1	.904	955

1974–75

Yuen skipped ahead and did a couple of seasons in the mid-'70s, when, even if the level of play was somewhat diluted by the large number of teams making up the NHL and WHA, there was at least a nice balance between offence and defence. The clutch-and-grab was young, so forwards could still freewheel, and goalie equipment was still of human rather than tractor-trailer proportion. All this meant that when you watched an NHL game during this period, you stood a 50-50 chance of seeing a 7-6 goalfest or a 2-1 defensive epic. Well, maybe not 50-50, because with the likes of Washington and Kansas City now in the league, you also stood a very good chance of seeing an 8-0 blow-out.

Eastern fans of a certain age remember hearing a lot around this time about Rogie Vachon out in the Fabulous Forum, where the L.A. Kings gambolled. But these were all only rumours, because their games were on TV at 10:30 or 11 o'clock, and you just plain never got to see 'em. But here we finally get a feel for just how good Vachon was, all decked out as he was in gold and purple. (Actually it was yellow and purple, but teams never say their colours include "yellow";

it's always "gold.") He'd been tending the nets for Los Angeles since early in the '71–72 season, when Montreal sent him west for four players, and in this campaign he backstopped the Kings to a 105-point finish and a .656 winning percentage – both club records that stand to this day. And don't be fooled, either, into thinking that these are the Marcel Dionne Kings; Dionne wouldn't arrive for another year. These Kings are of the Butch Goring–Juha Widing–Bob Nevin–Mike Murphy–Terry Harper–Bob Murdoch vintage, so you know Vachon was really good.

Looking just below Vachon, we're treated to the sight of a goaltending duet that could not possibly be more democratic or effective: Dan Bouchard and Phil Myre of the Atlanta Flames. As you can see, they both played exactly the same number of minutes, and they both were terrific. Bouchard and Myre earned a great deal of well-deserved admiration back in the mid-'70s for instantly making the Flames a respectable team and a tough opponent. A lot of people thought they'd challenge for the Stanley Cup soon, but of course it would not be them but their expansion cousins, the Islanders, who'd rise to the top. Already at the top is Bernie Parent, checking in here at number four. Fresh off the Flyers' first Cup the year before, when the Broad Street Bullies became the first expansion team to capture the Fabled Goblet, Parent gets terrific support en route to the team's second Cup victory. His teammates, when they're not otherwise occupied by brawling, cheap-shotting, and hooking and high-sticking their opponents, allow only 24.9 shots per game to get through to the great stand-up goalie. In fact, only one team has a stingier defence: the Sabres, who would face the Flyers in the Cup Final this year. Buffalo's main goalie this season is Gary Bromley, who plainly is not up to the challenge. Despite facing the fewest shots per game any regular is asked to handle this year, he posts a miserable .873 save percentage and finishes dead last in the perseverance parade. He'll be replaced in the playoffs by WHA refugee Gerry Desjardins, who'll help Buffalo to the Final, where he in turn will be replaced after freaking out and asking to be removed. Roger Crozier will step in, but Parent and the Flyers prove just too much. Some fans, and Bromley himself, have wondered why the Buffalo brain trust of Punch Imlach and Floyd Smith gave up on him. Now, alas, we can see why.

Keeping Bromley company down there at the bottom of the regulars' list is Eddie Giacomin. He had a pretty poor season here, which has to have been a reason why New York GM Emile Francis thought him expendable enough to trade away the following season. It seems like a logical move, but as we shall see, the Rangers will experience an unpleasant amount of blow-back. Now we direct your attention to the two Washington goalers, Ron Low and Michel Belhumeur. This Capital team, you may recall from our discussion of the most inept teams in hockey history, are dreadful, literally beyond compare. Their unfortunate netminding tandem is bombarded nightly with more than three dozen shots, scads of them unstoppable, and sure enough they don't stop a whole lot of them, thus condemning the aptly named Low and the inaptly named Belhumeur to a season in perseverance hell. But let's not forget that the Washington skaters weren't the only Capitals who were scraped from the bottom of the barrel; the Washington goalies were too, and it shows.

Finally, a word about the italics for Gary Smith and Ken Lockett of the Canucks. There is no record of who stopped how many shots in one period of each of three Vancouver games this season, so as many as eight or nine saves that Smith made might in fact have been made by Lockett, or vice versa.

1974–75
(minimum 1600 minutes played)

	GOALER, TEAM	MINS	SAVES-SHOTS	SH/GP	SVPCT	PERSEV
1	R Vachon, LA	3239	1521-1642	30.4	.926†	977
2	D Bouchard, Atl	2400	1178-1289	32.2	.914	968
3	Myre, Atl	2400	1139-1253	31.3	.909	961
4	B Parent, Phi	4041	1540-1677	24.9	.918	960
5	*Inness, Pit	3122	1512-1673	32.2	.904	957
6	K Dryden, Mtr	3320	1440-1589	28.7	.906	954
7t	A Esposito, Chi	4219	1841-2034	29.9	.905	953
7t	Wm Smith, NYI	3368	1477-1633	29.1	.904	953
7t	*G Simmons, Clf	2029	1055-1179	34.9	.895	953
10	E Johnston, StL	1800	803-896	29.9	.896	946
11	Gi Gilbert, Bos	3029	1341-1499	29.7	.895	944
12t	Ga Smith, Van	3828	1663-1860	29.2	.894	943
12t	McDuffe, KC	2100	1112-1260	36.0	.883	943
14	Maniago, Min	2129	1110-1259	35.5	.882	941
15	J Davidson, StL	2360	1123-1267	32.2	.886	940
16	Plasse, KC-Pit	2514	1252-1421	33.9	.881	938
17	*P LoPresti, Min	1964	994-1131	34.6	.879	936
18	Villemure, NYR	2470	1024-1154	28.0	.887	934
19t	G Meloche, Clf	2771	1332-1518	32.9	.877	932
19t	Favell, Tor	2149	1034-1179	32.9	.877	932
21	Rutherford, Det	3478	1573-1790	30.9	.879	930
22	Low, Was	2588	1418-1653	38.3‡	.857	922
23t	Belhumeur, Was	1812	958-1120	37.1	.855‡	917
23t	Giacomin, NYR	2069	818-938	27.2	.872	917
25	*Bromley, Buf	2787	986-1130	24.3†	.873	913

(534–1600 minutes played)

GOALER, TEAM	MINS	SAVES-SHOTS	SH/GP	SVPCT	PERSEV
*Resch, NYI	1432	643-702	29.4	.916	965
G Edwards, LA	1561	644-705	27.1	.913	959
*Herron, Pit-KC	1388	760-851	36.8	.893	954
G Desjardins, Buf	540	239-264	29.3	.905	954
R Crozier, Buf	1260	529-584	27.8	.906	952
*Y Belanger, StL	640	264-293	27.5	.901	947
*K Broderick, Bos	804	300-332	24.8	.904	945
*G McRae, Tor	1063	464-521	29.4	.891	940
MR Larocque, Mtr	1480	607-681	27.6	.891	937

GOALER, TEAM	MINS	SAVES-SHOTS	SH/GP	SVPCT	PERSEV
W Stephenson, Phi	639	244-273	25.6	.894	936
F Rivard, Min	707	355-405	34.4	.877	934
*Lockett, Van	912	376-424	27.9	.887	933
Du Wilson, Tor-NYR	1573	715-814	31.0	.878	930
R Brooks, Bos	967	368-416	25.8	.885	928
*W McKenzie, Det	740	363-421	34.1	.862	919

(1–533 minutes played)

GOALER, TEAM	MINS	SAVES-SHOTS	SH/GP	SVPCT	PERSEV
*Farr, Buf	213	103-117	33.0	.880	935
*Rb Johnson, Pit	476	261-301	37.9	.867	930
*P Hamel, Tor	195	110-128	39.4	.859	925
*Jh Adams II, Was	400	229-275	41.2	.833	901
*Veisor, Chi	460	193-229	29.9	.843	893
*Bullock, Van	60	21-25	25.0	.840	882
*M Dumas, Chi	121	36-43	21.3	.837	873
Rb Taylor, Phi	120	57-70	35.0	.814	873
Dg Grant, Det	380	142-176	27.8	.807	853
*T Richardson, Det	202	73-96	28.5	.760	808
*C Ridley, NYR	81	35-42	31.1	.694	746
All goalers	86400	39375-44232	30.7	.890	941

1975–76

The last full season Yuen reconstructed was 1975–76, the first year of the four-year reign atop the NHL of the Canadiens, a team that combined regular-season and play-off dominance like no other in the league's history. Ken Dryden was a big part of the Habs' utter superiority, although we thought at the time – and many others did, too – that Dryden had a pretty easy time of it back there and wasn't much of a factor; any decent goaler, we figured, would have prospered with the Canadiens of the late '70s. The unearthed stats, mocking us with numbers, tell us that we were very much mistaken.

At the same time that Montreal walked the earth, crushing all before it, a clever new species had begun to arise: the Islanders, scurrying safely away from the behemoth Habs, biding their time until they would replace the Canadiens as lords of all hockey. Here we see the first stirrings of the Isles' ascendancy in the form of Glenn Resch's league-best perseverance rating, not to mention Billy Smith's tie for fourth. Just before this season, in the '75 playoffs, the Isles made quite a splash by upsetting the big boys in New York, the Rangers, by two games to one in a preliminary-round series, thus birthing the incomparable rivalry between the two teams. In the next round, Long Island went on to rally from a 3-games-to-0 deficit to beat the Penguins, making them only the second team ever to get out of so deep a hole. The Isles then fell behind Philadelphia, again by three games to none but rallied back to tie that series as well. The

111

Flyers had to trundle Kate Smith onto the Spectrum ice to sing a live version of "God Bless America," their foolproof talisman, to save them the embarrassment of becoming the third team to fall to the upstart Islanders. Now, in '75–76, everyone was ready for the suburban club, but they came on strong anyway, and the Resch–Smith tandem was a huge part of their success.

Resch, then, wins the perseverance title, but only by a hair over Dryden, who had a marginally better save percentage but also slightly better protection from his defence. The two of them, though, were *miles* better than the rest of the league's goalies, kind of like the Gretzky-and-Lemieux-then-everyone-else phenomenon of the '80s and '90s. There's quite a long drop down to third place, but once you get there you find Dan Bouchard, one of the most underappreciated goalies of the era. Speaking of underappreciated goalies of the '70s, we also find Denis Herron of Kansas City – that's right, Kansas City – and Gilles Meloche of California on this list. Both had the misfortune of spending their career with some pretty crummy teams, but both were fine goalers. Elsewhere, Tony Esposito shows why he was one of the most respected keepers of the decade, Cesare Maniago guards the crease manfully in Minnesota, just like we remember, and Wayne Stephenson fills in skilfully for the injured Bernie Parent in Philadelphia, home of the two-time defending Cup champion Flyers.

There's John Davidson struggling a bit in his first season with New York, but the Ranger brain trust likes him enough to drop Eddie Giacomin, whose rights they owned for 15 years. This is one of the signal events in Ranger history. To this day, a lot of New Yorkers will tell you they stopped following hockey because of this very season. The waiving of Giacomin preceded by only two weeks the departure of two more beloved Blueshirts, Jean Ratelle and Brad Park, in a trade to the hated Bruins for the despised Phil Esposito and Carol Vadnais, and these two acts killed hockey fandom for a surprisingly large number of Gothamites.

The Giacomin affair was made even more dramatic by the fact that Detroit picked Giacomin up – and the Red Wings were due in to Madison Square Garden for their next game. Sure enough, he got the start for Detroit, and as he stood on the blue line for the national anthem, the Ranger fans roared for him and chanted his name for minutes on end. He stood there crying, and still the fans would not stop. Finally the game started, and of course the 36-year-old Giacomin turned aside 42 of 46 shots to lead the Wings to victory, the Garden fans, who are the loudest in hockey, chanting his name throughout: *Ed-die! Ed-die!*

Finally, have a look down the save-percentage column. After Resch and Dryden's stratospheric marks and the high ratings of the five men who follow them, you run across a string of pretty mediocre numbers. We're heading for the lowered goaltending standards of the '80s, when anyone attaining a .900 percentage in a season was worshipped like a deity, so rare was the achievement. The rigid lanes of North American hockey are starting to break down as Europeans begin to make inroads into the game. Shots are getting harder too, and the refs are allowing teams to clutch and grab in the foul wake of the Flyers' pollution of the game. And the sheer number of major-league teams – 18 in the NHL, 14 in the WHA, 32 in all – has drained the talent pool to a dry lakebed. All of this is making it harder and harder for the men behind the masks, and it's starting to show in the dropping save percentages. In this, the last season reconstructed by the indefatigable Yuen, we are witnessing the dawn of the Age of Air Hockey.

1975–76
(minimum 1600 minutes played)

	GOALER, TEAM	MINS	SAVES-SHOTS	SH/GP	SVPCT	PERSEV
1	Resch, NYI	2546	1126-1214	28.6	.928	975
2	K Dryden, Mtr	3580	1550-1671	28.0	.928†	974
3	D Bouchard, Atl	2671	1152-1265	28.4	.911	958
4t	A Esposito, Chi	4003	1877-2075	31.1	.905	956
4t	Wm Smith, NYI	2254	973-1071	28.5	.908	956
6	Maniago, Min	2704	1349-1500	33.3	.899	955
7	W Stephenson, Phi	3819	1610-1774	27.9	.908	954
8	Herron, KC	3620	1949-2192	36.3	.889	950
9	W Thomas, Tor	3684	1715-1911	31.1	.897	949
10	*Wolfe, Was	2134	1147-1295	36.4	.886	946
11	Plasse, Pit	3096	1456-1634	31.7	.891	944
12	R Vachon, LA	3060	1316-1476	28.9	.892	940
13t	G Meloche, Clf	2440	1111-1251	30.8	.888	939
13t	G Simmons, Clf	2360	1046-1177	29.9	.889	939
15	Rutherford, Det	2640	1221-1379	31.3	.885	938
16	*Y Belanger, StL	1763	844-957	32.6	.882	936
17t	Myre, Atl	2129	946-1069	30.1	.885	935
17t	J Davidson, NYR	3207	1554-1766	33.0	.880	935
19	G Desjardins, Buf	3280	1296-1457	26.7	.889	934
20	Giacomin, NYR-Det	1980	882-1001	30.3	.881	932
21	Gi Gilbert, Bos	3123	1184-1335	25.6†	.887	930
22t	P LoPresti, Min	1789	858-981	32.9	.875	929
22t	Ga Smith, Van	2864	1224-1391	29.1	.880	929
24	G Edwards, LA	1740	723-826	28.5	.875	923
25	E Johnston, StL	2152	886-1016	28.3	.872	919
26	Low, Was	2289	1219-1427	37.4‡	.854‡	917

(534–1599 minutes played)

GOALER, TEAM	MINS	SAVES-SHOTS	SH/GP	SVPCT	PERSEV
*Staniowski, StL	620	304-337	32.6	.902	956
MR Larocque, Mtr	1220	484-534	26.3	.906	950
Cheevers, Bos	900	380-421	28.1	.903	949
Inness, Pit-Phi	1332	670-755	34.0	.887	944
Lockett, Van	1436	673-756	31.6	.890	943
R Crozier, Buf	620	214-241	23.3	.888	927
*Reece, Bos	777	309-352	27.2	.878	923
Villemure, Chi	797	357-414	31.2	.862	914
Du Wilson, NYR	1080	471-547	30.4	.861	912

GOALER, TEAM	MINS	SAVES-SHOTS	SH/GP	SVPCT	PERSEV
W McKenzie, KC	1120	529-626	33.6	.845	901
Al Smith, Buf	840	257-300	21.4	.857	892

(1-533 minutes played)

GOALER, TEAM	MINS	SAVES-SHOTS	SH/GP	SVPCT	PERSEV
*Oleschuk, KC	60	48-52	52.0	.923	1010
*G Gratton, StL	265	137-148	33.5	.926	982
*C Ridley, Van	500	210-229	27.5	.917	963
B Parent, Phi	615	236-260	25.4	.908	950
G McRae, Tor	956	459-518	32.5	.886	940
Rb Taylor, Phi-Pit	318	154-176	33.2	.875	930
*Soetaert, NYR	273	149-173	38.0	.861	925
McDuffe, Det	240	133-155	38.7	.858	923
Belhumeur, Was	377	193-225	35.8	.858	917
*P Harrison, Min	307	148-176	34.4	.841	898
*Laxton, Pit	414	149-180	26.1	.828	871
*T Richardson, Det	60	29-36	36.0	.806	866
Dg Grant, Det	120	37-45	22.5	.822	860
Bromley, Buf	60	27-34	34.0	.794	851
Favell, Tor	160	55-70	26.2	.786	829
*Mrazek, Phi	6	1-2	20.0	.500	533
All goalers	86400	39027-43873	30.5	.890	940

1982–83

We pick up the goaling story again in '82–83, when the NHL finally started recording saves and shots as an official stat. This year, the Islander netminding tandem of Rollie Melanson and Billy Smith won the Jennings Trophy, which by now was given to the goaltenders whose team allowed the fewest goals, while the Vezina became an award voted to the one goalie believed to be the best. There was a kind of poetic justice in Melanson and Smith getting the Jennings, because they really *were* the two best goalers in the league. The sophomore Melanson was being groomed as the goalie of the Isles' future, but he was not deemed ready yet. After all, Smith was still great, and the club had won two straight Cups with the Hatchet Man in the nets. So Melanson rode the bench during the playoffs.

The general managers voted the Vezina to Pete Peeters this season, probably because he had the lowest goals-against average, naming him first on all 21 ballots. Melanson finished second in the voting. This reminds us just how long ago 1983 is, in some ways longer ago than 1963, because while even young fans know a little about Sawchuk, Plante, the Gumper, and their cohorts, what is there to know about Melanson, Peeters, Murray Bannerman? We were struck by this as we went through what we wrote in the original *Compendium* about the goalies of this period. We were obsessed with Glen Hanlon, Rejean Lemelin, Bob Froese, Bob Sauve, among others. The thing is, they were all pretty good at one point or another, as were Melanson,

Bannerman, Peeters, but how much is there to say about them now, and please don't take this personally if you're one of these goalies reading these words. This is the Age of Air Hockey we're looking at right here, with an average of almost eight goals per game, virtually no checking, and most defencemen doing weak Bobby Orr impersonations. The Islanders are just about the only team providing relief from the singlemindedness of the era, and it's probably no coincidence that they have just about the only goalie who is remembered as great: Smith, dirty, dangerous, and malicious as he was. And Grant Fuhr, of course, who was pretty much a one-man defence in attack-crazed Edmonton (he had a great rookie year in '81–82, but fell off this season). Most everywhere else, goalkeepers didn't make much of an impression, not that they could do anything about it, considering how little emphasis was placed on helping the goalie in those days. Look down the list and see what you remember of these guys.

The only rookie to rate high this year is Pelle Lindbergh, and even if this had been his only year in the NHL it would have marked him as the best European-trained goalie ever to play on these shores up to that time. His performance this season was hardly great; it's just that there had never been a halfway decent European goaler on the roster of a North American big-league club, hard as that is to believe today. Among the old-timers here, two doughty veterans did well: John Garrett and Tony Esposito. But for both, it would amount to the last hurrah. Others we like: Gilles Meloche, underrated throughout his career; Andy Moog, who paired with Fuhr in the Oiler nets so effectively; Mike Palmateer, the Popcorn Kid; ex-MVP Mike Liut; Glenn Resch, here a Devil; and Richard Brodeur. Before there was Martin Brodeur, there was King Richard, the man who led the sub-.500 Vancouver Canucks to the '81–82 Cup Final.

As we leave this season behind us, we ask you to glance over your shoulder and look, at the risk of turning into a pillar of salt, at the low save percentages of so many of the goalies here. Get used to it; it's going to be a long time before the goalkeepers get the upper hand again.

1982-83
(minimum 1600 minutes played)

	GOALER, TEAM	MINS	SAVES-SHOTS	SH/GP	SVPCT	PERSEV
1	R Melanson, NYI	2460	1094-1203	29.3	.909†	958
2	Wm Smith, NYI	2340	1081-1193	30.6	.906	957
3	M Bannerman, Chi	2460	1154-1281	31.2	.901	953
4t	Peeters, Bos	3611	1338-1480	24.6†	.904	945
4t	Hanlon, StL-NYR	1844	929-1046	34.0	.888	945
4t	Moog, Edm	2833	1363-1530	32.4	.891	945
7t	J Garrett, Qbc-Van	1887	896-1008	32.1	.889	942
7t	Re Lemelin, Clg	2211	1056-1189	32.3	.888	942
9t	G Meloche, Min	2689	1249-1409	31.4	.886	939
9t	D Edwards, Clg	2209	1106-1254	34.1	.882	939

GOALER, TEAM	MINS	SAVES-SHOTS	SH/GP	SVPCT	PERSEV
9t A Esposito, Chi	2340	1064-1199	30.7	.887	939
12 Beaupre, Min	2011	926-1046	31.2	.885	937
13 *Lindbergh, Phi	2333	942-1058	27.2	.890	936
14 Sevigny, Mtr	2130	918-1040	29.3	.883	932
15t Mio, NYR	2365	1020-1156	29.3	.882	931
15t St. Croix, Phi-Tor	1840	818-930	30.3	.881	931
17 A Jensen, Was	2358	1004-1139	29.0	.881	930
18 D Bouchard, Qbc	2947	1381-1578	32.1	.875	929
19t Liut, StL	3794	1680-1915	30.3	.877	928
19t Resch, NJ	3650	1689-1931	31.7	.875	928
21 P Riggin, Was	2161	890-1011	28.1	.880	927
22 Wamsley, Mtr	2583	1087-1238	28.8	.878	926
23 Palmateer, Tor	2965	1334-1531	31.0	.871	923
24t R Brodeur, Van	3291	1427-1635	29.8	.873	922
24t M Dion, Pit	2791	1304-1502	32.3	.868	922
26t Soetaert, Wpg	2533	1151-1325	31.4	.869	921
26t G Millen, Har	3520	1771-2053	35.0‡	.863	921
26t Fuhr, Edm	1803	841-970	32.3	.867	921
29 R Sauve, Buf	3110	1211-1390	26.8	.871	916
30 *Laskoski, LA	2277	1036-1209	31.9	.857	910
31t *G Stefan, Det	1847	806-945	30.7	.853	904
31t *Micalef, Det	1756	655-761	26.0	.861	904
33 Herron, Pit	1707	779-930	32.7	.838‡	892

(534-1599 minutes played)

GOALER, TEAM	MINS	SAVES-SHOTS	SH/GP	SVPCT	PERSEV
*B Hayward, Wpg	1440	697-786	32.7	.887	941
*Froese, Phi	1407	510-569	24.3	.896	937
Low, Edm-NJ	712	346-397	33.5	.872	927
*Ellacott, Van	555	267-308	33.3	.867	922
*Malarchuk, Qbc	900	446-517	34.5	.863	920
Veisor, Har	1280	697-815	38.2	.855	919
Mattsson, Min-LA	999	452-523	31.4	.864	917
Weeks, NYR	1040	423-491	28.3	.862	909
MR Larocque, Tor-Phi	955	434-510	32.0	.851	904
*J Cloutier, Buf	1390	491-572	24.7	.858	900
Gi Gilbert, Det	1137	480-565	29.8	.850	899
Staniowski, Wpg	827	350-415	30.1	.843	894
M Lessard, LA	888	364-432	29.2	.843	891
*M Moffat, Buf	673	221-270	24.1	.819	859

(1-533 minutes played)

GOALER, TEAM	MINS	SAVES-SHOTS	SH/GP	SVPCT	PERSEV
V Tremblay, Tor	40	25-27	40.5	.926	993
R Parent, Tor	40	20-22	33.0	.909	964
J Davidson, NYR	120	50-55	27.5	.909	955
S Baker, NYR	102	37-42	24.7	.881	922
Myre, Buf	300	130-151	30.2	.861	911
*Bernhardt, Clg	280	126-147	31.5	.857	910
*M Blake, LA	432	180-210	29.2	.857	906

GOALER, TEAM	MINS	SAVES-SHOTS	SH/GP	SVPCT	PERSEV
*M Holden, Mtr	87	36-42	29.0	.857	905
Ma Baron, Bos	516	199-232	27.0	.858	903
Heinz, StL	335	136-160	28.7	.850	898
Parro, Was	261	107-126	29.0	.849	897
Middlebrook, NJ-Edm	472	213-253	32.2	.842	895
*Rb Moore, Was	20	6-7	21.0	.857	892
Rutherford, Det	60	32-39	39.0	.821	886
*Romano, Pit	155	78-96	37.2	.812	874
Keans, LA	304	114-138	27.2	.826	871
Ricci, Pit	147	60-76	31.0	.789	941
S MacKenzie, NJ	130	53-68	31.4	.779	832
*Vernon, Clg	100	35-46	27.6	.761	807
*Caprice, Van	20	5-8	24.0	.625	665
All goalers	100800	44820-51200	30.5	.875	926

1983-84

It's Melanson and Smith again, and this year their 1-2 finish is even more impressive than it was in 1982-83. The Isles finally surrendered the Cup this season, though they went out like champions in getting all the way to their fifth Final in a row, and their swan song was so beautiful in large part because Melanson and Smith wrote the melody. All the excellence with which Islander goalkeepers had guarded the gates during the club's reign was brought to a thrilling *pas de deux* here by the youngster and the veteran, but all the extended metaphors you could have mustered wouldn't have convinced the GMs or the rest of the hockey world to vote an honour to the Long Island goalers. Hockey was sick of the Islanders and their anonymity; everyone wanted glamour, and they got it with the Oilers. So while Edmonton took the Cup and Gretzky took all the trophies for his offensive achievements, the GMs ignored the yesterday's-news Islanders and voted the Vezina to the glamorous rookie Tom Barrasso.

Barrasso had been very strong for Buffalo, but in reality he wasn't even the best *rookie* in the nets this season; Allan Bester was. The GMs had fallen in love with Barrasso's rock-bottom goals-against average, second best in the league, and they lavished their affection on the Boston-area boy by making him only the third rookie ever to receive the Vezina, and the first to win it since it became an elective honour. (In 1987, Ron Hextall became the second.) What made Barrasso so sexy, besides his low GAA and the fact that he was the first U.S. high-schooler to step directly into the league, was his brash poise. (And perhaps his receding hairline, which had to be the only one ever observed on a 19-year-old. These things appeal to general managers.) Barrasso played with a team whose style was notoriously conservative, tailored to be so by the confines of the small rink at the Aud. He faced just 26 and a half shots per game, and this was of immense help in keeping his GAA so low.

Allan Bester, on the other hand, received no such help. The Leafs were awful, and he had to face a whopping, league-high 37 shots per game. Naturally, his goals-against was high (4.35), and anyone with the insight to suggest that Bester was doing a good job was dismissed as a nut. In fact, Bester was fabulous, and how he managed to turn aside over 88% of the barrage levelled at him nightly at the Carlton-Street Shooting Gallery is a mystery. Two of his fellow Leaf goalies, the veterans Mike Palmateer and Rick St. Croix, were overwhelmed by the carpet-bombing, but another Leaf goalie, the rookie Ken Wregget, did quite well in his three games under the blazing guns of the Leafs' opponents. So there you go: the Leaf goalies for 1984–85 will be Bester and Wregget, right? Wrong. One of the reasons the Leafs were so bad for so long was their management's utter inability to recognize talent, or the inexplicable alacrity with which they stamped out talent wherever it sprouted on the barren tundra that was Maple Leaf hockey in the Harold Ballard years.

Here we see that Denis Herron, who was the worst goalie in the NHL the previous year after having been traded from Montreal to Pittsburgh, rebounds wonderfully after intense bombardment in the Penguin nets. Like Bester, Herron's grace under pressure was exemplary. Fuhr and Moog do very well this year in backstopping the Oilers to their first Cup. Incidentally, check out the list for those goalers who played 534 to 1,599 minutes. See Markus Mattsson? If you remember him at all, you probably remember him as a klutzy goaltender. But Mattsson had his moment of glory, and it came during this season. He was the goalie who stopped Wayne Gretzky's 51-game scoring streak.

Among those goalers whose perseverance ratings were low, Pelle Lindbergh's stands out the most. He had impressed as a rookie the year before, but part of being a rookie was (and, all too often, still is) having to undergo the inane tribal ritual of "the shave," in which the player is held down and has his pubic hair shaved off by his cheering teammates. For eons it was dismissed as being no more than a silly adolescent rite, but now, finally, most people see it for what it really is: an act of cruelty and a twisted, homophobic fantasy of homosexual rape. This season Lindbergh was subjected to the shave, and apparently his Flyer teammates were more brutal than usual. Instead of feeling as though he'd been accepted into the fold, the ostensible reason for the ritual, he was traumatized, and he said so in public. Resentful at what had been perpetrated on him and apparently alienated from his teammates, his performance nose-dived in this season, and he gave way to Bob Froese as the club's number one goaltender. Fortunately, Lindbergh's numbers would recover in '84–85.

1983–84
(minimum 1600 minutes played)

	GOALER, TEAM	MINS	SAVES-SHOTS	SH/GP	SVPCT	PERSEV
1	R Melanson, NYI	2019	1018-1128	33.5	.902†	958
2	Wm Smith, NYI	2279	1122-1252	33.0	.896	951
3	Re Lemelin, Clg	2568	1255-1405	32.8	.893	948
4	*Bester, Tor	1848	1009-1143	37.1‡	.883	945
5t	Herron, Pit	2028	1055-1193	35.3	.884	943
5t	Hanlon, NYR	2837	1337-1503	31.8	.890	943
7t	Fuhr, Edm	2625	1290-1461	33.4	.883	938
7t	*Barrasso, Buf	2475	979-1096	26.6	.893	938
9	M Bannerman, Ch	3335	1475-1663	30.0	.887	937
10	Moog, Edm	2212	1038-1177	31.9	.882	935
11t	*Froese, Phi	2863	1174-1324	27.7	.887	933
11t	Liut, StL	3425	1494-1691	29.6	.004	933
13	P Riggin, Was	2299	821-923	24.1†	.889	930
14	G Millen, Har	3583	1591-1812	30.3	.878	929
15	Keans, Bos	1779	697-789	26.6	.883	928
16t	Beaupre, Min	1791	846-969	32.5	.873	927
16t	D Bouchard, Qbc	3373	1341-1521	27.0	.882	927
18	Resch, NJ	2641	1238-1422	32.3	.871	924
19t	D Edwards, Clg	2303	1057-1214	31.6	.871	923
19t	A Jensen, Was	2414	875-992	24.7	.882	923
19t	Soetaert, Wpg	2536	1202-1384	32.7	.868	923
22t	G Stefan, Det	2600	1066-1218	28.1	.875	922
22t	*M Blake, LA	1634	772-890	32.7	.867	922
24	G Meloche, Min	2883	1320-1521	31.7	.868	921
25	Peeters, Bos	2868	1070-1221	25.5	.876	919
26	R Brodeur, Van	2107	919-1060	30.2	.867	917
27	R Sauve, Buf	2375	912-1050	26.5	.869	913
28	Sevigny, Mtr	2203	819-943	25.7	.869	911
29	Low, NJ	2218	971-1132	30.6	.858	909
30	Lindbergh, Phi	1999	828-963	28.9	.860	908
31	Palmateer, Tor	1831	834-983	32.2	.848‡	902
32	J Garrett, Van	1652	642-755	27.4	.850	896
33	Wamsley, Mtr	2333	832-976	25.1	.852	894

(534–1599 minutes played)

GOALER, TEAM	MINS	SAVES-SHOTS	SH/GP	SVPCT	PERSEV
*Hrudey, NYI	535	261-289	32.4	.903	957
*Romano, Pit	1020	551-629	37.0	.876	938
*Caprice, Van	1099	461-523	28.6	.881	929
A Esposito, Chi	1095	531-619	33.9	.858	914
Weeks, NYR	1361	575-665	29.3	.865	914
Ma Baron, LA	1211	541-628	31.1	.861	913
*Malarchuk, Qbc	1215	511-591	29.2	.865	913
M Dion, Pit	1553	795-933	36.0	.852	912
*B Hayward, Wpg	1530	735-859	33.7	.856	912
Mio, Det	1295	579-674	31.2	.859	911
Staniowski, Wpg-Har	1081	494-576	32.0	.858	911
St. Croix, Tor	939	449-529	33.8	.849	905
Mattsson, LA	1101	450-529	28.8	.851	899

GOALER, TEAM	MINS	SAVES-SHOTS	SH/GP	SVPCT	PERSEV
Micalef, Det	808	305-357	26.5	.854	899
Veisor, Har-Wpg	660	240-286	26.0	.839	882
Laskoski, LA	665	264-319	28.8	.828	876
Heinz, StL	1118	458-538	28.9	.814	862

(1–533 minutes played)

GOALER, TEAM	MINS	SAVES-SHOTS	SH/GP	SVPCT	PERSEV
*M Gosselin, Qbc	148	64-67	27.2	.955	1000
*R Mason, Was	120	43-46	23.0	.935	973
*Casey, Min	84	53-59	42.1	.898	969
*Wregget, Tor	165	114-128	46.5	.891	968
*Dowie, Tor	72	39-43	35.8	.907	967
*Janecyk, Chi	412	209-237	34.5	.882	939
*R Scott, NYR	485	224-253	31.3	.885	938
*Vanbiesbrouck, NYR	180	74-84	28.0	.881	928
M Lessard, LA	266	132-158	35.6	.835	895
Craig, Min	110	47-56	30.5	.839	890
V Tremblay, Pit	240	117-141	35.2	.832	889
*Penney, Mtr	240	96-115	28.7	.835	883
*Behrend, Wpg	351	152-184	31.5	.826	879
*B Ford, Qbc	123	57-70	34.1	.814	871
MR Larocque, StL	300	132-163	32.6	.810	864
*M Moffat, Bos	186	66-81	26.1	.815	858
*K Holland, Det	146	41-51	21.0	.804	839
*M Holden, Det	52	13-17	19.6	.765	797
*Vernon, Clg	11	2-6	32.7	.333	388
Parro, Was	1	0-0	–	–	–
All goalers	101914	44774-51277	30.2	.873	924

1984–85

Lindbergh overcomes the trauma of the previous year in Philadelphia, and now he stands in full glory atop the goaltending pinnacle. For once justice is served in the awarding of an NHL trophy, as the general managers vote him the Vezina. He plays more minutes than any goalie has since 1980–81, and through it all he maintains a high standard of excellence. The Flyers will make the Final this year, but their dependence on Lindbergh will eventually catch up with them. Exhausted and with his penchant for becoming dehydrated exacerbated by the late-May heat (this is where the practice of leaving a water bottle on top of the goal net got started), Lindbergh's play will deteriorate and he will be unable to last through the final round against Edmonton. Oddly, many commentators will blame Lindbergh for this, while Mike Keenan will escape criticism. What could Keenan have been thinking when he put Lindbergh in the nets for night after night of regular-season games? He knew that Bob Froese had proved himself a good goaler over the course of the previous two seasons, so why did he sit Froese out? It was a mindless move by Keenan – the first of

Keenan's many gaffes involving goaltenders over the years – and when Lindbergh finally flared out after playing almost every game for nine full months, Froese was rusty and ineffective when he was sent in to stem the Oiler tide in the last three games of the Final.

Right behind Lindbergh at the top of the perseverance charts is Andy Moog, and the Moog–Fuhr duet replaces Melanson–Smith as the best goaltending tandem in the NHL. Mike Liut, the overworked St. Louis guardian, prospers after a late-season trade to Hartford. Rejean Lemelin continues to do his bit to make Alberta a goalie-rich province, while Murray Bannerman and Denis Herron carry on their heroic play under difficult circumstances. Herron's effort is practically superhuman, as it had been the year before; his reward for this in '85–86, after the Pens acquire Gilles Meloche, will be a season-long exile to the AHL. It's probably fair to say that no goalie of the '70s and '80s got such a raw deal from so many different quarters as Herron. Glen Hanlon, too, is soon to get the shaft. After his fine '84–85 season with the Rangers, he will be rewarded with a demotion to Adirondack and New Haven.

Somewhat happier than these stories are those of the three rookies Kelly Hrudey, Roberto Romano, and John Vanbiesbrouck, though the happiness of each of their stories is somewhat mitigated by the unhappy stories of the goalies they displaced. Hrudey replaced Rollie Melanson as Billy Smith's partner, and while Melanson languished through an ineffective and injury-shortened year in Minnesota, robbed of the chance he had earned of being Smith's successor, Hrudey showed himself to be a superb netminder. He led all rookies in this campaign. Romano was fantastic facing the puck blizzard at the Igloo, but the Penguins were so bad and the future looked so bleak to him that he quit at the end of the year, deciding to become a vintner. Vanbiesbrouck, who had been the goaler the year before when the Tulsa Oilers won the CHL title despite the curious problem of not having a home rink or even a home city, was very good in the face of the frozen vulcanized monsoon that constantly lashed him. Each of these three youngsters learned at the elbow of veterans – Hrudey from Melanson (as well as from Smith, of course), Romano from Herron, Vanbiesbrouck from Hanlon – each of these three veterans was sent into temporary or permanent exile, and at least two of these three younger men would go on to enjoy long, prosperous careers that eclipsed those of their mentors.

Two veterans are burning out here – Glenn Resch and Richard Brodeur – and they settle to the forest floor, where they will eventually turn into mulch. Most curious of all is Doug Soetaert. He faced the fewest shots per game of any goaler this season, and yet his save percentage was the worst of any goaler. For this unique double, he truly deserved to finish last.

Goaltending

1984–85
(minimum 1600 minutes played)

	GOALER, TEAM	MINS	SAVES-SHOTS	SH/GP	SVPCT	PERSEV
1	Lindbergh, Phi	3858	1732-1926	30.0	.899†	949
2	Moog, Edm	2019	938-1049	31.2	.894	946
3	Liut, StL-Har	2660	1254-1411	31.8	.889	942
4t	Fuhr, Edm	2559	1260-1425	33.4	.884	940
4t	Re Lemelin, Clg	3176	1452-1635	30.9	.888	940
6t	*Hrudey, NYI	2335	1091-1232	31.7	.886	938
6t	M Bannerman, Chi	3371	1629-1844	32.8	.883	938
8	Herron, Pit	2193	1190-1360	37.2‡	.875	937
9t	*Romano, Pit	1629	853-973	35.8	.877	936
9t	Hanlon, NYR	2510	1263-1438	34.4	.878	936
9t	Beaupre, Min	1770	822-931	31.6	.883	936
12	*Vanbiesbrouck, NYR	2358	1177-1343	34.2	.876	933
13t	Wm Smith, NYI	2090	966-1099	31.6	.879	932
13t	Wamsley, StL	2319	965-1091	28.2	.885	932
14	G Meloche, Min	1817	833-948	31.3	.879	931
15	P Riggin, Was	3388	1304-1472	26.1	.886	929
16	B Hayward, Wpg	3481	1585-1809	31.2	.876	928
17	*Bernhardt, Tor	2182	968-1104	30.4	.877	927
18t	Barrasso, Buf	3248	1126-1270	23.5	.887	926
18t	*Janecyk, LA	3002	1296-1479	29.6	.876	926
20	D Bouchard, Qbc	1738	722-823	28.4	.877	925
21	*M Gosselin, Qbc	2020	776-887	26.3	.875	919
22	*Penney, Mtr	3252	1174-1341	24.7	.875	917
23	D Edwards, Clg	1691	742-857	30.4	.866	916
24	Micalef, Det	1856	848-984	31.8	.862	915
25t	Peeters, Bos	2975	1132-1304	26.3	.868	912
25t	G Stefan, Det	2635	1170-1360	31.0	.860	912
27	R Brodeur, Van	2930	1342-1570	32.2	.855	908
28t	Resch, NJ	2884	1197-1397	29.0	.857	905
28t	G Millen, Har-StL	3266	1334-1556	28.6	.857	905
28t	*Eliot, LA	1882	805-942	30.0	.855	905
31	Soetaert, Mtr	1606	530-621	23.2†	.853‡	892

(534–1599 minutes played)

GOALER, TEAM	MINS	SAVES-SHOTS	SH/GP	SVPCT	PERSEV
Froese, Phi	923	390-427	27.8	.913	960
Skorodenski, Chi	1396	698-773	33.2	.903	958
*R Mason, Was	661	260-291	26.4	.893	937
Bester, Tor	767	373-427	33.4	.874	929
Keans, Bos	1497	587-669	26.8	.877	922
A Jensen, Was	803	260-294	22.0	.884	921
Wregget, Tor	1278	645-748	35.1	.862	921
M Dion, Pit	553	272-315	34.2	.863	920
Weeks, Har	1397	609-700	30.1	.870	920
R Melanson, NYI	1567	730-843	32.3	.866	920
Sevigny, Qbc	1104	429-491	26.7	.874	918
*Behrend, Wpg	1173	536-623	31.9	.860	913
Low, NJ	1326	542-627	28.4	.864	912
*Caprice, Van	1523	693-815	32.1	.850	904
*Kampurri, NJ	645	295-349	32.5	.845	899

GOALER, TEAM	MINS	SAVES-SHOTS	SH/GP	SVPCT	PERSEV
R Sauve, Buf	1564	496-580	22.3	.855	892
St. Croix, Tor	628	260-314	30.0	.828	878

(1–533 minutes played)

GOALER, TEAM	MINS	SAVES-SHOTS	SH/GP	SVPCT	PERSEV
*Clifford, Chi	20	8-8	24.0	1.000	1040
*Pa Roy, Mtr	20	2-2	6.0	1.000	1010
Staniowski, Har	20	9-10	30.0	.900	950
J Cloutier, Buf	65	33-37	34.2	.892	949
*Sylvestri, Bos	102	46-52	30.6	.885	936
*Zanier, Edm	185	88-100	32.4	.880	934
Heinz, StL	70	23-26	22.3	.885	922
*Reaugh, Edm	60	29-34	34.0	.853	910
*M Holden, Wpg	213	89-104	29.3	.856	905
*M Sands, Min	139	74-88	38.0	.841	904
*B Ford, Pit	457	244-292	38.3	.836	900
Mio, Det	376	146-173	27.6	.844	890
J Garrett, Van	407	199-243	35.8	.819	879
*Daskalakis, Bos	289	117-141	29.3	.830	879
*Pang, Chi	60	18-22	22.0	.818	855
*D Jensen, Phi	60	23-30	30.0	.767	817
Ma Baron, Edm	33	7-9	16.4	.778	805
All goalers	102084	44706-51138	30.1	.874	924

1985–86

What is it about Billy Smith's understudies that makes them so good? This season the sophomore Islander Kelly Hrudey runs away with the perseverance title. Hrudey was excellent all season long, but in the final month he went on a tear and was virtually unbeatable. His fantastic performance gave the faded Isle defensive game some panache in an otherwise drab season. Smith, meanwhile, showed his age. By most goalies' standards, his season was just fine, but by his own standards it was an intimation of his career's mortality.

Grant Fuhr had another good season, as did several other netminders, at least in relation to John Vanbiesbrouck, who was somehow given the Vezina. Beezer spent many years as a good but not great goaler, usually ranking around 12th in the league, and he wouldn't join the league's elite until the early '90s. The GMs this season must have been clairvoyant to vote him the Vezina some seven or eight years before he actually deserved it. Meanwhile, Patrick Roy and Mike Vernon, the Hero Youths of the playoffs this year, didn't stink during the regular season, but they weren't all that good, either. This makes their springtime exploits – Roy's Canadiens beat Vernon's Flames in the Cup Final – all the more remarkable. Those two, along with Kirk McLean and the now-retired Vanbiesbrouck, were the only players on this list still active in 2000-01.

Pelle Lindbergh died in a car crash early this season, a terrible event still remembered with sadness in Philadelphia, and a much too early end to a promising career. The Flyers' starting job falls to Bob Froese, and he responds by showing that he is indeed one of the best goalers in the league, finishing with the second-best rating in the NHL. Oddly, many pundits around the league weren't impressed with him, despite his superb numbers. One whom we heard while the Flyers were slumping a bit at the three-quarters mark of the season, and he shall remain nameless, even after all these years, made this idiotic statement: "What's wrong with Philadelphia? I'll tell you in just one word – *goaltending*!" He wasn't the only one with such an unreasonably low opinion of Froese. Flyers' manager Bobby "Bob" Clarke slagged Frosty by giving the rookie Darren Jensen a shot at the starting position. Later, Clarke brought in Chico Resch – not much of a show of confidence in a goalie with a .909 save percentage in a league where .875 was the norm. At least the other GMs knew Froese's worth: they gave him second place in the season's Vezina balloting.

1985–86
(minimum 1600 minutes played)

	GOALER, TEAM	MINS	SAVES-SHOTS	SH/GP	SVPCT	PERSEV
1	Hrudey, NYI	2563	1316-1453	34.0	.906	962
2	Froese, Phi	2728	1153-1269	27.9	.909†	955
3	Fuhr, Edm	2184	1152-1295	35.6‡	.890	949
4t	Wamsley, StL	2517	1210-1354	32.3	.894	947
4t	Beaupre, Min	3073	1506-1688	33.0	.892	947
4t	Malarchuk, Qbc	2657	1216-1358	30.7	.895	947
7	Moog, Edm	2664	1314-1478	33.3	.889	945
8	R Sauve, Chi	2099	1070-1208	34.5	.886	943
9	G Millen, StL	2168	1006-1135	31.4	.886	939
10t	Romano, Pit	2684	1229-1388	31.0	.885	937
10t	A Jensen, Was	2437	1036-1165	28.7	.889	937
12	Vanbiesbrouck, NYR	3326	1439-1623	29.3	.887	935
13	Wm Smith, NYI	2308	1059-1202	31.2	.881	933
14	G Meloche, Pit	1989	879-998	30.1	.881	931
15	Barrasso, Buf	3561	1559-1773	29.9	.879	929
16	M Bannerman, Chi	2689	1335-1536	34.3	.869	926
17	Re Lemelin, Clg	3369	1556-1785	31.8	.872	925
18	Liut, Har	3282	1373-1571	28.7	.874	922
19	Peeters, Bos-Was	2506	1007-1151	27.6	.875	921
20	*Pa Roy, Mtr	2651	1034-1182	26.8	.875	919
21	D Edwards, Tor	2009	979-1139	34.0	.861	916
22t	D Bouchard, Wpg	1696	682-789	27.9	.864	911
22t	Janecyk, LA	2083	966-1128	32.5	.856	911
24	R Brodeur, Van	3541	1481-1721	29.2	.861	909
25t	Resch, NJ-Phi	1956	829-965	29.6	.859	908
25t	G Stefan, Det	2068	922-1077	31.2	.856	908
27	Keans, Bos	1757	674-781	26.7	.863	907
28t	M Gosselin, Qbc	1726	682-793	27.6	.860	906
28t	P Riggin, Was-Bos	2641	954-1104	25.1†	.864	906
30	*Chevrier, NJ	1862	808-951	30.6	.850	901
31	B Hayward, Wpg	2721	1151-1368	30.2	.841‡	892

(534–1599 minutes played)

GOALER, TEAM	MINS	SAVES-SHOTS	SH/GP	SVPCT	PERSEV
*D'Amour, Clg	560	278-310	33.2	.897	952
Hanlon, NYR	1170	543-608	31.2	.893	945
*Casey, Min	1402	696-787	33.7	.884	941
Soetaert, Mtr	1215	476-532	26.3	.895	939
*We Young, Van	1023	476-535	31.4	.886	938
*D Jensen, Phi	1436	665-753	31.5	.883	936
J Cloutier, Buf	872	377-426	29.3	.885	934
Wregget, Tor	1566	785-898	34.4	.874	932
*Vernon, Clg	921	365-417	27.2	.875	921
R Melanson, Min-LA	1571	710-821	31.4	.865	917
Bernhardt, Tor	1266	620-727	34.4	.853	910
Weeks, Har	1544	622-721	28.0	.863	909
Micalef, Det	565	290-342	36.3	.848	908
Eliot, LA	1481	677-798	32.3	.848	902
*M LaForest, Det	1383	623-737	32.0	.845	899
Penney, Mtr	990	375-447	27.1	.839	884
*Billington, NJ	902	405-482	32.1	.840	894
Mio, Det	788	370-453	34.5	.817	874

(1–533 minutes played)

GOALER, TEAM	MINS	SAVES-SHOTS	SH/GP	SVPCT	PERSEV
*R Mason, Was	16	5-5	18.8	1.000	1031
*Takko, Min	60	30-33	33.0	.909	964
*Ranford, Bos	240	96-106	26.5	.906	950
*S St. Laurent, NJ	188	98-111	35.4	.883	942
Skorodenski, Chi	60	39-45	45.0	.867	942
*Puppa, Buf	401	163-184	27.5	.886	932
*Kleisinger, NYR	191	95-109	34.2	.872	929
Lindbergh, Phi	480	176-199	24.9	.884	926
Sevigny, Qbc	468	209-242	31.0	.864	915
*Healy, LA	51	29-35	41.2	.829	897
Caprice, Van	308	127-155	30.2	.819	897
*D May, StL	184	73-86	28.0	.849	896
Herron, Pit	180	76-90	30.0	.844	894
*Daskalakis, Bos	120	53-63	31.5	.841	894
*K McLean, NJ	111	48-59	31.9	.814	867
Behrend, Wpg	422	178-219	31.1	.813	865
*R Scott, NYR	156	45-56	21.5	.804	839
*Pusey, Det	40	9-12	18.0	.750	780
Bester, Tor	20	3-5	15.0	.600	625
All goalers	101866	45480-52036	30.7	.874	925

1986–87

This season's newfound emphasis on conscientious defensive play works its magic on the goalkeeping stats as well. Over the previous four years, NHL goalers faced an average of about 30.3 shots per game, but this year they saw (or didn't see) only 29.6 shots. The tightened defences made the goalies' jobs a little easier, and they responded by registering a composite save percentage of .880, a considerable improvement over the previous four years' average of .874. These factors combined to drop GAAs around the league. Meanwhile, perseverance ratings soared by more than four points, from a four-year average of 925 to this season's 929. The worst rating for a regular, Billy Smith's 36th-place 913, would've been good enough for 22nd place in '85–86 and 26th or 27th place in each of the two seasons prior to that. The last-place goalies in prior seasons were always in the 890s. It's an encouraging sign: after the overproliferation of teams in the NHL-WHA war years and the chaos of the Age of Air Hockey that followed, the talent pool is at last deepening – in short, the game in general, after several sloppy, watered-down years, is finally on the upswing.

All season long, several commentators insisted that Ron Hextall, once everyone in the league had seen him once, would screw up in the Flyer nets. He never did, replying instead with the best rookie goaling performance since Grant Fuhr's in '81–82, though he lost out in the Calder Trophy voting to Luc Robitaille. But Hextall deservedly won the Vezina this season and was voted to the first All-Star team, a portent of many fine, if dangerously stick-swinging, seasons to come. His excellent performance here meant that GM Bobby "Bob" Clarke could indulge his inexplicable dislike of Bob Froese by trading him to the Rangers. Detroit lucked out by picking up Glen Hanlon, and he was an enormous help as the Wings adopted a close-checking belief system that spurred their huge improvement this year. The Wings shaved an incredible 141 goals off their goals-against and thus boosted their winning percentage from .250 to .488. Detroit had been awful for all but one or two of the previous 15 seasons, but this year they changed for good. The Red Wings have been strong ever since, and Hanlon was the man who got it all started. Elsewhere, Bob Sauve thrives in the busy crease at Chicago, and Allan Bester makes a triumphant return to the Leaf igloo, albeit in a back-up role. Kelly Hrudey and the aging Smith had a bad year on Long Island, even as Grant Fuhr and Andy Moog had a mediocre year in Edmonton, but at least Hrudey and Fuhr would atone with marvellous performances in the playoffs. It was Hrudey, you may remember – or maybe not, because it was so long ago – who held the fort during the Easter Epic, stopping 73 out of 75 shots as the Islanders outlasted the Capitals in a seven-period seventh game.

	GOALER, TEAM	MINS	SAVES-SHOTS	SH/GP	SVPCT	PERSEV
7t	*Takko, Min	2075	938-1057	30.6	.887	938
7t	Froese, Phi-NYR	1654	771-871	31.6	.885	938
9	B Hayward, Mtr	2178	855-957	26.4†	.893	937
10	Pa Roy, Mtr	2686	1073-1204	26.9	.891	936
11	Vernon, Clg	2957	1348-1526	31.0	.883	935
12t	Beaupre, Min	2622	1261-1435	32.8	.879	933
12t	R Melanson, LA	2734	1249-1417	31.1	.881	933
12t	Vanbiesbrouck, NYR	2656	1202-1363	30.8	.882	933
12t	Malarchuk, Qbc	3092	1336-1511	29.3	.884	933
12t	Wamsley, StL	2410	1068-1210	30.1	.883	933
12t	Re Lemelin, Clg	1735	727-821	28.4	.886	933
12t	M Gosselin, Qbc	1625	669-755	27.9	.886	933
19t	Liut, Har	3476	1435-1622	28.0	.885	931
19t	*Berthiaume, Wpg	1758	716-809	27.6	.885	931
19t	Peeters, Was	2002	821-928	27.8	.885	931
19t	Moog, Edm	2461	1072-1216	29.6	.882	931
23	Chevrier, NJ	3153	1563-1790	34.1‡	.873	930
24	Fuhr, Edm	2388	1011-1148	28.8	.881	929
25t	G Meloche, Pit	2343	986-1120	28.7	.880	928
25t	Keans, Bos	1942	800-908	28.1	.881	928
25t	M Bannerman, Chi	2059	978-1120	32.6	.873	928
28t	Wregget, Tor	3026	1395-1595	31.6	.875	927
28t	Hrudey, NYI	2634	1073-1218	27.7	.881	927
28t	*Reddick, Wpg	2762	1105-1254	27.2	.881	927
31t	Barrasso, Buf	2501	1046-1198	28.7	.873	921
31t	G Stefan, Det	2351	943-1078	27.5	.875	921
33	G Millen, StL	2482	1003-1149	27.8	.873	919
34	R Brodeur, Van	2972	1210-1388	28.0	.872	918
35	J Cloutier, Buf	2167	897-1034	28.6	.868‡	915
36	Wm Smith, NYI	2252	872-1004	26.7	.869	913

(534–1599 minutes played)

GOALER, TEAM	MINS	SAVES-SHOTS	SH/GP	SVPCT	PERSEV
Resch, Phi	867	393-435	30.1	.903	954
P Riggin, Bos-Pit	1501	617-701	28.0	.880	927
Romano, Pit-Bos	1498	653-746	29.9	.875	925
Weeks, Har	1367	535-613	26.9	.873	918
Caprice, Van	1390	552-641	27.7	.861	907
Eliot, LA	1404	584-687	29.4	.850	899
Soetaert, NYR	675	309-367	32.6	.842	896
*Billington, NJ	1114	480-569	30.6	.844	895
A Jensen, Was-LA	628	282-336	32.1	.839	893

(1–533 minutes played)

GOALER, TEAM	MINS	SAVES-SHOTS	SH/GP	SVPCT	PERSEV
Skorodenski, Chi	155	83-90	34.8	.922	980
*M Sands, Min	163	91-103	37.9	.883	948
M LaForest, Det	219	99-111	30.4	.892	943
*Terreri, NJ	286	151-172	36.1	.878	939
*S St. Laurent, Det	342	119-135	23.7	.881	921
*Dadswell, Clg	125	62-72	34.6	.861	919

1986–87
(minimum 1600 minutes played)

	GOALER, TEAM	MINS	SAVES-SHOTS	SH/GP	SVPCT	PERSEV
1	*R Hextall, Phi	3799	1739-1929	30.5	.902†	952
2	R Sauve, Chi	2660	1338-1497	33.8	.894	950
3t	Bester, Tor	1808	878-988	32.8	.889	943
3t	Hanlon, Det	1963	869-973	29.7	.893	943
5	*Ranford, Bos	2234	1012-1136	30.5	.891	942
6	*R Mason, Was	2536	1107-1244	29.4	.890	939

GOALER, TEAM	MINS	SAVES-SHOTS	SH/GP	SVPCT	PERSEV
*Daskalakis, Bos	97	44–51	31.5	.863	915
*R Scott, NYR	65	30–35	32.3	.857	911
*K McLean, NJ	160	62–72	27.0	.861	906
Janecyk, LA	420	188–222	31.7	.847	900
*We Young, Van	420	187–222	31.7	.842	895
*Guenette, Pit	113	44–52	27.6	.846	892
*Puppa, Buf	185	66–79	25.6	.835	878
*K Friesen, NJ	130	64–80	36.9	.800	862
*T Gamble, Van	60	18–22	22.0	.818	855
Penney, Wpg	327	108–133	24.4	.812	853
Sevigny, Qbc	144	45–56	23.3	.804	842
Bernhardt, Tor	20	4–7	21.0	.571	606
All goalers	102028	44236–50282	29.6	.880	929

1987–88

Every so often someone comes out on top in one of our statistical studies that makes us wonder whether we flunked sixth-grade math. This is one of those times. Look below and see who was the year's best goalie according to the perseverance index. That's right: Darren Pang. *Rookie* Darren Pang. We got this answer years ago, in fact, at the end of the '88 season, long before Panger became a likable, somewhat elfin colour commentator for ESPN. At the time, we thought we'd found the next Fuhr, the next Hextall – a young goalie who entered the league ready not only to start, but also to take his rightful place immediately among the best in pads. And though he did not win the Vezina or the Calder, he was chosen as the goaler on the NHL all-rookie team, a modest honour, but a sign of recognition nonetheless. Yet Pang never got much more of a chance to show his stuff: he played one more season with the Hawks, then his knee gave out and he had to hang up the waffle pad. His pro career wound up lasting just six years, but who knows how good he might've been had he stayed healthy? It would have been great, at the very least, to see such a little guy – Pang was 5'5", 155 pounds – do well while everyone else was touting the virtue of big, Dryden/Burke-size goalies. But this year, anyway, he had a terrific season. Hail, Panger.

Not to gainsay Pang's achievement, but this year's goaltending field is particularly weak; his winning perseverance mark of 950 is the second-lowest ever to take season honours, behind Pelle Lindbergh's 949 in '85. And yet . . . shame on us. We're certain that if this group of goalies was given the same equipment as today's goalies, and if they were put in the nets behind teams that emphasized backchecking and trapping like today's do, they'd be recording .920 save percentages and perseverances of 975, easy. And by the same token, give today's goalers '80s equipment and make them play behind casual defences, and we'd bet their save percentages and perseverances would plummet. Take Patrick Roy, who finished fourth here with a .900 save rate

and a 948 perseverance. In 2000, he finished with a .914 save percentage and a 958 perseverance – which was good for only 13th place. So there you go, and we beg Pang's pardon.

Along with Roy, Kelly Hrudey and Tom Barrasso are more famous names vainly nipping at Pang's heels. Barrasso is really coming into his own, but Buffalo fans are extremely frustrated with Scotty Bowman's regime at Memorial Auditorium. Under his direction the Sabres are bereft of personality, plummeting in the standings, and missing the playoffs consistently, something the team has not done since its earliest seasons a decade and a half before. The boos rain down fast and thick from the Aud's steeply pitched upper deck, and pretty soon the whole building resounds every night to the sound of the fans' disgust. Some of it is aimed at Barrasso, and the reclusive and short-tempered goalie reacts one night following a loss to Hartford by giving the crowd the finger. In a sense, he catches the bullet that Sabre fans were aiming at Bowman, but the rupture was complete. Early the next season, he was traded to Pittsburgh, where he would prosper as he never did in Buffalo.

Also here: up-one-year-down-the-next Pete Peeters, the consistently underrated Glen Hanlon and Allan Bester, a reanimated Billy Smith, and way down there in 20th place among 31 starters, Grant Fuhr, who this year became the first goaler ever to play more than 4,200 minutes. Despite his modest averages, Fuhr won the Vezina this season. He'd played a lot and "won" 40 games, although you'd think Gretzky, Kurri, Messier, and company maybe had a little to do with that, and so was voted the award. The voters were vindicated somewhat in the playoffs, however, as Fuhr helped the Oil to their fourth Cup in five years. Finally, look who's on the bottom of the starters' list: Rollie Melanson, now of the Kings. Alas, how the mighty have fallen.

1987–88 (minimum 1600 minutes played)						
	GOALER, TEAM	MINS	SAVES-SHOTS	SH/GP	SVPCT	PERSEV
1	*Pang, Chi	2548	1334–1497	35.3‡	.891	950
2	Hrudey, NYI	2751	1314–1467	32.0	.896	949
3t	Barrasso, Buf	3133	1484–1657	31.7	.896	948
3t	Pa Roy, Mtr	2586	1123–1248	29.0	.900†	948
5	G Stefan, Det	1854	824–920	29.8	.896	945
6t	Peeters, Was	1896	775–863	27.3	.898	944
6t	Wm Smith, NYI	2107	948–1061	30.2	.894	944
8	B Hayward, Mtr	2247	924–1031	27.5	.896	942
9	Vanbiesbrouck, NYR	3319	1510–1697	30.7	.890	941
10t	R Mason, Chi	2312	1192–1352	35.1	.882	940
10t	Hanlon, Det	2623	1147–1288	29.5	.891	940
12	Bester, Tor	1607	776–878	32.8	.884	938
13	Wamsley, StL–Clg	1891	846–954	30.3	.887	937
14	R Hextall, Phi	3560	1608–1816	30.6	.885	936
15	Re Lemelin, Bos	2828	1104–1242	26.4†	.889	933
16t	Berthiaume, Wpg	3010	1313–1489	29.7	.882	931

Goaltending

GOALER, TEAM	MINS	SAVES-SHOTS	SH/GP	SVPCT	PERSEV
16t Malarchuk, Was	2926	1184-1338	27.4	.885	931
18 Liut, Har	3532	1430-1617	27.5	.884	930
19t G Millen, StL	2854	1228-1395	29.3	.880	929
19t Fuhr, Edm	4304	1815-2061	28.7	.881	929
21t Wregget, Tor	3000	1487-1709	34.2	.870	927
21t Beaupre, Min	2288	1095-1256	32.9	.872	927
23t Vernon, Clg	3565	1498-1708	28.7	.877	925
23t Keans, Bos	1660	658-748	27.0	.880	925
25 *K McLean, Van	2380	1027-1174	29.6	.875	924
26 Takko, Min	1919	925-1068	33.4	.866	922
27 *Healy, LA	1869	867-1002	32.2	.865	919
28 R Sauve, NJ	1803	714-821	27.3	.870	915
29t Chevrier, NJ	2354	965-1113	28.4	.867	914
29t M Gosselin, Qbc	3002	1230-1419	28.4	.867	914
31 R Melanson, LA	2676	1202-1397	31.3	.860‡	913

(534–1599 minutes played)

GOALER, TEAM	MINS	SAVES-SHOTS	SH/GP	SVPCT	PERSEV
*Guenette, Pit	1092	521-582	32.0	.895	948
Casey, Min	663	306-347	31.4	.882	934
*S Burke, NJ	689	265-300	26.1	.883	927
*Brunetta, Qbc	1550	680-776	30.0	.876	926
Froese, NYR	1443	610-695	28.9	.878	926
*Puppa, Buf	874	408-469	32.2	.870	924
M LaForest, Phi	972	416-476	29.4	.874	923
G Meloche, Pit	1394	625-720	31.0	.868	920
P Riggin, Pit	1169	503-579	29.7	.869	918
Weeks, Har-Van	1468	586-672	27.5	.872	918
R Brodeur, Van-Har	1010	424-488	29.0	.869	917
*Pietrangelo, Pit	1207	519-599	29.8	.866	916
Caprice, Van	1250	539-626	30.0	.861	911
*Dadswell, Clg	1221	539-628	30.9	.858	910
Reddick, Wpg	1487	609-711	28.7	.857	904
J Cloutier, Buf	851	380-447	31.5	.850	903

(1–533 minutes played)

GOALER, TEAM	MINS	SAVES-SHOTS	SH/GP	SVPCT	PERSEV
Moog, Bos	360	163-180	30.0	.906	956
*A Raymond, Was	40	18-20	30.0	.900	950
Ranford, Edm	325	143-159	29.4	.899	948
*S St. Laurent, Det	294	132-148	30.2	.892	942
*Reaugh, Edm	176	100-114	38.9	.877	942
*Reese, Tor	249	111-128	30.8	.867	919
*Tugnutt, Qbc	284	107-123	26.0	.870	913
Janecyk, LA	303	142-165	32.7	.861	913
We Young, Phi	320	128-148	27.8	.865	911
R Scott, NYR	90	35-41	27.3	.854	899
Eliot, Det	97	47-56	34.6	.839	897
*Sidorkiewicz, Har	60	30-36	36.0	.833	893
*D May, StL	180	88-106	35.3	.830	889
Penney, Wpg	385	156-186	29.0	.839	887

GOALER, TEAM	MINS	SAVES-SHOTS	SH/GP	SVPCT	PERSEV
Riendeau, Mtr	36	17-22	36.7	.773	834
Skorodenski, Edm	61	18-25	24.6	.720	761
All goalers	102004	44901-51055	30.0	.879	930

1988–89

You'll definitely be surprised at the winner of the '88–89 perseverance race – Kari Takko. Never in a million years would anyone guess his name for this distinction, but here he is, helped no doubt by his having played just barely enough minutes to qualify as a regular goalie. Thus the Finnish North Star becomes the second European to cop the perseverance crown. The Uusikaupunki native had been a young star with Assat Pori in the Finnish league, then moved over to the North Stars for a six-year stint, plus another season with Edmonton. Then he went back home for six more years with Assat Pori, closing out his career in '97–98 with the Swedish club HV71 Jonkoping. Why can't our teams have names like that? Much better than the Minnesota "Wild."

Takko is our number one goaler of the year (rules are rules), but the more legitimate man for the title is Patrick Roy. He logs a huge .908 save percentage behind a rock-steady Canadiens defence that features rookie stud Eric Desjardins, and sure enough the Habs get to the Final. They come up against Calgary again, but this time the Flames will win, so let's look for their goaler on this list. We don't have to look far at all, because there he is, Mike Vernon, in sixth place. It's worth noting that the Flames and Canadiens wound up the regular season 1-2 in shots allowed per game; Calgary finished first, so it's fitting that they won the Cup. Even the post-season accolades involved this pair: Roy was the first-team All-Star, Vernon the second-teamer; Roy won the Vezina, Vernon was the runner-up.

With Vernon this year it was feast; in other years it's famine. Few goalies can look so terrific for several months in a row then look so inept for the next several months in a row, then look terrific again, and so on. Follow his progress over the years in these lists and you'll see the hills and valleys, as starkly evident as fans' playoff memories of his great performances and his daffy spells of whiffing on easy stick saves, allowing rink-length sliders to go through him and strike the ironwork, and making expansion-team pluggers look like the second coming of Cyclone Taylor.

The thing about Roy that we're reminded of here is how his success has had a double-edged effect on young French Canadians. His skill and charisma and quirkiness inspired many young Quebecois to take up the chest protector and make like Patrick, talking to the goalposts and popping their heads like the *tiqueur* in *bleu, blanc, et rouge*. The other, more insidious effect, especially after Martin Brodeur took the Devils' starting job in '93–94, was how Anglophone GMs

Goaltending

121

and journalists came to stereotype French Canadians as goaltenders, and mainly as goaltenders. It used to be that those Anglos stereotyped the Quebecois as fast, stylish, naturally talented skaters and scoring demons, great on offence but lacking the Protestant work ethic to be tough, gritty, and dependable in their own end like a good Ontario lad or those Western farmboys. Nonsense, of course, but that was the way people thought – a weird parallel to the prevailing opinion in the United States, where execs and journos fostered the racist idea that black players are innately gifted but lack the necessary discipline and smarts, which white players have, when the going gets tough. In both Canada and the United States, the notion of the majority, that the minority may be more talented but not as sharp or nose-to-the-grindstone as we are, seemed to recede in the '80s and into the '90s – but not entirely. With the success of Roy, it became okay for a lot of English-speakers to find a new pigeonhole for French-speaking players. Thus on draft days, anyone with a wide stick and a silent consonant in his name was snapped up in a hurry, and the number of French-Canadian forwards and defencemen dropped like a stone. Take a look at the perseverance lists around 2000 and you'll see it: French everywhere. What you don't see anymore is a whole lot of French on the roster of skaters. *Calice de tabernacle.*

Among the others, we hate to keep beating this drum, but there's Allan Bester, up high again. Jon Casey finally gets a regular job in Minnesota and does well. The same holds true for Daren Puppa, who finally gets a regular job in Buffalo and looks good as one of Barrasso's replacements. Mike Liut had a couple of very good seasons in his career, but we gotta say it, most of the time he was mediocre. This year he's downright bad. And Billy Smith's career ends here, not with a bang, but with a whimper.

Finally, look midway down the regulars' list, where you'll find Clint Malarchuk. He had just joined the Sabres from the Capitals and was goaling against St. Louis at the Aud. Blues forward Steve Tuttle came barrelling in through the slot when Buffalo defenceman Uwe Krupp grabbed him up high. Tuttle fell, his skate rose and sliced across the side of Malarchuk's neck, severing his jugular vein. Malarchuk's blood gushed out as if from a fountain, the ice pooling crimson, easily one of the most horrifying things ever seen at a hockey game. Fortunately, Malarchuk was at the end of the rink nearest the infirmary, and within less than a minute he was helped off, a towel held against his neck, the towel and his sweater drenched scarlet, as the stunned and silent crowd looked helplessly on. He was rushed to hospital, and his life was saved. The doctors who attended him later said that had Malarchuk been standing at the other end of the rink when the accident happened, 200 feet from the Zamboni doors instead of 10, he would have died. Meeting with reporters at the hospital the next day, Malarchuk said, "When I saw the blood, I flipped my mask off. It was incredible. As my heart would beat, it would squirt. I thought I was dying then." Two nights later, dressed in street clothes and his neck swathed in bandages, Malarchuk returned to the Aud. The applause from a prolonged ovation cascaded down to where he stood, as once again the rink attendants opened the Zamboni doors for him.

1988–89
(minimum 1600 minutes played)

	GOALER, TEAM	MINS	SAVES-SHOTS	SH/GP	SVPCT	PERSEV
1	Takko, Min	1603	824-917	34.3	.899	956
2	Pa Roy, Mtr	2744	1113-1226	26.8	.908†	953
3	Casey, Min	2961	1355-1506	30.5	.900	951
4	Bester, Tor	2460	1259-1415	34.5	.890	947
5	R Hextall, Phi	3756	1653-1855	29.6	.891	941
6	Vernon, Clg	2938	1133-1263	25.8	.897	940
7	Puppa, Buf	1908	853-960	30.2	.889	939
8t	Barrasso, Buf-Pit	2951	1518-1725	35.1‡	.880	938
8t	Weeks, Van	2056	844-946	27.6	.892	938
8t	K McLean, Van	2477	1039-1166	28.2	.891	938
11	*Sidorkiewicz, Har	2635	1073-1206	27.5	.890	935
12t	Vanbiesbrouck, NYR	3207	1465-1662	31.1	.881	933
12t	Hrudey, NYI-LA	3774	1711-1941	30.9	.882	933
14	Hanlon, Det	2092	928-1052	30.2	.882	932
15t	Peeters, Was	1854	702-790	25.6	.889	931
15t	Re Lemelin, Bos	2392	938-1058	26.5	.887	931
17	B Hayward, Mtr	2091	791-892	25.6	.887	929
18	Healy, LA	2699	1315-1507	33.5	.873	928
19t	Malarchuk, Was-Buf	2754	1132-1286	28.0	.880	927
19t	Fuhr, Edm	3341	1497-1710	30.7	.875	927
21t	Reddick, Wpg	2109	985-1129	32.1	.872	926
21t	G Millen, StL	3019	1238-1408	28.0	.879	926
23t	Pang, Chi	1644	794-914	33.4	.869	924
23t	*S Burke, NJ	3590	1586-1816	30.4	.873	924
25t	J Cloutier, Buf	1786	748-856	28.8	.874	922
25t	Wamsley, Clg	1927	700-795	24.8†	.881	922
25t	G Stefan, Det	2499	1119-1286	30.9	.870	922
26	M Gosselin, Qbc	2064	959-1105	32.1	.868	921
27	Moog, Bos	2482	946-1079	26.1	.877	920
28	Froese, NYR	1621	685-787	29.1	.870	919
29	Wregget, Tor-Phi	2018	957-1109	33.0	.863	918
30	Chevrier, Wpg-Chi	2665	1120-1290	29.0	.868	917
31	*Riendeau, StL	1842	724-832	27.1	.870	915
32	Liut, Har	2006	884-1026	30.7	.862‡	913

(534–1599 minutes played)

GOALER, TEAM	MINS	SAVES-SHOTS	SH/GP	SVPCT	PERSEV
*Pietrangelo, Pit	669	363-408	36.6	.890	951
*Tugnutt, Qbc	1367	673-755	33.1	.891	947
Beaupre, Min-Was	637	262-293	27.6	.894	940
*M Fitzpatrick, LA-NYI	1584	769-874	33.1	.880	935

GOALER, TEAM	MINS	SAVES-SHOTS	SH/GP	SVPCT	PERSEV
*Essensa, Wpg	1102	504-572	31.1	.881	933
*Hackett, NYI	662	290-329	29.8	.881	931
*Belfour, Chi	1148	530-604	31.6	.877	930
Ranford, Edm	1509	629-717	28.5	.877	925
M LaForest, Phi	933	433-497	32.0	.871	924
We Young, Pit	1150	581-673	35.1	.863	922
*Guenette, Pit	574	267-308	32.2	.867	921
R Mason, Qbc	1168	534-626	32.2	.853	907
Wm Smith, NYI	730	308-362	29.9	.852	902
R Sauve, NJ	720	275-331	27.6	.831	877

(1-533 minutes played)

GOALER, TEAM	MINS	SAVES-SHOTS	SH/GP	SVPCT	PERSEV
*D'Amour, Phi	19	13-13	44.2	1.000	1074
*Exelby, Mtr	3	1-1	20.0	1.000	1033
Janecyk, LA	30	20-22	44.0	.909	982
S St. Laurent, Det	141	82-91	38.7	.901	966
*T Gamble, Van	302	126-138	27.4	.913	959
*Whitmore, Har	180	86-96	32.0	.896	949
*Cheveldae, Det	122	65-74	36.4	.878	939
*Terreri, NJ	402	151-169	25.2	.893	936
Reese, Tor	486	245-285	35.2	.860	918
Eliot, Buf	67	36-43	38.5	.837	901
*Myllys, Min	238	116-138	34.8	.841	899
Brunetta, Qbc	226	97-116	30.8	.836	888
R Melanson, LA	178	90-109	36.7	.826	887
Berthiaume, Wpg	443	209-253	34.3	.826	883
*Waite, Chi	494	208-251	30.5	.829	879
Billington, NJ	140	55-65	27.9	.831	877
*T Draper, Wpg	120	54-66	33.0	.818	873
*Tabaracci, Pit	33	17-21	38.2	.810	873
*Wakaluk, Buf	214	74-89	25.0	.831	873
*Clifford, Chi	4	0-0	0.00	–	–
All goalers	101580	44744-50898	30.1	.879	929

1989–90

This is the year Edmonton arises from the ashes of Wayne Gretzky's departure to win the Stanley Cup. Mark Messier leads the way, making his name for all time as one of the most indomitable players ever to lace up a pair of skates. But Grant Fuhr wasn't in goal for the Oil when they lifted the Storied Silverware a fifth time at Northlands; he had suffered through a trying season that featured an appendectomy and surgical reconstruction of his shoulder, which he wound up reinjuring anyway. Bill Ranford came in to tend goal and did all right in the regular season (and very well in the playoffs, but that's not the story here). With Fuhr down and Patrick Roy very much up again, it's probably fair to say that this season marks the passing of the torch from Fuhr to Roy. Statistically, Fuhr may not have been the best goalie around, but certainly he was the best in the popular

mind, and for good reason: he kept the Oilers in games while everyone else on the team ran around the other end in a frenzy of goal hunger, and he was the number one goaler for Team Canada. But young Roy, with his one Cup, two trips to the Final, and, this year, his second-straight Vezina, becomes The Man. His .912 save percentage is gargantuan, especially in a year in which the league average stands at .881. He richly deserved the Vezina and the first team All-Star selection, and he got them both this year.

Who is that in second place? Mark Fitzpatrick?! We will encounter him again in the future, but here he is a healthy, promising sophomore in his first full season on the Island. In third place we find Daren Puppa, the oddly named but very promising Kirkland Lake, Ontario, native. Towering over the crossbar at 6'4", Puppa has exactly what GMs like: size. And while he uses it very well, and never better than this year, he will run into a string of injuries that will hamper his career for the next decade. This '89–90 season happens to be one of only two or three in which he stays healthy the entire campaign, and he finishes second to Roy in both the Vezina and post-season All-Star voting.

Elsewhere, Mike Liut goes to Washington and revives. Glenn Healy proves that even Billy Joel could play goal for the Islanders and win. Mike Vernon takes a voyage to the bottom of the perseverance sea. And just how long did Rejean Lemelin guard the nets for Boston? Was it, like, 27 years or something? We're glad to see Clint Malarchuk rebounding from his grievous injury of the previous season. He fell just four minutes short of qualifying as a regular. If Malarchuk had played those four extra minutes, his perseverance mark of 960 would have tied him with Roy for top honours.

Finally, we note here that the NHL made a little-noticed rule change prior to the start of this season: goalies were allowed to use leg pads 12 inches in width, up from 10 inches. The effect of that rule change was not felt this season, but starting next year, save percentages will go up and up. This rule change also touches off an arms race of sorts, as leg pads, catching gloves, blockers, shoulder pads, and even the sweaters themselves all get bigger and start having stiff little pieces sticking out all over the place. None of it is prohibited by the rule book, but the NHL, slow to act as always, does nothing to stem the tide of wider and wider goaling gear. At first, it's a relief for fans to see goalies making saves again, even getting some shutouts, too. But will the balance of power stabilize, or will it tip dangerously to one side? We shall see....

1989–90
(minimum 1600 minutes played)

	GOALER, TEAM	MINS	SAVES-SHOTS	SH/GP	SVPCT	PERSEV
1	Pa Roy, Mtr	3173	1388-1522	28.8	.912†	960
2t	M Fitzpatrick, NYI	2653	1318-1468	33.2	.898	953

GOALER, TEAM	MINS	SAVES-SHOTS	SH/GP	SVPCT	PERSEV
2t Puppa, Buf	3241	1452-1608	29.8	.903	953
4 Liut, Har-Was	2161	865-956	26.5	.905	949
5 Healy, NYI	2197	1076-1204	32.9	.894	948
6 Casey, Min	3407	1569-1752	30.9	.896	947
7 Wregget, Phi	2961	1388-1557	31.6	.891	944
8 Terreri, NJ	1931	891-1001	31.1	.891	943
9t *Essensa, Wpg	2035	876-983	29.0	.891	939
9t Moog, Bos	2536	1023-1145	27.1	.893	939
11 Beaupre, Was	2793	1209-1359	29.2	.890	938
12 Vanbiesbrouck, NYR	2734	1207-1361	29.9	.887	937
13t Re Lemelin, Bos	2310	892-1000	26.0	.892	935
13t *Cheveldae, Det	1600	752-853	32.0	.882	935
15 Ranford, Edm	3107	1293-1458	28.2	.887	934
16 Riendeau, StL	2551	1120-1269	29.8	.883	932
17 Bester, Tor	2206	1127-1292	35.1‡	.872	931
18 S Burke, NJ	2914	1278-1453	29.9	.880	929
19 K McLean, Van	3739	1581-1797	28.8	.880	928
20 We Young, Pit	2318	1102-1263	32.7	.873	927
21 Hrudey, LA	2860	1331-1525	32.0	.873	926
22 B Hayward, Mtr	1674	675-769	27.6	.878	924
23t G Millen, StL-Qbc-Chi	2900	1277-1465	30.3	.872	922
23t J Cloutier, Chi	2178	817-929	25.6	.879	922
25 Wamsley, Clg	1969	746-853	26.0	.875	918
26t Hanlon, Det	2290	1002-1156	30.3	.867	917
26t Berthiaume, Wpg-Min	1627	669-769	28.4	.870	917
28 Tugnutt, Qbc	1978	924-1076	32.6	.859	913
29t Sidorkiewicz, Har	2703	1038-1199	26.6	.866	910
29t Vernon, Clg	2795	974-1120	24.0†	.870	910
31 Chevrier, Chi-Pit	2060	840-986	28.7	.852‡	900

(534-1599 minutes played)

GOALER, TEAM	MINS	SAVES-SHOTS	SH/GP	SVPCT	PERSEV
Malarchuk, Buf	1596	824-913	34.3	.903	960
*M Richter, NYR	1320	620-686	31.2	.904	956
*Beauregard, Wpg	1079	507-566	31.5	.896	948
M LaForest, Tor	1343	676-763	34.1	.886	943
*Cu Joseph, StL	852	387-435	30.6	.890	941
Reddick, Edm	604	250-281	27.9	.890	936
S St. Laurent, Det	607	285-323	31.9	.882	936
Peeters, Phi	1140	529-601	31.6	.880	933
*Reese, Tor	1101	549-630	34.3	.871	929
Weeks, Van	1142	540-619	32.5	.872	927
*Hrivnak, Was	609	255-291	28.7	.876	924
*R Scott, LA	654	279-319	29.3	.875	923
Barrasso, Pit	1294	645-746	34.6	.865	922
R Mason, Was	822	337-385	28.1	.875	922
Pietrangelo, Pit	1066	503-580	32.6	.867	922
Fuhr, Edm	1081	462-532	29.5	.868	918
*S Gordon, Qbc	597	314-367	36.9	.856	917
Froese, NYR	812	309-354	26.2	.873	916

GOALER, TEAM	MINS	SAVES-SHOTS	SH/GP	SVPCT	PERSEV
*Mylnikov, Qbc	568	282-329	34.8	.857	915
M Gosselin, LA	1226	504-583	28.5	.864	912
Takko, Min	1012	410-478	28.3	.858	905

(1-533 minutes played)

GOALER, TEAM	MINS	SAVES-SHOTS	SH/GP	SVPCT	PERSEV
*Tanner, Qbc	60	27-30	30.0	.900	950
*Hoffort, Phi	329	140-159	29.0	.881	929
Brunetta, Qbc	191	86-99	31.1	.869	921
R Hextall, Phi	419	190-219	31.4	.868	920
*Whitmore, Har	442	157-183	24.8	.858	899
*Waite, Chi	183	78-92	30.2	.848	898
*Ing, Tor	182	88-106	34.9	.830	888
*Fiset, Qbc	342	164-198	34.7	.828	886
Guenette, Clg	119	42-50	25.2	.840	882
G Stefan, Det	359	123-147	24.6	.837	878
*Exelby, Edm	60	24-29	29.0	.828	876
*Jablonski, StL	208	81-98	28.2	.827	874
*T Draper, Wpg	359	126-152	25.4	.829	871
*Kolzig, Was	120	51-63	31.5	.810	862
*Myllys, Min	156	66-82	31.5	.805	857
*Greenlay, Edm	20	13-17	51.0	.765	850
*Stauber, LA	83	32-43	31.1	.744	796
*Racicot, Mtr	13	3-6	27.7	.500	546
All goalers	101771	44658-50702	29.9	.881	931

1990–91

This year's list is headed by the most prestigious group of goalies we've seen in a long time. The top seven are indisputably prominent (we're counting Bob Essensa as prominent because he was on his way to making a big name for himself, as well as the huge contract that became his albatross when he came a cropper in subsequent years). We're starting to feel *good* about goalies again, a hopeful sign that a proper balance between offence and defence is being restored.

But we must not slight Mike Richter by passing over him here. He wins the perseverance title in only his second full season (he had a strong 956 in 1,320 minutes the previous year) and starts the process by which he will team with John Vanbiesbrouck to form the best goalie tandem of the '90s and eventually take over as the Rangers' number one, even to the point of overtaking the sainted Eddie Giacomin as all-time leader in several team categories. This season he got jobbed out of the Vezina, with Belfour winning it and Roy the runner-up. (By the way, did you know that Richter took classes in political science, literature, and philosophy at Columbia during a couple of off-seasons?) In second, Ed Belfour, here with the Blackhawks, giving a preview of his steady play in the nets at the end of the decade. Fortunately, he's not giving a preview of his unsteady off-ice demeanour, like vomiting all over a police officer while being arrested. But those kinds of things happen in Dallas, not Chicago.

In third place we find our *bon ami* Roy, and in fourth, Tom Barrasso, the Stanley Cup-winning goalie. Can you believe that Barrasso backstopped the Pens to the Auld Goblet while facing 34.4 shots per game, the league high? Only three clubs in the 21-team NHL allowed more goals than Pittsburgh this season, but in complete contravention of hockey precedent, they won on offence, and without defence. Still, it wasn't *all* Lemieux, Jagr, and Francis. Barrasso was holding the fort well in the face of repeated counterattack.

This is Curtis Joseph's first full season – look for big things from him soon. Mike Liut returns to the bottom after a year near the top. Grant Fuhr has to sit out much of the season under suspension because he admitted he had used cocaine. (Thankfully, the NHL's antidrug program is a lot more enlightened now, and you don't get suspended for admitting you have a problem.) And who's that lurking down there among the part-timers at 195 minutes? Some Euro guy for Chicago, name of Dominik Hasek. The Blackhawks media guide says he was the Czechoslovakian League goalie of the year in '86, '87, '88, '89, and '90 and the league MVP, '88 through '90. Big deal. What does that make him, the next Jiri Crha?

1990–91
(minimum 1600 minutes played)

	GOALER, TEAM	MINS	SAVES-SHOTS	SH/GP	SVPCT	PERSEV
1	*M Richter, NYR	2596	1257-1392	32.2	.903	957
2	*Belfour, Chi	4127	1713-1883	27.4	.910†	955
3	Pa Roy, Mtr	2835	1234-1362	28.8	.906	954
4	Barrasso, Pit	2754	1414-1579	34.4	.896	953
5t	*Cu Joseph, StL	1710	785-874	30.7	.898	949
5t	Essensa, Wpg	2916	1343-1496	30.8	.898	949
7	Hrudey, LA	2730	1189-1321	29.0	.900	948
8	Healy, NYI	2999	1391-1557	31.2	.893	945
9t	Tugnutt, Qbc	3144	1639-1851	35.3‡	.886	944
9t	Berthiaume, LA	2119	969-1086	30.8	.892	944
11	Ranford, Edm	3415	1523-1705	30.0	.893	943
12t	Malarchuk, Buf	2131	971-1090	30.7	.891	942
12t	Vanbiesbrouck, NYR	2257	1028-1154	30.7	.891	942
12t	Moog, Bos	2844	1171-1307	27.6	.896	942
15	R Hextall, Phi	2035	876-982	29.0	.892	940
16t	Beaupre, Was	2572	982-1095	25.5†	.897	939
16t	Terreri, NJ	2970	1204-1348	27.2	.893	939
18t	Riendeau, StL	2671	1107-1241	27.9	.892	938
18t	*Ing, Tor	3126	1516-1716	32.9	.883	938
20	Casey, Min	3185	1292-1450	27.3	.891	937
21	Puppa, Buf	2092	911-1029	29.5	.885	935
22	Wamsley, Clg	1670	677-762	27.4	.888	934
23	*T Gamble, Van	2433	1016-1156	28.5	.879	926
24t	Cheveldae, Det	3615	1502-1716	28.5	.875	923
24t	Vernon, Clg	3121	1234-1406	27.0	.878	923
26	S Burke, NJ	1870	763-875	28.1	.872	919
27	K McLean, Van	1969	852-983	30.0	.867	917
28	Sidorkiewicz, Har	2953	1120-1284	26.1	.872	916
29	Re Lemelin, Bos	1829	730-841	27.6	.868	914
30	Liut, Was	1834	672-786	25.7	.855‡	898

(534–1599 minutes played)

GOALER, TEAM	MINS	SAVES-SHOTS	SH/GP	SVPCT	PERSEV
Peeters, Phi	1270	562-623	29.4	.902	951
Fuhr, Edm	778	341-380	29.3	.897	946
Hanlon, Det	862	392-438	30.5	.895	946
*Racicot, Mtr	975	427-479	29.5	.891	941
*Reaugh, Har	1010	426-479	28.5	.889	937
J Cloutier, Chi-Qbc	1232	616-701	34.1	.879	936
Pietrangelo, Pit	1311	628-714	32.7	.880	934
We Young, Pit	773	376-428	33.2	.879	934
B Hayward, Min	1473	597-674	27.5	.886	932
*Tabaracci, Wpg	1093	499-570	31.3	.875	928
*Wakaluk, Buf	630	257-292	27.8	.880	926
Hackett, NYI	1508	650-741	29.5	.877	926
*Beauregard, Wpg	836	368-423	30.4	.870	921
Reese, Tor	1430	603-695	29.2	.868	916
Takko, Min-Edm	648	304-353	32.7	.861	916
Wregget, Phi	1484	572-660	26.7	.867	911
*Whitmore, Har	850	327-379	26.8	.863	907
*JC Bergeron, Mtr	941	367-426	27.2	.862	907

(1–533 minutes played)

GOALER, TEAM	MINS	SAVES-SHOTS	SH/GP	SVPCT	PERSEV
*DelGuidice, Bos	10	7-7	42.0	1.000	1070
*Rhodes, Tor	60	25-26	26.0	.962	1005
Waite, Chi	60	26-28	28.0	.929	975
Fiset, Qbc	186	111-123	39.7	.902	969
*Hasek, Chi	195	85-93	28.6	.914	962
M Fitzpatrick, NYI	120	54-60	30.0	.900	950
*Tanner, Qbc	228	117-133	35.0	.880	938
*Hrivnak, Was	432	200-226	31.4	.885	937
*Jablonski, StL	492	203-228	27.8	.890	937
Myllys, Min	78	49-57	43.8	.860	933
G Millen, Chi	58	28-32	33.1	.875	930
Bester, Tor-Det	425	197-228	32.2	.864	918
Guenette, Clg	60	26-30	30.0	.867	917
*F Chabot, Mtr	108	39-45	25.0	.867	908
*Maneluk, NYI	140	79-94	40.3	.840	908
*Lorenz, NYI	80	31-36	27.0	.861	906
*Hoffort, Phi	39	17-20	30.8	.850	901
R Mason, Van	353	159-188	32.0	.846	899
Reddick, Edm	120	50-59	29.5	.8475	897
*Littman, Buf	36	15-18	30.0	.833	883
*N Foster, Bos	184	68-82	26.7	.829	874
*D Gagnon, Det	35	22-28	48.0	.786	866

GOALER, TEAM	MINS	SAVES-SHOTS	SH/GP	SVPCT	PERSEV
Chevrier, Det	108	44-55	30.6	.800	852
*Rs McKay, Har	35	12-15	25.7	.800	843
*Sc King, Det	45	9-11	14.7	.818	843
Weeks, Van	59	23-29	29.5	.793	842
*S Gordon, Qbc	485	177-225	27.8	.787	833
*McKichan, Van	20	6-8	24.0	.750	790
R Melanson, NJ	20	5-7	21.0	.714	749
All goalers	101897	44277-49973	29.4	.886	935

1991–92

This is a season in which defence reasserts itself. Teams average only 27.7 shots per game, way below the 29.4-to-30.7 range in force over the previous nine years. Seven regular netminders log save percentages above .900, another stark improvement over previous years, when it was a freak of nature if as many as two goalies barely breached the surface of a 90% save rate. Once again it's Patrick Roy spearheading the drive above .900, his .914 mark bettering his own .912 in '89–90 as the best since the NHL started keeping track of such things in '82–83. But Roy is not the best goaler this season – Curtis Joseph is. For while Roy plays behind a strong defence that limits the number and quality of shots taken against him, Joseph does not. He must stand up to a withering fusillade of rock-hard rubber in the St. Louis nets and like it, which apparently he does, for he records a heady .910 save percentage under these miserable conditions. It's a tremendous performance, one of several in Cujo's career, yet this year at least he finishes out of the running in All-Star and Vezina voting. Roy wins both, and finishing second in both is – we don't get this – Kirk McLean. Should have been Joseph and Bob Essensa.

In New York, Vanbiesbrouck responds to the Richter challenge, and their fruitful partnership helps propel the Rangers to first place in the Patrick Division and first overall in the whole league. Well, the arrival on Broadway of Mark Messier had a little something to do with it, too. But get this: the mere fact that they finish atop the six-team Patrick Division, let alone win the President's Trophy, gives them their first regular-season title since – drum roll, please – 1942! That's a 50-year wait.

Also earning kudos here is Mark Fitzpatrick of the Isles. At the start of the '90–91 season he developed eosinophilia-myalgia syndrome, an extremely debilitating and painful blood and muscle disorder, from which only 5% of those afflicted fully recover. The condition left Fitzpatrick severely weakened, and he almost quit hockey a couple of times, but each time he fought his way back. After another relapse in training camp before this campaign, he had a biopsy taken that showed the disease present and unabated. He took a few weeks off to condition himself, returned, and here he is, fifth best in the league.

Jeff Hackett also deserves credit, for his eighth-place finish as the fish in the barrel for the San Jose Sharks. We were skeptical when San Jose got a team, but their fans have turned out to be enthusiastic and loyal, and they've learned a fair bit about the game. But we'll bet they don't know who Julian Klymkiw was. Down among the scrubs we see a star of the future, Martin Brodeur, coming up. And we see the end of the line for Roland Melanson, once a star of the future for the Islanders, but here playing his last NHL games as a fill-in for the Canadiens.

1991–92 (minimum 1600 minutes played)

	GOALER, TEAM	MINS	SAVES-SHOTS	SH/GP	SVPCT	PERSEV
1	Cu Joseph, StL	3494	1778-1953	33.5	.910	966
2	Essensa, Wpg	2627	1281-1407	32.1	.910	964
3	Vanbiesbrouck, NYR	2526	1211-1331	31.6	.910	963
4	Pa Roy, Mtr	3935	1651-1806	27.5	.914†	960
5	M Fitzpatrick, NYI	1743	856-949	32.7	.902	956
6	M Richter, NYR	2298	1086-1205	31.5	.901	954
7	Hrudey, LA	3509	1719-1916	32.8	.897	952
8	Hackett, SJ	2314	1218-1366	35.4‡	.892	951
9	K McLean, Van	3852	1604-1780	27.7	.901	947
10	Malarchuk, Buf	1639	801-903	33.1	.887	942
11t	Belfour, Chi	2928	1109-1241	25.4†	.894	936
11t	Barrasso, Pit	3329	1506-1702	30.7	.885	936
11t	Ranford, Edm	3822	1743-1971	30.9	.884	936
11t	Terreri, NJ	3169	1342-1511	28.6	.888	936
15	Healy, NYI	1960	921-1045	32.0	.881	935
16t	Moog, Bos	3640	1531-1727	28.5	.887	934
16t	Vernon, Clg	3640	1636-1853	30.5	.883	934
18t	Cheveldae, Det	4236	1752-1978	28.0	.886	932
18t	Fuhr, Tor	3774	1703-1933	30.7	.881	932
18t	R Hextall, Phi	2668	1143-1294	29.1	.883	932
21	Puppa, Buf	1757	818-932	31.8	.878	931
22t	Beaupre, Was	3108	1269-1435	27.7	.884	930
22t	Whitmore, Har	2567	1137-1292	30.2	.880	930
22t	Casey, Min	2911	1236-1401	28.9	.882	930
25	Sidorkiewicz, Har	1995	829-940	28.3	.882	929
26	Wakaluk, Min	1905	770-874	27.5	.881	927
27	Tugnutt, Qbc-Edm	1707	739-855	30.1	.864	914
28	Wregget, Phi-Pit	1707	653-759	26.7	.860‡	905

(534–1599 minutes played)

GOALER, TEAM	MINS	SAVES-SHOTS	SH/GP	SVPCT	PERSEV
*G Hebert, StL	738	357-393	32.0	.908	962
*Roussel, Phi	922	397-437	28.4	.908	956
Beauregard, Wpg	1267	550-611	28.9	.900	948
*Fiset, Qbc	1133	572-646	34.2	.890	947
We Young, Pit	838	423-476	34.1	.889	945
*T Draper, Buf	1403	637-712	30.4	.895	945
Weeks, NYI-LA	1284	623-702	32.8	.887	942

GOALER, TEAM	MINS	SAVES-SHOTS	SH/GP	SVPCT	PERSEV
Billington, NJ	1363	568-637	28.0	.892	938
*Tabaracci, Wpg	966	418-470	29.2	.889	938
Reese, Tor-Clg	1000	443-500	30.0	.886	936
*Hasek, Chi	1014	369-413	24.4	.893	934
*Tanner, Qbc	796	348-394	29.7	.883	933
J Cloutier, Qbc	1345	624-712	31.8	.876	929
Myllys, SJ	1374	747-862	37.6	.867	929
Berthiaume, LA-Bos	1378	610-697	30.3	.875	926
*Irbe, SJ	645	317-365	34.0	.868	925
Liut, Was	1123	488-558	29.8	.875	924
Hrivnak, Was	605	239-274	27.2	.872	918
Wamsley, Clg-Tor	885	383-444	30.1	.863	913
T Gamble, Van	1009	445-518	30.8	.859	910
*Waite, Chi	877	293-347	23.7	.844	884

(1–533 minutes played)

GOALER, TEAM	MINS	SAVES-SHOTS	SH/GP	SVPCT	PERSEV
R LeBlanc, Chi	60	21-22	22.0	.955	991
*F Potvin, Tor	210	112-120	34.3	.933	990
*W Sharples, Clg	65	36-40	36.9	.900	962
*Flaherty, SJ	178	107-120	40.4	.892	959
Riendeau, StL-Det	244	114-127	31.2	.898	950
*Racicot, Mtr	436	196-219	30.1	.895	945
Re Lemelin, Bos	407	187-210	31.0	.890	942
Pietrangelo, Pit-Har	531	254-286	32.3	.888	942
G Millen, Det	487	190-212	26.1	.896	940
*DelGuidice, Bos	424	211-239	33.8	.883	939
*N Foster, Edm	439	163-183	25.0	.891	932
*M Brodeur, NJ	179	75-85	28.5	.882	930
R Melanson, Mtr	492	173-195	23.8	.887	927
Ing, Edm	463	219-252	32.7	.869	923
B Hayward, SJ	305	152-177	34.8	.859	917
*M O'Neill, Wpg	13	6-7	32.3	.857	911
*Littman, Buf	60	25-29	29.0	.862	910
*Goverde, LA	120	54-63	31.5	.857	910
*Jablonski, StL	468	221-259	33.2	.853	909
*Kidd, Clg	120	48-56	28.0	.857	904
*Lorenz, NYI	120	50-60	30.0	.833	883
*C Erickson, NJ	120	46-55	27.5	.836	882
*Sc King, Det	16	4-5	18.8	.800	831
*Bester, Det	31	7-9	17.4	.778	807
All goalers	115905	47566-53565	27.7	.888	934

1992–93

Curt Joseph, as he was known then by fans in St. Louis, logs his second-straight victory in the perseverance derby, this time by an enormous 12-point margin over his closest competitor, the rookie sensation Felix Potvin of Toronto, who Joseph will unseat as the Leafs' goalie in '98–99. Look at the high number of shots Joseph faced in the Blues nets, and also notice that he spent a lot of time in there. Overall, the league-wide shots average went way up from its depressed levels of the previous season, but five regular goalies still managed to conquer the .900 peak: Cujo, Felix the Cat, Beezer (who says players don't have good nicknames anymore?), Barrasso, and Eddie the Eagle (*damn* that Barrasso). You know who we would have voted for in the Vezina and All-Star balloting: Joseph and Potvin. But somehow Belfour and Barrasso got the votes. Good choices certainly, but not the best ones.

Bob Essensa continues to impress in Winnipeg, and Arturs Irbe emerges in San Jose, bringing glory to the Sharks and to Latvia. The notion of a foreign goalie no longer seems quite so weird as it did back in the days of Lindbergh and Takko. Indeed, we see Dominik Hasek, now a Sabre, lurking in the wings at Buffalo as Toronto-bound Daren Puppa and Buffalo-bound Grant Fuhr pass each other on the Queen E. Way, right around the Dixie Plaza exit. The year before, Hasek was with Chicago as the Blackhawks reached the Stanley Cup Final under Mike Keenan. The Penguins thrashed the Hawks, and one of the things that made the loss so bad was the way Keenan desperately shuffled Hasek and Belfour in and out of games – a clear sign of panic that did nothing for either goalie's confidence or for their teammates' confidence, though it certainly must have made the Pens feel good. Keenan is such a terrible handler of goalers, and we'll see more of it a bit later on. Darryl Sutter, who took over for Keenan after the Cup Final debacle, wasn't any better. "He flops around like some kind of fish," Sutter said of Hasek, and had him traded off to Buffalo.

Finally, you've probably noticed that these goalie perseverance lists are getting awfully long. It's nice to see "Otw" on 'em, but "TB"? Ugh. The league is getting too big, and there are now teams in cities that have nothing to do with hockey except that they can ante up the $50 million it takes to get a franchise. Furthermore, the schedule has now been increased to 84 games, as if there weren't enough regular-season games already, with four of these games at "neutral sites." Kings owner Bruce McNall is behind this scheme. In fact, one of his companies pockets some of the money for arranging the neutral sites. McNall is hailed as a visionary who will make the NHL a fabulously wealthy fixture in mainstream American sports, but soon he will go to jail for fraud.

1992–93
(minimum 1680 minutes played)

	GOALER, TEAM	MINS	SAVES-SHOTS	SH/GP	SVPCT	PERSEV
1	Cu Joseph, StL	3890	2006-2202	34.0	.911†	968
2t	*F Potvin, Tor	2781	1170-1286	27.8	.910	956
2t	Vanbiesbrouck, NYR	2757	1373-1525	33.2	.900	956
4t	Barrasso, Pit	3702	1699-1885	30.6	.901	952
4t	Belfour, Chi	4106	1703-1880	27.5	.906	952

	GOALER, TEAM	MINS	SAVES-SHOTS	SH/GP	SVPCT	PERSEV
6	Puppa, Buf-Tor	1785	842-938	31.5	.898	950
7	Essensa, Wpg	3855	1892-2119	33.0	.893	948
8	*Irbe, SJ	2074	1108-1250	36.2	.886	947
9t	*Soderstrom, Phi	2512	1184-1327	31.7	.892	945
9t	Pa Roy, Mtr	3595	1622-1814	30.3	.894	945
11t	Fuhr, Tor-Buf	3359	1544-1729	30.9	.893	944
11t	*Stauber, LA	1735	876-987	34.1	.888	944
11t	Hrudey, LA	2718	1377-1552	34.3	.887	944
14	M Richter, NYR	2105	1046-1180	33.6	.886	942
15t	Ranford, Edm	3753	1825-2065	33.0	.884	939
15t	R Hextall, Qbc	2988	1357-1529	30.7	.888	939
15t	Healy, NYI	2655	1170-1316	29.7	.889	939
18t	Cheveldae, Det	3880	1687-1897	29.3	.889	938
18t	Whitmore, Van	1817	764-858	28.3	.890	938
20t	Vernon, Clg	3732	1601-1804	29.0	.887	936
20t	K McLean, Van	3261	1431-1615	29.7	.886	936
20t	Terreri, NJ	2672	1173-1324	29.7	.886	936
23t	*Roussel, Phi	1769	822-933	31.6	.881	934
23t	Casey, Min	3476	1490-1683	29.1	.885	934
25t	Fiset, Qbc	1939	835-945	29.2	.884	932
25t	S Burke, Har	2656	1301-1485	33.5	.876	932
27	Beaupre, Was	3282	1349-1530	28.0	.882	928
28	Jablonski, TB	2268	1044-1194	31.6	.874	927
29t	Billington, NJ	2389	1032-1178	29.6	.876	925
29t	M Fitzpatrick, NYI	2253	936-1066	28.4	.878	925
31	Moog, Bos	3194	1189-1357	25.5†	.876	919
32	Hackett, SJ	2000	1044-1220	36.6‡	.856‡	917
33	Sidorkiewicz, Otw	3388	1487-1737	30.8	.856	907

(560–1679 minutes played)

GOALER, TEAM	MINS	SAVES-SHOTS	SH/GP	SVPCT	PERSEV
Hasek, Buf	1429	645-720	30.2	.896	946
M Gosselin, Har	867	442-499	34.5	.886	943
Blue, Bos	1322	533-597	27.1	.893	938
Wregget, Pit	1368	614-692	30.4	.887	938
Reese, Clg	1311	559-629	28.8	.889	937
Tugnutt, Edm	1338	674-767	34.4	.879	936
*G Hebert, StL	1210	556-630	31.2	.883	934
T Draper, Buf	664	303-344	31.1	.881	933
Wakaluk, Min	1596	706-803	30.2	.879	930
Tabaracci, Wpg-Was	1302	578-658	30.3	.878	929
Racicot, Mtr	1433	601-682	28.6	.881	929
Berthiaume, Otw	1326	644-739	33.4	.871	927
*JC Bergeron, TB	1163	503-574	29.6	.876	926
Hrivnak, Was-Wpg	1601	1677-773	29.0	.876	924
Waite, Chi	996	362-411	24.8	.881	922
Riendeau, Det	1193	458-522	26.3	.877	921
We Young, TB	1591	661-758	28.6	.872	920
Pietrangelo, Har	1373	672-783	34.2	.858	915
B Hayward, SJ	930	473-559	36.1	.846	906
Beauregard, Phi	802	346-405	30.3	.854	905

(1–559 minutes played)

GOALER, TEAM	MINS	SAVES-SHOTS	SH/GP	SVPCT	PERSEV
*D'Alessio, Har	11	3-3	16.4	1.000	1027
*F Chabot, Mtr	40	18-19	28.5	.947	995
*Flaherty, SJ	60	41-46	46.0	.891	968
*M Lenarduzzi, Har	168	78-87	31.1	.897	948
*Bales, Bos	25	9-10	24.0	.900	940
Knickle, LA	532	257-292	32.9	.880	935
*Trefilov, Clg	65	34-39	36.0	.872	932
*C Hirsch, NYR	224	102-116	31.1	.879	931
*Lorenz, NYI	157	68-78	29.8	.872	921
Wamsley, Tor	160	76-91	34.1	.835	892
J Cloutier, Qbc	154	55-65	25.3	.846	888
*M O'Neill, Wpg	73	28-34	27.9	.824	870
Weeks, Otw	249	114-144	34.7	.792	849
*Madeley, Otw	90	34-44	29.3	.773	822
*Goverde, LA	98	38-51	31.2	.745	797
*Kolzig, Was	20	5-7	21.0	.714	749
*Littman, TB	45	14-21	28.0	.667	713
*Dafoe, Was	1	0-0	--	--	--
All goalers	121875	55154-62327	30.7	.885	936

1993–94

John Vanbiesbrouck leaves New York after 11 seasons, joins the expansion Florida Panthers, and turns in the performance of his life. Thanks to Beezer's incredible work, the Panthers finish their inaugural season with a 33-34-17 record, just missing the playoffs, and the fourth-best goals-against record in the league. It's the best performance by an expansion team since the 1926–27 Rangers, and they weren't really an expansion team back then. So this year's Panthers can be called the hands-down best expansion team in NHL history, and most of that credit must go to Vanbiesbrouck.

But sadly for the Beezer, this is the magical year that the Rangers break the 54-year hex and win the Stanley Cup, and he's not there to share it. Mike Richter is in goal for both the regular season, when the Rangers allow two fewer goals than the Panthers yet finish first overall in the NHL, and for the playoffs. Finishing second to the Rangers in the overall standings are their trans-Hudson rivals, the Devils, and they'll also hook up in an unforgettable semi-final that features Messier's victory guarantee in game six and Matteau's goal in game seven overtime. The rookie sensation Martin Brodeur is the Devils goalie for all this – there he is in fifth place on the perseverance list, just behind his childhood hero, Roy.

We also find Hasek, now ensconced as the starter for the first time in his NHL career, in second place with a mighty .930 save percentage. Funny that Buffalo allowed only 27.7 shots when Hasek was between the pipes. In subsequent seasons, they just let everyone pour in on the Dominator. Hasek won the Vezina this year ahead of Vanbiesbrouck;

this is probably the only year we can say that Hasek didn't deserve the award, at least not quite as much as Beezer did. Mark Fitzpatrick, still recovering from EMS, is now Vanbiesbrouck's goaling partner in Miami. He does very well, though he doesn't play quite enough to qualify as a regular. But after the season he is arrested for kicking and grabbing his pregnant wife, and he must undergo a court-ordered counselling program. Fitzpatrick is hard to root against and hard to root for, all at once.

We haven't mentioned Sean Burke yet, and we ought to. He was pretty overrated as a young giant with the Devils in the late '80s, but now in Hartford he's starting to really excel. Keep an eye on him. And what's this "Dal" abbreviation? Not Darcy Wakaluk's fault, but the Minnesota North Stars have moved to Dallas, the first in a series of sickening franchise shifts we're going to have to endure. And there's Troy, N.Y., native Guy Hebert, backstopping the expansion Mighty Ducks of Anaheim. Hebert will stay with the team until March 2001, when he's finally waived. Guy Hebert, original Duck.

1993–94
(minimum 1680 minutes played)

	GOALER, TEAM	MINS	SAVES-SHOTS	SH/GP	SVPCT	PERSEV
1	Vanbiesbrouck, Fla	3440	1767-1912	33.3	.924	980
2	Hasek, Buf	3358	1443-1552	27.7	.930†	976
3t	Cu Joseph, StL	4127	2169-2382	34.6	.911	968
3t	Pa Roy, Mtr	3867	1795-1956	30.3	.918	968
5	*M Brodeur, NJ	2625	1133-1238	28.3	.915	962
6t	S Burke, Har	2750	1321-1458	31.8	.906	959
6t	Wakaluk, Dal	2000	890-978	29.3	.910	959
6t	F Potvin, Tor	3883	1823-2010	31.1	.907	959
9t	G Hebert, Ana	2991	1372-1513	30.4	.907	957
9t	Hrudey, LA	3713	2089-2219	35.9‡	.897	957
9t	M Richter, NYR	3710	1599-1758	28.4	.910	957
12t	Terreri, NJ	2340	1035-1141	29.3	.907	956
12t	Ranford, Edm	4070	2089-2325	34.3	.898	956
14t	Belfour, Chi	3998	1714-1892	28.4	.906	953
14t	Tugnutt, Ana-Mtr	1898	900-1000	31.6	.900	953
16	Roussel, Phi	3285	1579-1762	32.2	.896	950
17	R Hextall, NYI	3581	1617-1801	30.2	.898	948
18t	Barrasso, Pit	2482	1165-1304	31.5	.893	946
18t	Wregget, Pit	2456	1153-1291	31.5	.893	946
18t	Irbe, SJ	4412	1855-2064	28.1	.899	946
21	Moog, Dal	3121	1434-1604	30.8	.894	945
22	Puppa, TB	3653	1472-1637	26.9	.899	944
23	Fiset, Qbc	2798	1276-1434	30.8	.890	941
24	*Osgood, Det	2206	894-999	27.2	.895	940
25	Essensa, Wpg-Det	3914	1816-2051	31.4	.885	938
26	K McLean, Van	3128	1274-1430	27.4	.891	937
27	Fuhr, Buf	1726	801-907	31.5	.883	936
28t	Vernon, Clg	2798	1078-1209	25.9	.892	935
28t	Tabaracci, Was	1770	726-817	27.7	.889	935

	GOALER, TEAM	MINS	SAVES-SHOTS	SH/GP	SVPCT	PERSEV
30	Cheveldae, Det-Wpg	2360	1069-1212	30.8	.882	933
31	Casey, Bos	3192	1136-1289	24.2	.881	922
32	Beaupre, Was	2853	987-1122	23.6†	.880	919
33t	Billington, Otw	3319	1547-1801	32.6	.859‡	913
33t	Soderstrom, Phi	1736	735-851	29.4	.864	913
35	Whitmore, Van	1921	735-848	26.5	.867	911

(560–1679 minutes played)

GOALER, TEAM	MINS	SAVES-SHOTS	SH/GP	SVPCT	PERSEV
Stauber, LA	1144	641-706	37.0	.908	970
M Fitzpatrick, Fla	1603	771-844	31.6	.914	966
*Trefilov, Clg	623	279-305	29.4	.915	964
*McLennan, NYI	1287	578-639	29.8	.905	954
*Rhodes, Tor	1213	488-541	26.8	.902	947
*Thibault, Qbc	1504	685-768	30.6	.892	943
Hackett, Chi	1084	504-566	31.3	.890	943
*Brathwaite, Edm	982	465-523	32.0	.889	942
Reese, Clg-Har	1099	472-529	28.9	.892	940
Hrivnak, StL	970	494-563	34.8	.877	935
*Kidd, Clg	1614	667-752	28.0	.887	934
Blue, Bos	944	360-407	25.9	.885	928
Pietrangelo, Har	984	414-473	28.8	.875	923
*Madeley, Otw	1583	753-868	32.9	.868	922
Healy, NYR	1368	498-567	24.9	.878	920
*M O'Neill, Wpg	738	331-382	31.1	.866	918
Riendeau, Det-Bos	1321	473-546	24.8	.866	908
Jablonski, TB	834	320-374	26.9	.856	900
Waite, SJ	697	269-319	27.5	.843	889

(1–559 minutes played)

GOALER, TEAM	MINS	SAVES-SHOTS	SH/GP	SVPCT	PERSEV
Romano, Pit	125	53-56	26.9	.946	991
Wa Cowley, Edm	57	32-35	36.8	.914	976
*M Lenarduzzi, Har	21	11-12	34.3	.917	974
Shtalenkov, Ana	543	241-265	29.3	.909	958
JC Bergeron, TB	134	62-69	30.9	.899	950
We Young, TB	480	191-211	26.4	.905	949
J Cloutier, Qbc	475	208-232	29.3	.897	945
Sidorkiewicz, NJ	130	49-55	25.4	.891	933
Dopson, Pit	45	20-23	30.7	.870	921
*Kuntar, Mtr	302	114-130	25.8	.877	920
*Snow, Qbc	279	111-127	27.3	.874	920
T Draper, NYI	227	102-118	31.2	.864	916
*Dafoe, Was	230	88-101	26.3	.871	915
Knickle, LA	174	62-71	24.5	.873	914
Ing, Det	170	87-102	36.0	.853	913
*Kolzig, Was	224	108-128	34.3	.844	901
Racicot, Mtr	500	209-246	29.5	.850	899
*F Chabot, Mtr-Phi	130	54-64	29.5	.844	893
Beauregard, Wpg	418	177-211	30.3	.839	889
Reddick, Fla	80	37-45	33.8	.822	878

GOALER, TEAM	MINS	SAVES-SHOTS	SH/GP	SVPCT	PERSEV
M LaForest, Otw	182	79-96	31.6	.823	876
*Goverde, LA	60	30-37	37.0	.811	872
M Gosselin, Har	239	86-107	26.9	.804	849
*Muzzatti, Clg	60	27-35	35.0	.771	830
Berthiaume, Otw	1	0-2	120.0	.000	200
*Soucy, Chi	3	0-0	0.0	–	–
All goalers	132362	59090-66017	29.9	.895	945

1994–95

The lockout-shortened season, with only a 48-game schedule for each team. A lot of people deride this campaign as being somehow tainted, a shadow season, with the Cup champions, New Jersey, not quite "real" champions because the schedule was so short. Bollocks, we say! We saw a lot of games this year, and taken together they were the most intense regular-season matches we've ever seen. Every player knew that the abbreviated schedule meant every game counted, that losing, say, the third game of the season might really mean your team would miss the playoffs.

As a result, play was tight-checking all the way through, and spurred by the success of the Panthers' and Devils' anti-hockey the previous season, teams adopted the neutral-zone trap, further tightening things up – a process helped along in the early going by the rustiness of a lot of the players after the league locked them out for more than four months. All this meant that the average save percentage sky-rocketed up to .901, crossing the great divide for the first time in a generation.

These conditions were perfect for Dominik Hasek, and here he records a gaping 13-point victory over the rest of the field. Again he rings up a staggering .930 kick-out rate, which manages to make Detroit rookie Chris Osgood's .917 look puny by comparison. Kelly Hrudey's 968 perseverance mark would've been good enough to win most years and is five points better than everyone else here, but he still plays second fiddle to the Pride of Pardubice. Well, at least give Hrudey the second All-Star slot, eh, why don'tcha? But no – it goes to Ed Belfour, and that's the first ridiculous choice the writers and managers have made in a long time. Meanwhile, with a .900 save percentage now merely the average (remember when a .900 meant you were the best in the league?), we're starting to see all kinds of people stopping everything that comes near them. Jim Carey? Dominic Roussel? Stephane Fiset? It all seems kind of fishy, and what's with that new piece of leather stretching from the thumb of the catching glove back to the wrist? Is that *legal*? And do your shoulders really go all the way up to your earlobes?

1994–95
(minimum 960 minutes played)

	GOALER, TEAM	MINS	SAVES-SHOTS	SH/GP	SVPCT	PERSEV
1	Hasek, Buf	2416	1136-1221	30.3	.930†	981
2	Hrudey, LA	1894	1000-1099	34.8‡	.910	968
3t	S Burke, Har	2418	1125-1233	30.6	.912	963
3t	Osgood, Det	1087	455-496	27.4	.917	963
3t	Moog, Dal	1770	774-846	28.7	.915	963
6t	Vanbiesbrouck, Fla	2087	914-1000	28.7	.914	962
6t	Fiset, Qbc	1879	881-968	30.9	.910	962
8t	F Potvin, Tor	2144	1016-1120	31.3	.907	959
8t	Pa Roy, Mtr	2566	1230-1357	31.7	.906	959
8t	Roussel, Phi	1075	444-486	27.1	.914	959
11t	Wregget, Pit	2208	1101-1219	33.1	.903	958
11t	G Hebert, Ana	2092	1023-1132	32.4	.904	958
13	Kidd, Clg	2463	1063-1170	28.5	.909	956
14	Soderstrom, NYI	1350	647-717	31.9	.902	955
15	*J Carey, Was	1604	597-654	24.5	.913	954
16t	K McLean, Van	2374	1031-1140	28.8	.904	952
16t	Puppa, TB	2013	856-946	28.2	.905	952
18	Beaupre, Otw	2101	1025-1143	32.6	.897	951
19t	*Khabibulin, Wpg	1339	647-723	32.4	.895	949
19t	Cu Joseph, StL	1914	815-904	28.3	.902	949
21	Irbe, SJ	2043	945-1056	31.0	.895	947
22	Belfour, Chi	2450	897-990	24.2	.906	946
23	M Brodeur, NJ	2184	819-908	24.9	.902	944
24	*Lacher, Bos	1965	726-805	24.6	.902	943
25	M Richter, NYR	1993	787-884	26.6	.890	935
26t	Ranford, Edm	2203	1001-1134	30.9	.883	934
26t	R Hextall, Phi	1824	713-801	26.3	.890	934
28	Cheveldae, Wpg	1571	721-818	31.2	.881	933
29	Vernon, Det	1807	634-710	23.6†	.893	932
30	McLennan, NYI	1185	472-539	27.3	.876‡	921

(320–959 minutes played)

GOALER, TEAM	MINS	SAVES-SHOTS	SH/GP	SVPCT	PERSEV
Rhodes, Tor	760	370-404	31.9	.916	969
Thibault, Qbc	898	388-423	28.3	.917	964
Hackett, Chi	328	137-150	27.4	.913	959
*T Salo, NYI	358	171-189	31.7	.905	958
*Flaherty, SJ	852	411-455	32.0	.903	957
Tabaracci, Was-Clg	596	219-240	24.2	.912	953
Healy, NYR	888	342-377	25.5	.907	950
*Torchia, Dal	327	154-172	31.6	.895	948
*Shtalenkov, Ana	810	399-448	33.2	.891	946
Casey, StL	872	360-400	27.5	.900	946
We Young, Pit	497	228-255	30.8	.894	945
Tugnutt, Mtr	346	154-172	29.8	.895	945
M Fitzpatrick, Fla	819	325-361	26.4	.900	944
Kolzig, Was	724	275-305	25.3	.902	944
Terreri, NJ	734	278-309	25.3	.900	942
Reese, Har	477	208-234	29.4	.889	938

GOALER, TEAM	MINS	SAVES-SHOTS	SH/GP	SVPCT	PERSEV
Wakaluk, Dal	754	301-341	27.1	.883	928
Fuhr, Buf-LA	878	405-464	31.7	.873	926
Whitmore, Van	558	242-279	30.0	.867	917
Riendeau, Bos	565	194-221	23.5	.878	917
*Brathwaite, Edm	601	252-292	29.2	.863	912
JC Bergeron, TB	883	325-374	25.4	.869	911
Billington, Otw-Bos	845	329-380	27.0	.866	911
Stauber, LA-Buf	333	134-156	28.1	.859	906

(1–319 minutes played)

GOALER, TEAM	MINS	SAVES-SHOTS	SH/GP	SVPCT	PERSEV
*Muzzatti, Clg	10	8-8	48.0	1.000	1080
*Bales, Otw	3	1-1	20.0	1.000	1033
*Jaks, LA	40	23-25	37.5	.920	982
Barrasso, Pit	125	67-75	36.0	.893	953
Madeley, Otw	315	153-171	32.6	.895	949
*Storr, LA	263	135-152	34.7	.888	946
Waite, Chi	119	46-51	25.7	.902	945
*Fernandez, Dal	59	24-27	27.5	.889	935
*DeRouville, Pit	60	24-27	27.0	.889	934
*Trefilov, Clg	236	114-130	33.1	.877	932
*Sarjeant, StL	120	46-52	26.0	.885	928
*Dafoe, Was	187	69-80	25.7	.862	905
*Snow, Qbc	119	52-63	31.8	.825	878
*Jq Gage, Edm	99	33-40	24.2	.825	865
All goalers	75477	32891-36522	29.0	.901	949

1995–96

Hasek wins his second perseverance title in a row, and does so with the neat parlour trick of recording the league's highest save percentage while facing the highest average shots per game. Clearly his Sabre teammates have figured out that they don't have to bother protecting Hasek; they can just try to get down ice to score, which is not something they're very good at. This makes Buffalo just about the only team not playing the trap, probably because it's too complicated, although it could also be because it requires some lateral skating, which you can't do on double-runners.

Daren Puppa of the Tampa Bay Lightning, and our skin crawls every time we see those last three words, stays healthy and has a terrific season, as does Guy Hebert and the aging but still excellent Kelly Hrudey. For some unfathomable reason, however, none of these guys gets the Vezina or a post-season All-Star slot, nor do Khabibulin, Richter, Potvin, even Hackett. No, this year the Vezina and first-team spot were voted to . . . Jim Carey?! Hey, he was a likable fella, but he was also the lucky recipient of the biggest hype job hockey has seen in a long time, since, oh, Mark Messier's purported date with Madonna. A guy who

should have had a starting job and a shot at the Vezina a few years back, Allan Bester, winds up his NHL career this season in Dallas. Grant Fuhr finds himself in St. Louis under the goalie-killing direction of Mike Keenan. Iron Mike keeps Fuhr, who by now is no spring chicken, in the nets for a league-high 4,365 minutes. Sure enough, Fuhr's knee gives out early in the playoffs, and the Blues go down in the second round.

You see Stephane Fiset down the list there? Can't find him because you're looking for "Quebec"? Well, Quebec are no more, gone to Colorado, and that's particularly sad because Avalanche win the Cup this year. Poor Quebec, they put up with years of bad teams, then the Nordiques started to improve, and just as they got good they were sold out of town. This is the beginning of a very bad stretch for Canada, and for hockey as a whole.

Who was in goal when Colorado won the Cup? Patrick Roy, of course. This was the season he blew up on the Canadiens' bench after coach Mario Tremblay pulled him during an 11-1 loss to Detroit at the Forum. Roy had allowed 9 goals on 26 shots (imagine how much better his save percentage and perseverance would have been had he not played that night) and was upset that he had been left in so long on a night when he and his teammates clearly didn't have it. When Roy finally came off, he bawled out Tremblay and Habs president Ronald Corey, demanded a trade, and never played for Montreal again. The next day at a press conference, a sobbing Roy said there was no chance for reconciliation. "I really wanted it to end differently – not in a stupid way like this," he said. It was a dramatic, old-fashioned kind of departure, the kind you get these days only in international soccer. In North American sports all the tantrums and staredowns and ultimatums now come behind closed doors or through agents. It was great to see Roy's emotions right there, out in the open. And since only in Montreal (and Toronto) are the benches and the players on them not glassed in like fish in an aquarium, the volatile goalie could speak direct and face to face to the boss for everyone to see. The trade followed the press conference by two days, and in exchange for Roy, the Habs got Jocelyn Thibault. Patrick Roy is a tough act to follow, and Thibault did not really follow that act successfully. This year at least, Thibault was Roy's regular-season equal, but the Canadiens have never been the same since. We've seen many a team shoot itself in the foot before, but in all our years, this is the only time we've seen a franchise shoot itself in the head.

One good thing that happened in hockey this year: the neutral-site minstrel show was dropped, and the schedule was accordingly reduced from 84 to 82 games. Still way too long, but it's the first time in North American sports history that a major league's regular season was voluntarily shortened.

1995–96
(minimum 1640 minutes played)

	GOALER, TEAM	MINS	SAVES-SHOTS	SH/GP	SVPCT	PERSEV
1	Hasek, Buf	3417	1850-2011	35.3‡	.920†	979
2	Puppa, TB	3189	1474-1605	30.2	.918	969
3	G Hebert, Ana	3326	1663-1820	32.8	.914	968
4t	Hrudey, LA	2077	1101-1214	35.1	.907	965
4t	Khabibulin, Wpg	2914	1504-1656	34.1	.908	965
6t	M Richter, NYR	2396	1114-1221	30.6	.912	963
6t	F Potvin, Tor	4009	1943-2135	32.0	.910	963
6t	Hackett, Chi	2000	868-948	28.4	.916	963
9	S Burke, Har	3669	1844-2034	33.3	.907	962
10	Wregget, Pit	2132	1090-1205	33.9	.905	961
11	Barrasso, Pit	2799	1466-1626	34.9	.902	960
12	Pa Roy, Mtr-Col	3565	1632-1797	30.2	.908	959
13	Thibault, Col-Mtr	2892	1342-1480	30.7	.907	958
14	M Brodeur, NJ	4434	1781-1954	26.4	.911	956
15	R Hextall, Phi	3102	1180-1292	25.0	.913	955
16	Rhodes, Tor-Otw	2747	1215-1342	29.3	.905	954
17t	*C Hirsch, Van	2338	1026-1173	30.1	.903	953
17t	Fuhr, StL	4365	1948-2157	29.6	.903	953
19	Osgood, Det	2933	1084-1190	24.3	.911	951
20	Vanbiesbrouck, Fla	3178	1331-1473	27.8	.904	950
21	Moog, Dal	2228	995-1106	29.8	.900	949
22t	Belfour, Chi	2956	1238-1373	27.9	.902	948
22t	Healy, NYR	2564	1113-1237	28.9	.900	948
24t	J Carey, Was	4069	1478-1631	24.1	.906	946
24t	Fiset, Col	2107	909-1012	28.8	.898	946
24t	*Dafoe, LA	2666	1367-1539	34.6	.888	946
27	Wakaluk, Dal	1875	869-975	31.2	.891	943
28	Vernon, Det	1855	653-723	23.4†	.903	942
29t	Cheveldae, Wpg	1695	837-948	33.6	.883	939
29t	Kidd, Clg	2570	1011-1130	26.4	.895	939
30	Tabaracci, Clg	2391	970-1087	27.3	.892	938
31	M Fitzpatrick, Fla	1786	722-810	27.2	.891	937
32t	Terreri, NJ-SJ	2726	1250-1414	31.1	.884	936
32t	Cu Joseph, Edm	1936	860-971	30.1	.886	936
34	Ranford, Edm-Bos	4322	1817-2054	28.5	.885	932
35	Soderstrom, NYI	2590	1203-1370	31.7	.878	931
36	K McLean, Van	2645	1136-1292	29.3	.879	928
37	Beaupre, Otw-Tor	2106	926-1062	30.3	.872‡	922

(547–1639 minutes played)

GOALER, TEAM	MINS	SAVES-SHOTS	SH/GP	SVPCT	PERSEV
*Muzzatti, Har	1013	502-551	32.6	.911	965
Trefilov, Buf	1094	596-660	36.2	.903	963
Jablonski, Mtr-StL	1272	618-681	32.1	.907	961
*Fichaud, NYI	1234	591-659	32.0	.897	950
Bester, Dal	601	267-297	29.7	.899	948
Shtalenkov, Ana	1637	729-814	29.8	.896	945
Reese, Har-TB	1269	566-634	30.0	.893	943
McLennan, NYI	636	303-342	32.3	.886	940

GOALER, TEAM	MINS	SAVES-SHOTS	SH/GP	SVPCT	PERSEV
Snow, Phi	1437	579-648	27.1	.894	939
Kolzig, Was	897	360-406	27.2	.887	932
*S Bailey, Bos	571	233-264	27.7	.883	929
Flaherty, SJ	1137	597-689	36.4	.867	927
*Bales, Otw	1040	488-560	32.3	.871	925
Roussel, Phi-Wpg	741	274-312	25.3	.878	920
*Jq Gage, Edm	717	305-350	29.3	.871	920
Irbe, SJ	1112	522-607	32.8	.860	915
Billington, Bos	1380	515-594	25.8	.867	910
Lacher, Bos	671	240-284	25.4	.845	887
JC Bergeron, TB	595	208-250	25.2	.832	874

(1–546 minutes played)

GOALER, TEAM	MINS	SAVES-SHOTS	SH/GP	SVPCT	PERSEV
*Ram, NYR	27	9-9	20.0	1.000	1033
*S Langkow, Wpg	6	2-2	20.0	1.000	1033
Waite, Chi	31	8-8	15.5	1.000	1026
*J Willis, Dal	19	13-14	44.2	.929	1002
*Hodson, Det	163	64-67	24.7	.955	996
*Storr, LA	262	125-147	33.7	.918	974
Brathwaite, Edm	293	128-140	28.7	.907	955
*Tallas, Bos	60	26-29	29.0	.897	945
Blue, Buf	255	122-137	32.2	.891	944
*Schwab, NJ	331	107-119	21.6	.899	935
*B Racine, StL	230	89-101	26.3	.881	925
*S Shields, Buf	75	28-32	25.6	.875	918
*D Wilkinson, TB	200	90-105	31.5	.857	910
T Salo, NYI	523	215-250	28.7	.860	908
Casey, StL	395	155-180	27.3	.861	907
*Labrecque, Mtr	98	40-47	28.8	.851	899
*Mr Biron, Buf	119	54-64	32.3	.844	898
*Fernandez, Dal	249	102-121	29.2	.843	892
*Sarjeant, SJ	171	73-87	30.5	.839	890
T Draper, Wpg	34	11-14	24.7	.786	827
*Theodore, Mtr	9	1-2	13.3	.500	522
All goalers	129173	57808-64344	29.9	.898	948

1996–97

Now the Winnipeg Jets are gone, leaving behind a huge hole in the hearts of hockey fans not just in Manitoba but everywhere. Phoenix, where the Jets wash up, has a long history of minor-league and even WHA hockey, but let's face it: a team in Winnipeg makes sense; a team in Phoenix does not.

So it was in the late '90s, as events off the ice – mainly the de-Canadianization of the game, or more properly the de-Northernization of it – outstripped events on the ice. Thus great individual achievements like Dominik Hasek's total mastery of the nets were somewhat overshadowed. Here he wins his third-straight perseverance crown – matching Johnny Bower's feat of the late '60s – and his third Vezina in four years. He also becomes the first goalie to win the Hart Trophy since Jacques Plante in 1962. It's an entirely appropriate honour, because no player in recent memory, maybe ever, has been as valuable to his team as Hasek has been to Buffalo. It's virtually impossible to imagine the Sabres finishing first in their division, as they did this season, without the Dominator bailing them out time after time. If, for example, Hasek played his 4,037 minutes this year and logged a save percentage at the league average, .902, instead of at his ionospheric .930, things would have been much different for the Ice Herd. At a .902 rate, he would've allowed 214 goals, not 153, and the Sabres' overall goal difference would've tumbled from plus-29 to minus-32. Their winning percentage would have tumbled too, from .561 to somewhere well below .500, perhaps taking them out of a playoff berth. And there would have been further repercussions: this season Michael Peca won the Selke Trophy as best defensive forward, but if Hasek had been merely human, Peca wouldn't have looked so good; his plus-26 mark would surely have dropped several notches, like those of each Sabre.

Yet despite's Hasek's overarching greatness and his ability to make his teammates look so much better than they really were, many fans didn't think Hasek was so hot, because he'd never been on a Cup-winner. Those who questioned his true worth because of his regular-season achievements conveniently forgot that he was just as good in the playoffs. Most of the post-season success the Sabres had was, and continues to be, attributable to the Dominator. This season, Hasek got hurt in the first round against Ottawa, but Steve Shields filled in and helped the Sabres advance. The elusive nature of Hasek's groin injury and his mercurial temperament – the line between genius and insanity is a thin one – led some to believe that he was dogging it. When Jim Kelley, the venerable *Buffalo News* hockey columnist and president of the PHWA, suggested that this might be true, Hasek tried to slug him in the Sabres dressing room. Everyone soon apologized and Hasek returned, but Buffalo lost to perennial *bête noire* Philadelphia in the next round. The whole affair led to the firing of Buffalo's popular coach, Ted Nolan. Hasek felt Nolan gave him no support during the Kelley contretemps and, furthermore, did not know how to relate to the Sabres' European players. Early the next season, the Sabre fans booed Hasek constantly, but he carried on regardless, turning the catcalls to cheers through his near flawless play.

Hasek's single-mindedness, no matter the consequences or the unpopularity of his stand, is a quality he possesses that is not much remarked upon. In his last season in the Czech Republic, he played for Dukla Jihlava, an army-sponsored team. One night they were to play his hometown club, Tesla Pardubice, for whom he had guarded the nets for eight years. Pardubice were in last place and in danger of demotion from the top division. Hasek did not want to seal his beloved former club's doom and refused to

play, but he was ordered to go in. He did, but took himself off the ice after just 20 seconds. His punishment: two weeks' suspension from Dukla Jihlava, and two weeks' duty in the regular army. Hasek is a man of his convictions, consequences be damned.

The Red Wings, despite some shaky goaltending from Vernon and Osgood, won the Cup this year, their first since Terry Sawchuk backstopped them to the Hallowed Vase in 1955. Jim Carey, last year's Vezina winner, is traded from Washington to Boston, where he's exposed for what he really is, yet another one of those disposable local-boy Bruin goalies out of the Cleon Daskalakis–Matt DelGuidice mould. He finishes last in perseverance. Pittsburgh rookie Patrick Lalime sets a record by playing his first 16 NHL games without losing, or more accurately, without being in the nets when the Penguins lose. And Mike Milbury, in his first full season as the Islanders' general manager, is already generating the chaos that will characterize his inexplicably long tenure. During Milbury's regime, the Isles will go through a half-dozen ownership changes, most of them disastrous and one of them even resulting in a bank and wire fraud conviction for a would-be buyer of the team. But Milbury soldiers on, publicly insulting his players and their agents and making baffling personnel changes. He drafts young goalie after young goalie, anoints each of them his "goaltender of the future," then trades them after a season or two. Here he starts the season with Tommy Salo and Tommy Soderstrom, but he dumps Soderstrom for second-year man Eric Fichaud, a former number one draft choice whose French-Canadian heritage Milbury and various commentators constantly reference as proof of his can't-miss status. We'll keep an eye on the revolving door in the Isles' goal crease in the coming years. It will amuse us.

1996–97
(minimum 1640 minutes played)

	GOALER, TEAM	MINS	SAVES-SHOTS	SH/GP	SVPCT	PERSEY
1	Hasek, Buf	4037	2024-2177	32.4	.930†	984
2	Hackett, Chi	2473	1123-1212	29.4	.927	976
3	G Hebert, Ana	3863	1961-2133	33.1	.919	975
4	Pa Roy, Col	3698	1718-1861	30.2	.923	973
5	M Richter, NYR	3598	1784-1945	32.4	.917	971
6	*Lalime, Pit	2058	1065-1166	34.0	.913	970
7	M Brodeur, NJ	3838	1513-1633	25.5	.927	969
8t	S Burke, Har	2985	1426-1560	31.4	.914	966
8t	Vanbiesbrouck, Fla	3347	1454-1582	28.4	.919	966
10	F Potvin, Tor	4271	2214-2438	34.2‡	.908	965
11t	Fiset, LA	2482	1278-1410	34.1	.906	963
11t	Thibault, Mtr	3397	1651-1815	32.1	.910	963
13	M Fitzpatrick, Fla	1680	705-771	27.5	.914	960
14t	Dafoe, LA	2162	1066-1178	32.7	.905	959
14t	Cu Joseph, Edm	4089	1944-2144	31.5	.907	959

GOALER, TEAM	MINS	SAVES-SHOTS	SH/GP	SVPCT	PERSEV
14t Khabibulin, Phx	4091	1901-2094	30.7	.908	959
17 Wregget, Pit	2514	1247-1383	33.0	.902	957
18 Moog, Dal	2738	1023-1121	24.6	.913	954
19 T Salo, NYI	3208	1425-1576	29.5	.904	953
20t Kolzig, Was	1645	687-758	27.6	.906	952
20t Osgood, Det	2769	1069-1175	25.5	.910	952
22t Tabaracci, Clg-TB	3373	1418-1570	27.9	.903	950
22t *Fichaud, NYI	1759	806-897	30.6	.899	950
24 Belfour, Chi-SJ	2723	1186-1317	29.0	.901	949
25 Kidd, Clg	2979	1275-1416	28.5	.900	948
26t Snow, Phi	1884	737-816	26.0	.903	946
26t Fuhr, StL	4261	1747-1940	27.3	.901	946
28 C Hirsch, Van	2127	974-1090	30.7	.894	945
29t Vernon, Det	1952	703-782	24.0†	.899	939
29t Tugnutt, Otw	1991	789-882	26.6	.895	939
29t R Hextall, Phi	3094	1153-1285	24.9	.897	939
32 K McLean, Van	2581	1109-1247	29.0	.889	938
33 Hrudey, SJ	2631	1123-1263	28.8	.889	937
34t Irbe, Dal	1965	737-825	25.2	.893	935
34t Ranford, Bos-Was	3156	1343-1514	28.8	.887	935
36 Rhodes, Otw	2934	1080-1213	24.8	.890	932
37 J Carey, Was-Bos	3297	1311-1480	26.9	.886‡	931

(547–1639 minutes played)

GOALER, TEAM	MINS	SAVES-SHOTS	SH/GP	SVPCT	PERSEV
*S Shields, Buf	789	408-447	34.0	.913	969
*Cousineau, Tor	566	286-317	33.6	.902	958
Billington, Col	1200	531-584	29.2	.909	958
*Theodore, Mtr	821	455-508	37.1	.896	958
Shtalenkov, Ana	1079	487-539	30.0	.904	953
Healy, NYR	1357	573-632	27.9	.907	953
*Dunham, NJ	1013	413-456	27.0	.906	951
Wakaluk, Phx	782	347-386	29.6	.899	948
Terreri, SJ-Chi	1629	671-745	27.4	.901	946
*Schwab, TB	1462	645-719	29.5	.897	946
Essensa, Edm	879	365-406	27.7	.899	945
*Roloson, Clg	1618	682-760	28.2	.897	944
Jablonski, Mtr-Phx	813	410-462	34.1	.887	944
Muzzatti, Har	1591	724-815	30.7	.888	940
*Tallas, Bos	1244	518-587	28.3	.882	930
Casey, StL	707	259-299	25.4	.866	909

(1–546 minutes played)

GOALER, TEAM	MINS	SAVES-SHOTS	SH/GP	SVPCT	PERSEV
*Storr, LA	265	136-147	33.3	.925	981
Turek, Dal	263	120-129	29.4	.930	979
*Hodson, Det	294	106-114	23.3	.930	969
*DeRouville, Pit	111	60-66	35.7	.909	969
Trefilov, Buf	159	88-98	37.0	.898	960
Puppa, TB	325	136-150	27.7	.907	953
*Fountain, Van	245	121-135	33.1	.896	951
JC Bergeron, LA	56	31-35	37.5	.886	948
Waite, Chi	105	51-58	33.1	.879	935

GOALER, TEAM	MINS	SAVES-SHOTS	SH/GP	SVPCT	PERSEV
*Giguere, Har	394	177-201	30.6	.881	932
Barrasso, Pit	270	160-186	41.3	.890	929
*M Denis, Col	60	23-26	26.0	.885	928
*S Bailey, Bos	394	157-181	27.6	.867	913
Flaherty, SJ	359	171-202	33.8	.847	903
*Duffus, Phx	29	7-8	16.6	.875	903
Beaupre, Tor	110	50-60	32.7	.833	888
Cheveldae, Bos	93	28-33	21.3	.848	884
*D Wilkinson, TB	169	60-72	25.6	.833	876
Reese, NJ	139	52-65	28.1	.800	847
Bales, Otw	52	14-18	20.8	.778	812
*Schafer, Bos	77	19-25	19.5	.760	792
*Vokoun, Mtr	20	10-14	42.0	.714	784
M O'Neill, Ana	31	7-10	19.4	.700	732
Soderstrom, NYI	1	0-0	0.0	.000	0
All goalers	129720	57327-63543	29.4	.902	951

1997–98

It's Dominik Hasek, the perseverance champ for a record fourth consecutive year. In the real world, he becomes the first goaler ever to win the Hart Trophy two seasons in a row and captures his fourth Vezina in five years. For the second time in his career, the goalie with a spine like a Slinky notches the league's highest save percentage while facing the highest average shots per game. Priceless. Speaking of shots, note that the league average in that department has dwindled to 27 per game. This is the heyday of the neutral-zone trap, the left-wing lock, the clutch and grab, the video replay that disallows toe-in-the-crease goals, the Michelin Man goalie pads, and all the other forms of anti-hockey that afflict the late '90s.

Elsewhere on the perseverance rundown, Trevor Kidd, suddenly transformed into a good goalie, finishes second as a – gag – Carolina Hurricane. We were never overly fond of Hartford as an NHL city, but at least it was up north and the Whalers had some loyal fans. But what exactly is "Carolina"? We're not sure what city they started in or what city they play in now, but even if we did we couldn't place 'em on a map. Worse, no one in "Carolina" seems to care that they have a hockey team. The Carolina Hurricanes embody everything that's wrong with the NHL in the Bettman era.

Meanwhile in Washington, Olaf Kolzig, born in South Africa of German parents but who grew up in Canada, has a terrific season and leads the Capitals to the Cup Final, but Olie the Goalie and the Caps fall meekly to Detroit in a four-game series so boring even Wings coach Scotty Bowman acknowledges that no one is paying attention. Here's what Dave Bidini, author of the superb *Tropic of Hockey: My Search for the Game in Unlikely Places* as well as the foreword to this book, had to say about that particular Final:

The play volleyed from blue line to blue line. Both the Red Wings and Capitals were employing the trap, a form of hockey which is the athletic equivalent of playing Pong. *Hockey Night in Canada* announcers Bob Cole and Harry Neale, who had suffered through every playoff series of the post-season, sounded as if they were describing the action with their chins propped on their hands. Finally, two players I'd never heard of fenced for the puck and chipped it into the stands. The referee called a TV timeout and both teams drifted, heads lowered, towards their benches.

The Capitals had been in Washington almost a quarter-century when they reached their first Final, but such is the ignorance of hockey in the District of Columbia that when *The Washington Post* published a special Stanley Cup supplement to mark the occasion, the biggest article was devoted to explaining the meaning of "icing," "offside," and "puck." We're not kidding.

Patrick Roy is still finishing high on the lists, this year at number five. Late in the season, Roy attacked Detroit's Chris Osgood at Joe Louis Arena, trying to avenge a fight in the previous year's playoffs in which the Wings' Mike Vernon pummelled and bloodied Roy. Osgood gave as good as he got and went on to win the Cup. And out on Long Island, Milbury has given up on Eric Fichaud. Tommy Salo is the goalie of the future again. Or maybe it's Wade Flaherty.

As you can see, there was both good and bad in NHL hockey this season. But one event stands out as unforgettable: the hockey tournament at the '98 Olympics in Nagano, Japan. For the first time ever, the very best from each nation squared off, not on summertime rinks in Canada or the United States, but on neutral ice in winter. A lot of commentators whined that the 17-day break from NHL play would wreck the season, an astoundingly asinine opinion. What would you rather watch? Carolina vs. Tampa Bay, or Sweden vs. Russia? Phoenix-Anaheim, or Canada–United States? No contest. We've written elsewhere about this tournament, so we're not going to get into a whole thing here, but for taut drama and emotion, it couldn't be beat.

With so many of the internationals playing in North America, the hockey itself was infected with most of the same problems afflicting your typical NHL game: mid-ice tackling unpenalized by the refs, a clogged neutral zone, a paralyzing fear of getting caught up-ice that prevented forwards from committing deep, overlarge equipment that allowed goalies to plug the net without so much as flexing a muscle. But the *intensity* of each game was overwhelming, all the more so for the absence of much of the chippy stuff, because this, after all, was international play. (Brendan Shanahan, though, behaved like an idiot, blind-siding Slovaks wherever he found them).

Everyone believed that the final would involve Canada, the United States, and/or Russia, but Hasek stoned the Americans, kicking out 38 of 39 shots and ousting them in a quarter-final. Then the Czechs went to work on Team Canada in the semi-final. They held a 1-0 lead until the final minute, but Trevor Linden tied it. Hasek was not the reason Canada had such trouble scoring, the Czech Republic's close checking was. In the end, the game was decided by a penalty-shot contest, and here Hasek was unbelievable. He stopped all five Canadians (actually, Eric Lindros hit the post, but Hasek's incredible 360-degree barrel-roll move on him made it *look* like he got a piece of the puck), while down at the other end, Patrick Roy allowed Robert Reichel to score, the only one among four Czech shooters, but it was enough.

The Czech-Russia gold medal game was a stagnant, NHL-like affair with the teams splitting just 41 shots between them. Petr Svoboda got the only goal early in the third period, and Hasek didn't have to do much. The Czechs – with only 11 of their side on North American teams – were the world champions in the only true world championship hockey tournament ever held. (As if to underscore the supremacy of European hockey over the North American game, Finland beat Canada, 3-2, to earn the bronze.)

A couple of days later, the Czech team stood on a stage in Old Town Square in Prague, 130,000 of their countrymen cheering for them below. A 66-year-old told a *New York Times* reporter that on this day there were more people celebrating in the square, and with greater enthusiasm, than when World War II ended. A 19-year-old who arrived with the Czech flag draped over his shoulders after a three-hour train ride from a town near the German border said, "I came to see Hasek. I would like to say to him, 'Dominik, you are not a man. You are a god.'"

1997–98
(minimum 1640 minutes played)

	GOALER, TEAM	MINS	SAVES-SHOTS	SH/GP	SVPCT	PERSEV
1	Hasek, Buf	4220	2002-2149	30.6‡	.932†	983
2	Kidd, Car	2685	1141-1238	27.7	.922	968
3	Barrasso, Pit	3542	1434-1556	26.4	.922	966
4	Kolzig, Was	3788	1590-1729	27.4	.920	965
5	Pa Roy, Col	3835	1672-1825	28.6	.916	964
6	Hackett, Chi	3441	1394-1520	26.5	.917	961
7	Fiset, LA	3497	1570-1728	29.6	.909	958
8	Dafoe, Bos	3693	1464-1602	26.0	.914	957
9	Irbe, Van	1999	891-982	29.5	.907	956
10t	F Potvin, Tor	3864	1706-1882	29.2	.906	955
10t	M Brodeur, NJ	4128	1439-1569	22.8	.917	955
10t	Osgood, Det	3807	1465-1605	25.3	.913	955
13t	Belfour, Dal	3581	1223-1335	22.4	.916	953
13t	G Hebert, Ana	2660	1209-1339	30.2	.903	953
13t	T Salo, NYI	3461	1465-1617	28.0	.906	953
16t	R Hextall, Phi	2688	992-1089	24.3	.911	951
16t	Cu Joseph, Edm	4132	1720-1901	27.6	.904	951
18t	Moog, Mtr	2337	927-1024	26.3	.905	949
18t	Rhodes, Otw	2743	1041-1148	25.1	.907	949

	GOALER, TEAM	MINS	SAVES-SHOTS	SH/GP	SVPCT	PERSEV
20	M Richter, NYR	4143	1704-1888	27.3	.903	948
21	Vanbiesbrouck, Fla	3451	1473-1638	28.5	.899	947
22t	Khabibulin, Phx	4026	1651-1835	27.3	.900	945
22t	Snow, Phi-Van	2155	851-944	26.3	.901	945
24t	Tugnutt, Otw	2236	798-882	23.7	.905	944
24t	Shtalenkov, Ana	2049	921-1031	30.2	.893	944
24t	Thibault, Mtr	2652	1000-1109	25.1	.902	944
27	S Burke, Car-Van-Phi	2885	1220-1362	28.3	.896	943
28t	McLennan, StL	1658	558-618	22.4†	.903	940
28t	M Fitzpatrick, Fla-TB	2578	1106-1240	28.9	.892	940
30	Fuhr, StL	3274	1216-1354	24.8	.898	939
31	Tabaracci, Clg	2419	971-1087	27.0	.893	938
32t	Vernon, SJ	3564	1255-1401	23.6	.896	935
32t	Roloson, Clg	2205	887-997	27.1	.890	935
34	K McLean, Van-Car-Fla	2390	1046-1187	29.8	.881‡	931

(547-1639 minutes played)

GOALER, TEAM	MINS	SAVES-SHOTS	SH/GP	SVPCT	PERSEV
*Storr, LA	920	448-482	31.4	.929	982
Billington, Col	1162	543-588	30.4	.923	974
Flaherty, NYI	694	286-309	26.7	.926	970
Tallas, Bos	788	302-326	24.8	.926	968
*Skudra, Pit	851	315-341	24.0	.924	964
Essensa, Edm	825	369-404	29.4	.913	962
*S Shields, Buf	785	371-408	31.2	.909	961
Fichaud, NYI	807	382-422	31.4	.905	958
Dunham, NJ	773	303-332	25.8	.913	956
Waite, Phx	793	294-322	24.4	.913	954
Wregget, Pit	611	265-293	28.8	.904	952
*D Cloutier, NYR	551	225-248	27.0	.907	952
Terreri, Chi	1222	470-519	25.5	.906	948
Ranford, Was	1183	500-555	28.1	.901	948
*Hodson, Det	988	400-444	27.0	.901	946
Puppa, TB	1456	594-660	27.2	.900	945
Hrudey, SJ	1360	538-600	26.5	.897	941
*F Chabot, LA	554	238-267	28.9	.891	940
*Turek, Dal	1324	447-496	22.5	.901	939
Schwab, TB	821	330-370	27.0	.892	937
Healy, Tor	1068	400-453	25.4	.883	925

(1-546 minutes played)

GOALER, TEAM	MINS	SAVES-SHOTS	SH/GP	SVPCT	PERSEV
*Cousineau, Tor	17	9-9	31.8	1.000	1053
*Ri Parent, StL	12	1-1	5.0	1.000	1008
*Fernandez, Dal	69	33-35	30.4	.943	994
*Shulmistra, NJ	62	28-30	29.0	.933	982
*Moss, Clg	367	166-186	30.4	.892	943
*N Maracle, Det	178	57-63	21.2	.905	940
J Carey, Bos	496	201-225	27.2	.893	939

GOALER, TEAM	MINS	SAVES-SHOTS	SH/GP	SVPCT	PERSEV
Muzzatti, NYR-SJ	340	150-169	29.8	.888	937
*Askey, Ana	273	101-113	24.8	.894	935
*D Wilkinson, TB	311	131-148	28.7	.885	933
Trefilov, Chi	299	128-145	29.1	.883	931
*Weekes, Fla	485	215-247	30.6	.870	921
C Hirsch, Van	50	29-34	40.8	.853	921
Jablonski, Car	279	101-115	24.7	.878	919
Sidorkiewicz, NJ	20	7-8	24.0	.875	915
*Bierk, TB	433	180-210	29.1	.857	906
*Fountain, Car	163	58-68	25.0	.853	895
*S Langkow, Phx	137	50-60	26.3	.833	877
All goalers	129313	52667-58116	27.0	.906	951

1998-99

Five in a row for Hasek. His .937 save percentage is by far the highest ever recorded, aside from Jacques Plante's .942 in 1971. His 986 perseverance rating ties Johnny Bower's '64 mark as the second-best ever. He has opened the door wide for European goalies, and this year three of the top five are from across the pond: Hasek the Czech, Irbe the Latvian, Khabibulin the Russian. Within two years, two of Hasek's understudies on the Czech national team, Roman Turek and Roman Cechmanek, will rise to NHL prominence. This is getting to be a bit like the '50s and '60s, when the same guys would dominate the perseverance race, and we'd have to think of new things to say about them each year. Now it's true with Hasek. Fortunately, we come armed.

The signal event of the 1998-99 season, and probably the signal moment of the entire Bettman era, has already been summed up in two memorable words: No Goal. You no doubt know what we're referring to here, even you people from Dallas, not that any one of you would read a book about hockey. The travesty that ended the 1999 Cup Final – Brett Hull's clearly illegal goal, the uproar that followed it, and the NHL's fumbling efforts to back and fill to convince everyone that it really should have counted – all took place after we wrote our last book, *The Death of Hockey*, so we haven't had a chance to weigh in on the subject. If anything could have cemented the idea that hockey is being ushered to its deathbed by an inept administration of lawyers and businessmen who haven't the faintest notion of what our game is all about, the No Goal fiasco is it.

We're sure you recall the '99 Cup Final between the Stars and the Sabres, an unforgettable anxiety-drenched war between two teams that had to hack and hew endlessly not just to score a goal, but merely to gain a few feet of space simply to move the puck up-ice. It didn't make for anything remotely entertaining on the skills or creativity scale, but for tension, drama, courage, and sheer bitterness it was unsurpassed by any Final we've seen in more than a quarter century of watching them.

With Dallas up three games to two, it came down to game six in Buffalo, tied 1-1 at the end of regulation. Both teams, especially Dallas, were so physically battered that the Stars' team doctor later said the training rooms resembled battlefield triage units. Through one overtime, then two, and on into a third they played, with Hasek and Ed Belfour dependably stopping any rare attacker who somehow managed to machete his way through the gauntlet of sticks and gloves and bodies that stood between him and the net. Then, finally, in the third overtime period, Hull had the puck at the edge of the crease. His skates swivelled so that one was in the crease and one out as he slid the puck along the ice toward the net. The puck rebounded off a sprawling Hasek and came out beyond the crease at just the same moment that the Sabres' Brian Holzinger cruised between Hasek and Hull, although Holzinger missed the puck. Hull lifted his stick in the air, and now he was inside the crease, not in possession of the puck, his left skate blocking Hasek's glove hand as the biscuit skidded outside the crease. He then brought his stick down and, reaching behind himself, garnered the puck and shot it home.

Under the rules that were in force at the time – and make no mistake, they were bad rules – a mandatory video review should have followed. It would have revealed that the goal should not have counted, because Hull was standing in the crease when he got possession of the puck prior to shooting it into the net. As far as we could tell from our vantage point at the very top-most row of the Dallas end of the rink, that review was indeed undertaken – the two referees and two linesmen dutifully gathered at the sideboards by the scorer's bench to await word via phone from the video review judge upstairs, and dispersed after a brief conversation – but the goal was not reversed. (In fact, from our end the goal looked fine.) With the Dallas celebrants, cameramen, and photographers pouring onto the ice, Bettman and other league functionaries hauling out trophies, setting up tables, and rolling out red carpets, and the ESPN telecast as way, way over-schedule as so many other low-rated NHL playoff games had been in recent years, there was never any chance that the goal would be called back. Coach Lindy Ruff repaired to the Buffalo dressing room, watched the goal being replayed, and, along with the ESPN announcers, realized in horror that the goal was illegal. He raced back down the corridor and onto the carpet where Bettman stood, appealed to the commissioner to have the goal reviewed, but, Ruff says, Bettman simply turned away from him without even replying.

Way up in the top row we didn't know there was anything wrong with the goal yet. We simply looked on, stunned and heartbroken. It was amazing how quickly the building emptied out. As Bettman did his usual spiel in presenting the hardware, a few fans stood by their seats, but such was the monumental sense of bitterness in this series that some booed and even threw things at the Stars and

their small group of supporters, who were by now parading the Cup around and holding it aloft as if anyone there cared to see them. We finally shuffled out of the Marine Midland Arena (or was it by then the HSBC Arena?) with the huge, drained, silent throng, and as we hit the front doors in the big lobby, somebody listening on a transistor radio shouted out, "Now they're saying the goal shouldn't have counted." When we got to the car we heard Ruff and some other Sabres talking about what a shame it was that the Final should be decided by a phantom goal, and then we went to a bar – by now it was two in the morning – where we found one young guy raving about how Buffalo always gets screwed, how "they" will never let Buffalo win anything, how "they" will do whatever it takes to make sure Buffalo never fucking succeeds. On the television they had the CBC post-game show from the Dallas dressing room, and Brett Hull was telling Ron MacLean how great it felt to win the Stanley Cup, no one really letting on that his goal was unclean. At the same time, even long after we went to bed around 3:30, an outraged Ruff was still out on the sidewalk in front of the arena, talking to people about the goal that never was.

A couple of days later Ruff appeared at a rally attended by about 25,000 people in Niagara Square – more than showed up in Dallas for the Stars' victory parade – and started the famous No Goal chant. In New York, Bettman convened a press conference in which various NHL officials tried to rationalize the call, citing as precedent an early-season game in Phoenix that supposedly replicated what had happened in Buffalo, and in which there too the goal was allowed. No mention was made of the dozens, maybe hundreds, of perfectly fine goals, goals far more legitimate than Hull's, that were called back over the previous few seasons because of the league's asinine skate-in-the-crease rule. Colin Campbell, the league's chief hockey guy, tried to justify the call on the principle that Hull always had possession of the puck, and cited as proof the practice of awarding assists on goals that follow rebounds. If Player A, said Campbell, passes to Player B, and Player B takes a shot that the goalie kicks out, and the rebound goes to Player B and he shoots it into the net, we don't give an unassisted goal to Player B, do we? Player A gets an assist. Somehow, the league desperately reasoned, this meant that Player B always had possession of the puck, therefore Hull always had possession, so he was not in the crease illegally. This was plainly illogical. The relevant analogy, obviously, was that of a player entering the attacking zone, getting poke-checked so that the puck popped out of the zone for a moment, and that player then reaching back and dragging it back into the attacking zone. Clearly offside, because the player lost possession for an instant. Everyone has seen that call made a thousand times. That's exactly what Hull did, only he was entering the crease, not the attacking zone, but the same principle applied, or should have applied.

We were worried that Sabre fans were the only ones complaining, that we were being paranoid Buffalonians like the young guy in the bar, although when you're from as star-crossed a city as ours, it's very easy to believe that the reason you always fail is because greater powers are making certain you fail. But we were getting condolence calls from friends in Canada and in New York, and we were reading columns in out-of-town papers blasting Bettman and the NHL for the fiasco and their lame attempt to justify it. Then came the NHL awards show on CBC, and MacLean opened by taking pot-shot after pot-shot at the league and continued all night long, as the camera showed Ken Hitchcock and Bob Gainey shifting uncomfortably in their seats, making a game effort to laugh at the jokes but definitely anxious for the show to end so they could get the hell out of there. We even started to feel badly for the Stars; after all, it is merely the city they represent that is evil. They themselves were a great team with many likable players, and they'd performed courageously in reaching the Final, then absorbed a withering physical beating and battled on against a less talented but equally stubborn, infinitely wilful opponent. It wasn't their fault the referees and the league made a mistake; surely they didn't deserve to be belittled, but they were.

Then Wayne Gretzky, recently retired amid memorable fanfare in New York, walked out and announced that he thought the goal was perfectly good. It was perhaps the first public misstep the Great One, a grand master of public relations, had ever made. It was mystifying, but after a day's thought it became crystal clear: it wasn't a misstep at all. Gretzky knew exactly what he was doing: there was no upside to supporting the Sabres in the dispute; the upside lay entirely in supporting Bettman. Gretzky's new role was as the league's pure-as-snow goodwill ambassador, and Bettman, booed so loudly wherever he went that he could no longer afford to be introduced before the public, needed him badly. Gretzky, though we didn't know it at the time, was looking to get into the ownership side, and within a couple of years he had bought into the Phoenix franchise. Hence, Gretzky's pronouncement. After the CBC show, he was asked why he thought the goal was good. "Brett Hull's my friend," said the Wayner, "and he said the goal was good." We couldn't believe all this was happening, but it was. Meanwhile, the insufferable Dallas fans were posting all kinds of dim-witted yee-haw chest-thumping on the *Dallas Morning News* Web site, trying with the characteristic simple-minded grunting that passes for wit down there to prove wrong the opinion of the entire hockey world.

This was the low point for the NHL in our lifetime. Anything that transpired after that had to be an improvement. Fortunately, things did indeed improve. The toe-in-the-crease rule was abolished at the same press conference we described above, video reviews were sharply cut back, allowing fans to cheer when the puck went in the net rather than after three minutes of waiting around to see what the

video goal judge thought, referees started whistling down players who clutched, grabbed, and hooked, one of the reasons for Mario Lemieux's eventual return to the ice, and even though four new teams had entered the already grossly overextended league by 2000, the NHL announced that there was now a moratorium on expansion for the foreseeable future. That's all good, but the 1999 Cup Final was a terrible, terrible price to pay for it.

1998–99
(minimum 1640 minutes played)

	GOALER, TEAM	MINS	SAVES-SHOTS	SH/GP	SVPCT	PERSEV
1	Hasek, Buf	3817	1758-1877	29.5	.937†	986
2	G Hebert, Ana	4083	1949-2114	31.1	.922	974
3t	Irbe, Car	3643	1618-1753	28.9	.923	971
3t	Dafoe, Bos	4001	1667-1800	27.0	.926	971
5	Khabibulin, Phx	3657	1551-1681	27.6	.923	969
6	S Shields, SJ	2162	931-1011	28.1	.921	968
7t	Tugnutt, Otw	2508	930-1005	24.0	.925	965
7t	Fiset, LA	2403	1113-1217	30.4	.915	965
7t	Dunham, Nas	2472	1260-1387	33.7‡	.908	965
10	Pa Roy, Col	3648	1534-1673	27.5	.917	963
11	Brathwaite, Clg	1663	728-796	28.7	.915	962
12	*Vokoun, Nas	1954	945-1041	32.0	.908	961
13	M Richter, NYR	3878	1728-1898	29.4	.910	959
14	Cu Joseph, Tor	4001	1732-1903	28.5	.910	958
15t	S Burke, Fla	3402	1473-1624	28.6	.907	955
15t	Osgood, Det	3691	1505-1654	26.9	.910	955
17	Belfour, Dal	3536	1256-1373	23.3	.915	954
18t	Vernon, SJ	2831	1093-1200	25.4	.911	953
18t	Thibault, Mtr-Chi	3543	1526-1685	28.5	.906	953
20	Hackett, Chi-Mtr	3615	1466-1616	26.8	.907	952
21	Snow, Van	3501	1544-1715	29.4	.900	949
22t	Essensa, Edm	2091	878-974	27.9	.901	948
22t	T Salo, NYI-Edm	3718	1488-1647	26.6	.903	948
24t	Rhodes, Otw	2480	959-1060	25.6	.905	947
24t	M Brodeur, NJ	4239	1566-1728	24.5	.906	947
26t	Barrasso, Pit	2306	895-993	25.8	.901	944
26t	Schwab, TB	2146	1026-1152	32.2	.891‡	944
28	Kolzig, Was	3586	1384-1538	25.7	.900	943
29	Shtalenkov, Edm-Phx	2062	796-886	25.8	.898	941
30	Vanbiesbrouck, Phi	3712	1245-1380	22.3	.902	939
31	Ranford, TB-Det	1812	846-956	31.7	.885	938
32	*Skudra, Pit	1914	733-822	25.8	.892	935
33	Fuhr, StL	2193	738-827	22.6	.892	930
34	McLennan, StL	1763	570-640	21.8†	.891‡	927

(547–1639 minutes played)

GOALER, TEAM	MINS	SAVES-SHOTS	SH/GP	SVPCT	PERSEV
Roussel, Ana	884	441-478	32.4	.923	977
*Moss, Clg	550	272-295	32.2	.922	976
*D Cloutier, NYR	1097	521-570	31.2	.914	966

GOALER, TEAM	MINS	SAVES-SHOTS	SH/GP	SVPCT	PERSEV
*N Maracle, Det	821	348-379	27.7	.918	964
*Storr, LA	1525	663-724	28.5	.916	963
*M Legace, LA	899	400-439	29.3	.911	960
Roloson, Buf	911	418-460	30.3	.909	959
Puppa, TB	691	317-350	30.4	.906	956
Turek, Dal	1382	514-562	24.4	.915	955
M Fitzpatrick, Chi	1403	618-682	29.2	.906	955
Kidd, Car	1358	579-640	28.3	.905	952
Wregget, Clg	1590	645-712	26.9	.906	951
Tabaracci, Was	1193	480-530	26.7	.906	950
*Giguere, Clg	860	401-447	31.2	.897	949
*JS Aubin, Pit	756	276-304	24.1	.908	948
K McLean, Fla	1597	654-727	27.3	.900	945
Tallas, Bos	987	378-421	25.6	.898	941
Billington, Col	1086	440-492	27.2	.894	940
Flaherty, NYI	1048	438-491	28.1	.892	939
F Potvin, Tor-NYI	905	431-487	32.3	.885	939
Terreri, NJ	726	264-294	24.3	.898	938
Waite, Phx	898	349-390	26.1	.895	938
C Hirsch, Van	919	387-435	28.4	.890	937
R Hextall, Phi	1235	412-464	22.5	.888	926
*Theodore, Mtr	913	356-406	26.7	.877	921

(1–546 minutes played)

GOALER, TEAM	MINS	SAVES-SHOTS	SH/GP	SVPCT	PERSEV
S Gauthier, SJ	3	2-2	40.0	1.000	1067
Rosati, Was	28	12-12	25.7	1.000	1043
*Fernandez, Dal	60	27-29	29.0	.931	979
*M Denis, Col	217	101-110	30.4	.918	969
*Bt Johnson, StL	286	117-127	26.6	.921	966
*Mt Biron, Buf	281	110-120	25.6	.917	959
F Chabot, Mtr	430	172-188	26.2	.915	959
*Passmore, Edm	362	166-183	30.3	.907	958
*D Wilkinson, TB	253	116-129	30.6	.899	950
Fichaud, Nas	447	205-229	30.7	.895	946
Hodson, Det-TB	413	177-197	28.6	.898	946
Healy, Tor	546	230-257	28.2	.895	942
*Bierk, TB	59	19-21	21.4	.905	940
*Bach, LA	108	58-66	36.7	.879	940
*M Brochu, Was	120	49-55	27.5	.891	937
*C Mason, Nas	69	38-44	38.3	.864	927
*Ri Parent, StL	519	171-193	22.3	.886	923
*Cousineau, NYI	293	105-119	24.4	.882	923
*Weekes, Van	532	223-257	29.0	.868	916
Trefilov, Clg-Chi	187	189-104	33.4	.856	911
*Esche, Phx	130	43-50	23.1	.860	898
Reese, Tor	106	43-51	28.9	.843	891
*Garner, Clg	139	62-74	31.9	.838	891
*JM Pelletier, Phi	60	24-29	29.0	.828	876
*S Langkow, Phx	35	14-17	29.1	.824	872
J Carey, StL	202	66-76	22.6	.829	867
All goalers	134743	55869-61699	27.5	.906	951

1999–2000

Of all the goalies donning the pads in the National Hockey League today, Mike Vernon is perhaps the one we'd least expect to win a perseverance championship. Yet here he is, ending Hasek's five-year stranglehold on the title. Vernon's accomplishment is all the more remarkable in that he achieved it despite a mid-season trade from San Jose to Florida, thus becoming the first league-leader in perseverance to claim the crown having played for two teams in one season. The Panthers acquired Vernon after their number one, Trevor Kidd, went down injured with the same 966 perseverance rating that Vernon would wind up registering. Florida had awesome goaling this year (they started the campaign with Sean Burke in their nets but traded him away, and *he* had a great season), but it went for naught in the playoffs. Vernon notched a .912 save percentage against New Jersey in the first round, but Martin Brodeur had a .942, and out went the Panthers in a four-game sweep.

Hasek finished in a tie for second, incredible considering the nagging groin injury that sidelined him for much of the season and that bothered him when he did play. His early-season performance was that of a mortal, even an ordinary mortal, and there was much talk of Hasek's bad year. They were still saying that when he backstopped the Sabres to a March tear that got them into the final playoff spot.

Jean-Sebastien Aubin has a tremendous rookie season with Pittsburgh, although he is somehow relegated to foot-note status when commentators talk about the fine crop of rookies between the pipes this year: Brian Boucher in Philly, Marc Denis in Colorado, Roberto Luongo on the Island, Martin Biron in Buffalo. Aubin takes a seat when the Penguins get to the post-season, Ron Tugnutt getting the nod for the Pens' two-round run. Curtis Joseph turns in another fine year in Toronto, but finishes second in the Vezina voting to Olaf Kolzig – not a bad choice, but as you can see by the slim five perseverance points separating first from ninth on the 1999–2000 list, the honour could have gone to any of those nine men and we wouldn't complain. Well, we'd complain if it had gone to Ed Belfour, who led the league in save percentage and Dallas back to the Cup Final but who also got drunk at a motel, assaulted a security guard responding to a call from a woman in the same motel room as Belfour, was arrested by police, tried to bribe one of the arresting officers by offering him "a million dollars," then vomited all over the officer. A class act befitting the city of Dallas.

Look at the bottom of the list, see Byron Dafoe, and ask yourself why anyone cared that he held out at the start of this season. Typical Bruin goalie. Can you say "Ross Brooks"? "John Blue"? "Doug Keans"? There are players on this list from a team in Nashville; it does not even warrant our attention, or yours. Let's revisit the Islanders. The season before, Mike Milbury left goalie-of-the-future Eric Fichaud unprotected in the expansion draft and promptly lost him, traded goalie-of-the-future Tommy Salo to Edmonton, and acquired Toronto goalie-of-the-future Felix Potvin. This year he anoints number one draft choice Roberto Luongo goalie-of-the-future and trades Potvin to Vancouver for goalie-of-the-future Kevin Weekes. On Long Island, the future's so bright you've got to wear an air-sickness bag.

1999–2000
(minimum 1640 minutes played)

	GOALER, TEAM	MINS	SAVES-SHOTS	SH/GP	SVPCT	PERSEV
1	Vernon, SJ-Fla	2791	1265-1380	29.7	.917	966
2t	Hasek, Buf	2066	861-937	27.2	.919	964
2t	*JS Aubin, Pit	2789	1272-1392	29.9	.914	964
2t	Cu Joseph, Tor	3801	1696-1854	29.3	.915	964
5t	S Burke, Fla-Phx	2492	1124-1230	29.6	.914	963
5t	Belfour, Dal	3620	1494-1571	26.0	.919†	963
7	Theodore, Mtr	1655	659-717	26.0	.919	962
8t	Kolzig, Was	4371	1794-1957	26.9	.917	961
8t	Hackett, Mtr	3301	1411-1543	28.0	.914	961
10t	S Shields, SJ	3797	1664-1826	28.9	.911	959
10t	Dunham, Nas	3077	1438-1584	30.9	.908	959
10t	T Salo, Edm	4164	1713-1875	27.0	.914	959
13	Pa Roy, Col	3704	1499-1640	26.6	.914	958
14	*B Boucher, Phi	2038	725-790	23.3	.918	956
15t	Weekes, Van-NYI	3013	1472-1634	32.5‡	.901	955
15t	M Richter, NYR	3622	1642-1815	30.1	.905	955
15t	Thibault, Chi	3438	1521-1679	29.3	.906	955
18t	Storr, LA	2206	915-1008	27.4	.908	953
18t	G Hebert, Ana	3976	1639-1805	27.2	.908	953
18t	Brathwaite, Clg	3448	1506-1664	29.0	.905	953
18t	*Mr Biron, Buf	2229	898-988	26.6	.909	953
18t	Vokoun, Nas	1879	821-908	29.0	.904	953
23	M Brodeur, NJ	4312	1636-1797	25.0	.910	952
24t	Osgood, Det	3148	1223-1349	25.7	.907	949
24t	Turek, StL	3960	1341-1470	22.3†	.912	949
24t	Irbe, Car	4345	1683-1858	25.7	.906	949
27t	Fiset, LA	2592	1089-1208	28.0	.901	948
27t	F Potvin, NYI-Van	3239	1385-1538	28.5	.901	948
29t	Snow, Van	1712	699-775	27.2	.902	947
29t	Shtalenkov, Phx-Fla	1786	669-739	24.8	.905	947
31t	Tugnutt, Otw-Pit	2809	1099-1217	26.0	.903	946
31t	Lalime, Otw	2038	755-834	24.6	.905	946
33	Vanbiesbrouck, Phi	2950	1035-1143	23.2	.906	944
34	D Cloutier, TB	2492	1113-1258	30.3	.885‡	935
35	Dafoe, Bos	2307	916-1030	26.8	.889	934

(547–1639 minutes played)

GOALER, TEAM	MINS	SAVES-SHOTS	SH/GP	SVPCT	PERSEV
*M Denis, Col	1203	567-618	30.8	.917	969
Kidd, Fla	1574	740-809	30.8	.915	966
Fernandez, Dal	1353	555-603	26.7	.920	965
*R Luongo, NYI	1292	670-730	33.9	.904	961
Billington, Was	611	282-310	30.4	.910	960
*J Grahame, Bos	1344	554-609	27.2	.910	955
Passmore, Chi	1388	591-654	28.3	.904	951
Wregget, Det	1579	630-700	26.6	.900	944
Essensa, Phx	1573	646-719	27.4	.898	944
N Maracle, Atl	1618	758-852	31.6	.890	942
K McLean, NYR	1206	500-558	27.8	.896	942
*Fankhouser, Atl	920	402-451	29.4	.891	940
McLennan, StL	1009	308-341	20.3	.903	937
Ranford, Edm	785	360-407	31.1	.885	936
Healy, Tor	1164	468-527	27.2	.888	933
Tallas, Bos	1363	556-628	27.6	.886	931
Ri Parent, TB	698	310-353	30.3	.878	929
Roussel, Ana	988	393-445	27.0	.883	928
Rhodes, Atl	1561	702-803	30.9	.874	926
Roloson, Buf	677	245-277	24.5	.884	925
Barrasso, Pit-Otw	1288	500-568	26.5	.880	924
Terreri, NJ	649	262-299	27.6	.876	922
*S Langkow, Atl	765	340-395	31.0	.861	912
Skudra, Pit	922	326-374	24.3	.872	912
Fuhr, Clg	1205	459-536	26.7	.856	901
Hodson, TB	769	280-327	25.5	.856	899

(1–546 minutes played)

GOALER, TEAM	MINS	SAVES-SHOTS	SH/GP	SVPCT	PERSEV
*S Valiquette, NYI	193	111-117	36.4	.949	1009
Shulmistra, Fla	60	20-21	21.0	.952	987
*Minard, Edm	60	33-36	36.0	.917	977
Giguere, Clg	330	160-175	31.8	.914	967
*Bierk, TB	509	277-308	36.3	.899	960
Flaherty, NYI	182	74-81	26.7	.914	958
M Legace, Det	240	106-117	29.2	.906	955
*Nabokov, SJ	414	151-166	24.1	.910	950
M Fitzpatrick, Car	107	60-68	38.2	.882	946
*Esche, Phx	408	192-215	31.6	.893	946
Cousineau, LA	171	58-64	22.5	.906	944
*Hnilicka, NYR	86	39-44	30.7	.886	938
*Hurme, Otw	60	17-19	19.0	.895	926
Fichaud, Car	490	182-206	25.2	.883	926
Tabaracci, Atl-Col	119	44-50	25.2	.880	922
Fountain, Otw	16	5-6	22.5	.833	871
Puppa, TB	249	110-129	31.1	.853	905
Schwab, Van	269	99-115	25.7	.861	904
*Labbe, NYR	60	19-22	22.0	.864	900
*Kochan, TB	238	94-111	28.0	.847	893
*Michaud, Van	69	22-27	23.5	.815	854
*Lamothe, Chi	116	40-50	25.9	.800	843
All goalers	139118	57929-64053	27.6	.904	950

2000-01

We come at last to the new millennium's first full season, played out as we wrote this book, so if you are reading this a few years from now and find that we wrote some things here that sounded downright stupid, well, you just let us know – if you can find us down there in Mexico, that is, sipping margaritas on the beach, having absconded with all the profits our hockey expertise will have earned us. *¡Una bebida más, nuestra bonita rosita!*

One impression we had as we looked at the season's perseverance table was that the goaltending guard had changed. There's a new generation topping the creasekeepers' chart, headed by Mike Dunham of – swallow hard – the Nashville Predators. Dunham was the Preds' first selection in the expansion draft in 1998, and he endeared himself to us that day by noting that Nashville's newly unveiled sweater seemed to depict some kind of cat gagging on something or other. Beyond earning points for his facility with words and images, Dunham had already earned praise as Martin Brodeur's understudy at New Jersey; he built his reputation in the AHL with Albany River Rats, not far from his hometown of Johnson City, N.Y., next to Binghamton. That part of New York State is also the home of the highly competent, highly underrated Guy Hebert (from Troy, near Albany), which seems to presage the region becoming the new nursery of netminders, a kind of latter-day Winnipeg.

In any case, Dunham is hardly the only young whipper-snapper who excelled this season. In second place we find Roberto Luongo, one of Mike Milbury's recently discarded goalies of the future, now a Florida Panther. Luongo is technically a rookie, despite having played 24 games the previous year, yet there will be nary a peep from anyone that perhaps he should be considered for the Calder Trophy. (The same thing happened to Mike Richter in '91.) Part of the problem is that the Panthers were so awful this season – as we've already seen, Pavel Bure was not only fantastic, but their only skater of any ability whatever – that Luongo's performance was entirely overlooked. For those of you still unimpressed, compare Luongo's .920 save percentage and 970 perseverance rating with those of Florida's other goaler, Trevor Kidd, whom you'll find in 31st place, sporting .893 and 945 marks. Speaking of the dreary proliferation of poorly drawn big cats on hockey sweaters, just what is it that the panther is supposed to be doing on Florida's uniforms? Balancing on his hind legs? Conducting an orchestra?

Maybe it's snarling at the cat-like thing snarling on Minnesota's uniforms, which brings us to Manny Fernandez, another recent understudy getting his big chance with an expansion club, helping Jacques Lemaire's neutral-zone trappers to an encouraging inaugural season. Ron Tugnutt excels in the first-year nets of the Columbus Blue Jackets, a nice renascence for a journeyman goaler whose best days seemed long past, and Roman Cechmanek, Dom Hasek's understudy with the Czech national team, stages an impressive North American debut in the Flyers net. Phoenix's Sean Burke, no spring chicken he, has his best season ever, but his third-place finish here is bittersweet. He'd led the league all year long, carrying the Coyotes on his back the whole way, but both Burke and his teammates faltered in the final three weeks. He fell out of the lead just at the wire, and the Coyotes fell out of the playoff spot they'd occupied all year long in the season's 81st game. So how 'bout that – the top five goalers of the year all come from clubs that missed the playoffs. No wonder none of them were Vezina finalists. Seems you're not worth thinking about these days unless your team makes the post-season.

There are other fine performances here from goaltending's Fresh Young Things: Manny Legace, Patrick Lalime, Jean-Sebastien Giguere, Evgeni Nabokov – but we have to focus on Hasek, who by now has established himself as the most compelling goalie of our time, and we really mean that. So excellent, so head-and-shoulders above everyone else has Hasek been for so long, that this year, when he was merely one of the very best, a whole slew of commentators proclaimed that he was having a "poor season," that he was "past his prime." In Buffalo, which we like to think of as a bastion of hockey sophistication, the newspaper and radio reporters were openly touting the wisdom of trading Hasek "while the Sabres can still get something for him" and were convinced that young Martin Biron was ready to take over the starting job – a line of faulty reasoning picked up on and embraced by practically every fan who called in to the city's various open-line hockey shows on radio and TV. In January, Hasek sat on the bench for two straight games for the first time since he took over the Buffalo starting job from Grant Fuhr, which only further fuelled the commentators' bonfire of inanities. Well, look here: Hasek is still as good as any goaler in the league, a fact to which his sixth-place finish, just seven perseverance points off the pace, testifies. Moreover, Hasek's .921 save percentage is much, much better than Biron's .909. And finally, the Sabres, behind Hasek's supposedly diminished goaltending skills, won the Jennings Trophy this year. Yes, the Sabres tightened their defence this season, but many of the shots Hasek faced were difficult ones: deflections, odd-man rushes, and the like. Still, Hasek kicked out more than 92% of them.

The Dominator is the victim of the impossibly high expectations he himself created and lived up to for so many years – this is the first time he did not finish first or second in perseverance since 1993 – and that is why so many thought so little of his performance this season. Yet there is no question that despite the lockstep in which most hockey pundits marched this season in their premature dismissal of Hasek, Buffalo would surely have missed the playoffs without him, and they would've gotten nowhere in the post-season against Philadelphia and Pittsburgh. That the Sabres lost to the Pens in game seven overtime with Hasek performing no miracles but still playing dependably, superbly – in fact, flawlessly – was seen as a sign of failure by a shocking number of fans not just in Buffalo but all around the continent. How sad that we have come to *expect* miracles, and blame the miracle worker when he doesn't produce enough of them for us anymore. By the time this book is published, the Sabres may indeed have let Dominik Hasek go. If they did, it would rank as one of the stupidest moves any hockey club has ever made.

Last but not least, look who finished on the bottom of the list of regular goalers. Why, it's Mike Vernon, back with his hometown team in Calgary, scene of some of his greatest achievements and, of course, some of his worst. Now he adds another typically Vernonian achievement: he becomes the first man since Harry Lumley in 1955 to finish first in perseverance one season and last the next.

2000–01
(minimum 1640 minutes played)

	GOALER, TEAM	MINS	SAVES-SHOTS	SH/GP	SVPCT	PERSEV
1	Dunham, Nas	2810	1274-1381	29.5	.923†	972
2t	*R Luongo, Fla	2628	1226-1333	30.4	.920	970
2t	S Burke, Phx	3644	1628-1766	29.1	.922	970
4t	Fernandez, Min	2461	1055-1147	28.0	.920	966
4t	Tugnutt, Cmb	3129	1401-1528	29.3	.917	966
6	Hasek, Buf	3904	1589-1726	26.5	.921	965
7	Cechmanek, Phi	3431	1349-1464	25.6	.921	964
8	Legace, Det	2136	836-909	25.5	.920	962
9	Cu Joseph, Tor	4100	1744-1907	27.9	.915	961
10t	Lalime, Otw	2136	1499-1640	27.3	.914	959
10t	Giguere, Ana	2031	889-976	28.8	.911	959
12	*E Nabokov, SJ	3700	1447-1582	25.7	.915	957
13	Theodore, Mtr	3298	1405-1546	28.1	.909	956
14t	Pa Roy, Col	3585	1381-1513	25.3	.913	955
14t	Vokoun, Nas	2088	855-940	27.0	.910	955
16	Kolzig, Was	4279	1764-1941	27.2	.909	954
17	Brathwaite, Clg	2742	1075-1181	25.8	.910	953
18t	Rhodes, Atl	2072	1013-1129	32.7‡	.897	952
18t	Irbe, Car	4406	1767-1947	26.5	.908	952
20	McLennan, Min	2230	934-1032	27.8	.905	951
21t	Snow, Pit	2032	913-1014	29.9	.900	950
21t	Weekes, TB	3378	1565-1742	30.9	.898	950
23t	Osgood, Det	2834	1183-1310	27.7	.903	949
23t	Vanbiesbrouck, NYI-NJ	2630	1144-1270	29.0	.901	949
23t	Dafoe, Bos	2536	975-1076	25.5	.906	949
26	G Hebert, Ana-NYR	2950	1364-1521	30.9	.897	948
27	M Brodeur, NJ	4297	1596-1762	24.6	.906	947
28t	T Salo, Edm	4364	1677-1856	25.5	.904	946
28t	*M Denis, Col	1830	841-940	30.8	.895	946
28t	*Bt Johnson, StL	1744	613-676	23.3	.907	946
31t	Belfour, Dal	3687	1364-1508	24.5	.905	945
31t	Kidd, Fla	2354	1087-1217	31.0	.893	945
33t	Storr, LA	2498	1017-1131	27.2	.899	944
33t	M Richter, NYR	2635	1199-1343	30.6	.893	944
35	F Potvin, Van-LA	3416	1336-1485	26.1	.900	943
36t	Hnilicka, Atl	1879	846-951	30.4	.890	940
36t	Turek, StL	3232	1125-1248	23.2†	.901	940

	GOALER, TEAM	MINS	SAVES-SHOTS	SH/GP	SVPCT	PERSEV
38	Thibault, Chi	3844	1531-1711	26.7	.895	939
39	D Cloutier, TB-Van	1920	793-889	27.8	.892	938
40	JS Aubin, Pit	2050	866-973	28.5	.890	937
41	Essensa, Van	2059	762-854	24.9	.892	934
42	Vernon, Clg	2246	913-1034	27.6	.883‡	929

(547–1639 minutes played)

GOALER, TEAM	MINS	SAVES-SHOTS	SH/GP	SVPCT	PERSEV
*Turco, Dal	1266	492-532	25.2	.925	967
Billington, Was	660	290-317	28.8	.915	963
S Shields, SJ-Ana	1135	484-531	28.1	.911	958
Mr Biron, Buf	918	388-427	27.9	.909	955
N Maracle, Atl	753	363-406	32.4	.894	948
*Hurme, Otw	1296	509-563	26.1	.904	948
*Esche, Phx	1350	589-657	29.2	.896	945
*Aebischer, Col	1393	486-538	23.2	.903	942
K McLean, NYR	1220	568-639	31.4	.889	941
Terreri, NJ-NYI	895	333-372	24.9	.895	937
*Garon, Mtr	589	209-233	23.7	.897	937
*Raycroft, Bos	649	259-291	26.9	.890	935
Hackett, Mtr	998	423-477	28.7	.887	935
Passmore, LA-Chi	1058	406-457	25.9	.888	932
Roussel, ANA-Edm	1001	394-446	26.7	.883	928
*DiPietro, NYI	1083	452-515	28.5	.878	925
Skudra, Buf-Bos	1116	449-511	27.5	.879	924
Flaherty, NYI-TB	1135	461-525	27.8	.878	924
Healy, Tor	871	293-331	22.8	.885	923
B Boucher, Phi	1470	564-644	26.3	.876	920
Tallas, Chi	627	230-265	25.4	.868	910
Moss, Car	557	214-251	27.0	.853	898

(1–546 minutes played)

GOALER, TEAM	MINS	SAVES-SHOTS	SH/GP	SVPCT	PERSEV
C Hirsch, Was	20	8-8	24.0	1.000	1040
*LaBarbera, NYR	10	2-2	12.0	1.000	1020
Khabibulin, TB	123	63-69	33.7	.913	969
*Fankhouser, Atl	260	144-160	36.9	.900	962
J Hedberg, Pit	545	229-253	27.9	.905	952
*Gustafson, Min	239	87-97	24.4	.897	937
*Kiprusoff, SJ	154	46-51	19.9	.902	935
*C Mason, Nas	59	18-20	20.3	.900	934
Ri Parent, Pit	332	133-150	27.1	.887	932
Jq Gage, Edm	260	110-125	28.8	.880	928
Fichaud, Mtr	62	28-32	31.0	.875	927
*Ouellet, Phi	76	24-27	21.3	.889	924
Fountain, Otw	59	22-25	25.4	.880	922
*Holmqvist, NYR	119	61-71	35.8	.859	919
*Kochan, TB	314	120-138	26.4	.870	914
*J Grahame, Bos	471	183-211	26.9	.867	912
*Noronen, Buf	108	34-39	21.7	.872	908
*Yeremeyev, NYR	212	88-104	29.4	.846	895
Fiset, LA	318	110-129	24.3	.853	893

GOALER, TEAM	MINS	SAVES-SHOTS	SH/GP	SVPCT	PERSEV
*Mi Larocque, Chi	152	50-59	23.3	.847	886
Whitmore, Bos	203	76-94	27.8	.809	855
Bierk, Min	60	21-27	27.0	.778	823
*Naumenko, Ana	70	22-29	24.9	.759	800
*T Scott, LA	25	7-10	24.0	.700	740
*E Konstantinov, TB	0	0-0	—	—	—
All goalers	147516	61383-67957	27.6	.903	949

Perseverance Leaders

Now let us review. Thirty-five seasons' worth of perseverance stats have given us the following roll call of champions. The asterisks (*) alongside Ron Hextall and Darren Pang designate them as the only rookies to win perseverance titles; the italics for Johnny Bower's '65–66 numbers denote the estimates Edward Yuen had to make for that year's totals; the daggers (†) by Jacques Plante's mindboggling save percentage and perseverance rating in '70–71 designate those marks as all-time records for any regular goalie in those categories; and that double dagger (‡) next to Gump Worsley's shots-per-game figure in 1962–63 signals that as the highest any regular netminder has ever been forced to face during any one season. Step forth, o champions!

Perseverance champions, season by season				
SEAS GOALER, TEAM		SH/GP	SVPCT	PERSEV
'54–55: Worsley, NY		35.6	.916	975 (tie)
	H Lumley, Tor	27.2	.929	975 (tie)
'55–56: Worsley, NY		36.3	.922	982
'56–57: Gl Hall, Det		30.4	.927	977
'57–58: Worsley, NY		32.6	.929	983
'58–59: J Plante, Mtr		28.8	.925	973
'59–60: Bower, Tor		33.1	.919	974
'60–61: Bower, Tor		32.3	.923	976
'61–62: J Plante, Mtr		30.6	.923	974
'62–63: Worsley, NY		38.2‡	.914	978
'63–64: Bower, Tor		31.6	.933	986
'64–65: Bower, Tor		31.3	.924	976
'65–66: Bower, Tor		32.3	.930	984
'66–67: Sawchuk, Tor		35.0	.920	978
'70–71: J Plante, Tor		32.6	.942†	997†
'74–75: R Vachon, LA		30.4	.926	977
'75–76: Resch, NYI		28.6	.928	975
'82–83: R Melanson, NYI		29.3	.909	958
'83–84: R Melanson, NYI		33.5	.902	958
'84–85: Lindbergh, Phi		30.0	.899	949
'85–86: Hrudey, NYI		34.0	.906	962
'86–87: *R Hextall, Phi		30.5	.902	952
'87–88: *Pang, Chi		35.3	.891	950
'88–89: Takko, Min		34.5	.899	957
'89–90: Pa Roy, Mtr		28.8	.912	960

SEAS	GOALER, TEAM	SH/GP	SVPCT	PERSEV
'90–91:	M Richter, NYR	32.2	.903	957
'91–92:	Cu Joseph, StL	33.5	.910	966
'92–93:	Cu Joseph, StL	34.0	.911	968
'93–94:	Vanbiesbrouck, Fla	33.3	.924	980
'94–95:	Hasek, Buf	30.3	.930	981
'95–96:	Hasek, Buf	35.3	.920	979
'96–97:	Hasek, Buf	32.4	.930	984
'97–98:	Hasek, Buf	30.6	.932	983
'98–99:	Hasek, Buf	29.5	.937	986
'99–00:	Vernon, SJ-Fla	29.7	.917	966
'00–01:	Dunham, Nas	29.5	.923	972

Career Perseverance Leaders

Eon upon eon of complete single-season perseverance statistics can mean only one thing: career perseverance statistics. We present them in two sets, covering only those seasons in which we have a run of several consecutive years of stats. Therefore we'll look at goalies' career stats for the Original Six years reconstructed by Yuen, '54–55 through '66–67, and for the years that the NHL has kept official shots-and-saves figures, '82–83 through '00–01.

Before we start, we understand the impulse to regard these career stats as the be-all, end-all goaltending stat. But no! assiduously resist that impulse! Form cadres to participate in vigorous self-criticism sessions! Ardently pursue, dear comrades, correct thought! There is too much year-to-year variation in league-wide perseverance figures to take these career figures too literally. For example, in the mid-'80s, the average league-wide save percentage hovered around .875; by the late '90s, it had risen above .900. Thus any goalie who spent his career playing in the late '90s, no matter how mediocre he was, would have better save percentages and perseverance marks than even an excellent goaler who played in the mid-'80s. For this reason, we will not rank the goalies who appear in these lists.

Nevertheless, there is much here to enthrall and astound even the casual observer, young and old alike. Step right up, folks, and gaze upon the career perseverance stats of the nine goaltenders who played at least 12,000 minutes between 1954–55 and 1966–67. They are listed only with the teams they played for and the number of seasons they performed during this 13-year period; those whose careers began before '54–55 have a small degree symbol (°) appended to their number-of-seasons figure. Behold:

Career Perseverance, 1954–55 to 1966–67 (minimum 12,000 minutes played)					
GOALER, TEAM(S), SEASONS	MINS	SAVES-SHOTS	SH/GP	SVPCT	PRSV
Bower, NY-Tor, 11°	24738	12050-13084	31.7	.921	974
Worsley, NY-Mtr, 13°	36996	19198-21043	34.1	.912	969
Gl Hall, Det-Chi, 13°	45141	21029-22926	30.5	.917	968
J Plante, Mtr-NY, 11°	37904	17104-18637	29.5	.918	967

GOALER, TEAM(S), SEASONS	MINS	SAVES-SHOTS	SH/GP	SVPCT	PRSV
Sawchuk, Det-Bos-Det-Tor, 13°	37565	17128-18821	30.1	.910	966
C Hodge, Mtr, 9	13735	5869-6433	28.1	.912	959
E Johnston, Bos, 5	13524	7051-7842	34.8	.899	957
R Crozier, Det, 4	12057	5405-5979	29.8	.904	954
D Simmons, Bos-Tor-NY, 10	13930	6288-6966	30.0	.903	953

Johnny Bower has a substantial edge here, but remember too that he didn't generally shoulder the full-season load that other goalers of his day bore. Still, he looks awfully good. Behind Bower, all bunched closely together, are Worsley, Hall, Plante, and Sawchuk, rounding out the quintessential quintet of Golden Age goalkeeping. The only other backstops of the era to have played enough to qualify only barely did; Hodge, Johnston, and Simmons were given NHL auditions and stuck around for a while, but none of them ever got an extended starring role, and Crozier debuted late in the era. This list, therefore, shows us just how much of a stranglehold the same five men had on the goaltending jobs of the period. The sixth job was that of the Boston goalie, and as this list shows it was a job no one held for long. It's a strange fact that the Bruins, a team whose first quarter-century was distinguished by the legendary goaltending tenures of Cecil "Tiny" Thompson and Frankie "Mr. Zero" Brimsek, should have marked their next 20 years by going through an extended fallow period between the pipes, relieved only by Terry Sawchuk's two unhappy seasons in Beantown. Only with the emergence of Gerry Cheevers during the Orr-Esposito years could Boston boast of having a prominent goalie for any length of time – and you could argue that they've never had one since, though Andy Moog and Reggie Lemelin had pretty good runs many years later, even if each of those two earned more fame elsewhere.

Looking at this list makes us think once again of the short shrift accorded Bower and Worsley in the game's collective memory, where they are hailed as clown princes of the cord cottage but not quite up to the Olympian standards of Sawchuk, Hall, and Plante. Well, we beg, one last time, to differ. Bower and Worsley were every bit as good, and we'd like to see everyone recognize that once and for all. The only other thing we'd like to see, but which we fear we never will because the data simply aren't there, is Sawchuk's numbers from the sparkling dawn of his career. By all accounts he was unbeatable in his first four full seasons, '51 through '54, years that immediately precede the reliable reporting of shots-and-saves statistics, and also years in which the Red Wings garnered two Stanley Cups and four first-place finishes. Certainly if those four years were somehow factored into Sawchuk's career stats, he might well have finished higher, even highest of all the Golden Age goalies.

Now to the career stats of the 63 goalkeepers who have played at least 12,000 minutes since 1982–83. Those

goalies with one of these suckers (°) alongside their years-played figure had careers that began before '82–83, and those with an "x" before their name were active through the 2000–01 season.

Career Perseverance, 1982–83 to 2000–01
(minimum 12,000 minutes played)

GOALER, TEAM(S), SEASONS	MINS	SAVES-SHOTS	SH/GP	SVPCT	PRSV
x-Hasek, Chi-Buf, 11	29873	13762-14876	29.9	.925	975
x-G Hebert, StL-Ana-NYR, 10	27889	13093-14400	31.0	.909	961
x-Cu Joseph, StL-Edm-Tor, 12	38057	17635-19430	30.6	.908	959
x-Khabibulin, Wpg/Phx-TB, 6	16149	7317-8058	29.9	.908	958
x-F Potvin, Tor-NYI-Van-LA, 9	28722	13136-14501	30.3	.906	956
x-Pa Roy, Mtr-Col, 17	52693	22701-24988	28.5	.908	956
x-M Brodeur, NJ, 9	29354	11558-12674	25.9	.912	955
x-M Richter, NYR, 12	34294	15566-17215	30.1	.904	955
x-Dafoe, Was-LA-Bos, 9	17783	7612-8406	28.4	.906	954
x-Kolzig, Was, 10	19654	8018-8832	27.0	.908	953
x-Thibault, Qbc-Col-Mtr-Chi, 8	22168	9644-10670	28.9	.904	952
x-Osgood, Det, 8	22475	8878-9778	26.1	.908	951
x-Kidd, Clg-Car-Fla, 9	17717	7610-8427	28.5	.903	951
x-T Salo, NYI-Edm, 7	19796	8154-9010	27.3	.905	951
x-Fiset, Qbc/Col-LA, 12	21676	9911-11018	30.5	.900	950
x-Hackett, NYI-SJ-Chi-Mtr, 12	23724	10528-11688	29.6	.901	950
x-Belfour, Chi-SJ-Dal, 12	38860	15377-16967	26.2	.906	950
x-S Burke, NJ-Har/Car-Van-Phi-Fla-Phx, 13	35964	16354-18196	30.4	.899	949
x-Irbe, SJ-Dal-Van-Car, 10	26644	11443-12707	28.6	.901	948
x-Vanbiesbrouck, NYR-Fla-Phi-NYI-NJ, 19°	50115	22049-24541	29.4	.898	947
M Fitzpatrick, LA-NYI-Fla-TB-Chi-Car, 12	18329	8242-9195	30.1	.896	947
Hrudey, NYI-LA-SJ, 15	38082	18136-20310	32.0	.893	946
Puppa, Buf-Tor-TB, 15	23819	10472-11676	29.4	.897	946
x-Essensa, Wpg-Det-Edm-Van, 11	23865	10732-11985	30.1	.895	946
x-Snow, Qbc-Phi-Van-Pit, 8	13119	5486-6102	27.9	.899	946
x-Rhodes, Tor-Ott-Atl, 9	16570	6893-7666	27.8	.899	945
x-Tugnutt, Qbc-Edm-Ana-Mtr-Ott-Pit-Cmb, 13	24735	10827-12113	29.4	.894	943
R Hextall, Phi-Qbc-NYI-Phi, 13	34749	14633-16356	28.3	.895	942
Barrasso, Buf-Pit-Ott, 17	41760	18663-20939	30.1	.891	941

GOALER, TEAM(S), SEASONS	MINS	SAVES-SHOTS	SH/GP	SVPCT	PRSV
x-Terreri, NJ-SJ-Chi-NJ-NYI, 14	22368	9475-10618	28.5	.892	940
Tabaracci, Pit-Wpg-Was-Clg-Atl-Col, 11	15255	6340-7100	27.9	.893	939
Ranford, Bos-Edm-Bos-Was-TB-Det-Edm, 15	35936	16220-18262	30.5	.888	939
Moog, Edm-Bos-Dal-Mtr, 16°	39438	16709-18754	28.5	.891	939
Hanlon, StL-NYR-Det, 9°	18191	8416-9502	31.3	.886	938
Wregget, Tor-Phi-Pit-Clg-Det, 17	31663	14747-16664	31.6	.885	938
x-Healy, LA-NYI-NYR-Tor, 15	24256	10387-11710	29.8	.887	937
Wm Smith, NYI, 7°	14106	6356-7173	30.5	.886	937
Froese, Phi-NYR, 8	13451	5602-6296	28.1	.890	937
Casey, Min-Bos-StL, 12	23254	9907-11153	28.8	.888	936
M Bannerman, Chi, 5°	13914	6571-7444	32.1	.883	936
Malarchuk, Qbc-Was-°Bfl, 9	18910	8411-9497	30.1	.886	936
Fuhr, Edm-Tor-Buf-LA-StL-Clg, 18°	46098	20211-22810	29.7	.886	936
x-K McLean, NJ-Van-Car-Fla-NYR, 16	35090	14963-16867	28.8	.887	935
x-Vernon, Clg-Det-SJ-Fla-Clg, 18	43624	17420-19588	26.9	.889	934
Beaupre, Min-Was-Ott-Tor, 15°	33177	14536-16448	29.7	.884	933
Re Lemelin, Clg-Bos, 11°	23367	10088-11408	29.3	.884	933
R Melanson, NYI-Min-LA-NJ-Mtr, 9°	13717	6271-7120	31.1	.881	933
Cheveldae, Det-Wpg-Bos, 10	19171	8414-9530	29.8	.883	933
Peeters, Bos-Was-Phi, 8°	20122	7936-8961	26.7	.886	930
G Meloche, Min-Pit, 6°	13115	5892-6716	30.7	.877	929
Liut, StL-Was-Har, 10°	27233	11574-13150	29.0	.880	928
x-Billington, NJ-Ott-Bos-Col-Was, 13	16170	6726-7680	29.7	.877	927
Wamsley, Mtr-StL-Clg-Tor, 11°	20664	8590-9768	28.4	.879	927
G Millen, Har-StL-Qbc-Chi-Det, 10°	24337	10696-12217	30.1	.876	926
B Hayward, Wpg-Mtr-Min-SJ, 11	20025	8639-9881	29.6	.874	924
P Riggin, Atl/Clg-Was-Bos-Pit, 5°	13159	5090-5791	26.4	.879	923
R Sauve, Bfl-Chi-NJ, 7°	14332	6016-6877	28.8	.875	923
J Cloutier, Bfl-Chi-Qbc 7°	12826	5384-6162	28.8	.874	922
Weeks, NYR-Har-Van-NYI-LA-Ott, 11°	12967	5494-6302	29.2	.872	920

GOALER, TEAM(S), SEASONS	MINS	SAVES-SHOTS	SH/GP	SVPCT	PRSV
M Gosselin, Qbc-LA-Har, 9	12857	5420-6221	29.0	.871	920
G Stefan, Det, 8°	16213	6973-8031	29.7	.868	918
R Brodeur, Van-Har, 6°	15854	6803-7862	29.8	.865	915
Chevrier, NJ-Wpg-Chi-Pit-Det, 6	12202	5340-6185	30.4	.863	914

As we expected, this list is weighted heavily in favour of goalies of recent vintage, who are spending their careers in a time of bulging equipment, advanced technique, close checking, and the high save percentages that result from these developments. So hey, we love Byron Dafoe, but we don't really believe he's a better goaler than, say, Kelly Hrudey was. However, we can still draw water from this gurgling fount of information. There's Hasek, way out in front by a gaping 14 career perseverance points on a list in which no two other men are separated by more than three points. Guy Hebert is a surprise in second, mute testament to the anonymity in which any player toils if he's exiled to Anaheim. We rarely got to see him out there, stuck in the southwesternmost corner of the entire hockey world for the better part of a decade, though we noticed that he always put up very good numbers. We finally did get a good look at Hebert after he was acquired by the Rangers late in the '00–01 campaign, and he was a revelation to watch. His deep, spring-like crouch brought to mind Sawchuk himself, and he was always square to the puck. It's an interesting style, sort of a hybrid between the best of the old and of the new, and it's why Hebert has done so well for so long, even if few people have noticed.

Look down the list and find your favourite padmen, but save your glee or your high dudgeon for the next pair of lists, which we feel provide a more accurate measure of their performance. Please, allow us to explain. As if you have any choice in the matter.

Perseverance Plus/Minus

As we mentioned earlier, it's a little unfair to compare a goaler's performance in 1983 with another's performance in 2001. In order to get any kind of meaningful comparison, you have to measure each against the prevailing averages of the seasons in question. And we happen to have the league-wide save-percentage, shots-per-game, and perseverance averages for every one of these 35 seasons. So we devised a simple method for putting everyone on the same scale, whether they struggled through a goal-crazed, everyone-over-the-top season of the Gretzky-in-Edmonton era or gloried in a check-'em-till-they-drop campaign of Jacques Lemaire's most lascivious fantasies. All you do is take the netminder's perseverance mark from a given season and subtract from it the league-wide average perseverance for that season. We count only those seasons in which a goaler played enough to qualify as a regular. So, for example, let's take Bob Sauve, whom we once called the most underrated player in the NHL (our bad). In '82–83 he registered a 916 perseverance mark, 10 points below the league average of 926. The following year, his 913 was 11 below the NHL average, but he rebounded in '85 with a 943, 18 better than the average. So for those three years, you take Sauve's minus-10, minus-11, and plus-18, which gives him a minus-3, then add in the plus-21 and minus-15 for his final two years as a regular. Add them all together (–10–11+18+21–15) and you get a sum of plus-3. Now divide that by the five seasons Sauve spent as a regular during the years being measured, and you get an average of plus-0.6 – which means that over the five years Bob Sauve was a regular goalkeeper, his perseverance rating was an eyelash better than the league average. This method, ingenious as it is, thank you, smooths out the many bumps that varying annual averages leave in the statistical road. Everyone's on a level surface now.

Now to the numbers themselves, with a minimum of 12,000 minutes played and five seasons spent as a regular. For this stat, we'll rank the goalers according to their career totals above or below the perseverance average. First, the very short Original Six listing:

	Perseverance Plus/Minus, 1954–55 to 1966–67 (minimum 12,000 minutes played and five seasons as regular)	
	GOALER, TEAM (SEASONS AS REGULAR)	PRSV +/– AVG.
1	Bower, NY-Tor (8)	+13.8
2	Worsley, NY-Mtr (10)	+ 9.1
3	Gl Hall, Det-Chi (11)	+ 6.8
4	J Plante, Mtr-NY (11)	+ 4.8
5	Sawchuk, Det-Bos-Det-Tor (13)	– 0.3
6	D Simmons, Bos-Tor-NY (5)	– 4.4
7	E Johnston, Bos (5)	– 8.2

Johnny Bower stands alone as the premier goalie of the last seasons before expansion. In the eight years here for which he served as a regular, all with the Leafs, he finished every single season above the league perseverance average – a feat equalled by only one other netminder in all the years of the perseverance statistic. Unless and until someone can prove otherwise, from now on we regard Bower as the best of his time. You should too. And you should hold Lorne Worsley in similar high esteem. No other backstop we encounter in the three and a half decades of the perseverance stat flourished so grandly under such impossible conditions. The Gumper performed so heroically for so long under siege at the old Madison Square Garden, conditions that would've broken a lesser man after a season or two, and then had to struggle through injuries and demotion to get his richly deserved shot at the Cup in Montreal. He succeeded on all counts, and his marvellous record is distilled in the proud numbers he posts here.

Glenn Hall was called "Mr. Goalie" for his unstinting consistency, and what's not reflected here in his already impressive mark is the continued excellence he exhibited in the first years of expansion with St. Louis. The same must be said of Jacques Plante, who shows very well on this list, but whose performance in the '70s, which does not show up here, was truly mind-bending. If we can someday fill in the gaps in the statistical record and piece together the entirety of Jake the Snake's career, how much greater will his statistical showing be? Perhaps then, Plante would emerge as the best of a bygone era.

Terry Sawchuk's story, tragic in the classic Greek sense of greatness squandered by a fatal human flaw, has captured the imaginations of the hockey world in recent years. The full measure of his on-ice greatness is lost to us, because his greatest years went statistically unrecorded. Here he checks in just a hair's breadth beneath the league-wide average, but it's important to remember that equalling the league average over a long career is an achievement in and of itself, and besides, we know that Sawchuk was better than that. We take solace in knowing that on the last night of the last season measured here, the man who revelled in his own pain, who collected his own excised body parts, whose troubled soul tortured himself and many of those around him, felt the unparalleled joy of hoisting the Stanley Cup in victory while thousands cheered. For Terry Sawchuk, it was a brief, perfect respite of happiness and communion.

And now we move on to the perseverance plus-minus list for the current era. Active goalies get an "x" before their names. We're so nervous, we can barely read our cue cards. The envelope, please:

	Perseverance Plus/Minus, 1982–83 to 2000–01 (minimum 12,000 minutes played and five seasons as regular)	
	GOALER, TEAM (SEASONS AS REGULAR)	PRSV +/– AVG.
1	x-Hasek, Chi-Buf (8)	+28.0
2	x-Pa Roy, Mtr-Col (16)	+14.4
3	Wm Smith, NYI (6)	+12.0
4	x-Cu Joseph, StL-Edm-Tor (11)	+11.8
5	x-G Hebert, StL-Ana-NYR (8)	+11.5
6t	Hrudey, NYI-LA-SJ (13)	+10.8
6t	M Bannerman, Chi (5)	+10.8
8	Hanlon, StL-NYR-Det (7)	+ 9.0
9t	x-F Potvin, Tor-NYI-Van-LA (8)	+ 8.6
9t	x-Hackett, NYI-SJ-Chi-Mtr (8)	+ 8.6
11	x-Vanbiesbrouck, NYR-Fla-Phi-NYI-NJ (17)	+ 8.4
12	Puppa, Buf-Tor-TB (8)	+ 8.2
13	x-M Richter, NYR (11)	+ 7.8
14t	Barrasso, Buf-Pit-Otw (13)	+ 7.4
14t	x-Khabibulin, Wpg/Phx-TB (5)	+ 7.4
16	Malarchuk, Qbc-Was-Bfl (6)	+ 6.7
17	x-Terreri, NJ-SJ-Chi-NJ-NYI (5)	+ 5.8
18	x-Essensa, Wpg-Det-Edm-Van (7)	+ 5.6

GOALER, TEAM (SEASONS AS REGULAR)	PRSV +/– AVG.
19 Re Lemelin, Clg-Bos (9)	+ 5.3
20t x-S Burke, NJ-Har/Car-Van-Phi-Fla-Phx (12)	+ 5.0
20t x-Belfour, Chi-SJ-Dal (11)	+ 5.0
22 x-M Brodeur, NJ (8)	+ 4.8
23 x-Kolzig, Was (5)	+ 4.6
24 G Meloche, Min-Pit (5)	+ 4.4
25 x-Fiset, Qbc/Col-LA (8)	+ 4.2
26 Moog, Edm-Bos-Dal-Mtr (15)	+ 4.1
27 Casey, Min-Bos-StL (6)	+ 3.6
28t R Hextall, Phi-Qbc-NYI-Phi (11)	+ 2.7
28t x-Healy, LA-NYI-NYR-Tor (7)	+ 2.7
28t x-Dafoe, Was-LA-Bos (6)	+ 2.7
31 x-Irbe, SJ-Dal-Van-Car (8)	+ 2.6
32 x-Osgood, Det (8)	+ 2.5
33 Peeters, Bos-Was-Phi (7)	+ 2.1
34 x-Kidd, Clg-Car-Fla (5)	+ 1.6
35 x-T Salo, NYI-Edm (5)	+ 1.4
36 x-Thibault, Qbc/Col-Mtr-Chi (6)	+ 1.3
37 Fuhr, Edm-Tor-Buf-LA-StL-Clg (14)	+ 0.7
38 R Sauve, Buf-Chi-NJ (5)	+ 0.6
39 Beaupre, Min-Was-Otw-Tor (13)	− 0.2
40 Wregget, Tor-Phi-Pit-Clg-Det (9)	− 0.3
41 Liut, StL-Was-Har (9)	− 0.8
42 x-Tugnutt, Qbc-Edm-Ana-Mtr-Otw-Pit-Cmb (9)	− 1.4
43 Wamsley, Mtr-StL-Clg-Tor (9)	− 1.6
44 Ranford, Bos-Edm-Bos-Was-TB-Det-Edm (10)	− 2.0
45 B Hayward, Wpg-Mtr-Min-SJ (6)	− 2.7
46t Cheveldae, Det-Wpg-Bos (7)	− 3.0
46t x-Snow, Qbc-Phi-Van-Pit (5)	− 3.0
48 x-Rhodes, Tor-Otw-Atl (5)	− 3.2
49 G Millen, Har-StL-Qbc-Chi-Det (8)	− 3.5
50 x-Vernon, Clg-Det-SJ-Fla-Clg (15)	− 5.6
51 x-K McLean, NJ-Van-Car-Fla-NYR (11)	− 7.4
52 G Stefan, Det (7)	− 7.6
53 M Gosselin, Qbc-LA-Har (5)	− 8.8
54 R Brodeur, Van-Har (5)	−10.8
55 Chevrier, NJ-Wpg-Chi-Pit-Det (5)	−16.4

Here is the most compelling proof yet of Dominik Hasek's overarching greatness. Back at the beginning of this chapter we made the bold claim that Hasek would prove to be by far the best in the recorded history of goaltending. We made that claim before we knew anything about the career statistics we have since compiled, and back then we couldn't have imagined that Hasek would finish so astoundingly far ahead of everyone else. He is not the Dominator simply because he's the single biggest factor in any game he plays, but also, we now see, because his statistical dominance over time is so complete, so enormous, so, dare we say it, Gretzky-like. There is no one else to compare Hasek's statistical performance to: his margins of victory in various goaltending categories are so vast, they outstrip everything in hockey statistics except Wayne

Gretzky's margins of victory in various scoring categories.

Look at the goalies who finish in the second and third positions on this list: all-time greats, shoo-in Hall of Famers, Stanley Cup-winners Patrick Roy and Billy Smith. Yet they stand miles behind Hasek, nowhere even close to him, even as they lead more than 50 other regular National Hockey League goalkeepers, the cream of the professional crop. It beggars the imagination: Hasek is not just the only goalie besides Bower to finish above the median every year of his career; he has finished an *average* of 28 perseverance points better than the league-wide figure, season after season after season. If you don't believe in perseverance, consider this: Hasek's career save percentage of .925 is *13 points better than that of the next-highest goaler*, Martin Brodeur, and it's roughly *27 points better than the league average* over the same period. In a profession where statistical differences of two or three one-thousandths of a percentage point can mean everything, Hasek stands above his next closest competitors by five, six, even ten times that. He is the greatest goalie in the world, and according to all the evidence anyone has amassed, he is the greatest there ever was.

There are so many other admirable performances here. Roy, after finishing below the perseverance average in his rookie year (a year in which he nevertheless went on to goaltend the Habs to the Cup), has gone on to record 15 above-average seasons in a row. This list shows why he has been a hero for two generations of young goalies, belonging to two language groups, in two nations, on two different sides of the continent and everywhere in between. He is a winner through and through. In the third spot is Smith, the Hatchet Man, whose career we pick up in the middle of the Islanders' Stanley Cup dynasty. He was an evil player who thought nothing of injuring an opponent. But he was undeniably a superb goalie, one excellent enough to oust another fine goalie, Chico Resch, from the starting job, and one who mentored two fine young colleagues in the Isle nets, Rollie Melanson, whose career would ultimately not pan out, and Kelly Hrudey, whose career was long and accomplished. Smith was a fierce and ungracious competitor who during the playoffs skulked off to the dressing room rather than take part in series-ending handshake lines, but whose dedication to his job was such that he'd devise imaginative exercises to keep his reflexes sharp, like throwing a rubber ball against a wall and catching it for hours on end, like Steve McQueen in *The Great Escape*. Since retiring he has had a successful career as a goalie coach, mostly with the Florida Panthers, whose goalkeeping has been very good and accounts for just about all the success that team has had. Smith's numbers here are great, fitting for the man who guarded the nets for an Isles club that won 4 Cups in a row and an astonishing 19 straight playoff series, perhaps the best team ever to take the ice.

Next up at number four is Curtis Joseph, so beloved in Toronto and anywhere he's been. One of Mike Keenan's signal gaffes, so many of them involving goalies, was to jettison Joseph from St. Louis, a move that plunged that city's loyal hockey fans into mourning and outrage. Most of Toronto's recent success can be laid at the bladed feet of Cujo. Guy Hebert, whom we recently spoke about, comes next. He's the top-rated American netminder of them all, and a reminder that there are great, unsung heroes out there, playing in the game's dark, distant corners, awaiting the light of illuminating statistical measure, where they can shine at last. He is followed by Kelly Hrudey, whose work as a young Islander was so excellent that when it came time for Wayne Gretzky to assemble his dream team in Los Angeles, Hrudey was the guy he wanted in goal. Alongside Hrudey, Murray Bannerman, forgotten by most of the hockey world but still very fondly recalled in Chicago. Frankly, we were surprised to find him so high on the perseverance scale, but there he is, adorned in that beautiful face mask he had, done up in the same war-paint arrangement worn by Chief Blackhawk himself on the team's sweaters. Bannerman was only 31 when he retired from pro hockey in 1988. Too bad for all of us that we didn't see more of him.

Glen Hanlon is next. We liked him a lot back in the '80s, as you can tell from what we wrote several pages back in the year-by-year roundups. He was a tremendously underrated goalie who deserves to be remembered more often and with more respect than he is now, especially in New York and Detroit, where he really turned the tide on what had been deteriorating situations. Hopefully now, at least a few people will take notice of his unsung career. Felix Potvin and Jeff Hackett share the number nine spot. Potvin is a goalie of widely recognized promise who fell upon hard times, but who seems to have revived his career in Los Angeles. Hackett is a little-recognized journeyman, who, it turns out, is surprisingly good. It's going to be a tough haul for Hackett if he stays in Montreal, weird as it is to think that being in Montreal is a bad fate for a goalie; hopefully he'll be the one to help revive the Canadiens. At number 11 we encounter John Vanbiesbrouck, whose long career had been a model of consistency and, counterintuitively, increasing excellence. He spent his first seven years as a regular as a dependably above-average goaler, then improved to one of the very best in the league. Expansion came, and the Rangers went with Mike Richter while leaving Vanbiesbrouck exposed. He went to Florida and got even better, making the Panthers a team of historic proportions in an age when expansion was otherwise dreary and meaningless. As we write this, Beezer has just finished his distinguished career sitting on the bench in New Jersey.

Look down at the rest of this list, and there's so much to see. Daren Puppa, a fine goalie whose career has been marred and perhaps ended by injury. Mike Richter, the Ranger fans' darling and a paradigm of skill, intelligence, and good nature. Tom Barrasso, moody but a champion, and by far the best goalie in the three and a half decades of

Penguins history. Down, down the list we range, and find some we're a bit surprised to see so high, others we're a bit surprised to see so low. At numbers 20, 22, and 23 we come across Ed Belfour, Martin Brodeur, and Olaf Kolzig. All three are excellent, two of them Stanley Cup winners, even though Belfour really isn't, as we've already proven conclusively. But why aren't this troika ranked higher? Well, all three have spent their careers behind stingy, vigorously backchecking teams. It's kept their goal-against averages down and made them winners, but it's hurt their perseverance marks. So unlike a lot of people, we'll never buy the idea that Brodeur is really the best goaler around. We'd love to see how he'd do on a team that allows a fair number of shots. But we're sure Brodeur doesn't care; he'd rather be on a winner.

Down, down farther, past the witty Leaf Glenn Healy, who during the 2001 playoff series against New Jersey took the piss out of Randy McKay for getting into a late-game fight with Curtis Joseph by referring to McKay as "the guy with the cheesy 1970s porno sideburns"; down still farther, past Grant Fuhr, who was so marvellous with Edmonton but who hung on perhaps a few years too long as a vagabond backstop, which accounts for his relatively low ranking here; past Bill Ranford, whose early-career successes were balanced out by some late-career disappointments; past Garth Snow, he of the I-beam shoulder pads and size-200 sweater when oversized goalie equipment reached the zenith of Michelin Man absurdity in the late '90s; past Mike Vernon and Kirk McLean, the lowest-ranked active goalkeepers, on down to the very bottom of the list at number 55, you will find the very worst regular goaler of the era, Alain Chevrier of the Devs, Jets, Hawks, Pens, and Wings. So bad, and yet, what either of us wouldn't have given to be as good a goalie as Chevrier, to strap on the gear and go out there before thousands of people, to face the best hockey players in the world, to have our teammates skate past us and tap our leg pads, to make a difficult save and hear the fans applaud and see our defencemen give us an appreciative wink, to know that our families and friends back home are watching us on TV, the local boy made good, good enough to be a National Hockey League goaltender. What pride to be a link in that long, long chain, Chevrier to Hasek to Bower to Lumley, Joe Schaefer and Julian Klymkiw, Long John Henderson and Kenny Dryden, Glenn Hall and Patrick Roy and even Evgeni Konstantinov, to be joined with all the pain and joy and sorrow and glory in between.

WHA Perseverance

No discussion of modern-day goaltending would be complete without looking at the World Hockey Association. The WHA kept statistics on shots and saves for all seven years of its existence, and like all its stats, they were kept much better and in greater detail than the NHL's of the era.

Today you can have a close look at all the WHA's numbers in two fine books: *Same Game, Different Name: The World Hockey Association*, by Jack Lautier and Frank Polnaszek, and *The Complete Historical and Statistical Reference to the World Hockey Association, 1972–1979*, by Scott Adam Surgent. Polnaszek was the chief statistician of the league and later of the Hartford Whalers. He installed many sensible statistical practices years before they were adopted by the NHL: keeping track of the shots each goaltender faced, even when he is replaced in the middle of a period; crediting a goaler with only 59 minutes of play rather than 60 when he is pulled at the end of a game; and not charging a goal or a shot to his account when an empty-netter is scored. All of this has left us with a vivid fossil record of WHA goalkeeping, which we know will warm the hearts of that small remaining coterie of World Association loyalists out there.

First, we present the maverick league's top-10 single-season netminding performances, ranked by perseverance.

Top-10 WHA Single-Season Perseverance Ratings, 1972–73 to 1978–79

GOALER, TEAM	SEASON	MINS	SAVES-SHOTS	SH/GP	SVPCT	PERSEV
Curran, Min	'73–74	2382	1314-1444	36.4	.910	971
Cheevers, Cle	'72–73	3144	1546-1695	32.3	.912	966
*Curran, Min	'72–73	2540	1306-1437	33.9	.909	965
*J Garrett, Min	'73–74	2290	1277-1414	37.0	.903	965
Jm McLeod, Chi	'72–73	2996	1576-1742	34.9	.905	963
Cheevers, Cle	'74–75	3076	1596-1763	34.4	.905	963
Rutledge, Hou	'72–73	2163	1053-1161	32.2	.907	961
J Garrett, Min	'74–75	3294	1691-1871	34.1	.904	961
*M Dion, Ind	'75–76	1860	857-942	30.4	.910	960
D McLeod, Hou	'73–74	2971	1305-1432	28.9	.911	960

* Rookie

All of the top performances in the WHA come in the league's first years, and they bear a fairly close resemblance to the NHL's top performances of the same era. Goaltending numbers in the WHA deteriorated in the mid- and late '70s, a phenomenon that happens to coincide with the increasing presence of swirling European forwards in the league. It's interesting to note that while .900 save percentages were quite common in the first three years of the WHA, only two regulars (Michel Dion and Joe Daley) logged .900 save rates in '75–76, nobody did in the following two seasons, and only one (Richard Brodeur) managed it in '78–79.

Now here's the WHA career chart. Keep an eye on the famous NHL backstops on the list – Cheevers, Parent, Liut, Brodeur, et al. Their figures are intriguing. Finally, because WHA franchises tended to move around a lot, we've had to devise a special punctuation convention for this list. A slash between two cities' names, as in NY/NJ (New York/New Jersey) or Dn/Ot (Denver/Ottawa), denotes one club moving from one locale to another during a season.

Sometimes one of these transient clubs moved to a third location the next season, in which case we enclose the entire series within brackets to show that it's the same franchise, as in [NY/NJ–SD]. And if a club moved from one city to another between seasons, that's bracketed too, as in [Van–Cgy]. With this method, you'll know that Jim McLeod played with three teams during his WHA career: Chicago, New York–New Jersey, and Los Angeles–Michigan–Baltimore. Prepare yourselves, and all hail Mike Curran:

Career Perseverance Ratings, WHA, 1972–73 to 1978–79
(minimum 3,200 minutes played)

GOALER, TEAM(S), SEASONS	MINS	SAVES-SHOTS	SH/GP	SVPCT	PRSV
Curran, Min, 5	7377	3921-4344	35.3	.903	962
Cheevers, Cle, 4	11352	5612-6203	32.8	.905	959
Whidden, Cle, 4	5725	2807-3134	32.8	.896	950
Grahame, Hou, 4	8528	3839-4264	30.0	.900	950
J Garrett, Min-[Tor-Bir]-NE, 6	18919	9363-10473	33.2	.894	949
Newton, Chi-Dn/Ot-Cle, 4	6106	2978-3330	32.7	.894	949
Jk Norris, Alb/Edm-Phx, 4	11030	5063-5645	30.7	.897	948
C Abrahamsson, NE, 3	5739	2821-3163	33.1	.892	947
Jm McLeod, Chi-NY/NJ-[LA-Mi/Ba], 4	5175	2616-2940	34.1	.890	947
Corsi, Qbc, 3	3380	1681-1889	33.5	.890	946
Levasseur, Min-Edm-NE, 4	4916	2319-2600	31.7	.892	945
Rutledge, Hou, 6	10372	4721-5282	30.6	.894	945
Wakely, Wpg-SD-Cin-Hou-Bir, 7	19332	8884-9948	30.9	.893	945
R Brodeur, Qbc, 5	17101	8339-9376	32.9	.889	944
Junkin, [NY/NJ-SD], 2	3961	1935-2178	33.0	.888	943
G Gratton, [Ott-Tor], 3	9102	4449-5009	33.0	.888	943
Worthy, Edm, 3	4368	2217-2506	34.4	.885	942
S Aubry, Qbc-Cin, 5	7511	3657-4127	33.0	.886	941
Binkley, Ott-Tor, 4	4228	2045-2307	32.7	.886	941
M Dion, Ind-Cin, 5	8242	3664-4114	29.9	.891	941
J Daley, Wpg, 7	17835	8065-9067	30.5	.889	940
B Parent, Phi, 1	3653	1716-1936	31.8	.886	939
Landon, NE, 5	6695	3048-3434	30.8	.888	939
D Dryden, Chi-Edm, 5	13820	6274-7082	30.7	.886	937
Pe Donnelly, NY-Van-Qbc, 3	5559	2574-2918	31.5	.882	935
D McLeod, Hou-[Van-Clg]-Qbc-Edm, 6	18926	8075-9126	28.9	.885	933
W Wood, [Van-Clg]-[Tor-Bir], 5	5167	2436-2771	32.2	.879	933
An Brown, Ind, 3	4777	2260-2574	32.3	.878	932
Bromley, Clg-Wpg, 5	3489	1510-1713	29.5	.881	931
C Hebenton, Phx, 2	3209	1580-1809	33.8	.873	930
Mattsson, Qbc-Wpg, 2	3767	1726-1967	31.3	.877	930

GOALER, TEAM(S), SEASONS	MINS	SAVES-SHOTS	SH/GP	SVPCT	PRSV
Liut, Cin, 2	4396	1949-2219	30.3	.878	929
Gillow, LA-SD, 4	5713	2433-2766	29.0	.880	928
Larsson, Wpg, 3	3820	1802-2067	32.5	.872	926
Al Smith, NE, 5	15389	6669-7621	29.7	.875	925
P Hoganson, [LA-Mi/Ba]-NE-Cin-Ind, 5	7244	3355-3851	31.9	.871	924

GOALER, TEAM(S), SEASONS	MINS	SAVES-SHOTS	SH/GP	SVPCT	PRSV
Inness, Ind, 2	3459	1661-1912	33.2	.869	924
G Gardner, LA-Van, 2	4423	1973-2262	30.7	.872	924
N LaPointe, Cin, 3	4105	1879-2159	31.6	.870	923
Kurt, NY/NJ-Phx, 5	9932	4429-5119	30.9	.865	917
K Broderick, Edm-Qbc, 2	3938	1635-1894	28.9	.863	911

5.
Playoffs

The playoffs, common wisdom has it, are a whole 'nother thing. Action more intense . . . less room to manoeuvre . . . no margin for error . . . shooters and goaltenders both ascending to operatic heights of drama and heroism. Mmm. Well, maybe, or at least that's Stanley Cup action as seen through a romantic haze by nostalgists and dreamers. Playoff hockey always used to make the needles jump on the Intensity and Skill meters, and to a lesser extent it still does – mainly because unlike the derided, interminable regular seasons of the last five, ten, twenty years, there's something of value at stake in every game, and because the most talentless bottom third of the NHL's teams aren't around to drag down the level of hockey discourse. Unfortunately, the needles seem to hit the red zone less often nowadays, thanks to the prevailing attitude governing playoff officiating. You know the troglodyte mantra: "Let the players decide it." In other words: Mr. Referee, put your whistle in your pocket. Don't let the outcome of the game turn on a power-play goal resulting from a questionable grey-area call. A pretty sentiment, and we concur. We all want to see a team really *earn* the Cup, to have to pay a certain price in sacrifice and pain and sweat and blood and all that nifty, manful, guts-and-gallantry stuff. It ain't supposed to be the Ice Capades. We all want the

big hits as well as the pretty plays, some physicality as well as some finesse. The road to hell, of course, is paved with good intentions. Instead of an apotheosis of all the best hockey has to offer, the playoffs often provide the nadir in clutch-and-grab to the virtual exclusion of spectacular skilled play. Not only are borderline calls never made, but outright mugging and tackling are almost never called either. What the playoffs' monotonous shibboleth has inevitably, invariably, unalterably come to mean, of course, is "Let the *worst* players decide it." "Let the thugs decide it." "Let the absolute lowest common denominator decide it." Why this Bizarro World mentality has become so widely, acquiescently accepted among fans and media is a mystery for the ages. Why not *call* the holding, *call* the hooking, *call* the hacking and obstruction, and "let the *best* players decide it"? "Let the *skill* players decide it"? "Let the star players we pay to see play and demonstrate their amazing talent decide it"? Nah, who'd wanna see *that*.

The 2001 Final wasn't the worst playoff series of recent years by any means; there *was* some elbow room out there, we saw the occasional odd-man break, and by today's standards both sides played it tough but clean. Ironically, game seven was marred most by some very borderline calls in the closing minutes of a contest that was still close, at least on the scoreboard. Still, we stand our position – even as we admit that thrills nonetheless continue to be found at playoff time. Maybe it's not so much that today's playoff hockey is irredeemably bad by any means, it's just that it's so easy to see how it could be so much better.

What's undeniably true, at least, is that from the standpoint of statistical analysis, the playoffs are indeed a whole different animal. There's little if anything that can be derived from the tiny statistical sample of a seven-game series, let alone from a best-of-three or a two-games total-goals set, nor even from the twenty-plus games at least two teams are likely to play through to the awarding of the Stanley Cup, since they have no common opponents against which to make comparisons.

We can provide you some factoids out of all of it, though – some lists to conjure with, some bits of intriguing trivia; those will whet your appetite for the main course of our playoff section, which consists of more never-before-seen goaltender ratings. While we bake those to a fine golden-brown, here, nibble on these hors d'oeuvres . . .

All-Time Team Playoff Performance

Which team was the most impressive Stanley Cup champions – the team that won the Cup the most years in a row? The team that won the Cup with the most dominating playoff performance? The team that had to defeat the most opponents to win the Cup? The team that had to overcome the most adversity to win the Cup? The team that won the Cup to cap the most impressive regular-season performance? Now there's a tough call.

We all know the late '50s Canadiens are the only team to have won the Auld Mug five years in a row, and that the late '70s Habs and the early '80s Islanders are the only other teams to have won it four years running. Worth considering, though, is that the road to the Cup was a lot shorter Back When. The Montreal teams that won it all from 1956 to 1960 played only a semi-final and the Final in each of those years, and therefore won 10 consecutive playoff series in their Cup skein. The Montreal teams that dominated the disco era had to get past a quarter-final round, a semi, and the Final for each of their Cup triumphs, needing 12 straight playoff series victories for their four Cups. For the Islanders, the road was the longest of all, requiring that they swat aside a preliminary-round opponent in a perilous best-of-five set each year before advancing through the quarters and semis and finally on to the Cup. That means Isles won 16 straight playoff series, an unapproached achievement in itself, in order to earn the Cup four years straight, and they knocked off three more playoff opponents en route to the 1984 Final as well, before giving way to Edmonton.

Most Consecutive Playoff Series Won

TEAM	SEASONS	CONSECUTIVE SERIES WON	GAMES W-L DURING STREAK
New York Isl	'79–80 to '83–84	19	71-23 (.755)
Montreal Can	'75–76 to '79–80	13	51-12 (.810)
Montreal Can	'55–56 to '59–60	10	40-9 (.816)
Edmonton	'83–84 to '85–86	9	33-7 (.825)
Pittsburgh Pen	'90–91 to '92–93	9	36-14 (.720)
Detroit	'96–97 to '98–99	9	36-10 (.783)
Montreal Can	'67–68 to '70–71	9*	36-9 (.800)

* Montreal missed playoffs in '69–70.

That Isles-Oilers series reminds us of another confrontation you don't see often: a new Stanley Cup champion actually winning it by defeating the reigning Cup holder in the Final. The Avs did it in 2001 by dethroning the Devils, and that's the first time that's happened in 17 years and only the 14th time it's happened in the entire history of major-league professional competition for the Cup.

Defending Cup Champ Loses Final, since 1908

1917, PCHA Seattle Metropolitans defeated NHA Montreal Canadiens, 3 games to 1.

1925, PCHA Victoria Cougars defeated NHL Montreal Canadiens, 3 games to 1.

1926, NHL Montreal Maroons defeated WHL Victoria Cougars, 3 games to 1.

1929, Boston Bruins defeated New York Rangers, 2 games to 0.

1930, Montreal Canadiens defeated Boston Bruins, 2 games to 0.

1933, New York Rangers defeated Toronto Maple Leafs, 3 games to 1.

1947, Toronto Maple Leafs defeated Montreal Canadiens, 4 games to 2.

1954, Detroit Red Wings defeated Montreal Canadiens, 4 games to 3.

1956, Montreal Canadiens defeated Detroit Red Wings, 4 games to 1.

1962, Toronto Maple Leafs defeated Chicago Black Hawks, 4 games to 2.

1967, Toronto Maple Leafs defeated Montreal Canadiens, 4 games to 2.

1976, Montreal Canadiens defeated Philadelphia Flyers, 4 games to 0.

1984, Edmonton Oilers defeated New York Islanders, 4 games to 1.

2001, Colorado Avalanche defeated New Jersey Devils, 4 games to 3.

For the record, there have been 26 repeat winners of the Cup since 1908, starting with the Quebec Bulldogs of 1912 and '13, up to the Red Wings of '97 and '98.

If you're looking for the teams that combined regular-season and playoff excellence, the list might be longer than you expect. Since the NHL annexed the Stanley Cup in 1926, the best regular-season team has won the Cup a little less than half the time. You'd hardly know it, since by the time the playoffs conclude nowadays, the regular season is already a distant memory, and especially over the last 15 or 20 years the season slate has been widely denigrated as a thousand-game ordeal of meaningless exhibition games. That's an enormous shame, not to mention a pretty idiotic attitude. If the sports media and the fans themselves all hold the inarguably overlong regular season in such contempt, where do they get off complaining when the players go through the motions and treat regular-season games as meaningless? If the NHL doesn't like that perception, where does the league get off mulling the idea of adding even more teams to the playoff field, further undermining the regular season's value and credibility? In every other sport, the regular season title is a real honour, a respected achievement, as it should be. Here's the list of teams that have accomplished hockey's version of the double over the last 75 years.

Best Regular-Season Record and Stanley Cup in Same Year since 1926–27

SEASON	TEAM
1926–27	Ottawa Senators
1935–36	Detroit Red Wings
1936–37	Detroit Red Wings
1938–39	Boston Bruins
1940–41	Boston Bruins
1942–43	Detroit Red Wings
1943–44	Montreal Canadiens
1945–46	Montreal Canadiens
1947–48	Toronto Maple Leafs
1949–50	Detroit Red Wings
1951–52	Detroit Red Wings
1953–54	Detroit Red Wings
1954–55	Detroit Red Wings
1955–56	Montreal Canadiens
1957–58	Montreal Canadiens
1958–59	Montreal Canadiens
1959–60	Montreal Canadiens
1962–63	Toronto Maple Leafs
1965–66	Montreal Canadiens
1967–68	Montreal Canadiens
1968–69	Montreal Canadiens
1971–72	Boston Bruins
1972–73	Montreal Canadiens
1974–75	Philadelphia Flyers
1975–76	Montreal Canadiens
1976–77	Montreal Canadiens
1977–78	Montreal Canadiens
1980–81	New York Islanders
1981–82	New York Islanders
1983–84	Edmonton Oilers
1986–87	Edmonton Oilers
1988–89	Calgary Flames
1993–94	New York Rangers
1998–99	Dallas Stars*
2000–01	Colorado Avalanche

* Awarded Cup when league officials interrupted game six of Final with Dallas leading 3 games to 2.

A most impressive list of elite teams, and we salute them all. Except for the '75 Flyers, whom we still despise with the blinding, white-hot intensity of a thousand burning suns. And the '99 Stars, who never did actually win the Cup, but might have eventually. Anyway, 35 doubles in 75 years: maybe that's about the right proportion, amazingly enough – a fair, aesthetically pleasing balance between inevitability and vulnerability, between a cakewalk to an uncontested coronation and a fatal misstep in a post-season minefield. We would point out the odds of achieving it were a lot shorter when there were just six teams in the league. Only six teams in history, though, have done the double back-to-back, which you have to admit is an especially stunning achievement. The 1935–36 and 1936–37 Red Wings – Marty Barry, Larry Aurie, Herbie Lewis, Ebbie Goodfellow, Normie Smith, et al. – were the first to pull it off, and the Production Line Wings of '53–54 and '54–55 were the second. The late '60s Habs did it, and the early '80s Isles as well, but it's those two great Canadien dynasties of the 1950s and the 1970s that are the only clubs to have been both the best regular-season side and Cup champion an astounding three years in a row.

What's actually pretty rare, not surprisingly, is seeing the league's top two regular-season teams face off for the Preston Punchbowl. Once the NHL took sole control of Lord Stanley's silverware in 1926, the top two sides never met each other for the Cup until 1943. After that it became almost a biennial pairing until 1960, and following a 12-year absence of one-vs.-two Final match-ups, it was the pattern again through the '70s and '80s. The 2000–01 showdown between Colorado and New Jersey, though, was the first time since 1989 we've seen One meet Two.

Meetings of Top Two Regular-Season Teams in Stanley Cup Final, since 1926–27

SEASON	CUP WINNER	CUP RUNNER-UP
1942–43	1 Detroit Red Wings	2 Boston Bruins
1945–46	1 Montreal Canadiens	2 Boston Bruins
1946–47	2 Toronto Maple Leafs	1 Montreal Canadiens
1947–48	1 Toronto Maple Leafs	2 Detroit Red Wings
1951–52	1 Detroit Red Wings	2 Montreal Canadiens
1953–54	1 Detroit Red Wings	2 Montreal Canadiens

SEASON	CUP WINNER		CUP RUNNER-UP	
1954–55	1	Detroit Red Wings	2	Montreal Canadiens
1955–56	1	Montreal Canadiens	2	Detroit Red Wings
1959–60	1	Montreal Canadiens	2	Toronto Maple Leafs
1971–72	1	Boston Bruins	2	New York Rangers
1973–74	2	Philadelphia Flyers	1	Boston Bruins
1974–75	1	Philadelphia Flyers	2	Buffalo Sabres
1975–76	1	Montreal Canadiens	2	Philadelphia Flyers
1977–78	1	Montreal Canadiens	2	Boston Bruins
1983–84	1	Edmonton Oilers	2	New York Islanders
1984–85	2	Edmonton Oilers	1	Philadelphia Flyers
1988–89	1	Calgary Flames	2	Montreal Canadiens
2000–01	1	Colorado Avalanche	2	New Jersey Devils

Strange to note that in these pairings of top teams, number one has drubbed number two in 15 of 18 meetings for the Cup.

On the one hand, it's great to see excellence rewarded by getting through at least to the Final, if not the Cup itself. On the other hand, it's nice, once in a while anyway, to see a Cinderella side come from back in the pack and make a run at the Cup. Then again, two dark horses meeting for the Cup aren't better than one. One plucky overachiever is a good story; two are just a pair of mediocrities that leave us longing for a good team to watch. But it happens. Here, in contrast to the best-vs.-second-best list, are the lamest Final conflicts since 1926–27 . . .

Stanley's Receptacle? Raise your hands, you pretenders . . .

Yeah, who let *those* guys into the post-season party? Suddenly the clam paté tastes a little off. Luckily, we haven't been subjected to a sub-.400 playoff *poseur* in 13 years, and happily, the NHL went to a best-eight-in-conference qualifying format in 1993–94, precisely to avoid the spectacle of sub-.400 clubs from weak divisions roaming the post-season gala while .500-plus teams in strong divisions sat at home. That hasn't stopped 20 separate losing sides in just those last eight years from finding their way in; last season was the first since, ironically, 1992–93 that the post-season hasn't featured at least one sub-.500 team. Recent banter among NHL execs, though, suggests the number of teams qualifying for the playoffs be increased. This will inevitably come to pass, not because of any inherent unfairness in excluding very bad teams from Stanley Cup contention, but simply because it will mean more playoff receipts for more franchise owners – and it will inevitably allow the return of more clearly undeserving, declassé teams into what should be a tony post-season soirée, not to mention pushing the Final somewhere into August.

One thing mercifully absent from the 2001 playoffs was endless multiple overtime. What a rare thrill, what a strange tableau, what a special treat a second overtime, let alone a third, used to be. You got to see them about as often as you got to see a comet. They were every bit as memorable, and the tension was all but unbearable. In the NHL's

Worst Combined Winning Percentages by Finalists, Since 1926–27

SEASON	CUP WINNER	W PCT	CUP RUNNER-UP	W PCT	COMBINED W PCT
1991	Pittsburgh Penguins	.550	Minnesota North Stars	.425	.488
1938	Chicago Black Hawks	.385	Toronto Maple Leafs	.594	.490
1961	Chicago Black Hawks	.536	Detroit Red Wings	.471	.504
1953	Montreal Canadiens	.536	Boston Bruins	.493	.514
1942	Toronto Maple Leafs	.594	Detroit Red Wings	.438	.516

As you can see, the 14-25-9 Hawks of 1938 actually won the Cup. Urp. Dead-last in the standings both the year before and the year after, they were the beneficiaries of the short-series format that made it easier for weak teams; the Bruins, who had played nearly .700 hockey that season, tripped and fell in the semi-finals. The whole result was sufficiently nauseating that the Final was changed from a best-of-five format to a best-of-seven the next year, making the test a little longer and tougher. The '49 Leafs (22-25-9, .475) are, thankfully, the only other losing club to have taken hold of Hockey's Ultimate Prize. The Leafs, though, were a top-flight team through the late '40s; they won at a .612 pace over the two previous seasons and the two that followed, and this was their third-straight Cup victory. All this kind of invites the question, then: which were the worst teams to so much as qualify for a shot at Lord

first 71 years, only 57 playoff games needed a second overtime period, and a mere 19 required a third OT or beyond. Just since 1989, however, 50 games have gone into a second OT, 12 of them into a third, or a fourth, or a fifth. The '90s seemed to dish up at least one interminable overtime game every other night, as the goal-scoring talent on even the elite teams, painfully diluted by overexpansion, asphyxiated in the "let the players decide it" atmosphere that pervades the playoffs. What once set us alight with anticipation now too often just numbs us with boredom. *Another* OT? Screw it. We've gotta get up for work. Once again, the NHL has turned the rare into the commonplace, and excitement into tedium. And once again, the problem would utterly and instantly disappear if only the league would allow the rule book to do its work. We will say, though, that we'll tolerate however many OTs may head our way rather than be

Worst Playoff Qualifiers Since 1926–27

SEASON	TEAM	W-L-T	PCT	PLAYOFF RESULT
1988	Toronto Maple Leafs	21-49-10	.325	lost preliminary 4 games to 2
1940	New York Americans	15-29-4	.354	lost quarter-final 2 games to 1
1986	Toronto Maple Leafs	25-48-7	.356	won preliminary 2 games to 1
				lost quarter-final 4 games to 3
1945	Boston Bruins	16-30-4	.360	lost semi-final 4 games to 3
1978	Colorado Rockies	19-40-21	.369	lost preliminary 2 games to 0
1986	Vancouver Canucks	23-44-13	.369	lost preliminary 3 games to 0
1986	Winnipeg Jets	26-47-7	.369	lost preliminary 3 games to 0
1970	Oakland Seals	22-40-14	.382	lost quarter-final 4 games to 0
1969	Los Angeles Kings	24-42-10	.382	won quarter-final 4 games to 3
				lost semi-final 4 games to 0
1938	Chicago Black Hawks	14-25-9	.385	won quarter-final 2 games to 1
				won semi-final 2 games to 1
				won Stanley Cup Final 3 games to 1
1985	Minnesota North Stars	25-43-12	.388	won preliminary 2 games to 1
				lost quarter-final 4 games to 2
1985	New York Rangers	26-44-10	.388	lost preliminary 2 games to 1
1982	Los Angeles Kings	24-41-15	.394	lost preliminary 3 games to 1
1979	Vancouver Canucks	25-42-13	.394	lost preliminary 2 games to 1
1977	Chicago Black Hawks	26-43-11	.394	lost preliminary 2 games to 0
1970	Minnesota North Stars	19-35-22	.395	lost quarter-final 4 games to 2
1940	Detroit Red Wings	16-26-6	.396	won quarter-final 2 games to 1
				lost semi-final 2 games to 0
1977	Minnesota North Stars	23-39-18	.400	lost preliminary 2 games to 0

subjected to a single instance of the reprehensible, team-concept-abrogating, traditionless carnival gimmick of shoot-outs.

Playoff Games Decided in Overtime, by Number of Overtimes Needed

		OTGP	1 OT	2 OT	3 OT	4 OT	5 OT	6 OT
PCHA/ WCHL/WHL	'12–26	3	2	1	0	0	0	0
NHL	'18–38	45	24	12	5	2	0	2
NHL	'39–67	84	65	11	6	2	0	0
NHL	'68–88	179	162	15	1	1	0	0
NHL	'89–01	232	181	39	9	2	1	0
WHA	'73–79	20	20	0	0	0	0	0

Playoff overtime does, however, provide us a laboratory in which to test regular-season OT – and what a farce *that's* been for the last 18 years. Regular-season overtime is a venerable institution, pre-dating the NHL, played in several major leagues, and played in many different formats – to sudden death, to full time regardless of how many goals were scored, to 10 minutes, to 20, 30, 40, 60. In the WHL's final season, and in the NHL from 1928–29 until early in the 1942–43 campaign, it was a full-ten-minutes affair. The practice was terminated to accommodate wartime travel schedules, and for the next 40 years, a tie was a tie, and everyone understood that, and nobody minded. Like three periods instead of four quarters, the idea that a tie could be an acceptable result was part of hockey's unique identity, in contrast to the must-produce-a-winner mindset of the big three American sports.

In 1983, though, the NHL informed us fans that we actually *hate* ties – hey, thanks for setting us straight! We never even suspected! – and was reinstating overtime to help get rid of them. It would do this by having teams, tied at the end of regulation, play in a completely unprecedented format,

NHL Regular-Season Overtime

SEASONS	YEARS	GP	OTGP	PCT OT	OT W/L	PCT OTGP W/L	FORMAT
1928–29 to 1942–43	14.1	2769	637	.230	203	.320	10 minutes
1983–84 to 1998–99	16	14629	2696	.184	888	.329	5 minutes, sudden-death
1999–00 to 2000–01	2	2378	534	.225	236	.442	5 minutes, sudden-death, 4-on-4, losing team gets point

groundless anywhere in the game's heritage: a five-minute sudden-death mini-overtime. Huh. This unorthodox solution to a non-existent problem may have been based on extensive research that revealed eight playoff games that had required overtime in 1982 ended in five minutes or less. Of course, the fact that eight others that year needed more than five minutes, and that having even half that year's games decided that quickly was a statistical fluke by historical standards, apparently eluded them. The NHL plunged ahead, and over the next 16 seasons the mini-overtime, predictably, provided a winner and a loser in less than a third of the games in which it was used.

In 1999, the NHL informed us again how much we all hate ties, or, really, how *foreign* the concept is to people in Nashville and Carolina, and so it would plough right ahead once more and fix that. The owners' new directive was so loathsome and so transparent that it was inserted into the rule book without consulting the general managers – and whatever else you may think about that latter group, they do tend to exhibit a genuine sense of responsibility when it comes to protecting the integrity of the game on the ice. What the owners foisted upon us was the five-minute mini-overtime now played *four-on-four* – another abomination with absolutely no precedent or pedigree. Would basketball remove a player from the court in overtime? Would baseball remove a couple of players from the field in extra innings? Absurd. Worse yet, the incomprehensible, unconscionable subsidy of a point in the standings to the *losing team* after this sham – which in fact only exacerbated the very problem it was allegedly manufactured to solve. As you can see in the preceding table, while the undisciplined shinny of four-on-four indeed rendered a winner and a loser more frequently – though still far less than half the time – the promise of a point for losing actually *increased* the number of games that were tied after 60 minutes of regulation. Teams now play a stultifying game of shuffleboard instead of hockey, not just for the last five minutes or so of regulation to preserve a point, but for the *entire third period*, in order to *gain* a point even if they lose in OT. The NHL's move was instead plainly meant as a stalking horse for four-on-four hockey *all the time*, thus eventually reducing the number of players on every roster and the size of every team's payroll, and forever changing the fundamental nature of our game. Four-on-four. We spit on it.

Here, look at the following table. If what the NHL was really concerned about was seriously reducing the number of tie games, all it would have to do is what it could have done 18 years ago, and play ten minutes of overtime instead of five. The full-ten-minutes OT format of NHL regular-season play from '28–29 to '42–43 doesn't really apply here, since we haven't extracted the times of the initial goals in each of the 637 games that used OT in those years, nor tabulated how many of the 434 of those games that remained

tied wound up tied because both teams scored in OT. Besides, there's an entirely different psychology at work in playing a full 10 minutes than in playing a maximum 10 minutes in a sudden-death situation. What does apply is the WHA, which played 10 minutes of sudden death to break ties in all seven seasons of its existence, and NHL playoff OT, the results of which can be broken down to see how long it usually takes one team to score.

LEAGUE, FORMAT SEASONS	OTGP	DECIDED IN UNDER 10 MINUTES	PCT DECIDED IN UNDER 10 MINUTES
Sudden-Death Overtime Games Decided in Less Than 10 Minutes of OT			
NHL playoffs			
1918–38	45	13	.289
1939–67	84	43	.512
1968–88	179	130	.726
1989–2001	232	121	.522
WHA 1972–73 to 1978–79			
regular season	402	250	.622
playoffs	20	18	.900

The faster and more freely the goals come, of course, the more likely it is that a goal will be scored in any 10-minute segment, so the figures for the NHL playoffs of the 1970s and '80s and any WHA game are boosted a bit by that. But we'd bet our eye teeth that even in the midst of today's scoring drought, 10 minutes of sudden-death five-on-five would produce a winner and a loser significantly more often than five minutes of idiotic four-on-four.

We've gotten away, momentarily, from the Stanley Cup, but let's return to it for one last nosh before we dish up a humungous feast of playoff goaltending stats. The 2001 playoffs wound up being all about Ray Bourque and his quest for hockey's Holy Grail. At times, winding up for a slapper from the point with his white playoff beard trailing down the front of his armour, he actually looked a bit more like Don Quixote tilting at windmills, and you had to wonder if he'd ever realize his impossible dream. But sure enough, he was able to hug the Old Barrel at last, and there wasn't a dry seat in the house. Everybody Loves Raymond. And a more deserving player there's never been, all sarcasm aside. Which left us wondering, though, which venerable warhorse now becomes the sentimental favourite to have his name inscribed in silver? It turns out Ron Sutter and – eek! – Dave Andreychuk and Phil Housley are the active players of longest service never to be on a Cup winner. Having watched the latter pair rack up regular-season points in Buffalo for years, and then, annually, turn into an imperceptible vapour in the playoffs, we're not remotely surprised. In fact, we said more than a decade ago that no team with Phil Housley as a regular could ever win the Cup. Earlier, we

Most Seasons, No Cup

SKATERS	SKATERS (ACTIVE ONLY)	GOALTENDERS
Doug Mohns, 22	x – Dave Andreychuk, 19	John Vanbiesbrouck, 19
Dean Prentice, 22	x – Phil Housley, 19	Gilles Meloche, 18
Harry Howell, 21	x – Ron Sutter, 19	Don Beaupre, 17
Jean Ratelle, 21	x – James Patrick, 18	x – Kirk McLean, 16
Bill Gadsby, 20	x – Sylvain Cote, 17	Glen Hanlon, 15
Norm Ullman, 20	x – Kevin Dineen, 17	Kelly Hrudey, 15
x – Dave Andreychuk, 19	x – Ray Ferraro, 17	Reggie Lemelin, 15
x – Phil Housley, 19	x – Garry Galley, 17	Cesare Maniago, 15
x – Ron Sutter, 19	x – Kevin Hatcher, 17	Roger Crozier, 14
Dave Babych, 19	x – Steve Thomas, 17	Dan Bouchard, 14
Leo Boivin, 19	x – Scott Mellanby, 16	Greg Millen, 14
Dino Ciccarelli, 19	x – Adam Oates, 16	Gary Smith, 14
Mike Gartner, 19	x – Luc Robitaille, 15	
Dale Hunter, 19		

x – Active players

cited a few of the truly great players who never got their name there; here's a list of the guys who've played the longest without ever embracing it.

Add to that list any number of long-time stars and worthies – Marcel Dionne, Darryl Sittler, Russell Bowie, Pat LaFontaine, Brad Park, Dominik Hasek, Doug Bentley, Bernie Federko, Curtis Joseph, Mike Ramsey, Gil Perreault, Tom Dunderdale, Peter Stastny, Eddie Giacomin, Dale Hawerchuk, Dick Irvin, Dave Taylor, Bill Quackenbush, Chuck Rayner, Craig Ramsay, Michel Goulet, Roy Worters, Borje Salming, Mike Foligno, Herb Jordan, Rod Gilbert, Rick Middleton, and on and on . . . these are lesser players because they never played for, or may never play for, a Stanley Cup champion? Not in *our* book they're not.

Playoff Goaltending

The most important thing in playoff hockey is goaltending. So goes the old adage, and it makes sense, because after all, a hot goalie can carry you all the way to the Stanley Cup. We're going to concentrate on that principle in this chapter, thanks once again to that pioneering researcher, Edward Yuen, who compiled shot-and-save summaries for every post-season, starting in 1952 and going all the way up through 1983. As we said in Chapter Four, Yuen hit the library microfilm and used several daily newspapers, *The Hockey News*, and the annual NHL Guides to compile these figures, which no one had compiled before. With the stats provided by Yuen and by the league, which started keeping track of shots and saves only in the 1984 post-season, we can present a half-century of playoff goalkeeping using the only measures that really matter, save percentage and shots faced per game. And, of course, the stat we devised, perseverance, which, simply put,

combines six parts save percentage with one part shots-against. Even if you decide you don't like our perseverance statistic, pay attention instead to save percentage. Either way, it's all here, for the first time ever.

Having an uninterrupted run of 50 post-seasons to examine gives us a unique chance to watch goaltending strategies evolve from era to era. The differences between the goalers of one era and these of another are truly astonishing, just as the way hockey itself is played has changed so vastly. We recently watched tapes of two games from the 1959 Stanley Cup Final, Montreal vs. Toronto, and, like so many who complain about the current state of the game, we expected this vintage hockey to be far superior to what we see today. In some ways, it *was* superior: no hooking, no holding, no tripping, no gratuitous hitting after the puck carrier passed it away, no needless "finishing your check." Collisions were rare; indeed, the lightly padded, unhelmeted players of 1959 went out of their way to avoid collisions. When commentators discuss today's high rate of serious injury, they talk about how players "respected" one another in the olden days, keeping their sticks and elbows down. Watching the Habs and Leafs play for the Cup in '59, that seemed true – but the players also seemed to be avoiding contact out of self-preservation at least as much as anything else. Clearly, an unnecessary collision was not desirable, foremost because you could get hurt, and also because someone else could get hurt, which might in turn cause some real trouble.

The play itself, therefore, was open and flowing. But compared to today's standards, it was – and here's the bad part – unimaginative and unskilful. The prevailing tactic in 1959 was for one guy to pick up the puck, head over the other team's blue line, and get stopped trying to stickhandle past the one or two defenceman back. Passing? There was practically none, and the stringing together of more than two consecutive passes was a rare event indeed. What little passing there was consisted of short relays; a cross-ice, boards-to-boards pass was so rare as to elicit a breathless "Provost *rinkwide* to Bonin!" from Danny Gallivan. Even the vaunted Canadiens' power play barely passed the puck. Today we're used to the point men routinely exchanging the biscuit several times, then relaying it down to the men in the corners, then back up to the point again, all while the players are in motion. In 1959, one successful exchange between the point men was about all the mighty Habs dared before taking a shot. And the shot itself? Pretty much all anyone could manage, even the great Doug Harvey, was a strong wrist shot. Slap shots? They were very little in evidence. In fact, the only modern-looking slapper was the one Dick Duff fired past Jacques Plante in overtime of game three to give the Leafs their only win. Back then, the straight-bladed sticks with relatively stiff shafts may have made backhand passes easy, but they made every other shot and pass a laborious, difficult undertaking – so unlike today's sticks, with their craftily curved blades and whippy shafts that allow players to pass and shoot with snap and authority every time.

Whether you think the kind of hockey played in 1959 was better or worse than today's is a matter of taste. We'd say that, at it's best, it's much better here in the 21st century. But the biggest contrast of all definitely was in the goalkeeping. Whereas nowadays we have become used to sprawling goalers playing close to the ice, butterflying, pinwheeling, belly-flopping, and doing the splits in their lightweight head-to-toe padding, all the while playing deep in the crease, the netminders of the 1959 Final, the all-time greats Jacques Plante and Johnny Bower, did all they could to keep their feet. Readers old enough to know the melody to the Calgary Export Ale commercial ("Twas out in the West in '92/ That first we made our Calgary brew") will remember the days when the highest praise you could pay a netminder was to call him "a stand-up goalie" – the idea being that any goaler who stayed on his skates, no matter the chaos going on around him, would be able to stop any shot that came his way, mainly by coming way, way out to cut down the angles. Thus we watched as Bower and Plante, bare-faced and skimpily padded (even though those pads weighed roughly 35 pounds), kick out a shot, then labour mightily to stay on their feet. Bower especially married elements of the heroic and the comical in his efforts to stay atop his skates, clutching madly at the crossbar, flailing his arms, contorting his body desperately, all to keep from falling down. There was a lot of this, given that goalers faced more shots then than they do now, even if the shots were not as hard or as difficult to handle as today's. But we mustn't forget that in 1959 goalies were more or less buck-naked, and every shot had the potential to do grievous damage.

Goalies began to go down a bit more as time went on.

Stu Hackel, the hockey writer and former president of the Gump Worsley fan club, told us the following about the Gumper: "I saw him probably about 25 times in '62–63 between TV and going to the Garden, and there was absolutely no question as to how great he was. He was incredibly acrobatic for a tubby little guy, and the writers thought he flopped to the ice too much; he did, but he had no help and the quality – as well as the quantity – of scoring chances against him were astonishing, since the opponents could skate in on him at will. He played his angles very well also, but the image of him throwing his body – and bare face – at pucks that no one else could stop stays with me all these years later and became the standard by which I judged goaltenders for decades. Of course the game has changed, but back then, no one understood why he left his feet so often; perhaps he didn't have his acrobatics as well plotted out as Hasek, but he knew what he was doing. The better teams' goalies had fewer shots and fewer tough shots to stop. They didn't have to resort to flinging themselves at pucks."

It took a generation and the success of Tony Esposito, as well as the gymnastic acuity of Vladislav Tretiak, for the butterfly style to become the goaltending standard, but even as late as 1979, the idea was for goalers to keep standing. That'll be clear to anyone watching a replay of game seven of the '79 Bruins-Canadiens semi-final, when Don Cherry put too many men on the ice in the closing minutes. Both Gilles Gilbert and Ken Dryden played the angles way out of the net, and like Bower and Plante before them, their skates slipped out of control when pucks went past them, making them look like can-can dancers on an icy patch of Montmartre sidewalk. In the '80s, forwards got too fast and defence too sloppy for goalies to keep up. Save percentages plummeted. In the early '90s, goalies took to dropping to one knee with their stick paddle on the ice and finally became comfortable not standing up. Equipment ballooned to its present, bloated size, and voila! pucks stopped going in. In the mid-'90s teams started trapping and backchecking like mad, shot totals fell, and teams played days and days before anyone scored, which is pretty much where we are today. But we're getting a bit ahead of ourselves, so whaddya say we watch it all unfold before us, year by year, post-season by post-season, Stanley Cup by Stanley Cup.

In each of the following annual charts, playoff goaltenders are divided into two groups. First, there are the "regulars," who played a number of minutes equivalent to half that playoff year's shortest possible Cup-winning run (at least 240 minutes for those seasons in which a minimum of 8 games, or 480 minutes, was needed to win the Cup; at least 480 minutes today, when a minimum of 16 games, or 960 minutes, is needed). The second group consists of those goalies who did not reach that minimum threshold. Rookies are denoted by an asterisk, and those goalies who won the Stanley Cup that year are indicated by a †.

1952

Yuen's reconstruction of the playoff past begins here, or perhaps we should say sort of here. The shots for one Montreal-Boston semi-final game were not printed in the newspapers, and the NHL didn't keep game-summary sheets with that kind of detail until '59–60, so the record is incomplete. But we do have figures for each of Terry Sawchuk's games in this, the year that the Red Wings won the Stanley Cup in the minimum eight games, recording sweeps of Toronto and Montreal and birthing the Detroit tradition of throwing an octopus on the ice to represent the eight wins needed for the Cup. Through it all, Sawchuk allowed just five goals, including only two in the Final, establishing his reputation as the greatest goalie ever. That reputation can be disputed now that we have more detailed statistics than mere career shutouts to go by, but whatever anyone concludes about Sawchuk, this is clearly the greatest single playoff goalkeeping performance ever measured. It's a crime against suspense that nothing to come after for the next 50 years will surpass it, but there you go. Speaking of what-a-shame, you know that famous picture of Sugar Jim Henry, the black-eyed and bandaged Bruins goalie, bowing to shake hands with a dazed and bloodied Maurice Richard? That photo was taken after game seven of this year's semi-final, when Richard returned from a concussion to rush through the whole Bruins team and score the winning goal late in the game. After the handshake Richard went to the dressing room and collapsed, sobbing uncontrollably. All the best hockey stories end in tears.

(minimum 240 minutes played)

GOALER, TEAM	MINS	SAVES-SHOTS	SH/GP	SVPCT	PERSEV
Sawchuk, Det †	480	224-229	28.6	.978	1026
McNeil, Mtr	688	statistics unavailable			
J Henry, Bos	448	statistics unavailable			

(1–239 minutes played)

GOALER, TEAM	MINS	SAVES-SHOTS	SH/GP	SVPCT	PERSEV
Rollins, Tor	120	49-55	27.5	.891	937
Broda, Tor	120	46-53	26.5	.868	912

1953

The Canadiens fall behind Chicago in the semi-final, three games to two, prompting Gerry McNeil, nerves frayed, to bench himself "for the good of the team." Rookie Jacques Plante steps in and gets the Habs past the Hawks and to the Final against Boston. A refreshed McNeil returns to the nets with the final series tied at 1-1, and Montreal win the Cup in five. The Bruins would've done better had Sugar Jim Henry not sprained his ankle in game two. His replacement, Gord "Red" Henry, gets badly cut on the arm soon after going in and is ineffective the rest of the way.

(minimum 240 minutes played)

GOALER, TEAM	MINS	SAVES-SHOTS	SH/GP	SVPCT	PERSEV
J Henry, Bos	510	284-310	36.5	.916	977
Rollins, Chi	425	209-227	32.0	.921	974
McNeil, Mtr †	486	186-201	24.8	.925	967
*J Plante, Mtr †	240	84-91	22.8	.923	961
Sawchuk, Det	372	119-140	22.6	.850	877

(1–239 minutes played)

GOALER, TEAM	MINS	SAVES-SHOTS	SH/GP	SVPCT	PERSEV
*G Henry, Bos	163	74-85	31.3	.871	923

1954

Sawchuk returns to form, and the Red Wings go up three games to one against Montreal in the Final. Plante, despite playing well, is yanked for McNeil, who stops 55 of 56 over the next two contests to get the Canadiens to game seven. With the score tied 1-1 in the fifth minute of overtime in the decider at Olympia Stadium, the Wings' Tony Leswick bloops a harmless shot from 30 feet away – which Doug Harvey accidentally gloves down into his own net. "If Gerry McNeil had been taller," Butch Bouchard later remembers, "say, 6'2", it would have ticked his shoulder, maybe, but he was about 5'7". The puck dropped over his shoulder and into the goal." Poor McNeil – his .966 save percentage isn't quite good enough to win the Cup, and what's worse, he gets flak for being short.

(minimum 240 minutes played)

GOALER, TEAM	MINS	SAVES-SHOTS	SH/GP	SVPCT	PERSEV
Sawchuk, Det †	751	314-334	26.7	.940	985
J Plante, Mtr	480	193-207	25.9	.932	975
H Lumley, Tor	321	142-156	29.2	.910	959
J Henry, Bos	240	133-149	37.2	.893	955

(1–239 minutes played)

GOALER, TEAM	MINS	SAVES-SHOTS	SH/GP	SVPCT	PERSEV
McNeil, Mtr	190	86-89	28.1	.966	1013

1955

Plante and Sawchuk each have strong playoffs and are still standing in the Olympia for game seven of the Final. Detroit have the home-ice advantage thanks, in part, to the late-season game Montreal forfeited the previous month because of the Richard Riot. Sure enough, in game seven, the Wings outshoot the Rocket-less Habs 33-22 and outscore them 3-1, claiming their fourth Cup in five years – and their last until 1997. Sugar Jim Henry gets struck just under the eye during the semi-final with Montreal, finishes the game, but is found to have suffered a broken upper jaw. The injury forces Henry out of pro hockey for the next three years – he'll never play in the NHL again – and sets in motion a chain of events that will leave the Bruins without a dependable goalie for the next dozen years.

(minimum 240 minutes played)					
GOALER, TEAM	MINS	SAVES-SHOTS	SH/GP	SVPCT	PERSEV
J Plante, Mtr	639	310-341	32.0	.909	962
Sawchuk, Det †	660	281-307	27.9	.915	962
H Lumley, Tor	240	123-137	34.2	.898	955

(1-239 minutes played)					
GOALER, TEAM	MINS	SAVES-SHOTS	SH/GP	SVPCT	PERSEV
*C Hodge, Mtr	84	40-45	32.1	.889	942
J Henry, Bos	183	62-70	23.0	.886	924
*J Henderson, Bos	120	45-53	26.5	.849	893

1956

Glenn Hall mans the nets for Detroit in place of the departed Sawchuk, and the Wings overcome the stalwart Harry Lumley and the Leafs in the semi-final. But Plante and the Canadiens are too strong in the Final, and Montreal are off on their five-year Stanley Cup run.

(minimum 240 minutes played)					
GOALER, TEAM	MINS	SAVES-SHOTS	SH/GP	SVPCT	PERSEV
H Lumley, Tor	304	161-175	34.5	.920	978
J Plante, Mtr †	600	213-231	23.1	.922	961
Gl Hall, Det	604	279-307	30.5	.909	960

(1-239 minutes played)					
GOALER, TEAM	MINS	SAVES-SHOTS	SH/GP	SVPCT	PERSEV
*G Bell, NY	120	61-70	35.0	.871	930
Worsley, NY	180	85-99	33.0	.859	914

1957

Plante is clearly the class of the field this post-season as Canadiens roll over New York and Boston, five games apiece. Check the number of shots Gump Worsley faces; seems the Ranger defence of this era is as porous in the playoffs as it is in the regular season. And Hall does poorly in the Detroit nets, prompting Jack Adams to trade him to Chicago and reacquire Sawchuk.

(minimum 240 minutes played)					
GOALER, TEAM	MINS	SAVES-SHOTS	SH/GP	SVPCT	PERSEV
J Plante, Mtr †	616	249-266	25.9	.936	979
Worsley, NY	316	175-197	37.4	.888	951
*D Simmons, Bos	600	241-270	27.0	.893	938
Gl Hall, Det	300	114-129	25.8	.884	927

1958

Don Simmons is heroic in goal for Boston, the high-water

mark of his career. But with the Final tied at two games apiece and game five at the Forum in overtime, Rocket Richard beats Simmons with a screened 35-footer. Plante and the Habs go on to win their third Cup in a row.

(minimum 240 minutes played)					
GOALER, TEAM	MINS	SAVES-SHOTS	SH/GP	SVPCT	PERSEV
J Plante, Mtr †	618	299-319	31.0	.937	989
D Simmons, Bos	671	346-372	33.3	.930	986
Worsley, NY	365	190-218	35.8	.872	931
Sawchuk, Det	252	118-137	32.6	.861	916

(1-239 minutes played)					
GOALER, TEAM	MINS	SAVES-SHOTS	SH/GP	SVPCT	PERSEV
H Lumley, Bos	60	25-30	30.0	.833	883

1959

Montreal are dominant enough to win the Cup this year with Beliveau and Richard missing most of the playoffs through injury, and with Plante the least impressive of the four post-season goalers. Two playoff institutions begin here: Glenn Hall between the pipes for Chicago and Johnny Bower plying the crease for Toronto.

(minimum 240 minutes played)					
GOALER, TEAM	MINS	SAVES-SHOTS	SH/GP	SVPCT	PERSEV
Gl Hall, Chi	360	212-233	38.8	.910	975
H Lumley, Bos	436	208-228	31.4	.912	965
Bower, Tor	746	374-412	33.1	.908	963
J Plante, Mtr †	620	270-297	28.7	.909	957

1960

In the first post-season in which he wears his mask, Plante is superb as the Canadiens roll to their fifth-straight Cup, doing so in the minimum eight games, one of only two clubs (along with the '52 Wings) to sweep through the playoffs unbeaten.

(minimum 240 minutes played)					
GOALER, TEAM	MINS	SAVES-SHOTS	SH/GP	SVPCT	PERSEV
J Plante, Mtr †	489	211-222	27.2	.950	996
Bower, Tor	645	339-370	34.4	.916	974
Gl Hall, Chi	249	120-134	32.3	.896	949
Sawchuk, Det	405	169-188	27.9	.899	945

1961

Hall backstops the Black Hawks to the only Stanley Cup they have won since 1938. Bobby Hull supplies the firepower, as Detroit's Hank Bassen, who fills in for the injured Sawchuk in four games of the six-part Final, so eloquently attests: "I've never been afraid of what I do. But when Bobby blasts one, he puts the fear of God in you. You see that thing coming at you like a bullet, and your life flashes before your eyes."

(minimum 240 minutes played)					
GOALER, TEAM	MINS	SAVES-SHOTS	SH/GP	SVPCT	PERSEV
Gl Hall, Chi †	772	377-403	31.3	.935	988
Sawchuk, Det	465	209-227	29.3	.921	970
J Plante, Mtr	412	164-180	26.2	.911	955

(1-239 minutes played)					
GOALER, TEAM	MINS	SAVES-SHOTS	SH/GP	SVPCT	PERSEV
Bower, Tor	180	92-101	33.7	.911	967
H Bassen, Det	220	97-106	28.9	.915	963
*Maniago, Tor	145	57-63	26.1	.905	948

1962

Gump Worsley gets no help at all from the Ranger defence, yet sparkles anyway – business as usual for the Gumper. In the Final, Toronto's Bower goes down with an injury and is replaced by Don Simmons. He does pretty poorly, but the Leaf blue-line corps closes ranks protectively around him. Meanwhile, the Leaf forwards beat Hall on five straight shots to overcome a 3-2 deficit in game five, and Toronto are on their way to their first Cup in 11 years.

(minimum 240 minutes played)					
GOALER, TEAM	MINS	SAVES-SHOTS	SH/GP	SVPCT	PERSEV
Worsley, NY	384	236-257	40.2	.918	985
Bower, Tor †	579	277-298	30.9	.930	981
Gl Hall, Chi	720	376-407	33.9	.924	980
J Plante, Mtr	360	177-196	32.7	.903	958

(1-239 minutes played)					
GOALER, TEAM	MINS	SAVES-SHOTS	SH/GP	SVPCT	PERSEV
D Simmons, Tor	165	64-72	26.2	.889	933

1963

The aged Maple Leafs win again, and the legend of Punch Imlach's senior citizens is born. But in fact it's Bower's goalkeeping that wins the Cup for the Hogtown team; with goaling this good, it almost doesn't matter who you've got skating up front. The China Wall's 1002 perseverance mark is one of only five of 1000 or better registered by a regular goalie in the playoffs between 1952 and 2001.

(minimum 240 minutes played)					
GOALER, TEAM	MINS	SAVES-SHOTS	SH/GP	SVPCT	PERSEV
Bower, Tor †	600	299-315	31.5	.949	1002
Gl Hall, Chi	360	213-238	39.7	.895	961
J Plante, Mtr	300	126-140	28.0	.900	947
Sawchuk, Det	660	289-324	29.5	.892	941

1964

Three in a row for the Leafs, as once again Bower proves virtually impregnable. The first three games of the Final are tied or won in the last minute of play (two for Toronto, one for Detroit), and Bobby Baun scores in game six overtime on a cracked ankle, his long shot deflecting past Sawchuk off poor Bill Gadsby's stick. In game two of the Detroit-Chicago semi-final, Sawchuk gets hurt and the Wings are forced to go into the stands for a replacement, who turns out to be Central Leaguer Bob Champoux. The resulting delay on national TV riles fans and commentators. It's the last gasp for the emergency-goalkeeper concept; in the off-season, the NHL enacts a rule requiring teams to dress two goalies.

(minimum 240 minutes played)					
GOALER, TEAM	MINS	SAVES-SHOTS	SH/GP	SVPCT	PERSEV
Bower, Tor †	850	429-459	32.4	.935	989
C Hodge, Mtr	420	201-217	31.0	.926	978
Sawchuk, Det	695	323-354	30.6	.912	963
Gl Hall, Chi	408	206-228	33.5	.904	959

(1-239 minutes played)					
GOALER, TEAM	MINS	SAVES-SHOTS	SH/GP	SVPCT	PERSEV
*R Crozier, Det	108	53-58	32.2	.914	967
*Champoux, Det	40	14-18	27.0	.778	823
*DeJordy, Chi	20	7-9	27.0	.778	823

1965

At last, Worsley reaches the playoffs with a good team, and he's rewarded with his first Cup – but not without much anxiety. In the Final against Chicago, he gets hurt, and Charlie Hodge fills in very ably in games four, five, and six. But Toe Blake goes with Worsley for game seven because "I thought Gump would be less nervous than Charlie." Sure enough, Worsley stops all 20 shots in an easy 4-0 victory.

(minimum 240 minutes played)					
GOALER, TEAM	MINS	SAVES-SHOTS	SH/GP	SVPCT	PERSEV
Worsley, Mtr †	501	205-219	26.2	.936	980
Gl Hall, Chi	760	359-387	30.6	.928	979
C Hodge, Mtr †	300	123-133	26.6	.925	969
Bower, Tor	321	137-150	28.0	.913	960
*R Crozier, Det	420	167-190	27.1	.879	924

(1-239 minutes played)					
GOALER, TEAM	MINS	SAVES-SHOTS	SH/GP	SVPCT	PERSEV
Sawchuk, Tor	60	36-39	39.0	.923	988
*DeJordy, Chi	80	33-42	31.5	.786	838

1966

Roger Crozier, in defeat, wins the Conn Smythe Trophy in its second year of existence. It's a nice gesture, but really,

Gump Worsley was better. Game six is the setting for the most controversial ending to a Cup Final in NHL history until Brett Hull's "No Goal" of 1999. In overtime, Dave Balon's centring pass hits Henri Richard as the Pocket Rocket slides through the slot. The puck hits Richard in the leg and is swept into the net, perhaps by his hand. The goal stands and Montreal win the Cup, but to this day Detroit fans swear that Richard gloved it over the line.

(minimum 240 minutes played)					
GOALER, TEAM	MINS	SAVES-SHOTS	SH/GP	SVPCT	PERSEV
Worsley, Mtr †	600	270-290	29.0	.931	979
R Crozier, Det	666	279-305	27.5	.915	961
Gl Hall, Chi	347	162-184	31.8	.880	933

(1–239 minutes played)					
GOALER, TEAM	MINS	SAVES-SHOTS	SH/GP	SVPCT	PERSEV
*D Dryden, Chi	13	7-7	32.3	1.000	1054
Sawchuk, Tor	120	66-72	36.0	.917	977
H Bassen, Det	54	25-27	30.0	.926	976
Bower, Tor	120	67-75	37.5	.893	956

1967

The famous Cup triumph in which all 19 Toronto players were age 65 or older. Actually, seven of them were 36 or older, but the legend grows in the telling, eh? However, as we see here, the Leafs won entirely because of the tremendous work of Sawchuk (and Bower, too, in the three games he played in the Final before going down with a pulled muscle), who had to face nearly 40, count 'em, 40 shots per game. Montreal's Rogie Vachon, a 22-year-old out of Junior B, had a fine post-season, but neither he nor Gump Worsley, in the nets for the game six finale, could offset the artistry of the Toronto tandem. Next time you hear someone droning on mistily about Allan Stanley winning the draw and getting the puck to Red Kelly and then to Chief Armstrong for the clinching empty-netter, just remember: those guys were playing horrible defence, and they won only because Sawchuk and Bower were so awesome.

(minimum 240 minutes played)					
GOALER, TEAM	MINS	SAVES-SHOTS	SH/GP	SVPCT	PERSEV
Sawchuk, Tor †	568	350-375	39.6	.933	999
*R Vachon, Mtr	555	274-296	32.0	.926	979
Giacomin, NY	246	120-134	32.7	.896	950

(1–239 minutes played)					
GOALER, TEAM	MINS	SAVES-SHOTS	SH/GP	SVPCT	PERSEV
Bower, Tor †	155	98-103	39.9	.951	1018
Worsley, Mtr	80	43-45	33.8	.956	1012
Gl Hall, Chi	176	94-102	34.8	.922	980
DeJordy, Chi	184	94-104	34.0	.904	960

1968

The first expansion-era playoffs provide a festival of fine goaling, with Glenn Hall getting the Connie Smythe for helping the Blues past Philadelphia (in seven games) and Minnesota (also in seven games). In the Final against the Canadiens, St. Louis are outshot by 38-36, 36-19, 46-15, and 31-21, yet Hall lets only 10 get past him. The Blues lose in four, but by only a single goal in each game. Among those vanquished en route to the Final: the Flyers' Bernie Parent, who gives the rest of the league a piquant foretaste of things to come.

(minimum 360 minutes played)					
GOALER, TEAM	MINS	SAVES-SHOTS	SH/GP	SVPCT	PERSEV
Worsley, Mtr †	669	272-293	26.3	.928	972
DeJordy, Chi	662	357-391	35.4	.913	972
Giacomin, NY	360	184-201	33.5	.915	971
Maniago, Min	893	435-474	31.8	.918	971
Gl Hall, StL	1111	512-557	30.1	.919	969

(1–359 minutes played)					
GOALER, TEAM	MINS	SAVES-SHOTS	SH/GP	SVPCT	PERSEV
B Parent, Phi	355	206-214	36.2	.963	1023
*R Vachon, Mtr †	113	52-56	29.7	.929	978
Cheevers, Bos	240	128-143	35.8	.895	955
*Rutledge, LA	149	65-73	29.4	.890	939
*Favell, Phi	120	55-63	31.5	.873	926
Sawchuk, LA	280	121-139	29.8	.871	920
*S Martin, StL	73	16-21	17.3	.762	791

1969

Vachon takes over from Worsley during the semi-finals against Boston and fashions one of the best post-seasons of the last half-century. But he's not alone: the Bruins' Gerry Cheevers is almost as good, and so is Jacques Plante, who comes out of retirement and prods the Blues to a Cup Final rematch with Montreal. But the Canadiens have no love lost for their former teammate. "Plante talks about us," Jacques Laperriere offers ominously. "He talks too much." Says Yvan Cournoyer, "When I see those eyes looking out from behind the mask, I want my shots to come from cannons." Plante plays well in the Final, stopping 115 of 127, but the Canadiens sweep much more easily than they did in '68.

(minimum 360 minutes played)					
GOALER, TEAM	MINS	SAVES-SHOTS	SH/GP	SVPCT	PERSEV
R Vachon, Mtr †	507	241-253	29.9	.953	1002
Cheevers, Bos	572	284-300	31.5	.947	999
J Plante, StL	589	258-272	27.7	.949	995
Worsley, Mtr †	370	163-177	28.7	.921	969
Ga Smith, Oak	420	205-228	32.6	.899	953
*G Desjardins, LA	431	214-242	33.7	.884	940

(1–359 minutes played)					
GOALER, TEAM	MINS	SAVES-SHOTS	SH/GP	SVPCT	PERSEV
Gl Hall, StL	131	65-70	32.1	.929	982
*Villemure, NY	60	30-34	34.0	.882	939
Bower, Tor	154	80-91	35.5	.879	938
E Johnston, Bos	65	30-34	31.4	.882	935
B Parent, Phi	180	82-94	31.3	.872	925
Favell, Phi	60	31-36	36.0	.861	921
B Gamble, Tor	86	60-73	50.9	.822	907
Giacomin, NY	180	60-70	23.3	.857	896
Rutledge, LA	229	70-82	21.5	.854	889

1970

With Cheevers a steady presence in the nets, Boston roll to their first Cup since 1941. In game one of the Final, Jacques Plante gets knocked cold by a Fred Stanfield slap shot; on the way to hospital, he revives and announces, "The mask saved my life." Glenn Hall steps in and is immortalized in the endlessly replayed tape of an airborne Bobby Orr scoring the Cup-winning goal in overtime of game four. Elsewhere, don't blink: you'll miss the entire NHL post-season career of Les Binkley, which takes place here and is actually quite good. Rookie Tony Esposito does well too, coming off the famous 15-shutout season in which he was allegedly aided by a cleverly concealed apron that covered his five-hole when he dropped into the butterfly.

(minimum 360 minutes played)					
GOALER, TEAM	MINS	SAVES-SHOTS	SH/GP	SVPCT	PERSEV
Cheevers, Bos †	781	361-390	30.0	.926	976
Binkley, Pit	428	183-198	27.8	.924	971
*A Esposito, Chi	480	264-291	36.4	.907	968
Gl Hall, StL	421	202-223	31.8	.906	959

(1–359 minutes played)					
GOALER, TEAM	MINS	SAVES-SHOTS	SH/GP	SVPCT	PERSEV
Maniago, Min	180	95-101	33.7	.941	997
J Plante, StL	324	117-125	23.1	.936	975
Sawchuk, NY	80	51-57	42.8	.895	966
R Edwards, Det	206	108-119	34.7	.908	965
E Johnston, Bos †	60	35-39	39.0	.897	962
Ga Smith, Oak	248	121-134	32.4	.903	957
Worsley, Min	180	103-117	39.0	.880	945
*Wakely, StL	216	121-138	38.3	.877	941
*Al Smith, Pit	180	79-89	29.7	.888	937
Giacomin, NY	276	105-124	27.0	.847	892
R Crozier, Det	34	13-16	28.2	.812	860

1971

After making the most successful late-season debut in recorded history (see the '70–71 chart in Chapter Four), Ken Dryden makes a Cinderella run through the playoffs. The gangly law student stands up to the most fearsome attack of the age and beats the Bruins in seven, holds off the surprising North Stars in six, and gets Montreal to the last round against the Black Hawks in what proves to be the most compelling Cup Final of the post-'67 era. The Hawks are winning game seven, 2-0, when halfway through the game Jacques Lemaire fires a routine dump-in slapper from beyond the blue line. Esposito, who has been as good in the playoffs as Dryden, inexplicably loses it in the fog rising off the steamy Chicago Stadium ice, and the Habs are back in it. Henri Richard adds two more later to put Montreal in front, and with a minute left and the Hawks desperate to tie, Jim Pappin takes a cross-ice pass at the lip of the crease. He's about to tuck it home when Dryden's right leg shoots over from the other side of the goalmouth – an unbelievable save! Montreal win the Cup after a game seven that no one who saw will ever forget.

(minimum 360 minutes played)					
GOALER, TEAM	MINS	SAVES-SHOTS	SH/GP	SVPCT	PERSEV
A Esposito, Chi	1151	540-582	30.3	.928	978
*K Dryden, Mtr †	1221	648-709	34.8	.914	972
Giacomin, NY	759	292-320	25.3	.912	955
Maniago, Min	480	242-270	33.8	.896	953
Cheevers, Bos	360	173-194	32.3	.892	946

(1–359 minutes played)					
GOALER, TEAM	MINS	SAVES-SHOTS	SH/GP	SVPCT	PERSEV
J Plante, Tor	134	67-73	32.7	.918	972
B Parent, Tor	235	106-115	29.4	.922	971
Wakely, StL	180	80-87	29.0	.920	968
Worsley, Min	240	103-116	29.0	.888	936
Favell, Phi	120	52-60	30.0	.867	917
Gl Hall, StL	180	57-66	22.0	.864	900
B Gamble, Phi	120	55-67	33.5	.821	877
E Johnston, Bos	60	30-37	37.0	.811	872
*Villemure, NY	80	29-35	26.2	.829	872

1972

The Bruins win for the second time in three years, taking six games to beat the arch-rival Rangers, who are in their first Cup Final since 1950. Boston coach Tom Johnson goes back and forth between Ed Johnston and Gerry Cheevers, settling on Cheevers for the last two games – just as Emile Francis, who'd been shuttling Ed Giacomin and Gilles Villemure in and out of the Rangers nets, settles on Villemure for the last two.

(minimum 360 minutes played)					
GOALER, TEAM	MINS	SAVES-SHOTS	SH/GP	SVPCT	PERSEV
E Johnston, Bos †	420	191-204	29.1	.936	985

GOALER, TEAM	MINS	SAVES-SHOTS	SH/GP	SVPCT	PERSEV
Villemure, NYR	360	159-173	28.8	.919	967
Cheevers, Bos †	483	226-247	30.7	.915	966
K Dryden, Mtr	360	175-192	32.0	.911	965
Giacomin, NYR	600	249-276	27.6	.902	948
*J Caron, StL	499	224-250	30.1	.896	946

(1–359 minutes played)

GOALER, TEAM	MINS	SAVES-SHOTS	SH/GP	SVPCT	PERSEV
Ga Smith, Chi	120	67-70	35.0	.957	1015
Worsley, Min	194	98-105	32.5	.933	987
B Parent, Tor	243	135-148	36.5	.912	973
Rutherford, Pit	240	131-145	36.2	.903	964
Maniago, Min	238	119-131	33.0	.908	963
A Esposito, Chi	300	137-153	30.6	.895	946
G Desjardins, Chi	60	29-34	34.0	.853	910
*McDuffe, StL	60	31-38	38.0	.816	879
Wakely, StL	113	57-70	37.2	.814	876
J Plante, Tor	60	22-27	27.0	.815	860

1973

Not a great year for playoff goalkeeping. The Final, a rematch of '71 won by the Canadiens in six games over Chicago, produces a record 56 goals by both teams (33 by Montreal) and features an 8-7 travesty in game five. Dryden's final-round save percentage: .860. Esposito's: .831.

(minimum 360 minutes played)

GOALER, TEAM	MINS	SAVES-SHOTS	SH/GP	SVPCT	PERSEV
Favell, Phi	669	330-359	32.2	.919	973
K Dryden, Mtr †	1039	490-540	31.2	.907	959
A Esposito, Chi	895	406-452	30.3	.898	949
Giacomin, NYR	539	215-238	26.5	.903	948

(1–359 minutes played)

GOALER, TEAM	MINS	SAVES-SHOTS	SH/GP	SVPCT	PERSEV
Maniago, Min	309	138-147	28.5	.939	986
Villemure, NYR	61	29-31	30.5	.935	986
*Belhumeur, Phi	10	8-9	54.0	.889	979
Gi Gilbert, Min	60	36-40	40.0	.900	967
Ga Smith, Chi	65	39-44	40.6	.886	954
J Caron, StL	140	69-77	33.0	.896	951
E Johnston, Bos	160	78-87	32.6	.897	951
R Crozier, Buf	249	103-114	27.5	.904	949
D Dryden, Buf	120	62-71	35.5	.873	932
*W Stephenson, StL	160	86-100	37.5	.860	922
J Plante, Bos	120	53-63	31.5	.841	894
*R Brooks, Bos	20	8-11	33.0	.727	782

1974

Philadelphia become the first expansion team to win the Cup, beating Boston in six, as Bernie Parent, author of a 30-

save 1-0 shutout in the clincher, wins the Conn Smythe. In Montreal, Dryden sits out the year to clerk at a law firm, and Bunny Larocque fills in ably, but not ably enough.

(minimum 360 minutes played)

GOALER, TEAM	MINS	SAVES-SHOTS	SH/GP	SVPCT	PERSEV
B Parent, Phi †	1042	489-524	30.2	.933	983
A Esposito, Chi	584	287-315	32.4	.911	965
Gi Gilbert, Bos	977	445-488	30.0	.912	962
*MR Larocque, Mtr	364	170-188	31.0	.904	956
Giacomin, NYR	788	314-357	27.2	.880	925

(1–359 minutes played)

GOALER, TEAM	MINS	SAVES-SHOTS	SH/GP	SVPCT	PERSEV
G Edwards, LA	60	22-23	23.0	.957	995
Favell, Tor	181	104-114	37.8	.912	975
R Vachon, LA	240	89-96	24.0	.927	967
Myre, Atl	186	100-113	36.5	.885	946
*Veisor, Chi	80	40-45	33.8	.889	945
D Bouchard, Atl	60	22-26	26.0	.846	889
E Johnston, Tor	60	24-30	30.0	.800	850

1975

The Flyers beat the Sabres in six games for their second-straight Cup, and Parent wins the Conn Smythe once more, too. Goaltending, Buffalo's Achilles' heel all year long, comes back to bite the Sabres in the, er, heel again, as Gerry Desjardins implodes during the Final. Down two games to none, he allows three goals in game three's first five shots and takes himself out. Crozier comes in, and Buffalo win in overtime in the fog. Desjardins comes back for games four and five, gets bombarded, announces, "I hate this game," and gives way to Crozier for the finale, which the Flyers win, 2-0, with Parent making 32 saves, all of them easy. The goaltending star of the spring, though, is rookie Glenn "Chico" Resch, who goes in with Long Island down three games to none against the Pens and somehow emerges a four-games-to-three winner. He almost pulls it off again against the Flyers in the semi-final, rallying the Isles from three games down to even the series before Philly win the seventh.

(minimum 360 minutes played)

GOALER, TEAM	MINS	SAVES-SHOTS	SH/GP	SVPCT	PERSEV
*Resch, NYI	692	336-361	31.3	.931	983
*Inness, Pit	540	263-287	31.9	.916	970
K Dryden, Mtr	688	316-345	30.1	.916	966
B Parent, Phi †	922	352-381	24.8	.924	965
*G McRae, Tor	441	189-210	28.6	.900	948
A Esposito, Chi	472	244-278	35.3	.878	937
G Desjardins, Buf	760	266-309	24.4	.861	901

(1–359 minutes played)					
GOALER, TEAM	MINS	SAVES-SHOTS	SH/GP	SVPCT	PERSEV
R Vachon, LA	199	92-99	29.8	.929	979
W Stephenson, Phi †	123	47-51	24.9	.922	963
Ga Smith, Van	257	133-147	34.3	.905	962
R Crozier, Buf	292	136-150	30.8	.907	958
Giacomin, NYR	86	39-43	30.0	.907	957
Wm Smith, NYI	333	174-197	35.5	.883	942
*M Dumas, Chi	127	7-8	25.3	.875	917
*Lockett, Van	60	33-39	39.0	.846	911
Gi Gilbert, Bos	188	73-85	27.1	.859	904
J Davidson, StL	60	22-26	26.0	.846	889
E Johnston, StL	60	24-29	29.0	.828	876
Villemure, NYR	94	29-35	22.3	.829	866

1976

The Canadiens embark on another dynasty, this one to last four years, by going 12-1 in the playoffs, finishing with a final-round sweep of the Broad Street Bullies that elates goonery-hating fans across the continent. Parent gets hurt halfway through the post-season, but the Flyers get just as strong a performance from former Canadian Nats mainstay Wayne Stephenson the rest of the way.

(minimum 360 minutes played)					
GOALER, TEAM	MINS	SAVES-SHOTS	SH/GP	SVPCT	PERSEV
K Dryden, Mtr †	780	325-350	26.9	.929	973
W Thomas, Tor	587	326-360	36.8	.906	967
Cheevers, Bos	392	155-169	25.9	.917	960
R Vachon, LA	438	176-193	26.4	.912	956
W Stephenson, Phi	494	206-228	27.7	.904	950
B Parent, Phi	480	223-250	31.2	.892	944
Wm Smith, NYI	437	174-195	26.8	.892	937
G Desjardins, Buf	563	208-236	25.2	.881	923
Gi Gilbert, Bos	360	125-144	24.0	.868	908

(1–359 minutes played)					
GOALER, TEAM	MINS	SAVES-SHOTS	SH/GP	SVPCT	PERSEV
Staniowski, StL	206	123-130	37.9	.946	1009
D Bouchard, Atl	120	49-52	26.0	.942	986
Plasse, Pit	180	85-93	31.0	.914	966
Resch, NYI	357	176-194	32.6	.907	962
A Esposito, Chi	240	118-131	32.7	.901	955
G Edwards, LA	120	61-70	35.0	.871	930
C Ridley, Van	120	56-64	32.0	.875	928
G McRae, Tor	13	4-5	23.1	.800	838
Al Smith, Buf	17	2-3	10.6	.667	684

1977

Hey, it's the Popcorn Kid! Leaf rookie Mike Palmateer takes time out from road hockey games in front of his working-class high-rise to turn in the best performance of the post-season. Dryden and the Habs, meanwhile, go 12-2 – they're slipping a bit – and sweep the Bruins and a shaky Gerry Cheevers in the Final.

(minimum 360 minutes played)					
GOALER, TEAM	MINS	SAVES-SHOTS	SH/GP	SVPCT	PERSEV
*Palmateer, Tor	360	193-209	34.8	.923	982
K Dryden, Mtr †	849	302-324	22.9	.932	970
Wm Smith, NYI	580	275-302	31.2	.911	963
W Stephenson, Phi	532	187-210	23.7	.890	930
R Vachon, LA	520	236-272	31.4	.868	920
Cheevers, Bos	858	283-327	22.9	.865	904

(1–359 minutes played)					
GOALER, TEAM	MINS	SAVES-SHOTS	SH/GP	SVPCT	PERSEV
A Esposito, Chi	120	63-69	34.5	.913	971
Herron, Pit	180	102-113	37.7	.903	965
Resch, NYI	144	55-60	25.0	.917	958
B Parent, Phi	123	63-71	34.6	.887	945
P LoPresti, Min	77	43-49	38.2	.878	941
W Thomas, Tor	202	92-104	30.9	.885	936
E Johnston, StL	138	66-75	32.6	.880	934
Myre, Atl	120	41-46	23.0	.891	930
*D Edwards, Buf	300	108-123	24.6	.878	919
*Staniowski, StL	102	54-63	37.1	.857	919
G Simmons, LA	20	6-7	21.0	.857	892
G Desjardins, Buf	60	17-21	21.0	.809	845
D Bouchard, Atl	60	20-25	25.0	.800	842
Ga Smith, Min	43	11-15	20.9	.733	768
Gi Gilbert, Bos	20	4-7	21.0	.571	606

1978

Palmateer backstops the Leafs to a memorable seven-game quarter-final upset of the Islanders. But Dryden and the Canadiens, despite tumbling to a 12-3 record in the playoffs, prevail for their third-straight Cup, sweeping Boston again in the Final.

(minimum 360 minutes played)					
GOALER, TEAM	MINS	SAVES-SHOTS	SH/GP	SVPCT	PERSEV
Palmateer, Tor	795	348-380	28.7	.916	964
Resch, NYI	388	163-178	27.5	.916	962
K Dryden, Mtr †	919	332-361	23.6	.920	959
D Edwards, Buf	482	190-212	26.4	.896	940
B Parent, Phi	722	271-304	25.3	.891	934
Cheevers, Bos	731	265-300	24.6	.883	924

(1–359 minutes played)					
GOALER, TEAM	MINS	SAVES-SHOTS	SH/GP	SVPCT	PERSEV
Favell, Col	120	82-88	44.0	.932	1005
J Davidson, NYR	122	64-71	34.9	.901	960
Wm Smith, NYI	47	13-14	17.9	.929	958
Low, Det	240	124-141	35.2	.879	938

GOALER, TEAM	MINS	SAVES-SHOTS	SH/GP	SVPCT	PERSEV
D Bouchard, Atl	120	40-47	23.5	.851	929
R Grahame, Bos	202	59-66	19.6	.894	927
Rutherford, Det	180	75-87	29.0	.862	910
W Thomas, NYR	60	23-27	27.0	.852	897
A Esposito, Chi	242	98-117	29.0	.838	886
R Vachon, LA	120	40-51	25.5	.784	827

1979

John Davidson's nimble work between the pipes boosts the Studio 54–era Rangers to the Final, the highlight coming in a six-game semi-final upset of the hated Islanders. But the Canadiens (12-4 in the post-season, though that includes their narrow escape against Boston in game seven of their semi-final, thanks to Don Cherry's too-many-men-on-the-ice gaffe) take the Cup in five games. The Habs are so dominant that Dryden doesn't even have to be all that good. He retires, having had his name etched in silver six times in eight years of play.

(minimum 360 minutes played)

GOALER, TEAM	MINS	SAVES-SHOTS	SH/GP	SVPCT	PERSEV
J Davidson, NYR	1106	493-535	29.0	.921	970
Herron, Pit	421	197-221	31.5	.891	944
K Dryden, Mtr †	990	365-406	24.6	.899	940
Cheevers, Bos	360	122-137	22.8	.891	929

(1–359 minutes played)

GOALER, TEAM	MINS	SAVES-SHOTS	SH/GP	SVPCT	PERSEV
*Re Lemelin, Atl	20	15-15	45.0	1.000	1075
MR Larocque, Mtr †	20	9-9	27.0	1.000	1045
Wm Smith, NYI	315	137-147	28.0	.932	979
Resch, NYI	300	131-142	28.4	.923	970
Gi Gilbert, Bos	314	145-161	30.8	.901	952
A Esposito, Chi	243	112-126	31.1	.889	941
Palmateer, Tor	298	136-153	30.8	.889	940
*M Lessard, LA	126	64-73	34.8	.877	935
P Harrison, Tor	91	48-55	36.3	.873	933
*R Sauve, Buf	181	68-77	25.5	.883	926
Bromley, Van	180	80-94	31.3	.851	903
*Rb Moore, Phi	268	103-121	27.1	.851	896
W Stephenson, Phi	213	79-95	26.8	.832	876
D Bouchard, Atl	100	39-48	28.8	.812	860

1980

Now there are 16 teams in the playoffs, and the post-season starts to take on that interminable feel that will cost the game a lot of fans in the United States. Davidson shines again, along with, of all people, Bob Sauve. But this spring is really about Billy Smith and the Islanders, who start their four-year reign. Smith and Resch had exchanged the baton several times over the previous five years, the last three of

which reeked of disappointment and unrealized promise, but now Smith takes over the starting role at the start of the playoffs and skates with it. He doesn't blow anyone away, but he's more than good enough, and the Isles take rookie Pete Peeters and the Flyers in six to claim their first Cup.

(minimum 450 minutes played)

GOALER, TEAM	MINS	SAVES-SHOTS	SH/GP	SVPCT	PERSEV
J Davidson, NYR	541	267-288	31.9	.927	980
R Sauve, Buf	501	214-231	27.7	.926	973
Wm Smith, NYI †	1193	524-580	29.2	.903	952
*Peeters, Phi	799	343-380	28.5	.903	950
G Meloche, Min	564	252-286	30.4	.881	932
Cheevers, Bos	619	223-255	24.7	.875	916

(1–449 minutes played)

GOALER, TEAM	MINS	SAVES-SHOTS	SH/GP	SVPCT	PERSEV
Hanlon, Van	60	40-43	43.0	.930	1002
A Esposito, Chi	373	170-184	29.6	.924	973
Myre, Phi	384	185-201	31.4	.920	973
MR Larocque, Mtr	300	132-143	28.6	.923	971
*Crha, Tor	121	82-92	45.6	.891	967
Low, Edm	212	115-127	35.9	.906	965
Liut, StL	193	98-110	34.2	.891	948
Herron, Mtr	300	132-147	29.4	.898	947
D Edwards, Buf	360	152-169	28.2	.899	946
M Lessard, LA	207	103-117	33.9	.880	937
G Edwards, Min	337	158-180	32.0	.878	931
D Bouchard, Atl	241	103-117	29.1	.880	929
G Millen, Pit	300	138-159	31.8	.868	921
Palmateer, Tor	60	36-43	43.0	.837	909
Al Smith, Har	120	55-65	32.5	.846	900
Bromley, Van	180	57-68	22.7	.838	876
J Garrett, Har	60	32-40	40.0	.800	867
Resch, NYI †	120	34-43	21.5	.791	827
Veisor, Chi	60	19-25	25.0	.760	802
*Keans, LA	40	13-20	30.0	.650	700

1981

The Age of Air Hockey is now in full effect, so don't expect any great goalkeeping numbers. And indeed, there aren't any here. Pat Riggin rings up the best record, playing for the Flames in their first year in Calgary and, with Rejean Lemelin's help, getting them to the semi-finals. There they fall to Minnesota, who in turn fall to the Cup-retaining Islanders in five.

(minimum 450 minutes played)

GOALER, TEAM	MINS	SAVES-SHOTS	SH/GP	SVPCT	PERSEV
P Riggin, Clg	629	332-369	35.2	.900	958
G Meloche, Min	802	396-443	33.1	.894	949
Wm Smith, NYI †	994	391-433	26.7	.903	948
*St. Croix, Phi	541	223-250	27.7	.892	938

GOALER, TEAM	MINS	SAVES-SHOTS	SH/GP	SVPCT	PERSEV
D Edwards, Buf	503	221-249	29.7	.888	937
*Moog, Edm	526	238-270	30.8	.881	933
Liut, StL	685	299-349	30.6	.857	908
S Baker, NYR	826	329-384	27.9	.857	903

(1–449 minutes played)

GOALER, TEAM	MINS	SAVES-SHOTS	SH/GP	SVPCT	PERSEV
P Harrison, Tor	40	16-17	25.5	.941	984
Re Lemelin, Clg	366	207-229	37.5	.904	966
G Millen, Pit	325	159-178	32.9	.893	948
*R Melanson, NYI †	92	48-54	35.2	.889	948
D Bouchard, Qbc	286	141-160	33.6	.881	937
A Esposito, Chi	215	108-123	34.3	.878	935
R Vachon, Bos	164	88-104	38.0	.846	910
*Weeks, NYR	14	6-7	30.0	.857	907
*Beaupre, Min	360	154-180	30.0	.856	906
R Brodeur, Van	185	75-88	28.5	.852	900
M Lessard, LA	220	103-123	33.5	.837	893
*Sevigny, Mtr	180	71-84	28.0	.845	892
Plasse, Qbc	15	5-6	24.0	.833	873
Peeters, Phi	180	53-65	21.7	.815	851
*Crha, Tor	65	33-44	40.6	.750	818
MR Larocque, Tor	75	24-32	25.6	.750	793
Rutherford, LA	20	6-8	24.0	.750	790
*Ma Baron, Bos	20	9-12	36.0	.750	770
G Edwards, Edm	20	4-6	18.0	.667	697

1982

Richard Brodeur was a good WHA goaler but a pretty poor one in the NHL. However, this post-season he becomes King Richard, single-handedly propelling an abjectly mediocre Vancouver side through three rounds with an outstanding-for-the-era .930 save percentage, before being swept by the Isles in the Final. Smith is strong again for Long Island, but his young stablemate Roland Melanson seems emotionally hurt at being used for a couple of one-minute stints to give the skaters a rest and as an unwitting decoy when Coach Al Arbour deceptively hints within earshot of reporters that he might start. Nor does he get much of a hand from Smith. "Smitty's not the type to help you a lot. I can understand," he tells *The New York Times*. "Chico Resch used to talk to me." He also wishes that the Isles hire a goaltending coach, if only "they could see this is a kid of 21 who needs help." It's all very sad to see this in the midst of the Islanders' third-straight Cup Final; you can almost see Melanson losing his confidence before your very eyes. The Isles are about to jettison him for young phenom Kelly Hrudey, and Melanson will quickly bottom out away from the Island. "I worked hard all year," he concludes, "and right now it feels as if it's been taken away from me." On a happier note, there's the Nordiques' Dan Bouchard, hero of a 15-year-old Quebec City resident named Patrick Roy. When Roy was younger,

Bouchard gave him one of his goal sticks, and Roy slept with it every night. Something must have rubbed off on Roy, and then some.

(minimum 450 minutes played)

GOALER, TEAM	MINS	SAVES-SHOTS	SH/GP	SVPCT	PERSEV
R Brodeur, Van	1089	542-591	32.6	.917	971
Wm Smith, NYI †	1120	451-498	26.7	.906	950
D Bouchard, Qbc	677	319-357	31.6	.894	946
*M Bannerman, Chi	555	259-294	31.8	.881	934
Liut, StL	494	200-227	27.6	.881	927
M Lessard, LA	583	268-309	31.8	.867	920
*M Moffat, Bos	663	252-290	26.2	.869	913

(1–449 minutes played)

GOALER, TEAM	MINS	SAVES-SHOTS	SH/GP	SVPCT	PERSEV
A Esposito, Chi	381	176-192	30.2	.917	967
G Meloche, Min	184	79-87	28.4	.908	955
P Riggin, Clg	194	89-99	30.6	.899	950
M Dion, Pit	304	153-175	34.5	.874	932
Mio, NYR	443	199-227	30.7	.877	928
*Wamsley, Mtr	300	91-102	20.4	.892	926
P Harrison, Buf	26	8-9	20.8	.889	924
Soetaert, Wpg	120	54-62	31.0	.871	923
St. Croix, Phi	20	7-8	24.0	.875	915
J Garrett, Qbc	323	136-157	29.2	.867	915
*Fuhr, Edm	309	150-176	34.2	.852	909
*Weeks, NYR	127	52-61	28.8	.852	900
Beaupre, Min	60	23-27	27.0	.852	897
D Edwards, Buf	214	88-104	29.2	.846	895
Peeters, Phi	220	87-104	28.4	.837	884
Keans, LA	32	6-7	13.1	.857	879
Hanlon, StL	109	43-52	28.6	.827	875
*R Melanson, NYI †	64	22-27	25.3	.815	857
J Davidson, NYR	33	10-13	23.6	.769	809
Staniowski, Wpg	120	30-42	21.0	.714	749
R Vachon, Bos	20	2-3	9.0	.667	682

1983

Smith wins the Connie Smythe, and it's an apt choice: for the first time, he's the best goaler in the post-season. The New York press had long dubbed Smith the "best money goalie of all time." It's hard to argue with that, given that he is in goal for all four-straight Cup wins and will be for the unsurpassed 19 straight playoff-series wins the Isles will register before Edmonton finally beat them in the '84 Final. However, that sobriquet was coined by Mike Lupica, a famous *Daily News* sports columnist who knows next to nothing about hockey and writes about it with contempt on those few occasions he deigns to mention the game. Smith was great, but for a "money goalie," we'll take Bower or Plante over the Hatchet Man. Still, Smith was excellent here, especially in shutting down the young, high-powered Oilers in the Final on 122 of 128 shots, good for a whopping .953 save percentage.

This is the last season that Edward Yuen had to reconstruct. From '84 on, the NHL kept shot-and-save records for the playoffs, so starting with the next post-season we'll only present those goalies who played a minimum number of minutes. To find the shot-and-save records of all goalies from '84 on, consult the annual NHL Guides or look them up under individual goalies' entries in *Total Hockey: The Official Encyclopedia of the National Hockey League*.

(minimum 450 minutes played)					
GOALER, TEAM	MINS	SAVES-SHOTS	SH/GP	SVPCT	PERSEV
Wm Smith, NYI †	962	462-505	31.5	.915	967
Mio, NYR	480	264-296	37.0	.892	954
Moog, Edm	949	413-461	29.1	.896	944
R Sauve, Buf	545	208-236	26.0	.881	925
Peeters, Bos	1024	420-481	28.2	.873	920
M Bannerman, Chi	480	207-239	29.9	.866	916

(1–449 minutes played)					
GOALER, TEAM	MINS	SAVES-SHOTS	SH/GP	SVPCT	PERSEV
Soetaert, Wpg	20	10-10	30.0	1.000	1050
Fuhr, Edm	11	4-4	21.8	1.000	1036
R Sevigny, Mtr	28	10-10	21.4	1.000	1036
Palmateer, Tor	252	166-183	43.6	.907	980
Hanlon, NYR	60	42-47	47.0	.894	972
Liut, StL	240	133-148	37.0	.899	960
D Bouchard, Qbc	242	110-121	30.0	.909	959
A Esposito, Chi	311	144-162	31.3	.889	941
Wamsley, Mtr	152	56-63	24.9	.889	930
G Meloche, Min	319	134-152	28.6	.882	929
A Jensen, Was	139	66-76	32.8	.868	923
J Garrett, Van	60	26-30	30.0	.867	917
P Riggin, Was	101	49-57	33.9	.860	916
D Edwards, Clg	226	122-144	38.2	.847	911
Beaupre, Min	245	115-135	33.1	.852	907
R Brodeur, Van	193	73-86	26.7	.849	893
Re Lemelin, Clg	327	137-164	30.1	.835	886
R Melanson, NYI †	238	94-114	28.7	.825	872
*B Hayward, Wpg	160	59-73	27.4	.808	854
*Lindbergh, Phi	180	67-85	28.3	.788	835
Myre, Buf	57	21-28	29.5	.750	799
St. Croix, Tor	1	0-1	60.0	.000	100

1984

Grant Fuhr emerges as Edmonton's number-one goalie and leads the Oilers to a last-round rematch with the Islanders. But he goes down with an injury halfway through the Final and is replaced by Andy Moog, who finishes the job strongly. Nevertheless, take note of the 33.4 shots per game Fuhr must handle in the Edmonton nets.

That's the highest figure a Cup-winning goalie has faced since Ken Dryden's 34.8 in '71, and no victorious goaler has faced so many since.

(minimum 450 minutes played)					
GOALER, TEAM	MINS	SAVES-SHOTS	SH/GP	SVPCT	PERSEV
Liut, StL	714	332-361	30.3	.920	970
Fuhr, Edm †	883	447-491	33.4	.910	966
Wm Smith, NYI	1190	513-567	28.6	.905	952
*Penney, Mtr	871	322-354	24.4	.910	950
Beaupre, Min	782	340-380	29.2	.895	943
D Bouchard, Qbc	543	199-224	24.8	.888	930

1985

Edmonton steamroll over everyone before beating Philadelphia in five for their second-straight Cup in a year in which goaltending is pretty much irrelevant. Only Pelle Lindbergh puts up good numbers. Rookie Mario Gosselin sees lots of action as Quebec beat Montreal in the second overtime of game seven to reach the semi-finals, and the Canadiens' Steve Penney, who looked like the second coming of Ken Dryden in '84, plummets to earth with an all-too-mortal .867 save percentage.

(minimum 450 minutes played)					
GOALER, TEAM	MINS	SAVES-SHOTS	SH/GP	SVPCT	PERSEV
Lindbergh, Phi	1008	447-489	29.1	.914	963
Fuhr, Edm †	1064	465-520	29.3	.894	943
*M Gosselin, Qbc	1059	417-471	26.7	.885	930
Bannerman, Chi	906	472-544	36.0	.868	928
*Penney, Mtr	733	260-300	24.6	.867	908

1986

It's a battle of the rookies in the Final, and Patrick Roy's Canadiens prevail over Mike Vernon's Flames in five, though it's hardly surprising when you look at the records below. Roy, 20, thus becomes the youngest starting goalie to win the Cup and the youngest player ever to win the Conn Smythe. Greg Millen does much better than Rick Wamsley for St. Louis as the Blues get to game seven of an unforgettable semi-final against Calgary, and Ken Wregget, always a fairly clumsy goaler during the regular season, starts building a well-deserved reputation as a playoff stud.

(minimum 450 minutes played)					
GOALER, TEAM	MINS	SAVES-SHOTS	SH/GP	SVPCT	PERSEV
Millen, StL	586	298-327	33.5	.911	967
*Pa Roy, Mtr †	1218	465-504	24.8	.923	964
Wregget, Tor	607	290-322	31.8	.901	954
Peeters, Was	544	229-253	27.9	.905	952
Vanbiesbrouck, NYR	899	428-477	31.8	.897	950
Fuhr, Edm	541	244-272	30.2	.897	947

GOALER, TEAM	MINS	SAVES-SHOTS	SH/GP	SVPCT	PERSEV
*Vernon, Clg	1229	521-581	28.4	.897	944
Wamsley, StL	569	269-306	32.3	.879	933

1987

Easter Epic protagonist Kelly Hrudey, playoff specialist Ken Wregget, stick-swinging rookie Ron Hextall (who faces 768 shots, the most ever in a post-season), even Red Wing pylon Greg Stefan . . . all are better than Grant Fuhr this year except where it counts most – having Wayne Gretzky and friends down at the other end, scoring goals for you. To the Oilers' credit, they cut down dramatically on shots allowed and recapture the Cup in a terrific seven-game Final against Philly. Did you know that Edmonton, having gone up three games to one, led the Flyers by two goals in both games five and six, only to have the Flyers come back and win each time? Not shown here is Glen Hanlon's fantastic performance over 467 minutes; he logged a .943 save percentage and 991 perseverance as part of his one-man revival of the long-moribund Detroit organization, before going down with an injury.

(minimum 480 minutes played)					
GOALER, TEAM	MINS	SAVES-SHOTS	SH/GP	SVPCT	PERSEV
Hrudey, NYI	842	424-462	32.9	.918	973
Wregget, Tor	761	337-366	28.9	.921	969
*R Hextall, Phi	1540	697-768	29.9	.908	957
Stefan, Det	508	225-249	29.4	.904	953
Fuhr, Edm †	1148	462-509	26.6	.908	952
B Hayward, Mtr	708	276-308	26.1	.896	940
M Gosselin, Qbc	654	289-326	29.9	.887	936

1988

Goalkeeping bottoms out completely in this, the post-season of Edmonton's fourth Stanley Cup, featuring a four-and-a-half-game sweep of the Bruins thanks to that blown transformer across the street from a suddenly blacked-out Boston Garden. By 2001 Sean Burke had played 13 seasons in the NHL, but 1,001 of his 1,705 career playoff minutes come here, as the Devils make the playoffs on the last night of the season and roll all the way to the seventh game of the semi-finals before losing to Boston.

(minimum 480 minutes played)					
GOALER, TEAM	MINS	SAVES-SHOTS	SH/GP	SVPCT	PERSEV
Peeters, Was	654	291-325	29.8	.895	945
S Burke, NJ	1001	457-514	30.8	.889	940
G Millen, StL	600	214-252	25.2	.849	938
Re Lemelin, Bos	1027	383-428	25.0	.895	937
Fuhr, Edm †	1136	415-470	24.8	.883	924
Stefan, Det	531	203-235	26.6	.864	908
Vernon, Clg	515	176-210	24.5	.838	879

1989

Roy and Vernon meet in a final-round rematch, and this time it's the Flames and Vernon who emerge triumphant. Can't blame Roy, though – his .920 save percentage is a thing of beauty. At any rate, it's nice to see our old pal Alain Chevrier doing well in the post-season.

(minimum 480 minutes played)					
GOALER, TEAM	MINS	SAVES-SHOTS	SH/GP	SVPCT	PERSEV
Roy, Mtr	1206	484-526	26.2	.920	964
Barrasso, Pit	631	348-388	36.9	.897	958
Chevrier, Chi	1013	439-483	28.6	.909	957
Vernon, Clg †	1381	495-547	23.8	.905	945
R Hextall, Phi	886	396-445	30.1	.890	940
G Millen, StL	649	274-308	28.5	.890	937
Hrudey, LA	566	257-292	31.0	.880	932

1990

Ex-Bruin Bill Ranford has the post-season of his career, lifting Mark Messier's Gretzky-less Oilers to the Cup and earning the Conn Smythe Trophy for good measure. Edmonton's victims in the five-game Final are the Bruins and the old Oil goaler, Andy Moog.

(minimum 480 minutes played)					
GOALER, TEAM	MINS	SAVES-SHOTS	SH/GP	SVPCT	PERSEV
Ranford, Edm †	1401	612-671	28.7	.912	960
Pa Roy, Mtr	641	265-291	27.2	.911	956
Moog, Bos	1195	440-484	24.3	.909	950
Liut, Was	507	194-222	26.3	.874	918
G Millen, Chi	613	260-300	29.4	.867	916
Hrudey, LA	539	225-264	29.4	.852	901

1991

Tom Barrasso stands head and shoulders above the rest of his goaltending brethren as the high-risk Penguins pour down to the other end and fill their opponents' net with pucks. Pittsburghers know how much Barrasso meant to the Pens' two Stanley Cups, but outside of town their success is too often reduced to a matter of Lemieux-Jagr-and-everyone-else. Pittsburgh, no great shakes during the regular season with a .544 winning percentage, beat the extremely weak North Stars (regular-season winning percentage: .438) and Jon Casey in a six-game Final.

(minimum 480 minutes played)					
GOALER, TEAM	MINS	SAVES-SHOTS	SH/GP	SVPCT	PERSEV
Barrasso, Pit †	1175	578-629	32.1	.919	972
Hrudey, LA	798	345-382	28.7	.903	951
Pa Roy, Mtr	785	354-394	30.1	.898	949
Beaupre, Was	624	265-294	28.3	.901	948
Moog, Bos	1133	509-569	30.1	.895	945

GOALER, TEAM	MINS	SAVES-SHOTS	SH/GP	SVPCT	PERSEV
Fuhr, Edm	1019	437-488	28.7	.895	943
Casey, Min	1205	510-571	28.4	.893	941
Riendeau, StL	687	259-294	25.7	.881	924

1992

The Pens breeze to the Cup again during a post-season of steady but unspectacular netminding, sweeping past Chicago to cap an 11-game playoff winning streak. During the Final, Mike Keenan shuffles Ed Belfour and Dominik Hasek in and out of the Chicago nets in such a way as to maximize the Blackhawks' lack of confidence against the high-powered Penguins, another master stroke of motivational coaching from the mustachioed Borgia imitator behind the bench.

(minimum 480 minutes played)

GOALER, TEAM	MINS	SAVES-SHOTS	SH/GP	SVPCT	PERSEV
Barrasso, Pit †	1233	564-622	30.3	.907	957
Cheveldae, Det	597	252-277	27.8	.910	956
K McLean, Van	785	331-364	27.8	.909	956
Pa Roy, Mtr	686	282-312	27.3	.904	949
Ranford, Edm	909	433-484	31.9	.895	948
Belfour, Chi	949	359-398	25.2	.902	944
Moog, Bos	866	339-385	26.7	.881	925

1993

Roy wins the Smythe and does the job for the Canadiens as they surge past Los Angeles in a five-game Cup Final, which includes Marty McSorley's infamous illegal-stick penalty late in game two that saves the Habs' collective butt. Kelly Hrudey, who did so well for the Kings in the '91 playoffs, does not do well here; for all the wonderful regular-season skill he exhibited throughout his career, he was often not good in the post-season. Felix Potvin sees plenty of rubber as the Leafs get all the way to game seven of the semi-finals, and the Blues' Curt Joseph chimes in with the best playoff performance by a primary netminder since Rogie Vachon's in 1969.

(minimum 480 minutes played)

GOALER, TEAM	MINS	SAVES-SHOTS	SH/GP	SVPCT	PERSEV
Cu Joseph, StL	715	411-438	36.8	.938	1000
Pa Roy, Mtr †	1293	601-647	30.0	.929	979
Barrasso, Pit	722	335-370	30.7	.905	957
F Potvin, Tor	1308	574-636	29.2	.903	951
Hrudey, LA	1261	582-656	31.2	.887	939
K McLean, Van	754	327-369	29.4	.886	935
Healy, NYI	1109	465-524	28.3	.887	935

1994

The Rangers capture their first Stanley Cup since 1940, winning a game seven semi-final from the Devils in two overtimes and the silverware itself in a seven-game masterpiece over the Canucks. Mike Richter is strong throughout, but second-year man Martin Brodeur shines in the Devil nets, and Kirk McLean revives the old Vancouver tradition of a goalie enjoying a career post-season to carry a mediocre Canuck team to the Final. The most brilliant performance in this, the most well-goaltended playoffs in a quarter-century, is Dominik Hasek's in the seven-game opening-round loss to New Jersey. So much overtime is played, more than one full game's worth, that it allows Hasek to qualify. Just how bad were the Sabres to have had someone stop 95% of the shots he faced, yet still lose?

(minimum 480 minutes played)

GOALER, TEAM	MINS	SAVES-SHOTS	SH/GP	SVPCT	PERSEV
Hasek, Buf	484	248-261	32.4	.950	1004
K McLean, Van	1544	761-820	31.9	.928	981
M Brodeur, NJ	1171	493-531	27.2	.928	974
M Richter, NYR †	1417	574-623	26.4	.921	965
F Potvin, Tor	1124	474-520	27.8	.912	958
Casey, Bos	698	274-308	26.5	.890	934
Irbe, SJ	806	349-399	29.7	.875	924

1995

The lockout-shortened '95 season was like a giant playoff round, with all teams playing close-checking, trapping, worried hockey that was short on attacking creativity but long on drama. The post-season, though, was less memorable. Brodeur, the best stickhandling goalie ever to play the game – which no doubt contributes to his consistently low shots-against totals, like the 22.7 he faces here – has little trouble as the Devils sweep the Red Wings in the Final.

(minimum 480 minutes played)

GOALER, TEAM	MINS	SAVES-SHOTS	SH/GP	SVPCT	PERSEV
Belfour, Chi	1014	442-479	28.3	.923	970
M Brodeur, NJ †	1222	429-463	22.7	.927	964
Wregget, Pit	661	316-349	31.7	.905	958
R Hextall, Phi	897	395-437	29.2	.904	953
K McLean, Van	660	300-336	30.5	.893	944
Vernon, Det	1063	329-370	20.9	.889	924

1996

John Vanbiesbrouck is magnificent under a rain of plastic rats in leading the third-year Florida Panthers all the way to the Stanley Cup Final. But their luck runs out in the last round, where they're swept by the Colorado Avalanche, *né les Nordiques du Québec*. It's the only Cup victory for

Patrick Roy in which he does not win the Conn Smythe Trophy. Pittsburgh's Tom Barrasso and Ken Wregget take turns looking good in getting the Pens to the semi-finals, where, alas, they lose to Florida in seven.

(minimum 480 minutes played)					
GOALER, TEAM	MINS	SAVES-SHOTS	SH/GP	SVPCT	PERSEV
Vanbiesbrouck, Fla	1332	685-735	33.1	.932	987
Wregget, Pit	599	305-328	32.9	.930	985
Barrasso, Pit	558	311-337	36.2	.923	983
Belfour, Chi	666	300-323	29.1	.929	977
Pa Roy, Col †	1454	598-649	26.8	.921	966
R Hextall, Phi	760	292-319	25.2	.915	957
Casey, StL	747	342-378	30.4	.905	955
Osgood, Det	936	289-322	20.6	.898	932
M Richter, NYR	661	272-308	28.0	.883	930

1997

The war between the Red Wings and Avs begins, started by a late-season donnybrook that featured Roy and Mike Vernon trading haymakers. Roy is the better goalkeeper this post-season, but Vernon does pretty well himself, and Detroit dismiss Colorado in six and then sweep Philadelphia in the Final to win their first Cup in 42 years. The Flyers' Garth Snow and Ron Hextall (not shown here, but with a 937 perseverance mark in 444 minutes) are the only weak link in an exceptionally strong field of netminders.

(minimum 480 minutes played)					
GOALER, TEAM	MINS	SAVES-SHOTS	SH/GP	SVPCT	PERSEV
Pa Roy, Col	1034	521-559	32.4	.932	986
M Richter, NYR	939	455-488	31.2	.932	984
*S Shields, Buf	570	308-334	35.2	.922	981
G Hebert, Ana	534	237-255	28.7	.929	977
M Brodeur, NJ	659	249-268	24.4	.929	970
Vernon, Det †	1229	458-494	24.1	.927	967
Cu Joseph, Edm	767	369-405	31.7	.911	964
Snow, Phi	699	272-305	26.2	.892	935

1998

Detroit jettison Vernon and suffer no harm, as Chris Osgood does just about as well, enough for the Wings to repeat as Cup champions. They dispose of Washington in four extremely boring games in the Final – a sharp contrast to the semi-final, in which Olaf Kolzig and Dominik Hasek both are brilliant as the Caps prevail in six. Kolzig is just a bit better than Hasek in the series, but looking at their stratospheric numbers for this post-season reminds us when they're both this good, one goaler does not "outplay" the other, any more than one rainbow can be said to out-shine another; they're both miracles of nature, and the best

we can do is to look on in wonder and count ourselves lucky to be there.

(minimum 480 minutes played)					
GOALER, TEAM	MINS	SAVES-SHOTS	SH/GP	SVPCT	PERSEV
Kolzig, Was	1351	696-740	32.9	.941	995
Hasek, Buf	948	482-514	32.5	.938	992
Cu Joseph, Edm	716	296-319	26.7	.928	972
Osgood, Det †	1361	540-588	25.9	.918	962
Belfour, Dal	1039	368-399	23.0	.922	961
Fuhr, StL	616	269-297	28.9	.906	954
Rhodes, Otw	590	215-236	24.0	.911	951

1999

The year of the infamous "No Goal" Final, the nadir for a troubled NHL. Aside from the controversy, Hasek is superb, and Belfour is very strong while logging 1,544 playoff minutes, tying the all-time single-year record set by Vancouver's Kirk McLean in '94. Roy is no slouch either for his performance in leading the Avs to the semi-finals.

(minimum 480 minutes played)					
GOALER, TEAM	MINS	SAVES-SHOTS	SH/GP	SVPCT	PERSEV
Hasek, Buf	1217	551-587	28.9	.939	987
Pa Roy, Col	1173	598-650	33.2	.920	975
Belfour, Dal †	1544	574-617	24.0	.930	970
Dafoe, Bos	769	304-330	25.7	.921	964
Cu Joseph, Tor	1010	399-440	26.1	.907	950
Barrasso, Pit	788	315-350	26.6	.900	944
Fuhr, StL	790	274-305	23.2	.898	937

2000

Belfour and Brodeur hook up for an orgy of overtime in a well-played Final that New Jersey win in six games. But the goaltending has so much of an upper hand by now that save percentages in the high .920s are starting to look routine, even a bit disappointing, and multiple-overtime periods mundane. Anyway, it's nice to see Ron Tugnutt doing well.

(minimum 480 minutes played)					
GOALER, TEAM	MINS	SAVES-SHOTS	SH/GP	SVPCT	PERSEV
Tugnutt, Pit	747	376-398	32.0	.945	998
Cu Joseph, Tor	730	344-369	30.3	.932	983
Belfour, Dal	1443	606-651	27.1	.931	976
Pa Roy, Col	1039	400-431	24.9	.928	970
Osgood, Det	546	219-237	26.0	.924	967
M Brodeur, NJ †	1450	498-537	22.2	.927	964
*B Boucher, Phi	1184	444-484	24.5	.917	958
S Shields, SJ	696	287-323	27.8	.889	935

2001

This completes our 50-year record of playoff goaltending, and to mark the occasion we include the performance of all goalies in action this post-season. We find once more that you simply can't go by what many of the so-called experts say. Looking at the perseverance chart, you can see how the supposedly fabulous were in fact only just okay (Felix Potvin), and how the supposedly inept were in fact pretty good (Roman Turek). Remember, too, how Patrick Roy got lambasted in the press for his stickhandling miscue in game four of the Final, which allowed the Devils to get the equalizing goal en route to tying the series, 2-2. Roy was blamed for blowing everything for the Avs, even though his goalkeeping had been superb. Meanwhile, Martin Brodeur was playing pretty poorly, allowing soft shots to go in and generally failing to come up with the big save when needed – yet somehow he escaped criticism. Even after Colorado beat New Jersey in seven and Roy won an unprecedented, richly deserved third Conn Smythe, Devils detractors blamed the club's hubris, lack of discipline, lost scoring touch, you name it, but never – never – Brodeur's faulty goalkeeping. It's a fact that Jersey allowed just 20.2 shots per game, the lowest any club has permitted in the last half-century of playoffs. Sounds like good team discipline to us. But despite the easy time Brodeur had, he couldn't stop even 90% of what he faced. The weird thing is that the Devils had John Vanbiesbrouck on the bench, a goaler every bit as good as Brodeur and perhaps even Roy, yet he didn't see a single minute of post-season play. So while teary tribute was paid Ray Bourque for his great play over 22 years of Cup-less travail, no one said a word about Vanbiesbrouck, himself a veteran of 20 great years of Cup-less travail. Bourque lifted the Cup as the continent cheered; Vanbiesbrouck retired amid utter silence. Imagine what might have happened had Larry Robinson inserted Beezer in the faltering Brodeur's place for a game or two in the Final. Maybe he would've come up with a big save or two, and maybe the Devils would have won a game they otherwise lost, in which case New Jersey would have won the Cup, not Colorado. Maybe, but we'll never know.

(minimum 480 minutes played)

GOALER, TEAM	MINS	SAVES-SHOTS	SH/GP	SVPCT	PERSEV
Pa Roy, Col †	1451	581-622	25.7	.934	977
Cu Joseph, Tor	685	305-329	28.8	.927	975
Turek, StL	908	351-382	25.2	.919	961
Hasek, Buf	833	318-347	25.0	.916	958
J Hedberg, Pit	1123	439-482	25.8	.911	954
F Potvin, LA	812	328-361	26.7	.909	953
Belfour, Dal	671	252-277	24.8	.910	951
M Brodeur, NJ	1267	455-507	20.2	.897	931

(1-479 minutes played)

GOALER, TEAM	MINS	SAVES-SHOTS	SH/GP	SVPCT	PERSEV
*Bt Johnson, StL	62	34-36	34.8	.944	1003

GOALER, TEAM	MINS	SAVES-SHOTS	SH/GP	SVPCT	PERSEV
*Kiprusoff, SJ	149	74-79	31.8	.937	990
T Salo, Edm	406	172-187	27.6	.920	966
Irbe, Car	360	181-201	33.5	.900	956
*Nabokov, SJ	218	93-103	28.3	.903	950
Kolzig, Was	375	139-153	24.5	.908	949
Osgood, Det	365	143-158	26.0	.905	948
Essensa, Van	122	52-58	28.5	.897	944
Cechmanek, Phi	347	147-165	28.5	.891	938
Lalime, Otw	251	89-99	23.7	.899	938
D Cloutier, Van	117	48-57	29.2	.842	891

Career Playoff Perseverance

Now it's time to put together all the numbers compiled by Yuen and by the league. Below we present the career figures for all goalies who played at least 1,680 minutes (28 full games, or four seven-game playoff rounds) of playoff hockey between 1952 and 2001. Remember that you must take these figures with a grain of salt, because a goalie playing in 1980 will, on average, stop a lower percentage of shots than a goalie playing in 1960 or in 2000. One could make statistical adjustments to level the playing field for everyone, but we'll leave that for the next generation of stat freaks.

Nevertheless, the following table is fascinating and revealing. Each goalie is listed by his perseverance figure, with the teams he played for in the playoffs and the number of post-seasons in which he saw action. The names of active goalies are preceded by an "x." Linger, and admire the 50 years of work wrought by these men.

Career Playoff Perseverance

GOALER, TEAM(S), POST-SEASONS	MINS	SAVES-SHOTS	SH/GP	SVPCT	PRSV
Bower, Tor, 10	4350	2192-2374	32.7	.923	978
x-Kolzig, Was, 5	2395	1098-1184	29.7	.927	977
x-Hasek, Chi-Buf, 10	4517	2031-2188	29.1	.928	977
Maniago, Tor-Min, 6	2245	1086-1186	31.7	.916	969
J Plante, Mtr-StL-Tor-Bos, 16	6601	2813-3050	27.7	.922	969
J Davidson, StL-NYR, 5	1862	856-933	30.1	.917	968
Vanbiesbrouck, NYR-Fla-Phi, 11	3967	1895-2072	31.3	.915	967
x-Pa Roy, Mtr-Col, 15	13545	5878-6394	28.3	.919	967
B Parent, Phi-Tor-Phi, 9	4302	1927-2101	29.3	.917	966
Gl Hall, Det-Chi-StL, 15	6899	3348-3668	31.9	.913	966
x-Cu Joseph, StL-Edm-Tor, 10	5967	2763-3019	30.4	.915	966
Wregget, Tor-Phi-Pit, 8	3340	1632-1792	32.2	.911	964
Sawchuk, Det-Tor-LA-NYR, 14	5848	2670-2922	30.0	.914	964

GOALER, TEAM(S), POST-SEASONS	MINS	SAVES-SHOTS	SH/GP	SVPCT	PRSV
x-Belfour, Chi-Dal, 11	8639	3507-3815	26.5	.919	963
Worsley, NYR-Mtr-Min, 12	4079	1943-2133	31.4	.911	963
Palmateer, Tor, 5	1765	879-968	32.9	.908	963
Resch, NYI-Phi, 8	2044	906-991	29.1	.914	963
K Dryden, Mtr, 8	6846	2953-3227	28.3	.915	962
x-M Richter, NYR, 8	4515	2024-2226	29.6	.909	959
x-K McLean, Van, 7	4188	1936-2134	30.6	.907	958
x-F Potvin, Tor-LA, 5	4017	1788-1968	29.4	.909	958
x-M Brodeur, NJ, 8	6592	2407-2624	29.6	.917	957
R Vachon, Mtr-LA-Bos, 11	2876	1290-1423	29.7	.907	956
A Esposito, Chi, 14	6017	2867-3175	31.7	.903	956
Barrasso, Bfl-Pit-Ott, 13	6953	3218-3567	30.8	.902	953
Wm Smith, NYI, 13	7645	3326-3674	28.8	.905	953
x-Osgood, Det, 8	3989	1489-1633	24.6	.912	953
R Crozier, Det-Buf, 6	1769	751-833	28.3	.902	949
Cheevers, Bos, 10	5396	2220-2462	27.4	.902	947
Ranford, Bos-Edm-Bos-Was, 7	3110	1389-1548	29.9	.897	947
Hanlon, Van-StL-NYR-Det, 9	1756	791-883	30.2	.896	946
Fuhr, Edm-Buf-StL, 15	8044	3498-3897	29.1	.898	946
R Brodeur, Van-Har, 6	2009	934-1045	31.2	.894	946
R Hextall, Phi-Qbc-NYI-Phi, 9	5456	2391-2668	29.3	.897	945
Casey, Min-Bos-StL, 7	3743	1640-1832	29.4	.895	944
G Meloche, Min, 6	2464	1167-1310	31.9	.891	944
Giacomin, NYR, 9	3834	1577-1757	27.5	.898	943
Gi Gilbert, Min-Bos, 6	1919	828-925	28.9	.895	943
Hrudey, NYI-LA-SJ, 10	5162	2319-2602	30.2	.891	942
x-Vernon, Clg-Det-SJ-Fla, 14	8214	3154-3521	25.7	.896	939
R Sauve, Buf-Chi-NJ, 7	1850	777-872	28.3	.891	938
Liut, StL-Har-Was, 10	3814	1698-1913	30.1	.888	938
x-S Burke, NJ-Phi-Phx, 4	1705	760-858	30.2	.886	936
Moog, Edm-Bos-Dal-Mtr, 16	7452	3044-3421	27.5	.890	936
G Millen, Pit-StL-Chi, 8	3383	1488-1681	29.8	.885	935
Beaupre, Min-Was-Tor, 12	3943	1700-1920	29.2	.885	934
x-Irbe, SJ-Dal-Car, 5	1955	878-995	30.5	.882	933
D Edwards, Buf-Clg, 7	2302	1001-1133	29.5	.883	933
Re Lemelin, Atl/Clg-Bos, 12	3119	1374-1560	30.0	.881	931
M Gosselin, Qbc-LA, 4	1816	742-841	27.8	.882	929
D Bouchard, Atl-Qbc-Wpg, 12	2549	1076-1223	28.8	.880	928
x-Healy, LA-NYI-NYR-Tor, 7	1930	796-904	28.1	.881	927
M Bannerman, Chi, 5	2322	1122-1287	33.3	.872	927

GOALER, TEAM(S), POST-SEASONS	MINS	SAVES-SHOTS	SH/GP	SVPCT	PRSV
Peeters, Phi-Bos-Was, 10	4200	1708-1940	27.7	.880	927
Stefan, Det, 5	1681	691-790	28.2	.875	922
G Desjardins, LA-Chi-Buf, 5	1874	734-842	27.0	.872	917
B Hayward, Wpg-Mtr-Min, 8	1803	695-799	26.6	.870	914

Johnny Bower holds the best career playoff record among all goalies between 1952 and 2001. For us, he is the number one of them all, the man we'd rather have in our nets come the second season than any other goalkeeper. That might change in the near future if Olaf Kolzig or Dominik Hasek has a particularly good playoff in the next year or two, for they're the best of the active keepers and the only ones who can challenge the China Wall for the top spot. Look who comes next: Cesare Maniago, truly a fine goaler but one whose memory is unfairly neglected because he never played on a team good enough to win the Cup. Along with him, the immortal Jacques Plante, whose six Cup victories are matched only by Ken Dryden, and then comes John Davidson, who did so well for New York in his short post-season career – we'll take him more seriously next time he offers a colour comment. Then it's the two of the goalers involved in contrasting ways with the 2001 Final, John Vanbiesbrouck and Patrick Roy. Look again at Roy's figures: how has he kept up such a high level of excellence given all the playoff minutes he has played? No one has guarded the nets for even remotely as much time as Roy, yet here he is. If anyone wanted to call Patrick Roy the best playoff goaler of our time, we would not argue.

Next comes perhaps the finest goaler of the '70s, Bernie Parent. Right up there with him is Mr. Goalie himself, Glenn Hall, followed closely by hard-luck Curtis Joseph, who deserves better than merely to be close but never quite there. Ken Wregget is high on this list, the epitome of the goalie who raises his play for the playoffs. Then it's Terry Sawchuk, the man who, all the way back in 1952, set the standard no one has yet matched. And on down the list we go, past so many familiar names and vivid memories, past another of Roy's boyhood heroes, Rogie Vachon, past Bill Ranford, whose one great post-season was worth a Stanley Cup, past Ron Hextall, whose playoff career started so strongly but wound up to chants of "Swiss Cheese!" from Ranger fans, those masters of withering derision, past Pete Peeters, the first goalie to suffer having his name, simply his name, chanted by opposition fans who considered him shaky enough to be disturbed by hearing it, past Gerry Desjardins, who yanked himself from the nets in the Cup Final, saying "I hate this game," down to Bryan Hayward who maybe hated this game too. But they got to play for the Stanley Cup. How many of us wish we could have done the same thing?

Appendix

This appendix presents the complete year-by-year standings, scoring leaders, and playoff results for all professional major leagues. These leagues are included in the following material:

- ECHA – Eastern Canada Hockey Association, 1908–09
- NHA – National Hockey Association, 1909–10 to 1916–17
- PCHA – Pacific Coast Hockey Association, 1911–12 to 1923–24
- NHL – National Hockey League, 1917–18 to present
- WCHL – Western Canada Hockey League, 1921–22 to 1924–25
- WHL – Western Hockey League, 1925–26
- WHA – World Hockey Association, 1972–73 to 1978–79

Some leagues have, or have had, different franchises playing in the same city; such franchises are distinguished in the annual standings with the abbreviation for the team's nickname, in the playoff results with the team's full nickname, and in the scoring parades with the abbreviations noted at the end of each entry in the following list (teams sharing the same abbreviations can be distinguished from each other by the league in which they play). The professional major-league record of the following franchises is included:

Alberta Oilers	WHA 1972–73; *became* Edmonton Oilers. Alb
Anaheim Mighty Ducks	NHL 1993–94 to present. Ana
Atlanta Flames	NHL 1972–73 to 1979–80; *became* Calgary Flames. AtlF
Atlanta Thrashers	NHL 1999–2000 to present. AtlT
Baltimore Blades	WHA 1974–75; *were* Michigan Stags. Bal
Birmingham Bulls	WHA 1976–77 to 1978–79; *were* Toronto Toros. Bir
Boston Bruins	NHL 1924–25 to present. Bos
Boston	*See* New England Whalers.
Brooklyn Americans	NHL 1941–42; *were* New York Americans. Brk
Buffalo Sabres	NHL 1970–71 to present. Buf
Calgary Cowboys	WHA 1975–76 to 1976–77; *were* Vancouver Blazers. Clg
Calgary Flames	NHL 1980–81 to present; *were* Atlanta Flames. Clg
Calgary Tigers	WCHL 1921–22 to 1924–25, WHL 1925–26. Clg
California Seals	NHL 1967–68, Golden Seals 1970–71 to 1975–76; *became*

	Oakland Seals 1967–68 to 1969–70; *became* Cleveland Barons. Clf
Carolina Hurricanes	NHL 1997–98 to present; *were* Hartford Whalers. Car
Cherry Hill	*See* New Jersey Knights.
Chicago Blackhawks	*See* Chicago Black Hawks.
Chicago Black Hawks	NHL 1926–27 to 1984–85, Blackhawks 1985–86 to present. Chi
Chicago Cougars	WHA 1972–73 to 1974–75. Chi
Cincinnati Stingers	WHA 1975–76 to 1978–79. Cin
Cleveland Barons	NHL 1976–77 to 1977–78; *were* California Golden Seals; *absorbed by* Minnesota North Stars. Clv
Cleveland Crusaders	WHA 1972–73 to 1975–76. Clv
Cobalt Silver Kings	NHA 1909–10; *absorbed by* Quebec Bulldogs. Cbt
Colorado Avalanche	NHL 1995–96 to present; *were* Quebec Nordiques. ColA
Colorado Rockies	NHL 1976–77 to 1981–82; *were* Kansas City Scouts; *became* New Jersey Devils. ColR
Columbus Blue Jackets	NHL 2000–01 to present. Cmb
Dallas Stars	NHL 1993–94 to present; *were* Minnesota North Stars. Dal
Denver Spurs	WHA 1975–76; *became* Ottawa Civics. Den
Denver	*See* Colorado Rockies, Colorado Avalanche.
Detroit Cougars	NHL 1926–27 to 1929–30, Falcons 1930–31 to 1932–33, Red Wings 1933–34 to present. Det
Detroit Falcons	*See* Detroit Cougars.
Detroit Red Wings	*See* Detroit Cougars.
Detroit	*See* Michigan Stags.
East Rutherford	*See* New Jersey Devils.
Edmonton Eskimos	WCHL 1921–22 to 1924–25, WHL 1925–26. Edm
Edmonton Oilers	WHA 1973–74 to 1978–79, NHL 1979–80 to present; *were* Alberta Oilers. Edm
Florida Panthers	NHL 1993–94 to present. Fla
Greenville	*See* Carolina Hurricanes.
Haileybury	NHA 1909–10; *absorbed by* Montreal Canadiens. Hby
Hamilton Tigers	NHL 1920–21 to 1924–25; *were* Quebec Bulldogs; *became* New York Americans. Ham
Hartford Whalers	NHL 1979–80 to 1996–97; *were* New England Whalers; *became* Carolina Hurricanes. Har
Houston Aeros	WHA 1972–73 to 1977–78. Hou
Indianapolis Racers	WHA 1974–75 to 1978-79. Ind
Kansas City Scouts	NHL 1974–75 to 1975–76; *became* Colorado Rockies. KC
Los Angeles Kings	NHL 1967–68 to present. LA
Los Angeles Sharks	WHA 1972–73 to 1973–74; *became* Michigan Stags. LA
Miami	*See* Florida Panthers.
Michigan Stags	WHA 1974–75; *were* Los Angeles Sharks; *became* Baltimore Blades. Mch
Minneapolis	*See* Minnesota North Stars, Minnesota Fighting Saints.
Minnesota Fighting Saints	WHA 1972–73 to 1975–76, 1976–77. Min
Minnesota North Stars	NHL 1967–68 to 1992–93; *absorbed* Cleveland Barons; *became* Dallas Stars. MinNS
Minnesota Wild	NHL 2000–01 to present. MinW
Montreal Canadiens	NHA 1909–10 to 1916–17, NHL 1917–18 – present; *absorbed* Haileybury. MtrC
Montreal Maroons	NHL 1924–25 to 1937–38. MtrM
Montreal Shamrocks	ECHA 1908–09, NHA 1909–10. MtrS
Montreal Wanderers	ECHA 1908–09, NHA 1909–10 to 1916–17, NHL 1917–18. MtrW
Moose Jaw Sheiks	WCHL 1921–22; *were, became* Saskatoon Sheiks. MJ
Nashville Predators	NHL 1998–99 to present. Nas
New England Whalers	WHA 1972–73 to 1978–79; *became* Hartford Whalers. NE
New Jersey Devils	NHL 1982–83 to present; *were* Colorado Rockies. NJ
New Jersey Knights	WHA 1973–74; *were* New York Golden Blades, *became* San Diego Mariners. NJ
New Westminster Royals	PCHA 1911–12 to 1913–14; *became* Portland Rosebuds (PCHA). NW
New York Americans	NHL 1925–26 to 1940–41; *were* Hamilton Tigers; *became* Brooklyn Americans. NYA
New York Golden Blades	*See* New York Raiders.
New York Islanders	NHL 1972–73 to present. NYI
New York Raiders	WHA 1972–73, Golden Blades 1973–74; *became* New Jersey Knights. NY
New York Rangers	NHL 1926–27 to present. NYR
Northern Fusiliers	*See* 228th Battalion.
Oakland Seals	NHL 1967–68 to 1969–70; *were* California Seals, *became* California Golden Seals. Oak

Ottawa Civics	WHA 1975–76; *were* Denver Spurs. OtwC
Ottawa Nationals	WHA 1972–73; *became* Toronto Toros. OtwN
Ottawa Senators	ECHA 1908–09, NHA 1909–10 to 1916–17, NHL 1917–18 to 1930–31, 1932–33 to 1933–34; *became* St. Louis Eagles. Otw
Ottawa Senators	NHL 1992–93 to present. Otw
Philadelphia Blazers	WHA 1972–73; *became* Vancouver Blazers. Phi
Philadelphia Flyers	NHL 1967–68 to present. PhiF
Philadelphia Quakers	NHL 1930–31; *were* Pittsburgh Pirates. PhiQ
Phoenix Coyotes	NHL 1996–97 to present; *were* Winnipeg Jets. Phx
Phoenix Roadrunners	WHA 1974–75 to 1976–77. Phx
Pittsburgh Pirates	NHL 1925–26 to 1929–30; *became* Philadelphia Quakers. PitPi
Pittsburgh Penguins	NHL 1967–68 to present. PitPe
Portland Rosebuds	PCHA 1914–15 to 1917–18; *were* New Westminster Royals, *became* Victoria Aristocrats/ Cougars. Por
Portland Rosebuds	WHL 1925–26; *were* Regina Capitals. Por
Quebec Athletic	*See* Quebec Bulldogs.
Quebec Bulldogs	ECHA 1908–09, NHA 1910–11 to 1916–17, NHL 1919–20; *aka* Quebec Athletic, *absorbed* Cobalt Silver Kings; *became* Hamilton Tigers. QbcB
Quebec Nordiques	WHA 1972–73 to 1978–79, NHL 1979–80 to 1994–95; *became* Colorado Avalanche. Qbc (WHA), QbcN (NHL)
Raleigh	*See* Carolina Hurricanes.
Regina Capitals	WCHL 1921–22 to 1924–25; *became* Portland Rosebuds (WHL). Reg
Renfrew Creamery Kings	*See* Renfrew Millionaires.
Renfrew Millionaires	NHA 1909–10, Creamery Kings 1910–11. Rnf
San Diego Mariners	WHA 1974–75 to 1976–77; *were* New Jersey Knights. SD
San Jose Sharks	NHL 1991–92 to present. SJ
Saskatoon Crescents	*See* Saskatoon Sheiks.
Saskatoon Sheiks	WCHL 1921–22, 1922–23, Crescents 1923–24 to 1924–25, WHL 1925–26; *became, were* Moose Jaw Sheiks. Ssk
Seattle Metropolitans	PCHA 1915–16 to 1923–24. Sea

Spokane Canaries	PCHA 1916–17; *were* Victoria Senators/Aristocrats. Spo
Springfield	*See* New England Whalers.
St. Paul	*See* Minnesota Wild.
St. Louis Blues	NHL 1967–68 to present. StLB
St. Louis Eagles	NHL 1934–35; *were* Ottawa Senators (ECHA/NHA/NHL). StLE
Tampa Bay Lightning	NHL 1993–94 to present. TB
Toronto Arenas	*See* Toronto Blueshirts.
Toronto Blueshirts	NHA 1912–13 to 1916–17, NHL Arenas 1917–18 to 1918–19, St. Pats 1919–20 to 1925–26, Maple Leafs 1926–27 to present. TorB (NHA), Tor (NHL)
Toronto Maple Leafs	*See* Toronto Blueshirts.
Toronto Ontarios	*See* Toronto Tecumsehs. TorOn (1913–14), TorOS (1914–15)
Toronto Shamrocks	*See* Toronto Tecumsehs. TorOS (1914–15)
Toronto St. Pats	*See* Toronto Blueshirts.
Toronto Tecumsehs	NHA 1912–13, Ontarios 1913–14 to 1914–15, Shamrocks 1914–15. TorTe (1912–13)
Toronto Toros	WHA 1973–74 to 1975–76; *were* Ottawa Nationals, *became* Birmingham Bulls. Tor
Toronto	*See* 228th Battalion.
228th Battalion	NHA 1916–17; *aka* Northern Fusiliers. 228
Vancouver Blazers	WHA 1973–74 to 1974–75; *were* Philadelphia Blazers, *became* Calgary Cowboys. Van
Vancouver Canucks	NHL 1970–71 to present. Van
Vancouver Maroons	*See* Vancouver Millionaires.
Vancouver Millionaires	PCHA 1911–12 to 1921–22, Maroons 1922–23, WCHL 1924–25, WHL 1925–26. Van
Victoria Aristocrats	PCHA 1918–19 to 1919–20, Cougars 1920–21 to 1923–24, WCHL 1924–25, WHL 1925–26; *were* Portland Rosebuds (PCHA). VicC
Victoria Cougars	*See* Victoria Aristocrats.
Victoria Senators	PCHA 1911–12, Aristocrats 1912–13 to 1915–16; *became* Spokane Canaries. VicA
Washington Capitals	NHL 1974–75 to present. Was
Windsor	*See* Detroit Cougars.
Winnipeg Jets	WHA 1972–73 to 1978–79, NHL 1979–80 to 1995–96; *became* Phoenix Coyotes. Wpg

Individual players in the annual scoring parades are indicated by last name only if their last name is not shared by any other player in the entire history of either professional major-league hockey or Stanley Cup play (e.g., Selanne, Yzerman); a first name initial is added to distinguish players who share a last name (e.g., R Hull, Robert "Bobby" Hull; B Hull, Brett Hull); additional letters are added to distinguish players who share both a last name and a first initial (e.g., Mk Messier, Mark Messier; Mi Messier, Mitch Messier; Rea Cloutier, Real "Buddy" Cloutier; Rej Cloutier, Rejean Cloutier); if more than three letters are required, full first names are given (e.g., Carol "Cully" Wilson; Carey Wilson); if first names are identical, both first and middle initials are given (e.g., G A Adams, Greg A. Adams; G C Adams, Greg C. Adams); if names are entirely identical or no middle name is available, players are indicated with a roman numeral in order of their professional major-league or Stanley Cup debut (e.g., Rob Murray I, Robert J. "Bob" Murray; Rob Murray II, Robert F. "Bob" Murray; Rob Murray III, Rob Murray).

The top 6 scorers are listed for leagues of 3 or 4 teams; the top 8, for leagues of 5 to 7 seven teams; the top 10, for leagues of 8 to 12 teams; the top 12, for leagues of 13 to 18 teams; the top 14, for leagues of 19 to 25 teams; and the top 16 scorers, for leagues of 26 or more teams. If there are two or more players tied for the last spot on a scoring parade, the parade will be extended to accommodate the extra player or players.

The standings, scoring leaders, and playoff results for each season are prefaced with notes on significant changes in league structure, franchise location, playing conditions, roster regulations, equipment, rules, and playoff formats.

Each season's Stanley Cup champion is designated with an asterisk (*). Winners of the Avco World Trophy, representative of the championship of the WHA, are designated with an @ symbol.

Major-League Final Standings, 1908–09 to 2000–01

The Stanley Cup, originally donated in 1893 as a challenge trophy to be awarded to the best amateur hockey team in Canada, was administered by a trustee committee charged with determining which challenges would be accepted and the format and site of challenge games or series. Eleven of the first 13 Stanley Cup champions were representatives of the Amateur Hockey Association and its immediate successor, the Canadian Amateur Hockey League. Ottawa Senators of the CAHL, who had been Cup champions in 1903 and 1904, joined the new, rival Federal Amateur Hockey League in 1905 and again defended the Cup successfully. The CAHL and FAHL merged to form the Eastern Canada Amateur Hockey Association in 1906, establishing a single premiere hockey league among several rival circuits. The ECAHA, a league in which professional players competed alongside amateurs, was racked in 1908 by a continuing scandal in which several amateur players were charged with taking under-the-table payments. The clubs, made up exclusively of amateur players, withdrew from the league, which then dropped "Amateur" from its name and became a fully professional league. The member clubs of the reconstituted ECHA were Montreal Shamrocks, Montreal Wanderers, Ottawa Senators, and Quebec Athletic, more popularly known as Quebec Bulldogs. Joe Power was elected president of the league. Our record begins here.

ECHA 1908–09

At this time, the game resembled today's hockey only in that the game was played on ice, with players skating and trying to score goals by shooting a puck. A team consisted of seven players: a centre and two wingmen in front; a rover, who acted as a sort of mediary between offence and defence in much the same way that a midfielder does in soccer or lacrosse; a point (a defenceman who played in front and a bit to one side of the goaltender); a cover point (a defenceman who played farther up and to the other side of the goaltender); and the goaltender himself. The rinks were about 50 to 75 feet shorter and 10 to 20 feet narrower than today's standardized rinks, with much shorter dasher boards. There were no rinks with artificial ice (the first was built in Vancouver in 1911, with most other major-league cities not having one until 10 years later); the natural ice was slower and choppier than artificial ice and tended to become slushy or watery in warm weather. There were no markings on the ice, and the offside rule was the same as it was in rugby: that is, forward passing was illegal, and the puck always had to precede any attacking player. It was illegal for a goaler to leave his feet to make a save, as in field hockey, and it was illegal to kick the puck. Hooking was legal, and there was no limit to the length of sticks. One or two referees and no linesmen officiated the games, which consisted of two 30-minute halves, and sudden-death overtime if necessary. Goal judges, called umpires, stood on the ice behind the goals, which were simply two posts set in the ice with a net draped between them. The puck was placed on the ice for face-offs, and the referee would then call "Play." Penalized players were fined, but they were not sent off the ice unless they committed a match penalty. No substitutions were allowed during a game. If a player was lost to a match penalty during a game he could not be replaced; if he was lost to a first-half injury, the other team was likewise obligated to play a man short. The ECHA schedule was increased from 10 games to 12.

	W	L	T	PTS	GF	GA
Ottawa*	10	2	0	20	117	63
Montreal Wan	9	3	0	18	82	61
Quebec Bul	3	9	0	6	78	106
Montreal Sha	2	10	0	4	56	103

GOALSCORING LEADERS	GP	G
M Walsh, Otw	12	38
H Jordan, QbcB	12	29
Br Stuart, Otw	11	22
C Power, QbcB	12	22
Alb Kerr, Otw	9	20
Hyland, MtrS	11	18

Ottawa, as ECHA regular-season champion, won the Stanley Cup and twice defended it successfully before the start of the following season – defeating Ontario Professional League champion Galt, 15-4, at Ottawa, in a two-game total-goals series, and, two weeks later, defeating Alberta League champion Edmonton, 21-11, at Ottawa, in a two-game total-goals series.

NHA 1909–10

A struggle over the disposition of the Montreal Wanderers' franchise culminated in the ECHA reforming as the Canadian Hockey Association, from which Wanderers were excluded. A new rival professional league, the National Hockey Association, was formed around Wanderers. M. Doheney was elected president of the NHA. The CHA folded after two weeks of play; CHA clubs Montreal Shamrocks and Ottawa were absorbed into the NHA, joining Wanderers, Cobalt Silver Kings, Haileybury, Montreal Canadiens, and Renfrew Millionaires. Overtime was played variously as sudden-death and to a 10-minute limit.

	W	L	T	PTS	GF	GA
Montreal Wan*	11	1	0	22	91	41
Ottawa	9	3	0	18	89	66
Renfrew	8	3	1	17	96	54
Haileybury	4	8	0	8	77	83
Cobalt	4	8	0	8	79	104
Montreal Sha	3	8	1	7	52	95
Montreal Can	2	10	0	4	59	100

GOALSCORING LEADERS	GP	G
E Lalonde, MtrC-Rnf	11	38
E Russell, MtrW	12	31
T Smith, Cbt	10	24
Hyland, MtrW	11	24
M Walsh, Otw	11	23
H Clarke, Cbt	11	22
Le Patrick, Rnf	11	22
Gaul, Hby	12	22

Montreal Wanderers, as NHA regular-season champion, won the Stanley Cup and defended it successfully by defeating Ontario Professional League champion Berlin, 7-3, at Montreal, in a single-game challenge.

NHA 1910–11

T. Emmett Quinn was elected president and secretary of the NHA. Cobalt, Haileybury, and Montreal Shamrocks resigned from the league. Montreal Canadiens suspended operation, but a separate Montreal franchise, also called Canadiens, took over the contracts of the players of the former Canadiens team and those of Haileybury. The ECHA Quebec franchise was revived and took over the contracts of the Cobalt players. Renfrew Millionaires changed their nickname to Creamery Kings. A roster limit of 10 players under contract was established; a salary cap of $5,000 per team was also agreed upon unilaterally by the owners, but the players threatened to quit and form their own league. Game format was changed from two 30-minute halves to three 20-minute periods with 10-minute intermissions. Schedule increased to 16 games.

	W	L	T	PTS	GF	GA
Ottawa*	13	3	0	26	122	69
Montreal Can	8	8	0	16	66	62
Renfrew	8	8	0	16	91	101
Montreal Wan	7	9	0	14	73	88
Quebec Bul	4	12	0	8	65	97

GOALSCORING LEADERS	GP	G
M Walsh, Otw	16	37
Alb Kerr, Otw	16	32
Don Smith, Rnf	16	26
Ridpath, Otw	16	22
O Cleghorn, Rnf	16	20
E Lalonde, MtrC	16	19
Pitre, MtrC	16	19

Ottawa, as NHA regular-season champion, won the Stanley Cup and twice defended it successfully – first defeating Ontario Professional League champion Galt, 7-4, at Ottawa, in a single-game challenge, and second, three days later, defeating New Ontario League champion Port Arthur, 13-4, at Ottawa, in a single-game challenge.

NHA 1911–12

The franchises of Renfrew and of the first, suspended, Canadiens club were transferred to new ownership and were to play in Toronto, but as their rink was not ready the teams would not operate this season. Primarily as a cost-cutting measure, the rover position was dropped and the teams played six-man hockey. Teams were required to have at least nine players. The LeSueur goal net, introducing the crossbar, was approved as the NHA standard. The rule book was revised to include hooking, along with tripping, cross-checking, charging from behind, striking an opponent, throwing a stick to prevent a goal, and the use of foul language, as a major foul, penalized by ejection and a $5 fine, but with immediate substitution permitted for the penalized player. Substitution was allowed during any stoppage, but a player once removed could not re-enter the game; an injured player could be substituted for after 10 minutes. Overtime was played to sudden-death. The practice of identifying players with uniform numbering began. The O'Brien Trophy was designated as emblematic of the league championship. Schedule increased to 18 games.

	W	L	T	PTS	GF	GA
Quebec Bul*	10	8	0	20	81	79
Ottawa	9	9	0	18	99	93
Montreal Wan	9	9	0	18	95	96
Montreal Can	8	10	0	16	59	66

GOALSCORING LEADERS	GP	G
Er Ronan, Otw	18	35
Pitre, MtrC	18	27
E Russell, MtrW	18	27
Alb Kerr, Otw	18	25
O Cleghorn, MtrW	17	23
Jo Malone, QbcB	18	21

Quebec, as NHA regular-season champion, won the Stanley Cup and defended it successfully by defeating Maritime Professional League champion Moncton, 2 games to 0, at Quebec. Following the NHA Stanley Cup series, an NHA All-Star team played a three-game series against PCHA All-Stars at Vancouver and Victoria; the PCHA All-Stars won twice, the NHA All-Stars once.

PCHA 1911–12

A new professional league, the Pacific Coast Hockey Association, was founded by Frank and Lester Patrick; W. P. Irving was appointed president. The clubs were New Westminster Royals, Vancouver Millionaires, and Victoria Senators. The teams played seven-man hockey. The goal featured a crossbar. Goalers were permitted to leave their feet to make a stop. Substitution was allowed, but as there were only two spare players among the three clubs, it was rare. Penalized players were ruled off the ice, but immediate substitution for them was allowed, including a player who had been given a match penalty. Sudden-death overtime was played to break ties. A record of assists was to be kept. Vancouver's arena had the first artificial ice surface in Canada; the rink measured 210' by 85'. The schedule was 16

games, but if the final game of the season had no bearing on the standings it would not be played.

	W	L	T	PTS	GF	GA
New Westminster a	9	6	0	18	78	77
Vancouver	7	8	0	14	102	94
Victoria	7	9	0	14	81	90

a   Played all home games in Vancouver, as their own arena was still under construction.

GOALSCORING LEADERS	GP	G
E Lalonde, Van	15	27
Hyland, NW	15	26
Dunderdale, VicA	16	24
F Patrick, Van	15	23
Nichols, Van	15	19
Don Smith, VicA	16	19

New Westminster, the PCHA regular-season champion, did not challenge for the Stanley Cup. Following the NHA Stanley Cup series, a PCHA All-Star team played a three-game series against NHA All-Stars at Vancouver and Victoria; the PCHA All-Stars won twice, the NHA All-Stars once.

NHA 1912–13

Toronto Blueshirts and Toronto Tecumsehs joined the NHA. Midway through the season seven-man hockey was reinstituted, each team playing three games under this format, but after one week it was abandoned permanently in favour of the six-man game. Schedule increased to 20 games.

	W	L	T	PTS	GF	GA
Quebec Bul*	16	4	0	32	112	75
Montreal Wan	10	10	0	20	93	90
Ottawa	9	11	0	18	87	81
Montreal Can	9	11	0	18	83	81
Toronto Blu	9	11	0	18	86	95
Toronto Tecm	7	13	0	14	59	98

GOALSCORING LEADERS	GP	G
Jo Malone, QbcB	20	43
T Smith, QbcB	18	39
Hyland, MtrW	20	27
E Lalonde, MtrC	18	25
Nighbor, TorB	19	25
Pitre, MtrC	17	24
Broadbent, Otw	20	20
A Davidson, TorB	20	19
Don Smith, MtrC	20	19

Quebec, as NHA regular-season champion, retained the Stanley Cup and defended it successfully by defeating Maritime Professional League champion Sydney, 2 games to 0, at Quebec. Quebec then played PCHA regular-season champion Victoria in a best-of-three exhibition series at Victoria; Quebec lost, 2 games to 1, but did not lose possession of the Cup. The All-Star series between the PCHA and the NHA was expanded to six games, played at Winnipeg, Vancouver, and New Westminster; the PCHA All-Stars won four times, the NHA All-Stars twice.

PCHA 1912–13

Victoria Senators changed nickname to Aristocrats. C. E. Doherty of the New Westminster club was elected league president.

	W	L	T	PTS	GF	GA
Victoria	10	5	0	20	68	56
Vancouver	7	9	0	14	84	89
New Westminster	6	9	0	12	67	74

SCORING LEADERS	GP	G	A	P
Dunderdale, VicA	15	24	5	29
F Harris, Van	14	14	6	20
C Kendall, Van	16	16	6	20
F Patrick, Van	14	12	8	20
Le Patrick, VicA	15	14	5	19
F Taylor, Van	14	10	8	18

Victoria, the PCHA regular-season champion, played Quebec Bulldogs, NHA and Stanley Cup champion, in a best-of-three exhibition series at Victoria; Victoria won, 2 games to 1, but did not take possession of the Cup. The All-Star series between the PCHA and the NHA was expanded to six games, played at Winnipeg, Vancouver, and New Westminster; the PCHA All-Stars won four times, the NHA All-Stars twice.

NHA 1913–14

Toronto Tecumsehs changed nickname to Ontarios. Goal lines were painted on the ice between the goalposts. On face-offs, the referee was to drop the puck, rather than placing it on the ice and calling "Play," as had been the previous practice. Immediate substitution was allowed for injured players. Goaltenders' sticks were limited to three and one-half inches in width. The PCHA's practice of recording assists was officially adopted.

	W	L	T	PTS	GF	GA
Toronto Blu*	13	7	0	26	93	65
Montreal Can	13	7	0	26	85	65
Quebec Bul	12	8	0	24	111	73
Ottawa	11	9	0	22	65	71
Montreal Wan	7	13	0	14	102	125
Toronto Ont	4	16	0	8	61	118

SCORING LEADERS	GP	G	A	P
T Smith, QbcB	20	39	6	45
Go Roberts I, MtrW	20	31	13	44
Hyland, MtrW	18	30	12	42
A Davidson, TorB	20	23	13	36
J Walker, TorB	20	20	16	36
J MacDonald, TorOn	20	27	8	35
Jo Malone, QbcB	17	24	4	28
J Darragh, Otw	20	23	5	28
Don Smith I, MtrC	20	18	10	28

Toronto Blueshirts defeated Montreal Canadiens, 6-2, in a two-game total-goals special playoff series for first place. Blueshirts then defeated PCHA champion Victoria, 3 games to 0, at Toronto, to win the Stanley Cup.

PCHA 1913–14

Blue lines were introduced, dividing the ice surface into three zones. Forward passing was allowed in the centre zone only, and not across either blue line. Frank Patrick of the Vancouver club was elected league president, and Dr. C. E. Doherty was made honorary president.

	W	L	T	PTS	GF	GA
Victoria	10	5	0	20	80	67
New Westminster	7	9	0	14	75	81
Vancouver	6	9	0	12	76	83

SCORING LEADERS	GP	G	A	P
F Taylor, Van	16	24	15	39
Alb Kerr, VicA	16	20	11	31
Dunderdale, VicA	16	24	4	28
E Oatman, NW	14	22	5	27
K Mallen, NW	16	21	6	27
Nichols, Van	12	14	7	21

Victoria lost to NHA champion Toronto Blueshirts, 3 games to 0, at Toronto, in Stanley Cup series.

NHA 1914–15

Toronto Ontarios changed their nickname to Shamrocks midway through the season. The offside rule was waived for rebounds of shots on goal. Players were required to keep a distance of five feet from the players involved in a face-off.

	W	L	T	PTS	GF	GA
Montreal Wan a	14	6	0	28	127	82
Ottawa	14	6	0	28	74	65

	W	L	T	PTS	GF	GA
Quebec Bul	11	9	0	22	85	85
Toronto Blu	8	12	0	16	66	84
Toronto Ont/Sha a	7	13	0	14	76	96
Montreal Can	6	14	0	12	65	81

a Wanderers won forfeit of unplayed game with Shamrocks.

SCORING LEADERS	GP	G	A	P
T Smith, TorOS-QbcB	19	40	4	44
Pitre, MtrC	20	30	4	34
Go Roberts I, MtrW	19	29	5	34
S Cleghorn, MtrW	19	21	12	33
Hyland, MtrW	19	23	6	29
Broadbent, Otw	20	24	3	27
Carol Wilson, TorB	20	22	5	27
O Cleghorn, MtrW	15	21	5	26
Ru Crawford, QbcB	20	18	8	26

Ottawa defeated Montreal Wanderers, 4-1, in a two-game total-goals special playoff series for first place. Ottawa then lost to PCHA champion Vancouver, 3 games to 0, at Vancouver, in Stanley Cup series.

PCHA 1914–15

The New Westminster franchise moved to Portland and changed its nickname to Rosebuds. Body-checking within 10 feet of the boards was made illegal. The NHA practice of numbering players was adopted. Schedule increased to 18 games.

	W	L	T	PTS	GF	GA
Vancouver*	13	4	0	26	115	71
Portland	9	9	0	18	91	83
Victoria	4	13	0	8	64	116

SCORING LEADERS	GP	G	A	P
F Taylor, Van	16	23	22	45
Du Mackay, Van	17	33	11	44
Nighbor, Van	17	23	7	30
E Oatman, Por	18	22	8	30
Ra McDonald, Por	18	22	7	29
Dunderdale, VicA	17	17	10	27

Vancouver defeated NHA champion Ottawa, 3 games to 0, at Vancouver, to win the Stanley Cup.

NHA 1915–16

The Toronto Shamrocks franchise was dissolved. Regular-season sudden-death overtime was limited to 20 minutes. In response to incidents of players physically abusing referees and umpires during this and previous seasons, a rule was added requiring that officials would be locked in their dressing room between periods. Schedule increased to 24 games.

	W	L	T	PTS	GF	GA
Montreal Can*	16	7	1	33	104	74
Ottawa	13	11	0	26	78	72
Quebec Bul	10	12	2	22	91	98
Montreal Wan	10	14	0	20	90	116
Toronto Blu	9	14	1	19	97	98

SCORING LEADERS	GP	G	A	P
Pitre, MtrC	24	24	15	39
Jo Malone, QbcB	24	25	10	35
E Lalonde, MtrC	24	28	6	34
Keats, TorB	24	22	7	29
Cy Denneny, TorB	24	24	4	28
Go Roberts I, MtrW	21	18	7	25
Nighbor, Otw	23	19	5	24
Co Denneny, TorB	22	20	3	23
Ru Crawford, QbcB	22	18	5	23

Montreal Canadiens defeated PCHA champion Portland, 3 games to 2, at Montreal, to win the Stanley Cup.

PCHA 1915–16

Seattle Metropolitans joined the PCHA. William Foran, acting Stanley Cup trustee in the absence of trustee Philip Dansken ("P. D.") Ross, declared that the Cup was emblematic of the world championship and thus open to be won by either Portland or Seattle.

	W	L	T	PTS	GF	GA
Portland a	13	5	0	26	71	50
Vancouver	9	9	0	18	75	69
Seattle	9	9	0	18	68	67
Victoria a	5	13	0	10	74	102

a Played one home game at Seattle.

SCORING LEADERS	GP	G	A	PTS
F Taylor, Van	18	22	13	35
B Morris, Sea	18	23	9	32
Tobin, Por	18	21	8	29
Alb Kerr, VicA	18	16	10	26
Le Patrick, VicA	18	13	11	24
Ld Cook, Van	18	18	3	21
Nichols, Van-VicA	12	13	8	21
E Oatman, Por	18	11	10	21

Portland lost to NHA champion Montreal Canadiens, 3 games to 2, at Montreal, in Stanley Cup series.

NHA 1916–17

The 228th Battalion of the Canadian Army, also known as the Northern Fusiliers, comprised largely of athletes from the Toronto region and Northern Ontario, joined the NHA. Emmett Quinn resigned as president of the NHA and Major Frank Robinson was appointed as his successor. In response to incidents of stick-throwing as a defensive tactic, a rule was added to award a goal when a stick was thrown in an attempt to prevent a goal from being scored. A split-season format was instituted to determine the league champion. Early in the second-half schedule, the 228th Battalion was ordered overseas, requiring the cancellation of their remaining games, and Toronto Blueshirts' remaining games were dropped from the schedule as well. The two half-seasons were each 10 games long, decreasing the schedule to 20 games.

1ST HALF	W	L	T	PTS	GF	GA
Montreal Can a	7	3	0	14	58	38
Ottawa b	7	3	0	14	56	41
228th Battalion b	6	4	0	12	70	57
Toronto Blu	5	5	0	10	50	45
Montreal Wan	3	7	0	6	56	72
Quebec Bul	2	8	0	4	43	80
2ND HALF	W	L	T	PTS	GF	GA
Ottawa a	8	2	0	16	63	22
Quebec Bul c	8	2	0	16	54	46
Montreal Can	3	7	0	6	31	42
Toronto Blu d	2	2	0	4	14	16
Montreal Wan c	2	8	0	4	38	65
228th Battalion e	0	4	0	0	3	12

a Awarded first place on goal difference.
b Ottawa defeated 228th Battalion 8-0, but were charged with loss, and 228th Battalion credited with win, because Ottawa used an ineligible player.
c Won forfeit of unplayed game with 228th Battalion.
d Franchise suspended operation during season.
e Includes two losses in unplayed, forfeited games; franchise folded during season.

SCORING LEADERS	GP	G	A	P
Jo Malone, QbcB	19	41	7	48
Nighbor, Otw	19	41	2	43
O Cleghorn, MtrW	18	28	4	32
E Lalonde, MtrC	18	27	5	32
J Darragh, Otw	20	26	5	31
Gerard, Otw	19	17	9	26
D Ritchie, QbcB	19	17	8	25
Pitre, MtrC	20	22	2	24

First-half champion Montreal Canadiens defeated second-half champion Ottawa, 7-6, in two-game total-goals NHA championship series. Canadiens lost to PCHA champion Seattle, 3 games to 1, at Seattle, in Stanley Cup series.

PCHA 1916–17

The Victoria franchise moved to Spokane and changed its nickname to Canaries. Schedule increased to 24 games.

	W	L	T	PTS	GF	GA
Seattle*	16	8	0	32	125	80
Vancouver	14	9	0	28	131	124
Portland	9	15	0	18	114	112
Spokane	8	15	0	16	89	143

SCORING LEADERS	GP	G	A	PTS
B Morris, Sea	24	37	17	54
Go Roberts I, Van	23	43	10	53
Foyston, Sea	24	36	12	48
R Stanley, Van	23	28	18	46
R Irvin, Por	23	35	10	45
Du Mackay, Van	23	22	11	33

Seattle defeated NHA champion Montreal Canadiens, 3 games to 1, at Seattle, to win the Stanley Cup.

NHL 1917–18

The Quebec franchise suspended operation. Racked by disorganization, charges of game-fixing, and an inability to establish authority over the member clubs and individual players, and desiring to manoeuvre in such a way as to remove Toronto Blueshirts owner Eddie Livingstone from the league, the representatives of the Montreal Canadiens, Montreal Wanderers, and Ottawa franchises dissolved the association and reorganized as the National Hockey League. NHA secretary Frank Calder was elected president and secretary of the NHL. The Blueshirts franchise was placed under new ownership and changed its nickname to Arenas. The PCHA rule permitting a goaler to leave his feet to make a save was adopted. The rule limiting regular-season sudden-death overtime to 20 minutes was relaxed. The split-season format was retained. Two weeks into the first half, the Wanderers' rink burned down and the franchise withdrew from the league. The first-half schedule of 14 games and the modified second-half schedule of 8 games increased the season schedule to 22 games.

1ST HALF	W	L	T	PTS	GF	GA
Montreal Can a	10	4	0	20	81	47
Toronto a	8	6	0	16	71	75
Ottawa	5	9	0	10	67	79
Montreal Wan b	1	5	0	2	17	35
2ND HALF	W	L	T	PTS	GF	GA
Toronto*	5	3	0	10	37	34
Ottawa	4	4	0	8	35	35
Montreal Can	3	5	0	6	34	37

a Won forfeit of unplayed game with Montreal Wanderers.
b Includes two losses in unplayed, forfeited games; franchise folded during season.

SCORING LEADERS	GP	G	A	P
Jo Malone, MtrC	20	44	4	48
Cy Denneny, Otw	20	36	10	46
Noble, Tor	20	30	10	40
E Lalonde, MtrC	14	23	7	30
Co Denneny, Tor	21	20	9	29
H Cameron, Tor	21	17	10	27
Pitre, MtrC	20	17	6	23

Second-half champion Toronto defeated first-half champion Canadiens, 10-7, in two-game total-goals NHL championship series at Toronto and Montreal. Toronto defeated PCHA champion Vancouver, 3 games to 2, at Toronto, to win the Stanley Cup.

PCHA 1917–18
The Spokane franchise was dropped from the league. Penalties were to be served for three minutes with no substitution allowed. Schedule decreased to 18 games. A playoff system was instituted in which the first- and second-place teams would play each other for the league championship.

	W	L	T	PTS	GF	GA
Seattle	11	7	0	22	67	65
Vancouver	9	9	0	18	70	60
Portland	7	11	0	14	63	75

SCORING LEADERS	GP	G	A	PTS
F Taylor, Van	18	32	11	43
B Morris, Sea	18	20	12	32
Go Roberts I, Sea	18	20	3	23
E Oatman, Por	18	11	10	21
Dunderdale, Por	18	14	6	20
Du Mackay, Van	18	10	8	18

Vancouver defeated Seattle, 3-2, in two-game total-goals PCHA championship series at Vancouver and Seattle. Vancouver lost to NHL champion Toronto, 3 games to 2, at Toronto, in Stanley Cup series.

NHL 1918–19
The PCHA innovation of the blue lines was adopted; they were drawn 20 feet from centre ice. The PCHA rule allowing forward passing in the centre zone was also adopted. Kicking the puck was made legal, but only in the centre zone. As in the PCHA, minor penalties were to be served for three minutes with no substitution allowed; major penalties were to be served for five minutes with no substitution. The practice of recording assists was permanently adopted. The point and cover-point players were now referred to as defencemen. A split-season schedule of two 10-game halves was installed, but the second half had to be curtailed to

accommodate the directive of the Stanley Cup trustees regarding the dates of the Cup series. With two weeks left to play in the second half, Toronto withdrew from the remainder of the schedule, and all games remaining on the NHL schedule were cancelled.

1ST HALF	W	L	T	PTS	GF	GA
Montreal Can	7	3	0	14	57	50
Ottawa	5	5	0	10	39	40
Toronto	3	7	0	6	43	49
2ND HALF	**W**	**L**	**T**	**PTS**	**GF**	**GA**
Ottawa	7	1	0	14	32	14
Montreal Can	3	5	0	6	31	28
Toronto	2	6	0	4	22	43

SCORING LEADERS	GP	G	A	PTS
E Lalonde, MtrC	17	23	10	33
O Cleghorn, MtrC	18	21	6	27
Nighbor, Otw	18	18	9	27
Cy Denneny, Otw	18	18	6	24
Pitre, MtrC	17	14	4	18
A Skinner, Tor	16	12	5	17

First-half champion Montreal defeated second-half champion Ottawa, 4 games to 1, in NHL championship series. The Stanley Cup series between Montreal and PCHA champion Seattle, tied at 2-2-1, at Seattle, was abandoned because of the influenza epidemic. No Cup-holder was declared.

PCHA 1918–19
The Portland franchise was moved to Victoria and changed its nickname to Aristocrats, which had been the name of the former PCHA Victoria franchise. A delayed penalty system was adopted, ensuring neither team could be down more than one man at any time. Schedule increased to 20 games.

	W	L	T	PTS	GF	GA
Vancouver	12	8	0	24	72	55
Seattle	11	9	0	22	66	46
Victoria	7	13	0	14	44	81

SCORING LEADERS	GP	G	A	PTS
F Taylor, Van	20	23	13	36
B Morris, Sea	20	22	7	29
F Harris, Van	20	19	6	25
Foyston, Sea	18	15	4	19
Du Mackay, Van	17	9	9	18
E Oatman, VicC	18	11	5	16
Carol Wilson, Sea	18	11	5	16
R Stanley, Van	20	10	6	16

Seattle defeated Vancouver, 7-5, at Seattle and Vancouver, in a two-game total-goals PCHA championship series. The

Appendix

Stanley Cup series between Seattle and NHL champion Montreal, tied at 2-2-1, at Seattle, was abandoned because of the influenza epidemic. No Cup-holder was declared.

NHL 1919–20

The Quebec franchise was reactivated; its players, who had been distributed to the other NHL clubs prior to the start of the 1917–18 season, were returned to Bulldogs. Toronto Arenas changed their nickname to St. Pats. Schedule increased to 24 games.

1ST HALF	W	L	T	PTS	GF	GA
Ottawa	9	3	0	18	59	23
Montreal Can	8	4	0	16	62	51
Toronto	5	7	0	10	52	62
Quebec Bul	2	10	0	4	44	81
2ND HALF	W	L	T	PTS	GF	GA
Ottawa*	10	2	0	20	62	41
Toronto	7	5	0	14	67	44
Montreal Can	5	7	0	10	67	62
Quebec Bul	2	10	0	4	47	96

SCORING LEADERS	GP	G	A	PTS
Jo Malone, QbcB	24	39	10	49
E Lalonde, MtrC	23	37	9	46
Nighbor, Otw	23	26	15	41
Cy Denneny, Otw	24	24	12	36
J Darragh, Otw	23	22	14	36
Noble, Tor	24	24	9	33

Ottawa, as champion of both halves of the regular season, was declared NHL champion. Ottawa defeated PCHA champion Seattle, 3 games to 2, at Ottawa, to win the Stanley Cup.

PCHA 1919–20

Schedule increased to 22 games.

	W	L	T	PTS	GF	GA
Seattle	12	10	0	24	59	55
Vancouver	11	11	0	22	75	65
Victoria	10	12	0	20	57	71

SCORING LEADERS	GP	G	A	PTS
Dunderdale, VicC	22	26	7	33
Foyston, Sea	22	26	3	29
F Harris, Van	22	14	11	25
E Oatman, VicC	22	11	14	25
Go Roberts I, Van	22	16	3	19
A Skinner, Van	22	15	2	17

Seattle defeated Vancouver, 7-3, at Seattle and Vancouver, in a two-game total-goals PCHA championship series. Seattle

lost to NHL champion Ottawa, 3 games to 2, at Ottawa and Toronto, in the Stanley Cup series.

NHL 1920–21

The Quebec franchise moved to Hamilton and changed its nickname to Tigers.

1ST HALF	W	L	T	PTS	GF	GA
Ottawa	8	2	0	16	49	23
Toronto	5	5	0	10	39	47
Montreal Can	4	6	0	8	37	51
Hamilton	3	7	0	6	34	38
2ND HALF	W	L	T	PTS	GF	GA
Toronto	10	4	0	20	66	53
Montreal Can	9	5	0	18	75	48
Ottawa*	6	8	0	12	48	52
Hamilton	3	11	0	6	58	94

SCORING LEADERS	GP	G	A	PTS
E Lalonde, MtrC	24	32	11	43
Dye, Ham-Tor	24	35	5	40
Cy Denneny, Otw	24	34	5	39
Jo Malone, Ham	20	28	9	37
Nighbor, Otw	24	19	10	29
Noble, Tor	24	19	8	27
H Cameron, Tor	24	18	9	27
Prodgers, Ham	24	18	9	27

First-half champion Ottawa defeated second-half champion Toronto, 7-0, at Ottawa and Toronto, in a two-game total-goals NHL championship series. Ottawa defeated PCHA champion Vancouver, 3 games to 2, at Vancouver, to win the Stanley Cup.

PCHA 1920–21

Victoria Aristocrats changed their nickname to Cougars. A game was declared a tie after 60 minutes of sudden-death overtime. Schedule increased to 24 games.

	W	L	T	PTS	GF	GA
Vancouver	13	11	0	26	86	79
Seattle	12	11	1	25	77	68
Victoria	10	13	1	21	72	88

SCORING LEADERS	GP	G	A	PTS
Frederickson, VicC	21	20	12	32
F Harris, Van	24	15	17	32
Foyston, Sea	23	26	4	30
JJ Adams, Van	24	17	12	29
Jm Riley, Sea	24	23	5	28
A Skinner, Van	24	20	4	24
B Morris, Sea	24	11	13	24

Vancouver defeated Seattle, 13-2, at Vancouver and Seattle, in a two-game total-goals PCHA championship series. Vancouver lost to NHL champion Ottawa, 3 games to 2, at Vancouver, in the Stanley Cup series.

NHL 1921–22

The NHL abandoned the split-season format and adopted the PCHA playoff system. Minor penalties were reduced to two minutes. Regular-season sudden-death overtime was limited to 20 minutes. Goaltenders were permitted to pass the puck forward as far as their own blue line.

	W	L	T	PTS	GF	GA
Ottawa	14	8	2	30	106	84
Toronto*	13	10	1	27	98	97
Montreal Can	12	11	1	25	88	94
Hamilton	7	17	0	14	88	105

SCORING LEADERS	GP	G	A	PTS
Broadbent, Otw	24	32	14	46
Cy Denneny, Otw	22	27	12	39
Dye, Tor	24	31	7	38
H Cameron, Tor	24	18	17	35
Jo Malone, Ham	24	24	7	31
Co Denneny, Tor	24	19	9	28

Toronto defeated Ottawa, 5-4, at Toronto and Ottawa, in a two-game total-goals NHL championship series. Toronto defeated PCHA champion Vancouver, 3 games to 2, at Toronto, to win the Stanley Cup.

PCHA 1921–22

Regular-season sudden-death overtime was limited to 20 minutes. The penalty shot was introduced, to be awarded to attacking puck carriers who were deliberately tripped while approaching the opponents' goal; the shot had to be taken from behind a spot on the ice 28 feet in front of the net. The point and cover-point players were now referred to as defencemen.

	W	L	T	PTS	GF	GA
Seattle	12	11	1	25	65	64
Vancouver	12	12	0	24	77	68
Victoria	11	12	1	23	61	71

SCORING LEADERS	GP	G	A	PTS
JJ Adams, Van	24	26	4	30
Du Mackay, Van	24	14	12	26
Frederickson, VicC	24	15	10	25
B Morris, Sea	24	14	10	24
Foyston, Sea	24	16	7	23
Jm Riley, Sea	24	16	2	18

Vancouver defeated Seattle, 2-0, at Seattle and Vancouver, in a two-game total-goals PCHA championship series. Vancouver defeated WCHL champion Regina, 5-2, at Vancouver and Regina, in a two-game total-goals series to decide which team would meet the NHL champion for the Stanley Cup. Vancouver lost to NHL champion Toronto, 3 games to 2, at Toronto, in the Stanley Cup series.

WCHL 1921–22

A new professional league, the Western Canada Hockey League, was formed; E. L. Richardson of the Calgary club was appointed league president. The clubs were Calgary Tigers, Edmonton Eskimos, Regina Capitals, and Saskatoon Sheiks. The teams played six-man hockey. Regular-season sudden-death overtime was played to break ties, but was limited to 40 minutes. A new playoff system was devised, in which the second- and third-place teams played off for the right to meet the first-place team. Due to poor attendance in Saskatoon, Sheiks played their last four home games in Moose Jaw. The schedule was 24 games.

	W	L	T	PTS	GF	GA
Edmonton a	14	9	1	29	106	74
Regina a	14	9	1	29	92	67
Calgary	14	10	0	28	75	62
Saskatoon/Moose Jaw	5	19	0	10	67	137

a Edmonton defeated Regina, 11-2, at Edmonton, in a special one-game playoff for first place.

SCORING LEADERS #	GP	G	A	P
Keats, Edm	25	31	24	55
E Arbour, Edm	24	27	6	33
J Simpson, Edm	25	21	12	33
G Hay, Reg	25	21	11	32
R Stanley, Clg	24	26	5	31
R Irvin, Reg	20	21	7	28

Includes special playoff game.

Regina defeated Calgary, 2-1, at Calgary and Regina, in a two-game total-goals WCHL semi-final. Regina defeated Edmonton, 3-2, at Regina and Edmonton, in a two-game total-goals WCHL championship series. Regina lost to PCHA champion Vancouver, 5-2, at Vancouver and Regina, in a two-game total-goals series to decide which team would meet the NHL champion for the Stanley Cup.

Appendix

NHL 1922–23

	W	L	T	PTS	GF	GA
Ottawa*	14	9	1	29	77	54
Montreal Can	13	9	2	28	73	61
Toronto	13	10	1	27	82	88
Hamilton	6	18	0	12	81	110

SCORING LEADERS	GP	G	A	PTS
Dye, Tor	22	26	11	37
Cy Denneny, Otw	24	21	10	31
JJ Adams, Tor	23	19	9	28
W Boucher, MtrC	24	23	4	27
O Cleghorn, MtrC	24	19	7	26
M Roach, Ham	23	17	8	25

Ottawa defeated Montreal, 3-2, at Montreal and Ottawa, in a two-game total-goals NHL championship series. Ottawa defeated PCHA champion Vancouver, 3 games to 1, at Vancouver, in a series to decide which team would meet the WCHL champion for the Stanley Cup. Ottawa defeated WCHL champion Edmonton, 2 games to 0, at Vancouver, to win the Stanley Cup.

PCHA/WCHL 1922–23

The PCHA and WCHL agreed to play an interlocking schedule of 24 interleague games. In effect, this made the two leagues one league of two divisions. The standings are presented as they appear below to reflect the reality of the arrangement.

Sheiks returned to Saskatoon. Vancouver Millionaires changed their nickname to Maroons. The PCHA eliminated the rover position, and all PCHA and WCHL teams played six-man hockey. An anti-defence rule was devised, making it illegal for a team to use more than three skaters on defence, and requiring all skaters to be advancing toward the opponents' goal when not backchecking or in the neutral zone; violation earned a two-minute penalty. Kicking the puck was made legal anywhere on the ice but not to score a goal. WCHL regular-season overtime was limited to 20 minutes. Schedules increased to 30 games.

By this point, rules in the east and west were nearly identical, with the primary exception of the western leagues' legalization of kicking the puck, the penalty shot, and the delayed penalty system.

PCHA	W	L	T	PTS	GF	GA
Vancouver	17	12	1	35	116	88
Victoria	16	14	0	32	94	85
Seattle	15	15	0	30	100	106
WCHL	W	L	T	PTS	GF	GA
Edmonton	19	10	1	39	112	90
Regina	16	14	0	32	93	97
Calgary	12	18	0	24	91	106
Saskatoon	8	20	2	18	91	125

SCORING LEADERS	GP	G	A	PTS
Frederickson, VicC	30	39	16	55
A Gagne, Edm	29	22	21	43
Du Mackay, Van	30	28	12	40
Keats, Edm	25	24	13	37
G Hay, Reg	30	28	8	36
E Lalonde, Ssk	29	30	4	34
H Oliver, Clg	29	25	7	32
L Cook, Van	30	19	11	30

Vancouver defeated Victoria, 5-3, at Victoria and Vancouver, in a two-game total-goals PCHA championship series. Vancouver lost to NHL champion Ottawa, three games to one, at Vancouver, in a series to decide which team would meet the WCHL champion for the Stanley Cup. Edmonton defeated Regina, 4-3, at Regina and Edmonton, in a two-game total-goals WCHL championship series. Edmonton lost to NHL champion Ottawa, two games to none, at Vancouver, in the Stanley Cup series.

NHL 1923–24

The Prince of Wales Trophy was designated as emblematic of the league championship, replacing the O'Brien Trophy.

	W	L	T	PTS	GF	GA
Ottawa	16	8	0	32	74	54
Montreal Can*	13	11	0	26	59	48
Toronto	10	14	0	20	59	85
Hamilton	9	15	0	18	63	68

SCORING LEADERS	GP	G	A	PTS
Cy Denneny, Otw	21	22	1	23
W Boucher, MtrC	23	16	6	22
A Joliat, MtrC	24	15	5	20
Dye, Tor	19	17	2	19
G Boucher, Otw	21	14	5	19
W Burch, Ham	24	16	2	18

Montreal defeated Ottawa, 5-2, at Montreal and Ottawa, in a two-game total-goals NHL championship series. Montreal defeated PCHA champion Vancouver, 2 games to 0, at Montreal, in a series to decide which team would meet the WCHL champion for the Stanley Cup. Montreal defeated WCHL champion Calgary, 2 games to 0, at Montreal and Ottawa, to win the Stanley Cup.

PCHA/WCHL 1923–24

Saskatoon Sheiks changed their nickname to Crescents. Goalie pads were limited to 12" in width, and goaltenders were prohibited from going behind their net. The PCHA and WCHL interlocking schedule was increased to 48 interleague games, but team schedules remained at 30 games.

PCHA	W	L	T	PTS	GF	GA
Seattle	14	16	0	28	84	99
Vancouver	13	16	1	27	87	80
Victoria	11	18	1	23	78	103
WCHL	**W**	**L**	**T**	**PTS**	**GF**	**GA**
Calgary	18	11	1	37	83	71
Regina	17	11	2	36	83	67
Saskatoon	15	12	3	33	91	73
Edmonton	11	15	4	26	69	81

SCORING LEADERS	GP	G	A	PTS
W Cook, Ssk	30	26	14	40
H Oliver, Clg	27	22	12	34
A Duncan, Van	30	21	10	31
G Hay, Reg	25	20	11	31
Keats, Edm	29	19	12	31
Frederickson, VicC	30	19	8	27
R Stanley, Reg	30	15	11	26
Du Mackay, Van	28	21	4	25

Vancouver defeated Seattle, 4-3, at Vancouver and Seattle, in a two-game total-goals PCHA championship series. Calgary defeated Regina, 4-2, at Regina and Calgary, in a two-game total-goals WCHL championship series. Calgary defeated PCHA champion Vancouver, 2 games to 1, at Vancouver, Calgary, and Winnipeg, to earn a bye into the Stanley Cup series; Vancouver was not eliminated. Vancouver lost to NHL champion Montreal Canadiens, 2 games to 1, at Montreal, in a series to decide which team would meet WCHL champion Calgary for the Stanley Cup. Calgary lost to NHL champion Montreal Canadiens, 2 games to 0, at Montreal and Ottawa, in the Stanley Cup series.

NHL 1924–25

Boston Bruins and Montreal Maroons joined the NHL. The 1918–19 rule that legalized kicking the puck in the neutral zone, which had apparently been done away with later, was reinstated. The WCHL playoff system was adopted. Schedule increased to 30 games.

	W	L	T	PTS	GF	GA
Hamilton	19	10	1	39	90	60
Toronto	19	11	0	38	90	84
Montreal Can	17	11	2	36	93	56
Ottawa	17	12	1	35	83	66
Montreal Mar	9	19	2	20	45	65
Boston	6	24	0	12	49	119

SCORING LEADERS	GP	G	A	PTS
Dye, Tor	29	38	6	44
Cy Denneny, Otw	28	27	15	42
A Joliat, MtrC	24	29	11	40
H Morenz, MtrC	30	27	7	34
W Boucher, MtrC	30	18	13	31
JJ Adams, Tor	27	21	8	29
Burch, Ham	27	20	4	24
Rd Green, Ham	30	19	4	23

At the conclusion of the regular season the Hamilton players went on strike, saying they had been paid to play a 24-game schedule but had been obligated to play 30 games, and that they had not been offered additional pay for any playoff games; they refused to continue unless they were paid for the playoffs. NHL president Frank Calder suspended all of the Hamilton players and ruled that the winner of the Toronto–Montreal Canadiens series would be declared NHL champion.

Montreal Canadiens defeated Toronto, 5-2, at Montreal and Toronto, in a two-game total-goals NHL championship series. Montreal Canadiens lost to WCHL champion Victoria, 3 games to 1, at Victoria and Vancouver, in the Stanley Cup series.

WCHL 1924–25

Seattle dropped out of the PCHA. The PCHA was dissolved, and the two remaining teams, Vancouver and Victoria, joined the WCHL. The playoff system was revised, matching the second- and third-place teams in a two-game total-goals semi-final, and the semi-final winner against the first-place team in a two-game total-goals series for the WCHL championship. In the Stanley Cup Final, Victoria made complete line changes while play was in progress, the first time the tactic had been tried; it was the outgrowth of the more liberal substitution rules long in force in the PCHA. Schedule decreased to 28 games.

	W	L	T	PTS	GF	GA
Calgary	17	11	0	34	96	80
Saskatoon	16	11	1	33	102	75
Victoria*	16	12	0	32	84	63
Edmonton	14	13	1	29	97	109
Vancouver	12	16	0	24	91	102
Regina	8	20	0	16	82	123

SCORING LEADERS	GP	G	A	PTS
Du Mackay, Van	28	27	6	33
H Oliver, Clg	24	20	13	33

SCORING LEADERS	GP	G	A	PTS
Keats, Edm	28	23	9	32
W Cook, Ssk	27	22	10	32
Frederickson, VicC	28	22	8	30
F Boucher, Van	27	16	12	28
Briden, Edm	28	17	6	23
G Hay, Reg	20	16	6	22

Victoria defeated Saskatoon, 6-4, at Victoria and Saskatoon, in a two-game total-goals WCHL semi-final. Victoria defeated Calgary, 3-1, at Calgary and Victoria, in a two-game total-goals WCHL championship series. Victoria defeated NHL champion Montreal Canadiens, three games to one, at Victoria and Vancouver, to win the Stanley Cup.

NHL 1925–26

Pittsburgh Pirates joined the NHL. The Hamilton franchise moved to New York and changed its nickname to Americans. Goalie pads were limited to 12" in width, as in the WCHL. A version of the PCHA delayed-penalty system was adopted, ensuring that neither team could be down more than two men at any time. An anti-defence rule was devised, making it illegal for a team to have more than two defence players behind their own blue line. Ragging the puck, except while short-handed, would incur a stoppage and face-off. A team could not dress more than 12 players for a game, nor after December 31 have more than 14 players under contract. A salary cap was unilaterally instituted by the owners, limiting each team's player payroll to $35,000. Schedule increased to 36 games.

	W	L	T	PTS	GF	GA
Ottawa	24	8	4	52	77	42
Montreal Mar*	20	11	5	45	91	73
Pittsburgh Pir	19	16	1	39	82	70
Boston	17	15	4	38	92	85
New York Ame	12	20	4	28	68	89
Toronto	12	21	3	27	92	114
Montreal Can	11	24	1	23	79	108

SCORING LEADERS	GP	G	A	PTS
N Stewart, MtrM	36	34	8	42
Cy Denneny, Otw	36	24	12	36
C Cooper, Bos	36	28	3	31
Herberts, Bos	36	26	5	31
H Morenz, MtrC	31	23	3	26
A Joliat, MtrC	35	17	9	26
JJ Adams, Tor	36	21	5	26
Burch, NYA	36	22	3	25
Re Smith, Otw	28	16	9	25
Nighbor, Otw	35	12	13	25

Montreal Maroons defeated Pittsburgh, 6-4, at Pittsburgh and Montreal, in a two-game total-goals NHL semi-final. Montreal Maroons defeated Ottawa, 2-1, at Montreal and Ottawa, in a two-game total-goals NHL championship series. Montreal Maroons defeated WHL champion Victoria, 3 games to 1, at Montreal, to win the Stanley Cup.

WHL 1925–26

The WCHL changed its name to the Western Hockey League. The Regina franchise moved to Portland and changed its nickname to Rosebuds, which had been the name of the former PCHA Portland franchise. Regular-season sudden-death overtime was limited to 10 minutes. Schedule increased to 30 games.

	W	L	T	PTS	GF	GA
Edmonton	19	11	0	38	94	77
Saskatoon	18	11	1	37	93	64
Victoria	15	11	4	34	68	53
Portland	12	16	2	26	84	110
Calgary	10	17	3	23	71	80
Vancouver	10	18	2	22	64	90

SCORING LEADERS	GP	G	A	PTS
W Cook, Ssk	30	31	13	44
R Irvin, Por	30	31	5	36
A Gagne, Edm	29	21	11	32
Co Denneny, Ssk	30	17	15	32
G Hay, Por	30	19	12	31
Keats, Edm	29	20	10	30
H Oliver, Clg	29	13	12	25
Frederickson, VicC	29	16	8	24

Victoria defeated Saskatoon, 4-3, at Saskatoon and Victoria, in a two-game total-goals WHL semi-final. Victoria defeated Edmonton, 5-3, at Victoria and Vancouver, in a two-game total-goals WHL championship series. Victoria lost to NHL champion Montreal Maroons, 3 games to 1, at Montreal, in the Stanley Cup series.

NHL 1926–27

The WHL folded, leaving the NHL as the only professional major-league. Chicago Black Hawks, Detroit Cougars, and New York Rangers joined the NHL; most of the former WHL players were signed by the 10 NHL teams, with Chicago retaining most of the former Portland players and Detroit retaining most of the Victoria players. The NHL split into two five-team divisions. Toronto St. Pats changed their nickname to Maple Leafs. The neutral zone was enlarged by redrawing the blue lines 60 feet from each goal line. Holding, tripping, loafing offside, offside interference, and preventing a goal by kneeling or lying on the ice (except by the goaltender) were classified as minor fouls, punishable by a two-minute penalty. Holding or tripping to prevent a goal, hooking, cross-checking, boarding, charging from behind, excessive force in checking the goaltender, interference by a substitute before the replaced player had exited the ice, fighting, attempting to injure, abusive language directed at an official, throwing the stick (except in instances where a goal was to be awarded), and a third violation for loafing offside, were classified as major fouls, punishable by a 5-minute penalty; a second major was punishable by a 10-minute penalty, and a third by ejection from the game. Deliberately injuring an opponent was classified as a match foul, punishable by ejection and obligating the penalized player's team to play short-handed for 20 minutes. A related system of fines and suspensions was also in place. Schedule increased to 44 games, each team to play 6 games against each intra-division opponent and 4 against each team in the other division.

CANADIAN DIVISION	W	L	T	PTS	GF	GA
Ottawa*	30	10	4	64	86	69
Montreal Can	28	14	2	58	99	67
Montreal Mar	20	20	4	44	71	68
New York Ame	17	25	2	36	82	91
Toronto	15	24	5	35	79	94
AMERICAN DIVISION	W	L	T	PTS	GF	GA
New York Ran	25	13	6	56	95	72
Boston	21	20	3	45	97	89
Chicago	19	22	3	41	115	116
Pittsburgh Pir	15	26	3	33	79	108
Detroit a	12	28	4	28	76	105

a   Played all home games in Windsor, as their own arena was still under construction.

SCORING LEADERS	GP	G	A	PTS
W Cook, NYR	44	33	4	37
R Irvin, Chi	43	18	18	36
H Morenz, MtrC	44	25	7	32
Frederickson, Bos-Det	41	18	13	31
Dye, Tor	41	25	5	30
I Bailey, Tor	42	15	13	28
F Boucher, NYR	44	13	15	28
Burch, NYA	43	19	8	27
H Oliver, Bos	42	18	6	24
Keats, Bos-Det	42	16	8	24

Quarter-finals (two games, total goals): Montreal Canadiens defeated Montreal Maroons, 2 goals to 1.

Boston defeated Chicago, 10 goals to 5.

Semi-finals (two games, total goals): Ottawa defeated Montreal Canadiens, 5 goals to 1.

Boston defeated New York Rangers, 3 goals to 1.

Stanley Cup Final (best of three): Ottawa defeated Boston, 2 games to 0, with two ties.

NHL 1927–28

The Art Ross goal-net design was approved as the NHL standard. Forward passing was permitted within the defending and neutral zones, but not across either blue line; offside was waived for shots rebounding off the goaltender. Kicking the puck was permitted in the defending zone. A goal could not be scored if directed or deflected in by the body or skates of an attacking player. Deliberately picking up the puck (except by the goaltender), and shooting the puck over the boards and out of play to force a stoppage, was made punishable by a minor penalty. The length of sticks, previously unlimited, was limited to 53 inches. Goalie pads were limited to 10" in width, and the blade of goalie sticks was limited to 14¾". The Prince of Wales Trophy was awarded to the team finishing first in the American Division; the O'Brien Trophy was returned to service and awarded to the team finishing first in the Canadian Division.

CANADIAN DIVISION	W	L	T	PTS	GF	GA
Montreal Can	26	11	7	59	116	48
Montreal Mar	24	14	6	54	96	77
Ottawa	20	14	10	50	78	57
Toronto	18	18	8	44	89	88
New York Ame	11	27	6	28	63	128
AMERICAN DIVISION	W	L	T	PTS	GF	GA
Boston	20	13	11	51	77	70
New York Ran*	19	16	9	47	94	79
Pittsburgh Pir	19	17	8	46	67	76
Detroit	19	19	6	44	88	79
Chicago	7	34	3	17	68	134

SCORING LEADERS	GP	G	A	PTS
H Morenz, MtrC	43	33	18	51
A Joliat, MtrC	44	28	11	39
F Boucher, NYR	44	23	12	35
G Hay, Det	42	22	13	35
N Stewart, MtrM	41	27	7	34
A Gagne, MtrC	44	20	10	30
F Cook, NYR	44	14	14	28
W Carson, Tor	32	20	6	26
Finnigan, Otw	38	20	5	25
W Cook, NYR	43	18	6	24
Keats, Bos-Det	38	14	10	24

Quarter-finals (two games, total goals): Montreal Maroons defeated Ottawa, 3 goals to 1.

New York Rangers defeated Pittsburgh, 6 goals to 4.

Semi-finals (two games, total goals): Montreal Maroons defeated Montreal Canadiens, 3 goals to 2.

New York Rangers defeated Boston, 5 goals to 2.

Stanley Cup Final (best of five): New York Rangers defeated Montreal Maroons, 3 games to 2, at Montreal.

NHL 1928–29

Forward passing was permitted from the neutral zone across the blue line into the attacking zone, as long as no offensive player preceded the puck into the attacking zone; forward passing within the attacking zone was still forbidden. Regular-season overtime was changed to a 10-minute, non-sudden-death format, to be played in its entirety regardless of how many goals were scored. The playoff format was revised, matching first-place teams in a best-of-five series for the NHL championship, second-place teams and third-place teams in a two-game total-goals series to determine the participants for a best-of-three semi-final, and the semi-final winner against the NHL champion in a best-of-three series for the Stanley Cup.

CANADIAN DIVISION	W	L	T	PTS	GF	GA
Montreal Can	22	7	15	59	71	43
New York Ame	19	13	12	50	53	53
Toronto	21	18	5	47	85	69
Ottawa	14	17	13	41	54	67
Montreal Mar	15	20	9	39	67	65

AMERICAN DIVISION	W	L	T	PTS	GF	GA
Boston*	26	13	5	57	89	52
New York Ran	21	13	10	52	72	65
Detroit	19	16	9	47	72	63
Pittsburgh Pir	9	27	8	26	46	80
Chicago a	7	29	8	22	33	85

a Played one or more home games at Fort Erie and Windsor.

SCORING LEADERS	GP	G	A	PTS
I Bailey, Tor	44	22	10	32
N Stewart, MtrM	44	21	8	29
C Cooper, Det	43	18	9	27
H Morenz, MtrC	42	17	10	27
A Blair, Tor	44	12	15	27
F Boucher, NYR	44	10	16	26
H Oliver, Bos	43	17	6	23
W Cook, NYR	43	15	8	23
Jm Ward, MtrM	43	14	8	22
Finnigan, Otw	44	15	4	19
Gainor, Bos	39	14	5	19
E Shore, Bos	39	12	7	19
D Cox, Tor	42	12	7	19
G Hay, Det	42	11	8	19
Re Smith, MtrM	41	10	9	19

Third-place teams (two games, total goals): Toronto defeated Detroit, 7 goals to 2.
Second-place teams (two games, total goals): New York Rangers defeated New York Americans, 1 goal to 0.
First-place teams (best of five): Boston defeated Montreal Canadiens, 3 games to 0.
Semi-final (best of three): New York Rangers defeated Toronto, 2 games to 0.
Stanley Cup Final (best of three): Boston defeated New York Rangers, 2 games to 0.

NHL 1929–30

Teams were permitted to dress 15 players for a game. Kicking the puck was permitted in all zones. Forward passing was permitted anywhere on the ice except across either blue line, and players could precede the puck into the attacking zone. After 66 games had been played, the offside rule, forbidding players from preceding the puck into the attacking zone, was reinstituted for the remaining 154 games.

CANADIAN DIVISION	W	L	T	PTS	GF	GA
Montreal Mar	23	16	5	51	141	114
Montreal Can*	21	14	9	51	142	114
Ottawa a	21	15	8	50	138	118
Toronto	17	21	6	40	116	124
New York Ame	14	25	5	33	113	161

AMERICAN DIVISION	W	L	T	PTS	GF	GA
Boston	38	5	1	77	179	98
Chicago	21	18	5	47	117	111
New York Ran	17	17	10	44	136	143
Detroit	14	24	6	34	117	133
Pittsburgh Pir b	5	36	3	13	102	185

a Played one home game at Atlantic City.
b Played one home game at Atlantic City and one home game at Fort Erie.

SCORING LEADERS	GP	G	A	PTS
Weiland, Bos	44	43	30	73
F Boucher, NYR	42	26	36	62
Clapper, Bos	44	41	20	61
W Cook, NYR	44	29	30	59
H Kilrea, Otw	44	36	22	58
N Stewart, MtrM	44	39	16	55
H Morenz, MtrC	44	40	10	50
Himes, NYA	44	28	22	50
Lamb, Otw	44	29	20	49
Gainor, Bos	42	18	31	49

Third-place teams (two games, total goals): New York Rangers defeated Ottawa, 6 goals to 3.
Second-place teams (two games, total goals): Montreal Canadiens defeated Chicago, 3 goals to 2.
First-place teams (best of five): Boston defeated Montreal Maroons, 3 games to 1.
Semi-final (best of three): Montreal Canadiens defeated New York Rangers, 2 games to 0.
Stanley Cup Final (best of three): Montreal Canadiens defeated Boston, 2 games to 0.

NHL 1930–31

The Pittsburgh franchise played its home games in Philadelphia and changed its nickname to Quakers. Detroit Cougars changed their nickname to Falcons. Forward passing was again permitted from the neutral zone across the blue line into the attacking zone, providing no offensive player preceded the puck into the attacking zone; forward passing from the defending zone across the blue line into the neutral zone was still forbidden. The Stanley Cup Final was changed to a best-of-five format. In the last minute of the second game of the playoff series between Boston and Montreal Canadiens, Boston coach Art Ross pulled his goaler, Tiny Thompson, from the net in favour of an extra attacker; it was the first time the tactic had been tried in pro hockey. The move failed to produce the tying goal.

CANADIAN DIVISION	W	L	T	PTS	GF	GA
Montreal Can*	26	10	8	60	129	89
Toronto	22	13	9	53	118	99
Montreal Mar	20	18	6	46	105	106
New York Ame	18	16	10	46	76	74
Ottawa	10	30	4	24	91	142
AMERICAN DIVISION	W	L	T	PTS	GF	GA
Boston	28	10	6	62	143	90
Chicago	24	17	3	51	108	78
New York Ran	19	16	9	47	106	87
Detroit	16	21	7	39	102	105
Philadelphia Qua	4	36	4	12	76	184

SCORING LEADERS	GP	G	A	PTS
H Morenz, MtrC	39	28	23	51
Goodfellow, Det	44	25	23	48
C Conacher, Tor	37	31	12	43
W Cook, NYR	43	30	12	42
I Bailey, Tor	40	23	19	42
J Primeau, Tor	38	9	32	41
N Stewart, MtrM	42	25	14	39
F Boucher, NYR	44	12	27	39
Weiland, Bos	44	25	13	38
F Cook, NYR	44	18	17	35
A Joliat, MtrC	43	13	22	35

Third-place teams (two games, total goals): New York Rangers defeated Montreal Maroons, 8 goals to 1.

Second-place teams (two games, total goals): Chicago defeated Toronto, 4 goals to 3.

First-place teams (best of five): Montreal Canadiens defeated Boston, 3 games to 2.

Semi-final (best of three): Chicago defeated New York Rangers, 2 games to 0.

Stanley Cup Final (best of five): Montreal Canadiens defeated Chicago, 3 games to 2.

NHL 1931–32

The Ottawa and Pittsburgh franchises suspended operation, and their players were loaned to the remaining eight teams as distributed in an allotment draft. The deliberate screening by an attacking player of the opponent's goaltender was made illegal, and goaltenders were prohibited from holding the puck to obtain a stoppage or throwing the puck forward; infractions would incur a stoppage and face-off. Referee hand signals were unofficially introduced. The definition of an assist was modified and made official. The owners unilaterally agreed on a roster limit of 14 players exclusive of goaltenders, set a salary cap of $75,000 per team, and set the maximum player salary at $7,500, or a maximum of $4,000 per year for players under multi-year contract. Schedule increased to 48 games.

The playoff semi-final was changed to a two-game total-goals format. A format of 20-minute, sudden-death overtime periods was approved for the playoffs. The American Hockey League issued a challenge for the Stanley Cup; the challenge was ignored by the NHL, which considered the AHL an "outlaw" league. Cup trustee Foran initially declared that as the NHL refused to meet the challenge, the Stanley Cup would not be awarded but, after conferring with NHL president Calder, allowed for Cup games in 1932 with the AHL challenge to be postponed one year.

CANADIAN DIVISION	W	L	T	PTS	GF	GA
Montreal Can	25	16	7	57	128	111
Toronto*	23	18	7	53	155	127
Montreal Mar	19	22	7	45	142	139
New York Ame	16	24	8	40	95	142
AMERICAN DIVISION	W	L	T	PTS	GF	GA
New York Ran	23	17	8	54	134	112
Chicago	18	19	11	47	86	101
Detroit	18	20	10	46	95	108
Boston	15	21	12	42	122	117

SCORING LEADERS	GP	G	A	PTS
Hv Jackson, Tor	48	28	25	53
J Primeau, Tor	46	13	37	50
H Morenz, MtrC	48	24	25	49
C Conacher, Tor	44	34	14	48
W Cook, NYR	48	34	14	48
D Trottier, MtrM	48	26	18	44
Re Smith, MtrM	43	11	33	44
A Siebert, MtrM	48	21	18	39
Clapper, Bos	48	17	22	39
A Joliat, MtrC	48	15	24	39

Third-place teams (two games, total goals): Montreal Maroons defeated Detroit, 3 goals to 1.

Second-place teams (two games, total goals): Toronto defeated Chicago, 6 goals to 2.

First-place teams (best of five): New York Rangers defeated Montreal Canadiens, 3 games to 1.
Semi-final (two games, total goals): Toronto defeated Montreal Maroons, 4 goals to 3.
Stanley Cup Final (best of five): Toronto defeated New York Rangers, at New York, Boston, and Toronto, 3 games to 0.

NHL 1932–33

The Ottawa franchise was reactivated, and players still under contract to Ottawa were returned by the other teams. While a goaltender served his own penalty, another skater was officially allowed to take his place in goal, but not to use goaltending equipment. The salary cap was lowered to $70,000 per team. The NHL avoided the AHL's pending Stanley Cup challenge when the AHL disbanded.

CANADIAN DIVISION	W	L	T	PTS	GF	GA
Toronto	24	18	6	54	119	111
Montreal Mar	22	20	6	50	135	119
Montreal Can	18	25	5	41	92	115
New York Ame	15	22	11	41	91	118
Ottawa	11	27	10	32	88	131
AMERICAN DIVISION	W	L	T	PTS	GF	GA
Boston	25	15	8	58	124	88
Detroit	25	15	8	58	111	93
New York Ran*	23	17	8	54	135	107
Chicago	16	20	12	44	88	101

SCORING LEADERS	GP	G	A	PTS
W Cook, NYR	48	28	22	50
Hv Jackson, Tor	48	27	17	44
Northcott, MtrM	48	22	21	43
Re Smith, MtrM	48	20	21	41
Haynes, MtrM	48	16	25	41
A Joliat, MtrC	48	18	21	39
M Barry, Bos	48	24	13	37
F Cook, NYR	48	22	15	37
N Stewart, MtrM	47	18	18	36
H Morenz, MtrC	48	14	21	35
J Gagnon, MtrC	48	12	23	35
E Shore, Bos	48	8	27	35
F Boucher, NYR	47	7	28	35

Third-place teams (two games, total goals): New York Rangers defeated Montreal Canadiens, 8 goals to 5.
Second-place teams (two games, total goals): Detroit defeated Montreal Maroons, 5 goals to 2.
First-place teams (best of five): Toronto defeated Boston, 3 games to 2.
Semi-final (two games, total goals): New York Rangers defeated Detroit, 6 goals to 3.
Stanley Cup Final (best of five): New York Rangers defeated Toronto, 3 games to 1.

NHL 1933–34

Detroit Falcons changed their nickname to Red Wings. Teams were prohibited from stationing more than three players, including the goaltender, inside their defending zone. The definition of an assist was again modified. Two referees would officiate each game, replacing the one referee and one linesman arrangement. The salary cap was lowered to $65,000 per team. A special exhibition game was played in February between Toronto and a team of NHL All-Stars, to benefit Toronto player Ace Bailey, seriously injured during a game in December.

CANADIAN DIVISION	W	L	T	PTS	GF	GA
Toronto	26	13	9	61	174	119
Montreal Can	22	20	6	50	99	101
Montreal Mar	19	18	11	49	117	122
New York Ame	15	23	10	40	104	132
Ottawa	13	29	6	32	115	143
AMERICAN DIVISION	W	L	T	PTS	GF	GA
Detroit	24	14	10	58	113	98
Chicago*	20	17	11	51	88	83
New York Ran	21	19	8	50	120	113
Boston	18	25	5	41	111	130

SCORING LEADERS	GP	G	A	PTS
C Conacher, Tor	42	32	20	52
J Primeau, Tor	45	14	32	46
F Boucher, NYR	48	14	30	44
M Barry, Bos	48	27	12	39
C Dillon, NYR	48	13	26	39
N Stewart, MtrM	47	21	17	38
Hv Jackson, Tor	38	20	18	38
A Joliat, MtrC	48	22	15	37
Re Smith, MtrM	47	18	19	37
P Thompson, Chi	48	20	16	36

Third-place teams (two games, total goals): Montreal Maroons defeated New York Rangers, 2 goals to 1.
Second-place teams (two games, total goals): Chicago defeated Montreal Canadiens, 4 goals to 3.
First-place teams (best of five): Detroit defeated Toronto, 3 games to 2.
Semi-final (two games, total goals): Chicago defeated Montreal Maroons, 6 goals to 2.
Stanley Cup Final (best of five): Chicago defeated Detroit, 3 games to 1.

NHL 1934–35

The Ottawa franchise played its home games in St. Louis and changed its nickname to Eagles. The goal crease was introduced, established as eight feet by five feet. A version of the PCHA penalty shot rule was introduced; the shot had to be taken from inside a circle 20 feet in diameter, centred 38 feet in front of the goal, and the goaltender was required to stay within a foot of his goal line. The owners unilaterally agreed to lower the salary cap to $62,500 per team, and set the maximum player salary at $7,000.

CANADIAN DIVISION	W	L	T	PTS	GF	GA
Toronto	30	14	4	64	157	111
Montreal Mar*	24	19	5	53	123	92
Montreal Can	19	23	6	44	110	145
New York Ame	12	27	9	33	100	142
St. Louis Eag	11	31	6	28	86	144

AMERICAN DIVISION	W	L	T	PTS	GF	GA
Boston	26	16	6	58	129	112
Chicago	26	17	5	57	118	88
New York Ran	22	20	6	50	137	139
Detroit	19	22	7	45	127	114

SCORING LEADERS	GP	G	A	PTS
C Conacher, Tor	47	36	21	57
S Howe, StLE-Det	50	22	25	47
Aurie, Det	48	17	29	46
F Boucher, NYR	48	13	32	45
Hv Jackson, Tor	42	22	22	44
H Lewis, Det	47	16	27	43
A Chapman, NYA	47	9	34	43
M Barry, Bos	48	20	20	40
Schriner, NYA	48	18	22	40
N Stewart, MtrM	47	21	18	39
P Thompson, Chi	48	16	23	39

Third-place teams (two games, total goals): New York Rangers defeated Montreal Canadiens, 6 goals to 5.
Second-place teams (two games, total goals): Montreal Maroons defeated Chicago, 1 goal to 0.
First-place teams (best of five): Toronto defeated Boston, 3 games to 1.
Semi-final (two games, total goals): Montreal Maroons defeated New York Rangers, 5 goals to 4.
Stanley Cup Final (best of five): Montreal Maroons defeated Toronto, 3 games to 0.

NHL 1935–36

The Ottawa franchise was dissolved, and its players distributed to the remaining eight teams in an allotment draft. Fines were added for incidents of stick-swinging and for leaving the bench to join an altercation on the ice. A special exhibition game was played in February, to benefit Montreal Canadiens player Nels Crutchfield, seriously injured the previous September. The playoff semi-final was changed back to a best-of-three format.

CANADIAN DIVISION	W	L	T	PTS	GF	GA
Montreal Mar	22	16	10	54	114	106
Toronto	23	19	6	52	126	106
New York Ame	16	25	7	39	109	122
Montreal Can	11	26	11	33	82	123

AMERICAN DIVISION	W	L	T	PTS	GF	GA
Detroit*	24	16	8	56	124	103
Boston	22	20	6	50	92	83
Chicago	21	19	8	50	93	92
New York Ran	19	17	12	50	91	96

SCORING LEADERS	GP	G	A	PTS
Schriner, NYA	48	19	26	45
M Barry, Bos	48	21	19	40
P Thompson, Chi	45	17	23	40
C Conacher, Tor	44	23	15	38
Thoms, Tor	48	23	15	38
Re Smith, MtrM	47	19	19	38
Romnes, Chi	48	13	25	38
A Chapman, NYA	47	10	28	38
H Lewis, Det	45	14	23	37
Northcott, MtrM	48	15	21	36

Third-place teams (two games, total goals): New York Americans defeated Chicago, 7 goals to 5.
Second-place teams (two games, total goals): Toronto defeated Boston, 8 goals to 6.
First-place teams (best of five): Detroit defeated Montreal Maroons, 3 games to 0.
Semi-final (best of three): Detroit defeated New York Americans, 2 games to 1.
Stanley Cup Final (best of five): Detroit defeated Toronto, 3 games to 1.

NHL 1936–37

The Pittsburgh franchise was finally dissolved. Assists were limited to two per goal. As part of a reciprocal agreement, the playing rules of the NHL were adopted as official by the Canadian Amateur Hockey Association, the Amateur Athletic Association of the United States, and the British Ice Hockey Association. Montreal Canadiens were granted first rights to sign any French-Canadian amateur player. The playoff series between second-place teams and between third-place teams were changed to a best-of-three format.

CANADIAN DIVISION	W	L	T	PTS	GF	GA
Montreal Can	24	18	6	54	115	111
Montreal Mar	22	17	9	53	126	110
Toronto	22	21	5	49	119	115
New York Ame	15	29	4	34	122	161

AMERICAN DIVISION	W	L	T	PTS	GF	GA
Detroit*	25	14	9	59	128	102
Boston	23	18	7	53	120	110

	W	L	T	PTS	GF	GA
New York Ran	19	20	9	47	117	106
Chicago	14	27	7	35	99	131

SCORING LEADERS	GP	G	A	PTS
Schriner, NYA	48	21	25	46
C Apps, Tor	48	16	29	45
M Barry, Bos	48	17	27	44
Aurie, Det	45	23	20	43
Hv Jackson, Tor	46	21	19	40
J Gagnon, MtrC	48	20	16	36
Gracie, MtrM	47	11	25	36
N Stewart, Bos-NYA	43	23	12	35
P Thompson, Chi	47	17	18	35
Cowley, Bos	46	13	22	35

Third-place teams (best of three): New York Rangers defeated Toronto, 2 games to 0.
Second-place teams (best of three): Montreal Maroons defeated Boston, 2 games to 1.
First-place teams (best of five): Detroit defeated Montreal Canadiens, 3 games to 2.
Semi-final (best of three): New York Rangers defeated Montreal Maroons, 2 games to 0.
Stanley Cup Final (best of five): Detroit defeated New York Rangers, 3 games to 2.

NHL 1937–38

Shooting the puck from the defending zone into the attacking zone while at equal strength was made an infraction, incurring a stoppage and a face-off in the offending team's zone. A penalty shot was to be awarded if any defending player other than the goaltender fell on the puck within 10 feet of the goal. A substitute was allowed to serve a major penalty assessed to a goaltender; goaltenders still had to serve their own minor penalties, but a teammate taking up the position was allowed to use a goaltender's stick and glove. The definition of an assist was again modified. A special exhibition game was played in November between a team comprising Montreal Canadiens and Maroons stars and a team of NHL All-Stars, to benefit the family of Canadiens player Howie Morenz, who had died the previous March.

CANADIAN DIVISION	W	L	T	PTS	GF	GA
Toronto	24	15	9	57	151	127
New York Ame	19	18	11	49	110	111
Montreal Can	18	17	13	49	123	128
Montreal Mar	12	30	6	30	101	149
AMERICAN DIVISION	W	L	T	PTS	GF	GA
Boston	30	11	7	67	142	89
New York Ran	27	15	6	60	149	96
Chicago*	14	25	9	37	97	139
Detroit	12	25	11	35	99	135

SCORING LEADERS	GP	G	A	PTS
Drillon, Tor	48	26	26	52
C Apps, Tor	47	21	29	50
P Thompson, Chi	48	22	22	44
G Mantha, MtrC	47	23	19	42
C Dillon, NYR	48	21	18	39
Cowley, Bos	48	17	22	39
Schriner, NYA	48	21	17	38
Thoms, Tor	48	14	24	38
Cl Smith, NYR	48	14	23	37
N Stewart, NYA	48	19	17	36
N Colville, NYR	45	17	19	36

Third-place teams (best of three): Chicago defeated Montreal Canadiens, 2 games to 1.
Second-place teams (best of three): New York Americans defeated New York Rangers, 2 games to 1.
First-place teams (best of five): Toronto defeated Boston, 3 games to 0.
Semi-final (best of three): Chicago defeated New York Americans, 2 games to 1.
Stanley Cup Final (best of five): Chicago defeated Toronto, 3 games to 1.

NHL 1938–39

The Montreal Maroons franchise suspended operation. The divisional format was dropped. Teams were allowed to dress 15 players exclusive of the goaltender. The penalty shot rule was modified, allowing the shooter to skate in and shoot, rather than shooting from a stationary position. One referee and one linesman would officiate each game, replacing the two-referee arrangement. The sponsorship of amateur clubs by NHL teams was approved. The first-place team would receive the Prince of Wales Trophy, the second-place team the O'Brien Trophy, and the two teams would meet in a best-of-seven series in the first round of the playoffs; the third-place team would meet the fourth-place team, and the fifth-place team would meet the sixth-place team, in a best-of-three series. The Stanley Cup Final was changed to a best-of-seven format.

	W	L	T	PTS	GF	GA
Boston*	36	10	2	74	156	76
New York Ran	26	16	6	58	149	105
Toronto	19	20	9	47	114	107
New York Ame	17	21	10	44	119	157
Detroit	18	24	6	42	107	128
Montreal Can	15	24	9	39	115	146
Chicago	12	28	8	32	91	132

SCORING LEADERS	GP	G	A	PTS
H Blake, MtrC	48	24	23	47
Schriner, NYA	48	13	31	44

	GP	G	A	PTS
Cowley, Bos	34	8	34	42
Cl Smith, NYR	48	21	20	41
M Barry, Det	48	13	28	41
C Apps, Tor	44	15	25	40
T Anderson, NYA	48	13	27	40
Gottselig, Chi	48	16	23	39

Fifth-place vs. Sixth-place (best of three): Detroit defeated Montreal Canadiens, 2 games to 1.
Third-place vs. Fourth-place (best of three): Toronto defeated New York Americans, 2 games to 0.
First-place vs. Second-place (best of seven): Boston defeated New York Rangers, 4 games to 3.
Semi-final (best of three): Toronto defeated Detroit, 2 games to 1.
Stanley Cup Final (best of seven): Boston defeated Toronto, 4 games to 1.

NHL 1939–40

An All-Star exhibition game was played in October, to benefit the family of Canadiens player Babe Siebert, who had died the previous August.

	W	L	T	PTS	GF	GA
Boston	31	12	5	67	170	98
New York Ran*	27	11	10	64	136	77
Toronto	25	17	6	56	134	110
Chicago	23	19	6	52	112	120
Detroit	16	26	6	38	90	126
New York Ame	15	29	4	34	106	140
Montreal Can	10	33	5	25	90	167

SCORING LEADERS	GP	G	A	PTS
M Schmidt, Bos	48	22	30	52
Dumart, Bos	48	22	21	43
Bauer, Bos	48	17	26	43
Drillon, Tor	43	21	19	40
Cowley, Bos	48	13	27	40
B Hextall Sr., NYR	48	24	15	39
N Colville, NYR	48	19	19	38
S Howe, Det	46	14	23	37

Fifth-place vs. Sixth-place (best of three): Detroit defeated New York Americans, 2 games to 1.
Third-place vs. Fourth-place (best of three): Toronto defeated Chicago, 2 games to 0.
First-place vs. Second-place (best of seven): New York Rangers defeated Boston, 4 games to 2.
Semi-final (best of three): Toronto defeated Detroit, 2 games to 0.
Stanley Cup Final (best of seven): New York Rangers defeated Toronto, 4 games to 2.

NHL 1940–41

Flooding the ice between periods was made mandatory. The anti-defence rule was amended to allow three defending skaters to enter their own zone ahead of the attacking opponents. Sticks made of material other than wood were made legal, although it would be decades before such sticks were used in an NHL game. The fines for players leaving the bench to join an altercation on the ice were resumed at half their previous cost, after apparently having been discontinued.

	W	L	T	PTS	GF	GA
Boston*	27	8	13	67	168	102
Toronto	28	14	6	62	145	99
Detroit	21	16	11	53	112	102
New York Ran	21	19	8	50	143	125
Chicago	16	25	7	39	112	139
Montreal Can	16	26	6	38	121	147
New York Ame	8	29	11	27	99	186

SCORING LEADERS	GP	G	A	PTS
Cowley, Bos	46	17	45	62
B Hextall Sr., NYR	48	26	18	44
Drillon, Tor	42	23	21	44
C Apps, Tor	41	20	24	44
Ln Patrick, NYR	48	20	24	44
S Howe, Det	48	20	24	44
N Colville, NYR	48	14	28	42
Wiseman, Bos	48	16	24	40

Fifth-place vs. Sixth-place (best of three): Chicago defeated Montreal Canadiens, 2 games to 1.
Third-place vs. Fourth-place (best of three): Detroit defeated New York Rangers, 2 games to 1.
First-place vs. Second-place (best of seven): Boston defeated Toronto, 4 games to 3.
Semi-final (best of three): Detroit defeated Chicago, 2 games to 0.
Stanley Cup Final (best of seven): Boston defeated Detroit, 4 games to 0.

NHL 1941–42

New York Americans changed their name to Brooklyn Americans. A second linesman was added to the officiating crew for each game. Face-off circles, 20 feet in diameter, were introduced, one placed at centre ice, and one each centred on spots 40 feet apart and 20 feet out from the goal lines; the penalty shot circles were removed and replaced by a penalty shot line 28 feet in front of the goal. Penalty shots were classified as major, for incidents in which a puck carrier is tripped from behind with only the goaltender to beat, incurring an opportunity to skate in from the penalty shot line all the way to the goalmouth before shooting, and minor, for all other penalty shot infractions, incurring a shot from the penalty shot line. A minor penalty shot was to be awarded when a minor penalty was assessed to a goaltender.

	W	L	T	PTS	GF	GA
New York Ran	29	17	2	60	177	143
Toronto*	27	18	3	57	158	136
Boston	25	17	6	56	160	118
Chicago	22	23	3	47	145	155
Detroit	19	25	4	42	140	147
Montreal Can	18	27	3	39	134	173
Brooklyn	16	29	3	35	133	175

SCORING LEADERS	GP	G	A	PTS
B Hextall Sr., NYR	48	24	32	56
Ln Patrick, NYR	47	32	22	54
Grosso, Det	48	23	30	53
P Watson, NYR	48	15	37	52
S Abel, Det	48	18	31	49
H Blake, MtrC	47	17	28	45
Thoms, Chi	47	15	30	45
Drillon, Tor	48	23	18	41
C Apps, Tor	38	18	23	41
T Anderson, Brk	48	12	29	41

Fifth-place vs. Sixth-place (best of three): Detroit defeated Montreal Canadiens, 2 games to 1.
Third-place vs. Fourth-place (best of three): Boston defeated Chicago, 2 games to 1.
First-place vs. Second-place (best of seven): Toronto defeated New York Rangers, 4 games to 2.
Semi-final (best of three): Detroit defeated Boston, 2 games to 0.
Stanley Cup Final (best of seven): Toronto defeated Detroit, 4 games to 3.

NHL 1942–43

The Brooklyn franchise suspended operation. Schedule increased to 50 games.

On November 21, after 21 league games had been played, regular-season overtime was discontinued; the number of players a team was allowed to dress for a game, exclusive of goaltenders, was reduced to 14, and the requirement that a team dress a minimum of 12 players was eliminated. NHL president Calder died in February; Mervyn "Red" Dutton was named managing director of the league. The playoff format was revised, matching the first- and third-place teams, and the second- and fourth-place teams, in a best-of-seven semi-final series; the winners of each series would play a best-of-seven series for the Stanley Cup.

	W	L	T	PTS	GF	GA
Detroit*	25	14	11	61	169	124
Boston	24	17	9	57	195	176
Toronto	22	19	9	53	198	159
Montreal Can	19	19	12	50	181	191
Chicago	17	18	15	49	179	180
New York Ran	11	31	8	30	161	253

SCORING LEADERS	GP	G	A	PTS
D Bentley, Chi	50	33	40	73
Cowley, Bos	48	27	45	72
M Bentley, Chi	47	26	44	70
Ln Patrick, NYR	50	22	39	61
L Carr, Tor	50	27	33	60
WJ Taylor, Tor	50	18	42	60
B Hextall Sr., NYR	50	27	32	59
H Blake, MtrC	48	23	36	59

Semi-finals (best of seven): Detroit defeated Toronto, 4 games to 2.

Boston defeated Montreal Canadiens, 4 games to 1.
Stanley Cup Final (best of seven): Detroit defeated Boston, 4 games to 0.

NHL 1943–44

The centre red line, conceived by New York Rangers coach Frank Boucher, was introduced; forward passing from the defending zone across the blue line as far as centre ice was now legal. Two-line passes were illegal, unless the player receiving such a pass was in the same zone as the passer at the moment the pass was made. All anti-defence rules were eliminated; all skaters were again allowed to enter their own zone at any time. The league agreed to co-operate with independent interests seeking to establish a hockey hall of fame. Managing director Dutton suggested the league employ an official statistician, but the matter was deferred; following the Stanley Cup series, Dutton accepted the league presidency on a temporary basis.

	W	L	T	PTS	GF	GA
Montreal Can*	38	5	7	83	234	109
Detroit	26	18	6	58	214	177
Toronto	23	23	4	50	214	174
Chicago	22	23	5	49	178	187
Boston	19	26	5	43	223	268
New York Ran	6	39	5	17	162	310

SCORING LEADERS	GP	G	A	PTS
H Cain, Bos	48	36	46	82
D Bentley, Chi	50	38	39	77
L Carr, Tor	50	36	38	74
Liscombe, Det	50	36	37	73
Lach, MtrC	48	24	48	72

SCORING LEADERS	GP	G	A	PTS
Cl Smith, NYR	50	23	49	72
Cowley, Bos	36	30	41	71
Mosienko, Chi	50	32	38	70

Semi-finals (best of seven): Montreal Canadiens defeated Toronto, 4 games to 1.

Chicago defeated Detroit, 4 games to 1.

Stanley Cup Final (best of seven): Montreal Canadiens defeated Chicago, 4 games to 0.

NHL 1944–45

	W	L	T	PTS	GF	GA
Montreal Can	38	8	4	80	228	121
Detroit	31	14	5	67	218	161
Toronto*	24	22	4	52	183	161
Boston	16	30	4	36	179	219
Chicago	13	30	7	33	141	194
New York Ran	11	29	10	32	154	247

SCORING LEADERS	GP	G	A	PTS
Lach, MtrC	50	26	54	80
M Richard, MtrC	50	50	23	73
H Blake, MtrC	49	29	38	67
Cowley, Bos	49	25	40	65
T Kennedy, Tor	49	29	25	54
Mosienko, Chi	50	28	26	54
Carveth, Det	50	26	28	54
DeMarco, NYR	50	24	30	54
Cl Smith, NYR	50	23	31	54

Semi-finals (best of seven): Toronto defeated Montreal Canadiens, 4 games to 2.

Detroit defeated Boston, 4 games to 3.

Stanley Cup Final (best of seven): Toronto defeated Detroit, 4 games to 1.

NHL 1945–46

	W	L	T	PTS	GF	GA
Montreal Can*	28	17	5	61	172	134
Boston	24	18	8	56	167	156
Chicago	23	20	7	53	200	178
Detroit	20	20	10	50	146	159
Toronto	19	24	7	45	174	185
New York Ran	13	28	9	35	144	191

SCORING LEADERS	GP	G	A	PTS
M Bentley, Chi	47	31	30	61
G Stewart, Tor	50	37	15	52
H Blake, MtrC	50	29	21	50

SCORING LEADERS	GP	G	A	PTS
Cl Smith, NYR	50	26	24	50
M Richard, MtrC	50	27	21	48
Mosienko, Chi	40	18	30	48
DeMarco, NYR	50	20	27	47
Lach, MtrC	50	13	34	47

Semi-finals (best of seven): Montreal Canadiens defeated Chicago, 4 games to 0.

Boston defeated Detroit, 4 games to 1.

Stanley Cup Final (best of seven): Montreal Canadiens defeated Boston, 4 games to 1.

NHL 1946–47

Although the NHL had been the sole professional major-league since 1926 and had produced all Stanley Cup champions since that year, the Stanley Cup was still, under the terms of its donation, officially a challenge trophy; originally emblematic of the hockey champions of Canada, it had come to be designated as the trophy for the champion hockey club of the world. At least one other league since 1926 had submitted a formal challenge, although it was turned down. P. D. Ross, who had been one of the Cup trustees since the trophy was first presented in 1893, now turned over "full authority to determine and amend . . . conditions of competition for the Stanley Cup" to the NHL; his abrogation of the trusteeship's authority and jurisdiction transformed the Cup from the supreme symbol of all of hockey to the supreme symbol of the NHL. Henceforward, any rival major league would first have to obtain the NHL's consent before being allowed to challenge for the Stanley Cup. The WHA, 26 years later, would ask for such consent and have it denied; had the Cup remained in the control of an independent trustee, the WHA's request, as well as any a European champion might have made, would instead have been considered by a neutral authority.

Clarence S. Campbell was elected president of the NHL after the retirement of "Red" Dutton. Following a review by a rules committee headed by Frank Boucher, the playing rules for the NHL, CAHA, AAU, and BIHA were again amended and standardized. Teams were again permitted to dress 15 players for a game, exclusive of goaltenders. The size of the goal crease was reduced to seven feet by three feet. Sticks had to be made of wood. A minor penalty would be incurred by a goaltender, and a match misconduct by any other player, using an oversized stick. The use of pads or protectors made of any material likely to cause injury to an opponent was prohibited. Players were required to keep a distance of 10 feet from the players involved in a face-off. Goals were allowed if deflected off the body or skates of an attacking player, but not if deliberately directed across the goal line by any means except the stick. Icing would be waved off if it resulted from an attempt at an onside pass and the puck was first recovered by the intended recipient.

Infractions incurring a minor penalty, requiring the offending player's team to play two full minutes shorthanded, included charging, cross-checking, holding, hooking, interference, slashing, tripping, elbowing, delay of game by shooting the puck out of play, face-off violation, falling on the puck, carrying the stick above shoulder height, roughing, fighting (if in retaliation), ragging the puck at even strength, leaving the penalty box early, and the goaltender holding the puck to obtain a stoppage or throwing the puck forward.

Infractions incurring a major penalty included charging from behind, charging or cross-checking the goaltender in his crease, cross-checking or hooking or high-sticking resulting in injury to an opponent, fighting (if instigator), and throwing the stick (except in instances where the rules called for a goal to be awarded).

Falling on or holding the puck in the goal crease, or tripping an opposing puck carrier who has only the goaltender to beat, incurred a penalty shot. Shooters were permitted to skate in all the way to the goalmouth before shooting on all penalty shots; the puck was placed at the attacking zone blue line to begin all penalty shot attempts.

Kicking or attempting to injure an opponent incurred a match penalty, for which the offending player would be ejected, and require his team to play short-handed for five minutes. Deliberately injuring an opponent so as to prevent him from returning to the game incurred a match penalty, for which the offending player would be ejected, and require his team to play short-handed for 20 minutes. Infractions incurring a game misconduct, for which the offending player would serve 10 minutes but not require his team to play short-handed, included leaving the bench to join an altercation on the ice, verbal or physical abuse of an official, and receiving a second major penalty in one game. A second misconduct in one game for abusing an official or a third major penalty in one game incurred a match misconduct, for which the offending player would be ejected but would not require his team to play short-handed.

Goaltenders were no longer required to serve their own minor or game misconduct penalties; a penalty shot was awarded when a goaltender incurred a major penalty. A goaltender incurring a second major penalty in one game was to receive a match misconduct; he would be replaced not by a back-up goaltender but by another teammate, who would be allowed to don full goaltending equipment.

Referee hand signals were standardized. The definition of an assist was again modified. Players were for the first time guaranteed a predetermined payment for playoff participation. The schedule increased to 60 games.

	W	L	T	PTS	GF	GA
Montreal Can	34	16	10	78	189	138
Toronto*	31	19	10	72	209	172

	W	L	T	PTS	GF	GA
Boston	26	23	11	63	190	175
Detroit	22	27	11	55	190	193
New York Ran	22	32	6	50	167	186
Chicago	19	37	4	42	193	274

SCORING LEADERS	GP	G	A	PTS
M Bentley, Chi	60	29	43	72
M Richard, MtrC	60	45	26	71
WJ Taylor, Det	60	17	46	63
M Schmidt, Bos	59	27	35	62
T Kennedy, Tor	60	28	32	60
D Bentley, Chi	52	21	34	55
Bauer, Bos	58	30	24	54
R Conacher, Det	60	30	24	54

Semi-finals (best of seven): Montreal Canadiens defeated Boston, 4 games to 1.

Toronto defeated Detroit, 4 games to 1.

Stanley Cup Final (best of seven): Toronto defeated Montreal Canadiens, 4 games to 2.

NHL 1947–48

The first annual All-Star Game for the benefit of the players' pension fund and various charities was played before the season began; the All-Stars defeated Stanley Cup champion Toronto. The offside rule allowing a two-line pass if the player receiving the pass was onside at the moment the pass was made was rescinded, but reinstated before the halfway point of the season. At the same time, the icing rule was modified, icing to be waived off if the result of an attempt at an onside pass and the puck first recovered by any member of the attacking team. An attempt was made to make the raising of the stick by a goal scorer, long a widespread spontaneous reaction, an official and mandatory signal for a goal. The National Hockey League Pension Society was established. The Montreal Maroons franchise, in suspension since 1938, was officially terminated.

	W	L	T	PTS	GF	GA
Toronto*	32	15	13	77	182	143
Detroit	30	18	12	72	187	148
Boston	23	24	13	59	167	168
New York Ran	21	26	13	55	176	201
Montreal Can	20	29	11	51	147	169
Chicago	20	34	6	46	195	225

SCORING LEADERS	GP	G	A	PTS
Lach, MtrC	60	30	31	61
H O'Connor, NYR	60	24	36	60
D Bentley, Chi	60	20	37	57
G Stewart, Tor-Chi	61	27	29	56
M Bentley, Chi-Tor	59	26	28	54

SCORING LEADERS	GP	G	A	PTS
N Poile, Tor-Chi	58	25	29	54
M Richard, MtrC	53	28	25	53
C Apps, Tor	55	26	27	53

Semi-finals (best of seven): Toronto defeated Boston, 4 games to 1.

Detroit defeated New York Rangers, 4 games to 2.

Stanley Cup Final (best of seven): Toronto defeated Detroit, 4 games to 0.

NHL 1948–49

	W	L	T	PTS	GF	GA
Detroit	34	19	7	75	195	145
Boston	29	23	8	66	178	163
Montreal Can	28	23	9	65	152	126
Toronto*	22	25	13	57	147	161
Chicago	21	31	8	50	173	211
New York Ran	18	31	11	47	133	172

SCORING LEADERS	GP	G	A	PTS
R Conacher, Chi	60	26	42	68
D Bentley, Chi	58	23	43	66
S Abel, Det	60	28	26	54
T Lindsay, Det	50	26	28	54
J Conacher, Det-Chi	59	26	23	49
Ronty, Bos	60	20	29	49
H Watson, Tor	60	26	19	45
Reay, MtrC	60	22	23	45
Bodnar, Chi	59	19	26	45

Semi-finals (best of seven): Detroit defeated Montreal Canadiens, 4 games to 3.

Toronto defeated Boston, 4 games to 1.

Stanley Cup Final (best of seven): Toronto defeated Detroit, 4 games to 0.

NHL 1949–50

Painting the ice surface white was made mandatory. An annual intra-league draft was established; each team was allowed to protect 30 players, and unprotected players could be claimed by another team for $25,000 each. Teams were permitted to dress 17 players for a game exclusive of the goaltender. When a goaltender incurred a major penalty, the penalty would be served by a teammate. Schedule increased to 70 games.

	W	L	T	PTS	GF	GA
Detroit*	37	19	14	88	229	164
Montreal Can	29	22	19	77	172	150
Toronto	31	27	12	74	176	173

	W	L	T	PTS	GF	GA
New York Ran	28	31	11	67	170	189
Boston	22	32	16	60	198	228
Chicago	22	38	10	54	203	244

SCORING LEADERS	GP	G	A	PTS
T Lindsay, Det	69	23	55	78
S Abel, Det	69	34	35	69
G Howe, Det	70	35	33	68
M Richard, MtrC	70	43	22	65
Ronty, Bos	70	23	36	59
R Conacher, Chi	70	25	31	56
D Bentley, Chi	64	20	33	53
Peirson, Bos	57	27	25	52

Semi-finals (best of seven): Detroit defeated Toronto, 4 games to 3.

New York Rangers defeated Montreal Canadiens, 4 games to 1.

Stanley Cup Final (best of seven): Detroit defeated New York Rangers, 4 games to 3, at Detroit and Toronto.

NHL 1950–51

The O'Brien Trophy was retired from service. A playoff semi-final game in Toronto ended in a tie when the game was terminated by Sunday curfew laws.

	W	L	T	PTS	GF	GA
Detroit	44	13	13	101	236	139
Toronto*	41	16	13	95	212	138
Montreal Can	25	30	15	65	173	184
Boston	22	30	18	62	178	197
New York Ran	20	29	21	61	169	201
Chicago	13	47	10	36	171	280

SCORING LEADERS	GP	G	A	PTS
G Howe, Det	70	43	43	86
M Richard, MtrC	65	42	24	66
M Bentley, Chi	67	21	41	62
S Abel, Det	69	23	38	61
M Schmidt, Bos	62	22	39	61
T Kennedy, Tor	63	18	43	61
T Lindsay, Det	67	24	35	59
Sloan, Tor	70	31	25	56

Semi-finals (best of seven): Montreal Canadiens defeated Detroit, 4 games to 2.

Toronto defeated Boston, 4 games to 1, with 1 tie.

Stanley Cup Final (best of seven): Toronto defeated Montreal Canadiens, 4 games to 1.

NHL 1951–52

The size of the goal crease was increased to 8 feet by 4 feet; face-off circles were enlarged to 30 feet in diameter. All-Star Game format changed from All-Stars vs. Stanley Cup champion to two competing teams of All-Stars.

	W	L	T	PTS	GF	GA
Detroit*	44	14	12	100	215	133
Montreal Can	34	26	10	78	195	164
Toronto	29	25	16	74	168	157
Boston	25	29	16	66	162	176
New York Ran	23	34	13	59	192	219
Chicago	17	44	9	43	158	241

SCORING LEADERS	GP	G	A	PTS
G Howe, Det	70	47	39	86
T Lindsay, Det	70	30	39	69
Lach, MtrC	70	15	50	65
Raleigh, NYR	70	19	42	61
Si Smith, Tor	70	27	30	57
B Geoffrion, MtrC	67	30	24	54
Mosienko, Chi	70	31	22	53
S Abel, Det	62	17	36	53

Semi-finals (best of seven): Detroit defeated Toronto, 4 games to 0.

Montreal Canadiens defeated Boston, 4 games to 3.
Stanley Cup Final (best of seven): Detroit defeated Montreal Canadiens, 4 games to 0.

NHL 1952–53

Teams were allowed to dress 16 players exclusive of the goaltender at home, and 15 players exclusive of the goaltender on the road. At the end of the regular season, the Cleveland Barons of the American Hockey League issued a challenge for the Stanley Cup in the event Cleveland won the AHL championship. The challenge was refused by the NHL, as Cleveland had not yet secured their league's championship and the AHL was not considered a major league.

	W	L	T	PTS	GF	GA
Detroit	36	16	18	90	222	133
Montreal Can*	28	23	19	75	155	148
Boston	28	29	13	69	152	172
Chicago	27	28	15	69	169	175
Toronto	27	30	13	67	156	167
New York Ran	17	37	16	50	152	211

SCORING LEADERS	GP	G	A	PTS
G Howe, Det	70	49	46	95
T Lindsay, Det	70	32	39	71
M Richard, MtrC	70	28	33	61
W Hergesheimer, NYR	70	30	29	59

SCORING LEADERS	GP	G	A	PTS
Delvecchio, Det	70	16	43	59
Ronty, NYR	70	16	38	54
Prystai, Det	70	16	34	50
L Kelly, Det	70	19	27	46

Semi-finals (best of seven): Boston defeated Detroit, 4 games to 2.

Montreal Canadiens defeated Chicago, 4 games to 3.
Stanley Cup Final (best of seven): Montreal Canadiens defeated Boston, 4 games to 1.

NHL 1953–54

The intra-league draft rules were amended, limiting each team to protecting 18 skaters and two goaltenders; the claiming price was reduced to $15,000. Teams were allowed to dress 16 players exclusive of the goaltender for all games. All-Star Game format changed back to All-Stars vs. Stanley Cup champion.

	W	L	T	PTS	GF	GA
Detroit*	37	19	14	88	191	132
Montreal Can	35	24	11	81	195	141
Toronto	32	24	14	78	152	131
Boston	32	28	10	74	177	181
New York Ran	29	31	10	68	161	182
Chicago	12	51	7	31	133	242

SCORING LEADERS	GP	G	A	PTS
G Howe, Det	70	33	48	81
M Richard, MtrC	70	37	40	77
T Lindsay, Det	70	26	36	62
B Geoffrion, MtrC	54	29	25	54
Olmstead, MtrC	70	15	37	52
L Kelly, Det	62	16	33	49
Reibel, Det	69	15	33	48
Sandford, Bos	70	16	31	47
Mackell, Bos	67	15	32	47

Semi-finals (best of seven): Detroit defeated Toronto, 4 games to 1.

Montreal Canadiens defeated Boston, 4 games to 0.
Stanley Cup Final (best of seven): Detroit defeated Montreal Canadiens, 4 games to 3.

NHL 1954–55

Teams were allowed to dress 18 players exclusive of the goaltender for games until December 1, and 16 players exclusive of the goaltender thereafter. Player numbers were required to be displayed on skate boots. The Zamboni was introduced on March 10 at the Montreal Forum.

	W	L	T	PTS	GF	GA
Detroit* a	42	17	11	95	204	134
Montreal Can a	41	18	11	93	228	157
Toronto	24	24	22	70	147	135
Boston	23	26	21	67	169	188
New York Ran	17	35	18	52	150	210
Chicago b	13	40	17	43	161	235

a Detroit won forfeit of game with Montreal Canadiens; game stopped after first period with score at 4-1 for Detroit and forfeited to Detroit 4-1.
b Played six home games at St. Louis, one home game at Omaha, and one home game at St. Paul.

SCORING LEADERS	GP	G	A	PTS
B Geoffrion, MtrC	70	38	37	75
M Richard, MtrC	67	38	36	74
J Beliveau, MtrC	70	37	36	73
Reibel, Det	70	25	41	66
G Howe, Det	64	29	33	62
G Sullivan, Chi	69	19	42	61
Olmstead, MtrC	70	10	48	58
Si Smith, Tor	70	33	21	54
K Mosdell, MtrC	70	22	32	54

Semi-finals (best of seven): Detroit defeated Toronto, 4 games to 0.

Montreal Canadiens defeated Boston, 4 games to 1.
Stanley Cup Final (best of seven): Detroit defeated Montreal Canadiens, 4 games to 3.

NHL 1955–56

Teams were allowed to dress 17 players exclusive of the goaltender. Officials' solid-coloured sweaters changed to black and white vertical stripe pattern.

	W	L	T	PTS	GF	GA
Montreal Can*	45	15	10	100	222	131
Detroit	30	24	16	76	183	148
New York Ran	32	28	10	74	204	203
Toronto	24	33	13	61	153	181
Boston	23	34	13	59	147	185
Chicago a	19	39	12	50	155	216

a Played four home games at St. Louis and one home game at Omaha.

SCORING LEADERS	GP	G	A	PTS
J Beliveau, MtrC	70	47	41	88
G Howe, Det	70	38	41	79
M Richard, MtrC	70	38	33	71
Olmstead, MtrC	70	14	56	70
Sloan, Tor	70	37	29	66
A Bathgate, NYR	70	19	47	66
B Geoffrion, MtrC	59	29	33	62
Reibel, Det	68	17	39	56

Semi-finals (best of seven): Montreal Canadiens defeated New York Rangers, 4 games to 1.

Detroit defeated Toronto, 4 games to 1.
Stanley Cup Final (best of seven): Montreal Canadiens defeated Detroit, 4 games to 1.

NHL 1956–57

A minor penalty expired once an opponent scored, and the player serving the penalty was allowed to return to the ice. Officials' hand signals were again standardized.

	W	L	T	PTS	GF	GA
Detroit	38	20	12	88	198	157
Montreal Can*	35	23	12	82	210	155
Boston	34	24	12	80	195	174
New York Ran	26	30	14	66	184	227
Toronto	21	34	15	57	174	192
Chicago	16	39	15	47	169	255

SCORING LEADERS	GP	G	A	PTS
G Howe, Det	70	44	45	89
T Lindsay, Det	70	30	55	85
J Beliveau, MtrC	69	33	51	84
A Bathgate, NYR	70	27	50	77
Litzenberger, Chi	70	32	32	64
M Richard, MtrC	63	33	29	62
D McKenney, Bos	69	21	39	60
R Moore, MtrC	70	29	29	58

Semi-finals (best of seven): Boston defeated Detroit, 4 games to 1.

Montreal Canadiens defeated New York Rangers, 4 games to 1.
Stanley Cup Final (best of seven): Montreal Canadiens defeated Boston, 4 games to 1.

NHL 1957–58

The newly formed NHL Players' Association filed suit against the NHL and its six clubs; the NHL refused to recognize the association, but conceded to a minimum player salary of $7,000 per season, pension and hospitalization benefits, and a larger share of playoff revenues, and the suit was dropped.

	W	L	T	PTS	GF	GA
Montreal Can*	43	17	10	96	250	158
New York Ran	32	25	13	77	195	188
Detroit	29	29	12	70	176	207
Boston	27	28	15	69	199	194
Chicago	24	39	7	55	163	202
Toronto	21	38	11	53	192	226

SCORING LEADERS	GP	G	A	PTS
R Moore, MtrC	70	36	48	84
M Richard, MtrC	67	28	52	80
A Bathgate, NYR	65	30	48	78
G Howe, Det	64	33	44	77
Horvath, Bos	67	30	36	66
Litzenberger, Chi	70	32	30	62
Mackell, Bos	70	20	40	60
J Beliveau, MtrC	55	27	32	59
Delvecchio, Det	70	21	38	59

Semi-finals (best of seven): Montreal Canadiens defeated Detroit, 4 games to 0.

Boston defeated New York Rangers, 4 games to 2.

Stanley Cup Final (best of seven): Montreal Canadiens defeated Boston, 4 games to 2.

NHL 1958–59

	W	L	T	PTS	GF	GA
Montreal Can*	39	18	13	91	258	158
Boston	32	29	9	73	205	215
Chicago	28	29	13	69	197	208
Toronto	27	32	11	65	189	201
New York Ran	26	32	12	64	201	217
Detroit	25	37	8	58	167	218

SCORING LEADERS	GP	G	A	PTS
R Moore, MtrC	70	41	55	96
J Beliveau, MtrC	64	45	46	91
A Bathgate, NYR	70	40	48	88
G Howe, Det	70	32	46	78
Litzenberger, Chi	70	33	44	77
B Geoffrion, MtrC	59	22	44	66
G Sullivan, NYR	70	21	42	63
A Hebenton, NYR	70	33	29	62
D McKenney, Bos	70	32	30	62
Sloan, Tor	59	27	35	62

Semi-finals (best of seven): Montreal Canadiens defeated Chicago, 4 games to 2.

Toronto defeated Boston, 4 games to 3.

Stanley Cup Final (best of seven): Montreal Canadiens defeated Toronto, 4 games to 1.

NHL 1959–60

	W	L	T	PTS	GF	GA
Montreal Can*	40	18	12	92	255	178
Toronto	35	26	9	79	199	195
Chicago	28	29	13	69	191	180
Detroit	26	29	15	67	186	197
Boston	28	34	8	64	220	241
New York Ran	17	38	15	49	187	247

SCORING LEADERS	GP	G	A	PTS
R Hull, Chi	70	39	42	81
Horvath, Bos	68	39	41	80
J Beliveau, MtrC	60	34	40	74
A Bathgate, NYR	70	26	48	74
H Richard, MtrC	70	30	43	73
G Howe, Det	70	28	45	73
B Geoffrion, MtrC	59	30	41	71
D McKenney, Bos	70	20	49	69

Semi-finals (best of seven): Montreal Canadiens defeated Chicago, 4 games to 0.

Toronto defeated Detroit, 4 games to 2.

Stanley Cup Final (best of seven): Montreal Canadiens defeated Toronto, 4 games to 0.

NHL 1960–61

Teams were allowed to dress 16 players exclusive of the goaltender.

	W	L	T	PTS	GF	GA
Montreal Can	41	19	10	92	254	188
Toronto	39	19	12	90	234	176
Chicago*	29	24	17	75	198	180
Detroit	25	29	16	66	195	215
New York Ran	22	38	10	54	204	248
Boston	15	42	13	43	176	254

SCORING LEADERS	GP	G	A	PTS
B Geoffrion, MtrC	64	50	45	95
J Beliveau, MtrC	69	32	58	90
F Mahovlich, Tor	70	48	36	84
A Bathgate, NYR	70	29	48	77
G Howe, Det	64	23	49	72
Ullman, Det	70	28	42	70
L Kelly, Tor	64	20	50	70
R Moore, MtrC	57	35	34	69

Semi-finals (best of seven): Chicago defeated Montreal Canadiens, 4 games to 2.

Detroit defeated Toronto, 4 games to 1.

Stanley Cup Final (best of seven): Chicago defeated Detroit, 4 games to 2.

NHL 1961–62

Penalty shots were required to be taken by the player against whom the foul was committed; if the infraction incurring the penalty shot was not committed against any individual player, the shot had to be taken by a player on the ice at the time the foul was committed.

	W	L	T	PTS	GF	GA
Montreal Can	42	14	14	98	259	166
Toronto*	37	22	11	85	232	180
Chicago	31	26	13	75	217	186
New York Ran	26	32	12	64	195	207
Detroit	23	33	14	60	184	219
Boston	15	47	8	38	177	306

SCORING LEADERS	GP	G	A	PTS
R Hull, Chi	70	50	34	84
A Bathgate, NYR	70	28	56	84
G Howe, Det	70	33	44	77
Mikita, Chi	70	25	52	77
F Mahovlich, Tor	70	33	38	71
Delvecchio, Det	70	26	43	69
Backstrom, MtrC	66	27	38	65
Ullman, Det	70	26	38	64

Semi-finals (best of seven): Toronto defeated New York Rangers, 4 games to 2.

Chicago defeated Montreal Canadiens, 4 games to 2.
Stanley Cup Final (best of seven): Toronto defeated Chicago, 4 games to 2.

NHL 1962–63

Goaltenders were prohibited from skating past their own blue lines.

	W	L	T	PTS	GF	GA
Toronto*	35	23	12	82	221	180
Chicago	32	21	17	81	194	178
Montreal Can	28	19	23	79	225	183
Detroit	32	25	13	77	200	194
New York Ran	22	36	12	56	211	233
Boston	14	39	17	45	198	281

SCORING LEADERS	GP	G	A	PTS
G Howe, Det	70	38	48	86
A Bathgate, NYR	70	35	46	81
Mikita, Chi	65	31	45	76
F Mahovlich, Tor	67	36	37	73
H Richard, MtrC	67	23	50	73
J Beliveau, MtrC	69	18	49	67
Bucyk, Bos	69	27	39	66
Delvecchio, Det	70	20	44	64

Semi-finals (best of seven): Toronto defeated Montreal Canadiens, 4 games to 1.

Detroit defeated Chicago, 4 games to 2.

Stanley Cup Final (best of seven): Toronto defeated Detroit, 4 games to 1.

NHL 1963–64

The universal amateur draft was established, allowing NHL teams to claim rights to any amateur player at least 17 years of age and not already sponsored by an NHL team.

	W	L	T	PTS	GF	GA
Montreal Can	36	21	13	85	209	167
Chicago	36	22	12	84	218	169
Toronto*	33	25	12	78	192	172
Detroit	30	29	11	71	191	204
New York Ran	22	38	10	54	186	242
Boston	18	40	12	48	170	212

SCORING LEADERS	GP	G	A	PTS
Mikita, Chi	70	39	50	89
R Hull, Chi	70	43	44	87
J Beliveau, MtrC	68	28	50	78
A Bathgate, NYR-Tor	71	19	58	77
G Howe, Det	69	26	47	73
Wharram, Chi	70	39	32	71
M Oliver, Bos	70	24	44	68
Goyette, NYR	67	24	41	65

Semi-finals (best of seven): Toronto defeated Montreal Canadiens, 4 games to 3.

Detroit defeated Chicago, 4 games to 3.
Stanley Cup Final (best of seven): Toronto defeated Detroit, 4 games to 3.

NHL 1964–65

The minimum age of players eligible for the amateur draft was raised to 18. Body contact prior to face-offs was made illegal. Teams were required to provide their own back-up goaltender for playoff games and have him present and dressed on the bench.

	W	L	T	PTS	GF	GA
Detroit	40	23	7	87	224	175
Montreal Can*	36	23	11	83	211	185
Chicago	34	28	8	76	224	176
Toronto	30	26	14	74	204	173
New York Ran	20	38	12	52	179	246
Boston	21	43	6	48	166	253

SCORING LEADERS	GP	G	A	PTS
Mikita, Chi	70	28	59	87
Ullman, Det	70	42	41	83
G Howe, Det	70	29	47	76

SCORING LEADERS	GP	G	A	PTS
R Hull, Chi	61	39	32	71
Delvecchio, Det	68	25	42	67
Provost, MtrC	70	27	37	64
R Gilbert, NYR	70	25	36	61
Pilote, Chi	68	14	45	59

Semi-finals (best of seven): Chicago defeated Detroit, 4 games to 3.

Montreal Canadiens defeated Toronto, 4 games to 2.
Stanley Cup Final (best of seven): Montreal Canadiens defeated Chicago, 4 games to 3.

NHL 1965–66

Teams were required to have two goaltenders dressed for each regular-season game. The maximum length for sticks was increased to 55 inches.

	W	L	T	PTS	GF	GA
Montreal Can*	41	21	8	90	239	173
Chicago	37	25	8	82	240	187
Toronto	34	25	11	79	208	187
Detroit	31	27	12	74	221	194
Boston	21	43	6	48	174	275
New York Ran	18	41	11	47	195	261

SCORING LEADERS	GP	G	A	PTS
R Hull, Chi	65	54	43	97
Mikita, Chi	68	30	48	78
Rb Rousseau, MtrC	70	30	48	78
J Beliveau, MtrC	67	29	48	77
G Howe, Det	70	29	46	75
Ullman, Det	70	31	41	72
Delvecchio, Det	70	31	38	69
Nevin, NYR	69	29	33	62

Semi-finals (best of seven): Montreal Canadiens defeated Toronto, 4 games to 0.

Detroit defeated Chicago, 4 games to 2.
Stanley Cup Final (best of seven): Montreal Canadiens defeated Detroit, 4 games to 2.

NHL 1966–67

The sponsorship of amateur clubs by NHL teams was ended. Immediate substitution was allowed for coincidental major penalties. The length of intermissions was standardized at 15 minutes.

	W	L	T	PTS	GF	GA
Chicago	41	17	12	94	264	170
Montreal Can	32	25	13	77	202	188
Toronto*	32	27	11	75	204	211

	W	L	T	PTS	GF	GA
New York Ran	30	28	12	72	188	189
Detroit	27	39	4	58	212	241
Boston	17	43	10	44	182	253

SCORING LEADERS	GP	G	A	PTS
Mikita, Chi	70	35	62	97
R Hull, Chi	66	52	28	80
Ullman, Det	68	26	44	70
Wharram, Chi	70	31	34	65
G Howe, Det	69	25	40	65
Rb Rousseau, MtrC	68	19	44	63
P Esposito, Chi	69	21	40	61
Goyette, NYR	70	12	49	61

Semi-finals (best of seven): Toronto defeated Chicago, 4 games to 2.

Montreal Canadiens defeated New York Rangers, 4 games to 0.
Stanley Cup Final (best of seven): Toronto defeated Montreal Canadiens, 4 games to 2.

NHL 1967–68

Six new clubs joined the NHL: California Seals (based in Oakland), Los Angeles Kings, Minnesota North Stars (based in Minneapolis), Philadelphia Flyers, Pittsburgh Penguins, and St. Louis Blues. An expansion draft was devised to stock the new clubs. The NHL split into two six-team divisions, the established teams in the east, the expansion teams in the west. California Seals changed their name to Oakland Seals in December. The maximum curvature of stick blades was limited to one and a half inches. The minimum age of players eligible for the amateur draft was raised to 20. The Prince of Wales Trophy was awarded to the team finishing first in the East Division; the Clarence S. Campbell Bowl was introduced, awarded to the team finishing first in the West Division.

The playoff format was revised, matching the first- and third-place teams, and the second- and fourth-place teams, within divisions, in best-of-seven quarter-final series; and the winners of the first-vs.-third-place series and the winners of the second-vs.-fourth-place series, within divisions in best-of-seven semi-final series. The winners of each semi-final series would play a best-of-seven series for the Stanley Cup. Schedule increased to 74 games.

EAST DIVISION	W	L	T	PTS	GF	GA
Montreal Can*	42	22	10	94	236	167
New York Ran	39	23	12	90	226	183
Boston	37	27	10	84	259	216
Chicago	32	26	16	80	212	222
Toronto	33	31	10	76	209	176
Detroit	27	35	12	66	245	257

WEST DIVISION	W	L	T	PTS	GF	GA
Philadelphia Fly	31	32	11	73	173	179
Los Angeles	31	33	10	72	200	224
St. Louis Blu	27	31	16	70	177	191
Minnesota NSt	27	32	15	69	191	226
Pittsburgh Pen	27	34	13	67	195	216
California/Oakland	15	42	17	47	153	219

SCORING LEADERS	GP	G	A	PTS
Mikita, Chi	72	40	47	87
P Esposito, Bos	74	35	49	84
G Howe, Det	74	39	43	82
Ratelle, NYR	74	32	46	78
R Gilbert, NYR	73	29	48	77
R Hull, Chi	71	44	31	75
Ullman, Det-Tor	71	35	37	72
Delvecchio, Det	74	22	48	70
Bucyk, Bos	72	30	39	69
Wharram, Chi	74	27	42	69

Quarter-finals (best of seven): Montreal Canadiens defeated Boston, 4 games to 0.

St. Louis Blues defeated Philadelphia Flyers, 4 games to 3.

Chicago defeated New York Rangers, 4 games to 2.

Minnesota North Stars defeated Los Angeles, 4 games to 3.

Semi-finals (best of seven): Montreal Canadiens defeated Chicago, 4 games to 1.

St. Louis Blues defeated Minnesota North Stars, 4 games to 3.

Stanley Cup Final (best of seven): Montreal Canadiens defeated St. Louis Blues, 4 games to 0.

NHL 1968–69

Schedule increased to 76 games. All-Star Game format changed from All-Stars vs. Stanley Cup champion to East Division All-Stars vs. West Division All-Stars.

EAST DIVISION	W	L	T	PTS	GF	GA
Montreal Can*	46	19	11	103	271	202
Boston	42	18	16	100	303	221
New York Ran	41	26	9	91	231	196
Toronto	35	26	15	85	234	217
Detroit	33	31	12	78	239	221
Chicago	34	33	9	77	280	246
WEST DIVISION	W	L	T	PTS	GF	GA
St. Louis Blu	37	27	14	88	204	157
Oakland	29	36	11	69	219	251
Philadelphia Fly	20	35	21	61	174	225
Los Angeles	24	42	10	58	185	260
Pittsburgh Pen	20	45	11	51	189	252
Minnesota NSt	18	43	15	51	189	270

SCORING LEADERS	GP	G	A	PTS
P Esposito, Bos	74	49	77	126
R Hull, Chi	74	58	49	107
G Howe, Det	76	44	59	103
Mikita, Chi	74	30	67	97
K Hodge Sr., Bos	75	45	45	90
Cournoyer, MtrC	76	43	44	87
Delvecchio, Det	72	25	58	83
Berenson, StLB	76	35	47	82
J Beliveau, MtrC	69	33	49	82
F Mahovlich, Det	76	49	29	78
Ratelle, NYR	75	32	46	78

Quarter-finals (best of seven): Montreal Canadiens defeated New York Rangers, 4 games to 0.

St. Louis Blues defeated Philadelphia Flyers, 4 games to 0.

Boston defeated Toronto, 4 games to 0.

Los Angeles defeated Oakland, 4 games to 3.

Semi-finals (best of seven): Montreal Canadiens defeated Boston, 4 games to 2.

St. Louis Blues defeated Los Angeles, 4 games to 0.

Stanley Cup Final (best of seven): Montreal Canadiens defeated St. Louis Blues, 4 games to 0.

NHL 1969–70

The maximum curvature of stick blades was limited to one inch.

EAST DIVISION	W	L	T	PTS	GF	GA
Chicago	45	22	9	99	250	170
Boston*	40	17	19	99	277	216
Detroit	40	21	15	95	246	199
New York Ran	38	22	16	92	246	189
Montreal Can	38	22	16	92	244	201
Toronto	29	34	13	71	222	242
WEST DIVISION	W	L	T	PTS	GF	GA
St. Louis Blu	37	27	12	86	224	179
Pittsburgh Pen	26	38	12	64	182	238
Minnesota NSt	19	35	22	60	224	257
Oakland	22	40	14	58	169	243
Philadelphia Fly	17	35	24	58	197	225
Los Angeles	14	52	10	38	168	290

SCORING LEADERS	GP	G	A	PTS
R Orr, Bos	76	33	87	120
P Esposito, Bos	76	43	56	99
Mikita, Chi	76	39	47	86
Goyette, StLB	72	29	49	78
Tkaczuk, NYR	76	27	50	77
Ratelle, NYR	75	32	42	74
Berenson, StLB	67	33	39	72
Parise, MinNS	74	24	48	72

SCORING LEADERS	GP	G	A	PTS
G Howe, Det	76	31	40	71
F Mahovlich, Det	74	38	32	70
Balon, NYR	76	33	37	70
J McKenzie, Bos	72	29	41	70

Quarter-finals (best of seven): Chicago defeated Detroit, 4 games to 0.

St. Louis Blues defeated Minnesota North Stars, 4 games to 2.

Boston defeated New York Rangers, 4 games to 2.

Pittsburgh Penguins defeated Oakland, 4 games to 0.

Semi-finals (best of seven): Boston defeated Chicago, 4 games to 0.

St. Louis Blues defeated Pittsburgh, 4 games to 2.

Stanley Cup Final (best of seven): Boston defeated St. Louis Blues, 4 games to 0.

NHL 1970–71

Buffalo Sabres and Vancouver Canucks joined the NHL and were assigned to the East Division; Chicago moved to the West Division. An expansion draft was again used to stock the new clubs. Oakland Seals changed their name to California Golden Seals. Teams were obligated to wear base light-coloured sweaters at home and base dark-coloured sweaters on the road. The maximum curvature of stick blades was limited to half an inch. A new, but redundant, rule was approved, assessing a delay of game penalty for deliberately shooting the puck out of play; such a rule had already existed since 1927–28.

The playoff format was revised, matching the winners of the first-vs.-third-place series and the winners of the second-vs.-fourth-place series across divisions in best-of-seven semi-final series. The winners of each semi-final series would play a best-of-seven series for the Stanley Cup. Schedule increased to 78 games.

EAST DIVISION	W	L	T	PTS	GF	GA
Boston	57	14	7	121	399	207
New York Ran	49	18	11	109	259	177
Montreal Can*	42	23	13	97	291	216
Toronto	37	33	8	82	248	211
Buffalo	24	39	15	63	217	291
Vancouver	24	46	8	56	229	296
Detroit	22	45	11	55	209	308

WEST DIVISION	W	L	T	PTS	GF	GA
Chicago	49	20	9	107	277	184
St. Louis Blu	34	25	19	87	223	208
Philadelphia Fly	28	33	17	73	207	225
Minnesota NSt	28	34	16	72	191	223
Los Angeles	25	40	13	63	239	303
Pittsburgh Pen	21	37	20	62	221	240
California	20	53	5	45	199	320

SCORING LEADERS	GP	G	A	PTS
P Esposito, Bos	78	76	76	152
R Orr, Bos	78	37	102	139
Bucyk, Bos	78	51	65	116
K Hodge Sr., Bos	78	43	62	105
R Hull, Chi	78	44	52	96
Ullman, Tor	73	34	51	85
Cashman, Bos	77	21	58	79
J McKenzie, Bos	65	31	46	77
Keon, Tor	76	38	38	76
J Beliveau, MtrC	70	25	51	76
F Stanfield, Bos	75	24	52	76
Tkaczuk, NYR	77	26	49	75

Quarter-finals (best of seven): Montreal Canadiens defeated Boston, 4 games to 3.

Chicago defeated Philadelphia Flyers, 4 games to 0.

New York Rangers defeated Toronto, 4 games to 2.

Minnesota defeated St. Louis Blues, 4 games to 2.

Semi-finals (best of seven): Montreal Canadiens defeated Minnesota, 4 games to 0.

Chicago defeated New York Rangers, 4 games to 3.

Stanley Cup Final (best of seven): Montreal Canadiens defeated Chicago, 4 games to 3.

NHL 1971–72

Teams were allowed to dress 17 players and 2 goaltenders. A game misconduct penalty was to be assessed to a third player entering an altercation.

The playoff format was revised, matching the first- and fourth-place teams, and the second- and third-place teams, within divisions, in a best-of-seven quarter-final series; the winners of the first-vs.-fourth-place series and the winners of the second-vs.-third-place series, across divisions in a best-of-seven semi-final series. The winners of each semi-final series would play a best-of-seven series for the Stanley Cup.

EAST DIVISION	W	L	T	PTS	GF	GA
Boston*	54	13	11	119	330	204
New York Ran	48	17	13	109	317	192
Montreal Can	46	16	16	108	307	205
Toronto	33	31	14	80	209	208
Detroit	33	35	10	76	261	262
Buffalo	16	43	19	51	203	289
Vancouver	20	50	8	48	203	297

WEST DIVISION	W	L	T	PTS	GF	GA
Chicago	46	17	15	107	256	166
Minnesota NSt	37	29	12	86	212	191
St. Louis Blu	28	39	11	67	208	247
Pittsburgh Pen	26	38	14	66	220	258
Philadelphia Fly	26	38	14	66	200	236
California	21	39	18	60	216	288
Los Angeles	20	49	9	49	206	305

SCORING LEADERS	GP	G	A	PTS
P Esposito, Bos	76	66	67	133
R Orr, Bos	76	37	80	117
Ratelle, NYR	63	46	63	109
Hadfield, NYR	78	50	56	106
R Gilbert, NYR	73	43	54	97
F Mahovlich, MtrC	76	43	53	96
R Hull, Chi	78	50	43	93
Cournoyer, MtrC	73	47	36	83
Bucyk, Bos	78	32	51	83
R Clarke, PhiF	78	35	46	81
Lemaire, MtrC	77	32	49	81
F Stanfield, Bos	78	23	56	79

Quarter-finals (best of seven): Boston defeated Toronto, 4 games to 1.

Chicago defeated Pittsburgh Penguins, 4 games to 0.

New York Rangers defeated Montreal Canadiens, 4 games to 2.

St. Louis Blues defeated Minnesota North Stars, 4 games to 3.

Semi-finals (best of seven): Boston defeated St. Louis Blues, 4 games to 0.

New York Rangers defeated Chicago, 4 games to 0.

Stanley Cup Final (best of seven): Boston defeated New York Rangers, 4 games to 2.

NHL 1972–73

Prior to the season, a team of Canadian NHL All-Stars played an eight-game exhibition series against the Soviet National Team, at Montreal, Toronto, Winnipeg, Vancouver, and Moscow; the NHL All-Stars won the "Summit Series" 4 games to 3 with 1 tie.

Two more expansion clubs joined the NHL: Atlanta Flames, assigned to the West Division, and New York Islanders (based in Nassau, Long Island), assigned to the East Division. An expansion draft was again used to stock the new clubs. The minimum width of stick blades was reduced to two inches.

EAST DIVISION	W	L	T	PTS	GF	GA
Montreal Can*	52	10	16	120	329	184
Boston	51	22	5	107	330	235
New York Ran	47	23	8	102	297	208
Buffalo	37	27	14	88	257	219
Detroit	37	29	12	86	265	243
Toronto	27	41	10	64	247	279
Vancouver	22	47	9	53	233	339
New York Isl	12	60	6	30	170	347
WEST DIVISION	W	L	T	PTS	GF	GA
Chicago	42	27	9	93	284	225
Philadelphia Fly	37	30	11	85	296	256
Minnesota NSt	37	30	11	86	254	230

	W	L	T	PTS	GF	GA
St. Louis Blu	32	34	12	76	233	251
Pittsburgh Pen	32	37	9	73	257	265
Los Angeles	31	36	11	73	232	245
Atlanta Fla	25	38	15	65	191	239
California	16	46	16	48	213	323

SCORING LEADERS	GP	G	A	PTS
P Esposito, Bos	78	55	75	130
R Clarke, PhiF	78	37	67	104
R Orr, Bos	63	29	72	101
MacLeish, PhiF	78	50	50	100
Lemaire, MtrC	77	44	51	95
Ratelle, NYR	78	41	53	94
M Redmond, Det	76	52	41	93
Bucyk, Bos	78	40	53	93
F Mahovlich, MtrC	78	38	55	93
Pappin, Chi	76	41	51	92
M Dionne, Det	77	40	50	90
D Hull, Chi	78	39	51	90
H Martin, Chi	78	29	61	90

Quarter-finals (best of seven): Montreal Canadiens defeated Buffalo, 4 games to 2.

Chicago defeated St. Louis Blues, 4 games to 1.

New York Rangers defeated Boston, 4 games to 1.

Philadelphia Flyers defeated Minnesota, 4 games to 2.

Semi-finals (best of seven): Montreal Canadiens defeated Philadelphia Flyers, 4 games to 1.

Chicago defeated New York Rangers, 4 games to 1.

Stanley Cup Final (best of seven): Montreal Canadiens defeated Chicago, 4 games to 2.

WHA 1972–73

A new professional league, the World Hockey Association, was founded by Gary Davidson and Dennis Murphy; Davidson was named league president. The clubs were Alberta Oilers (based in Edmonton), Chicago Cougars, Cleveland Crusaders, Houston Aeros, Los Angeles Sharks, Minnesota Fighting Saints (based in Minneapolis), New England Whalers (based in Boston), New York Raiders, Ottawa Nationals, Philadelphia Blazers, Quebec Nordiques, and Winnipeg Jets. Teams were stocked by signing players from the NHL, minor pro leagues, amateur hockey, and Europe. The WHA rules were essentially identical to those of the NHL, but added a 10-minute sudden-death overtime to regular-season games tied at the end of 60 minutes. The schedule was 78 games. Avco World Trophy champions are designated with @.

EASTERN DIVISION	W	L	T	PTS	GF	GA
New England @	46	30	2	94	318	263
Cleveland	43	32	3	89	287	239

	W	L	T	PTS	GF	GA
Philadelphia	38	40	0	76	288	305
Ottawa Nat	35	39	4	74	279	301
Quebec	33	40	5	71	276	313
New York	33	43	2	68	303	334
WESTERN DIVISION	**W**	**L**	**T**	**PTS**	**GF**	**GA**
Winnipeg	43	31	4	90	285	249
Houston	39	35	4	82	284	269
Los Angeles	37	35	6	80	259	250
Alberta a	38	37	3	79	269	256
Minnesota a	38	37	3	79	250	269
Chicago	26	50	2	54	245	295

a Minnesota defeated Alberta, 4-2, at Calgary, in special one-game playoff for final playoff berth.

SCORING LEADERS	**GP**	**G**	**A**	**PTS**
An Lacroix, Phi	78	50	74	124
R Ward, NY	77	51	67	118
Lawson, Phi	78	61	45	106
T Webster, NE	77	53	50	103
R Hull, Wpg	63	51	52	103
Beaudin, Wpg	78	38	65	103
C Bordeleau, Hou	78	47	54	101
Caffery, NE	74	39	61	100
Labossiere, Hou	77	36	60	96
Carleton, OtwN	76	42	49	91

Quarter-finals (best of seven): New England defeated Ottawa, 4 games to 1.

Winnipeg defeated Minnesota, 4 games to 1.

Cleveland defeated Philadelphia, 4 games to 0.

Houston defeated Los Angeles, 4 games to 2.

Semi-finals (best of seven): New England defeated Cleveland, 4 games to 1.

Winnipeg defeated Houston, 4 games to 0.

Avco World Trophy Final (best of seven): New England defeated Winnipeg, 4 games to 1.

NHL 1973–74

EAST DIVISION	**W**	**L**	**T**	**PTS**	**GF**	**GA**
Boston	52	17	9	113	349	221
Montreal Can	45	24	9	99	293	240
New York Ran	40	24	14	94	300	251
Toronto	35	27	16	86	274	230
Buffalo	32	34	12	76	242	250
Detroit	29	39	10	68	255	319
Vancouver	24	43	11	59	224	296
New York Isl	19	41	18	56	182	247
WEST DIVISION	**W**	**L**	**T**	**PTS**	**GF**	**GA**
Philadelphia Fly*	50	16	12	112	273	164
Chicago	41	14	23	105	272	164

	W	L	T	PTS	GF	GA
Los Angeles	33	33	12	78	233	231
Atlanta Fla	30	34	14	74	214	238
Pittsburgh Pen	28	41	9	65	242	273
St. Louis Blu	26	40	12	64	206	248
Minnesota NSt	23	38	17	63	235	275
California	13	55	10	36	195	342

SCORING LEADERS	**GP**	**G**	**A**	**PTS**
P Esposito, Bos	78	68	77	145
R Orr, Bos	74	32	90	122
K Hodge sr, Bos	76	50	55	105
Cashman, Bos	78	30	59	89
R Clarke, PhiF	77	35	52	87
R Martin, Buf	78	52	34	86
S Apps, PitPe	75	24	61	85
D Sittler, Tor	78	38	46	84
L MacDonald, PitPe	78	43	39	82
B Park, NYR	78	25	57	82
D Hextall, Min	78	20	62	82
F Mahovlich, MtrC	71	31	49	80
Mikita, Chi	76	30	50	80

Quarter-finals (best of seven): Boston defeated Toronto, 4 games to 0.

Philadelphia Flyers defeated Atlanta Flames, 4 games to 0.

New York Rangers defeated Montreal Canadiens, 4 games to 2.

Chicago defeated Los Angeles, 4 games to 1.

Semi-finals (best of seven): Boston defeated Chicago, 4 games to 2.

Philadelphia Flyers defeated New York Rangers, 4 games to 3.

Stanley Cup Final (best of seven): Philadelphia Flyers defeated Boston, 4 games to 3.

WHA 1973–74

The New England franchise moved to Hartford but retained its name. The Philadelphia franchise moved to Vancouver, but retained its nickname. The Ottawa franchise moved to Toronto and changed its nickname to Toros. Alberta Oilers changed their name to Edmonton Oilers. New York Raiders changed their nickname to Golden Blades; midway through the season, the franchise moved to Cherry Hill, New Jersey, and changed its name to New Jersey Knights.

EASTERN DIVISION	**W**	**L**	**T**	**PTS**	**GF**	**GA**
New England	43	31	4	90	291	260
Toronto	41	33	4	86	304	272
Cleveland	37	32	9	83	266	264
Chicago	38	35	5	81	271	273

	W	L	T	PTS	GF	GA
Quebec	38	36	4	80	306	280
New York/New Jersey	32	42	4	68	268	313
WESTERN DIVISION	**W**	**L**	**T**	**PTS**	**GF**	**GA**
Houston @	48	25	5	101	318	219
Minnesota	44	32	2	90	332	275
Edmonton	38	37	3	79	268	269
Winnipeg	34	39	5	73	264	296
Vancouver	27	50	1	55	278	345
Los Angeles	25	53	0	50	239	339

SCORING LEADERS	GP	G	A	PTS
M Walton, Min	78	57	60	117
An Lacroix, NY/NJ	78	31	80	111
G Howe, Hou	70	31	69	100
R Hull, Wpg	75	53	42	95
W Connelly, Min	78	42	53	95
Carleton, Tor	76	42	49	91
Bry Campbell, Van	76	27	62	89
Lawson, Van	78	50	38	88
S Bernier, Qbc	74	37	49	86
L Lund, Hou	75	33	53	86

Quarter-finals (best of seven): Chicago defeated New England, 4 games to 3.

Houston defeated Winnipeg, 4 games to 0.

Toronto defeated Cleveland, 4 games to 1.

Minnesota defeated Edmonton, 4 games to 1.

Semi-finals (best of seven): Chicago defeated Toronto, 4 games to 3.

Houston defeated Minnesota, 4 games to 2.

Avco World Trophy Final (best of seven): Houston defeated Chicago, 4 games to 0.

NHL 1974–75

Two more expansion clubs joined the NHL: Kansas City Scouts and Washington Capitals. An expansion draft was again used to stock the new clubs.

The NHL realigned into two nine-team conferences: the Prince of Wales Conference, containing the Charles Adams and James Norris Divisions, and the Clarence Campbell Conference, containing the Lester Patrick and Conn Smythe Divisions. All-Star Game format changed from East Division vs. West Division to Prince of Wales Conference vs. Clarence Campbell Conference.

A bench minor penalty was to be imposed if a penalized player did not proceed directly to the penalty box.

Schedule increased to 80 games. Twelve teams would qualify for playoffs; division winners received first-round byes, second- and third-place clubs would be seeded and play best-of-three preliminary round.

PRINCE OF WALES CONFERENCE

ADAMS DIVISION	W	L	T	PTS	GF	GA
Buffalo	49	16	15	113	354	240
Boston	40	26	14	94	345	245
Toronto	31	33	16	78	280	309
California	19	48	13	51	212	316
NORRIS DIVISION	**W**	**L**	**T**	**PTS**	**GF**	**GA**
Montreal Can	47	14	19	113	293	181
Los Angeles	42	17	21	105	269	185
Pittsburgh Pen	37	28	15	89	326	289
Detroit	23	45	12	58	259	335
Washington	8	67	5	21	181	446

CLARENCE CAMPBELL CONFERENCE

PATRICK DIVISION	W	L	T	PTS	GF	GA
Philadelphia Fly*	51	18	11	113	293	181
New York Ran	37	29	14	88	319	276
New York Isl	33	25	22	88	264	221
Atlanta Fla	34	31	15	83	243	233
SMYTHE DIVISION	**W**	**L**	**T**	**PTS**	**GF**	**GA**
Vancouver	38	32	10	86	271	254
St. Louis Blu	35	31	14	84	269	267
Chicago	37	35	8	82	268	241
Minnesota NSt	23	50	7	53	221	341
Kansas City	15	54	11	41	184	328

SCORING LEADERS	GP	G	A	PTS
R Orr, Bos	80	46	89	135
P Esposito, Bos	79	61	66	127
M Dionne, Det	80	47	74	121
G Lafleur, MtrC	70	53	66	119
P Mahovlich, MtrC	80	35	82	117
R Clarke, PhiF	80	27	89	116
R Robert, Buf	74	40	60	100
R Gilbert, NYR	76	36	61	97
G Perreault, Buf	68	39	57	96
R Martin, Buf	68	52	43	95
Lemaire, MtrC	80	36	56	92
Ratelle, NYR	79	36	55	91

Preliminaries (best of three): Toronto defeated Los Angeles, 2 games to 1.

Chicago defeated Boston, 2 games to 1.

Pittsburgh Penguins defeated St. Louis Blues, 2 games to 0.

New York Islanders defeated New York Rangers, 2 games to 1.

Quarter-finals (best of seven): Buffalo defeated Chicago, 4 games to 1.

Philadelphia Flyers defeated Toronto, 4 games to 0.

Montreal Canadiens defeated Vancouver, 4 games to 1.

New York Islanders defeated Pittsburgh Penguins, 4 games to 3.

Semi-finals (best of seven): Buffalo defeated Montreal Canadiens, 4 games to 2.

Philadelphia Flyers defeated New York Islanders, 4 games to 3.
Stanley Cup Final (best of seven): Philadelphia Flyers defeated Buffalo, 4 games to 2.

WHA 1974–75

Prior to the season, a team of WHA All-Stars played an eight-game exhibition series against the Soviet National Team, at Quebec, Toronto, Winnipeg, Vancouver, and Moscow; the Soviets won the "International Series" 4 games to 1 with 3 ties.

Two new expansion clubs joined the WHA: Indianapolis Racers and Phoenix Roadrunners. An expansion draft was used to stock the new clubs. The New Jersey franchise moved to San Diego and changed its nickname to Mariners. The Los Angeles franchise moved to Detroit and changed its name to Michigan Stags; midway through the season, the Michigan franchise moved to Baltimore and changed its nickname to Blades.

EASTERN DIVISION	W	L	T	PTS	GF	GA
New England	43	30	5	91	274	279
Cleveland	35	40	3	73	236	258
Chicago	30	47	1	61	261	312
Indianapolis	18	57	3	39	216	338
WESTERN DIVISION	W	L	T	PTS	GF	GA
Houston @	53	25	0	106	369	247
San Diego	43	31	4	90	326	268
Minnesota	42	33	3	87	308	279
Phoenix	39	31	8	86	300	265
Michigan/Baltimore	21	53	4	46	205	341
CANADIAN DIVISION	W	L	T	PTS	GF	GA
Quebec	46	32	0	92	331	299
Toronto	43	33	2	88	349	304
Winnipeg	38	35	5	81	332	293
Vancouver	37	39	2	76	256	270
Edmonton	36	38	4	76	279	279

SCORING LEADERS	GP	G	A	PTS
An Lacroix, SD	78	41	106	147
R Hull, Wpg	78	77	65	142
S Bernier, Qbc	76	54	68	122
U Nilsson, Wpg	78	26	94	120
L Lund, Hou	78	33	75	108
W Rivers, SD	78	54	53	107
Hedberg, Wpg	65	53	47	100
G Howe, Hou	75	34	65	99
W Dillon, Tor	77	29	66	95
M Walton, Min	75	48	45	93
Houle, Qbc	64	40	52	92
M Tardif, Qbc	76	50	39	89

Quarter-finals (best of seven): Quebec defeated Phoenix, 4 games to 1.
Minnesota defeated New England, 4 games to 2.
Houston defeated Cleveland, 4 games to 1.
San Diego defeated Toronto, 4 games to 2.
Semi-finals (best of seven): Quebec defeated Minnesota, 4 games to 2.
Houston defeated San Diego, 4 games to 0.
Avco World Trophy Final (best of seven): Houston defeated Quebec, 4 games to 0.

NHL 1975–76

NHL teams played an eight-game mid-season exhibition series, called Super Series 76, against touring Soviet teams, going 1-3-1 against Soviet Central Army and 1-2-0 against Wings of the Soviet.

PRINCE OF WALES CONFERENCE						
ADAMS DIVISION	W	L	T	PTS	GF	GA
Boston	48	15	17	113	313	237
Buffalo	46	21	13	105	339	240
Toronto	34	31	15	83	294	276
California	27	42	11	65	250	278
NORRIS DIVISION	W	L	T	PTS	GF	GA
Montreal Can*	58	11	11	127	337	174
Los Angeles	38	33	9	85	263	265
Pittsburgh Pen	35	33	12	82	339	303
Detroit	26	44	10	62	226	300
Washington	11	59	10	32	224	394
CLARENCE CAMPBELL CONFERENCE						
PATRICK DIVISION	W	L	T	PTS	GF	GA
Philadelphia Fly	51	13	16	118	348	209
New York Isl	42	21	17	101	297	190
Atlanta Fla	35	33	12	82	262	237
New York Ran	29	42	9	67	262	333
SMYTHE DIVISION	W	L	T	PTS	GF	GA
Chicago	32	30	18	82	254	261
Vancouver	33	32	15	81	271	272
St. Louis Blu	29	37	14	72	249	290
Minnesota NSt	20	53	7	47	195	303
Kansas City	12	56	12	36	190	351

SCORING LEADERS	GP	G	A	PTS
G Lafleur, MtrC	80	56	69	125
R Clarke, PhiF	76	30	89	119
G Perreault, Buf	80	44	69	113
W Barber, PhiF	80	50	62	112
Larouche, PitPe	76	53	58	111
Ratelle, NYR-Bos	80	36	69	105
P Mahovlich, MtrC	80	34	71	105
J Pronovost, PitPe	80	52	52	104
D Sittler, Tor	79	41	59	100
S Apps, PitPe	80	32	67	99

SCORING LEADERS	GP	G	A	PTS
Potvin, NYI	78	31	67	98
B Trottier, NYI	80	32	63	95

Preliminaries (best of three): Buffalo defeated St. Louis Blues, 2 games to 1.

New York Islanders defeated Vancouver, 2 games to 0.

Toronto defeated Pittsburgh Penguins, 2 games to 1.

Los Angeles defeated Atlanta Flames, 2 games to 0.

Quarter-finals (best of seven): Boston defeated Los Angeles, 4 games to 3.

Philadelphia Flyers defeated Toronto, 4 games to 3.

Montreal Canadiens defeated Chicago, 4 games to 0.

New York Islanders defeated Buffalo, 4 games to 2.

Semi-finals (best of seven): Montreal Canadiens defeated New York Islanders, 4 games to 2.

Philadelphia Flyers defeated Boston, 4 games to 1.

Stanley Cup Final (best of seven): Montreal Canadiens defeated Philadelphia Flyers, 4 games to 0.

WHA 1975–76

The Baltimore and Chicago franchises dropped out of the WHA. Two new expansion clubs joined the league: Cincinnati Stingers and Denver Spurs. An expansion draft was used to stock the new clubs. The Vancouver franchise moved to Calgary and changed its nickname to Cowboys. Early in the season, the Denver franchise moved to Ottawa and changed its nickname to Civics. Midway through the season, the Ottawa franchise folded and dropped out of the WHA. Five weeks later, the Minnesota franchise folded and dropped out of the WHA.

Schedule increased to 80 games, but the mid-season withdrawal of two clubs forced four of the remaining clubs to play 81 games.

EASTERN DIVISION	W	L	T	PTS	GF	GA
Indianapolis	35	39	6	76	245	247
Cleveland	35	40	5	75	273	279
New England	33	40	7	73	255	290
Cincinnati	35	44	1	71	285	340
WESTERN DIVISION	**W**	**L**	**T**	**PTS**	**GF**	**GA**
Houston	53	27	0	106	341	263
Phoenix	39	35	6	84	302	287
San Diego	36	38	6	78	303	290
Minnesota #	30	25	4	64	211	212
Denver/Ottawa Civ#	14	26	1	29	134	172
CANADIAN DIVISION	**W**	**L**	**T**	**PTS**	**GF**	**GA**
Winnipeg @	52	27	2	106	345	254
Quebec	50	27	4	104	371	316
Calgary	41	35	4	86	307	282
Edmonton	27	49	5	59	268	345
Toronto	24	52	5	53	335	398

Franchise folded during season.

SCORING LEADERS	GP	G	A	PTS
M Tardif, Qbc	81	71	77	148
R Hull, Wpg	80	53	70	123
Rea Cloutier, Qbc	80	60	54	114
U Nilsson, Wpg	78	38	76	114
Ftorek, Phx	80	41	72	113
C Bordeleau, Qbc	74	37	72	109
Hedberg, Wpg	76	50	55	105
Houle, Qbc	81	51	52	103
S Bernier, Qbc	70	34	68	102
G Howe, Hou	78	32	70	102
An Lacroix, SD	80	29	72	101
Nedomansky, Tor	81	56	42	98

Preliminaries (best of five): New England defeated Cleveland, 3 games to 0.

San Diego defeated Phoenix, 3 games to 2.

Quarter-finals (best of seven): Winnipeg defeated Edmonton, 4 games to 0.

New England defeated Indianapolis, 4 games to 3.

Houston defeated San Diego, 4 games to 2.

Calgary defeated Quebec, 4 games to 1.

Semi-finals (best of seven): Winnipeg defeated Calgary, 4 games to 1.

Houston defeated New England, 4 games to 3.

Avco World Trophy Final (best of seven): Winnipeg defeated Houston, 4 games to 0.

NHL 1976–77

The California franchise moved to Cleveland and changed its nickname to Barons. The Kansas City franchise moved to Denver and changed their name to Colorado Rockies.

A game misconduct penalty was to be assessed to a player who was the instigator in a fight.

PRINCE OF WALES CONFERENCE						
ADAMS DIVISION	**W**	**L**	**T**	**PTS**	**GF**	**GA**
Boston	49	23	8	106	312	240
Buffalo	48	24	8	104	301	220
Toronto	33	32	15	81	301	285
Cleveland	25	42	13	63	240	292
NORRIS DIVISION	**W**	**L**	**T**	**PTS**	**GF**	**GA**
Montreal Can*	60	8	12	132	387	171
Los Angeles	34	31	15	83	271	241
Pittsburgh Pen	34	33	13	81	240	252
Washington	24	42	14	62	221	307
Detroit	16	55	9	41	183	309
CLARENCE CAMPBELL CONFERENCE						
PATRICK DIVISION	**W**	**L**	**T**	**PTS**	**GF**	**GA**
Philadelphia Fly	48	16	16	112	323	213
New York Isl	47	21	12	106	288	193
Atlanta Fla	34	34	12	80	264	265
New York Ran	29	37	14	72	272	310

SMYTHE DIVISION	W	L	T	PTS	GF	GA
St. Louis Blu	32	39	9	73	239	276
Minnesota NSt	23	39	18	64	240	310
Chicago	26	43	11	63	240	298
Vancouver	25	42	13	63	235	294
Colorado Rck	20	46	14	54	226	307

SCORING LEADERS	GP	G	A	PTS
G Lafleur, MtrC	80	56	80	136
M Dionne, LA	80	53	69	122
S Shutt, MtrC	80	60	45	105
MacLeish, PhiF	79	49	48	97
G Perreault, Buf	80	39	56	95
T Young, MinNS	80	29	66	95
Ratelle, Bos	78	33	61	94
L McDonald, Tor	80	46	44	90
D Sittler, Tor	73	38	52	90
R Clarke, PhiF	80	27	63	90
P McNab, Bos	80	38	48	86
Goring, LA	78	30	55	85
L Robinson, MtrC	77	19	66	85

Preliminaries (best of three): Buffalo defeated Minnesota North Stars, 2 games to 0.

New York Islanders defeated Chicago, 2 games to 0.

Toronto defeated Pittsburgh Penguins, 2 games to 1.

Los Angeles defeated Atlanta Flames, 2 games to 0.

Quarter-finals (best of seven): Boston defeated Los Angeles, 4 games to 2.

Philadelphia Flyers defeated Toronto, 4 games to 2.

Montreal Canadiens defeated St. Louis Blues, 4 games to 0.

New York Islanders defeated Buffalo, 4 games to 0.

Semi-finals (best of seven): Montreal Canadiens defeated New York Islanders, 4 games to 2.

Boston defeated Philadelphia Flyers, 4 games to 0.

Stanley Cup Final (best of seven): Montreal Canadiens defeated Boston, 4 games to 0.

WHA 1976–77

The Toronto franchise moved to Birmingham, Alabama, and changed its nickname to Bulls. The Cleveland franchise suspended operations, and its players were distributed to the other clubs; the franchise was moved to St. Paul, reactivated, changed its name to Minnesota Fighting Saints, and was stocked with most of the players who had performed for the earlier Minnesota franchise the previous season. Midway through the season, the new Minnesota franchise dropped out of the WHA.

Schedule remained at 80 games, but the mid-season withdrawal of one club forced eight of the remaining clubs to play 81 games.

EASTERN DIVISION	W	L	T	PTS	GF	GA
Quebec @	47	31	3	97	353	295
Cincinnati	39	37	5	83	354	303
Indianapolis	36	37	8	80	276	305
New England	35	40	6	76	275	290
Birmingham	31	46	4	66	289	309
Minnesota #	19	18	5	43	136	129

WESTERN DIVISION	W	L	T	PTS	GF	GA
Houston	50	24	6	106	320	241
Winnipeg	46	32	2	94	366	291
San Diego	40	37	4	84	284	283
Edmonton	34	43	4	72	243	304
Calgary	31	43	7	69	252	296
Phoenix	28	48	4	60	281	383

\# Franchise folded during season.

SCORING LEADERS	GP	G	A	PTS
Rea Cloutier, Qbc	76	66	75	141
Hedberg, Wpg	68	70	61	131
U Nilsson, Wpg	71	39	85	124
Ftorek, Phx	80	46	71	117
An Lacroix, SD	81	32	82	114
M Tardif, Qbc	62	49	60	109
R Leduc, Cin	81	52	55	107
C Bordeleau, Qbc	72	32	75	107
Stoughton, Cin	81	52	52	104
Napier, Bir	80	60	36	96
D Sobchuk, Cin	81	44	52	96
S Bernier, Qbc	74	43	53	96

Quarter-finals (best of seven): Quebec defeated New England, 4 games to 1.

Houston defeated Edmonton, 4 games to 1.

Indianapolis defeated Cincinnati, 4 games to 0.

Winnipeg defeated San Diego, 4 games to 3.

Semi-finals (best of seven): Quebec defeated Indianapolis, 4 games to 1.

Winnipeg defeated Houston, 4 games to 2.

Avco World Trophy Final (best of seven): Quebec defeated Winnipeg, 4 games to 3.

NHL 1977–78

John A. Ziegler Jr. was elected NHL president after the retirement of Clarence Campbell.

Teams challenging the legality of an opponent's stick were to be assessed a minor penalty if the stick was found to be legal.

NHL teams played a five-game mid-season exhibition series, called Super Series 78, against a touring Soviet team, Spartak Moscow, going 2-3-0.

ADAMS DIVISION	W	L	T	PTS	GF	GA
Boston	51	18	11	113	333	218
Buffalo	44	19	17	105	288	215
Toronto	41	29	10	92	271	237
Cleveland	22	45	13	57	230	325

NORRIS DIVISION	W	L	T	PTS	GF	GA
Montreal Can*	59	10	11	129	359	183
Detroit	32	34	14	78	252	266
Los Angeles	31	34	15	77	243	245
Pittsburgh Pen	25	37	18	68	254	321
Washington	17	49	14	48	195	321

CLARENCE CAMPBELL CONFERENCE

PATRICK DIVISION	W	L	T	PTS	GF	GA
New York Isl	48	17	15	111	334	210
Philadelphia Fly	45	20	15	105	296	200
Atlanta Fla	34	27	19	87	274	252
New York Ran	30	37	13	73	279	280

SMYTHE DIVISION	W	L	T	PTS	GF	GA
Chicago	32	29	19	83	230	220
Colorado Rck	19	40	21	59	257	305
Vancouver	20	43	17	57	239	320
St. Louis Blu	20	47	13	53	195	304
Minnesota NSt	18	53	9	45	218	325

SCORING LEADERS	GP	G	A	PTS
G Lafleur, MtrC	79	60	72	132
B Trottier, NYI	77	46	77	123
D Sittler, Tor	80	45	72	117
Lemaire, MtrC	76	36	61	97
D Potvin, NYI	80	30	64	94
Bossy, NYI	73	53	38	91
T O'Reilly, Bos	77	29	61	90
G Perreault, Buf	79	41	48	89
R Clarke, PhiF	71	21	68	89
L McDonald, Tor	74	47	40	87
W Paiement, ColR	80	31	56	87
S Shutt, MtrC	80	49	37	86
Gillies, NYI	80	35	50	85

Preliminaries (best of three): Buffalo defeated New York Rangers, 2 games to 1.

Philadelphia Flyers defeated Colorado Rockies, 2 games to 0.

Toronto defeated Los Angeles, 2 games to 1.

Detroit defeated Atlanta Flames, 2 games to 0.

Quarter-finals (best of seven): Boston defeated Chicago, 4 games to 0.

Philadelphia Flyers defeated Buffalo, 4 games to 1.

Montreal Canadiens defeated Detroit, 4 games to 1.

Toronto defeated New York Islanders, 4 games to 3.

Semi-finals (best of seven): Montreal Canadiens defeated Toronto, 4 games to 0.

Boston defeated Philadelphia Flyers, 4 games to 1.

Stanley Cup Final (best of seven): Montreal Canadiens defeated Boston, 4 games to 2.

WHA 1977–78

The Calgary, Phoenix, and San Diego franchises dropped out of the WHA. During the season, both Czechoslovakia and the Soviet national "B" team played one game against each WHA club, the result of which counted in the standings.

WHA teams also played mid-season exhibition games against touring Soviet and European teams, going 1-5-0 against the Soviet national team, 0-2-0 against the Soviet national "B" team, 4-1-0 against Sweden, and 2-3-0 against Finland.

	W	L	T	PTS	GF	GA
Winnipeg @	50	28	2	102	381	270
New England	44	31	5	93	335	269
Houston	42	34	4	88	296	302
Quebec	40	37	3	83	349	347
Edmonton	38	39	3	79	309	307
Birmingham	36	41	3	75	287	314
Cincinnati	35	42	3	73	298	332
Indianapolis	24	51	5	53	267	353
Soviet "B"	3	4	1	7	27	36
Czechoslovakia	1	6	1	3	21	40

SCORING LEADERS	GP	G	A	PTS
M Tardif, Qbc	78	65	89	154
Rea Cloutier, Qbc	73	56	73	129
U Nilsson, Wpg	73	37	89	126
Hedberg, Wpg	77	63	59	122
R Hull, Wpg	77	46	71	117
An Lacroix, Hou	78	36	77	113
Ftorek, Phx	80	59	50	109
K Nilsson, Wpg	80	42	65	107
G Howe, NE	76	34	62	96
Mk Howe, NE	70	30	61	91

Preliminaries (best of seven): Winnipeg defeated Birmingham, 4 games to 1.

New England defeated Edmonton, 4 games to 1.

Quebec defeated Houston, 4 games to 2.

Semi-final (best of seven): New England defeated Quebec, 4 games to 1.

Avco World Trophy Final (best of seven): Winnipeg defeated New England, 4 games to 0.

NHL 1978–79

The Cleveland and Minnesota franchises merged; the contracts of all Cleveland players were bought by

Appendix

Minnesota, and the franchise would play all home games in Minneapolis and be transferred to the Adams Division.

The minimum age of players eligible for the amateur draft was lowered to 19.

The NHL All-Star Game was replaced for this season by the best-of-three Challenge Cup series between Team NHL and the Soviet Union, played at New York; the Soviets defeated the NHL 2 games to 1. NHL teams also played a four-game mid-season exhibition series, called Super Series 79, against a touring Soviet team, Wings of the Soviet, going 1-2-1.

PRINCE OF WALES CONFERENCE

ADAMS DIVISION	W	L	T	PTS	GF	GA
Boston	43	23	14	100	316	270
Buffalo	36	28	16	88	280	263
Toronto	34	33	13	81	267	252
Minnesota NSt	28	40	12	68	257	289

NORRIS DIVISION	W	L	T	PTS	GF	GA
Montreal Can*	52	17	11	115	337	204
Pittsburgh Pen	36	31	13	85	281	279
Los Angeles	34	34	12	80	292	286
Washington	24	41	15	63	273	338
Detroit	23	41	16	62	252	295

CLARENCE CAMPBELL CONFERENCE

PATRICK DIVISION	W	L	T	PTS	GF	GA
New York Isl	51	15	14	116	358	214
Philadelphia Fly	40	25	15	95	281	248
New York Ran	40	29	11	91	316	292
Atlanta Fla	41	31	8	90	327	280

SMYTHE DIVISION	W	L	T	PTS	GF	GA
Chicago	29	35	15	73	244	277
Vancouver	25	42	13	63	217	291
St. Louis Blu	18	50	12	48	249	348
Colorado Rck	15	53	12	42	210	331

SCORING LEADERS	GP	G	A	PTS
B Trottier, NYI	76	47	87	134
M Dionne, LA	80	59	71	130
G Lafleur, MtrC	80	52	77	129
Bossy, NYI	80	69	57	126
R MacMillan, AtlF	79	37	71	108
Gy Chouinard, AtlF	80	50	57	107
D Potvin, NYI	73	31	70	101
B Federko, StLB	74	31	64	95
D Taylor, LA	78	43	48	91
Gillies, NYI	75	35	56	91
Maruk, MinNS-Was	78	31	59	90
D Sittler, Tor	70	36	51	87
Goring, LA	80	36	51	87

Preliminaries (best of three): Pittsburgh Penguins defeated Buffalo, 2 games to 1.

Philadelphia Flyers defeated Vancouver, 2 games to 1.

New York Rangers defeated Los Angeles, 2 games to 0.

Toronto defeated Atlanta Flames, 2 games to 0.

Quarter-finals (best of seven): Boston defeated Pittsburgh Penguins, 4 games to 0.

New York Islanders defeated Chicago, 4 games to 0.

Montreal Canadiens defeated Toronto, 4 games to 1.

New York Rangers defeated Philadelphia Flyers, 4 games to 1.

Semi-finals (best of seven): Montreal Canadiens defeated Boston, 4 games to 3.

New York Rangers defeated New York Islanders, 4 games to 2.

Stanley Cup Final (best of seven): Montreal Canadiens defeated New York Rangers, 4 games to 1.

WHA 1978-79

The Houston franchise dropped out of the WHA. Early in the season, the Indianapolis franchise dropped out of the WHA.

Both Czechoslovakia and a Soviet all-star team played one game against each remaining WHA club, the results of which counted in the standings. A game between Edmonton and touring Finland also counted.

The annual WHA all-star game was replaced by a three-game series between a WHA all-star team and Dynamo Moscow, the WHA team winning 3 games to 0. WHA teams also played mid-season exhibition games against touring Soviet and European teams, going 3-1-0 against Dynamo Moscow, 3-0-0 against Sweden, and 1-1-0 against Finland.

EASTERN DIVISION	W	L	T	PTS	GF	GA
Edmonton	48	30	2	98	340	266
Quebec	41	34	5	87	288	271
Winnipeg @	39	35	6	84	307	306
New England	37	34	9	83	298	287
Cincinnati	33	41	6	72	274	284
Birmingham	32	42	6	70	286	311
Indianapolis #	5	18	2	12	78	130
Soviet Union	4	1	1	9	27	20
Czechoslovakia	1	4	1	3	14	33
Finland	0	1	0	0	4	8

\# Franchise folded during season.

SCORING LEADERS	GP	G	A	PTS
Rea Cloutier, Qbc	77	75	54	129
Ftorek, Phx	80	39	77	116
W Gretzky, Ind-Edm	60	46	64	110
Mk Howe, NE	77	42	65	107
K Nilsson, Wpg	78	39	68	107
M Lukowich, Wpg	80	65	34	99
M Tardif, Qbc	74	41	55	96
An Lacroix, Hou	78	32	56	88

SCORING LEADERS	GP	G	A	PTS
P Sullivan, Wpg	80	46	40	86
Ruskowski, Wpg	75	20	66	86

Preliminary (best of three): New England defeated Cincinnati, 2 games to 1.
Semi-finals (best of seven): Edmonton defeated New England, 4 games to 3.

Winnipeg defeated Quebec, 4 games to 0.
Avco World Trophy Final (best of seven): Winnipeg defeated Edmonton, 4 games to 2.

NHL 1979–80

The WHA folded, again leaving the NHL as the only professional major league. Four of the WHA franchises – Edmonton Oilers, New England Whalers, Quebec Nordiques, and Winnipeg Jets – joined the NHL. The four ex-WHA clubs were allowed to keep two skaters and two goaltenders, but the contracts of the rest of their players reverted to the NHL clubs that last held them, as did the contracts of those players who had been employed by the two disbanded WHA clubs. An expansion draft was then used to stock the four ex-WHA clubs. The New England Whalers changed the team's name to Hartford Whalers.

Helmets were made mandatory equipment for any new player, but left optional for players with NHL experience. The minimum age of players eligible for the amateur draft was lowered to 18.

NHL teams played a nine-game mid-season exhibition series, called Super Series 80, against touring Soviet teams, going 2-3-0 against Soviet Central Army and 1-2-1 against Dynamo Moscow. Preliminary round playoff series changed to best-of-five format. The NHL retained its two-conference, four-division structure, but the new schedule was balanced, and playoff positions were awarded to the 16 teams with the highest point totals, regardless of division. In effect, the divisional structure was irrelevant, and to reflect the reality of the situation, the standings appear as presented below, with divisional assignment indicated in an additional column.

Appendix

	D	W	L	T	PTS	GF	GA
Philadelphia Fly	P	48	12	20	116	327	254
Buffalo	A	47	17	16	110	318	201
Montreal Can	N	47	20	13	107	328	240
Boston	A	46	21	13	105	310	234
New York Isl*	P	39	28	13	91	281	247
Minnesota NSt	A	36	28	16	88	311	253
Chicago	S	34	27	19	87	241	250
New York Ran	P	38	32	10	86	308	284
Atlanta Fla	P	35	32	13	83	282	269
St. Louis Blu	S	34	34	12	80	266	278
Toronto	A	35	40	5	75	304	327
Los Angeles	N	30	36	14	74	290	313

	D	W	L	T	PTS	GF	GA
Pittsburgh Pen	N	30	37	13	73	251	303
Hartford	N	27	34	19	73	303	312
Vancouver	S	27	37	16	70	256	281
Edmonton	S	28	39	13	69	301	322
Washington	P	27	40	13	67	261	293
Detroit	N	26	43	11	63	268	306
Quebec Nor	A	25	44	11	61	248	313
Winnipeg	S	20	49	11	51	214	314
Colorado Rck	S	19	48	13	51	234	308

D – Divisional affiliation
A – Adams Division
N – Norris Division
P – Patrick Division
S – Smythe Division

SCORING LEADERS	GP	G	A	PTS
M Dionne, LA	80	53	84	137
W Gretzky, Edm	79	51	86	137
G Lafleur, MtrC	74	50	75	125
G Perreault, Buf	80	40	66	106
M Rogers, Har	80	44	61	105
B Trottier, NYI	78	42	62	104
Simmer, LA	64	56	45	101
Stoughton, Har	80	56	44	100
D Sittler, Tor	73	40	57	97
Bl MacDonald, Edm	80	46	48	94
B Federko, StLB	79	38	56	94
A MacAdam, MinNS	80	42	51	93
K Nilsson, AtlF	80	40	53	93
Bossy, NYI	75	51	41	92
Middleton, Bos	80	40	52	92

Preliminaries (best of five): Philadelphia Flyers defeated Edmonton, 3 games to 0.

Buffalo defeated Vancouver, 3 games to 1.
Montreal Canadiens defeated Hartford, 3 games to 0.
Boston defeated Pittsburgh Penguins, 3 games to 2.
New York Islanders defeated Los Angeles, 3 games to 1.
Minnesota North Stars defeated Toronto, 3 games to 0.
Chicago defeated St. Louis Blues, 3 games to 0.
New York Rangers defeated Atlanta Flames, 3 games to 1.
Quarter-finals (best of seven): Philadelphia Flyers defeated New York Rangers, 4 games to 1.

Buffalo defeated Chicago, 4 games to 0.
Minnesota North Stars defeated Montreal Canadiens, 4 games to 3.
New York Islanders defeated Boston, 4 games to 1.
Semi-finals (best of seven): Philadelphia Flyers defeated Minnesota North Stars, 4 games to 1.

New York Islanders defeated Buffalo, 4 games to 2.
Stanley Cup Final (best of seven): New York Islanders defeated Philadelphia Flyers, 4 games to 2.

NHL 1980–81

The Atlanta franchise moved to Calgary but retained its nickname.

The maximum length for sticks was increased to 58 inches.

	D	W	L	T	PTS	GF	GA
New York Isl*	P	48	18	14	110	355	260
St. Louis Blu	S	45	18	17	107	352	281
Montreal Can	N	45	22	13	103	332	232
Los Angeles	N	43	24	13	99	337	290
Buffalo	A	39	20	21	99	327	250
Philadelphia Fly	P	41	24	15	97	313	249
Calgary	P	39	27	14	92	329	298
Boston	A	37	30	13	87	316	272
Minnesota NSt	A	35	28	17	87	291	263
Chicago	S	31	33	16	78	304	315
Quebec Nor	A	30	32	18	78	314	318
Vancouver	S	28	32	20	76	289	301
New York Ran	P	30	36	14	74	312	317
Edmonton	S	29	35	16	74	328	327
Pittsburgh Pen	N	30	37	13	73	302	345
Toronto	A	28	37	15	71	322	367
Washington	P	26	36	18	70	286	317
Hartford	N	21	41	18	60	292	372
Colorado Rck	S	22	45	13	57	258	344
Detroit	N	19	43	18	56	252	339
Winnipeg	S	9	57	14	32	246	400

SCORING LEADERS	GP	G	A	PTS
W Gretzky, Edm	80	55	109	164
M Dionne, LA	80	58	77	135
K Nilsson, AtlF	80	49	82	131
Bossy, NYI	79	68	51	119
D Taylor, LA	72	47	65	112
P Stastny, QbcN	77	39	70	109
Simmer, LA	65	56	49	105
M Rogers, Har	80	40	65	105
B Federko, StLB	78	31	73	104
J Richard, QbcN	78	52	51	103
Middleton, Bos	80	44	59	103
B Trottier, NYI	73	31	72	103
Maruk, Was	80	50	47	97
W Paiement, Tor	77	40	57	97

Preliminaries (best of five): New York Islanders defeated Toronto, 3 games to 0.

St. Louis Blues defeated Pittsburgh Penguins, 3 games to 2.

Edmonton defeated Montreal Canadiens, 3 games to 0.
New York Rangers defeated Los Angeles, 3 games to 1.
Buffalo defeated Vancouver, 3 games to 0.
Philadelphia Flyers defeated Quebec Nordiques, 3 games to 2.

Calgary defeated Chicago, 3 games to 0.

Minnesota North Stars defeated Boston, 3 games to 0.

Quarter-finals (best of seven): New York Islanders defeated Edmonton, 4 games to 2.

New York Rangers defeated St. Louis Blues, 4 games to 2.
Minnesota North Stars defeated Buffalo, 4 games to 1.
Calgary defeated Philadelphia Flyers, 4 games to 3.

Semi-finals (best of seven): New York Islanders defeated New York Rangers, 4 games to 0.

Minnesota North Stars defeated Calgary, 4 games to 2.

Stanley Cup Final (best of seven): New York Islanders defeated Minnesota North Stars, 4 games to 1.

NHL 1981–82

The league returned to an unbalanced schedule and realigned teams within divisions.

PRINCE OF WALES CONFERENCE

ADAMS DIVISION	W	L	T	PTS	GF	GA
Montreal Can	46	17	17	109	360	223
Boston	43	27	10	96	323	285
Buffalo	39	26	15	93	307	273
Quebec Nor	33	31	16	82	356	345
Hartford	21	41	18	60	264	351

PATRICK DIVISION	W	L	T	PTS	GF	GA
New York Isl*	54	16	10	118	385	250
New York Ran	39	27	14	92	316	306
Philadelphia Fly	38	31	11	87	325	313
Pittsburgh Pen	31	36	13	75	310	337
Washington	26	41	13	65	319	338

PRINCE OF WALES CONFERENCE

NORRIS DIVISION	W	L	T	PTS	GF	GA
Minnesota NSt	37	23	20	94	346	288
Winnipeg	33	33	14	80	319	332
St. Louis Blu	32	40	8	72	315	349
Chicago	30	38	12	72	332	363
Toronto	20	44	16	56	298	380
Detroit	21	47	12	54	270	351

SMYTHE DIVISION	W	L	T	PTS	GF	GA
Edmonton	48	17	15	111	346	288
Vancouver	30	33	17	77	290	286
Calgary	29	34	17	75	334	345
Los Angeles	24	41	15	63	314	369
Colorado Rck	18	49	13	49	241	362

SCORING LEADERS	GP	G	A	PTS
W Gretzky, Edm	80	92	120	212
Bossy, NYI	80	64	83	147
P Stastny, QbcN	80	46	93	139
Maruk, Was	80	60	76	136
B Trottier, NYI	80	50	79	129
D Savard, Chi	80	32	87	119
M Dionne, LA	78	50	67	117
Rb Smith, Min	80	43	71	114

SCORING LEADERS	GP	G	A	PTS
Ciccarelli, Min	76	55	51	106
D Taylor, LA	78	39	67	106
G Anderson, Edm	80	38	67	105
Hawerchuk, Wpg	80	45	58	103
M Rogers, NYR	80	38	65	103
N Broten, Min	73	38	60	98

Preliminaries (best of five): Quebec Nordiques defeated Montreal Canadiens, 3 games to 2.

New York Islanders defeated Pittsburgh Penguins, 3 games to 2.

New York Rangers defeated Philadelphia Flyers, 3 games to 1.

Chicago defeated Minnesota North Stars, 3 games to 1.

St. Louis Blues defeated Winnipeg, 3 games to 1.

Los Angeles defeated Edmonton, 3 games to 2.

Vancouver defeated Calgary, 3 games to 0.

Quarter-finals (best of seven): Quebec Nordiques defeated Boston, 4 games to 3.

New York Islanders defeated New York Rangers, 4 games to 2.

Chicago defeated St. Louis Blues, 4 games to 2.

Vancouver defeated Los Angeles, 4 games to 1.

Semi-finals (best of seven): New York Islanders defeated Quebec Nordiques, 4 games to 0.

Vancouver defeated Chicago, 4 games to 1.

Stanley Cup Final (best of seven): New York Islanders defeated Vancouver, 4 games to 0.

NHL 1982–83

The Colorado franchise moved to East Rutherford, New Jersey, and changed its name to New Jersey Devils; the club was reassigned to the Patrick Division. Winnipeg were reassigned to the Smythe Division.

Teams were permitted to dress 18 skaters and 2 goaltenders.

NHL teams played a six-game mid-season exhibition series, called Super Series 83, against a touring Soviet all-star team, going 2-4-0.

PRINCE OF WALES CONFERENCE

ADAMS DIVISION	W	L	T	PTS	GF	GA
Boston	50	20	10	110	327	228
Montreal Can	42	24	14	98	350	286
Buffalo	38	29	13	89	318	285
Quebec Nor	34	34	12	80	343	336
Hartford	19	54	7	45	261	403

PATRICK DIVISION	W	L	T	PTS	GF	GA
Philadelphia Fly	49	23	8	106	326	240
New York Isl*	42	26	12	96	302	226

	W	L	T	PTS	GF	GA
Washington	39	25	16	94	306	283
New York Ran	35	35	10	80	306	287
New Jersey	17	49	14	48	230	338
Pittsburgh Pen	18	53	9	45	257	394

PRINCE OF WALES CONFERENCE

NORRIS DIVISION	W	L	T	PTS	GF	GA
Chicago	47	23	10	104	338	268
Minnesota NSt	40	24	16	96	321	290
Toronto	28	40	12	68	293	330
St. Louis Blu	25	40	15	65	285	316
Detroit	21	44	15	57	263	344

SMYTHE DIVISION	W	L	T	PTS	GF	GA
Edmonton	47	21	12	106	424	315
Calgary	32	34	14	78	321	317
Vancouver	30	35	15	75	303	309
Winnipeg	33	39	8	74	311	333
Los Angeles	27	41	12	66	308	365

SCORING LEADERS	GP	G	A	PTS
W Gretzky, Edm	80	71	125	196
P Stastny, QbcN	75	47	77	124
D Savard, Chi	78	35	86	121
Bossy, NYI	79	60	58	118
M Dionne, LA	80	56	51	107
Pederson, Bos	77	46	61	107
Mk Messier, Edm	77	48	58	106
Goulet, QbcN	80	57	48	105
G Anderson, Edm	72	48	56	104
K Nilsson, Clg	80	46	58	104
Kurri, Edm	80	45	59	104
L McDonald, Clg	80	66	32	98
Middleton, Bos	80	49	47	96
Coffey, Edm	80	29	67	96

Preliminaries (best of five): Boston defeated Quebec Nordiques, 3 games to 1.

Buffalo defeated Montreal Canadiens, 3 games to 0.

New York Islanders defeated Washington, 3 games to 1.

New York Rangers defeated Philadelphia Flyers, 3 games to 0.

Chicago defeated St. Louis Blues, 3 games to 1.

Minnesota North Stars defeated Toronto, 3 games to 1.

Edmonton defeated Winnipeg, 3 games to 0.

Calgary defeated Vancouver, 3 games to 1.

Quarter-finals (best of seven): Boston defeated Buffalo, 4 games to 3.

New York Islanders defeated New York Rangers, 4 games to 2.

Chicago defeated Minnesota North Stars, 4 games to 1.

Edmonton defeated Calgary, 4 games to 1.

Semi-finals (best of seven): New York Islanders defeated Boston, 4 games to 2.

Edmonton defeated Chicago, 4 games to 0.
Stanley Cup Final (best of seven): New York Islanders defeated Edmonton, 4 games to 0.

NHL 1983–84
Regular-season overtime reinstituted in five-minute sudden-death format.

PRINCE OF WALES CONFERENCE

ADAMS DIVISION	W	L	T	PTS	GF	GA
Boston	49	25	6	104	336	261
Buffalo	48	25	7	103	315	257
Quebec Nor	42	28	10	94	360	278
Montreal Can	35	40	5	75	286	295
Hartford	28	42	10	66	288	320
PATRICK DIVISION	**W**	**L**	**T**	**PTS**	**GF**	**GA**
New York Isl	50	26	4	104	357	269
Washington	48	27	5	101	308	226
Philadelphia Fly	44	26	10	98	350	290
New York Ran	42	29	9	93	314	304
New Jersey	17	56	7	41	231	350
Pittsburgh Pen	16	58	6	38	254	390

PRINCE OF WALES CONFERENCE

NORRIS DIVISION	W	L	T	PTS	GF	GA
Minnesota NSt	39	31	10	88	345	344
St. Louis Blu	32	41	7	71	293	316
Detroit	31	42	7	69	298	323
Chicago	30	42	8	68	277	311
Toronto	26	45	9	61	303	387
SMYTHE DIVISION	**W**	**L**	**T**	**PTS**	**GF**	**GA**
Edmonton*	57	18	5	119	446	314
Calgary	34	32	14	82	311	314
Vancouver	32	39	9	73	306	328
Winnipeg	31	38	11	73	340	374
Los Angeles	23	44	13	59	309	376

SCORING LEADERS	GP	G	A	PTS
W Gretzky, Edm	74	87	118	205
Coffey, Edm	80	40	86	126
Goulet, QbcN	75	56	65	121
P Stastny, QbcN	80	46	73	119
Bossy, NYI	67	51	67	118
Pederson, Bos	80	39	77	116
Kurri, Edm	64	52	61	113
B Trottier, NYI	68	40	71	111
B Federko, StLB	79	41	66	107
Middleton, Bos	80	47	58	105
Hawerchuk, Wpg	80	37	65	102
Mk Messier, Edm	73	37	64	101
G Anderson, Edm	80	54	45	99
R Bourque, Bos	78	31	65	96

Preliminaries (best of five): Montreal Canadiens defeated Boston, 3 games to 0.

Quebec Nordiques defeated Buffalo, 3 games to 0.

New York Islanders defeated New York Rangers, 3 games to 2.

Washington defeated Philadelphia Flyers, 3 games to 0.

Minnesota North Stars defeated Chicago, 3 games to 2.

St. Louis Blues defeated Detroit, 3 games to 1.

Edmonton defeated Winnipeg, 3 games to 0.

Calgary defeated Vancouver, 3 games to 1.

Quarter-finals (best of seven): Montreal Canadiens defeated Quebec Nordiques, 4 games to 2.

New York Islanders defeated Washington, 4 games to 1.

Minnesota North Stars defeated St. Louis Blues, 4 games to 3.

Edmonton defeated Calgary, 4 games to 3.

Semi-finals (best of seven): New York Islanders defeated Montreal Canadiens, 4 games to 2.

Edmonton defeated Minnesota North Stars, 4 games to 0.

Stanley Cup Final (best of seven): Edmonton defeated New York Islanders, 4 games to 1.

NHL 1984–85

PRINCE OF WALES CONFERENCE

ADAMS DIVISION	W	L	T	PTS	GF	GA
Montreal Can	41	27	12	94	309	262
Quebec Nor	41	30	9	91	323	275
Buffalo	38	28	14	90	290	237
Boston	36	34	10	82	303	287
Hartford	30	41	9	69	268	318
PATRICK DIVISION	**W**	**L**	**T**	**PTS**	**GF**	**GA**
Philadelphia Fly	53	20	7	113	348	241
Washington	46	25	9	101	322	240
New York Isl	40	34	6	86	345	312
New York Ran	26	44	10	62	295	345
New Jersey	22	48	10	54	264	346
Pittsburgh Pen	24	51	5	53	276	385

PRINCE OF WALES CONFERENCE

NORRIS DIVISION	W	L	T	PTS	GF	GA
St. Louis Blu	37	31	12	86	299	288
Chicago	38	35	7	83	309	299
Detroit	27	41	12	66	313	357
Minnesota NSt	25	43	12	62	268	321
Toronto	20	52	8	48	253	358
SMYTHE DIVISION	**W**	**L**	**T**	**PTS**	**GF**	**GA**
Edmonton*	49	20	11	109	401	298
Winnipeg	43	27	10	96	358	332
Calgary	41	27	12	94	363	302
Los Angeles	34	32	14	82	339	326
Vancouver	25	46	9	59	284	401

SCORING LEADERS	GP	G	A	PTS
W Gretzky, Edm	80	73	135	208
Kurri, Edm	73	71	64	135
Hawerchuk, Wpg	80	53	77	130
M Dionne, LA	80	46	80	126
Coffey, Edm	80	37	84	121
Bossy, NYI	76	58	59	117
Ogrodnick, Det	79	55	50	105
D Savard, Chi	79	38	67	105
B Federko, StLB	76	30	73	103
Gartner, Was	80	50	62	102
Bre Sutter, NYI	72	42	60	102
P MacLean, Wpg	79	41	60	101
Nicholls, LA	80	46	54	100
M Lemieux, PitPe	73	43	57	100
Tonelli, NYI	80	42	58	100
P Stastny, QbcN	75	32	68	100

Preliminaries (best of five): Montreal Canadiens defeated Boston, 3 games to 2.

Quebec Nordiques defeated Buffalo, 3 games to 2.

Philadelphia Flyers defeated New York Rangers, 3 games to 0.

New York Islanders defeated Washington, 3 games to 2.

Minnesota North Stars defeated St. Louis Blues, 3 games to 0.

Chicago defeated Detroit, 3 games to 0.

Edmonton defeated Los Angeles, 3 games to 0.

Winnipeg defeated Calgary, 3 games to 1.

Quarter-finals (best of seven): Quebec Nordiques defeated Montreal Canadiens, 4 games to 3.

Philadelphia Flyers defeated New York Islanders, 4 games to 1.

Chicago defeated Minnesota North Stars, 4 games to 2.

Edmonton defeated Winnipeg, 4 games to 0.

Semi-finals (best of seven): Philadelphia Flyers defeated Quebec Nordiques, 4 games to 2.

Edmonton defeated Chicago, 4 games to 2.

Stanley Cup Final (best of seven): Edmonton defeated Philadelphia Flyers, 4 games to 1.

NHL 1985–86

Chicago Black Hawks changed their nickname "retroactively" to Blackhawks.

The Presidents' Trophy was instituted to reward the team with the best regular-season record. Substitutions were allowed in the event of coincidental minor penalties. Maximum length of stick increased to 60 inches. An increase in eye injuries led to a stricter interpretation of high-sticking rules.

NHL teams played a ten-game mid-season exhibition series, called Super Series 86, against touring Soviet teams, going 1-5-0 against Soviet Central Army and 1-2-1 against Dynamo Moscow.

PRINCE OF WALES CONFERENCE

ADAMS DIVISION	W	L	T	PTS	GF	GA
Quebec Nor	43	31	6	92	330	289
Montreal Can*	40	33	7	87	330	280
Boston	37	31	12	86	311	288
Hartford	40	36	4	84	332	302
Buffalo	37	37	6	80	296	291

PATRICK DIVISION	W	L	T	PTS	GF	GA
Philadelphia Fly	53	23	4	110	335	241
Washington	50	23	7	107	315	272
New York Isl	39	29	12	90	327	284
New York Ran	36	38	6	78	280	276
Pittsburgh Pen	34	38	8	76	313	305
New Jersey	28	49	3	59	301	374

PRINCE OF WALES CONFERENCE

NORRIS DIVISION	W	L	T	PTS	GF	GA
Chicago	39	33	8	86	351	350
Minnesota NSt	38	33	9	85	327	305
St. Louis Blu	37	34	9	83	302	291
Toronto	25	48	7	57	311	386
Detroit	17	57	6	40	266	415

SMYTHE DIVISION	W	L	T	PTS	GF	GA
Edmonton	56	17	7	119	426	310
Calgary	40	31	9	89	354	315
Winnipeg	26	47	7	59	295	372
Vancouver	23	44	13	59	282	333
Los Angeles	23	49	8	54	284	389

SCORING LEADERS	GP	G	A	PTS
W Gretzky, Edm	80	52	163	215
M Lemieux, PitPe	79	48	93	141
Coffey, Edm	79	48	90	138
Kurri, Edm	78	68	63	131
Bossy, NYI	80	61	62	123
P Stastny, QbcN	76	41	81	122
D Savard, Chi	80	47	69	116
Naslund, MtrC	80	43	67	110
Hawerchuk, Wpg	80	46	59	105
N Broten, MinNS	80	29	76	105
Goulet, QbcN	75	53	51	104
G Anderson, Edm	72	54	48	102
B Federko, StLB	80	34	68	102
Tr Murray, Chi	80	45	54	99

Preliminaries (best of five): Hartford defeated Quebec Nordiques, 3 games to 0.

Montreal Canadiens defeated Boston, 3 games to 0.

New York Rangers defeated Philadelphia Flyers, 3 games to 2.

Washington defeated New York Islanders, 3 games to 0.

Toronto defeated Chicago, 3 games to 0.

St. Louis Blues defeated Minnesota North Stars, 3 games to 2.

Edmonton defeated Vancouver, 3 games to 0.

Calgary defeated Winnipeg, 3 games to 0.

Quarter-finals (best of seven): Montreal Canadiens defeated Hartford, 4 games to 3.

New York Rangers defeated Washington, 4 games to 2.

St. Louis Blues defeated Toronto, 4 games to 3.

Calgary defeated Edmonton, 4 games to 3.

Semi-finals (best of seven): Montreal Canadiens defeated New York Rangers, 4 games to 1.

Calgary defeated St. Louis Blues, 4 games to 3.

Stanley Cup Final (best of seven): Montreal Canadiens defeated Calgary, 4 games to 1.

NHL 1986–87

The goal crease was enlarged by surrounding the existing 8' x 4' rectangle with a 47-square-foot semi-circle 6 feet in radius from the centre of the goal line.

Delayed offside introduced; play no longer automatically ruled offside when puck enters attacking zone preceded by a player of the attacking side, providing puck is first intercepted by defender and players of offending team leave opponent's defensive zone directly and before affecting play. A new, but redundant, rule was added, imposing at least an extra minor penalty on a player "instigating" a fight.

The NHL All-Star Game was replaced for this season by the two-game Rendez-Vous '87 series between Team NHL and the Soviet Union, played at Quebec; each team won once, the Soviets outscoring the NHL 8 goals to 7.

Preliminary round playoff series changed to best-of-seven format.

PRINCE OF WALES CONFERENCE

ADAMS DIVISION	W	L	T	PTS	GF	GA
Hartford	43	30	7	93	287	270
Montreal Can	41	29	10	92	277	241
Boston	39	34	7	85	301	276
Quebec Nor	31	39	10	72	267	276
Buffalo	28	44	8	64	280	308

PATRICK DIVISION	W	L	T	PTS	GF	GA
Philadelphia Fly	46	26	8	100	310	245
Washington	38	32	10	86	285	278
New York Isl	35	33	12	82	279	281
New York Ran	34	38	8	76	307	323
Pittsburgh Pen	30	38	12	72	297	290
New Jersey	29	45	6	64	293	368

PRINCE OF WALES CONFERENCE

NORRIS DIVISION	W	L	T	PTS	GF	GA
St. Louis Blu	32	33	15	79	281	293
Detroit	34	36	10	78	260	274
Chicago	29	37	14	72	290	310
Toronto	32	42	6	70	286	319
Minnesota NSt	30	40	10	70	296	314

SMYTHE DIVISION	W	L	T	PTS	GF	GA
Edmonton*	50	24	6	106	372	284
Calgary	46	31	3	95	318	289
Winnipeg	40	32	8	88	279	271
Los Angeles	31	41	8	70	318	341
Vancouver	29	43	8	66	282	314

SCORING LEADERS	GP	G	A	PTS
W Gretzky, Edm	79	62	121	183
Kurri, Edm	79	54	54	108
M Lemieux, PitPe	63	54	53	107
Mk Messier, Edm	77	37	70	107
Dg Gilmour, StLB	80	42	63	105
Ciccarelli, MinNS	80	52	51	103
Hawerchuk, Wpg	80	47	53	100
Goulet, QbcN	75	49	47	96
T Kerr, PhiF	75	58	37	95
R Bourque, Bos	78	23	72	95
Rn Francis, Har	75	30	63	93
D Savard, Chi	70	40	50	90
Yzerman, Det	80	31	59	90
J Mullen, Clg	79	47	40	87
Poddubny, NYR	75	40	47	87
B Trottier, NYI	80	23	64	87

Preliminaries (best of seven): Quebec Nordiques defeated Hartford, 4 games to 2.

Montreal Canadiens defeated Boston, 4 games to 0.

Philadelphia Flyers defeated New York Rangers, 4 games to 2.

New York Islanders defeated Washington, 4 games to 3.

Toronto defeated St. Louis Blues, 4 games to 2.

Detroit defeated Chicago, 4 games to 0.

Edmonton defeated Los Angeles, 4 games to 1.

Winnipeg defeated Calgary, 4 games to 2.

Quarter-finals (best of seven): Montreal Canadiens defeated Quebec Nordiques, 4 games to 3.

Philadelphia Flyers defeated New York Islanders, 4 games to 3.

Detroit defeated Toronto, 4 games to 3.

Edmonton defeated Winnipeg, 4 games to 0.

Semi-finals (best of seven): Philadelphia Flyers defeated Montreal Canadiens, 4 games to 2.

Edmonton defeated Detroit, 4 games to 1.

Stanley Cup Final (best of seven): Edmonton defeated Philadelphia Flyers, 4 games to 3.

NHL 1987–88

A Stanley Cup Final game in Boston was ended during the second period with the score tied due to a power failure.

PRINCE OF WALES CONFERENCE

ADAMS DIVISION	W	L	T	PTS	GF	GA
Montreal Can	45	22	13	103	298	238
Boston	44	30	6	94	300	251
Buffalo	37	32	11	85	283	305
Hartford	35	38	7	77	249	267
Quebec Nor	32	43	5	69	271	306

PATRICK DIVISION	W	L	T	PTS	GF	GA
New York Isl	39	31	10	88	308	267
Washington	38	33	9	85	281	249
Philadelphia Fly	38	33	9	85	292	292
New Jersey	38	36	6	82	295	296
New York Ran	36	34	10	82	300	283
Pittsburgh Pen	36	35	9	81	319	316

CLARENCE CAMPBELL CONFERENCE

NORRIS DIVISION	W	L	T	PTS	GF	GA
Detroit	41	28	11	93	322	269
St. Louis Blu	34	38	8	76	278	294
Chicago	30	41	9	69	284	328
Toronto	21	49	10	52	273	345
Minnesota NSt	19	48	13	51	242	349

SMYTHE DIVISION	W	L	T	PTS	GF	GA
Calgary	48	23	9	105	397	305
Edmonton*	44	25	11	99	363	288
Winnipeg	33	36	11	77	292	310
Los Angeles	30	42	8	68	318	359
Vancouver	25	46	9	59	272	320

SCORING LEADERS	GP	G	A	PTS
M Lemieux, PitPe	77	70	98	168
W Gretzky, Edm	64	40	109	149
D Savard, Chi	80	44	87	131
Hawerchuk, Wpg	80	44	77	121
L Robitaille, LA	80	53	58	111
P Stastny, QbcN	76	46	65	111
Mk Messier, Edm	77	37	74	111
J Carson, LA	80	55	52	107
Loob, Clg	80	50	56	106
Goulet, QbcN	80	48	58	106
Bullard, Clg	79	48	55	103
Yzerman, Det	64	50	52	102
Kurri, Edm	80	43	53	96
Muller, NJ	80	37	57	94

Preliminaries (best of seven): Montreal Canadiens defeated Hartford, 4 games to 2.

Boston defeated Buffalo, 4 games to 2.

New Jersey defeated New York Islanders, 4 games to 2.

Washington defeated Philadelphia Flyers, 4 games to 3.

Detroit defeated Toronto, 4 games to 2.

St. Louis Blues defeated Chicago, 4 games to 1.

Calgary defeated Los Angeles, 4 games to 1.

Edmonton defeated Winnipeg, 4 games to 1.

Quarter-finals (best of seven): Boston defeated Montreal Canadiens, 4 games to 1.

New Jersey defeated Washington, 4 games to 3.

Detroit defeated St. Louis Blues, 4 games to 1.

Edmonton defeated Calgary, 4 games to 0.

Semi-finals (best of seven): Boston defeated New Jersey, 4 games to 3.

Edmonton defeated Detroit, 4 games to 1.

Stanley Cup Final (best of seven): Edmonton defeated Boston, 4 games to 0, with one tie.

NHL 1988–89

NHL teams played a 14-game mid-season exhibition series, called Super Series 89, against touring Soviet teams, going 2-4-1 against Soviet Central Army and 4-2-1 against Dynamo Riga.

PRINCE OF WALES CONFERENCE

ADAMS DIVISION	W	L	T	PTS	GF	GA
Montreal Can	53	18	9	115	315	218
Boston	37	29	14	88	289	256
Buffalo	38	35	7	83	291	299
Hartford	37	38	5	79	299	290
Quebec Nor	27	46	7	61	269	342

PATRICK DIVISION	W	L	T	PTS	GF	GA
Washington	41	29	10	92	305	259
Pittsburgh Pen	40	33	7	87	347	349
New York Ran	37	35	8	82	310	307
Philadelphia Fly	36	36	8	80	307	285
New Jersey	27	41	12	66	281	325
New York Isl	28	47	5	61	265	325

CLARENCE CAMPBELL CONFERENCE

NORRIS DIVISION	W	L	T	PTS	GF	GA
Detroit	34	34	12	80	313	316
St. Louis Blu	33	35	12	78	275	285
Minnesota NSt	27	37	16	70	258	278
Chicago	27	41	12	66	297	335
Toronto	28	46	6	62	259	342

SMYTHE DIVISION	W	L	T	PTS	GF	GA
Calgary*	54	17	9	117	354	226
Los Angeles	42	31	7	91	376	335
Edmonton	38	34	8	84	325	306
Vancouver	33	39	8	74	251	253
Winnipeg	26	42	12	64	300	355

SCORING LEADERS	GP	G	A	PTS
M Lemieux, PitPe	76	85	114	199
W Gretzky, LA	78	54	114	168
Yzerman, Det	80	65	90	155
Nicholls, LA	79	70	80	150
Rb Brown II, PitPe	68	49	66	115
Coffey, PitPe	75	30	83	113
J Mullen, Clg	79	51	59	110

Appendix

SCORING LEADERS	GP	G	A	PTS
Kurri, Edm	76	44	58	102
J Carson, Edm	80	49	51	100
L Robitaille, LA	78	46	52	98
Hawerchuk, Wpg	75	41	55	96
D Quinn, PitPe	79	34	60	94
Mk Messier, Edm	72	33	61	94
Ge Gallant, Det	76	39	54	93

Preliminaries (best of seven): Montreal Canadiens defeated Hartford, 4 games to 0.

Boston defeated Buffalo, 4 games to 1.

Philadelphia Flyers defeated Washington, 4 games to 2.

Pittsburgh Penguins defeated New York Rangers, 4 games to 0.

Chicago defeated Detroit, 4 games to 2.

St. Louis Blues defeated Minnesota North Stars, 4 games to 1.

Calgary defeated Vancouver, 4 games to 3.

Los Angeles defeated Edmonton, 4 games to 3.

Quarter-finals (best of seven): Montreal Canadiens defeated Boston, 4 games to 1.

Philadelphia Flyers defeated Pittsburgh Penguins, 4 games to 3.

Chicago defeated St. Louis Blues, 4 games to 1.

Calgary defeated Los Angeles, 4 games to 0.

Semi-finals (best of seven): Montreal Canadiens defeated Philadelphia Flyers, 4 games to 2.

Calgary defeated Chicago, 4 games to 1.

Stanley Cup Final (best of seven): Calgary defeated Montreal Canadiens, 4 games to 2.

NHL 1989–90

PRINCE OF WALES CONFERENCE

ADAMS DIVISION	W	L	T	PTS	GF	GA
Boston	46	25	9	101	289	232
Buffalo	45	27	8	98	286	248
Montreal Can	41	28	11	93	288	234
Hartford	38	33	9	85	275	268
Quebec Nor	12	61	7	31	240	407

PATRICK DIVISION	W	L	T	PTS	GF	GA
New York Ran	36	31	13	85	279	267
New Jersey	37	34	9	83	295	288
Washington	36	38	6	78	284	275
New York Isl	31	38	11	73	281	288
Pittsburgh Pen	32	40	8	72	318	359
Philadelphia Fly	30	39	11	71	290	297

CLARENCE CAMPBELL CONFERENCE

NORRIS DIVISION	W	L	T	PTS	GF	GA
Chicago	41	33	6	88	316	294
St. Louis Blu	37	34	9	83	295	279
Toronto	38	38	4	80	337	358

	W	L	T	PTS	GF	GA
Minnesota NSt	36	40	4	76	284	291
Detroit	28	38	14	70	288	323

SMYTHE DIVISION	W	L	T	PTS	GF	GA
Calgary	42	23	15	99	348	265
Edmonton*	38	28	14	90	315	283
Winnipeg	37	32	11	85	298	290
Los Angeles	34	39	7	75	338	337
Vancouver	25	41	14	64	245	306

SCORING LEADERS	GP	G	A	PTS
W Gretzky, LA	73	40	102	142
Mk Messier, Edm	79	45	84	129
Yzerman, Det	79	62	65	127
M Lemieux, PitPe	59	45	78	123
B Hull, StLB	80	72	41	113
Nicholls, LA-NYR	79	39	73	112
P Turgeon, Buf	80	40	66	106
LaFontaine, NYI	74	54	51	105
Coffey, PitPe	80	29	74	103
Sakic, QbcN	80	39	63	102
Oates, StLB	80	23	79	102
L Robitaille, LA	80	52	49	101
Rn Francis, Har	80	32	69	101
Bellows, MinNS	80	55	44	99

Preliminaries (best of seven): Boston defeated Hartford, 4 games to 3.

Montreal Canadiens defeated Buffalo, 4 games to 2.

New York Rangers defeated New York Islanders, 4 games to 1.

Washington defeated New Jersey, 4 games to 2.

Chicago defeated Minnesota North Stars, 4 games to 3.

St. Louis Blues defeated Toronto, 4 games to 1.

Los Angeles defeated Calgary, 4 games to 2.

Edmonton defeated Winnipeg, 4 games to 3.

Quarter-finals (best of seven): Boston defeated Montreal Canadiens, 4 games to 1.

Washington defeated New York Rangers, 4 games to 1.

Chicago defeated St. Louis Blues, 4 games to 3.

Edmonton defeated Los Angeles, 4 games to 0.

Semi-finals (best of seven): Boston defeated Washington, 4 games to 0.

Edmonton defeated Chicago, 4 games to 2.

Stanley Cup Final (best of seven): Edmonton defeated Boston, 4 games to 1.

NHL 1990–91

Goal lines, blue lines, and all defensive zone face-off circles and markings were moved one foot farther out from the end boards.

ADAMS DIVISION	W	L	T	PTS	GF	GA
Boston	44	24	12	100	299	264
Montreal Can	39	30	11	89	273	249
Buffalo	31	30	19	81	292	278
Hartford	31	38	11	73	238	276
Quebec Nor	16	50	14	46	236	354
PATRICK DIVISION	W	L	T	PTS	GF	GA
Pittsburgh Pen*	41	33	6	88	342	305
New York Ran	36	31	13	85	297	265
Washington	37	36	7	81	258	258
New Jersey	32	33	15	79	272	264
Philadelphia Fly	33	37	10	76	252	267
New York Isl	25	45	10	60	223	290

CLARENCE CAMPBELL CONFERENCE

NORRIS DIVISION	W	L	T	PTS	GF	GA
Chicago	49	23	8	106	284	211
St. Louis Blu	47	22	11	105	310	250
Detroit	34	38	8	76	273	298
Minnesota NSt	27	39	14	68	256	266
Toronto	23	46	11	57	241	318
SMYTHE DIVISION	W	L	T	PTS	GF	GA
Los Angeles	46	24	10	102	340	254
Calgary	46	26	8	100	344	263
Edmonton	37	37	6	80	272	272
Vancouver	28	43	9	65	243	315
Winnipeg	26	43	11	63	260	288

SCORING LEADERS	GP	G	A	PTS
W Gretzky, LA	78	41	122	163
B Hull, StLB	78	86	45	131
Oates, StLB	61	25	90	115
Recchi, PitPe	78	40	73	113
J Cullen, PitPe-Har	78	39	71	110
Sakic, QbcN	80	48	61	109
Yzerman, Det	80	51	57	108
Fleury, Clg	79	51	53	104
MacInnis, Clg	78	28	75	103
S Larmer, Chi	80	44	57	101
Roenick, Chi	79	41	53	94
R Bourque, Bos	76	21	73	94
Coffey, PitPe	76	24	69	93
Janney, Bos	77	26	66	92

Preliminaries (best of seven): Boston defeated Hartford, 4 games to 2.

Montreal Canadiens defeated Buffalo, 4 games to 2.

Pittsburgh Penguins defeated New Jersey, 4 games to 3.

Washington defeated New York Rangers, 4 games to 2.

Minnesota North Stars defeated Chicago, 4 games to 2.

St. Louis Blues defeated Detroit, 4 games to 3.

Los Angeles defeated Vancouver, 4 games to 2.

Edmonton defeated Calgary, 4 games to 3.

Quarter-finals (best of seven): Boston defeated Montreal Canadiens, 4 games to 3.

Pittsburgh Penguins defeated Washington, 4 games to 1.

Minnesota North Stars defeated St. Louis Blues, 4 games to 2.

Edmonton defeated Los Angeles, 4 games to 2.

Semi-finals (best of seven): Pittsburgh Penguins defeated Boston, 4 games to 2.

Minnesota North Stars defeated Edmonton, 4 games to 1.

Stanley Cup Final (best of seven): Pittsburgh Penguins defeated Minnesota North Stars, 4 games to 2.

NHL 1991–92

A new club, San Jose Sharks, joined the NHL, assigned to the Smythe Division; an expansion draft was used to stock the new club.

The goal crease is now defined by the semi-circle added in 1986–87; the rectangular crease is eliminated but for five-inch-long vestigial corner markings, and the crease and the area inside the net are painted light blue.

A major and a game misconduct penalty were to be imposed for checking from behind into the boards. New but redundant rules were added penalizing unnecessary contact with the goaltender. A goal was to be disallowed if the puck entered the net while a player of the attacking team was in contact with the goal crease line, was standing in the goal crease, or had his stick in the goal crease. Video replay was introduced as a tool to assist referees in goal/no-goal situations. A time clock recorded tenths of a second in the last minute of each regulation and overtime period.

Regular season was suspended due to a players' strike on April 1, 1992. Play resumed April 12, 1992.

PRINCE OF WALES CONFERENCE

ADAMS DIVISION	W	L	T	PTS	GF	GA
Montreal Can	41	28	11	93	267	207
Boston	36	32	12	84	270	275
Buffalo	31	37	12	74	289	299
Hartford	26	41	13	65	247	283
Quebec Nor	20	48	12	52	255	318
PATRICK DIVISION	W	L	T	PTS	GF	GA
New York Ran	50	25	5	105	321	246
Washington	45	27	8	98	330	275
Pittsburgh Pen*	39	32	9	87	343	308
New Jersey	38	31	11	87	289	259
New York Isl	34	35	11	79	291	299
Philadelphia Fly	32	37	11	75	252	273

CLARENCE CAMPBELL CONFERENCE

NORRIS DIVISION	W	L	T	PTS	GF	GA
Detroit	43	25	12	98	320	256
Chicago	36	29	15	87	257	236
St. Louis Blu	36	33	11	83	279	266

	W	L	T	PTS	GF	GA
Minnesota NSt	32	42	6	70	246	278
Toronto	30	43	7	67	234	294
SMYTHE DIVISION	**W**	**L**	**T**	**PTS**	**GF**	**GA**
Vancouver	42	26	12	96	285	250
Los Angeles	35	31	14	84	287	296
Edmonton	36	34	10	82	295	297
Winnipeg	33	32	15	81	251	244
Calgary	31	37	12	74	296	305
San Jose	17	58	5	39	219	359

SCORING LEADERS	GP	G	A	PTS
M Lemieux, PitPe	64	44	87	131
K Stevens, PitPe	80	54	69	123
W Gretzky, LA	74	31	90	121
B Hull, StLB	73	70	39	109
L Robitaille, LA	80	44	63	107
Mk Messier, NYR	79	35	72	107
Roenick, Chi	80	53	50	103
Yzerman, Det	79	45	58	103
Leetch, NYR	80	22	80	102
Oates, StLB-Bos	80	20	79	99
Hawerchuk, Buf	77	23	75	98
Recchi, PitPe-PhiF	80	43	54	97
P Turgeon, Buf-NYI	77	40	55	95
Sakic, QbcN	69	29	65	94

Preliminaries (best of seven): Montreal Canadiens defeated Hartford, 4 games to 3.

Boston defeated Buffalo, 4 games to 3.

New York Rangers defeated New Jersey, 4 games to 3.

Pittsburgh Penguins defeated Washington, 4 games to 3.

Detroit defeated Minnesota North Stars, 4 games to 3.

Chicago defeated St. Louis Blues, 4 games to 2.

Vancouver defeated Winnipeg, 4 games to 3.

Edmonton defeated Los Angeles, 4 games to 2.

Quarter-finals (best of seven): Boston defeated Montreal Canadiens, 4 games to 0.

Pittsburgh Penguins defeated New York Rangers, 4 games to 2.

Chicago defeated Detroit, 4 games to 0.

Edmonton defeated Vancouver, 4 games to 2.

Semi-finals (best of seven): Pittsburgh Penguins defeated Boston, 4 games to 0.

Chicago defeated Edmonton, 4 games to 0.

Stanley Cup Final (best of seven): Pittsburgh Penguins defeated Chicago, 4 games to 0.

NHL 1992–93

Gil Stein was elected NHL president after the resignation of John Ziegler. In February 1993, Gary Bettman was named NHL commissioner, replacing Stein.

Two more expansion clubs joined the NHL: Ottawa Senators, assigned to the Adams Division, and Tampa Bay Lightning, assigned to the Norris Division. An expansion draft was used to stock the new clubs.

The number and length of time-outs were increased to accommodate television broadcasters. Helmets were made optional for skaters, but no new player nor helmeted veteran stopped wearing one. No substitutions were allowed in the event of coincidental minor penalties with both teams at full strength. High-sticking was redefined from shoulder height to waist height. A minor penalty was to be imposed for diving. A game misconduct penalty was to be imposed for instigating a fight.

Each team played two games at neutral sites: Hamilton and Saskatoon each hosted four neutral-site games, Cleveland, Milwaukee, and Sacramento two, and Atlanta, Birmingham, Cincinnati, Dallas, Halifax, Indianapolis, Miami, Oklahoma City, Phoenix, and Providence one each. Schedule increased to 84 games.

PRINCE OF WALES CONFERENCE

ADAMS DIVISION	W	L	T	PTS	GF	GA
Boston	51	26	7	109	332	268
Quebec Nor	47	27	10	104	351	300
Montreal Can*	48	30	6	102	326	280
Buffalo	38	36	10	86	335	297
Hartford	26	52	6	58	284	369
Ottawa	10	70	4	24	202	395
PATRICK DIVISION	**W**	**L**	**T**	**PTS**	**GF**	**GA**
Pittsburgh Pen	56	21	7	119	367	268
Washington	43	34	7	93	325	286
New York Isl	40	37	7	87	335	297
New Jersey	40	37	7	87	308	299
Philadelphia	36	37	11	83	319	319
New York Ran	34	39	11	79	304	308

CLARENCE CAMPBELL CONFERENCE

NORRIS DIVISION	W	L	T	PTS	GF	GA
Chicago	47	25	12	106	279	230
Detroit	47	28	9	103	369	280
Toronto	44	29	11	99	288	241
St. Louis Blu	37	36	11	85	282	278
Minnesota NSt	36	38	10	82	272	293
Tampa Bay	23	54	7	53	245	332
SMYTHE DIVISION	**W**	**L**	**T**	**PTS**	**GF**	**GA**
Vancouver	46	29	9	101	346	278
Calgary	43	30	11	97	322	282
Los Angeles	39	35	10	88	338	340
Winnipeg	40	37	7	87	322	320
Edmonton	26	50	8	60	242	337
San Jose	11	71	2	24	218	414

SCORING LEADERS	GP	G	A	PTS
M Lemieux, PitPe	60	69	91	160
LaFontaine, Buf	84	53	95	148

SCORING LEADERS	GP	G	A	PTS
Oates, Bos	84	45	97	142
Yzerman, Det	84	58	79	137
Selanne, Wpg	84	76	56	132
P Turgeon, NYI	83	58	74	132
Mogilny, Buf	77	76	51	127
Dg Gilmour, Tor	83	32	95	127
L Robitaille, LA	84	63	62	125
Recchi, PhiF	84	53	70	123
Sundin, QbcN	80	47	67	114
K Stevens, PitPe	72	55	56	111
P Bure, Van	83	60	50	110
Tocchet, PitPe	80	48	61	109

Preliminaries (best of seven): Buffalo defeated Boston, 4 games to 0.

Montreal Canadiens defeated Quebec Nordiques, 4 games to 2.

Pittsburgh Penguins defeated New Jersey, 4 games to 1.

New York Islanders defeated Washington, 4 games to 2.

St. Louis Blues defeated Chicago, 4 games to 0.

Toronto defeated Detroit, 4 games to 3.

Vancouver defeated Winnipeg, 4 games to 2.

Los Angeles defeated Calgary, 4 games to 2.

Quarter-finals (best of seven): Montreal Canadiens defeated Buffalo, 4 games to 0.

New York Islanders defeated Pittsburgh Penguins, 4 games to 3.

Toronto defeated St. Louis Blues, 4 games to 3.

Los Angeles defeated Vancouver, 4 games to 2.

Semi-finals (best of seven): Montreal Canadiens defeated New York Islanders, 4 games to 1.

Los Angeles defeated Toronto, 4 games to 3.

Stanley Cup Final (best of seven): Montreal Canadiens defeated Los Angeles, 4 games to 1.

NHL 1993–94

Two more expansion clubs joined the NHL: Mighty Ducks of Anaheim, assigned to the Pacific Division, and Florida Panthers, based in Miami, assigned to the Atlantic Division. An expansion draft was again used to stock the new clubs. The Minnesota franchise moved to Dallas and changed its nickname to Stars. Conferences and divisions were renamed to reflect U.S. geography. Teams were realigned.

Goals directed in by a stick below the height of the crossbar were allowed to stand.

Each team played between two and seven games at one or more neutral sites: Minneapolis hosted six neutral-site games, Orlando five, Cleveland, Hamilton, Phoenix, and Sacramento four, and Halifax and Saskatoon two each.

Playoff format changed to qualify top eight teams in each conference; teams were seeded 1 through 8 within conference, with division winners automatically seeded 1 and 2, and the preliminary round pitting 1 versus 8, 2 versus 7, 3 versus 6, and 4 versus 5.

EASTERN CONFERENCE

NORTHEAST DIVISION	W	L	T	PTS	GF	GA
Pittsburgh Pen	44	27	13	101	299	285
Boston	42	29	13	97	289	252
Montreal Can	41	29	14	96	283	248
Buffalo	43	32	9	95	282	218
Quebec Nor	34	42	8	76	277	292
Hartford	27	48	9	63	227	288
Ottawa	14	61	9	37	201	397

ATLANTIC DIVISION	W	L	T	PTS	GF	GA
New York Ran*	52	24	8	112	299	231
New Jersey	47	25	12	106	306	220
Washington	39	35	10	88	277	263
New York Isl	36	36	12	84	282	264
Florida	33	34	17	83	233	233
Philadelphia Fly	35	39	10	80	294	314
Tampa Bay	30	43	11	71	224	251

WESTERN CONFERENCE

CENTRAL DIVISION	W	L	T	PTS	GF	GA
Detroit	46	30	8	100	356	275
Toronto	43	29	12	98	280	243
Dallas	42	29	13	97	286	265
St. Louis Blu	40	33	11	91	270	283
Chicago	39	36	9	87	254	240
Winnipeg	24	51	9	57	245	344

PACIFIC DIVISION	W	L	T	PTS	GF	GA
Calgary	42	29	13	97	302	256
Vancouver	41	40	3	85	279	276
San Jose	33	35	16	82	252	265
Anaheim	33	46	5	71	229	251
Los Angeles	27	45	12	66	294	322
Edmonton	25	45	14	64	261	305

SCORING LEADERS	GP	G	A	PTS
W Gretzky, LA	81	38	92	130
Fedorov, Det	82	56	64	120
Oates, Bos	77	32	80	112
Dg Gilmour, Tor	83	27	84	111
P Bure, Van	76	60	47	107
Roenick, Chi	84	46	61	107
Recchi, PhiF	84	40	67	107
Shanahan, StLB	81	52	50	102
Andreychuk, Tor	83	53	46	99
Jagr, PitPe	80	32	67	99
B Hull, StLB	81	57	40	97
E Lindros, PhiF	65	44	53	97
Brind'Amour, PhiF	84	35	62	97
P Turgeon, NYI	69	38	56	94
R Sheppard, Det	82	52	41	93
Modano, Dal	76	50	43	93

SCORING LEADERS	GP	G	A	PTS
Reichel, Clg	84	40	53	93
Rn Francis, PitPe	82	27	66	93

Preliminaries (best of seven): New York Rangers defeated New York Islanders, 4 games to 0.

    Washington defeated Pittsburgh Penguins, 4 games to 2.

    New Jersey defeated Buffalo, 4 games to 3.

    Boston defeated Montreal Canadiens, 4 games to 3.

    San Jose defeated Detroit, 4 games to 3.

    Vancouver defeated Calgary, 4 games to 3.

    Toronto defeated Chicago, 4 games to 2.

    Dallas defeated St. Louis Blues, 4 games to 0.

Quarter-finals (best of seven): New York Rangers defeated Washington, 4 games to 1.

    New Jersey defeated Boston, 4 games to 2.

    Toronto defeated San Jose, 4 games to 3.

    Vancouver defeated Dallas, 4 games to 1.

Semi-finals (best of seven): New York Rangers defeated New Jersey, 4 games to 3.

    Vancouver defeated Toronto, 4 games to 1.

Stanley Cup Final (best of seven): New York Rangers defeated Vancouver, 4 games to 3.

NHL 1994–95

NHL management locked out the players in a labour dispute before the scheduled start of the season. The dispute was not resolved until January 1995, forcing the cancellation of 468 regular-season games and delaying the start of the season until January 19.

    Schedule decreased to 48 intra-conference games.

EASTERN CONFERENCE

NORTHEAST DIVISION	W	L	T	PTS	GF	GA
Quebec Nor	30	13	5	65	185	134
Pittsburgh Pen	29	16	3	61	181	158
Boston	27	18	3	57	150	127
Buffalo	22	19	7	51	130	119
Hartford	19	24	5	43	127	141
Montreal Can	18	23	7	43	125	148
Ottawa	9	34	5	23	117	174
ATLANTIC DIVISION	**W**	**L**	**T**	**PTS**	**GF**	**GA**
Philadelphia Fly	28	16	4	60	150	132
New Jersey*	22	18	8	52	136	121
Washington	22	18	8	52	136	120
New York Ran	22	23	3	47	139	134
Florida	20	22	6	46	115	127
Tampa Bay	17	28	3	37	120	144
New York Isl	15	28	5	35	126	158

WESTERN CONFERENCE

CENTRAL DIVISION	W	L	T	PTS	GF	GA
Detroit	33	11	4	70	180	117
St. Louis Blu	28	15	5	61	178	135
Chicago	24	19	5	53	156	115
Toronto	21	19	8	50	135	146
Dallas	17	23	8	42	136	135
Winnipeg	16	25	7	39	157	177
PACIFIC DIVISION	**W**	**L**	**T**	**PTS**	**GF**	**GA**
Calgary	24	17	7	55	163	135
Vancouver	18	18	12	48	153	148
San Jose	19	25	4	42	129	161
Los Angeles	16	23	9	41	142	174
Edmonton	17	27	4	38	136	183
Anaheim	16	27	5	37	125	164

SCORING LEADERS	GP	G	A	PTS
Jagr, PitPe	48	32	38	70
E Lindros, PhiF	46	29	41	70
Zhamnov, Chi	48	30	35	65
Sakic, QbcN	47	19	43	62
Rn Francis, PitPe	44	11	48	59
Fleury, Clg	47	29	29	58
Coffey, Det	45	14	44	58
Renberg, PhiF	47	26	31	57
LeClair, MtrC-PhiF	46	26	28	54
Mk Messier, NYR	46	14	39	53
Oates, Bos	48	12	41	53
Nicholls, Chi	48	22	29	51
Tkachuk, Wpg	48	22	29	51
B Hull, StLB	48	29	21	50
Nieuwendyk, Clg	46	21	29	50
Fedorov, Det	42	20	30	50
Forsberg, QbcN	47	15	35	50

Preliminaries (best of seven): New York Rangers defeated Quebec Nordiques, 4 games to 2.

    Philadelphia Flyers defeated Buffalo, 4 games to 1.

    Pittsburgh Penguins defeated Washington, 4 games to 3.

    New Jersey defeated Boston, 4 games to 1.

    Detroit defeated Dallas, 4 games to 1.

    San Jose defeated Calgary, 4 games to 3.

    Vancouver defeated St. Louis Blues, 4 games to 3.

    Chicago defeated Toronto, 4 games to 3.

Quarter-finals (best of seven): Philadelphia Flyers defeated New York Rangers, 4 games to 0.

    New Jersey defeated Pittsburgh Penguins, 4 games to 1.

    Detroit defeated San Jose, 4 games to 0.

    Chicago defeated Vancouver, 4 games to 0.

Semi-finals (best of seven): New Jersey defeated Philadelphia Flyers, 4 games to 2.

    Detroit defeated Chicago, 4 games to 1.

Stanley Cup Final (best of seven): New Jersey defeated Detroit, 4 games to 0.

NHL 1995–96

The Quebec franchise moved to Denver, changed its name to Colorado Avalanche, and was reassigned to the Pacific Division.

The ice inside the net was again painted white.

Schedule increased to 82 games.

EASTERN CONFERENCE

NORTHEAST DIVISION	W	L	T	PTS	GF	GA
Pittsburgh Pen	49	29	4	102	362	284
Boston	40	31	11	91	282	269
Montreal Can	40	32	10	90	265	248
Hartford	34	39	9	77	237	259
Buffalo	33	42	7	73	247	262
Ottawa	18	59	5	41	191	291

ATLANTIC DIVISION	W	L	T	PTS	GF	GA
Philadelphia Fly	45	24	13	103	282	208
New York Ran	41	27	14	96	272	237
Florida	41	31	10	92	254	234
Washington	39	32	11	89	234	204
Tampa Bay	38	32	12	88	238	248
New Jersey	37	33	12	86	215	202
New York Isl	22	50	10	54	229	315

WESTERN CONFERENCE

CENTRAL DIVISION	W	L	T	PTS	GF	GA
Detroit	62	13	7	131	325	181
Chicago	40	28	14	94	273	220
Toronto	34	36	12	80	247	252
St. Louis Blu	32	34	16	80	219	248
Winnipeg	36	40	6	78	275	291
Dallas	26	42	14	66	227	280

PACIFIC DIVISION	W	L	T	PTS	GF	GA
Colorado Avl*	47	25	10	104	326	240
Calgary	34	37	11	79	241	240
Vancouver	32	35	15	79	278	278
Anaheim	35	39	8	78	234	247
Edmonton	30	44	8	68	240	304
Los Angeles	24	40	18	66	256	302
San Jose	20	55	7	47	252	357

SCORING LEADERS	GP	G	A	PTS
M Lemieux, PitPe	70	69	92	161
Jagr, PitPe	82	62	87	149
Sakic, ColA	82	51	69	120
Rn Francis, PitPe	77	27	92	119
Forsberg, ColA	82	30	86	116
E Lindros, PhiF	73	47	68	115
P Kariya, Ana	82	50	58	108
Selanne, Wpg-Ana	79	40	68	108
Mogilny, Van	79	55	52	107
Fedorov, Det	78	39	68	107
Weight, Edm	82	25	79	104
W Gretzky, LA-StLB	80	23	79	102
Mk Messier, NYR	74	47	52	99

SCORING LEADERS	GP	G	A	PTS
P Nedved, PitPe	80	45	54	99
Tkachuk, Wpg	76	50	48	98
LeClair, PhiF	82	51	46	97

Preliminaries (best of seven): Philadelphia Flyers defeated Tampa Bay, 4 games to 2.

Pittsburgh Penguins defeated Washington, 4 games to 2.

New York Rangers defeated Montreal Canadiens, 4 games to 2.

Florida defeated Boston, 4 games to 1.

Detroit defeated Winnipeg, 4 games to 2.

Colorado Avalanche defeated Vancouver, 4 games to 2.

Chicago defeated Calgary, 4 games to 0.

St. Louis Blues defeated Toronto, 4 games to 2.

Quarter-finals (best of seven): Florida defeated Philadelphia Flyers, 4 games to 2.

Pittsburgh Penguins defeated New York Rangers, 4 games to 1.

Detroit defeated St. Louis Blues, 4 games to 3.

Colorado Avalanche defeated Chicago, 4 games to 2.

Semi-finals (best of seven): Florida defeated Pittsburgh Penguins, 4 games to 3.

Colorado Avalanche defeated Detroit, 4 games to 2.

Stanley Cup Final (best of seven): Colorado Avalanche defeated Florida, 4 games to 0.

NHL 1996–97

The Winnipeg franchise moved to Phoenix, and changed its nickname to Coyotes.

Four L-shaped positioning marks were added to the face-off dots in each defensive zone.

Play ruled offside if puck shot into attacking zone preceded by a player of the attacking side; if judged a deliberate offside, face-off to take place in offending team's defensive zone. Maximum length of stick increased to 63 inches.

EASTERN CONFERENCE

NORTHEAST DIVISION	W	L	T	PTS	GF	GA
Buffalo	40	30	12	92	237	208
Pittsburgh Pen	38	36	8	84	285	280
Ottawa	31	36	15	77	226	234
Montreal Can	31	36	15	77	249	276
Hartford	32	39	11	75	226	256
Boston	26	47	9	61	234	300

ATLANTIC DIVISION	W	L	T	PTS	GF	GA
New Jersey	45	23	14	104	231	182
Philadelphia Fly	45	24	13	103	274	217
Florida	35	28	19	89	221	201
New York Ran	38	34	10	86	258	231
Washington	33	40	9	75	214	231
Tampa Bay	32	40	10	74	217	247
New York Isl	29	41	12	70	240	250

WESTERN CONFERENCE

CENTRAL DIVISION	W	L	T	PTS	GF	GA
Dallas	48	26	8	104	252	198
Detroit*	38	26	18	94	253	197
Phoenix	38	37	7	83	240	243
St. Louis Blu	36	35	11	83	236	239
Chicago	34	35	13	81	223	210
Toronto	30	44	8	68	230	273
PACIFIC DIVISION	W	L	T	PTS	GF	GA
Colorado Avl	49	24	9	107	277	205
Anaheim	36	33	13	85	245	233
Edmonton	36	37	9	81	252	247
Vancouver	35	40	7	77	257	273
Calgary	32	41	9	73	214	239
Los Angeles	28	43	11	67	214	268
San Jose	27	47	8	62	211	278

SCORING LEADERS	GP	G	A	PTS
M Lemieux, PitPe	76	50	72	122
Selanne, Ana	78	51	58	109
P Kariya, Ana	69	44	55	99
LeClair, PhiF	82	50	47	97
W Gretzky, NYR	82	25	72	97
Jagr, PitPe	63	47	48	95
Sundin, Tor	82	41	53	94
Palffy, NYI	80	48	42	90
Rn Francis, PitPe	81	27	63	90
Shanahan, Har-Det	81	47	41	88
Tkachuk, Phx	81	52	34	86
Forsberg, ColA	65	28	58	86
P Turgeon, MtrC-StLB	78	26	59	85
Yzerman, Det	81	22	63	85
Mk Messier, NYR	71	36	48	84
Modano, Dal	80	35	48	83

Preliminaries (best of seven): New Jersey defeated Montreal Canadiens, 4 games to 1.

Buffalo defeated Ottawa, 4 games to 3.

Philadelphia Flyers defeated Pittsburgh Penguins, 4 games to 1.

New York Rangers defeated Florida, 4 games to 1.

Colorado Avalanche defeated Chicago, 4 games to 2.

Edmonton defeated Dallas, 4 games to 3.

Detroit defeated St. Louis Blues, 4 games to 2.

Anaheim defeated Phoenix, 4 games to 3.

Quarter-finals (best of seven): New York Rangers defeated New Jersey, 4 games to 1.

Philadelphia Flyers defeated Buffalo, 4 games to 1.

Colorado Avalanche defeated Edmonton, 4 games to 1.

Detroit defeated Anaheim, 4 games to 0.

Semi-finals (best of seven): Philadelphia Flyers defeated New York Rangers, 4 games to 1.

Detroit defeated Colorado Avalanche, 4 games to 2.

Stanley Cup Final (best of seven): Detroit defeated Philadelphia Flyers, 4 games to 0.

NHL 1997–98

The Hartford franchise moved to Raleigh, North Carolina, changed its name to Carolina Hurricanes, and played its home games in Greensboro.

All-Star Game format changed from Eastern Conference versus Western Conference to North America versus the World (All-Stars born in North America versus those born elsewhere).

EASTERN CONFERENCE

NORTHEAST DIVISION	W	L	T	PTS	GF	GA
Pittsburgh Pen	40	24	18	98	228	188
Boston	39	30	13	91	221	194
Buffalo	36	29	17	89	211	187
Montreal Can	37	32	13	87	235	208
Ottawa	34	33	15	83	193	200
Carolina	33	41	8	74	200	219
ATLANTIC DIVISION	W	L	T	PTS	GF	GA
New Jersey	48	23	11	107	225	166
Philadelphia Fly	42	29	11	95	242	193
Washington	40	30	12	92	219	202
New York Isl	30	41	11	71	212	225
New York Ran	25	39	18	68	197	231
Florida	24	43	15	63	203	256
Tampa Bay	17	55	10	44	151	269

WESTERN CONFERENCE

CENTRAL DIVISION	W	L	T	PTS	GF	GA
Dallas	49	22	11	109	242	167
Detroit*	44	23	15	103	250	196
St. Louis Blu	45	29	8	98	256	204
Phoenix	35	35	12	82	224	227
Chicago	30	39	13	73	192	199
Toronto	30	43	9	69	194	237
PACIFIC DIVISION	W	L	T	PTS	GF	GA
Colorado Avl	39	26	17	95	231	205
Los Angeles	38	33	11	87	227	225
Edmonton	35	37	10	80	215	224
San Jose	34	38	10	78	210	216
Calgary	26	41	15	67	217	252
Anaheim	26	43	13	65	205	261
Vancouver	25	43	14	64	224	273

SCORING LEADERS	GP	G	A	PTS
Jagr, PitPe	77	35	67	102
Forsberg, ColA	72	25	66	91
P Bure, Van	82	51	39	90
W Gretzky, NYR	82	23	67	90
LeClair, PhiF	82	51	36	87
Palffy, NYI	82	45	42	87
Rn Francis, PitPe	81	25	62	87

SCORING LEADERS	GP	G	A	PTS
Selanne, Ana	73	52	34	86
Jsn Allison, Bos	81	33	50	83
Stumpel, LA	77	21	58	79
Bondra, Was	76	52	26	78
Fleury, Clg	82	27	51	78
Oates, Was	82	18	58	76
Brind'Amour, PhiF	82	36	38	74
Sundin, Tor	82	33	41	74
Recchi, MtrC	82	32	42	74

Preliminaries (best of seven): Ottawa defeated New Jersey, 4 games to 2.

Montreal Canadiens defeated Pittsburgh Penguins, 4 games to 2.

Buffalo defeated Philadelphia Flyers, 4 games to 1.

Washington defeated Boston, 4 games to 2.

Dallas defeated San Jose, 4 games to 2.

Edmonton defeated Colorado Avalanche, 4 games to 3.

Detroit defeated Phoenix, 4 games to 2.

St. Louis Blues defeated Los Angeles, 4 games to 0.

Quarter-finals (best of seven): Washington defeated Ottawa, 4 games to 1.

Buffalo defeated Montreal Canadiens, 4 games to 0.

Dallas defeated Edmonton, 4 games to 1.

Detroit defeated St. Louis Blues, 4 games to 2.

Semi-finals (best of seven): Washington defeated Buffalo, 4 games to 2.

Detroit defeated Dallas, 4 games to 2.

Stanley Cup Final (best of seven): Detroit defeated Washington, 4 games to 0.

NHL 1998–99

Another expansion club, Nashville Predators, joined the NHL, assigned to the Central Division. An expansion draft was again used to stock the new club. The league went to a two-conference, six-division arrangement, and clubs were realigned within divisions.

Goal lines, blue lines, and all defensive zone face-off circles and markings were moved two feet farther out from the end boards. Size of the goal crease was reduced by "chopping off" the ends of the semi-circle, one foot out from the goal posts. Two referees officiated in some games (20 for each team).

Playoff format changed to seed division winners 1, 2, and 3 automatically.

EASTERN CONFERENCE

NORTHEAST DIVISION	W	L	T	PTS	GF	GA
Ottawa	44	23	15	103	239	179
Toronto	45	30	7	97	268	231
Boston	39	30	13	91	214	181

	W	L	T	PTS	GF	GA
Buffalo	37	28	17	91	207	175
Montreal Can	32	39	11	75	184	209
ATLANTIC DIVISION	**W**	**L**	**T**	**PTS**	**GF**	**GA**
New Jersey	47	24	11	105	248	196
Philadelphia Fly	37	26	19	93	231	196
Pittsburgh Pen	38	30	14	90	242	225
New York Ran	33	38	11	77	217	227
New York Isl	24	48	10	58	194	244
SOUTHEAST DIVISION	**W**	**L**	**T**	**PTS**	**GF**	**GA**
Carolina	34	30	18	86	210	202
Florida	30	34	18	78	210	228
Washington	31	45	6	68	200	218
Tampa Bay	19	54	9	47	179	292

WESTERN CONFERENCE

CENTRAL DIVISION	W	L	T	PTS	GF	GA
Detroit	43	32	7	93	245	202
St. Louis Blu	37	32	13	87	237	209
Chicago	29	41	12	70	202	248
Nashville	28	47	7	63	190	261
PACIFIC DIVISION	**W**	**L**	**T**	**PTS**	**GF**	**GA**
Dallas*	51	19	12	114	236	168
Phoenix	39	31	12	90	205	197
Anaheim	35	34	13	83	215	206
San Jose	31	33	18	80	196	191
Los Angeles	32	45	5	69	189	222
NORTHWEST DIVISION	**W**	**L**	**T**	**PTS**	**GF**	**GA**
Colorado Avl	44	28	10	98	239	205
Edmonton	33	37	12	78	230	226
Calgary	30	40	12	72	211	234
Vancouver	23	47	12	58	192	258

SCORING LEADERS	GP	G	A	PTS
Jagr, PitPe	81	44	83	127
Selanne, Ana	75	47	60	107
P Kariya, Ana	82	39	62	101
Forsberg, ColA	78	30	67	97
Sakic, ColA	73	41	55	96
Yashin, Otw	82	44	50	94
E Lindros, PhiF	71	40	53	93
Fleury, Clg	75	40	53	93
LeClair, PhiF	76	43	47	90
Demitra, StLB	82	37	52	89
M Straka, PitPe	80	35	48	83
Sundin, Tor	82	31	52	83
Modano, Dal	77	34	47	81
Jsn Allison, Bos	82	23	53	76
Amonte, Chi	82	44	31	75
L Robitaille, LA	82	39	35	74
Yzerman, Det	80	29	45	74
Brind'Amour, PhiF	82	24	50	74

Preliminaries (best of seven): Pittsburgh Penguins defeated New Jersey, 4 games to 3.

Buffalo defeated Ottawa, 4 games to 0.

Boston defeated Carolina, 4 games to 2.

Toronto defeated Philadelphia Flyers, 4 games to 2.

Dallas defeated Edmonton, 4 games to 0.

Colorado Avalanche defeated San Jose, 4 games to 2.

Detroit defeated Anaheim, 4 games to 0.

St. Louis Blues defeated Phoenix, 4 games to 3.

Quarter-finals (best of seven): Toronto defeated Pittsburgh Penguins, 4 games to 2.

Buffalo defeated Boston, 4 games to 2.

Dallas defeated St. Louis Blues, 4 games to 2.

Colorado Avalanche defeated Detroit, 4 games to 2.

Semi-finals (best of seven): Buffalo defeated Toronto, 4 games to 1.

Dallas defeated Colorado Avalanche, 4 games to 3.

Stanley Cup Final (best of seven): Dallas defeated Buffalo, 4 games to 2.

NHL 1999–2000

Another expansion club, Atlanta Thrashers, joined the NHL, assigned to the Southeast Division. An expansion draft was again used to stock the new club.

Regular-season overtime format changed to four skaters and a goaltender per side. Teams that lost in overtime were awarded a bonus point in the standings for having been tied at end of regulation. Zero-tolerance crease infringement rule relaxed to "no harm, no foul" status. Two referees officiated in most games (25 home games, 25 away games, for each team).

EASTERN CONFERENCE

NORTHEAST DIVISION	W	L	T	OL	PTS	GF	GA
Toronto	45	30	7	3	100	246	222
Ottawa	41	30	11	2	95	244	210
Buffalo	35	36	11	4	85	213	204
Montreal Can	35	38	9	4	83	196	194
Boston	24	39	19	6	73	210	248
ATLANTIC DIVISION	**W**	**L**	**T**	**OL**	**PTS**	**GF**	**GA**
Philadelphia Fly	45	25	12	3	105	237	179
New Jersey*	45	29	8	5	103	251	203
Pittsburgh Pen	37	37	8	6	88	241	236
New York Ran	29	41	12	3	73	218	246
New York Isl	24	49	9	1	58	194	275
SOUTHEAST DIVISION	**W**	**L**	**T**	**OL**	**PTS**	**GF**	**GA**
Washington	44	26	12	2	102	227	194
Florida	43	34	6	6	98	244	209
Carolina	37	35	10	0	84	217	216
Tampa Bay	19	54	9	7	54	204	310
Atlanta Thr	14	61	7	4	39	170	313

WESTERN CONFERENCE

CENTRAL DIVISION	W	L	T	OL	PTS	GF	GA
St. Louis Blu	51	20	11	1	114	248	165
Detroit	48	24	10	2	108	278	210
Chicago	33	39	10	2	78	242	245
Nashville	28	47	7	7	70	199	240
PACIFIC DIVISION	**W**	**L**	**T**	**OL**	**PTS**	**GF**	**GA**
Dallas	43	29	10	6	102	211	184
Los Angeles	39	31	12	4	94	245	228
Phoenix	39	35	8	4	90	232	228
San Jose	35	37	10	7	87	225	214
Anaheim	34	36	12	3	83	217	227
NORTHWEST DIVISION	**W**	**L**	**T**	**OL**	**PTS**	**GF**	**GA**
Colorado Avl	42	29	11	1	96	233	201
Edmonton	32	34	16	8	88	226	212
Vancouver	30	37	15	8	83	227	237
Calgary	31	41	10	5	77	211	256

SCORING LEADERS	GP	G	A	PTS
Jagr, PitPe	63	42	54	96
P Bure, Fla	74	58	36	94
Recchi, PhiF	82	28	63	91
P Kariya, Ana	72	42	44	86
Selanne, Ana	79	33	52	85
O Nolan, SJ	78	44	40	84
Amonte, Chi	82	43	41	84
Modano, Dal	77	38	43	81
Sakic, ColA	60	28	53	81
Yzerman, Det	78	35	44	79
Shanahan, Det	78	41	37	78
Roenick, Phx	75	34	44	78
LeClair, PhiF	82	40	37	77
V Bure, Clg	82	35	40	75
Demitra, StLB	71	28	47	75
L Robitaille, LA	71	36	38	74

Preliminaries (best of seven): Philadelphia Flyers defeated Buffalo, 4 games to 1.

Pittsburgh Penguins defeated Washington, 4 games to 1.

Toronto defeated Ottawa, 4 games to 2.

New Jersey defeated Florida, 4 games to 0.

San Jose defeated St. Louis Blues, 4 games to 3.

Dallas defeated Edmonton, 4 games to 1.

Colorado Avalanche defeated Phoenix, 4 games to 1.

Detroit defeated Los Angeles, 4 games to 0.

Quarter-finals (best of seven): Philadelphia Flyers defeated Pittsburgh Penguins, 4 games to 2.

New Jersey defeated Toronto, 4 games to 2.

Dallas defeated San Jose, 4 games to 1.

Colorado Avalanche defeated Detroit, 4 games to 1.

Semi-finals (best of seven): New Jersey defeated Philadelphia Flyers, 4 games to 3.

Dallas defeated Colorado Avalanche, 4 games to 3.

Stanley Cup Final (best of seven): New Jersey defeated Dallas, 4 games to 2.

NHL 2000–01

Two more expansion clubs joined the NHL: Columbus Blue Jackets, assigned to the Central Division, and Minnesota Wild (based in St. Paul), assigned to the Northwest Division. An expansion draft was again used to stock the new clubs.

Two referees and two linesmen officiated all games.

EASTERN CONFERENCE

NORTHEAST DIVISION	W	L	T	OL	PTS	GF	GA
Ottawa	48	25	9	4	109	274	205
Buffalo	46	31	5	1	98	218	184
Toronto	37	34	11	5	90	232	207
Boston	36	38	8	8	88	227	249
Montreal Can	28	46	8	6	70	206	232

ATLANTIC DIVISION	W	L	T	OL	PTS	GF	GA
New Jersey	48	22	12	3	111	295	195
Philadelphia Fly	43	28	11	3	100	240	207
Pittsburgh Pen	42	31	9	3	96	281	256
New York Ran	33	44	5	1	72	250	290
New York Isl	21	54	7	3	52	185	268

SOUTHEAST DIVISION	W	L	T	OL	PTS	GF	GA
Washington	41	31	10	4	96	233	211
Carolina	38	35	9	3	88	212	225
Florida	22	47	13	9	66	200	246
Atlanta Thr	23	47	12	2	60	211	289
Tampa Bay	24	52	6	5	59	201	280

WESTERN CONFERENCE

CENTRAL DIVISION	W	L	T	OL	PTS	GF	GA
Detroit	49	24	9	4	111	253	202
St. Louis Blu	43	27	12	5	103	249	195
Nashville a	34	39	9	3	80	186	200
Chicago	29	45	8	5	71	210	246
Columbus	28	45	9	6	71	190	233

PACIFIC DIVISION	W	L	T	OL	PTS	GF	GA
Dallas	48	26	8	2	106	241	187
San Jose	40	30	12	3	95	217	192
Los Angeles	38	31	13	3	92	252	228
Phoenix	35	30	17	3	90	214	212
Anaheim	25	46	11	5	66	188	245

NORTHWEST DIVISION	W	L	T	OL	PTS	GF	GA
Colorado Avl	52	20	10	4	118	270	192
Edmonton	39	31	12	3	93	243	222
Vancouver	36	35	11	7	90	239	238
Calgary	27	40	15	4	73	197	236
Minnesota Wld	25	44	13	5	68	168	210

a Played one "home" game and one "away" game in Japan.

SCORING LEADERS	GP	G	A	PTS
Jagr, PitPe	81	52	69	121
J Sakic, ColA	82	54	64	118
Elias, NJ	82	40	56	96
J Allison, Bos	82	36	59	95
Kovalev, PitPe	79	44	51	95
Straka, PitPe	82	27	68	95
P Bure, Fla	82	59	33	92
Weight, Edm	82	25	65	90
Forsberg, ColA	73	27	62	89
Palffy, LA	73	38	51	89
L Robitaille, LA	82	37	51	88
Yashin, Otw	82	40	48	88
Guerin, Edm-Bos	85	40	45	85
Modano, Dal	81	33	51	84
Mogilny, NJ	75	43	40	83
P Turgeon, StLB	79	30	52	82
Oates, Was	81	13	69	82

Preliminaries (best of seven): Toronto defeated Ottawa, 4 games to 0.

Buffalo defeated Philadelphia Flyers, 4 games to 2.
Pittsburgh Penguins defeated Washington, 4 games to 3.
New Jersey defeated Carolina, 4 games to 2.
St. Louis Blues defeated San Jose, 4 games to 2.
Los Angeles defeated Detroit, 4 games to 2.
Dallas defeated Edmonton, 4 games to 2.
Colorado Avalanche defeated Vancouver, 4 games to 0.

Quarter-finals (best of seven): Pittsburgh Penguins defeated Buffalo, 4 games to 3.

New Jersey defeated Toronto, 4 games to 3.
St. Louis Blues defeated Dallas, 4 games to 0.
Colorado Avalanche defeated Los Angeles, 4 games to 3.

Semi-finals (best of seven): New Jersey defeated Pittsburgh Penguins, 4 games to 1.

Colorado Avalanche defeated St. Louis Blues, 4 games to 1.

Stanley Cup Final (best of seven): Colorado Avalanche defeated New Jersey, 4 games to 3.

Acknowledgements

We hope you've found our selective statistical tour of the game's history both entertaining and enlightening. Not to back away an inch from any of our methods or conclusions, but we'd caution you not to take the numbers with deadly seriousness any more than the tone of our banter suggests you should. This isn't particle physics; it's just hockey. In a sense, the stats and our ratings are just an excuse for us to yammer on about the game we love, and, especially, to bring to life some of the great players and teams of the past.

Preparing a statistical treatise, Sir Francis Galton, the 19th-century British scientist, wrote, "I have a great subject to write upon, but feel keenly my literary incapacity to make it easily intelligible without sacrificing accuracy and thoroughness." As the founder of eugenics, it might have been better had his work remained unintelligible. If, despite our own literary incapacity, you've found anything in the book you're holding informative or at least thought-provoking, then we, and you, owe a great debt of gratitude to many people who've contributed in one way or another to this volume.

What more, though, can we say about Edward Yuen? His amazing research on raw goaltending statistics forms the foundation for massive sections of this book. Regardless of what you think about the way we interpret those numbers, we and every fan should be grateful to him for his most magnanimous gift of that data and its long-delayed exposition.

Ernie Fitzsimmons, president of the Society for International Hockey Research, and Bob Duff, fellow SIHR member, were invaluable in sharing with us the results of their immense and painstaking original hockey archaeology. Both of them, time and again, enthusiastically dug up, tabulated, and provided for us the most obscure player stats and league totals from the dawn of the pro game through the late 1920s. It is incumbent on us to state, however, that not a single word of this book has any official endorsement from nor in any way represents any official position of SIHR.

Benny Ercolani, NHL Chief Statistician, was equally essential and every bit as affable and prompt in looking up boxloads of more recent minutiae, and compiling team and league totals too *outré* even for the NHL Web site.

Dan Diamond spearheaded that landmark of ice game scholarship, *Total Hockey*; not only did the existence of that mammoth tome and its wealth of raw data make our work easier, but our biceps measurements have increased by

20% from constantly removing and replacing it on our bookshelves. We're indebted to all of the many researchers who contributed to *Total Hockey*'s statistical database. Dan also graciously gave his permission to run an updated version of our study of Team Degeneration from *Total Hockey*'s first edition.

Doug Norris, Web master of *The Goaltender Home Page*, the Internet's pre-eminent repository on the art and science of goaltending, is a great believer in our Perseverance Index rating. He's been updating the raw totals and ratings in that category annually since the debut of the original *Compendium*, and saved us many hours of number-crunching with his congenial blessing to use his own calculations.

Dave Bidini – author of *Tropic of Hockey* and *On a Cold Road*, rhythm guitarist of venerable Canadian rockers The Rheostatics, and personal friend of the authors – honoured us deeply with his embarrassingly flattering Foreword. Far, far too kind. Although every word is true.

David Johnston, our agent at Livingston Cooke, handled everything as always with unfailing diplomacy and precision, and continues to be a huge pleasure with whom to work and to talk hockey.

Jonathan Webb at McClelland & Stewart brought the project on board, and displayed exemplary patience when we failed sometimes to be perhaps as quick as we, er, otherwise might have been.

Rudy Mezzetta put tremendous hard work into editing our manuscript when it finally came in a mere 150% longer than was called for in the contract.

Several volumes of hockey statistics and lore and a number of Internet Web sites have proven indispensable to our research as well, and we offer this thumbnail bibliography/Webography for those of you interested in the game's history, statistics, and school of Correct Thought:

Coleman, Charles V. *The Trail of the Stanley Cup*. Dubuque, Iowa / Sherbrooke, Quebec: National Hockey League / Kendall/Hunt Publications / Progressive Publications: 1964/1976.

Cruise, David, and Alison Griffiths. *Net Worth*. Toronto: Viking, 1991.

Diamond, Dan, ed. *Total Hockey: The Official Encyclopedia of the National Hockey League*. New York: Total Sports, 2000.

Dryden, Ken. *The Game*. New York / Toronto: Times Books / Macmillan of Canada, 1983.

Fitsell, J. W. *Hockey's Captains, Colonels and Kings*. Erin, Ontario: The Boston Mills Press, 1987.

Fischler, Stan, and Shirley Walton Fischler. *The Hockey Encyclopedia*. New York: Macmillan Publishing, 1983.

Hollander, Zander, and Hal Bock, eds. *The Complete Encyclopedia of Hockey*. New York: Associated Features Inc. / The New American Library, Inc., 1983.

Huff, Darrell, and Irving Geis. *How to Lie with Statistics*. New York: W. W. Norton & Company, 1954.

Lautier, Jack, and Frank Polnaszek. *Same Game, Different Name*. Southington, Conn.: Glacier Publishing, 1996.

MacFarlane, Brian. *Everything You Always Wanted to Know About Hockey*. New York: Charles Scribner's Sons, 1973.

Moriarty, Tim. *Hockey's Hall of Fame*. New York: Avon Books, 1974.

The National Hockey League Official Guide & Record Book. Kingston, N.Y.: Total Sports, 2001.

Percival, Lloyd. *The Hockey Handbook*. Toronto: Copp Clark Publishing, 1960.

Podnieks, Andrew. *Shooting Stars: Photographs from the Portnoy Collection at the Hockey Hall of Fame*. Toronto: Doubleday Canada Ltd., 1998.

Stein, Gil. *Power Plays*. Seacaucus, N.J.: Birch Lane Press / Carol Publishing, 1997.

Surgent, Scott Adam. *The Complete Historical and Statistical Reference to the World Hockey Association, 1972-79*. Tempe, Ariz.: Xaler Press, 1995.

Above and Beyond Hockey
  members.aol.com/SportNet6/index.htm
The Goaltender Home Page
  ucsu.colorado.edu/~norrisdt/goalie.html
The Hockey Almanac
  www.geocities.com/Colosseum/Dugout/4128
Hockey Sandwich www.hockeysandwich.com
HockeyZonePlus www.hockeyzoneplus.com
The Internet Hockey Database www.hockeydb.com
North American Pro Hockey
  www.ottawavalleyonline.com/sites/tomking_01
National Hockey League Fans Association
  www.nhlfa.com
Society for International Hockey Research www.sihr.org
Spector's Hockey
  hometown.aol.com/dblspector/default.html

In a project of such scope and duration as this, a full accounting of the contributions of all the many individuals and organizations that helped make this volume possible would take up a small book of its own. So we can only mention by name the following friends, family, colleagues, associates, hockey fans, and members of the hockey media, and thank them all for their various but always significant provisions of cooperation, information, promotion, assistance, inspiration, enthusiasm, and/or moral support:

The members of the American–Canadian Hockey Union; Colleen and Pat Blizniak; Ann and Pat Bogucki; Lino, Butch, and Sylvio Brusco; Garry Collins and Lisa Green; François

Coulombe; Rich Dean; Ralph Dinger; Ron diOrio; James Duplacey; Lauren Ehret; Stu Hackel; Jean Hayward; Morey Holzman; Audrey and George Jepson; Kevin Jordan; Barbara and Dr. Cliff Kobland; Joe Lapointe; Keith Lenn; Gary Meagher; John Murphy; Jim Boone and Jim Spendlove of the National Hockey League Fans' Association; Jackie and Dave O'Connor; Georgie Pierce; Ruth and Robert Reif; Donna and Bob Reigstad; Tom Reigstad; Lyle Richardson; Miles Seligman; Lew Serviss; the many members of the Society for International Hockey Research it was our pleasure to meet in Montreal; SportNet; Sports Information and Research; Jan and Jon Stoberl; Ruth, Bill, Rick, and Wayne Stoeckert; Dorce Stojanovski; and Linda Willen.

On a more personal note, Jeff thanks Adam Moss, Rob Hoerberger, and everyone at *The New York Times Magazine* for discreetly looking the other way while obscure hockey books piled up rampartlike at his desk; Frances Winopol Klein and Irwin Klein for everything they've meant and done and imparted over the years, and, just the same, Phyllis Prussin and her family, Adam, David, and Laura. Thanks, too, to Manny Winopol for his repeated explanations of how the Canadian electoral system works, something that can never be explained enough. Special thanks to Asher Klein and Grace Klein for all the help, love, and good times they offered, and trenchant analysis, too, as when they accompanied one of the authors to the Molson Centre to see the Rangers play the Canadiens and tried to start the chant "Let's go, Rangers! Let's suck, Montreal!" Keen is the insight of the young. And finally to Danya Reich, the most beautiful, smartest, funniest, coolest rec-league basketball player in the world.

Karl, meanwhile, offers his undying thanks to his resolutely wondrous wife Beth for, well, everything, but here in particular for her performance as sharp-eyed critic, tireless editorial assistant, and social facilitator; to Jonathan Storm, to Dr. Sarah Bohrer and her husband Mark, and to Jessica Coyle and her husband John, for their affectionate tolerance of their stepdad's many eccentricities and his less-than-profitable obsession with the ice game; and to Fred, his bestest pal, who makes him laugh every single day.

And as always, the authors thank each other.

JZK, NYC / KER, Buffalo
June, 2001